The Prentice Hall

Real Estate Investor's Encyclopedia

Frank J. Blankenship, Ph.D.

PRENTICE HALL
Englewood Cliffs, New Jersey 07632

Prentice-Hall International (UK) Limited, *London*
Prentice-Hall of Australia Pty. Limited, *Sydney*
Prentice-Hall Canada, Inc., *Toronto*
Prentice-Hall Hispanoamericana, S.A., *Mexico*
Prentice-Hall of India Private Limited, *New Delhi*
Prentice-Hall of Japan, Inc., *Tokyo*
Simon & Schuster Asia Pte. Ltd., *Singapore*
Editora Prentice-Hall do Brasil, Ltda., *Rio de Janeiro*

© 1989 *by*

PRENTICE-HALL, Inc.

Englewood Cliffs, NJ

10 9 8 7 6 5 4 3 2 1

Library of Congress Cataloging-in-Publication Data

Blankenship, Frank J., 1921–
    The Prentice Hall real estate investor's encyclopedia / by Frank
J. Blankenship.
        p.   cm.
    ISBN 0-13-712837-1
    1. Real estate business—Dictionaries.   2. Real estate investment—
Dictionaries.   3. Real property—Dictionaries.   I. Title.
II. Title: Real estate investor's encyclopedia.
HD 1365.BSS 1989
333.33'03–dc20   89-34240
                                                                                      CIP

ISBN 0-13-712837-1
ISBN 0-13-713827-x (pbk)

PRENTICE HALL
BUSINESS & PROFESSIONAL DIVISION
A division of Simon & Schuster
Englewood Cliffs, New Jersey 07632

Printed in the United States of America

This book is dedicated to the thousands of REALTORS® and Realtor Associates who work seven days a week, night and day to provide their best professional assistance to the public through continuous education and their devotion to a strict code of ethics.

NOTICE TO READER

This encyclopedia is regarded as authoritative and accurate in its coverage of the subject matter. The author is not a Certified Public Accountant or Attorney and does not profess to offer professional advice reserved for these authorities. Suggestions and advice offered are based upon long years of practical experience as a REALTOR® and real estate appraiser and should not be accepted as the final word for specific situations requiring professional advice.

Note on the *Code of Ethics*, NATIONAL ASSOCIATION OF REALTORS®, reproduced on pages 416–420:

The NATIONAL ASSOCIATION OF REALTORS® reserves exclusively unto itself the right to officially comment on and interpret the CODE and particular provisions thereof. For the NATIONAL ASSOCIATION's official interpretations of the CODE, see INTERPRETATIONS OF THE CODE OF ETHICS; NATIONAL ASSOCIATION OF REALTORS®.

ABOUT THE AUTHOR

Dr. Frank J. Blankenship received a B.S. degree from the University of Maryland in 1954, an M.B.A. degree from the Harvard Graduate School of Business in 1956, and a Ph.D. degree (Business Administration-Real Estate) from the California Coast University in 1982.

For eighteen years, Dr. Blankenship was an active Real Estate Broker and practitioner of the real estate appraising profession. He currently holds the designation of Senior Appraiser (IFAS) with the National Association of Independent Fee Appraisers. He continues to be active with the Salt Lake City Chapter. Before his retirement, he was also active with the American Association of Certified Appraisers and held the designation of Certified Appraiser Consultant (CAC). He continues to serve as President of All Points Appraisal Service, Salt Lake City, Utah.

Dr. Blankenship has served as Assistant Chairman, Education Committee, Utah Association of REALTORS® and as contributing author to the *Salt Lake Realtor,* a monthly publication of the Salt Lake Board. He has also served on the Utah State Committee for Real Estate Licensing Requirements. He is the author of *The Prentice Hall Appraisal Deskbook,* 1986.

From 1972 to 1985, Dr. Blankenship served as Adjunct Professor of Finance, Westminster College at Salt Lake, where he taught graduate and undergraduate courses in Marketing, Finance, Investments, and Real Estate. He is a former advisor, Real Estate Studies, at that institution.

Dr. Blankenship was listed in the Marquis *Who's Who in the West 1986/87* and *1988/89* editions.

INTRODUCTION

The Prentice Hall Real Estate Investor's Encyclopedia is an exhaustive compilation of every term you may encounter in real estate investing. It has been arranged in an easy to use A-to-Z format with each term cross referenced to other terms related to the same subject or situation.

Each listing begins with a concise definition of the term, written in an easy-to-understand language. This is followed with advice to the investor to include an expanded explanation of the use of the term in everyday investing situations. Liberal use of illustrations and examples are utilized to expand your understanding of the subject. Where use of the term could enhance an investing situation, suggested uses and proper employment are outlined. Numerous checklists are provided for the investor. Where use of the term can result in undesirable situations, suggestions for avoidance are covered.

This encyclopedia is more than a dictionary or simplified list of terms. It also provides timely tips for maximizing an investment situation. For instance, the term "Amortization Schedule" defines the term, provides a simple mathematical illustration of a typical loan amortization schedule, and shows how a change in the method of making monthly payments can significantly reduce the overall cost and pay-out period. This one tip could result in thousands of dollars of saving on your next real estate purchase.

Many tips are provided for successful and profitable management of real properties. You are provided sample lease and rental agreements that protect you, the investor, as well as your tenants, thereby avoiding costly litigation, legal problems, and expenses. Under "Reserves for Replacement" the problem of keeping your property in first-class condition is addressed. Suggested methods of repair scheduling of maintenance and equipment maintenance are shown as well as the procedure for assuring the availability of funds for these tasks.

Numerous references are made to tax implications, including changes in the taxability of real estate investments occasioned by the 1986 Tax Act. You are provided guidance to minimize tax liabilities in the purchase, management, and eventual sale of acquired properties. More importantly, you are provided guidance for periodic assessment of the status of your investments and their profitability.

If you are a new investor in real estate, you will find numerous tips on the procedures of purchasing and acquiring properties, how to avoid problems of "the Offer" and "the Closing" of the deal. You are provided numerous tips on reading financial reports and how to find potential problems not directly revealed. Suggested additions to State approved agreements and forms used in the purchase, sale and closing of real estate transactions are illustrated to help you avoid problems and misunderstandings.

If you are an experienced real estate investor, you will find that this book is an easy way to refresh and sharpen your memory. The references to tax changes, which over the years alters the way of doing business, will assure that you are kept current and that each of your investments is producing the maximum after-tax return.

This book contains several terms associated with estate planning, wills, trusts, and the probate of a decedent's estate. It provides suggestions for continuing management of real estate investments after death, reduction of estate and inheritance taxes, and assurance that your estate is distributed in accordance with your wishes. It also addresses the problem of the changing portfolio and its affect on prior estate planning.

In compiling *The Prentice Hall Real Estate Investor's Encyclopedia*, the author has drawn upon his extensive background as a real estate salesman, broker, investor, certified real estate appraiser, small business consultant and teacher. Where professional advice is important, you are advised how to select a qualified counselor, such as an attorney, accountant or real estate appraiser. Particular attention has been devoted to the review of appraisal reports and the selection of qualified real estate appraisers.

The Prentice Hall Real Estate Investor's Encyclopedia contains a wealth of useful data for the novice as well as the seasoned real estate investor and practitioner. No accounting, legal or real estate office will be complete without this comprehensive reference.

CONTENTS

TERMS INCLUDED IN THIS BOOK

A   1

Abandonment • Abrogate • Abstract of Title • Accelerated Cost Recovery • Accelerated Depreciation • Acceleration Clause • Accounts Payable • Accounts Receivable • Accredited Residential Manager (ARM) • Accretion • Accrual Method • Accrued Depreciation • Acknowledgment • Acre Feet • Active Income • Actual Possession • Ad Valorem • Add-On Mortgage • Adjustable Rate Mortgage • Administrator (ix) • Adverse Possession • Advertising • After-Tax Return • Agent • Agreement of Sale • Air Easement/Lease • Air Rights • Allodial System of Ownership • Alluvium • Amenities • American Institute of Real Estate Appraisers (AIREA) • American Land Title Association (ALTA) • Amortization Schedule • Anchor Tenant • Annexation • Annual Constant • Annual Exclusion • Annual Percentage Rate (APR) • Annuity • Anti-Churning Rules • Apartment Building • Appraisal Report • Appraiser • Appreciation • Appurtenances • Appurtenant Easement • Architect • Arm's Length Transaction • Asking Price • Assessed Value • Assessment • Assessment Lien • Assets • Assignment, Agreement of Sale • Assignment of Contract • Assignment of Mortgage • Assumable Mortgage • Assumption Agreement • Authorization to Sell • Automatic Renewal Clause • Average

B   47

Balance Sheet • Balloon Payment • Band of Investment • Bank • Bankruptcy • Bartering • Base Line • Basis Cost • Bath Designations • Beneficiary • Bill of Sale • Binder Check • Blanket Mortgage • Blended Interest Rate • Blind Trust • Blockbusting • Blue Sky Laws • Board of Equalization • Book Depreciation • Boot • Break-Even Point • Bridge Loan • British Thermal Unit (BTU) • Broker • Buildable Units • Building Codes • Building Costs • Building Residuals • Bullet Loan • Bundle of Rights • Buyer's Market

C 71

Capacity of the Parties • Capacity to Contract • Capital Appreciation • Capital Gains Taxes • Capitalization of Income • Capitalization Rate • Cash Flow • Cash Throw Off • Cash versus Accrual Accounting • Caveat Emptor • Certificate • Certificate of No Defense • Certificate of Occupancy • Certificate of Reasonable Value (CRV) • Certificate of Release • Certificate of Sale • Certified Property Manager (CRM) • Certified Real Estate Broker (CRB) • Cession Deed • Chain • Chain of Title • Chattel Mortgage • Chattels • Chronological Age • Class Life System • Cleaning Deposit • Clifford Trust • Closing Costs • Cloud on the Title • Codicil • Co-Insurance • Collateralized Mortgage Obligation (CMO) • Color of Title • Combination Trust • Commercial Loan • Commingle • Commission • Commission Down • Commitment Letter • Committed Institutional Warehousing • Committed Technical Warehousing • Community Development Block Grant • Community Property • Comparable Market Value • Comparative Sales Approach • Compass Call • Competent Party • Completion Bond • Component Depreciation • Compound Interest • Condemnation • Conditional Sale • Condominium • Consistent Use Theory • Construction Draw • Construction Loan • Construction Permit • Constructive Eviction • Constructive Notice • Constructive Possession • Constructive Receipt • Constructive Value • Contingency Fund • Contingent Fee Basis • Continuity of Operation • Contract • Contract Price • Contract Rate • Contract Rent • Contractor's Lien • Controllable Expenses • Conventional Loan • Conversion • Convertible Debenture • Cooperative Apartment • Co-Ownership • Corporate Deed Form • Corporation • Correction Deed • Correlation • Co-Tenant • Counter Offer • Covenant • Creative Financing • Cubic Foot Method of Estimating Cost • Cul de Sac • Culinary Water • Curable Physical Deterioration • Curtsey Rights

D 127

Date of Possession • Debenture • Debt Service • Declaration of Complaint • Declaration of No Set-Off • Declining Balance Method of Depreciation • Dedication of Land • Deed • Deed of Reconveyance • Deed of Restriction • Deep Lot Evaluation • Default • Defeasance • Defeasance Clause • Defeasible • Defendant • Deferred Maintenance • Deficiency Judgment • De Minimus PUD • Demographics • Depreciation • Depreciation Recapture • Depth Tables • Deterioration • Development Costs • Disclosure • Discounted Paper • Disintermediation • Dispossess • Distinct Possession • Distraint • Distressed Property • District • Double Declining Balance • Double Scoop • Dower Rights • Down Payment Float • Due on Sale Clause • Duplex • Duress • Dutch Roof

E 153

Earnest Money • Earnest Money Contract • Earnest Money Deposit • Earnest Money Receipt and Exchange Agreement • Earnest Money Receipt and Offer to Lease • Earnest Money Receipt and Offer to Purchase • Easement • Economic Depreciation • Economic Life • Economic Obsolescence • Economic Rent • Economic Value • Effective Age • Effective Gross Income • Egress • Electrical Equipment • Ellwood Premise • Emblements • Eminent Domain • Encroachment • Encumbrances • Engineering Breakdown Method in Appraising • Equitable Title • Equity Buildup • Equity Trust • Escalation Clause • Escalator Loan • Escheat • Escrow • ESOPS • Estate at Sufferance • Estate at Will • Estate Planning • Estate Taxes • Estate Tax Lien • Estoppel Certificate • Eviction • Excess Rent • Exchange • Exclusive Agency • Exclusive Right to Sell • Exculpatory Clause • Executor(ix) • Executor's Deed • Extender Clause • Extrapolation

F 193

Fair Market Value • Farmer's Home Administration • Feasibility Study • Federal Home Loan Mortgage Corporation (Freddie Mac) • Federal Housing Administration • Federal National Mortgage Association (FNMA) • Federal Savings and Loan Insurance Corporation (FSLIC) • Fee Simple Title • Fee Tail Estate • Fenestration • FHA-Insured Loan • Fiduciary • Finder's Fee • Fire Insurance • First Right of Refusal • Fixed Expense • Fixtures, Electrical • Fixtures, Plumbing • Flat • Floating Rate Loan • Floor Load • Forces Affecting Value • Foreclosure • Fourplex • Fraud • Freehold Estate • Free Lease • Free Piece • Front Foot • Functional Obsolescence • Future Estate • Future Event Down Payment • Future Sweat • Future Value of One • Future Value of One per Period

G 217

Gable • General Mortgage • General Partner • Gift Taxes • Glue Deal • Government National Mortgage Association (GNMA) • Graduated Lease • Graduated Payment Mortgages • Grandfather Clause • Grant Deed • Grantee • Grantor • Gray Water Waste • Grazing Lease • Greenbelt Tax Classification • Gross Income • Gross National Product (GNP) • Gross Potential Income • Gross Rent Multiplier • Ground Rent • Guardian

H   231

Habendum Clause • Hangout • Hazard Insurance • Heating, Ventilating and Air
Conditioning (HVAC) • Hereditaments • Highest and Best Use • Hip Roof • Holding
Cost • Holding Period • Holdover Tenant • Holographic Will • Homeowner's
Association • Homeowner's Insurance • Homestead • Homestead Tax Exemption •
Hoskold Method • Hostile Possession • Housing and Urban Development (HUD) •
Hypothecate

I   243

IFA Appraiser • IFAC Appraiser • IFAS Appraiser • Implied Easement • Implied
Warranty Doctrine • Impounds • Improvements • Imputed Interest • Inchoate • Income
Approach to Value • Income Multiplier • Income Stream • Income Tax • Incurable
Depreciation • Individual Metering • Industrial Building • Industrial Park • Industrial
Property • Inflation • Ingress • Inheritance Taxes • Installment Land Contract •
Installment Payment • Insulation • Insulation "R" Value • Insurable Interest •
Insurable • Insurance • Insurance Value • Interest Computing • Interest-Only Loan •
Internal Rate of Return (IRR) • Interpolation • Inter Vivoce Trust • Intestate •
Investment Income • Inwood Method • Irrigation Water

J   275

Joint Tenancy • Joint Ventures • Judgment • Junior Lien • Junior Mortgage

K   281

Kicker

L   285

Laches • Land Identification Methods • Landlord • Land Residual • Land Rights
Reserved by Government • Late Payment Charge • Law of Contracts • Law of Principal
and Agent • Lease • Leaseback • Lease Guarantee Insurance • Leasehold Insurance •
Lease Rights • Legal Description • Legality of Object • Letter of Intent • Letters
Testamentary • Leverage • Liabilities • Liability Insurance • License • Lien Waiver •
Life Estate • Life Estate pur Autre Vie • Life Tenant • Limited Liability • Limited

Partnership • Line of Credit • Link • Liquid Assets • Liquidated Damages • Lis Pendens • Listing Contract • Listing Price • Litigation • Living Trust • Loan Assumption • Loan Broker • Loan Ratio • Loan Window • Lock-in Period • Locus Sigilli • Loft Building • Long-Term Gains • Lot Improvements • Lot Release System

M   313

Mack Truck Factor • MAI Appraiser • Mansard Roof • Manufactured Housing • Market Data Approach to Value • Market Rent • Market Survey • Market Value • Master Limited Partnership • Master Metering • Master Plan • Mean • Mechanical Equipment • Mechanic's Lien • Medical Office Building • Meridian • Metes and Bounds • Mill Rate • Mineral Lease • Mini-Warehouse • Mixed-Use Property • Mobile Home • Mobile Home Park • Modular Housing • Month-to-Month • Monument • Mortgage • Mortgage Commitment • Mortgage Company • Mortgage Constant • Mortgage Equity Technique • Mortgage Note • Mortgage Package • Mortgage Refinancing • Multiple Listing Service • Muniments • Mutual Savings Bank

N   339

National Association of Independent Fee Appraisers (NAIFA) • National Association of REALTOR® • Necessity Easement • Net Income • Net Income After Taxes • Net Income Multiplier • Net Lease • Net Rent Multiplier • Net Spendable Income • Neutron Bomb Analysis • Nonapparent Easement • Nonassumable Loan • Noncash Expense • Nonconforming Use • Normal Maintenance • No Springing Interest • Notary • Note • Notice of Contract • Notice of Default • Notice of Lien • Notorious Possession • Novation • Nuisance Rent Raise

O   353

Obsolescence • Offer • Offeree • Office Building • Old Spanish Law • One-Party Listing • On-Site Manager • Open End Mortgage • Open-Listing • Operating Expense • Operating Statement • Option • Other Income • Overage Rent • Overall Rate of Return (OAR) • Overimprovement • Owner's Equity

P   371

Parcel • Parole Evidence Rule • Partial Release Clause • Party Wall • Passive Income • Patent Claim • Payables • Payback Period • Pension Plans • Percentage Lease •

Percolation Test • Performance Bond • Periodic Estate • Personal Property • Physical Depreciation • Physical Life • Piggy Back Loan • Plaintiff • Planned Unit Development (PUD) • Pledged Savings • Plot Plan • Plottage • Plumbing Equipment • Points • Police Powers • Policy Binder • Possession Before Closing • Power of Attorney • Power of Eminent Domain • Prepayment Penalty • Prepayment Provision • Prescription • Prescriptive Easements • Present Value of One • Present Value of One per Period • Prime Rate • Principal of Anticipation • Principal of Balance • Principal of Change • Principal of Competition • Principal of Conformity • Principal of Contribution • Principal of Substitution • Principal of Supply and Demand • Principal of Surplus Productivity • Private Investor • Private Mortgage Insurance • Private Offering • Probate • Professional Office Building • Pro-Forma Analysis • Profits a Prendre • Profit Sharing Plans • Property Improvement • Property Management • Property Rights • Prospectus • Proximate Cause • Purchase Money Mortgage • Pyramiding

Q   405

Qualifications of the Appraiser • Quit Claim Deed

R   411

Range of Values • Real Estate • Real Estate Agent • Real Estate Board • Real Estate Investment Trust (REIT) • Real Estate Mortgage Investment Conduit (REMIC) • Real Property • REALTOR® • Recapture • Recapture Rate • Receivables • Recital • Reconciliation • Reconveyance Deed • Recording • Rectangular Survey • Recycled Real Estate • Redemption Rights • Red Herring • Redlining • Referee's Deed in Partition • Refinance • Regression Technique • Regulation "Z" • Release of Earnest Money • Release of Lien • Release or Satisfaction of Mortgage • Reliction • Remainder Man • Remaining Economic Life • Rent • Rent Schedule • Rentable Square Footage • Rental Deposit • Rental Income Insurance • Replacement Cost • Repossession Lists • Reproduction Cost • Reserves for Replacement • Residual Techniques • Restrictive Covenants • Return of Investment • Return On Investment • Revenue Stamps • Reverse Mortgage • Reversioner • Review Appraiser • Right of First Refusal • Right of Survivorship • Right of Way (ROW) • Rights of Ownership • Riparian Rights • Risk Versus Return • RM Appraiser • Rod • Roll Over Loan • Row House • Rule of ¼ • Rule of 3 • Rule of 5 • Rule of 78's • Rules of Contractual Construction

S   453

Safe Harbor Rules • Safe Rate • Sale and Buyback • Sale and Leaseback • Sale of Leased Property • Sale Proceeds • Sales Price • Salvage Value • Sandwich Lease •

Sanitary Sewer • Satisfaction Piece • Savings and Loan Associations • Scrap Value •
Seasoned Mortgage Loan • Second Feet • Second Mortgage • Secondary Mortgage
Market • Section • Securities Commission • Securities Exchange Commission (SEC) •
Security Deposit • Separate Metering • Separate Property • Septic System • Sheriff's
Deed • Short-Term Financing • Short-Term Gains • Sinking Fund • Small Claims
Court • Society of Real Estate Appraisers • Special Assessment • Special Warranty
Deed • Specific Performance • Spot Zoning • Square Footage • SRA Appraiser •
SREA Appraiser • SRPA Appraiser • Statute of Frauds • Stick-Built House • Storm
Sewer • Straight-Line Cost Recovery • Straight-Line Depreciation • Subchapter "S"
Corporation • Subcontractor • Subcontractor Lien • Subdivision • Subject-to Clause •
Sublease • Subordinate Debenture • Subordination • Subscription Agreement •
Sufferance Lease • Sum of Digits • Super-Six Magic Numbers • Supoena Duces
Tecum • Survey • Sweat Equity • Syndicated Equity Pools • Syndicate Vehicles •
Syndication

T   485

Take-Out Letter • Tax Deed • Taxfree Trades • Tax Lien • Tax Reform Act of 1986
(TRA) • Tax Rolls • Tax Sale • Tax Shelter • Tenancy at Sufferance • Tenancy at
Will • Tenancy by the Entireties • Tenancy from Month to Month • Tenancy from Year to
Year • Tenancy in Common • Tenant • Tenant Caretakers • Tenant Selection Criteria •
Tenements • Terminal Shape • Testamentary Trust • Thin Corporation • Three-Party
Blanket • Time Is of the Essence Clause • Time-Sharing Ownership • Title Insurance •
Title Report • Torrens System • Town House • Township • Tract Housing • Trading
Area Analysis • Triple Net Lease • Trust • Trust Account • Trust Deed • Trustee •
Trustor • Twenty-Four Hour Contingency Clause

U   509

Unit in Place Method • Units of Comparison • Useful Life • Useful Square Footage •
Usufructuary Right • Utilities • Utility Value

V   515

VA Loan • Vacancy Factor • Valuable Consideration • Valuation • Value • Value in
Use • Variable Expense • Vender's Lien • Vertical Revitalization • Visible Possession •
Void Contract • Voidable Contract

W   523

Warehouse • Warranty Deed • Water Rights • Water Table • Water Master • Well Permit • White Water Waste • Will • Will of Decent • Working Capital • Wrap Around Mortgage • Writ of Eviction

Y   531

Yield • Yield on Equity • Yield on Value

Z   535

Zero Down Technique • Zero Lot Line • Zoning • Zoning Codes • Zoning Variances

A

Abandonment
Abrogate
Abstract of Title
Accelerated Cost Recovery
Accelerated Depreciation
Acceleration Clause
Accounts Payable
Accounts Receivable
Accredited Residential Manager (ARM)
Accretion
Accrual Method
Accrued Depreciation
Acknowledgment
Acre Feet
Active Income
Actual Possession
Ad Valorem
Add-on Mortgage
Adjustable Rate Mortgage
Administrator (ix)
Adverse Possession
Advertising
After-Tax Return
Agent
Agreement of Sale
Air Easement/Lease
Air Rights
Allodial System of Ownership
Alluvium
Amenities
American Institute of Real Estate Appraisers (AIREA)

American Land Title Association (ALTA)
Amortization Schedule
Anchor Tenant
Annexation
Annual Constant
Annual Exclusion
Annual Percentage Rate (APR)
Annuity
Anti-Churning Rules
Apartment Building
Appraisal Report
Appraiser
Appreciation
Appurtenances
Appurtenant Easement
Architect
Arm's Length Transaction
Asking Price
Assessed Value
Assessment
Assessment Lien
Assets
Assignment, Agreement of Sale
Assignment of Contract
Assignment of Mortgage
Assumable Mortgage
Assumption Agreement
Authorization to Sell
Automatic Renewal Clause
Average

A

ABANDONMENT

1. The act of a tenant by which he leaves a leased property prior to the termination of a lease and without the consent of the owner. Such abandonment does not relieve the lessee from payment of all rents due during the remainder of the term of the lease.
2. The act of a real estate broker by which he fails to follow up on an offer for listed property or to act on behalf of the owner to procure a sale. Where such acts occur, another broker may proceed to negotiate a sale, after first determining that the original broker has indeed abandoned the listing. In this case, first broker may have lost all claim for a commission, even though the listing was active at the time of the sale.[1]

INVESTOR ADVICE

In the first case described above, once you, the owner, have determined that your property has been abandoned, should you immediately inspect said property. It is advised that this inspection be conducted in association with at least one other person. Where considerable damages have been done to the property, over and above fair wear and tear, it may be necessary to seek relief through court action and a witness may be required to verify your claim of damages. The inspection should record:

- All damages other than fair wear and tear. If extensive damages are found, pictures should be taken to show the extent of the damages. Be sure to include pictorial coverage of such items as carpet stains, holes in walls, broken glass, and damaged electrical and plumbing fixtures.

- Check all utilities and appliances to determine operating condition as of the date of abandonment. If furniture or other household items were provided, it is essential that a complete inventory be taken during the inspection and the inventory list acknowledged by each of the persons in the inspection party. *NOTE:* When leasing property which includes furnishings and equipment, most landlords recommend that an inventory of equipment and furnishings be jointly taken by landlord and tenant prior to occupancy. This document is dated and signed by both parties and serves as an official agreement of the property's status at the time of possession.

When initial property status and final status documents are presented to the court, there can be little argument as to damages caused by the tenant.

- Take prompt action to restore the property to rentable condition and to procure a new tenant. If reasonably prompt action is not taken to procure a new tenant and thus mitigate the loss due to abandonment, the courts may not award the full loss.[2]

SEE ALSO: LEASE.

ABROGATE

Abrogate is a legal term meaning cancelled or annulled.

INVESTOR ADVICE
This term is often applied to terms contained in the earnest money receipt and offer to purchase agreement and the subsequent closing of the deal. Legally, the initial agreement (offer and acceptance) is *abrogated* at the conclusion of the closing activity. It is assumed that all terms of the initial agreement have been included in the closing documents, which are signed by both buyer and seller.

CAUTION! Closing the deal may not abrogate the Earnest Money Agreement. Insist upon buyer inspection prior to closing.

In certain instances, the courts have refused to rule that the initial agreement was completely abrogated. For instance, concealed defects in the property, *which a normal buyer is not expected to be able to identify,* can be held applicable if the initial agreement specified that the item in question was to be in good condition, workable, etc.

For example, an agreement stating, "Buyer warrants that all electrical, mechanical, and plumbing equipment is in good and serviceable order at the time of closing" might prove to be a mitigating circumstance in the buyer's favor. Some of these conditions would be evident to a prudent and careful buyer during his preclosing inspection, but holes in the heating chamber of the furnace would not. If a hidden condition such as this was found to exist after the closing, the seller could be held liable under the original agreement (offer and acceptance).

SEE ALSO: EARNEST MONEY RECEIPT and OFFER TO PURCHASE.

ABSTRACT OF TITLE

A condensed summary of all official recorded facts pertaining to the title to land. The abstract begins with the first ownership by government grant or other basis and each succeeding fact pertaining thereto. It includes such items as transfers of ownership, mortgages, releases of mortgages, liens, tax sales, redemption from tax sales, foreclosure actions, chattel mortgages, recorded leases, Lis Pendens and execution notices, etc. It must trace the ownership back to an undisputable source.

All official data is shown by date and place of record (book and page). It also indicates the names of parties to the actions.

Abstracts of title are made by attorneys or others authorized by law to perform such services. At the conclusion of the abstract document, the abstractor provides a certificate to indicate his/her opinion as to the status of the title. He/she may also list any specific areas which were not researched and indicate why this was not performed.

In most cases the abstractor's actions are those of updating an original document to reflect changes since the last abstract work was performed. He/she researches any open items of the original abstract to determine their current status and adds documentation to cover new items. In the United States most abstracts are rather voluminous documents which date from the sixteenth and seventeenth century. The physical size of a typical abstract of title may include as many as 200 to 300 pages. The use of title abstracts is limited, since most mortgage lenders require title insurance, *which includes the abstracting action plus a guarantee of title accuracy.* Some title companies will allow a discount on the title insurance policy if the seller surrenders his/her abstract of title record. This assures the title company that all future sellers will not have access to the abstract and at the same time eases their job of research for policy issuance.

INVESTOR ADVICE

When preparing to purchase real property, you would be advised to include a statement in the earnest money agreement that the seller is to provide title insurance. Most earnest money agreements, approved by the various states, specify that the owner will provide good and clear title. However, the only guarantee of prompt relief in the event of future revelations of clouds on the title is through insurance. While relief may be possible by proof of abstractor negligence/error or by recourse to the seller, these actions require court actions and considerable expense and time.

> **CAUTION** An abstract of title provides only an opinion as to the status of the property title. *Title insurance guarantees* that the title is as listed in the policy.

SEE ALSO: EARNEST MONEY RECEIPT AND OFFER TO PURCHASE, LIS PENDENCE, and SATISFACTION PIECE.

ACCELERATED COST RECOVERY

This term refers to the method by which cost of real estate and other business properties are depreciated in less than the normal lifetime in order to reduce income taxes. The Internal Revenue Service refers to this as "The Accelerated Cost Recovery System" or ACRS.

EXAMPLE

Mr. Smith purchased an apartment house for $130,000. The land value is $30,000. The expected lifetime of the property is estimated to be twenty years. Straight-line depreciation would allow:

$$\$100,000/20 = \$5,000/year$$

If a method known as double declining balance is used, the following depreciation schedule would apply:

Year	Value at Beg. Year	Dec. Bal. Factor	Dept. Allowance
1	$100,000	$1/20 \times 2 = 10\%$	$10,000
2	90,000	$1/20 \times 2 = 10\%$	9,000
3	81,000	$1/20 \times 2 = 10\%$	8,100
4	72,000	$1/20 \times 2 = 10\%$	7,200
	Etc.		

There are other methods of accelerated depreciation which are applicable in certain cases. Those most often used are single declining balance and sum of the digits.

INVESTOR ADVICE

The allowable depreciation on all real and other business property drastically changed by enactment of the Tax Reform Act of 1986. You are advised to become acquainted with the provisions of the Tax Reform Act of 1986 or to seek the advice of a competent tax authority. The act requires both residential and nonresidential properties to be depreciated using the straight line method. Further, the recovery periods were extended to 271/2 years for residential property and to 311/2 years for nonresidential.

Section 202 of the 1986 act also established Asset Classes, Recovery Periods, and Depreciation Methods for personal properties. The cost of these personal properties are to be recovered over three-, five-, seven-, ten-, fifteen- and twenty-year periods, based on the type of property involved. The depreciation method allowed for three-, five-, seven- and ten-year properties is 200% (double) declining balance with a switch in later years to straight line to maximize depreciation. (*NOTE:* The switch to straight line would be made at the point at which the double declining balance rate is less than the straight line rate.) The allowable depreciation method for fifteen- and twenty-year properties is 150% declining balance with a switch to straight line to maximize depreciation.

Cars and light trucks are listed in the five-year class. Other items of equipment are classified in accordance with Section 202 of the tax act.

NOTICE As a real estate buyer, you should be aware of the requirement that 80% or more of rental income must be from dwelling units to be classified as residential. Hotels and motels do not qualify for residential classification.

Section 206 of the 1986 tax reform act provides for an increased expensing deduction. A taxpayer may elect for this in lieu of the normal depreciation method under ARCS. Effective January 1, 1987, and thereafter, property placed in service may be expensed during the taxable year up to a maximum of $10,000. Qualifying property is depreciable property that is placed in use in a trade or business. This provision is modified as follows:

- If the property placed in use exceeds $200,000, the credit is reduced dollar-for-dollar by the excess amount over $200,000.

- Married persons filing separately are limited to $10,000 each.

- The amount expensed cannot exceed the taxable income received from the business or trade.

- Any conversion of the property to personal use prior to the end of the normal recovery period is subject to recapture of income over that allowable under ACRS for the applicable period.

SEE ALSO: DOUBLE DECLINING BALANCE METHOD, and SUM OF THE DIGITS METHOD

ACCELERATED DEPRECIATION

See ACCELERATED COST RECOVERY

ACCELERATION CLAUSE

A clause or provision, often contained in a mortgage note or real estate contract, which provides for accelerated payment of the balance due in event of certain pre-scribed events, such as resale, sale on contract, or failure to make payments as required. Generally, when this provision is invoked, the balance due at that point is immediately due and payable. The purpose of such provisions is to encourage the buyer to avoid the specified events.

TYPICAL ACCELERATION CLAUSE

Non-Assumption Agreement: This transaction is subject to a non-assumption agreement, reference to which is made, provisions of which include the right of lender, in the event security for this transaction, or any interest therein, is conveyed, or contracted to be conveyed, to any third person(s) or corporation(s), to (1) declare immediately due and payable any remaining balance owing, or (2) require thereafter payment of interest (Annual Percentage Rate) equal to the then prevailing interest rate offered by the lender.

INVESTOR ADVICE

The acceleration clause, in event of resale, is becoming standard in all non-government backed mortgage loans. This assures the lender that the mortgagor will not sell the mortgaged property on a contract without the lender's permission or opportunity to adjust the rate of interest to that applicable at the time of the resale. If your property is proposed for sale with assumption of the existing mortgage, you should review the mortgage note provisions prior to listing it for sale to assure that the mortgage will not be called and due immediately after the closure of the sale. The principal of acceleration of debt is now well established in common law.[3] Any attempt to subvert the intent of an acceleration clause can result in extreme legal consequences.

> **ASSUME NOTHING** Never sign an agreement to purchase and presume that the existing mortgage is assumable. Make your offer subject to lender's permission to assume.

If a seller is reluctant to reveal personal mortgage information your offer to purchase his property should be made *subject to* your satisfactory review of the mortgage terms, prior to closing.

Similarly, where property is being purchased on a contract (owner financing), you must assure yourself that the underlying mortgage, if any, will not be called upon resale or the interest rate adjusted upwards to current rates. *This applies regardless of who remains responsible for the mortgage payment after the sale is concluded.* Even though the seller will be responsible for any increase in the interest rate or payment of the mortgage in full where called, it may place him in an untenable financial position. Regardless of who is responsible, it may require you, the buyer, to refinance the property, in order to prevent foreclosure by a lender who desires to enforce the non-assumption provision.

SEE ALSO: CONTRACT, MORTGAGE, MORTGAGE NOTE, and MORTGAGE REFINANCING.

ACCOUNTS PAYABLE

An accounting term meaning bills for goods and services delivered, but not paid. These are assumed to be due in six months or less. Debts with later due dates would normally be listed under "Long-Term Debt."

INVESTOR ADVICE

When purchasing a going operation, you will want assurance that there are no outstanding bills for goods and services at the time of closing, except where carefully studied and accepted as a part of the down payment.

Payables represent debts of the business. Even where the seller is willing to allow them to be assumed, you must be careful to ensure the operation is not overburdened with debt, particularly payables. Too much current debt can seriously effect operating efficiency and cash flow control.

CHECKLIST FOR PAYABLES EXAMINATION

- The total payables should not exceed one-twelfth of the annual purchases or payments for goods and services (one month's payables).

- Obtain all supplier's approvals prior to assuming existing payable debts.

- If the seller agrees to clear all payable debts at closing, obtain positive written proof that this was accomplished. *NOTE:* A good method of accomplishing this is to have the closing agency make all required payments from the seller's proceeds.

- If you have agreed to assume existing debt, obtain a payment schedule in writing from each supplier.

SEE ALSO: CASH FLOW and WORKING CAPITAL.

ACCOUNTS RECEIVABLE

An accounting term meaning accounts billed for goods or services delivered but not paid by the customer—expected income.

INVESTOR ADVICE
When purchasing a going operation or business, you should be extremely careful about buying receivables. These items can vary in value from zero to 100%. Most advisors would recommend leaving all receivables for the seller to collect, or at best buying them only at a substantial discount after study of the past payment history of each account. Good accounts with good credit history can be accepted at face value. Accounts with late payment histories should be discounted sufficiently to compensate for excessive payment delays or rejected altogether.

Another approach to this problem is to have the closing agency keep a certain dollar amount of the seller's proceeds in escrow, until all accounts on the books have been collected or a specified time has elapsed. This will assure that any receivable losses are absorbed by the seller.

SEE ALSO: ASSETS and WORKING CAPITAL.

ACCREDITED RESIDENTIAL MANAGER (ARM)

The title of Accredited Residential Manager is awarded to those members of the National Association of Realtors who have proven their ability to manage real property through specified course studies, examination, and other specified requirement.

INVESTOR ADVICE
Where the size of the property or your personal time limitations dictate management by someone other than yourself or with assistance of an on-site manager, it is recommended that applicants for the management position possess the ARM designation. You should be aware that the ARM designation alone does not assure good management, but it does indicate a recognized ability to manage. This, in addition to proper recommendations of other property owners, will provide a positive indication of the applicants ability.

SEE ALSO: NATIONAL ASSOCIATION OF REALTORS®.

ACCRETION

In real estate parlance, accretion is the addition to a land parcel by alluvial action, that is the deposits of sand, silt or other matter by water. The net result is a free increase in land size. Accretion is also the result of the permanent lowering of a body of water, thereby increasing useful land.

INVESTOR ADVICE

If you should purchase land adjoining a stream or lake it is advised that you carefully read the legal description of the property prior to its purchase. Where doubt exists as to the actual original and present boundaries, a survey may be required.

SEE ALSO: ALLUVIUM.

ACCRUAL METHOD

A method of accounting in which receipts and expenditures are recorded as they occur, regardless of whether the monies are actually received or paid out. The accrual method is differentiated from the cash method of accounting in which items of income or expenses are not recorded until the income is actually received or the bills actually paid.

INVESTOR ADVICE

If you are buying a business or operation where the current and past profitability is important to the evaluation, you must ascertain if accrual accounting or cash accounting is used in the financial record keeping. An operation on the accrual system can show a large profit without sufficient cash to continue. This is particularly true where inventories are substantial or sales are made on credit. All of the indicated profit may be tied up in these latter two accounts, leaving little working capital.

On the other hand, if cash accounting is employed, you should be careful to determine the exact amount of bills unpaid since there will be no record of these debts shown in the books.

SEE ALSO: CASH FLOW and CASH VERSUS ACCRUAL ACCOUNTING.

ACCRUED DEPRECIATION

Each taxable year after purchase of a depreciable asset the purchaser is allowed to deduct from income an applicable amount referred to as depreciation allowance. This process continues during the lifetime of the asset or until it is fully depreciated. Each year additional depreciation is taken, which is added to all prior depreciation taken to obtain a sum known as "accrued depreciation."

In the event the asset is sold, the accrued depreciation is deducted from the cost in determining the current cost base. The selling price less the base cost equals the capital gains attributed to the asset held for business purposes. The tax form, filed each year, lists each asset purchased, date of purchase, cost, total years over which the asset will be depreciated, type of depreciation, accrued depreciation to date, and book or remaining depreciation to be taken.

INVESTOR ADVICE

The total allowable depreciation becomes a non-cash expense to the business and a source of cash to the operation. Your ability to make required mortgage payments or obtain a required rate of return on your investment can be greatly enhanced by the depreciation cash flow.

In preparing a proforma income or proforma cash flow analysis for a proposed purchase, it is important that you obtain an accurate list of depreciable assets and are fully informed as to the maximum tax relief possible. For this purpose, the current owner's list may not be accurate as all fully depreciated assets will not appear on the depreciation schedule.

These assets, when purchased, may have value and a useful remaining life. They may also be eligible for additional depreciation to you, the new owner.

SEE ALSO: CAPITAL GAINS, BASE COST, CASH FLOW, and PRO FORMA ANALYSES.

ACKNOWLEDGMENT

The action by which a person who has executed (signed) a legal instrument acknowledges to an authorized officer, such as a Notary, that he/she executed the document. Forms of acknowledgment and method of execution vary from state to state. The requirements for those persons authorized to acknowledge legal instruments also varies. The following general form of acknowledgment is one typically used in most of the states.

Any document which is to be recorded in the official records of a legal jurisdiction (County etc.) must be an original document and acknowledged before a competent authority.

SAMPLE ACKNOWLEDGMENT

State of _____) ss
County of _____)
Before me personally appeared _____ to me well known and known to me to be the person described in and who executed the foregoing instrument, and acknowledged to and before me that he/she executed said instrument for the purposes therein expressed.
WITNESS my hand and official seal, this ____ day of _____ A.D. 19___.

_____
Notary Public

(Notary Seal)   State of _____
                                  My Commission Expires _____
                                  _____

INVESTOR ADVICE

You should be aware that an instrument notarized by a person having an interest in the transaction or closely related to the person executing the document is illegal. Similarly, an instrument notarized by a officer located outside his/her prescribed jurisdiction is not legally binding.

Before accepting a deed, mortgage, or other document as official you should determine that the person executing the document had the authority to do so. For example, if an officer of a corporation executed the document, was board action necessary to authorize the sale? If the seller is married, does the sale require both husband and wife to sign?

SEE ALSO: CERTIFICATE, NOTARY, and LOCUS SIGILLI.

ACRE FEET

A measure of water which indicates an amount equal to an area of 43,560 ft^2 covered one foot deep.

INVESTOR ADVICE

In arid areas of the western United States, land is of little value without water, irrigation, and/or culinary. Water rights are measured in one of the following ways:

- Acre-feet;

- Second-feet of water flow; and

- Right to drill a well(s) of certain size and capacity.

SEE ALSO: CULINARY WATER, IRRIGATION WATER, SECOND FEET, and WATER RIGHTS.

ACTIVE INCOME

A term originating in the Tax Reform Act of 1986, which classifies income from labor or active participation in management as active income. All other income is "passive income" or "investment income."

INVESTOR ADVICE

The significance of the three new designations of income is the manner in which losses in one operation or source can be deducted from gains in another.

Real estate investors are no longer able to write off losses on rental properties against their income from their work or profession. Prior to the 1986 act, a dollar of real estate investment loss was as good as a dollar of gain—the loss saved taxes on salary income, which was as good as real income to the investor.

Real estate investments must now stand or fall on their own merits. Losses are no longer attractive to the high income investor.

SEE ALSO: INVESTMENT INCOME, PASSIVE INCOME, and TAX REFORM ACT OF 1986.

ACTUAL POSSESSION

The physical possession or occupation of a land parcel by which a claimant attempts to obtain good title by means of adverse possession. Actual possession might be proven by one or more of the following: (1) building a home or other structure; (2) building fences; and (3) planting crops or orchards, any or all of which was conducted without notice from the legal owner to quit the premises. In order to establish a claim of adverse possession, the courts require that the acts of actual possession must leave no doubt in the mind of an ordinary person as to the adequacy of the acts or that the owner had denied title to the property.

In some states the claimant *must* pay the real property taxes for at least seven years, although such payment is not normally the controlling factor.

INVESTOR ADVICE

Owners of real property must constantly be aware of those who would use their property without permission. This usage often appears innocent. A good example is the passage of children and others through the property in effecting a short cut to schools, their homes, or other locations. Another example would be the use of driveways by unauthorized persons to or through the property as a convenience to themselves. Failure to erect barriers or post public notice will, after a time period, prevent the owner from closing the right-of-way to public use.

SEE ALSO: ADVERSE POSSESSION, CONSTRUCTIVE POSSESSION, HOSTILE POSSESSION, and PRESCRIPTION.

AD VALOREM

A Latin term meaning, "In accordance with the value." Thus, real estate taxes are ad valorem taxes since the actual tax levied is a rate, which applies to all similar properties, but is based upon its assessed value.

INVESTOR ADVICE

Ad valorem taxes are seldom based on the actual full value of the property, but rather on the assessed value. The tax rate, quoted in mills (one-thousandth of a dollar) is then applied to the assessed value to obtain the actual taxes.

EXAMPLE

A certain property is appraised by the tax assessor's office as $100,000. The state directive requires all properties be assessed at 80% of real value. The tax rate for this tax district is 98 mills ($0.0098). What is the tax to be paid?

Assessed Value = $100,000 x 0.80 = $80,000

Taxes Due = $80,000 x 0.0098 = $784

SEE ALSO: ASSESSED VALUE, MILL RATE, and TAX ROLLS (COUNTY).

ADD-ON MORTGAGE

The add-on mortgage is an additional loan on which the interest rate is based; which, in turn, is based upon the rate being charged on the original mortgage amount. It is often referred to as interest-on-interest. The formula for the interest on an add-on mortgage is:

$$I = PYr \left(1 + Yr\right) \quad \text{where:}$$

I = Add on interest rate
P = Loan amount
Y = Term of the loan in years
r = Interest rate on original loan (expressed as a decimal)

EXAMPLE

Mr. Jones borrows an additional $10,000 for four years using a 9% + 9% add on mortgage. How much interest will Mr. Jones pay over the four-year period?

$$I = \$10,000 \times 4 \times .09 \,(1 + 4 \times .09)$$

$$= \$3,600 \,(1 + .36) = \$4,896$$

Based on simple interest or Annual Percentage Rate (APR), the 9%+9% interest rate is about 12.2%. Prior to the passage of truth in lending laws, add-on interest was quoted as a means of disguising the real simple interest rate.

INVESTOR ADVICE

Where relatively small amounts of additional capital are required, the add-on interest rates are tolerable. Since the additional loan is a junior mortgage, you would expect to pay a higher rate than that of the first mortgage. If large amounts are required, you should examine the possibility of refinancing, since the refinance charges plus current interest may be less than amounts paid by the add-on method.

SEE ALSO: PIGGY-BACK LOANS.

ADJUSTABLE RATE MORTGAGE

An adjustable rate mortgage is variable interest rate mortgage in which the interest payable is tied to some well-known economic indicator. Normally, the rate is adjusted at designated periods and has a maximum and minimum rate specified.

INVESTOR ADVICE

An example of an adjustable rate mortgage would be one that specifies that the interest rate would be fixed at the end of each calendar year at a rate equal to the average prime rate for the last day of the past three months plus 1.5%. What would be the rate fixed at the end of 1988 if the following prime rates were in effect?

Prime rate in October = 9.0%
Prime rate in November = 9.5%
Prime rate in December = 8.5%

$$\text{Average} = (9.0 + 9.5 + 8.5)/3 = 9.0\%$$

$$1989 \text{ Interest Rate} = 9.0\% + 1.5\% = 10.5\%$$

SEE ALSO: VARIABLE RATE MORTGAGE.

ADMINISTRATOR (ix)

The title of a person, appointed by a probate court, to settle the estate of a deceased person who died intestate (without a valid will) or one who failed to provide for an executor(ix) in his will. Even though the will may have appointed an executor(ix), he/she may, at the time of the descedent's death, be dead or unable to perform due to health or other valid reasons, which would require court appointment of an administrator(ix).

INVESTOR ADVICE

You and your spouse should have a will, regardless of the size of your estate. Where a number of properties are owned, it is very important that the wills be revised after each new acquisition or sale or that instructions be contained within the will to deal with all real estate holdings as a class of assets.

Where considerable property is owned, consideration of a living trust is in order. In the event of death, the remaining trustees could continue to operate the properties without any interference of the probate process. Where the trust is a revocable one, there will be no loss of control of the property in the trust as you, the trustor and presumably also a trustee, can manage the property as if it was titled in your own name.

In setting up a living trust, care should be exercised in the decision to establish the trust as revocable or non-revocable. The revocable feature would allow more flexibility but also keeps the property in an estate taxable position. By setting up the trust as a non-revocable one, estate taxes can be avoided. Consult your attorney before making this very important decision.

SEE ALSO: EXECUTOR(IX), LIVING TRUST, and CLIFFORD TRUST.

ADVERSE POSSESSION

The occupancy of real estate without consent of the title holder. Such occupancy may result in transfer of title to the occupant if continued without owner protest and long enough to meet the state's time requirements.

A claim of title by adverse possession does not require that the occupant reside on the property: Fencing or other acts of possession may suffice.

For a claim of adverse possession to prevail all states require:

- Continuous possession for the required number of years;

- Exclusive occupancy—not shared with the owner;

- Possession must be actual, not constructive; and

- Possession must have been without owner protest.

INVESTOR ADVICE

Investors in real estate must protect their rights to their properties by preventing adverse possession or any attempts at such. This is particularly true of right-of-ways and the establishment of thruways by the public.

> **EXAMPLE** In the case of Shultz v. Atkins, in Utah, the establishment of an easement by perscription indicated that the use of the easement constituted "some actual invasion or infringement of the rights of the owner for a perscribed time."[4]

SEE ALSO: ACTUAL POSSESSION, CONSTRUCTIVE POSSESSION, HOSTILE POSSESSION, and PRESCRIPTION.

ADVERTISING

The act of bringing one's name, company, product or business to public attention. Advertising may be by printed material, radio, television, word of mouth, or any other means that will accomplish the purpose of:

- Promoting the name of the company or product;

- Causing the public to become aware;

- Producing business prospects;

- Creating knowledge and goodwill; and

- Increasing sales and profits.

INVESTOR ADVICE

Real estate investors will have many opportunities and needs for advertising. They may be as simple as a card or sign on the property saying "For Rent," or involve more elaborate and expensive procedures. Maximum profitability can only be achieved by minimum vacancy factors.

You, as a property owner, must determine the most effective and economical means of advertising your property for rent.

SUGGESTIONS FOR LOW-COST ADVERTISING

- When notified that a tenant plans to leave, advise all remaining tenants of the coming vacancy. They may have a friend or relative looking for this type of property.

- Post a notice on all available local bulletin boards found in groceries, drug stores, university book stores, and similar establishments.

- Place a sign on the property.

- Use church bulletins and other free advertising media.

- Advertise by word of mouth.

- Use "Nickel Want Ads" and similar low cost publications.

SEE ALSO: ON-SITE MANAGER.

AFTER-TAX RETURN

This term refers to total income received less expenses (cash and non-cash), less income taxes, divided by the current value of the property. After-tax return differs from after-tax return on (the initial) investment in that the denominator of the equation is *current value* (cost + capital gains).

EXAMPLE

Mr. Byer purchased an apartment house for $100,000. At the end of the first year of ownership he reports the following:

Income from Rents		$16,000
Other Income		500
	Total Income	$16,500
Expenses		4,500
Net Income before Taxes		$12,000
Income taxes		2,000
Net Income after Taxes		$10,000

Return on (initial) Investment: $10,000/$100,000 = 10%

Mr. Byer had the property appraised at the end of the year and determined the current market value to be $120,000. The after-tax return was therefore:

After-Tax Return: $10,000/120,000 = 8.3\%$

The after-tax return is less than the return on the initial investment since Mr. Byer has more invested than he did at the beginning of the year. Now he has his original $100,000 invested plus $20,000 of capital gains.

You should never make the mistake of thinking in terms of the higher return based upon initial investment. After all, if the investment is sold, what would Mr. Byer have in his pocket—$120,000 (assuming no selling costs). Return must, therefore, be calculated on the total investment to date.

SEE ALSO: GROSS POSSIBLE INCOME, NET INCOME, and NET LEASE.

AGENT

A person or persons appointed by a principal to perform specified or general tasks on behalf of that principal. Any person who has the authority to act for him/herself may appoint an agent to act on his/her behalf. The appointment itself constitutes the establishment of an agency.

The power granted to an agent may be general in nature or very specific. The power of attorney to sell an automobile would be an example of a specific agency. The appointment of a property manager would be a general agency.

An agency may be established for any legal purpose. The agent thus appointed has certain obligations to his principal among which are:

- To faithfully perform his/her duties;

- To act as an impartial agent with no personal interest influencing his/her duties;

- To use reasonable skill and care in performance of his/her duties;

- To make full disclosure to his/her principal regarding the facts of all transactions; and

- To operate within the scope of his/her appointed agency.

INVESTOR ADVICE

If you find it necessary to appoint an agent for any reason, you should use care to assure the competence and honesty of the one to be appointed. The agency assignment should not be overly general in nature but limited to a scope that can be supervised and managed by you, the principal. The following is an example of a simple agent appointment.

POWER OF ATTORNEY

KNOW ALL MEN BY THESE PRESENTS, that I, _____, of the city of _____, have made, constituted and appointed, and by these presents do make, constitute and appoint _____ , _____ of _____ , my true and lawful attorney. Giving and granting unto my said attorney full power, and authority to do and perform all and every act and thing whatsoever, requisite and necessary to be done, as to all intents and purposes as I might or could do, if personally present; hereby ratifying and confirming all that my said attorney shall lawfully do or cause to be done by virtue thereof.

IN WITNESS WHEREOF I have hereunto set my hand and seal, this _____ day of _____, in the year of our Lord one thousand nine hundred and eighty-eight.

Signed, sealed and delivered in the presence of

_____

_____   _____
                 (SEAL)

STATE OF   ) SS.
COUNTY OF   )

I, _____, a Notary Public of the State of _____, do certify that _____, whose name is signed to the writing above, bearing the date of _____, has this day acknowledged the same before me. Given under my hand this _____ day of _____, 1988.
My Commission Expires:
                    _____
                                 Notary

SEE ALSO: FIDUCIARY, and STATUTE OF FRAUDS.

AGREEMENT OF SALE

An agreement of sale is a written document and legal contract between seller(s) and buyer(s). It is normally prepared by the agent of the seller, a real estate broker, in the form of an Earnest Money Receipt and Offer to Purchase (often referred to simply as "The Earnest Money"). The broker, in most states is authorized to prepare this legal form, which has been approved for use within the state.

INVESTOR ADVICE

Most earnest money forms used in various states have an admonishment to the signers to the effect, "This is a legally binding instrument. Be sure you fully understand it before signing. If in doubt, consult your attorney."

There are a number of things about the agreement of sale that you must know before attempting to buy or sell real estate.

1. The Statute of Frauds in every state requires that an agreement of sale for real estate must be in writing. There can be no other verbal or otherwise agreement to the sale.
2. The principals involved, buyer and seller, must be competent to sign.
3. There must be a consideration, normally cash deposited in escrow with a broker, pending the closing of the transaction.

EARNEST MONEY SALES AGREEMENT
EARNEST MONEY RECEIPT

Legend   Yes(X)   No(O)

DATE: __November 15, 1988__

The undersigned Buyer(s) __James A. & Shirley P. Homebuyer__ hereby deposits with Brokerage as EARNEST MONEY, the amount of __two thousand and 00/100__ Dollars ($ __2,000.00__), in the form of __Personal Check on Key Bank of Utah.__ which shall be deposited in accordance with applicable State Law.

__Reliable Realtors   487-9944__   Received by _Frank G. Blankenship_
Brokerage   Phone Number   _agent_

OFFER TO PURCHASE

1. PROPERTY DESCRIPTION The above stated EARNEST MONEY is given to secure and apply on the purchase of the property situated at __2425 S.__ __Greenway Dr.__ in the City of __Salt Lake City__ County of __Salt Lake__ , Utah, subject to any restrictive covenants, zoning regulations, utility or other easements or rights of way, government patents or state deeds of record approved by Buyer in accordance with Section G. Said property is owned by __Mavis M. Occupant__ as sellers, and is more particularly described as: __Lot 24, Greenway Subdivision No 1.__

CHECK APPLICABLE BOXES:

☐ **UNIMPROVED REAL PROPERTY**   ☐ Vacant Lot   ☐ Vacant Acreage   ☐ Other _____
☒ **IMPROVED REAL PROPERTY**   ☐ Commercial   ☒ Residential   ☐ Condo   ☐ Other _____

(a) **Included Items.** Unless excluded below, this sale shall *include* all fixtures and any of the items shown in Section A if presently attached to the property. The following personal property shall also be included in this sale and conveyed under separate Bill of Sale with warranties as to title: __Built in__ __bookcases in Family Room, all window treatments as installed.__

(b) **Excluded Items.** The following items are specifically *excluded* from this sale: __Fireplace screen and tools located__ __in upstairs fireplace.__

(c) **CONNECTIONS, UTILITIES AND OTHER RIGHTS.** Seller represents that the property includes the following improvements in the purchase price:

☐ public sewer ☐ connected   ☐ well ☐ connected ☐ other   ☒ electricity ☒ connected
☐ septic tank ☐ connected   ☒ irrigation water / secondary system   ☐ ingress & egress by private easement
☐ other sanitary system _____   # of shares __1__ Company __Olympus__   ☒ dedicated road ☐ paved
☒ public water ☒ connected   ☒ TV antenna ☒ master antenna ☒ prewired   ☒ curb and gutter
☐ private water ☐ connected   ☒ natural gas ☒ connected   ☐ other rights _____

(d) **Survey.** A certified survey ☐ shall be furnished at the expense of _____ prior to closing, ☒ shall not be furnished.

(e) **Buyer Inspection.** Buyer has made a visual inspection of the property and subject to Section 1 (c) above and 6 below, accepts it in its present physical condition, except: __Buyer reserves the right to make a final inspection of the property__ __jut prior to closing and at the convenience of seller.__

2. PURCHASE PRICE AND FINANCING. The total purchase price for the property is __One hundred thousand and 00/00__ Dollars ($ __100,000.00__) which shall be paid as follows:

$ __2,000.00__ which represents the aforedescribed EARNEST MONEY DEPOSIT:

$ __28,000.00__ representing the approximate balance of CASH DOWN PAYMENT at closing.

$ _____ representing the approximate balance of an existing mortgage, trust deed note, real estate contract or other encumbrance to be assumed by buyer, which obligation bears interest at _____ % per annum with monthly payments of $ _____
which include: ☐ principal; ☐ interest; ☐ taxes; ☐ insurance; ☐ condo fees; ☐ other _____ .

$ _____ representing the approximate balance of an additional existing mortgage, trust deed note, real estate contract or other encumbrances to be assumed by Buyer, which obligation bears interest at _____ % per annum with monthly payments of $ _____
which include: ☐ principal; ☐ interest; ☐ taxes; ☐ insurance; ☐ condo fees; ☐ other _____ .

$ __70,000.00__ representing balance, if any, including proceeds from a new mortgage loan, or seller financing, to be paid as follows: __from proceeds__ __of a new loan to be applied for at 1st Federal Savings & Loan after__ __this offer is accepted.__

$ _____ Other _____

$ __100,000__   **TOTAL PURCHASE PRICE**

If Buyer is required to assume an underlying obligation (in which case Section F shall also apply) and/or obtain outside financing, Buyer agrees to use best efforts to assume and/or procure same and this offer is made subject to Buyer qualifying for and lending institution granting said assumption and/or financing. Buyer agrees to make application within _____ days after Seller's acceptance of this Agreement to assume the underlying obligation and/or obtain the new financing at an interest rate not to exceed __11.5__ %. If Buyer does not qualify for the assumption and/or financing within __15__ days after Seller's acceptance of this Agreement, this Agreement shall be voidable at the option of the Seller upon written notice. Seller agrees to pay up to __No__ mortgage loan discount points, not to exceed $ _____ . In addition, seller agrees to pay $ __No__ to be used for Buyer's other loan costs.

Page two of a four page form   Seller's Initials (X)( )   Date _11-14-88_   Buyer's Initials (X)( )   Date _11-15-88_

Figure 1

3. CONDITION AND CONVEYANCE OF TITLE. Seller represents that Seller ☒ holds title to the property in fee simple ☐ is purchasing the property under a real estate contract. Transfer of Seller's ownership interest shall be made as set forth in Section S. Seller agrees to furnish good and marketable title to the property, subject to encumbrances and exceptions noted herein, evidenced by ☒ a current policy of title insurance in the amount of purchase price ☐ an abstract of title brought current, with an attorney's opinion (See Section H).

4. INSPECTION OF TITLE. In accordance with Section G, Buyer shall have the opportunity to inspect the title to the subject property prior to closing. Buyer shall take title subject to any existing restrictive covenants, including condominium restrictions (CC & R's). Buyer ☐ has ☐ has not reviewed any condominium CC & R's prior to signing this Agreement.

5. VESTING OF TITLE. Title shall vest in Buyer as follows: _James A. & Shirley P. Homebuyer as Joint Owners with Full Rights of Survivorship._

6. SELLERS WARRANTIES. In addition to warranties contained in Section C, the following items are also warranted: _Furnace, air conditioner and all kitchen appliances as installed to be in good working condition._ Exceptions to the above and Section C shall be limited to the following: _Warranty to be as of the date of buyer's final inspection._

7. SPECIAL CONSIDERATIONS AND CONTINGENCIES. This offer is made subject to the following special conditions and/or contingencies which must be satisfied prior to closing: _Loan to be applied for by the buyer is to be approved and granted._

8. CLOSING OF SALE. This Agreement shall be closed on or before _December 15_, 19 _88_ at a reasonable location to be designated by Seller, subject to Section Q. Upon demand, Buyer shall deposit with the escrow closing office all documents necessary to complete the purchase in accordance with this Agreement. Prorations set forth in Section R shall be made as of ☐ date of possession ☒ date of closing ☐ other _____

9. POSSESSION. Seller shall deliver possession to Buyer on _December 15 '88_ unless extended by written agreement of parties.

10. AGENCY DISCLOSURE. At the signing of this Agreement the listing agent _Orville C. Jones_ represents (x) Seller ( ) Buyer, and the selling agent _Frank J. Blankenship_ represents ( ) Seller (x) Buyer. Buyer and Seller confirm that prior to signing this Agreement written disclosure of the agency relationship(s) was provided to him/her. (x) ( ) Buyer's initials ( ) ( ) Seller's initials.

11. GENERAL PROVISIONS. UNLESS OTHERWISE INDICATED ABOVE, THE GENERAL PROVISION SECTIONS ON THE REVERSE SIDE HEREOF HAVE BEEN ACCEPTED BY THE BUYER AND SELLER AND ARE INCORPORATED INTO THIS AGREEMENT BY REFERENCE.

12. AGREEMENT TO PURCHASE AND TIME LIMIT FOR ACCEPTANCE. Buyer offers to purchase the property on the above terms and conditions. Seller shall have until _10 AM_ (AM/PM) _11-16_, 19 _88_, to accept this offer. Unless accepted, this offer shall lapse and the Agent shall return the EARNEST MONEY to the Buyer.

James A. Homebuyer	_11-15-88_	141 Cherry St., SLC	272-6730	355-54-1829
(Buyer's Signature)	(Date)	(Address)	(Phone)	(SSN/TAX ID)
Shirley P. Homebuyer	_11-15-88_	141 Cherry St., SLC	272-6730	402-15-1276
(Buyer's Signature)	(Date)	(Address)	(Phone)	(SSN/TAX ID)

CHECK ONE

☒ ACCEPTANCE OF OFFER TO PURCHASE: Seller hereby ACCEPTS the foregoing offer on the terms and conditions specified above.

☐ REJECTION. Seller hereby REJECTS the foregoing offer. _____ (Seller's initials)

☐ COUNTER OFFER. Seller hereby ACCEPTS the foregoing offer SUBJECT TO the exceptions or modifications as specified below or in the attached Addendum, and presents said COUNTER OFFER for Buyer's acceptance. Buyer shall have until _____ (AM/PM) _____, 19 ___ to accept the terms specified below.

Marvis M. Occupant	_11-16-88_	_11:00 AM_	_2425 S. Greenway_	_849-3481_	_265-15-981_
(Seller's Signature)	(Date)	(Time)	(Address)	(Phone)	(SSN/TAX ID)
(Seller's Signature)	(Date)	(Time)	(Address)	(Phone)	(SSN/TAX ID)

CHECK ONE:

☐ ACCEPTANCE OF COUNTER OFFER. Buyer hereby ACCEPTS the COUNTER OFFER

☐ REJECTION. Buyer hereby REJECTS the COUNTER OFFER. _____ (Buyer's Initials)

☐ COUNTER OFFER. Buyer hereby ACCEPTS the COUNTER OFFER with modifications on attached Addendum.

(Buyer's Signature)	(Date)	(Time)	(Buyer's Signature)	(Date)	(Time)

DOCUMENT RECEIPT

State Law requires Broker to furnish Buyer and Seller with copies of this Agreement bearing all signatures. (One of the following alternatives must therefore be completed).

A. ☒ I acknowledge receipt of a final copy of the foregoing Agreement bearing all signatures:

SIGNATURE OF SELLER   SIGNATURE OF BUYER

Marvis M. Occupant _11-18-88_   _James A. Homeowner_ _11-18-88_
                      Date   Date
_____   _____
Date   Date

B. ☐ I personally caused a final copy of the foregoing Agreement bearing all signatures to be mailed on _____, 19 ___ by Certified Mail and return receipt attached hereto to the ☐ Seller ☐ Buyer. Sent by _____

Page three of a four page form

Figure 1 continued

4. The closing agency, broker, lawyer, or land title company can not add or delete any terms not specifically provided for in the agreement, without the written approval of both parties to the sale.

5. The agents involved are limited in their authority to that specifically instructed by their agency appointment or instructions of their principal.

6. An offer to purchase may be withdrawn by the buyer at any time before being accepted by the seller and such acceptance communicated to the buyer.

7. Any addition, deletion, or change to the agreement, made by the seller constitutes a rejection of the initial offer and a counter-offer. To complete the agreement, the buyer must then accept the changes made by the seller.

8. The closing date, contained in the offer, is not absolutely binding on either party; however each is bound to a "best effort." If a specific date must be met as a condition of the sale the offer must state; "Time is of the essence." If the closing is not made by or on the date stipulated, the contract is null and void.

9. The Earnest Money Agreement is *not* the final document closing the transaction; however, once the final closing has been made, the Earnest Money Agreement is said to have been abrogated. Any dispute between the parties after that time can rarely reference the terms of that agreement, except in the case of fraud, hidden defects that a normal buyer would not be able to ascertain, or existence of implied warranty.

10. If the consideration, deposited in escrow, is not in the form of cash, the offer must specifically indicate what form; in other words, personal check, postdated check, personal note, etc.

11. It is not unusual for the buyer to stipulate that the offer is valid only if certain events occur. These events or conditions are normally outlined in the agreement as "subject to." For instance, it is normal to say, "This offer is subject to the buyer obtaining a mortgage." The agreement might also state, "This offer is subject to the buyer's satisfactory final inspection of the property, prior to closing." This latter requirement can assure the buyer that the property remains in good condition, certain required repairs were completed, or that all appliances and mechanical equipment are still in good and serviceable condition at close. Regardless of the wordage of the agreement, it is wise for any buyer to inspect the property just prior to closing.

12. Perhaps the most important caveat concerns the avoidance of ambiguities in the offer. Nothing should be left for interpretation of others. Where any doubt can arise, the offer should clearly state the intent of the parties. A most common problem in this regard is the listing of personal property to be included in the real estate sale. One party considers an item, such as book shelves, to be real estate; the other considers it personal property. A dispute arises when the buyer occupies the premises and finds that the shelves have been removed.

Figure 1 is an example of an agreement of sale properly executed by buyer, seller, and selling agent, who prepared the document and whose brokerage is holding the earnest money in escrow.

SEE ALSO: AGENT, CAVEAT EMPTOR, EARNEST MONEY DEPOSIT, and PERSONAL PROPERTY.

AIR EASEMENT/LEASE

An air easement is created when the owner of a property agrees not to build a structure, of a specified type, height, or location on his land for a specified period, in order to assure a neighbor's enjoyment of sun and air benefits to his own property. This lease may be for a specified period or in perpetuity. Such leases are said to constitute an easement on the owner's property for the benefit of the neighbor.

INVESTOR ADVICE

If you are planning a new building to utilize solar energy, you must assure the continuance of sunshine to the property. In some locations, restrictive covenants prevent a neighbor from obstructing the sun from other existing neighbor's buildings. If such restrictions are not in force, it will be necessary to obtain a light/air easement from those neighbors who have the capacity to obstruct the normal radiation pattern to your property.

Protection from possible obstructions are normally only required in the areas 90 degrees east and 90 degrees west of a true south line, or a portion thereof.

SEE ALSO: AIR RIGHTS, EASEMENTS, and LEASE.

AIR RIGHTS

Air rights involve the right to the use and enjoyment of space above the ground level. In some locations, where land has become extremely valuable, owners of property have found a ready market for unused space above the ground level. These rights sold are usually for such above ground uses as highways or railroads and constitute so-called vertical subdivisions. Several such subdivisions are currently in existence in New York, Boston, and Chicago.

Access for construction and maintenance of supporting pillars and supports are easements on the ground level property.

Air rights can be sold or leased by the owner of the ground, just as in the case of mineral rights below the surface.

INVESTOR ADVICE

Many opportunities for development exist in areas not previously utilizing air rights. If you are looking for an excellent down-town location, where land is very expensive, you may find the leasing or purchase of air rights more competitive than the outright purchase of land parcels.

A good example of such innovative thinking is a situation in New York, where a very desirable property was occupied by an old church. The church members did not have the means to construct a new building nor the desire to give up their prestigious location. An enterprising developer proposed building a new structure on the property to provide a ground-level church and parking facility, with the provision that the space above the site could be vertically developed. The air rights thus obtained were about half as expensive as the outright purchase of a ground site.

> **BUY AIR RIGHTS** They may be more economical than land in the same location.

SEE ALSO: AIR EASEMENT/LEASE.

ALLODIAL SYSTEM OF OWNERSHIP

This term refers to that system of land ownership, prevailing in U.S. law, which recognizes the principle of individual ownership of land, without any proprietary or other control of a government or sovereign. This differs from the ancient feudal system in which the individual was, for services rendered, granted use of land but did not have title.

Although the land owner in the United States may have clear title, the property is still subject to state taxes, the exercise of police power, eminent domain, and escheat. These limitations were established and are enforced for the mutual good of the community as a whole.

INVESTOR ADVICE

In the U.S. most land titles tend to follow colonial laws. Many closely follow old English law. In the Southwest, evidence of old Spanish law is also apparent. Louisiana ownership laws, meanwhile, have their roots in Napoleonic law.

While most private ownership in this country can be traced to grants by monarchs who were responsible for settlement of various parts of the United States, much of Western U.S. private ownership had its beginning in federal grants, mining claims, or homesteads.

Prior to obtaining ownership to any property, it is advisable that you carefully consider how title is to be taken. There is no set right or wrong way to accept title to property, but your financial position, age, and other conditions may dictate *a better way,* based on your attorney's recommendations.

SEE ALSO: EMINENT DOMAIN, ESCHEAT, and POLICE POWER.

ALLUVIUM

This is sand or soil deposited upon land by the action of water flow or wave movement. The building up of land from alluvium is known as accretion.

INVESTOR ADVICE

Several states have established common law practices with regard to ownership of land formed by alluvial action. In Utah, ownership requires that it be shown that the land build-up was gradual and imperceptible. This means that accreation must be imperceptible, although it may be perceptible after a long period of time.[5] Riparian ownership of the alluvian addition, under the doctrine of accretion, results in changes to the original boundary line and the riparian owner acquires title to the addition.[6]

SEE ALSO: ACCRETION, and RIPARIAN RIGHTS.

AMENITIES

Amenities are those tangible and intangible additions to a property that increase its desirability and value. Examples of amenities in an apartment house might be:

1. *Tangibles*—Tennis courts, swimming pool, washer and dryer availability, meeting rooms, and playgrounds.
2. *Intangibles*—Location, public transportation stop nearby, reputation, and management.

INVESTOR ADVICE

If you wish to minimize the vacancy factor on your rental properties and achieve maximized return on investment, it is important that you provide amenities comparable to or better than other properties offered to the public. You should be aware of the fact that the appraised value of a property may be greatly increased over that of a similar property which does not offer the same amenities.

SEE ALSO: ADVERTISING, ECONOMIC VALUE, and PERSONAL PROPERTY.

AMERICAN INSTITUTE OF REAL ESTATE APPRAISERS (AIREA)

This organization is a division of the National Association of Realtors®, founded in 1928. It is the oldest professional appraisal organization in the United States. The AIREA confers two designations upon its members. (1) Residential Member (RM) on those meeting the requirements of the Institute and deemed qualified to appraise residential properties, and (2) Member Appraisal Institute (MAI) for those members qualified to appraise all types of properties.

For many years, only institute members were considered to be qualified real estate appraisers. Now several other appraisal organizations, such as The Society of Real Estate Appraisers and The National Association of Independent Fee Appraisers, have achieved recognizable status with banks and other institutions.

INVESTOR ADVICE

Before purchasing property, you should have a qualified appraisal made for your consideration. In this regard, extreme care should be exercised in the acceptance of values provided by appraisers having no designation, or designation from an appraisal organizations with minimum requirements for award of designations.

Even though the appraiser has a quality designation, it does not guarantee his/her competence to perform. The best assurance of a quality report is by consideration of appraiser designation, your own personal experience and, above all, the recommendations of other property owners, who have used that appraiser in the past.

SEE ALSO: SOCIETY OF REAL ESTATE APPRAISERS, and NATIONAL ASSOCIATION OF INDEPENDENT FEE APPRAISERS.

AMERICAN LAND TITLE ASSOCIATION (ALTA)

An organization dedicated to improved practices and standards in the examination of titles to land. Its membership consists of attorneys and other state approved organizations specializing in title search. Member organizations issue policies protecting both buyers, sellers, and lenders. ALTA lender's policies are more comprehensive in their coverage (see below).

The owner's policy provides for insurance against such risks as:

• Most matters covered in public records;

• Lack of capacity of the parties;

• Lack of authority of parties; and

• Failure to deliver instruments of title.

Risks normally excluded from the owner's policy are:

• Nonpublic record matters;

• Zoning problems;

• Water and mineral rights; and

• Unrecorded mechanic liens.

The lender's policy provides all coverages of the owner's policy plus protection against:

- Unrecorded mechanic liens;

- Unrecorded physical easements;

- Facts a correct survey would reveal;

- Water and mineral rights; and

- Rights of parties in possession (including tenants and buyers under unrecorded documentation).[7]

INVESTOR ADVICE

You are advised to require sellers to provide you with an ALTA owner's policy. Where new buildings are being purchased, it would also be advisable to inquire as to the availability of insurance against mechanic liens.

Where new construction or major modification has recently occurred, it is not unusual for some mechanic liens to be missing from the official records at the time of closing. Most states permit subcontractors 60 days after completion of their last work to record liens representing unpaid bills. Contractors are often provided 90 or more days after completion of their last work to record their unpaid invoices. Without mechanic lien coverage, it is possible that you may inherit unpaid bills of the former owner with little recourse other than making the payments yourself.

To fully understand the term "last work performed" you must realize that this means "the last time the mechanic appeared on the property and did anything." Although the plumbing might have been installed 150 days ago, if the plumber came back and only turned a valve his last work date is considered to be that of his or her last appearance.

SEE ALSO: CLOUD ON THE TITLE, and CONTRACTOR'S LIEN.

AMORTIZATION SCHEDULE

An amortization schedule consists of equal periodic debt payments required to amortize a loan over a given period. For each of these periods the following is shown:

- Amount of each equal payment;
- Amount applied to interest due for that period;
- Remainder of payment applied to principal payment; and
- Balance due after that payment.

EXAMPLE

Mr. Smith borrows $2,000 for home improvements to be repaid in 12 equal payments with 12% interest. This will require periodic payments of $177.70/month to amortize the loan. The amortization table would appear as follows:

(1) Payment No.	(2) Payment Amt.	(3) Interest	(4) Principal	(5) Balance Due
				$2000.00
1	$177.70	$20.00	$157.70	1842.30
2	"	18.42	159.28	1683.02
3	"	16.83	160.87	1522.12
4	"	15.22	162.48	1359.67
5	"	13.60	164.10	1195.57
6	"	11.96	165.74	1029.83
7	"	10.30	167.40	862.43
8	"	8.62	169.08	693.35
9	"	6.93	170.77	522.58
10	"	5.23	172.47	350.11
11	"	3.50	174.70	175.91
12	$177.67*	1.76	175.91	0

*Difference due to rounding.

In the given example, Column 3 is the interest for the period based on the previous balance at the end of the last period. Column 4 is the payment less the interest amount in Column 3. Column 5 is the amount still owed after application of the payment in Column 4.

INVESTOR ADVICE
Substantial savings can be made in the payment of long-term loans by reducing the pay-out period, say from thirty years to twenty years. This, of course, will require slightly larger monthly payments but it is well worth it.

EXAMPLE

A $50,000 loan borrowed at 12% for thirty years requires a monthly payment of $514.31. If the pay-out period is reduced to twenty years, the payment is only $550.54 or $36.23 more per month—a twenty year total of $8,695.94. This additional amount will save:

10 years x 12 payments x $514.31 = $61,717.20

or a net savings of:

$61,717.20 — $8,695.94 = $53,021.26

Recently lenders have begun to offer a new method of payment. This is based upon no monthly increase, but semi-monthly payments of one-half of the monthly requirement. Since some equity is paid in the middle of the month, there is a small reduction in the total interest paid and a corresponding increase in equity payment.

A typical thirty-year loan, if paid semi-monthly can be fully amortized in a little over 20 years—the exact payout period is dictated by the interest rate. Higher interest rates generate higher savings and a faster pay-out.

Where this type of loan payment is offered, the borrower can expect to pay a small additional process charge to compensate the lender for his extra administrative work. A semi-monthly payment loan is usually offered at a lower interest rate as the lender is exposed for a shorter period of time and has a lower risk.

SEE ALSO: ANNUAL CONSTANT, and ANNUAL PERCENTAGE RATE (APR).

ANCHOR TENANT

A major tenant, well known to the public, who is expected to draw shoppers and other tenants to the developed area is an anchor tenant. An anchor tenant may be deemed essential for the initial success of developments such as a shopping center or a professional building. He/she is usually the first lessee in a new development and, as an incentive to lease, is provided more favorable terms/benefits than future tenants.

While the term usually refers to commercial lessees, it can also apply to well known personalities who are one of the first to lease space in a prestigious apartment house.

INVESTOR ADVICE

In planning a new development, you would be wise to delay construction until at least one anchor tenant has been signed. Normally, you will begin the leasing process by soliciting "letters of intent to lease" from prospective tenants. This procedure will perform two worthwhile functions: (1) It will give your sales staff something to crow about until leases are signed; and (2) it will provide prospective tenants a reservation on required space without having to actually sign a lease.

Once one or more attractive anchor tenants are found and sufficient other tenants are assured, firm leases can be signed and construction begun.

SEE ALSO: LEASE, NET LEASE, OVERAGE RENT, RENT SCHEDULE, RENTABLE SQUARE FOOTAGE, and TENANT SELECTION CRITERIA.

ANNEXATION

The addition of real property to a larger unit or municipality constitutes annexation.

INVESTOR ADVICE

When considering unincorporated land for development, it often appears that annexation to an adjacent municipality is a distinct possibility. Where the land parcel lies adjacent to more than one incorporated area, a choice may even be possible.

Your decision to annex the land will be based on several considerations, including:

- Ability to improve services, water, sewer, etc. to your development;
- Salability of the property as annexed versus non-annexed;
- Tax level after annexation versus current taxes;
- Availability of water and other services from selected municipality and their costs;
- Allowable zoning;
- Relative cooperation expected from building approval officials; and
- Potential for tax relief as an incentive to annex to a certain municipality.

EXAMPLE

Mr. Jones has recently acquired a thirty-acre tract of land to be developed into residential home sites. The site lies between two small cities, either of which would be happy to annex the property and acquire the additional tax base.

After reviewing these considerations for annexation, Mr. Jones determines that most of the considerations are equal for the two annexing possibilities; however, city "A" would not be able to offer sanitary sewers. If the property is annexed into city "B," a 1,000-foot sewer trunk-line would have to be installed, as well as sewers within the development.

The cost of the sewer system would be slightly more than the cost of individual septic tank systems for each lot. Mr. Jones reasoned that sewer systems would be more acceptable to builders and would allow him to offer the lots at a slightly higher price. He decided to apply for annexation into city "B."

SEE ALSO: BUILDING CODES, RESTRICTIVE COVENANTS, and ZONING.

ANNUAL CONSTANT

An annual constant is a factor, which when multiplied by the amount borrowed, will show the cost per year for borrowing money. The factor includes the interest rate plus the additional amount required to amortize the loan.

INVESTOR ADVICE

Annual constants are normally quoted to the nearest whole percent. For instance, if the bank charged 9.5% and the loan was taken for a period of *about* 20 years. The annual constant would be quoted as 11% (0.11) and would require about 20 years and 1 month to amortize. The annual constant is no longer used as federal truth in lending laws now require accurate simple interest rates to be quoted to potential borrowers.

Recently, the time required to pay off a loan and the annual percentage (simple interest rate) have become more important. If a constant is mentioned at all, it is usually that figure, which when multiplied by the original loan amount, provides the annual cost of the loan. This constant is called the *annual loan or mortgage constant.*

EXAMPLE

A loan for 20 years at 10% would have the following factors based on method of payment:

Annual—0.11746

Monthly—0.11580

Thus a $40,000 loan at 10% for 20 years would have a monthly cost of:

$40,000 x .11580/12 = $386.00

The amount required to amortize a loan can be easily determined by reference to mortgage/loan tables or by use of any of the small hand-held financial calculators. To use either of these, the following data will be required:

- Amount of the loan;
- Simple interest rate (APR); and
- Time desired to pay off the loan.

SEE ALSO: ANNUAL PERCENTAGE RATE (APR), and MORTGAGE CONSTANT.

ANNUAL EXCLUSION

The amount of federal income tax allowable each year for free gifts. Additional amounts given to any one person or institution are taxable at the current gift tax rates.

INVESTOR ADVICE

Proper estate planning by systematic gifts to others can substantially reduce estate taxes and at the same time distribute assets to those selected to receive them.

As your estate grows, good conservation and planning become increasingly important. Your CPA and/or attorney can you assist in making the proper decisions.

EXAMPLE

Mr. and Mrs. Jones have amassed an estate of several million dollars. They have four children, all of whom are married. Under existing tax laws both Mr. and Mrs. Jones can each make a tax-free gift of $10,000 per person. Thus, by systematic giving, their estate can be reduced by:

$$\$10,000 \times 4 \text{ Children} = \$40,000/\text{year}$$

By also giving like amounts to their grandchildren, their estate and resultant estate taxes can be significantly reduced by the time of their death.

Amounts given in the period three years before death are deemed to be gift "in contemplation of death" and are taxable in the estate of the descendent.

SEE ALSO: ESTATE PLANNING.

ANNUAL PERCENTAGE RATE (APR)

A rate, required by federal law, to be quoted in all consumer loan transactions, APR represents simple annual interest, or:

Annual Interest Charge/Amount Owed

Consumer loans, which were formally quoted as percent/year charged on the unpaid balance, must now also indicate the APR rate. Where the total interest charged on the loan is added to the loan amount, the APR will often be almost double the percentage formerly quoted.

INVESTOR ADVICE

When you review your loan papers at closing, you may be surprised to note the quoted APR to be a rate slightly higher than the mortgage rate. The reason for this is that the lender has charged you a point or two for initiation of the mortgage. Since this is paid at closing, it raises the effective (APR) interest rate.

SEE ALSO: COMPOUND INTEREST, MORTGAGE CONSTANT, PRESENT VALUE OF ONE, and PRESENT VALUE OF $1/PERIOD.

ANNUITY

Annuity is defined as the equal periodic payment of principal and interest for a specified period of time. Thus, a retired person might purchase an annuity from an insurance company which would guarantee a certain payment/month for a specified period of time. In mathematical terms an annuity can be defined as "The Present Value of Dollars/period at an indicated percentage rate for a specified period of time."

EXAMPLE

Mr. Grey deposits $100,000 in the bank at a guaranteed rate of 9%/annum with payments to be an annuity for fifteen years. Using the financial calculator we find the factor (representing $1/period) for such an annuity is:

0.01014

The amount of money deposited will provide a monthly annuity of:

0.01014 x $100,000 = $1,014.27/mo.

INVESTOR ADVICE

A mortgage is nothing more than an annuity payable at the prescribed rate and number of periods. The depositor in this case is the lender, and the payer is the mortgagor. The amount deposited is the present value or initial amount of the mortgage and the annuity is the amount of monthly payment.

A recent lender innovation is the reverse mortgage, which provides a monthly annuity payable to the real estate owner. The amount of the annuity is determined by the value of the property (down payment) and the interest rate payable by the lender. The annuity payments can be a set amount for a predetermined number of years or varying amounts payable until the payments plus interest equal the beginning value of the property.

SEE ALSO: REVERSE MORTGAGE, and PRESENT VALUE OF ONE PER PERIOD.

ANTI-CHURNING RULES

The Economic Recovery Tax Act of 1981 (ERTA) made substantial changes to depreciation rules. In particular it prevented owners of pre-1981 investment properties involving syndication sales activities from using the newly authorized accelerated depreciation methods. Several provisions contained in the act were known as "Anti-Churning Rules."

The Tax Reform Act of 1986 again modified the Accelerated Cost Recovery System (ACRS), bringing new complications for the real estate investor. Many taxpayers are now subject to three sets of rules:

(1) the old system based on "useful life" for properties placed in use prior to 1981 and those covered by the prior anti-churning rules;
(2) The original ACRS rules, which apply to investment properties placed into service after 1980 but prior to 1987; and
(3) The new ACRS rules of the 1986 Tax Reform Act.

INVESTOR ADVICE

Unless you are a CPA or legally trained in tax law, it is advisable that you discuss the tax implications of any purchase or investment in an existing real estate syndicate with your tax advisor.

SEE ALSO: ACCELERATED DEPRECIATION, and REAL ESTATE INVESTMENT TRUSTS (REITS).

APARTMENT BUILDING

A residential building containing three or more units is called an apartment. A structure housing only two units is called a duplex. An "apartment" may also be a land parcel containing more than one building.

INVESTOR ADVICE

Apartments and apartment complexes are normally the highest utilization of land zoned for residential use. The number of allowable units is strictly controlled by local zoning authorities. You are advised to consult your local zoning officials before buying development land or planning new construction.

SEE ALSO: COOPERATIVE APARTMENTS, CONDOMINIUM, DUPLEX, and FLAT.

APPRAISAL REPORT

A written or oral statement of value submitted to a client by a real estate appraiser is called an appraisal report. The report will vary in length depending upon the needs stated by the client. A written report normally contains all facts affecting the value reported, and will have been arrived at by consideration of one or more approaches to value.

Most professional appraisal organizations specify those minimum requirements for classification as a satisfactory report.

The Federal Home Loan Bank Board has also established minimum criteria acceptable for loan documentation by member banks. These criteria are listed in Memorandum R41c, dated September 11, 1986, and later modified. The regulation specifies that each written report must:

1. Be totally self contained so that when read by a third party, the appraiser's logic, reasoning, judgement, and analyses in arriving at a final conclusion indicate to the reader the reasonableness of the market value reported.
2. Identify, via a legal description, the real estate being appraised.
3. Identify the property rights being appraised.
4. Describe all salient features of the property being appraised.
5. State that the purpose of the appraisal is to estimate market value as defined in Memorandum R41c.
6. Set forth the effective date of the value conclusion(s) and the date of the report.
7. Set forth all relevant data and the analytical process followed by the appraiser in arriving at the highest and best use conclusion.
8. Set forth the appraisal procedures followed, the data considered, and the reasoning that supports the analyses, opinions, and conclusions arrived at by the appraiser. The analytical process followed by the appraiser must be presented so that:
   (a) It includes a complete explanation of all comparable data, adjustments utilized in the analysis together with appropriate market support for each adjustment, and;
   (b) It contains descriptive information for all comparable data presented with sufficient detail to demonstrate the transactions were conducted under the terms and conditions of the definition of value being estimated or have been adjusted to meet such conditions; have a highest and best equivalent to the best use of the subject property, and; are physically and economically comparable to the subject property.
9. Set forth all assumptions and limiting conditions that effect the analyses, opinions, and conclusions in the report; however, such assumptions and limiting conditions must not result in either a non-market value estimate or one so

limited in scope that the final product will not represent a complete appraisal. A summary of all such assumptions and limiting conditions must be presented in one physical location within the appraisal.

10. Include a manually signed certification by the appraiser that is similar in content to the following form:

I certify that, to the best of my knowledge and belief:

- The statements of fact contained in this report are true and correct.

- The reported analyses, opinions, and conclusions are limited only by the reported assumptions and limiting conditions, and are my personal, unbiased professional analyses, opinions, and conclusions.

- I have no present or prospective interest in the property that is the subject of this report, and I have no personal interest or bias with respect to the parties involved.

- My compensation is not contingent on any action or event resulting from the analyses, opinions, and conclusions in, or the use of this report.

- My analyses, opinions, and conclusions were developed, and this report has been prepared, in accordance with the standards and reporting requirements of the Federal Home Loan Bank Board.

- I have made a personal inspection of the property that is the subject of this report. (If more than one person signs the report, this certification must clearly specify which individual did, and which individual did not, make the personal inspection of the appraised property.)

- No one provided significant professional assistance to the person signing the report. (If there are exceptions, the name of each individual providing significant professional assistance must be stated.)

INVESTOR ADVICE

You should *never* accept an appraisal that has not been made by a competent appraiser known to you or well recommended, or one that is not complete, as established by minimum criteria of the leading professional appraisal organizations.

SEE ALSO: COST APPROACH TO VALUE, INCOME APPROACH TO VALUE, and MARKET APPROACH TO VALUE.

APPRAISER

One who regularly engages in the business of estimating the value of property is called an appraiser. In addition, there are many who call themselves appraisers and participate in this activity in conjunction with other related occupations. A professional appraiser of real estate is one who is a member of one or more of the major professional organizations, has been certified by that organization(s) as competent to evaluate certain types of property and, in addition, has a minimum of three full years of experience in his profession.

INVESTOR ADVICE

Before hiring an appraiser to perform an evaluation of property in which you are interested, first ascertain that he or she is a designated member of one of major appraisal organizations (AIREA, SREA, or NAIFA). Second, be certain that he or she is certified to appraise the kind of property in which you have an interest. Third, ask for references from people for whom he/she has appraised similar property. Finally, be sure that she/he is familiar with the subject type of property and area in which it is located.

An excellent residential appraiser may not be capable of appraising commercial or income property. A good appraiser may be capable of appraising your type of property but may be unfamiliar with the area in which it is located. Make sure your selected appraiser meets the above four criteria.

SEE ALSO: AMERICAN INSTITUTE OF REAL ESTATE APPRAISERS, NATIONAL ASSOCIATION OF INDEPENDENT FEE APPRAISERS, and SOCIETY OF REAL ESTATE APPRAISERS.

APPRECIATION

Appreciation is the increase in value of real estate, due to inflation, cost of construction, scarcity, increased demand, or other economic factors. Normally, a significant appreciation occurs over a period of time and results in a capital gain to the owner when the property is sold.

INVESTOR ADVICE

It is seldom that you should consider the purchase of real estate unless some appreciation in value can be anticipated—at least an amount to compensate for inflation. Even though the property may be income-producing and possibly offer some tax shelter to other income, that income alone is unlikely to be sufficiently high to justify the financial risk and management effort required.

It is not unusual to see an unsophisticated investor buy real estate that has an after-tax return less than high-grade industrial bonds or even guaranteed certificates of deposit. This type of buyer purchases real estate because someone told him/her that it was a good deal or because he or she knew someone else who did well on investments in real estate.

WHAT PROPERTY SHOULD BE PURCHASED? The property should provide *an after-tax return equal to the bank safe rate plus enough more to justify the additional risk taken and compensation for your time spent in managing it.*

EXAMPLE

Mr. Banks was informed by his real estate agent that a certain apartment house was available at an attractive price. The property was producing about $7,000 clear profit after all expenses and depreciation. The agent indicated that the property could be purchased for approximately $100,000.

Mr. Banks realized that a $7,000 per year annual income on a $100,000 investment would indicate a return of:

$$\$7,000/\$100,000 = 7\%$$

He was currently earning 8% on his guaranteed certificates of deposit.

Mr. Banks also realized that property in the subject area had been steadily appreciating in value. He estimated the value of the property at the end of an assumed five-year holding period would be about $150,000. This would indicate a capital gain of $50,000 that would not be received until the property was sold. He quickly performed an investment analysis, which indicated that the potential capital gain would represent a compound return of about 7% per year and that:

The total return on the investment would be:

Income Return	7.0%/yr.
Capital Gains	7.0%/yr.
Total Return	14.0%/yr.

The extra 6% earned by the investment over his current certificate return would appear to justify the additional risk. He decided to buy the apartment house.

SEE ALSO: CAPITAL GAINS, CASH FLOW, ON-SITE MANAGER, RESERVES FOR REPLACE-MENT, and RETURN ON INVESTMENT.

APPURTENANCES

The incidental rights and values attached to real estate and passed with the land at the time of sale are appurtenances. Such items might include easements on adjacent property, right-of-ways, sheds, barns, and orchards.

INVESTOR ADVICE

You should also be aware that appurtenances can have negative as well as positive value. A barn useful in farming operations would have a positive value, while a barn located on development property and required to be removed for planned development might have negative value.

An old apartment house producing income and located on a lot planned for imme-diate development would have negative value, while the same apartment located on the same lot to be held for a period of time prior to development would have positive value, since it would produce some income during the holding period. Thus what one investor would consider as having positive value, another might consider a negative factor.

In purchasing real estate, you must consider your intended use and timing in determining if appurtenances have real value to you.

SEE ALSO: APPURTENANT EASEMENT.

APPURTENANT EASEMENT

An appurtenant easement is one, usually on adjacent property, which enhances the value of the subject property. An example would be a right-of-way over an adjacent owner's property which increases the value of the subject by providing improved access.

INVESTOR ADVICE

Where appurtenant easements are to be transferred with the property being sold, you should carefully ascertain the length of time that the easement is valid. A right-of-way which vanishes with time may seriously effect the value of the property.

SEE ALSO: APPURTENANCES.

ARCHITECT

A person who designs real estate structures and provides specifications for the project is called an architect. Normally, it is also the architect's job to supervise the construction of the structure to assure conformance with the plans and specifications.

Architect fees are often based on a percentage of the estimated cost.

INVESTOR ADVICE

It is wise to utilize the services of a competent architect in construction of other than small standard structures. A good architect can save you thousands of dollars by assuring contractor conformance with plans and specifications, detecting substandard contractor performance and by prompt issuance of change orders, where and if they become necessary.

WARNING! Architects tend to pay more attention to aesthetics than profitability. Both are desirable.

The architect performs five major functions:

1. Discusses the owner's needs and desires and prepares plans to meet those requirements at minimum cost.
2. Designs the structure to include size and basic characteristics, mechanical and electrical systems, and materials to be used.
3. Prepares construction bid documentation to include drawings, specifications, bidding requirements, and proposed agreements between contractor(s) and the owner.
4. Provides the owner with suggested construction firms to be solicited for bidding, assists in the evaluation of bids received, and the awarding of contract(s).
5. Provides overview supervision of contractors during the construction phase.

Most qualified architects are members of their professional society, The American Institute of Architects. As is the case of real estate appraisers, membership in a recognized society is not complete proof of competence. Before selecting your architect, you should ask for references of his satisfied clients and verify their opinions of his work.

SEE ALSO: CONTRACTOR'S LIEN, CONSTRUCTION LOAN, PERFORMANCE BOND, and RESTRICTIVE COVENANTS.

ARM'S LENGTH TRANSACTION

An arm's length transaction is one between parties where the price represents the normal consideration for the property sold, unaffected by special or creative financing, or sales concessions granted by anyone associated with the sale, and one in which neither of the parties were unduly influenced by any persons or circumstances.

Inherent in this definition is the supposition that the price was paid to the seller in cash. Any other terms or considerations would constitute a sales concession.

INVESTOR ADVICE

As a buyer of real estate, you will often have the opportunity to review property appraisals which will list comparable properties sold. The appraiser should indicate a buyer and seller for each sale and certify that all sales were arm's length transactions. He or she should also indicate the terms of the sale.

????? Was the sales price the real selling price, or did the seller make some concessions?

Where a sale was for other than cash, an adjustment downward in the selling price is required to compensate for terms more favorable than cash.

EXAMPLE

An appraisal includes, as a comparable, a property which was sold on a contract calling for interest on the balance due at 8%. The going rate of interest at the time of sale was 10%. The selling price was $68,000, with $8,000 down and the balance at the end of a set number of years. Loan payments were to reflect a twenty year pay-out.

The owner had, in effect, discounted the selling price by the amount of the interest lost. The amount lost can be calculated as follows:

Monthly payments @ 10%	$579.01
Monthly payments @ 8%	501.86
Lost Interest	$ 77.15

The present value of $77.15/mo for five years, with money valued @ 10% = $3,631. Say: $3,600. The true selling price was not $68,000, as reported, but actually ($68,000 - 3,600) $64,400 on a cash basis.

SEE ALSO: APPRAISER, FAIR MARKET VALUE, and MARKET APPROACH TO VALUE.

ASKING PRICE

Robert Johnsich[8] defines asking price as the original listed price of a property offered for sale. Actually, asking price is more than this narrow definition. It is *the* price asked for a property in the early selling stages. It need not be a realtor listed price, but a price advertised to the public.

INVESTOR ADVICE

Since your desire in selling a property is to achieve a maximum selling price, you should never use the term asking price. It is prima facie evidence that you do not expect to receive this price and are willing to take less. Even if this is a fact, it should not be advertised. Better, you should keep the buyer guessing.

A sophisticated buyer will assume that any price quoted is an "asking price" but cannot be sure. Who knows, maybe the seller has listed the property at his rock-bottom price to encourage a fast sale.

Some investors just assume they can acquire the property at less than the "asking price" and will make a low-ball offer and wait for the seller to make a counter-offer. Where the seller is assured that the buyer is ready, willing, and able to buy, his counter offer will most likely be at his lowest acceptable price.

At best, price negotiations for the purchase of real estate is a "poker game" with each player keeping his cards close to his vest. The buyer tries to obtain the property at the minimum cost, whereas the seller is anxious to obtain the highest selling price possible. As in the game of poker, experience is a great teacher and the longer you work at it, the better negotiator you will become.

SEE ALSO: COUNTER OFFER, FAIR MARKET VALUE, OFFER, and LISTING PRICE.

ASSESSED VALUE

The assessed value is established by a governmental tax authority as a basis for calculation of the actual taxes due. Generally, the assessed value is a percentage of the appraised fair market value; however, some states dictate that the assessed value should be the same as current fair market value. The taxes actually assessed by a board of equalization or other authority is determined by multiplying the appraised value by an assessment factor which is, in turn, multiplied by the established mill rate (cost per thousand of assessed value).

EXAMPLE

The following tax mill rates have been established for all properties in a designated area:

Tax District	Mill Rate
School District	.0091810
County General Fund	.0029160
County Bond Int. & Sink	.0005280
Flood Control	.0003120
Co. Govt. Immunity	.0000170
County Health	.0002510
County Library	.0007200
Co. Municipal Svc.	.0020670
Planetarium	.0000400
Mosquito Abatement	.0000400
Sanitary	.0014950
Water Conservancy	.0004000
Tax Administration Levy	.0005000
Total Tax Rate	.0184670

Property Value:

Land	$ 40,000
Improvements	100,000
Total Value	$140,000

Assessed Value @ 80% $112,000

Total Taxes: $112,000 x .0184670 = $2,068.30

INVESTOR ADVICE

You should never accept a tax assessment without questioning the value established for your property. Tax assessors are seldom able to hire as many appraisers as they need or of a quality that assures accurate valuations. Periodic adjustments to assessed values are often based on cursory exterior inspections of the property or in-office adjustments based on inflation rates in the general area.

> **ASSESSED VALUES ARE NOT NECESSARILY FAIR MARKET VALUES** Check current sales prices against the tax assessments for that property to determine the accuracy of local assessments.

Investment property is often appraised by tax appraisers by use of the "income approach" and assumed rental rates. The condition of your property may be such that you cannot charge the going rate, thus your property is of less value than appraised.

Since tax appraisers are not usually certified as good residential appraisers, it is not unlikely that they will do a very poor job in appraising investment property. As an active real estate investor, you are probably more qualified to establish the current fair market value than employees of the tax assessor.

Most tax authorities notify property owners of the assessed values on their property and the proposed tax to be assessed. This notice is received two or three months before the taxes are actually due. Included on the notice will usually be found a statement similar to the following:

BOARD OF EQUALIZATION

Challenges of the assessed valuation must be made to the County Board of Equalization, 4th Floor, City and County Building, during the time and on a date listed below. Failure to do so, at this time forfeits your right to any relief from excessive or erroneous valuations.
June 2, 9:00AM - 4:00PM
June 4, 9:00AM - 4:00PM

If the assessed value on your property appears unreasonably high and the additional taxes sufficient to make it worth your effort to appeal, the following steps are advised:

• Collect as much current sales data on properties in your area as possible. Your Realtor should be very helpful in helping you gather this data. If this collected data appears to support your opinions:

  ° Have the property appraised by a qualified real estate appraiser.

  ° Take all supportive evidence to the Board of Equalization and present your story.

In some areas, such as Utah, errors in assessment are so numerous and outlandish that a whole new industry has sprung up to serve the needs of property owners. There are several companies that will take your case to the Board of Equalization together with collected substantiating data, including a current appraisal. The charge for this service is usually 50% of the tax savings.

SEE ALSO: AD VALOREM, ASSESSMENT, BOARD OF EQUALIZATION, FAIR MARKET VALUE, and MILL RATE.

ASSESSMENT

The process of determining a property owner's portion of governmental expenses to be levied is called an assessment. This is usually based on the appraised fair market value as of a certain date, multiplied by an assessment factor. This value is then multiplied by a tax rate/thousand (Mill Rate) to determine the actual taxes payable.

Special assessments can also be levied for payment of special projects such as streets, curbs, and sidewalks that supposedly increase the property value. These special assessments are usually based on a cost/front foot of owned property.

INVESTOR ADVICE

It is interesting to note that the assessment process and methods used to calculate taxes payable can be determined in many ways. Regardless of the process chosen, the amount to be raised is dependent upon two more or less fixed factors: (1) By the size of the tax base—the value of property that can be taxed; and (2) by the dollar needs of the governmental agency.

One could use the fair market value of the entire tax base divided into the dollar needs to determine the tax rate per thousand. A simple example would be:

Total Fair Market Tax Base $1,000,000
Governmental Needs/yr. $ 10,000

Tax Rate: $10,000 / 1,000 = $10/thousand of fair market value

Another approach would be to assess all properties at 50% of their fair market value. Using the above situation:

Total Fair Market Tax Base: $1,000,000
Assessed Value @ 50%: $500,000

Tax Rate: $10,000 / 500 = $20/thousand of Assessed Value

In either of the above cases, the taxes payable would be the same for a particular property—$20 x half value or $10 x full value.

When special assessments are made for streets, curbs, sidewalks, etc., taxing authorities normally provide for payment of the assessment over a period of years, say five or more, with a low rate of interest chargeable for those who elect to pay over the extended period. If no interest is charged, the authority might provide an incentive for immediate payment by offering a discount for full payment by specified dates.

> **CHECK BEFORE YOU PAY** If the penalty for slow payment is less than you can make by investing, why not use the assessment money instead of borrowing?

You should never be in a rush to pay special assessments, particularly if a nominal interest charge is applicable. It would be more advisable to invest that money in other worthwhile projects and use the tax money at a no-interest or low-interest rate as long as possible.

A $1,000 assessment bearing no interest and not paid, is an additional income of $100, when money is worth 10% per annum.

SEE ALSO: AD VALOREM, ASSESSED VALUE, FRONT FOOT, and MILL RATE.

ASSESSMENT LIEN

An assessment lien is the official notification of a special assessment due, filed and recorded by the taxing authority as a matter of official record. At the same time, a letter of notification is sent to the property owner at his current official address. When the property is sold, this lien, if not paid, will be indicated in the title search. The seller must pay the lien in full to clear the title or, if permitted by law, it may be knowingly assumed by the buyer.

INVESTOR ADVICE
Insist upon title insurance when buying real estate. Read the title insurance report carefully to be sure that the closing will clear all assessment and other liens or that your assumption of indebtedness is identified as a part of the offer to purchase. Your signature on the closing papers will relieve the seller of any lien obligations not cleared at the time of closing.

SEE ALSO: ASSESSMENT, LIEN, TITLE INSURANCE, and TITLE REPORT.

ASSETS

Resources acquired to assist in accomplishing company goals: such as cash, bonds, stocks, receivables, property etc. are known as assets. In accounting, total assets exactly equals total liabilities plus net worth. In other words, all assets belong to someone, be it the owners, suppliers, or other lenders.

INVESTOR ADVICE

Nothing can be accomplished without assets, which are obtained by work-producing profits and/or finished goods, contribution by owners, borrowing, and delays in payment to suppliers for supplies received.

Your initial investment success will depend upon your ability to acquire the necessary assets. While borrowing may be necessary, it demands a good credit rating evidenced by your existing assets and/or your ability to acquire additional assets through other means.

The old adage, "To make rabbit soup, you must first catch a rabbit," was never more true than when starting a real estate investment portfolio.

> **BEWARE** "No money down" schemes rarely work. Don't believe the fast talkers who sell "Get Rich Quick" books.

There are numerous books and seminars professing to show how to buy real estate with nothing down, minimum down, or 100% financing. All of these schemes are suspect and involve one or more of the following:

- Using seller financing in combination with second mortgage loans;

- Working with appraisals that show the property value to be far in excess of the purchase price;

- Borrowing additional capital by second and third mortgages on current real estate holdings; and/or

- Making false statements to prospective lenders.

Some investors have succeeded in using one or more of the above techniques, but only in a time period of rapid inflation, scarcity of available properties, or other similar circumstances.

Often the use of these techniques succeeds in building a "house of cards" which begins to fall at the first sign of a poor economy or the inability to maintain 100% occupancy in all properties.

SEE ALSO: LIABILITIES.

ASSIGNMENT, AGREEMENT OF SALE

The transfer of a buyer's rights in a fully accepted offer whereby purchase has been accepted by the seller but is prior to the actual close of the transaction constitutes assignment.

EXAMPLE

You make an offer for the purchase of a new condominium under construction and located in a very desirable location. The offer is accepted by the seller and scheduled to be closed when the unit is completed.

Mr. Big hears about the project too late to make a purchase. All units were sold in the first week. Mr. Big offers you a $10,000 profit for your agreement interest. You have your attorney prepare an assignment of the contract to purchase and execute it in favor of Mr. Big. You receive your earnest money deposit plus a $10,000 profit from Mr. Big.

SEE ALSO: EARNEST MONEY, OFFER TO PURCHASE, and TRUST ACCOUNT.

ASSIGNMENT OF CONTRACT

The sale, trade or other transfer of a valid real estate land contract from one owner to another is an assignment of contract.

INVESTOR ADVICE

Real estate contracts can be transferred from one party to another in the same manner as a mortgage. This is a common occurance in the case of sellers, who provide their own financing to facilitate a sale. If you are the holder of a real estate contract and find that you need cash, you can probably find a buyer. Seasoned contracts are usually sold quite easily, but at a discount to provide the buyer with a higher yield than the interest rate cited in the original contract.

Figure 2 shows an example of a typical form used to transfer ownership of the contract.

It is usually not necessary to record this transfer; however, a notice of interest in the subject property should be recorded by the buyer to put the public on notice of his financial interest in the property. You should also notify the contractor of the sale and the address to which future payments should be made.

SEE ALSO: NOTICE OF CONTRACT.

ASSIGNMENT OF MORTGAGE

The act of transferring ownership of a mortgage and note (debt) from one person (assignor) to another (assignee) is known as assignment of mortgage. This transfer has no effect upon the terms, conditions, and amount owed, as originally agreed between the lender and the mortgagor.

INVESTOR ADVICE

You may have the opportunity to trade for or buy an existing mortgage at a price which will yield substantially more than the going rate for new instruments of the same quality. The debt owed is said to be purchased at discount. Such items, when purchased at discount, are like bonds purchased in the same manner. Their yield is greater than the interest rates specified.

When purchasing mortgages, you should closely consider the following:

• Has the mortgagor paid his obligations regularly and on time? Is he up to date in his payments?

• Will the yield on the investment, purchased at discount, be adequate compensation for the risk taken?

"THIS IS A LEGALLY BINDING CONTRACT IF NOT UNDERSTOOD, SEEK COMPETENT ADVICE."

ASSIGNMENT OF CONTRACT

THIS AGREEMENT, made in the City of ......SAlt Lake........, State of Utah on the ...23rd.... day of
...February........., 19.89.. by and between ....Arthur..S...Bowman..

hereinafter referred to as the assignors, and ......Basic..Realty..Incorporated..................................
hereinafter referred to as the assignees,

WITNESSETH:

WHEREAS, under date of ...January..30..., 19 87..., ...Oscar..L...&..Bertha..Sommers...........
...., as sellers, entered into a Uniform Real Estate Contract with
...Mary..A...&..Buford..J...Witosky...,
as buyers, of ...Salt..Lake Utah, which contract is delivered herewith, wherein and whereby the said sellers
agreed to sell and the said buyers agreed to purchase, upon the terms, conditions, and provisions therein set
forth, all that certain land, with the buildings and improvements thereon, erected, situate, lying and being in
the County of .....Davis................, State of Utah, and more particularly described as follows:

Lot 2034 Mountain Heights Subdivision

to which agreement in writing, reference is hereby made for all of the terms, conditions and provisions
thereof, and

WHEREAS, the assignees desire to acquire from the assignors all of the right, title and interest of the
assignors in said property above described as evidenced by said written agreement.

NOW, THEREFORE, it is hereby mutually agreed as follows:

1. That the assignors in consideration of the Payment of Ten Dollars and other good and valuable
consideration, the receipt of which is hereby acknowledged, assign to the assignees, all their right, title and
interest in and to said above described property as evidenced by the aforesaid Uniform Real Estate Contract
of ....Jan..30............, 19 87... concerning the above described property.

2. That to induce the assignees to pay the said sum of money and to accept the said contract, and the
rights obligation pursuant thereto the assignors hereby represent to the assignees as follows:

   a. That the assignors have duly performed all the conditions of the said contract.

   b. That the contract is now in full force and effect and that the unpaid balance of said contract is
   $ 79,456.23.., with interest paid to the ....1st............ day of ....February........., 19.89...
   c. That said contract is assignable.

3. That in consideration of the assignors executing and delivering this agreement, the assignees covenant with the assignors as follows:

   a. That the assignees will duly keep, observe and perform all of the terms, conditions and provisions
   of the said agreement that are to be kept, observed and performed by the assignors.

   b. That the assignees will save and hold harmless the assignors of and from any and all actions, suits,
   costs, damages, claims and demands whatsoever arising by reason of an act or omission of the
   assignees.

IN WITNESS WHEREOF, The parties hereto have hereunto set their hands and seals the day and year
first above written.

_____
ASSIGNORS

_____
WITNESS

_____
WITNESS

_____
ASSIGNEES
Pres., Basic Realty Inc.

Figure 2

ASSIGNMENT OF MORTGAGE

KNOW THAT _Frank H. Arnold_ , assignor, in consideration of $ _10.00_ dollars, paid by _Elmo T. Skuggins_ , assignee, hereby assigns unto the assignee, _Elmo T. Skuggins_ , a certain mortage made by _Jasper T. Jones_ , given to secure payment of the sum of $_50,000.00_ dollars and interest, dated the 1st day of _March_ , 19_85_, recorded on the _2nd_ day of _March_ 19_85_ in the office of the _Recorder_ , of the County of _Salt Lakw_ , in book _101_ , at page _210_ , covering the following described property.

(Insert Legal Description Here)

Lot 224, Evergreen Subdivision

TOGETHER with the note or obligation described in said mortgage and the moneys due and to become due thereon with interest.

TO HAVE AND TO HOLD the same unto the assignee and to his successors, legal representatives and assigns of the assignee for ever.

FURTHER, the assignor covenants that there is now owing upon said mortgage, without offset or defense of any kind, the principal sum of $_38,450.28_ dollars, with interest thereon at _7.0_% per annum from the _1st_ day of _March_ , nineteen hundred _85_ .

IN WITNESS WHEREOF, the assignor has duly executed this assignment the _22_ day of _February_ , 19 _89_ .

Frank H. Arnold
Assignor

State of _Utah_) ss
County of _Salt Lake_)

Before me personally appeared _Frank H. Arnold_ , to me well known and known to me to be the person described in and who executed the foregoing instrument, and acknowledged to and before me that he/she executed said instrument for the purposes therein expressed.

WITNESS my hand and official seal, this _22_ day of February ___ , A.D. 19 _89_ .

Rose M. Schwartz
Rose M. Schwartz
Notary Public

(Notary Seal)

State of _Utah_
My Commission Expires
May 15, 1994

Figure 2 continued

- Did the assignor provide an acknowledged assignment of mortgage, an estoppel certificate signed and acknowledged by the mortgagor, a transfer of casualty insurance to you, all original notes and documentation endorsed to you, and show evidence that the assignment had been promptly recorded?

Figures 2 and 3 show typical forms used in the assignment of an existing mortgage.

Mortgage assignment or sale is a standard procedure in the mortgage industry. Few savings and loans or mortgage companies have the assets to continue lending money without some method of acquiring additional cash.

These institutions usually use their own money to make loans and then bundle them in amounts attractive (several million dollars) to large investors for periodic sales. Typical investors are insurance companies, pension plans and real estate investment trusts. When a bundle is sold, the original lender often maintains the records and services the loans for their buyers. Thus, you may have a loan to a local savings and loan, which is now owned by an insurance company. You are unaware of this fact, as you continue to send your payments to the same place and, of course, none of the original terms have changed.

It is not unusual for a mortgage company to be servicing ten, twenty, thirty or more times the dollar amount of loans that they have in assets. Servicing loans for others can be quite profitable. A fee of 1/2% or more of the balance due, is charged the loan owner each year.

SEE ALSO: CERTIFICATE OF ESTOPPEL, MORTGAGEE, MORTGAGOR, and MORTGAGE NOTE.

ASSUMABLE MORTGAGE

An existing mortgage loan on a property, which can be assumed by a buyer without change in terms of payment, interest, or qualification to assume is an assumable mortgage.

INVESTOR ADVICE

The definition given is the strict definition of an assumable mortgage. There are some variations considered by many as assumable, however these variations do not meet the strict qualifications of the definition. These may include:

- A loan in which the buyer is allowed to assume with existing payment conditions and interest, but is required to qualify to assume; or

- A loan which can be assumed at the option of the lender, who may or may not change the terms of payment and interest.

Many buyers attempt to circumvent the non-assumable provisions of the loan by not informing the lender of the change in property ownership.

This will work only for a short period, until the lender becomes aware of the sale, and immediately triggers the inevitable acceleration clause.

Some will ask, "But what if the seller agrees to pay off the loan, in the event it is called and thus convert the assumption to a contract sale?" This sounds reasonable, but you must consider the possibility that the seller may not have the financial ability to perform at the time the loan is called, thereby putting the ball back into your court.

Most advisors will recommend that non-assumable loans not be assumed.

EXAMPLE

Mr. Ellis purchased Mr. Robert's residence for $125,000. The residence had an outstanding, non-assumable loan in the amount of $75,000 with interest at 8%. The going interest rates on new mortgages were 10%.

Mr. Roberts said he would accept $50,000 in cash and let Mr. Ellis assume the loan—they just wouldn't let the mortgage company know about it. If, for any reason, the loan was called, Mr. Roberts would pay off the mortgage and convert the $75,000 due to a contract.

When Mr. Ellis had the property insurance changed to show him as owner, a copy of the change was sent to the bank, which immediately called the loan for payment. When Mr. Roberts was informed, he stated that it would be impossible for him to pay off the loan at this time. In fact, he was in the process of Chapter 7 bankruptcy.

Mr. Ellis was forced to refinance the property at a 10% interest rate, which increased his payments from $550 plus taxes and insurance of $150/mo. to $658 plus taxes and insurance. In addition, Mr. Ellis had to pay the following fees:

Mortgage Origination Fee @ 1.5%	$1,125
Appraisal Fee	200
Title Policy to Lender	670
Recording Fees	20
Total	$2,015

When Mr. Ellis approached his attorney about suing Mr. Roberts, he was told they could probably win the case, but that it would take a year to get to court and any amount awarded would result in a judgment that probably couldn't ever be collected.

SEE ALSO: ACCELERATION CLAUSE, MORTGAGE, and TRUST NOTE.

ASSUMPTION AGREEMENT

An assumption agreement is one between two parties whereas the party of the second part agrees to assume a debt or other obligation primarily resting with the party of the first part. Assumption agreements are common when purchasing property and existing mortgages are assumed by the buyer. These agreements can also be used to transfer remaining leasehold interests.

INVESTOR ADVICE

Where property is being purchased and existing mortgages assumed, a very careful reading of the mortgage note and/or Trust Deed provisions is in order.

Since 1970 most lending institutions have inserted a "non-assumption" clause in their notes. This clause usually makes the total obligation due and payable upon sale of the property to anyone not specifically approved by the lender. Thus the lender has the option of calling the note due or reaching a new agreement with the buyer—usually at a higher interest rate.

There is seldom a case where the assumption of an existing mortgage action can utilize a standard form. Where an assumption is permitted by the lender, written agreement from that lender will be required before the property can be closed.

SEE ALSO: CONVENTIONAL LOANS, FHA LOANS, LEASE RIGHTS, and VA LOANS.

AUTHORIZATION TO SELL

Another name for a listing, wherein the broker is authorized by the seller to sell the described property for the listed price and terms is authorization to sell. The listing usually provides for payment of the stipulated commission for any sale, during the term of the listing, for any price and conditions for which the owner agrees.

INVESTOR ADVICE

See the suggestions and sample form in Investor Advice under "Listings."
SEE ALSO: EXCLUSIVE RIGHT TO SELL, and LISTING.

AUTOMATIC RENEWAL CLAUSE

This is a clause in a formal lease agreement that provides for an automatic renewal of the lease for a like period, when neither the lessor or lessee notifies the other party of any intent to change or cancel the existing agreement. Thus a one year lease would automatically be renewed for an additional year.

INVESTOR ADVICE

If you should purchase a property in which valid leases are in effect, you should carefully read each lease agreement, in force at the time of purchase, to be certain of actions required prior to the termination of each lease. Failure to recognize automatic renewal provisions may lock you into another lease without an opportunity to adjust rental rates.

The inclusion of an automatic renewal clause is not advised, as this would, in effect, double the time stated in the basic agreement. If some flexibility is desired, wording similar to the following is advised:

POSSESSION AFTER EXPIRATION
It is mutually agreed that should the Tenant, after the expiration of this lease with permission of the Landlord, remain in possession of said premises without written agreement or notification by the Landlord or a change in said rental as to said possession, such possession shall not be deemed a renewal of this lease for the whole term or any part thereof and the Tenant shall be regarded as a Tenant from month to month at a monthly rental payable in advance, equivalent to the last monthly installment hereunder. Moreover, this extended possession, shall be subject to all other terms of this lease.

You should be aware of the fact that some states, that permit extensions of written leases, limit time extensions to the length of the original lease or one year, which ever is shorter.
SEE ALSO: LEASE, MONTH-TO-MONTH LEASE, and TENANCY AT WILL.

AVERAGE

An average is mathematical term defined as the sum of a number of values divided by the number of those values.

INVESTOR ADVICE

Averages are often alluded to in various discussions and represent an indication of what might be expected when considering statistical data. The term is often confused with arithmetic mean.

A typical failure of the average person to fully understand these terms can be illustrated with the following real estate situation.

EXAMPLE

You are considering the purchase of a lot zoned for an office building. Your appraiser cites seven comparable properties sold in the past year and concludes that the subject property is valued at $3.34 per square foot, which was the average of the seven values. The appraiser lists the comparable sales, after adjustments, as follows:

Sale No.	Adjusted Value/ft²
1	$0.50
2	2.50
3	2.60
4	2.80
5	3.00
6	4.00
7	8.00

Your review of the appraisal indicates that the lowest and highest values appear to have been influenced by some situation, for which normal adjustments for differences were apparently not adequate. You also note that the mean value is $2.80, which is considerably lower than the appraiser's value.

The mean value, which strikes out the lowest value and the highest value repeatedly, until a middle value is found, appears more realistic in real life. Single highs and lows can unduly influence averages. Averages can be deceiving.

One is reminded of the cavalry troop traveling across the unfamiliar Western plains. When they came to a river, the captain in charge consulted his map and found that the *average* depth was two feet. Unfortunately, most of the troop drowned crossing the river at a point where the actual depth was twenty feet.

SEE ALSO: MEAN.

ENDNOTES

[1] (1) Mammen v. Snodgrass, 13 Ill. App. 2d 538 (1957). (2) Jackson v. North Western Life Insurance Co., 133 F.2d 111 (N.C., 1943).

[2] (1) Sommer v. Kridel, 378 A.2d 767 (N.J., 1977). (2) Condor Corp. v. Arlen Realty and Development Co., 529 F.2d 87 (Minn., 1976).

[3] (1) Gunther v. White, 489 S. W. 2d (Tenn., 1973). (2) Crockett v. First Federal Savings & Loan Association of Charlotte, 224 S.E.2d 580 (N.C., 1976). (3) Medovi v. American Savings and Loan Association, 133 Cal. Rptr. 63 (1976).

[4] Shultz v. Atkins, 554 P.2d 205 (Utah, 1976).

[5] Utah State Road Commission v. Hardy Salt Company, 26 Utah 2d 143, 486 P.2d 391 (1971).

[6] Hinckley v. Peay, 22 Utah 21, 60 P. 1012 (1900).

[7] B. E. Tsagris, *Real Estate License Examination Study Manual,* State of California Real Estate Division, Sacramento, Calif., 1974, pp. 187-88.

[8] John Robert Johnsich, *Modern Real Estate Dictionary* (San Francisco: Canfield Press, 1975), p. 15.

B

Balance Sheet
Balloon Payment
Band of Investment
Bank
Bankruptcy
Bartering
Base Line
Basis Cost
Bath Designations
Beneficiary
Bill of Sale
Binder Check
Blanket Mortgage
Blended Interest Rate
Blind Trust
Blockbusting

Blue Sky Laws
Board of Equalization
Book Depreciation
Boot
Break-Even Point
Bridge Loan
British Thermal Unit (BTU)
Broker
Buildable Units
Building Codes
Building Costs
Building Residual
Bullet Loan
Bundle of Rights
Buyer's Market

B

BALANCE SHEET

A balance sheet is a financial report listing all assets, liabilities, and net worth (owner's equity).

INVESTOR ADVICE

The balance sheet is one of two important financial statements which indicate the operating condition of a real estate company. It should not be taken as strictly accurate, since it is prepared in accordance *with good accounting practices.* It does not necessarily represent the true value of the operation.

Accounting practices require the following, which distort the true picture:

- Land is carried at cost, but may be worth more or less than that shown at the end of the accounting period.

- Buildings and equipment are carried at cost less accumulated depreciation. Since most operations take the maximum depreciation allowed by law (accelerated depreciation), the book value very often is less than the real value.

- Some equipment may be fully depreciated and not show on the report at all, but will still have value. Thus the value shown is understated.

- Where the accrual method of accounting is used, accounts receivable are carried at full value, but may be worth anywhere from 0 to 100% of the amount shown.

- If the operation utilizes the cash method of accounting, receivables may be due and payables owed, but neither will appear on the balance sheet.

Figure 4 shows a balance sheet for a real estate trust as reported by the accountants. Figure 5 shows a revision of those accounting figures as the result of an analysis by a potential buyer, who has taken the various distortion points into consideration.

BALANCE SHEET

Investors Real Estate Trust

Current Assets		*Current Liabilities*	
Cash	$ 500.00	Accts. Payable	$ 535.00
Bonds	10,000.00		
Total	$ 10,500.00		

Receivables		*Long-Term Debt*	
Supp'r Disc.	$60.00	Mortgage	$ 55,425.00

Land
Apt. Lot $60,000.00

Improvements
6 Unit Apt. $100,000.00

Equipment		*Owner's Equity*	$116,195.00
Appliances	$650.00		
Window Cvrs.	$820.00		
Other	$125.00		
Total	$1,595.00		

		Total Liabilities &	
Total Assets	$172,155.00	Owner's Equity	$172,155.00

Figure 4

BALANCE SHEET

Investors Real Estate Trust (Revised)

Current Assets		*Current Liabilities*	
Cash	$ 500.00	Accts. Payable $	535.00
Bonds	10,000.00		
Total	$10,500.00		

Receivables		*Long-Term Debt*	
Supl'r Disc.	$25.00*	Mortgage	$55,425.00

Land
Apt. Lot $75,000.00**

Improvements
6 Unit Apt. $115,000.00**

Equipment		Owner's Equity	$147,585.00
Appliances	$950.00#		
Window Cvrs.	820.00#		
Other	1,250.00#		
Total	$3,020.00		

		Total Liabilities &	
Total Assets	$203,545	Owner's Equity	$203,545.00

* $35 not collectable
** Revised per Appraisal of J. Banks 10-26-88
# Revised per personal inspection and appraisal

Figure 5

SEE ALSO: ACCELERATED DEPRECIATION, ACCOUNTS PAYABLE, and ACCOUNTS .

BALLOON PAYMENT

A lump sum payment due on a mortgage or other obligation in addition to regular periodic payments is termed a balloon payment. The balloon payment may be the final payment in liquidating a mortgage.

EXAMPLE

You sell your apartment house to Mr. Grey for $100,000, with $20,000 down and the balance payable in equal monthly installments, based on a twenty-year amortization, and with a further provision that the balance be paid in full at the end of five years or less. The interest rate is to be 10%. Your financial calculator shows that an $80,000 mortgage ($100,000 selling price less $20,000 down payment) at 10% interest for twenty years will require a monthly payment of $772.02.

Mr. Grey makes his monthly payments as required and at the end of five years the balance due on the mortgage, as shown on the amortization schedule, is $71,841.75. This indicates that Mr.Grey made total payments of:

$$60 \text{ Mo. } \times \$772.02 = \$46,321.20$$

of which:

$$\$80,000 - \$71,841.75 = \$8,158.25$$

was principal payment and the remainder was interest at 10%.

SEE ALSO: COMPOUND INTEREST, MORTGAGE CONSTANT, MORTGAGE EQUITY TECHNIQUE, and PRESENT VALUE OF ONE/PERIOD.

BAND OF INVESTMENT

A band of investment is a technique utilized by appraisers and investors to determine the weighted rate of return on an income property. In arriving at the overall rate, each source of funds is weighted in relationship to its proportion of the overall investment.

INVESTOR ADVICE

EXAMPLE

Let us assume that an 80% mortgage is available to purchase a property at a rate of 9%. Based upon the risk involved in buying and operating the property, you feel that you must have a minimum return of 12% on invested capital. What is the overall rate that the property must return to justify the purchase?

	Portion of value	Interest rate	Weighted value
Mortgage	80%	9%	0.072
Equity	20%	12%	0.024
Property	100%	Risk Rate	0.96 or 9.6%

Thus, a $100,000 property would be required to produce an after tax return of 0.096 x $100,000 = $9,600.

The band of investment technique can also be used to determine the equity rate of a property with known mortgage and income after taxes.

The preferred and more accurate method of determining the equity rate of return is by analysis of the market. This involves the abstraction of a recapture rate from an observed overall rate.

EXAMPLE

An income-producing property recently sold for $950,000 and produced a net annual income of $103,300.

The remaining economic life of the property is estimated to be 35 years. Land value is estimated to be $190,000. What is the indicated rate of return as shown by this market sale?

Overall Rate = $103,300 /950,000 = .11
Recapture Rate for Building: 1 / 35 yrs. = 0.029
Building Value = $950,000 - $190,000 = $760,000
Ratio of Building to Total Value: $760,000 / $950,000 = .80
Recapture of Building Value: .80 x 0.029 = .023
Investment Rate = .11 - .023 = .087, or 8.7%

If your goal is to acquire a portfolio of investment properties, you should become intimately acquainted with all of the techniques of calculating return versus risk. You cannot rely on others to evaluate prospective purchases as they will either have vested interests in the possible sale or know little about scientific investing techniques.

It has been estimated that few small real estate investors know much about the calculation of investment return. Most just invest hoping for good results, and do so primarily because they know someone who did well with their investments.

SEE ALSO: MORTGAGE EQUITY TECHNIQUE, MORTGAGE CONSTANT, AFTER-TAX RETURN, and OVERALL RETURN.

BANK

A bank is a financial institution chartered by the Federal Government (federal banks) or by one of the various states (state bank) and authorized to perform bank functions. In real estate parlance, the term "bank" is much more liberal and refers to any lending institution empowered to make real estate loans.

This broad definition includes federal and state savings and loans and the many mortgage institutions who use their own money to make mortgage loans and then resell the mortgage package to a secondary source such as the FNMA, GNMA, VA, FHA, insurance companies, and pension plans.

INVESTOR ADVICE

If you are seeking a mortgage loan, your prime interest will be in the rate offered, with a secondary interest in the quality and speed of service offered. You will probably care less about the safety of their depositor's money.

Another very important consideration to you, as a real estate investor, is the percentage of value that the lending institution can loan. Federal and state banks are usually limited to maximum loans of 80% of appraised value. Mortgage companies can probably lend a greater percentage, particularly if private mortgage insurance or government insurance (VA or FHA) is available. The pledged savings approach may also increase the loan/value percentage.

If you are looking for a place to deposit escrow funds and moneys set aside for taxes, insurance, redecoration, and replacement of equipment, you will be primarily interested in the security of your funds and secondarily in the interest rate offered.

Federal banks and savings and loans offer each depositor up to $100,000 insurance on their deposits. State organizations may or may not offer some type of insurance. There is no certainty that state institutions can guarantee the safety of depositor funds in times of a down economy. It is highly recommended that your real estate investment cash be deposited only in federally insured institutions.

When all considerations are evaluated, the ultimate choice of your bank is "the bank that gives you the best service."

SEE ALSO: FEDERAL HOUSING ADMINISTRATION, FEDERAL NATIONAL MORTGAGE ASSOCIATION (FNMA), GOVERNMENT NATIONAL MORTGAGE ASSOCIATION (GNMA), MORTGAGE COMPANIES, PLEDGED SAVINGS, and VETERAN'S ADMINISTRATION.

BANKRUPTCY

Bankruptcy is a legal procedure wherein a person or other legal entity (trust, corporation, or partnership) is protected from otherwise harsh treatment at the hands of its creditors and those creditors, in turn, are protected against additional losses due to actions of the debtor.

INVESTOR ADVICE

If you contemplate leasing a property to someone or providing financing for a property to be sold, you would normally ascertain the buyer or lessee's personal character and financial status. This can be done with credit bureau checks and/or examination of qualified (audited) personal financial statements or personal income tax returns filed with the IRS.

The following is a list of indicators of potential credit problems:

- A record of bankruptcy within the past 7 years.

- A credit history indicating "slow to pay";

- Evidence of judgments filed and currently unsettled; and/or

- Statements of former landlords indicating unsatisfactory tenancy.

SEE ALSO: LEASE RIGHTS, TENANT SELECTION CRITERIA, and VACANCY FACTOR.

BARTERING

Bartering is a method of obtaining desired properties in exchange for other properties or services, without the expenditure of significant amounts of money.

INVESTOR ADVICE

The Tax Reform Act of 1986 left intact the previous laws concerning property exchanges. This provision allows the effective sale of a property with large capital gains while delaying taxes on those gains.

When investment property is traded, the gains in the old property reduce the base cost of the new property. Thus taxes will not have to be paid until the new property is sold.

EXAMPLE

You purchased an apartment house in 1960 for $50,000 and in 1987 you traded this property for a warehouse worth $500,000. The seller of the warehouse took your apartment, now appraised for $100,000 and carried back a purchase mortgage for $400,000.

Your base cost for the warehouse will be the $500,000 purchase price less your capital gains in the apartment ($100,000 - $50,000 paid) or $450,000.

Had you sold the apartment outright, you would have had a minimum tax bill, under the 1986 tax law, of:

$$28\% \times \$50,000 = \$14,000$$

This delay of the $14,000 tax obligation, if invested at 10% will produce $1,400 of additional investment income/year —$1,064 after taxes.

Please note, you have not avoided this tax, but merely made it payable at some time in the future. However, if the property is disposed of in the future, no tax will be due at that time if, once again, the property is traded. Taxes on capital gains are payable only when cash or its equivalent is received.

SEE ALSO: BASIS COST, CAPITAL GAINS, EXCHANGE, and FUTURE VALUE OF ONE/PERIOD.

BASE LINE

An imaginary east-west line used by surveyors in locating property by the rectangular or government survey method is called a baseline. This method was adopted by the Federal Government in 1785 and is the primary method of property identification west of the Mississippi River.

INVESTOR ADVICE

If you are planning to purchase tracts of land for investment purposes, it would be helpful to be conversant with the rectangular survey nomenclature.

Land parcels described by this method are referenced to a named base line (east-west) and meridian (north-south).

EXAMPLE

A property might be described as:

All of section 27, Township 1E, Range 2S,
Salt Lake Base and Meridian.

This indicates that it is a parcel of land one mile square (a full section) containing 640 acres and located in the first township east of the meridian and two townships south of the base line.

A township contains thirty-six sections, as indicated in Figure 6. Smaller parcels may be described in a similar manner but with other descriptive additions such as:

S 1/2, NE 1/4, NE 1/4, Sect 27,
T 1E, R 2S, SL Base & Meridian

This description would outline a twenty-acre parcel, located in the NE quarter of the described section 27. To locate the parcel, we would first divide the section into quarters, then divide the NE quarter of that section once again into quarters and lastly this "quarter of a quarter" in half from north to south.

The described parcel is the south half of this last subdivision. Figure 7 shows this twenty acre parcel.

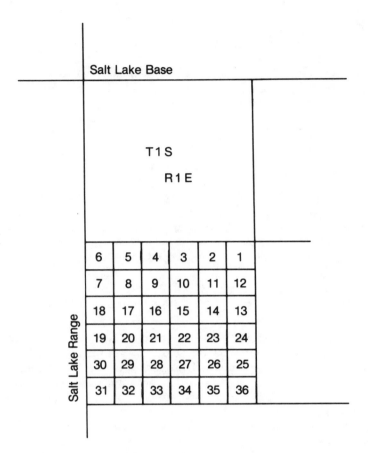

Figure 6

Section 27

NW ¼	
SW ¼	SE ¼

Figure 7

SEE ALSO: MERIDIAN, and RECTANGULAR SURVEY.

BASIS COST

The value of real property for tax purposes is termed basis cost. This is normally computed as the purchase price, plus improvements, less accumulated depreciation taken. In some cases, where accelerated depreciation methods have been employed, all depreciation over and above straight-line will be recaptured if the property is sold before it is completely depreciated.

INVESTOR ADVICE

EXAMPLE

Mr. Brown purchased an office building in 1985 for $125,000. Shortly after its purchase, he built new carports for each apartment and paved the driveway. The cost of this addition was $30,000. During the holding period, Mr. Brown took $7,500 depreciation on the original structure and $3,000 on the improvements.

In 1988, he sold the apartment complex for $175,000. What is Mr. Brown's cost basis for calculating long-term capital gains?

$$\$125,000 + \$30,000 - (\$7,500 + \$3000) = \$144,500 \text{ Basis Cost}$$

You must keep complete and accurate records of all improvements made to investment properties, as well as depreciation taken for tax purposes. Normal maintenance costs do not increase the cost basis. Even better, normal maintenance expenses can be written off in the year in which the work is accomplished. The addition of aluminum siding would be an example of an improvement, not maintenance. The cost of the siding must be depreciated over an applicable period.

Because of this tax provision, you may wish to carefully consider the timing on some required maintenance jobs. For instance, to repaint a building would be an expense and immediately tax deductible. If this work is completed in December, your tax could be reduced for the current year. If the job is delayed until January, you could not recover the tax savings for almost a year.

SEE ALSO: IMPROVEMENTS, and NORMAL MAINTENANCE.

BATH DESIGNATIONS

Residential real estate advertisements indicate the number of baths, in what has become more or less a standard manner. Bath designations in most areas of the U.S. are as follows:

Full Bath—A room containing a tub (with or without a shower), commode, and lavatory.
3/4 Bath—A room containing a shower stall, commode, and lavatory.
1/2 Bath—A room containing a commode and lavatory.

If the advertisement contains a "+" after a bath designation, it usually means something extra—double lavatory, jacuzzi tub, or, in the case of a full bath, both tub and shower stall.

INVESTOR ADVICE

Residences without adequate baths will seriously restrict the potential income and salability of the property. Usually homes or apartments with inadequate bath facilities are considered as functionally obsolescent. It is rarely possible to correct such deficiencies due to limited space originally provided for the bath facilities. Bathrooms are also very expensive to remodel because removal of the old is often necessary prior to construction of the new. It is not unusual for remodeled baths to cost two to three times that of the same facility in new construction.

In spite of the cost of modernizing old baths or adding new ones, this expense can usually be justified by the increased value of the property and the ability to raise rents sufficiently to help alleviate the expense.

When considering the purchase of older residential properties as an investment, you must carefully consider the bath situation and the potential need for modernization. You should also check the current plumbing codes. The modernization may have to extend well beyond the bathroom area in order to meet current codes.

SEE ALSO: CONSTRUCTION PERMIT, ECONOMIC OBSOLESCENCE, and FUNCTIONAL OBSOLESCENCE.

BENEFICIARY

A benficiary is:

(1) One who is designated to receive the proceeds or benefits derived from something, such as a trust or will; or

(2) The lender designated in a Trust Deed.

INVESTOR ADVICE

When you elect to place income property in a trust, the trust instrument (prepared by your attorney) will indicate who is to receive the income generated by the trust property.

Based upon your individual tax situation, you may elect one of several designations, some of which are as follows:

- Designate yourself as beneficiary of income;

- Designate your children, parents, or others as beneficiaries; and/or

- Require income to be accumulated in the trust for reinvestment.

The establishment of testamentary trusts, which are initiated after death of the trustor, are usually for the purpose of providing proper management of assets. Beneficiaries of this trust may be the surviving spouse or others. The trust may also provide for the eventual demise of the trust and designate certain individuals as "remaindermen" to receive the assets of the trust.

SEE ALSO: MORTGAGE, MORTGAGOR, TRUST, TRUSTEE, TRUSTOR, TRUST DEED, and REMAINDERMEN.

BILL OF SALE

An official document transferring personal property to another is termed a bill of sale.

INVESTOR ADVICE

When you purchase or sell real estate, it is normal to transfer certain personal property to the new owner. In the case of an apartment house, these items might be carpets, draperies, appliances, etc. In the sale of land, it might be unharvested crops.

To avoid any uncertainties or legal questions in the future, you should be sure that all clearly personal items and any other items that could be considered personal by either party are officially transferred to the new owner by a bill of sale. This document

𝔅ill of 𝔖ale

(WITH WARRANTIES)

𝔎now all 𝔐en by 𝔗hese 𝔓resents:

That ....Elias M. Howe..

....

the SELLER , for and in consideration of the sum of:

............Ten..DOLLARS

to .... in hand paid by ....James L. Morrison...........................

....,

the BUYER , the receipt whereof is hereby acknowledged, has   bargained, sold, assigned
and transferred, and by these presents do   bargain, sell, assign and transfer unto said
BUYER   that certain personal property now at

........4498 S. Morning Drive, Salt Lake City, Utah.................................

.......Salt Lake.................................... County, State of .....Utah................................,

particularly described as follows:

        1 Kelvinator Refrigerator
        1 RCA Gas Range
        1 RCA Disposall
        1 Sears Water Softener
        2 Sets for Fireplaces
        1 Set Bookshelves

    And the Seller   upon the consideration recited above warrants ownership of and good title
to said property, the right to sell the same and that there are no liens, encumbrances or charges
thereon or against the same and to defend the title and possession transferred to the BUYER
against all lawful claims.

    In Witness Whereof,   have hereunto set his   hand   this
.......22nd..... day of .....February....................., 19..89

                Witness: _Elias M. Howe_

    Mary Stubbins

Figure 8

is just as important as the deed to the real property. Problems occur in the understanding of the definition of personal property. One person may think of certain items as real estate, while another would consider it personal property.

> **DON'T FORGET** The bill of sale is the only proof of ownership for personal property. Demand it when you buy: Give it when you sell.

The law defines real estate as the land plus all other things *attached with intent to remain.* It is this item of intent that is often in dispute. You might have thought an item was attached with intent to remain, while the other party did not. Be safe. Spell out your intentions in the offer to purchase and include all personal items in a bill of sale.

If those personal items to be transferred with the real estate are clearly defined in the earnest money document, the closing authority will automatically include them on a bill of sale, similar to that shown in Figure 8. This will be signed by the seller at the closing and give you official title to the items listed.

SEE ALSO: CHATTELS, CHATTEL MORTGAGE, PERSONAL PROPERTY, and REAL ESTATE.

BINDER CHECK

A binder check is one to be deposited as earnest money to bind an offer to purchase. The check can be written on a personal account, a business account, or be a certified bank draft.

INVESTOR ADVICE

The REALTOR®, accepting a check as earnest money, must assure that the seller is aware of the type of earnest money proffered. In fact, he or she should spell out the earnest money type in the written language of the offer. In the event the check is not honored by the bank upon which it is drawn, the seller and buyer must be promptly informed in order that the discrepancy can be quickly corrected or the deal cancelled.

While cash or a cashier's check would be preferable to a brokerage, it is unusual for a buyer to carry that kind of money with him/her, when he/she goes in search of property. Normally, the buyer deposits *a check* with the selling broker, which is drawn on the buyer's personal account or that of his or her company.

Remember, it is the REALTOR'S® duty to notify both buyer and seller of the type of earnest money received by him/her for deposit in the realtor's escrow account. The REALTOR® does not certify in the earnest money agreement that the check is good, but only that it was received by him/her for prompt deposit in his/her trust account. The REALTOR® has a duty to inform both parties to the contract if the check is subsequently determined to be valueless and the contract in jeopardy.

It is quite possible that when a check has been proffered as a binder and subsequently found worthless, financial damages could have been suffered by the seller. Damages for such redress could be sought through the courts.

In real estate law, the selling agent has earned his/her fee for bringing a "willing buyer and seller together." Although it is standard procedure for the commission to be paid at the closing, the money due was earned when both signatures were placed on the earnest money agreement.

A failed sales leaves the seller liable for the commission. He also may have lost another good buyer during the time taken to determine that the earnest money check was bad—a substantial total loss.

SEE ALSO: CONTRACT, EARNEST MONEY AGREEMENT, OFFER TO PURCHASE, and TRUST ACCOUNT.

BLANKET MORTGAGE

A blanket mortgage, sometimes referred to as a general mortgage, is one covering more than one property. It may even cover all properties owned by a mortgagor.

INVESTOR ADVICE

When borrowing money every effort should be made to avoid a blanket mortgage. The transfer of any of the properties so covered becomes most difficult, as the mortgage appears as a lien on them. While it is possible to sell a property so covered, it can only be accomplished by agreement of the lender and the filing of appropriate mortgage release documents. In some cases, the lender may demand partial payment on the mortgage prior to providing the required release, particularly where the lender feels that his or her security for the loan is diminished by the sale of the subject property.

Blanket mortgages are common in the purchase of land for development purposes; however, the sale of developed lots can be expedited by a lot release clause in the trust note. This clause provides for an automatic release of lien on a lot by payment of a stipulated amount to the mortgage holder.

SEE ALSO: LIEN, LOT RELEASE SYSTEM, MORTGAGE, and TRUST NOTE.

BLENDED INTEREST RATE

A blended interest rate is the effective interest rate paid on two or more mortgages on the same property.

EXAMPLE

You purchase a property for $100,000, which has an existing assumable first mortgage of $50,000 at 8.0% interest. In order to acquire the property, you will require an additional $20,000 loan and request this from the first mortgage lender.

After having the property appraised, the lender determines that his or her institution can increase its commitment on the property to the required $70,000 if an overall or blended rate of 10% can be obtained. What interest rate must the second mortgage of $20,000 bear if a blended rate of 10% is to be obtained?

```
Given:
1st Mortgage =  $50,000/$70,000 = .7143 of total
2nd Mortgage = $20,000/$70,000 = .2857 of total

.7143 x Rate of 8.0%    =    .0571
.2857 x Rate (2nd Mtg)  =   .0429  (.1000 - .0571)
100% of Mtg.            = 10% rate

Solving for the 2nd Mortgage Rate, we have:
.2857 x Rate = .0429
Rate = .0429/.2857 = .1502 or 15.02%
        Say: 15%
```

INVESTOR ADVICE

A blended interest rate is often more advantageous than canceling an old mortgage and obtaining a new one for the total cash required. If the existing lender is not willing to advance the required additional funds at a blended rate, you should explore the possibilities of a second mortgage with another lender who is willing to assume the old loan and grant a second or piggy-back loan for the additional required funds.

This action will accomplish the desired objective and result in one payment to one agency at a blended interest rate, which preserves the old (advantageous) interest rate on the first mortgage loan.

SEE ALSO: SECOND MORTGAGE.

BLIND TRUST

A blind trust is one which contains assets of a trustor, and is managed by trustees who take no direction from the trustor.

INVESTOR ADVICE

Public officials, having control of legislative and other regulatory bodies or having the ability to influence procurement policy, often use the blind trust procedure to prevent any real or apparent conflict of interest.

Once the assets are in trust, the owner (trustor) no longer has any control over the assets until such time as the trust is vested to the original owner. The trustees are empowered to buy, sell, trade, and manage these assets until such time as the trust is abolished. The trustor, who establishes the trust has no power or influence over the trustee's decisions.

EXAMPLE

Mr. Big was appointed by the governor of his state as State Highway Commissioner. The commission was, at the time, actively planning a new freeway to the south of Capital City. One of the potential routes would go through property owned by Mr. Big. The highway would substantially increase the value of the property.

Mr. Big placed his property in a blind trust to avoid any potential conflict or apparent of interest. The trust would be in effect until such time as Mr. Big ceased to be the State Highway Commissioner.

SEE ALSO: INTER VIVOCE TRUST, and TRUSTEE.

BLOCKBUSTING

Blockbusting is a procedure in which an organization will acquire, or assist a person or group of persons to acquire, property in a high income neighborhood that normally would not be attainable to those persons, based upon their own financial ability.

The introduction of lower income persons into the neighborhood causes all other property values in that neighborhood to decline. This process is usually undertaken in residential areas, where the occupant-owners are very meticulous in the selection of their neighborhood.

INVESTOR ADVICE

You should avoid buying property in a location where blockbusting has occurred or is in the process of occuring. Similarly, extreme care must be exercised in selection of tenants for apartments for two reasons:

(1) You cannot afford to have an occupant who may cause a mass exodus at the first opportunity, and

(2) You must be careful that your selection practices do not violate the Fair Housing statutes.

You may reject an applicant where you have information which would indicate a financial inability to carry out the terms of the lease or where prior landlords have indicated the tenant failed to properly care for the property. You may not reject a tenant solely on the basis of race or national origin.

SEE ALSO: LEASE RIGHTS, NUISANCE RENT RAISE, and TENANT SELECTION CRITERIA.

BLUE SKY LAWS

Laws enacted by the various states to regulate the sale of securities are called blue sky laws. These laws are subordinate to and supplement federal laws enforced by the Securities Exchange Commission (SEC).

INVESTOR ADVICE

State blue sky laws and federal security regulations have been enacted to protect the public. In the real estate industry these regulations are applicable to investment corporations, limited partnerships, and real estate investment trusts.

Should you contemplate initiating any of the above, it is imperative that you seek the advice of legal counsel, familiar with both state and federal requirements.

In preparing your prospectus and/or advertising brochures, you must make sure that no breech of federal or state laws occur. You will also want to organize the operation in such a way that your investors will be able to minimize personal income taxes on their investment.

SEE ALSO: CORPORATIONS, LIMITED PARTNERSHIPS, PARTNERSHIPS, and REAL ESTATE INVESTMENT TRUSTS.

BOARD OF EQUALIZATION

The board of equalization is the official organization within a county, which sits to hear appeals of property owners who feel their property has been incorrectly assessed.

INVESTOR ADVICE

You are probably the best authority on the value of your own property. If you receive a notification of assessment which appears to be too high relative to other properties in the area, you have the right to appeal to the board of equalization.

The time allowed for appeals and the manner of appeal is strictly controlled. Your tax notice will indicate your right to appeal any assessment which you deem unfair. This right is indicated on the official notice in more or less the following manner:

BOARD OF EQUALIZATION

Challenges of the assessed valuation must be made to the County Board of Equalization, 4th Floor, City and County Building, during the time and on a date listed below. Failure to do so at this time forfeits your right to any relief from excessive or erroneous valuations.

June 2, 9:00AM - 4:00PM
June 4, 9:00AM - 4:00PM

SEE ALSO: ASSESSED VALUE.

BOOK DEPRECIATION

Book depreciation differs from real depreciation in that it is the total of all depreciation taken for tax purposes and carried on the books as a liability off-set to asset purchased value.

EXAMPLE

Under ARCS rule, you have taken, as an expense of doing business, $40,000 in depreciation against an improvement which cost $100,000. The book depreciation therefore, is $40,000 and the basis cost of that improvement has been reduced by that depreciation amount. Your books now show the basis cost to be:

$$\$100,000 - \$40,000 = \$60,000$$

This does not mean that the improvement is four-tenths worn out ($40,000/$100,000). In actuality, it may be almost as good as new.

INVESTOR ADVICE

In the example, the base cost was indicated to be $60,000. This is not necessarily the base cost for tax purposes. Where property is sold before being fully depreciated, depreciation taken over and above straight-line may be subject to recapture.

EXAMPLE

You purchased a certain piece of equipment in 1985 for $10,000. IRS regulations sets a ten-year lifetime for this type of equipment. You sell the equipment in 1988. Accelerated depreciation at that time was $5,000. How much of this value must be recaptured in calculating basis cost? What is the correct tax basis cost?

Straight Line Dep./yr = $10,000/10 = $1,000
Allowable for period held = $1,000 x 3 = $3,000
Recapture Amount = $5,000 — $3,000 = $2,000
Tax Basis = $10,000 — $3,000 = $7,000

Any amount received for the sale, in excess of $7,000, would be treated as a capital gain.

Where other than straight-line depreciation has been taken, tax implications should be considered prior to signing the sales agreement.

SEE ALSO: ACCELERATED COST RECOVERY, ACCELERATED DEPRECIATION, BASIS COST, and STRAIGHT-LINE COST RECOVERY.

BOOT

That extra something of value received as an incentive to make a trade is called a boot. In tax language it is anything given or received which cannot be considered as "like property."

INVESTOR ADVICE

Any boot received in a transaction, whether it be cash, loan relief, other property, or anything of value is considered as taxable gain, under Section 1031 of the IRS code.

EXAMPLE

Mr. Farmer trades his farm, with a basis cost of $200,000, for an office building in town. The office building was appraised for $225,000. The trade provided for the new owner of the farm to assume an existing mortgage of $15,000. Under current IRS regulations the value of the mortgage assumed (an assumption of a liability) is considered as boot. What is Mr. Farmer's realized taxable gain?

Value of Property Received	$225,000
Mtg. on Property Exchanged	15,000
Total Consideration	$240,000
Less: Cost basis	200,000
Taxable Gain Realized	$ 40,000

You should be aware of these tax implications in the sale of property. If a property is sold and the new owner assumes the existing loan, you are considered to have received cash equal to the amount of the loan assumed and from which you have been relieved of all liability.

SEE ALSO: ASSIGNMENT OF MORTGAGE, ASSUMABLE MORTGAGE, MORTGAGE, and TRADE OF PROPERTY.

BREAK-EVEN POINT

The break-even point is the point in time where increasing income from an investment property equals the operating expenses. The break-even point is most often expressed in terms of cash flow rather than actual profitability. When actual profitability is considered, that portion of the monthly mortgage payment which reduces the debt would also be considered as income.

INVESTOR ADVICE

In analyzing the profitability of a new project through pro-forma calculations, the point in time at which the project breaks even is very important. Until that point is reached, the investor must continue to pump funds into the investment or take funds from previously set aside reserves.

A new project, whether it be an apartment house, a shopping center, an industrial center, or almost any other income-producing entity, cannot be expected to be profitable from day one. Generally, some time will be required to reach 100% occupancy.

You should expect problems in this regard and not be too surprised when the projected break-even point is not on schedule. A contingency plan should be made for just such an event.

Figure 9 illustrates the pro-forma statement of a typical apartment project. You will note that the operation does not reach a break-even point (profit) until the fourth quarter of 1988, although a slight profit is made the prior quarter.

Perhaps a more important revelation is the break-even point in cash flow—the place where the income will cover the out-of-pocket expenses. You will note that this occurs in the second quarter of 1988 and before real profitability. The reason for this is that one expense, depreciation, is a non-cash expense.

SEE ALSO: CASH FLOW, DATE OF POSSESSION, DEBT SERVICE, NON-CASH EXPENSE, and TRIPLE NET LEASE.

PROFORMA INCOME ANALYSIS
Brookside Apartments

	1988				1989			
	1st Qtr	2nd Qtr	3rd Qtr	4th Qtr	1st Qtr	2nd Qtr	3rd Qtr	4th Qtr
Rental Income	1,000	3,000	6,000	8,000	10,000	12,000	12,000	12,000
Expenses								
Taxes	1,000	1,000	1,000	1,000	1,000	1,000	1,000	1,000
Lights, Common Areas	100	100	100	100	100	100	100	100
Yard Maintenance		120	120	60		120	120	60
On-Site Management	600	600	600	600	600	600	600	600
Snow Removal	100				100			
Insurance	1,000	1,000	1,000	1,000	1,000	1,000	1,000	1,000
Depreciation	3,125	3,125	3,125	3,125	3,125	3,125	3,125	3,125
Total Expense	5,925	5,945	5,945	5,885	5,925	5,945	5,945	5,885
Profit	(4,925)	(2,945)	55	2,115	4,075	6,055	6,055	6,115
Add Back Non-Cash Exp (Dep)	3,125	3,125	3,125	3,125	3,125	3,125	3,125	3,125
Cash Flow	(1,800)	180	3,180	5,240	7,200	9,180	9,180	9,240

Figure 9

BRIDGE LOAN

A bridge loan is an intermediate loan to provide funds on a temporary basis for new construction, rehabilitation of an existing project, addition of new units, or similar needs. This type of loan is usually taken for a relatively short term, say less than two years. The bridge loan is repaid when permanent long-term financing is provided or the property is sold.

INVESTOR ADVICE
Intermediate loans may make good sense in several cases, such as:

- The project is expected to be sold at the conclusion of new additions or remodeling.

- The current mortgage situation is very tight and it is expected that better rates will be available in a few months.

- Time is needed to get a new addition completed and fully rented, thus presenting a better risk to a lender at that later date.

- You need immediate funds to rehabilitate a property prior to placing it on the market for sale.

- A number of existing leases will expire in the near future. A bridge loan will allow for time to acquire new leasing at higher rates thereby presenting a better financial picture to a long-term lender.

- A need exists to free locked-in equity for other short-term purposes, or until the property can be sold or traded.

SEE ALSO: CONSTRUCTION LOAN, MORTGAGE COMPANIES, and SECOND MORTGAGE.

BRITISH THERMAL UNIT (BTU)

A British thermal unit is a unit of heat equal to 252 calories or the amount required to raise the temperature of one pound of water one degree Fahrenheit. The capacity of mechanical heating and cooling equipment is often quoted in BTU's or BTU's/hour.

INVESTOR ADVICE
While capacity to provide or remove a number of BTU's per hour is important, you would be wise to inquire as to the energy efficiency of any mechanical heating or cooling device. One air conditioner of a certain size may use 50% more electricity than another having the same capacity.

Normally, the higher the efficiency of the unit, the more it costs. A higher cost may be justified if the pay-back period from decreased fuel consumption is attractive.

SEE ALSO: ECONOMIC OBSOLESCENCE, ECONOMIC LIFE, and PAY- BACK PERIOD.

BROKER

A person licensed by the state, to list, sell, and lease real estate is called a broker. The broker hires and supervises the activities of real estate agents licensed to him or her, maintains a trust fund for escrow moneys deposited to blind sales contracts, collects all commissions earned by the agency, and pays his/her agents in accordance with the broker/agent agreement. A broker is fully responsible for the action of all agents licensed to him/her.

INVESTOR ADVICE

A broker may or may not be a REALTOR®.[1] You should be wary of any broker who feels it unnecessary to join his or her professional organization. Most properties listed for sale and sold in your locality are through the local board of realtors and its multi-list services. Only REALTORS® and their agents have legal access to this service.

DOES YOUR BROKER STEAL A broker who is not a member of the NAR has no right to REALTOR® data. If your broker has a current listing book, it was stolen.

SEE ALSO: CERTIFIED REAL ESTATE BROKER, and NATIONAL ASSOCIATION OF REALTORS®.[2]

BUILDABLE UNITS

Buildable units are the total number of living units which can be legally constructed on a land parcel. The authorized number is usually based on a minimum square footage (s.f.) for the first few units plus a lesser requirement for each additional unit.

EXAMPLE

You have a parcel of land containing 22,500 s.f. zoned for apartments. The zoning regulations require 10,000 s.f. for the first four units and 2,500 s.f. for each additional unit. How many units can be built on this property?

22,500 - 10,000 = 10,500 left after the first 4 authorized units.
10,500 / 2,500 = 4+ additional units.
The total number of units that would be authorized is eight units.

INVESTOR ADVICE

Although the example indicates that eight units could be legally constructed, this does not consider the specific plot plan, set-back requirements, easements, parking spaces, and, in some cases, a requirement for a percentage of the land to be landscaped.

Before committing to build or buy a parcel of property to build on, carefully check the zoning and other restrictive covenants. A difference of one or two buildable units can mean the difference between a successful and an unsuccessful investment.

SEE ALSO: RESTRICTIVE COVENANTS, PLOT PLAN, ZONING, and ZONING VARIANCES.

BUILDING CODES

Building codes are minimum standards of construction established by federal, state and local governments to assure building conformance, safety, and quality. Building codes can be comprehensive or minimal.

The requirement for building permits and mandatory inspections during construction is legislated to assure conformance with building codes and construction practices established by local law.

INVESTOR ADVICE

Standard plans and costs figures provided by other than local contractors and architects are subject to significant cost variances. To assure that cost quotations are accurate, they should be prepared by local professionals who are knowledgeable in local building codes and requirements.

SEE ALSO: BUILDING COSTS, BUILDING PERMITS, and RESTRICTIVE COVENANTS.

BUILDING COSTS

Building costs are the costs per square foot to construct a building of a certain quality, shape, and size. Costs quoted by real estate appraisers, contractors, and architects usually do not include appliances, fixtures, floor coverings, window treatments, the cost of land, landscaping, utility connection fees, and similar items.

INVESTOR ADVICE

You should be aware of the fact that square-foot costs can vary substantially from those quoted by various professionals. For instance, a residence of 1500 s.f. quoted as costing about $50/s.f. would be in substantial error if the home included a two-story brick chimney at a cost of $3000. The cost would then be $52/s.f. or an increase in the quoted figure of 4%.

Similarly, a home designed with several outward and inward changes in wall direction can substantially increase the cost over a standard box-like structure. Prices generally quoted are for the *standard* building.

> **DON'T BUY** pretty buildings with lots of fancy add-ons. Look for a basic utility that produces a better return on your investment.

Also overlooked in estimating the cost of buildings is the cost of ditches to be dug for utilities and then back filled. These may extend into the city streets and require repaving as well as ditch costs. Sewer, water, and other connection fees may also be substantial, particularly for multi-unit or commercial structures which require sprinkler systems.

SEE ALSO: BUILDING CODES, BUILDING PERMITS, CUBIC FOOT METHOD OF ESTIMATING COST, CULINARY WATER, EASEMENTS, IRRIGATION WATER, and RESTRICTIVE COVENANTS.

BUILDING RESIDUAL

A building residual is an appraisal technique in which the value of a building is obtained by subtracting the land value (usually determined by the market approach) from the total value of the improved property. The total value is usually obtained by capitalizing the income from the property (income approach).

EXAMPLE

An owner of a certain office building is determined to produce a net operating income of $28,000/yr. The normal rate of return in this area for the subject type of building is 9.0% A recent appraisal of the building lot indicates a value of $70,000. What is the building value?

Total Value = Income/Rate of Return

    Total Value = $28,000 / .09 = $311,111

Building Value = Total Value - Land Value

Building Value = $311,111 - $70,000 = $241,111

    Round to $241,000

The total value of a property should not exceed the sum of the land and building values. When an appraiser has determined land and building values separately and by different methods, he or she may make an erroneous assumption that the sum of those two is the total value.

Thus, the appraiser has failed to recognize that the building is an over-improvement on the land or is possibly not utilizing the land at its highest and best value. While the cost or reproduction value of a building is a legitimate appraisal technique, its improper use can result in an error in computing total fair market value.

In the example, if the appraiser had used the cost approach to determine the building value at say, $400,000 and added this to the known land value of $70,000, he or she would have erroneously concluded that the total value was $470,000.

SEE ALSO: CAPITALIZATION OF INCOME, COST APPROACH TO VALUE, FAIR MARKET VALUE, HIGHEST & BEST USE, INCOME APPROACH TO VALUE, INCOME MULTIPLIER, MARKET DATA APPROACH, and LAND RESIDUAL TECHNIQUE.

BULLET LOAN

A bullet loan is a mortgage loan with a very short maturity period—"fast as a speeding bullet." Such loans normally provide for periodic payments covering interest and little or no amortization of the loan principal. Whereas first mortgage loans are usually granted for fifteen to thirty years, high-risk commercial project loans may result from the lender's desire to limit his exposure to a shorter period, say five years.

INVESTOR ADVICE

Bullet loans are acceptable only as a last resort. The short term provided may not permit a project to reach a break-even or profitable position by the expiration date of the loan. A higher interest rate loan, with provisions for early pay-off may be a better alternative.

SEE ALSO: BALLOON PAYMENT, BREAK-EVEN POINT, COMMITTED INSTITUTIONAL WAREHOUSING, COMMITTED TECHNICAL WAREHOUSING and INTEREST-ONLY LOAN.

BUNDLE OF RIGHTS

This is an ownership concept that considers an owner's rights as a bundle of sticks, in which each stick represents a specific right of ownership. These rights are:

- The right to use the property;

- The right to sell the property;

- The right to lease the property;

- The right to give the property away; and

- The right to enter the property at will.

INVESTOR ADVICE

Ownership, in absolute fee simple, includes the listed bundle of rights, which are limited by the four powers reserved by government. These powers are:

- Power of taxation;

- Police power;

- Power of eminent domain; and

- Power of escheat.

SEE ALSO: FEE SIMPLE TITLE, EMINENT DOMAIN, and POWER OF ESCHEAT.

BUYER'S MARKET

A market condition in which there is an excess number of properties for sale versus the number of buyers is termed a buyer's market.

INVESTOR ADVICE

The best buys for an investment portfolio can be made in periods of a buyer's market. Sellers, unable to move their properties at normal value, will often reduce the price, provide seller financing, or offer other incentives to one willing to buy their property.

Although properties are offered at attractive prices during a buyer's market, income property will probably suffer increased loss in value due to increased vacancies or reduced rental rates to maintain a reasonable percentage of occupancy. Thus, the lower selling price will be somewhat justified by the reduced income.

A good investor will not buy for the short term, but will make his/her buying decision based on expected market conditions at some future date. The investor may be happy to accept reduced income and even a negative cash flow for the near term in order to achieve expected long-term capital gains.

EXAMPLE

Mr. and Mrs. Black are both employed and have considerable surplus cash to invest for the future. Their REALTOR® informs them of an excellent apartment house, which has been on the market for about a year, but was recently reduced to sell. He estimates that the property can be purchased for about $200,000. Current net income is less than normal at $12,000/yr., indicating an overall return from income of 6%.

Mr. Black is aware of several large firms planning to relocate to his city, which would greatly increase the value of real estate. He is confident that the subject apartment would be worth a minimum of $250,000 at the end of a five-year holding period. What would be the Internal Rate of Return (IRR) on the $200,000 investment, based on these assumptions and facts?

IRR = PV of Cash Flow + PV of Selling Price @ a rate that causes the above sum to equal the investment

Using his hand-held financial calculator, Mr. Black finds his projected rate of return to be 10%. This return actually would be slightly higher, after depreciation and other tax savings were considered. Mr. & Mrs. Black decided to buy.

SEE ALSO: CASH FLOW, CAPITAL GAINS, and INTERNAL RATE OF RETURN.

ENDNOTES

[1]The registered trademark of the National Association of Realtors. All persons designated as REALTORS® are members of their national, state, and local real estate boards and are sworn to a strict standard of conduct in their associations with the general public.

[2]*Ibid.*

C

Capacity of the Parties
Capacity to Contract
Capital Appreciation
Capital Gains Taxes
Capitalization of Income
Capitalization Rate
Cash Flow
Cash Throwoff
Cash versus Accrual Accounting
Caveat Emptor
Certificate
Certificate of No Defense
Certificate of Occupancy
Certificate of Reasonable Value (CRV)
Certificate of Release
Certificate of Sale
Certified Property Manager
Certified Real Estate Broker
Cession Deed
Chain
Chain of Title
Chattel Mortgage
Chattels
Chronological Age
Class Life System
Cleaning Deposit
Clifford Trust
Closing Costs
Cloud on the Title
Codicil
Co-Insurance
Collateralized Mortgage Obligation
   (CMO)
Color of Title
Combination Trust
Commercial Loan
Commingle
Commission
Commission Down
Commitment Letter
Committed Institutional Warehousing
Committed Technical Warehousing
Community Development Block Grant
Community Property
Comparable Market Value
Comparative Sales Approach

Compass Call
Competent Party
Completion Bond
Component Depreciation
Compound Interest
Condemnation
Conditional Sale
Condominium
Consistent Use Theory
Construction Draw
Construction Loan
Construction Permit
Constructive Eviction
Constructive Notice
Constructive Possession
Constructive Receipt
Constructive Value
Contingency Fund
Contingent Fee Basis
Continuity of Operation
Contract
Contract Price
Contract Rate
Contract Rent
Contractor's Lien
Controllable Expense
Conventional Loan
Conversion
Convertible Debenture
Cooperative Apartment
Co-Ownership
Corporate Deed Form
Corporation
Correction
Correlation
Co-Signer
Cost Approach to Value
Co-Tenant
Counter Offer
Covenant
Creative Financing
Cubic Foot Method of Estimating Cost
Cul de Sac
Culinary Water
Curable Physical Deterioration
Curtsey Rights

C

CAPACITY OF THE PARTIES

The legal competence of all parties to enter into a legal contractual action is termed capacity of the parties.

INVESTOR ADVICE
See *Investor Advice* under "Capacity to Contract."

SEE ALSO: CAPACITY TO CONTRACT, CONTRACT, and POWER OF ATTORNEY.

CAPACITY TO CONTRACT

Capacity to contract is defined as having the competence to enter into a contractual arrangement. This implies that the person is:

- Of legal age;
- Of sound mind; and
- Legally authorized to enter into the transaction through ownership or by legal authority of the owner(s).

INVESTOR ADVICE
A contract between parties, when either does not have the legal capacity to contract is unenforceable. Before entering into a contract with a very young or very elderly person it is wise to question that person's capacity to contract.

Lack of capacity due to questionable ownership will be revealed in the title search, but age and mental capacity can only be determined by you or other individuals having an interest in the transaction.

Problems involving capacity to contract can occur in any situation but are most often found in the following circumstances:

- Property is sold by parties having joint ownership, where one or more are reluctant to conclude the transaction that the others have negotiated.

- Property is owned by a corporation, where one or more principals assume they have the right to sell but do not, due to restrictions of the corporate charter.

- Properties which are a part of an estate in probate or never cleared through the probate system which then gets bogged down. The usual case is a surviving spouse who attempts to sell a property, which was legally his or hers after the death of his/her partner. The required documents were never filed to officially remove the deceased's name from the title.

- Children of property owners attempt to block the sale of property by claiming the elderly owner is not mentally competent.

- Property is sold by a person having less than full fee title—for instance, lifetime interest only.

SEE ALSO: ABSTRACT OF TITLE, CONTRACTS, and POWER OF ATTORNEY.

CAPITAL APPRECIATION

Capital appreciation is the increase in value of a property due to economic factors, which would result in capital gains if the property was sold.

INVESTOR ADVICE

Before offering a property for sale, you should carefully consider the potential for capital gains and the resultant tax consequences. A trade for like property may be more advantageous than an outright sale.

Capital appreciation can occur as the result of events controlled by the owner, or economic situations over which the owner has no control.

EXAMPLE

Mr. Green purchased an office building in 1980 for $500,000. Shortly after the purchase, Mr. Green remodeled the property to provide more but smaller office suites. This work cost an additional $100,000. The result was a significant increase in net income.

In 1988, a real estate broker approached Mr. Green about selling the building to the broker's client, a real estate investment trust. The broker indicated that the current net income of $75,000 would support a sales price of about $900,000, since his investor was willing to accept an overall yield (based on income only) as low as 8%. The trust expected to hold the property for at least ten years, during which time they expected the property to continue to appreciate in value.

Mr. Green's basis cost was:

Purchase Price	$500,000
Remodeling Cost	100,000
Total Cost	$600,000

A sale at the proposed $900,000 would show a capital appreciation, for the five-year holding period, of:

Proposed Sales Price	$900,000
Total Cost	600,000
Capital Appreciation	$300,000 or 50%

This appreciation was due to two factors: (1) Mr. Green's foresight in remodeling the property; and (2) the improving economic situation in the area.

While the capital appreciation was $300,000, the taxable gains would be even greater since Mr. Green's basis cost had been reduced by the amount of depreciation taken during his holding period.

SEE ALSO: BARTERING, BASIS COST, CAPITAL GAINS TAXES, DEPRECIATION, and RECAPTURE.

CAPITAL GAINS TAXES

Capital gains taxes are income taxes payable on a sale of property for more than its basis cost.

INVESTOR ADVICE

The basis cost (purchase price plus improvements minus depreciation taken) may be inaccurate for tax purposes, if the property has been depreciated by any of the various accelerated methods.

EXAMPLE

Mr. Smith purchased a warehouse in 1980 for $300,000. He elected accelerated depreciation and upon the sale of the property in 1988 had taken $100,000 in depreciation. He received $400,000 for the property. What would be the amount of gain taxable?

Purchase Cost	$300,000
Less: Depreciation Taken	−180,000
Basis Cost	$120,000

Since Mr. Smith had elected to take accelerated depreciation and sold the property before it was fully depreciated, all depreciation over straight-line must be recaptured.

Depreciation Taken	$180,000
Straight-line Allowed:	
8 years on 25-year basis	96,000
Dep. Recapture	$ 84,000

Mr. Smith's capital gains would be calculated as follows:

Purchase Cost	$300,000
Less: Depreciation Taken	180,000
Plus: Dep. Recapture	84,000
Taxable Gain	$204,000

Under the Tax Reform Act of 1986, short- and long-term capital gains are taxed as ordinary income (maximum 28% rate, beginning in 1988); however, beginning in 1987 both short- and long-term capital losses may be used to offset income on a dollar for dollar basis.

Investments in real estate, usually classified as a "passive activity," prevent you from writing off passive losses against "active income." Passive losses can only be written off against passive income. If you have no passive income, the loss may be carried forward to offset income of that activity in future years.

This drastic provision will be phased in over a five-year period. Losses can continue to be written off as follows:

1987:   You may write off 65% of your losses against non-
         sheltered (active) income.
1988:   You may write off 40%.
1989:   You may write off 20%.
1990:   You may write off 10%.

This phase-in period applies only to properties purchased prior to passage of the 1986 act. There are exceptions applicable to the first $25,000 loss from rental realty, low-income housing, and working interests in oil and gas properties.

SEE ALSO: BASIS COST, LONG-TERM GAINS, SHORT-TERM GAINS, and TAX RECOVERY ACT OF 1986 (TRA).

CAPITALIZATION OF INCOME

This term refers to an appraisal technique for determining value by dividing the net income by an appropriate percentage rate, known as "the capitalization rate."

INVESTOR ADVICE

When you review an appraisal in which income has been capitalized, you should carefully examine the justification of the capitalization rate employed. Any value may be obtained by adjusting the capitalization rate—the higher the rate, the lower the value and vice versa.

EXAMPLE

An income property has a net income of $15,000 per year. If a 10% capitalization rate is used, the value becomes:

$$V = \text{Income/Rate}$$

$$V = \$15,000/.10 = \$150,000$$

Had the appraiser selected a higher rate, say 12%, the value becomes:

$$V = \$15,000/.12 = \$125,000$$

Had the appraiser selected a lower rate, say 8%, the value would be:

$$V = \$15,000/.08 = \$187,500$$

A proper capitalization rate will have been derived by the band of investment or other approved technique, using current data from the market-place. Thus, the current value of mortgages and the size of the mortgage will have been considered along with the investor risk and amount of investment.

SEE ALSO: BAND OF INVESTMENT, CAPITALIZATION RATE, INCOME APPROACH TO VALUE, and YIELD ON INVESTMENT.

CAPITALIZATION RATE

The capitalization rate is the percentage rate by which the net income is divided to determine value.

INVESTOR ADVICE

The most accurate method of determining value is by the direct capitalization method, where the rate has been determined from recent comparable sales data. In this method, actual net income is divided by the cash sales price to determine the overall rate (OAR). The following illustration uses the formula:

Income/Sales Price = OAR

Comparable No.	Net Income	Sales Price	OAR
1	$150,000	$1,650,000	.091
2	200,000	2,100,000	.095
3	230,000	2,447,000	.094
4	283,500	3,000,000	.095
5	175,000	1,900,000	.092
6	191,000	2,000,000	.096
		Average OAR	.094

Approximately 9.4%

To assure that the rate is accurate, the appraiser would have to select his comparables so that the land/building ratios are similar; the comparables have approximately the same economic life; and more importantly, the net income figures are accurate. It is not unusual for sellers to *conveniently* forget some expense items, such as reserves for replacement, in order to show a higher rate of net income.

SEE ALSO: CAPITALIZATION OF INCOME, INCOME APPROACH TO VALUE, and MARKET APPROACH TO VALUE.

CASH FLOW

Cash flow is gross income, less all cash expenses, less debt service—spendable cash.

INVESTOR ADVICE

EXAMPLE

A certain income property has a monthly income of $1,500. Cash expenses average $400 per month. Mortgage payments (debt service) are $787.25/mo., plus taxes and insurance of $165.30. What is the average cash flow?

Total Income		$1,500.00
Less:		
Expenses	$400.00	
Mortgage	–787.25	
Taxes & Ins.	167.30	
Cash Flow/Cash Throwoff	$145.45/mo.	

Actual income from the property will equal the cash flow, less non-cash depreciation expenses, less reserves set aside for redecoration expenses and equipment replacements, plus the equity portion of the debt service payments.

SEE ALSO: DEBT SERVICE, GROSS INCOME, and NET INCOME.

CASH THROWOFF

Cash throwoff is another name for cash flow.

INVESTOR ADVICE
Cash flow or throw off is the figure shown before income taxes are computed. When taxes are deducted, the amount of cash left is generally referred to as "net spendable income."

SEE ALSO: CASH FLOW, DEBT SERVICE, and NET INCOME AFTER TAXES.

CASH VERSUS ACCRUAL ACCOUNTING
Cash accounting records receipts and expenditures as the cash is actually received or paid out. Accrual accounting, on the other hand, records receipts when earned and expenditures as they occur.

INVESTOR ADVICE
If you purchase a going operation with accounting records utilizing the accrual basis, it becomes immediately evident what is owed and what is yet to be received since the records contain all transactions. Buying a going operation that uses the cash accounting method is more difficult to evaluate, since many transactions will be missing. The company may have many bills outstanding and little or no payments or cash due in.

If a cash accounting operation is to be purchased, make sure that the seller provides you with a current list of all bills outstanding. He should also furnish you with an agreement to assume the liability for all bills outstanding as of the date of transfer. An even better arrangement is to have all outstanding bills paid by the closing agency and deducted from the seller's proceeds.

SEE ALSO: ACCOUNTS PAYABLE, ACCOUNTS RECEIVABLE, ASSETS, and LIABILITIES.

CAVEAT EMPTOR
This term is a Latin phrase meaning, "Let the Buyer Beware." This legal concept applies in many real estate transactions.

INVESTOR ADVICE
In real estate, the rule of caveat emptor applies to anything which you as an ordinary person should have seen or known about, had you applied average intelligence and due diligence to the transaction.

EXAMPLE

You can expect a court to award damages to you for a leaky roof which had been hidden by the seller's recent redecoration and constituted a deliberate attempt to conceal the condition. You cannot expect relief for a broken window which was there at the time of purchase and which you failed to see upon inspection.

Repairs noted in an earnest money receipt and offer-to-purchase, which specified that the seller would correct certain deficiencies but did not, may not be enforceable after the transaction has closed if you failed to perform the necessary pre-closing inspection. The earnest money agreement is said to have been abrogated at the time of the closing.

SEE ALSO: ABROGATE, EARNEST MONEY RECEIPT, and OFFER-TO- PURCHASE.

CERTIFICATE
A certificate is a written document attesting to a fact, qualification, or promise. It may also be a license.

SEE ALSO: CERTIFICATE OF NO DEFENSE, CERTIFICATE OF OCCUPANCY, CERTIFICATE OF REASONABLE VALUE (CRV), CERTIFICATE OF RELEASE, and CERTIFICATE OF SALE.

CERTIFICATE OF NO DEFENSE

A certificate of no defense is a written document showing the total due on a mortgage which is being sold or transferred. This is also referred to as "a declaration of no set-off."

INVESTOR ADVICE

This item is seldom used since it is superceded by a more effective instrument, the title search, which fully discloses the status of all mortgage loans.

SEE ALSO: TITLE INSURANCE, and TITLE REPORT.

CERTIFICATE OF OCCUPANCY

A certificate issued by a municipality certifying that a property is fit for occupancy and meets all of the municipal codes and requirements is called a certificate of occupancy.

INVESTOR ADVICE

Your local realtor can advise you in regards to certificates of occupancy. Some localities require that these certificates be issued each time a property is built, remodeled, or sold. This requirement assures compliance with construction and health codes.

In some localities, the certificate is a part of the construction permit which is signed by the inspector who performs the final inspection.

SEE ALSO: CONSTRUCTION PERMIT, and LICENSE.

CERTIFICATE OF REASONABLE VALUE (CRV)

A certificate of reasonable value is issued by the Veterans Administration attesting to the appraised value of a property. This certificate is a prerequisite to obtaining a VA loan.

INVESTOR ADVICE

A VA loan cannot be granted or a home sold for more than the CRV, unless a qualified veteran certifies that he or she is aware of the appraised value and desires to purchase it anyway. The amount of the sale over and above the CRV must be paid by the veteran at closing. Figure 10 shows the CRV form issued by the VA.

SEE ALSO: VA LOAN.

CERTIFICATE OF RELEASE

A certificate of release is issued by a lending institution certifying that a mortgage has been paid in full—also known as "satisfaction of mortgage."

INVESTOR ADVICE

When you receive a certificate of release, sometimes referred to as a satisfaction piece, check to see that the lender has:

VA Veterans Administration	**CERTIFICATE OF REASONABLE VALUE**	1. CASE NUMBER

2. PROPERTY ADDRESS (Include ZIP code and county)	3. LEGAL DESCRIPTION	4. TITLE LIMITATIONS AND RESTRICTIVE COVENANTS:
325 North Elmwood Ave Anytown, USA	Lot 26, Hardwood Height Subdivision, Section 1	Utility Easement 5.0 ft wide across South side. ☐ CONDOMINIUM ☐ PLANNED UNIT DEVELOPMENT

5. NAME AND ADDRESS OF FIRM OR PERSON MAKING REQUEST/APPLICATION (Include ZIP code)	6. REMAINING ECONOMIC LIFE OF PROPERTY IS ESTIMATED TO BE NOT LESS THAN (Enter number of years) 40 years YEARS

Lowcost Mortgage Corp
121 S. Howell Drive, Suite 210
Anytown, USA

7. ESTIMATED REASONABLE VALUE OF PROPERTY $ 78,200	8. EXPIRATION DATE June 15, 1989
9. ADMINISTRATOR OF VETERANS AFFAIRS BY (Signature of authorized agent) *James T. House*	
10. DATE ISSUED Dec 15, 1988	11. VA OFFICE Salt Lake City

GENERAL CONDITIONS

(NOTE: THE VETERANS ADMINISTRATION DOES NOT ASSUME ANY RESPONSIBILITY FOR THE CONDITION OF THE PROPERTY. THE CORRECTION OF ANY DEFECTS NOW EXISTING OR THAT MAY DEVELOP WILL BE THE RESPONSIBILITY OF THE PURCHASER.)

1. This certificate will remain effective as to any written contract of sale entered into by an eligible veteran within the validity period indicated.
2. This dwelling conforms with the Minimum Property Requirements prescribed by the Administrator of Veterans Affairs.
3. The aggregate of any loan secured by this property plus the amount of any assessment consequent on any special improvements as to which a lien or right to a lien shall exist against the property, except as provided in Item 13 below, may not exceed the reasonable value in Item 7 above.
4. Proposed construction shall be completed in accordance with the plans and specifications identified below, relating to both onsite and offsite improvements upon which this valuation is based and shall otherwise conform fully to the VA Minimum Property Requirements. Satisfactory completion must be evidenced by either
   A. VA Final Compliance Inspection Report (VA Form 26-1839), or
   B. VA Acceptance of FHA Compliance Inspection Reports or other evidence of completion under FHA supervision applicable to proposed construction.
5. By contracting to sell property, as proposed construction or existing construction not previously occupied, to a veteran purchaser who is to be assisted in the purchase by a loan made, guaranteed, or insured by VA, the builder or other seller agrees to place any downpayment received by the seller or agent of the seller in a special trust account as required by section 1806 of title 38, U.S. Code.
6. The VA guaranty is subject to and conditioned upon the lending institution's compliance, at the time of the making, increasing, extending or renewing of the proposed loan, with section 102 of P.L. 93-234, "Flood Disaster Protection Act of 1973."

12. PURCHASER'S NAME AND ADDRESS (Complete mailing address, Include ZIP code)	13. EXCEPTIONS TO GENERAL CONDITION NUMBER 3 ABOVE
George I. Veteran Room 121 Low Quality Motel 101 Main Street Anytown, USA	☐ ENERGY CONSERVATION IMPROVEMENTS—The buyer may wish to contact the local utility company or a qualified person or firm for a home energy audit. If energy-related improvements are suggested, your mortgage may be increased to include the following: Thermostats, water heaters, heating/cooling systems, attic insulation, insulation for floors and foundation walls, weather-stripping/caulking, storm windows and storm doors. The mortgage may be increased by (a) up to $2,000 without a separate determination of the value of the energy-related improvements; (b) up to $3,500 if supported by a value determination by a designated appraiser; or (c) more than $3,500 subject to a value determination by VA or HUD, as applicable, and subsequent endorsement of the certificate of reasonable value or HUD conditional commitment. ☐ OTHER (Cite and explain in Item 25 below)

SPECIFIC CONDITIONS (Applicable when checked or completed)

14. THE REASONABLE VALUE ESTABLISHED HEREIN FOR THE RELATED PROPERTY IS	15. PROPOSED CONSTRUCTION TO BE COMPLETED (Identify plans, specifications and exhibits)
☒ BASED UPON OBSERVATION OF THE PROPERTY IN ITS "AS IS" CONDITION ☐ PREDICATED UPON COMPLETION OF PROPOSED CONSTRUCTION (If checked complete Item 15) ☐ PREDICATED UPON COMPLETION OF REPAIRS LISTED IN ITEM 17	

16. INSPECTIONS REQUIRED	17. REPAIRS TO BE COMPLETED
☐ FHA COMPLIANCE INSPECTIONS FOR PROPOSED CONSTRUCTION ☒ VA COMPLIANCE INSPECTIONS ☐ LENDER TO CERTIFY	None
18. NAME OF COMPLIANCE INSPECTOR *Thomas Manager*	

19. HEALTH AUTHORITY APPROVAL—Execution of VA Form 26-6395 by the Health Authority (or Health Authority form or letter) indicating approval of the individual: ☐ WATER SUPPLY ☒ SEWAGE DISPOSAL SYSTEM	20. ☐ This document is subject to the provisions of Executive Orders 11246 and 11375, and the Rules and Regulations of the Secretary of Labor in effect this date, and 38 CFR 36.4390 through 36.4393, and also the provisions of the certification executed by the builder, sponsor or developer named herein which is on file in this office.

21. ☒ WOOD DESTROYING INSECT INFORMATION — EXISTING CONSTRUCTION — The seller shall, at no cost to the veteran-purchaser, prior to settlement, obtain a written statement from a qualified pest control operator reporting wood destroying insect information using VA Form 26-8850 or other form acceptable to VA. The veteran-purchaser will acknowledge receipt of a copy of the statement in Item 14 of VA Form 26-8850. PROPOSED CONSTRUCTION — VA Form 26-8375, Termite Soil Treatment Guarantee, is required.

22. WARRANTY ☐ (If checked, complete Item 23)	23. NAME OF WARRANTOR	24. ☐ Since this property is located in a special Flood Hazard Area as established by FEMA, flood insurance will be required in accordance with 38 CFR 36.4326. (Check if applicable)

25. OTHER REQUIREMENTS

       None

Figure 10

- Acknowledged the document;
- Recorded the document;
- Clearly indicated the mortgagor and mortgagee; and
- Properly identified the legal description of the property which the mortgage covered.

If the document is correct but has not been recorded, you should take the release to the local county recorder's office and have it made a part of the public record. Without this action, a title search of the property will show the mortgage as still outstanding.

After the document recording work has been completed, the document will be returned to you indicating the book and page of recordation. Once recorded, it is not necessary for you to retain the document.

SEE ALSO: RELEASE OF MORTGAGE, and SATISFACTION PIECE.

CERTIFICATE OF SALE

A certificate of sale is issued to a buyer of property sold by court order and is sometimes referred to as a sheriff's deed.

INVESTOR ADVICE

A certificate of sale or sheriff's deed is not a clear title to the property described. All properties sold as a result of court orders can be redeemed by the former owner within a stipulated time period and by satisfaction of all debts and costs which initiated court action. Your attorney can advise you as to the specific requirements in your state.

SEE ALSO: SHERIFF'S DEED.

CERTIFIED PROPERTY MANAGER

A certified property manager is a member of the National Association of REALTORS® who has been awarded the CPM designation, after successfully passing the required courses and meeting the minimum standards of practical experience.

INVESTOR ADVICE

When selecting a manager for your rental properties, you can depend upon the qualifications of those having been awarded the CPM designation. While others may also be qualified, you will have to depend solely upon the recommendations of their clients. A member of the National Association of REALTORS® with the CPM designation has sworn to uphold the standards and code of ethics of this prestigious organization and has been found to be a competent manager by a committee of his or her peers.

SEE ALSO: NATIONAL ASSOCIATION OF REALTORS.

CERTIFIED REAL ESTATE BROKER

A certified real estate broker is a member of the National Association of REALTORS® who has been awarded the CRB designation after successfully passing all required courses and meeting the minimum time in service requirements.

INVESTOR ADVICE

Brokers are those who have been certified and licensed by their state as competent to employ and supervise real estate salespeople and operate a real estate business. They may or may not be a member of a national, state and local boards of REALTORS®.

SHERIFF'S DEED

This Indenture, Made this ...23rd...... day of ....September.............. A.D. 1989, between Quick D. McGaw .... Sheriff of Salt Lake County, State of Utah, party of the first part, and First Mortgage Corp .... party of the second part.

WITNESSETH, WHEREAS, In and by a certain judgment and decree made and entered by the District Court of the Third Judicial District (Salt Lake County) of the State of Utah on the ...15th. day of .....February....... A.D. 1989, in a certain action then pending in said Court, wherein ......First Mortgage Corp. ....Of Salt Lake City, Utah..

.... Plaintiff....and ......Jasper P. Deadbeat........................

....

....

....

.... Defendant......

it was among other things ordered and adjudged that all and singular the premises in said judgment, and hereinafter described should be sold at public auction, by and under the direction of the Sheriff of Salt Lake County, State of Utah, in the manner required by law; that either of the parties to said action might become purchaser at such sale, and that said Sheriff should execute the usual certificates and deeds to the purchaser as required by law.

AND WHEREAS, The Sheriff did, at the hour of 12 o'clock noon, on the ...20th... day of ....March.............. A.D. 1989 at the west front door of the County Court House in the City and County of Salt Lake, State of Utah, after due public notice had been given, as required by law and said judgment, duly sell at public auction, agreeable to law and said judgment, the premises and property in said judgment and hereinafter described at which sale said premises and property were fairly struck off and sold to ....First Mortgage Corp. ....

....for the sum of ..Fifty Thousand and 00/100.........

.... Dollars, it being the highest bidder and that being the highest sum bid at said sale.

AND WHEREAS, Said ....First Mortgage Corp. .... thereupon paid to the said Sheriff said sum of money so bid, and said Sheriff thereupon made and issued the usual certificate in duplicate of such sale in due form, and delivered one thereof to said purchaser, and caused the other to be filed in the office of the County Recorder of the County of Salt Lake, State of Utah.

AND WHEREAS, More than six months have elapsed since the day of said sale, and no redemption of the property so sold has been made.

AND WHEREAS, Said ....First Mortgage Corp. .... purchaser as aforesaid did, on the ...22nd day of ....September....... A.D....., sell assign and transfer said Certificate of Sale and all his rights thereunder to ......Boyd G. Investor..

the said party of the second part, and duly authorized said Sheriff to make a deed for said premises, in pursuance of said sale to said ..Boyd G. Investor...

Now This Indenture Witnesses, That the said party of the first part, Sheriff as aforesaid, in order to carry into effect said sale in pursuance of said judgment and of the law, and also in consideration of the premises and of the money so bid and paid by the said ....First Mortgage Corp. ....

the receipt whereof is hereby acknowledged, has granted, sold, conveyed, and by these presents does grant, sell and convey and confirm unto the said party of the second part, its successors and assigns forever, the following described real estate lying and being in the City and County of Salt Lake, State of Utah, being all the right, title, claim and interest of the above named defendants of, in and to the following described property, to-wit:

Lot 254, Sunnyside Acres No 1.

Together with all and singular the tenements, hereditaments, and appurtenances thereunto belonging or in anywise appertaining, to have and to hold the same unto said party of the second part, its successors and assigns forever.

IN WITNESS WHEREOF, Said party of the first part has hereunto set his hand and seal the day and year first above written.

Signed, Sealed and Delivered in presence of

....   *Quick D. McGaw*   (SEAL)
                                                                        Sheriff of Salt Lake County, Utah

STATE OF UTAH,   }
County of Salt Lake. } ss.

On the 23rd day of .....September...., 1989, before me ...Mary Southworth.............. a Notary Public in and for the County of Salt Lake, State of Utah, personally appeared ...Quick D. McGaw.......... .... Sheriff of Salt Lake County, State of Utah, personally known to me to be the person described in and who executed the foregoing instrument, who acknowledged to me that he executed the same as such Sheriff, freely and voluntarily, and for the uses and purposes therein mentioned.

WITNESS my hand and notarial seal, this ...23rd... day of .....September......, 1989

My commission expires ...June 1, 1991   *Mary Southworth*
                                                        Notary Public, Residing in Salt Lake City, Utah.

Figure 11

Members of the NAR who have been awarded the CRB designation are certified after completion of a number of advanced management courses and the completion of a minimum number of years as an active broker. The CRB designation is awarded by the local chapter after examination by a committee of the broker's peers.

SEE ALSO: NATIONAL ASSOCIATION OF REALTORS®.

CESSION DEED

A special deed form used to transfer private property to a government agency is a cession deed. An example of such a transaction would be the deeding of a right-of-way or strip of property to the city for road improvement.

INVESTOR ADVICE

It is not unusual for property descriptions to read "to the center of the street." The following is an example of such a deed description:

Beginning at a point 33.0' South and 170.0' East of the Northwest corner of SW 1/4 of the SW 1/4 of Section 27, T 1 South, R 1 East, Salt Lake base and Meridian and continuing North 165.25, thence East 68.0', thence South 165.25 feet to the center of 3300 South Street, thence West 68.0' to the point of beginning. Contains 0.258 Acres.

Where the street has been in existence for many years, the use of the land occupied by the street (33,0' X 68.0'= 0.052 acres) cannot be recovered. Your property taxes may be reduced if this land is deeded to the city. If the above property was valued at $10/s.f., the reduced assessment would be:

$$33.0' \times 68.0' \times \$10/\text{s.f.} = \$22,440$$

No special deed form is used for this transfer. Usually a quit claim deed is used however, the use of a warranty deed would not be out of order.

SEE ALSO: ASSESSMENTS, and QUIT CLAIM DEED.

CHAIN

A chain is a surveyor's unit of measurement consisting of four rods, each containing twenty-five links. A chain is 66.0 feet in length. The chain is useful in land measurement since ten square chains equals one acre. Size calculations are made by simply multiplying length by width and pointing off one place (dividing by 10).

EXAMPLE

A rectangular piece of property is measured by the surveyor and found to be 14.5 chains X 23.8 chains. What is the included acreage of the parcel?

$$(14.5 \text{ ch.} \times 23.8 \text{ ch.}) / 10 = 34.51 \text{ acres}$$

INVESTOR ADVICE

Modern legal descriptions of land parcels are recorded in feet and hundreds of feet. You will find many older descriptions which employ chains, rods, and links. These units can be converted to feet by use of the following table:

1 Acre = 43,560 square feet
1 Chain = 66.0 feet
4 Rods = 1 chain
1 Rod = 16.5 feet
25 Links = 1 rod
1 Link = 7.92 inches

CHAIN OF TITLE

A chain of title is a chronological history of all conveyances and encumbrances affecting a land title. This history begins with the first patent or grant and continues to the current date.

INVESTOR ADVICE

An abstract of title is a complete history of a title chain. Most abstracts are now superceded by short summaries of a title search noting the current status of title, and then become a component part of a title insurance policy.

Complete abstracts, over the years, have become too cumbersome for practical use. It is not unusual for an abstract to contain 2,000–3,000 pages of documentation and certificates.

SEE ALSO: ABSTRACT OF TITLE, and TITLE INSURANCE.

CHATTEL MORTGAGE

A written mortgage or lien used to secure a loan on personal property, such as furniture and fixtures, is called a chattel mortgage.

INVESTOR ADVICE

If you transfer personal property and take back a mortgage for the remainder owed, you should obtain a chattel mortgage for all personal property transferred with the real estate. A real estate mortgage does not place a lien on personal property.

Figure 12 shows a typical form used by sellers of personal property, appliances etc., to retain ownership until such time as the chattel mortgage has been paid in full.

Check with your attorney to determine if chattel mortgages must be recorded to be valid in your state.

SEE ALSO: BILL OF SALE, CHATTELS, and PERSONAL PROPERTY.

CHATTELS

Chattels are personal property. All that is attached to real estate with intent to remain is real estate. All other items are chattels.

INVESTOR ADVICE

Be sure that a bill of sale is issued to transfer title to all personal property at the same time that the real estate is transferred by deed. If any doubt exists as to whether an item is real estate or personal property, have that item placed on the bill of sale.

SEE ALSO: BILL OF SALE, CHATTEL MORTGAGE, and PERSONAL PROPERTY.

CHRONOLOGICAL AGE

Chronological age is the actual age of a structure, as measured by the calendar.

$ 782.50   February 21,   19 89

   For value received __We__, the subscriber_S_, with{ residence / office x }at No._1234 N. Broadway_____Street, in
__Rapid City, N. Mex_____promise__ to pay to __Hardwood Furniture & Appliances__
or order, the sum of __Seven hundred eighty-two__ Dollars, payable in installments, as follows: The first payment
of _Fifty ($50.00)_____Dollars on the __1st_day of __April_____19_89_
and thereafter_ $50.00 per month until principal and interest are paid in full.

payable at the office of said _Hardwood Furniture_ in_ Rapid City, N.Mex_____, with interest
at the rate of_21.0_per cent per_Annum from _Feb 21, 1989____, both before and after judgment, until fully
paid, and a reasonable attorney's fee if placed in the hands of an attorney for collection. This note is given for the following described personal property this day sold to the maker_s_ hereof by_ Hardwood Furniture & Appliances____
to-wit: _1- 25" Sony TV model BX5247-98C_

And it is fully understood and agreed that the ownership, title and right of possession of said property above mentioned, and for
which this note is given, shall not pass from said _Hardwood Furniture & Appl_ or the assignee or holder of this note,
until this note is paid in full; and that should the maker_s_ hereof, at any time before this note is paid in full, attempt to sell or
otherwise dispose of said property, or to remove the same from the premises above noted as the _residence_ of said maker_s_
without the written consent of the holders of this note, or of for any other cause the holders of this note deem themselves insecure
even before the maturity of this note, then and in that case the holders of this note shall have the right to declare this note due,
and it shall be lawful for the said holders of this note to take immediate possession of said property wherever found, and to sell
the same at public or private sale, and without notice to maker_S_, and from the proceeds of such sale pay the balance then due
on said note, together with all costs for the taking and selling of said property, or they may, without sale, endorse the true value
of the property on the note, and the subscriber_S agree_ to pay on this note any balance due thereon after such endorsement
as damages and rental for said property.

Donna P. Smith
Joseph R. Smith

No._1475_

Figure 12

INVESTOR ADVICE

You may determine the chronological age of a structure by inspection of the public records of building permits and tax assessments. Chronological age is not too important in determining the value of a building. The effective age is more critical.

We have all seen ten-year-old homes that, due to hard wear, appear to be twenty years old. Similarly, some twenty-year-old homes, having been well maintained, appear to be less than ten years old.

SEE ALSO: CURABLE DEPRECIATION, EFFECTIVE AGE, and INCURABLE DEPRECIATION.

CLASS LIFE SYSTEM

The Class Life Asset Depreciation Range (ADR), set up by IRS regulations in 1971, allowed taxpayers to take as a reasonable allowance for depreciation, an amount based on any period of years selected by them within a range specified for designated classes of assets.

INVESTOR ADVICE

The ADR system was modified by the Tax Reform Act of 1986 and the Accelerated Cost Recovery System (ACRS). These changes are summarized as follows:

New ACRS Class	Old Mid-point Life
3 yr. Prop.	4 yr. or less
5 yr. Prop.	4 yr. but < 10
7 yr. Prop.	10 yr. but < 16
10 yr. Prop.	16 yr. but < 20

SEE ALSO: ACCELERATED COST RECOVERY SYSTEM (ACRS), and DEPRECIATION.

CLEANING DEPOSIT

A cleaning deposit is made with the landlord by a tenant to guarantee that on lease termination the property will be left in a clean and sanitary condition. Most leases provide for return of the cleaning deposit after the property has been inspected and found satisfactory.

INVESTOR ADVICE

It is most important that your lease *clearly outlines what is expected of the tenant* at the time he or she vacates the property. Some localities require cleaning deposits to be kept in a trust account to assure availability to exiting tenants.

In the event a tenant does not comply with the lease provisions, you should document that failure to comply with a dated written note of the inspection. This note should be witnessed and signed by a party who inspected the property with you—the on-site manager is a good person to use for this task.

If possible, color photographs showing the condition of the property, which resulted in the cleaning deposit forfeiture, should be taken at the time of the inspection. With this documentation you will be able to support your allegations of forfeited cleaning deposit.

SEE ALSO: LEASE, and TRUST ACCOUNT.

CLIFFORD TRUST

A Clifford trust is established by a grantor (parent) for ten years or more with the income from the trust directed as payable to minor children. The assets, often income-producing properties, are returned to the grantor at the end of the ten-year or greater period. The purpose of the trust is to shift real estate investment income from the high-taxed parent to lower-taxed children, while maintaining full management control.

INVESTOR ADVICE

The Tax Reform Act of 1986 abolished income-shifting breaks for Clifford trusts (inter vivoce). If the property placed in the trust reverts to the grantor or his/her spouse at any time, the income is taxable to the grantor. This rule does not apply if the reversion is only after death of the income beneficiary, who is a lineal descendent of the grantor. In other words, if the child dies, the parent(s) gets the property back.

Some tax savings can be made by transferring income-producing real estate by gift to children over fourteen years of age, or assets which will not produce income or capital gains until after a child is fourteen or more years old. The income will be taxed in accordance with the new rules but may still produce a net family income tax savings.

SEE ALSO: GIFT TAXES, INTER VIVOCE, and TRUSTS.

CLOSING COSTS

Closing costs are those paid by buyers and sellers which are attributable to the transfer of real property. Some of the costs often paid by the seller are:

- Realtor fees;
- Title policy premium for policy to buyer;
- Points paid to a lender to grant a VA or FHA loan;
- Property and other taxes to date of transfer;
- One half of the escrow fees to the closing agency; and
- Certain recording fees.

Some of the costs often collected from the buyer at closing are:

- Mortgage origination fees;
- One to two months taxes in advance;
- Cost of one-year insurance policy;
- One to two months' insurance in advance;
- Title policy premium for policy to mortgagee;
- One-half of the escrow fees to the closing agency;
- Certain recording fees; and
- Appraisal fees.

INVESTOR ADVICE

When preparing an earnest money receipt and offer to purchase, you should make sure that the party responsible for payment of closing costs, which are not obviously those of the seller or buyer, is clearly designated.

> **EXAMPLE OF WORDING:** "Buyer and Seller agree to split the closing fee of $100 equally."

These costs may not be clearly identifiable to the closing officer. It is often possible to get the selling party to agree to pay certain buyer costs. If he/she truly wants to sell, he/she may even agree to pay all or most of the closing costs.

SEE ALSO: AMERICAN LAND TITLE ASSOCIATION (ALTA), FHA LOAN, POINTS, and VA LOAN.

CLOUD ON THE TITLE

A cloud on the title is any claim or uncertainty regarding the clear title to a property. Clouds on the title are cleared by quit claim deeds, payments of sums owed, or by court actions. Problems with a title are often discovered as a result of title abstract work.

INVESTOR ADVICE

Clouds on a title may include any number of problems, including:

- Contractor and sub-contractor liens;
- Judgment(s) against the property owner;
- Incomplete probate work on the estate of a deceased former owner;
- Existence of a life estate, dower, and/or curtsey rights;
- Apparent unpaid mortgages and loans—usually still on the records due to failure of the property owner to record a satisfaction piece;
- Tax liens;
- Special assessments which are unpaid; and
- Divorce claims.

Some clouds on a title may not be discovered by the title abstractor. Title insurance is the only guaranteed protection from unknown liabilities or later discoveries.

SEE ALSO: ABSTRACT OF TITLE, CONTRACTOR'S LIENS, JUDGMENT, LIENS, SPECIAL ASSESSMENTS, and TITLE POLICY.

CODICIL

A codicil is a modification of a previously executed will. The codicil may be an addition, deletion, or change of desire on the part of the maker.

INVESTOR ADVICE

Everyone, regardless of financial status, should have a valid will to assure that their estate is settled in accordance with their personal desires. To die intestate is to invoke the will provided by the state for all who fail to provide a valid will of their own.

Lack of a will can cause undue delays in probation of the estate and unnecessary expense. Lengthy settlements can also produce asset deterioration and financial loss.

A codicil is the easiest way to modify an existing will to provide for disposition of newly acquired real estate or to bring the will up to date after sale of some of your assets.

> **MAKE YOUR WILL PERPETUAL:** If all real estate holdings are treated as one asset, your will need not change as properties are bought and sold.

If you are a trader, who is constantly changing your real estate holdings, you may wish to provide for the disposition of your properties by some type of generalized direction or by the establishment of a testamentary trust to receive the real property at your death.

SEE ALSO: ADMINISTRATOR (IX), ESTATE TAXES, EXECUTOR (IX), INHERITANCE TAXES, INTESTATE, TRUST, and PROBATE.

CO-INSURANCE

Fire protection in most areas of the United States is such that a 100% loss to property is rarely suffered. Accordingly, most policies provide 100% coverage if the owner covers his property for a minimum of 80% of value. If the owner fails to provide 80% coverage, a full loss is shared between the property owner and the insurer. The owner is then a co-insurer.

INVESTOR ADVICE

The following example indicates the insurer's liability in a case of full loss to a property not 80% covered:

EXAMPLE

Mr. Jones insured his $600,000 warehouse for $450,000 or 75% of value. The policy contains an 80% co-insurance clause. He suffers a $200,000 loss. What is the insurer's liability?

The formula for calculating the liability is:

Ins'r Liab. = Loss x [Ins. carried / (Co-Ins % X Prop. Val.)]
Ins'r Liab. = $200,000 X [$450,000 / (80% X $600,000)]
Ins'r Liab. = $200,000 x 94% = $187,500

The basic reason for any insurance is to cover a potential loss that you, the owner, cannot afford to cover yourself. You must decide what losses you can afford and balance this against the cost of insurance.

When your property is mortgaged, you may have no alternative but to carry a full 80% of value as required by the loan agreement. If the property is virtually free and clear, you may decide to provide less coverage.

SEE ALSO: HAZARD INSURANCE, and MORTGAGE.

COLLATERALIZED MORTGAGE OBLIGATION (CMO)

Collateralized mortgage obigations are real estate investment bonds, which are backed by mortgage bonds held by the issuing agency.

INVESTOR ADVICE

In the past few years several investment firms have begun to issue real estate income bonds which are backed by the Government National Mortgage Association (GNMA) and Freddy Mac mortgage bonds. The interest paid to the investment firm is that representing the yield on the original bonds, which is passed on to the collateralized-bond buyer. The investment firm issuing the collateralized bonds earns a fee from their discount purchase of the government guaranteed mortgage bonds.

Since these bonds issued by GNMA etc., are only available in large denominations, the collateralization procedure makes it possible for the small investor to participate in these government-backed mortgage programs.

Collateralized mortgage obligation bonds are sold to small investors in $1,000 denominations. Most brokerages require a minimum purchase of five bonds.

SEE ALSO: FEDERAL HOME LOAN MORTGAGE CORPORATION (FREDDY MAC), and GOVERNMENT NATIONAL MORTGAGE ASSOCIATION (GNMA).

COLOR OF TITLE

Color of title is a property title that contains some defect which renders it invalid. While it has the appearance of a title, it is not legal and is said to be a "color of title."

EXAMPLES

Some examples of color of titles include:

- A duly signed and executed deed by a person not having the authority to transfer or sell the property;
- A deed which transfers property to another to avoid payment of debt;
- A deed which transfers property in contemplation of a lawsuit; and
- A deed signed by a person having less than full free title.

INVESTOR ADVICE

Title insurance is your best assurance of a valid title free of future difficulties.
SEE ALSO: ACKNOWLEDGMENT, FREE SIMPLE TITLE, and TITLE INSURANCE.

COMBINATION TRUST

A combination trust is one of three types of real estate investment trusts (REITs).

Combination trusts are set up to provide participants an opportunity to share in equity and mortgage income. The other two types of combination trusts, Equity and Income, provide the investor with only one method of participation.

INVESTOR ADVICE

The Tax Reform Act of 1986 placed certain restrictions on "passive income" derived from REITS. You are advised to consult your accountant and attorney before investing in any of the three types of real estate investment trusts. These types, again, are:

- Equity trusts which invest their capital in real estate that is expected to provide rental income and possible capital gains when the property is sold.

- Mortgage trusts which invest their capital in mortgage-backed loans on real estate. Income is derived from the interest charged on the loans.

- Combination trusts as described in this definition.

SEE ALSO: REAL ESTATE INVESTMENT TRUSTS (REITS).

COMMERCIAL LOAN

A commercial loan is made by a commercial bank or other institution for the purpose of buying land, other commercial property, or a business, but not a residential home.

INVESTOR ADVICE

Lending institutions are authorized to make commercial loans, and make them after a detailed study of the purpose, participants in the project, and estimated value of the business or property to be acquired with the commercial loan. Interest rates are usually several points higher than for a corresponding residential mortgage loan, due to the increased risk involved.

The Small Business Administration directs a program of assistance to small business owners by guaranteeing loans made to them by local commercial banks.

Business owners often require capital to start a new business, to finance the growth of existing businesses, and/or to provide lines of credit to supplement working capital. Real estate investors may also find it advantageous to secure commercial loans for remodeling, purchasing new equipment, or other needs, without disturbing existing mortgage loans or securing second mortgages.

If you are to be a successful applicant for a commercial loan, you should be well prepared to support your request. You should have a valid and well-developed business plan, a pro forma income statement and balance sheet for the start-up date plus one year afterwards. These should be backed up with pro forma cash flow charts to show the adequacy of initial capitalization and funding.

If the loan is on an existing business, you should be prepared to provide actual accounting figures and tax returns for one, two, or three years previous. Where modernization, new equipment acquisitions, or purpose of the new money is expected to change the income picture, pro forma statements showing the expected changes would be in order.

Where it is proposed to purchase real estate or build on existing holdings, a current appraisal of the property should be submitted. One caution here—before ordering an appraisal, make sure that the appraiser selected is acceptable to the proposed lender.

A written resumé for the major participant(s) in a start-up operation is also recommended, since the success of the new venture will largely depend upon the background and experience of the proposed operators.

SEE ALSO: MACK TRUCK FACTOR, NEUTRON BOMB ANALYSIS and PRO FORMA ANALYSIS.

COMMINGLE

To commingle is to mix funds of one type of ownership with those of another.

INVESTOR ADVICE

A real estate broker is forbidden to commingle earnest money funds in his or her real estate trust with those of his or her agency. The broker is also responsible for the prompt deposit of those funds when received. Lawyers, title companies, and others having a fiduciary responsibility for the funds of others are similarly controlled by law.

In those states which follow old Spanish law authorizing separte property ownership, care must be exercised to prevent commingling of joint income with that of the separate propety. The penalty for such commingling is loss of the separate property status.

In thses states described, property and income can be classified as separate (his or hers) or joint. Separate property is that property which the person had at the time of marriage or inherited after marriage. Income from this separate property, if carefully accounted for, is classified as separate.

Income earned by either party during the period of a marriage is classified as community property, regardless of who earned it.

SEE ALSO: COMMUNITY PROPERTY, OLD SPANISH LAW, SEPARATE PROPERTY, and TRUST ACCOUNT.

COMMISSION

Commission is the fee charged by real estate brokerages for listing, selling, and leasing real estate.

INVESTOR ADVICE

Prior to July 1987, it was difficult for real estate buyers to determine who their realtor represented—the buyer or the seller. In July 1987 the National Association of Realtors promulgated regulations regarding realtor/buyer relationships. Now, a realtor must advise a potential buyer, in writing, of his options of having the realtor represent the buyer or the seller. This must be done prior to showing property to the client. Commissions are paid by the party being represented.

Figure 13 shows the form now employed by realtors to notify prospective real estate buyers as to their rights.

SEE ALSO: AGENCY and MULTIPLE LISTING SERVICE.

COMMISSION DOWN

A purchase arrangement in which a real estate agent or broker purchases property, using his/her commission due on the sale as a down payment, is termed commission down.

INVESTOR ADVICE

Commission down is a good deal for the real estate person, but of doubtful advantage to the seller. Since the commission due is in the vicinity of 5–7%, it is usually insufficient security to justify a contract or mortgage commitment for the remainder of the selling price, the two exceptions being VA or FHA financing guaranteed by the federal government.

A commission down sale generally means that the sale is seller-financed or possibly an assumption of existing mortgage with a purchase-money mortgage (second mortgage) taken back by the seller.

EXAMPLE

Mr. Farmer had his apartment house listed for sale for over a year with no offers. His realtor, understanding his desire for a quick sale, made the following offer:

NOTICE TO PROSPECTIVE
REAL ESTATE PURCHASERS

As a prospective purchaser you should know that:
- Generally, the listing and cooperating ("selling") brokers are the agents of the seller.
- Their fiduciary duties of loyalty and faithfulness are owed to their client (the seller).
- While neither broker is your agent, they are able to provide you with a variety of valuable market information and assistance in your decision-making process.

For example, a real estate broker representing the seller can:
- Provide you with information about available properties and sources of financing.
- Show you available properties and describe their attributes and amenities.
- Assist you in submitting an offer to purchase.

Both the listing broker and the cooperating broker are obligated by law to treat you honestly and fairly. They must:
- Present all offers to the seller promptly.
- Respond honestly and accurately to questions concerning the property.
- Disclose material facts the broker knows or reasonably should know about the property.
- Offer the property without regard to race, creed, sex, religion or national origin.

You can, if you feel it necessary, obtain agency representation of a lawyer or a real estate broker, or both.

If you choose to have a real estate broker represent you as your agent, you should:
- Enter into a written contract that clearly establishes the obligations of both parties.
- Specify how your agent will be compensated.

If you have any questions regarding the roles and responsibilities of real estate brokers, please do not hesitate to ask.

I have received, read and understand the information in this "Notice to Prospective Real Estate Purchasers."

Mary J. & George L. Smithers
Name of Prospective Purchaser:

Mary J. Smithers   George L. Smithers
Signature:

Address:
56 N. Albermarl Dr   St Louis, Mo.

Telephone: Date:
804-255-9807   2-24-89

I certify that I have provided the Prospective Purchaser named above with a copy of this "Notice to Prospective Purchasers."

Edward M. Simms, Salesman, Drake Realty Inc.
Name of Broker or Sales Agent:

Edward M. Simms.
Signature:

2-24-59
Date:

Figure 13

1. Purchase price $150,000 as currently listed:
2. Listing commission of 7% as down payment;
3. Assumption of current assumable mortgage of $120,000; and
4. Seller to take back a second mortgage for the balance due, payable in ten years.

Mr. Farmer accepted the offer and the following financial arrangements were finalized:

Purchase Price	$150,000
Less: Downpayment	10,500
Less: Mortgage Assumed	120,000
Second Mortgage Taken Back	$ 19,500

If you wish to dispose of a property at all costs, this type of arrangement is one alternative. This situation suggests a consideration of the following questions:

- If the buyer can only afford a 5–7% down payment, is he/she financially strong enough to maintain his contract or mortgage payments?

- If the economy turns downward, what incentive has the buyer to continue his/her payments on a propety now worth less that he/she paid for it? The buyer has nothing invested to lose.

If you are forced to recover the property at a later date, the resale may be at a price lower than the original sale. There will be nothing left over after the expense of the resale to compensate you for your interest and other losses.
SEE ALSO: ASSUMPTION AGREEMENT, CASH FLOW, and PURCHASE MONEY MORTGAGE.

COMMITMENT LETTER
A commitment letter is provided by a financial institution and commits that institution to provide financing for a project. This could be for purchase of existing property, interim construction financing, or a long-term mortgage.

INVESTOR ADVICE
It is inadvisable to proceed with a project without a firm commitment of needed funds. Wherever possible, it is advisable to have a firm commitment on interest rates as well.

This is particularly true of new construction, which may take a year or so to complete. To proceed with such a project on the assumption that upon completion financing will be available at acceptable rates can result in failure to meet income projections. A failure to meet income projections can be disastrous where public participation through limited partnership sales or corporate stock sales are required.
SEE ALSO: COMMITTED INSTITUTIONAL WAREHOUSING, COMMITTED TECHNICAL WAREHOUSING and LIMITED PARTNERSHIPS.

COMMITTED INSTITUTIONAL WAREHOUSING
A standby loan commitment, usually for a one- or two-year duration, which is made to a commmercial lender by a mortgage banker to back that lender's agreement to provide long-term financing on a commercial project is a committed institutional

warehouse. The source of the required funds to be provided by a mortgage banker may have already been determined at the time the commitment is made, or may be identified at a later date.

INVESTOR ADVICE

Due to the turn-around time required to build a project and deliver instruments to the commercial lender's permanent investor, economic conditions may be such that the permanent investor is unwilling to provide the funds when required. The warehoused funds will provide interim financing until another investor can be found.

Before initiating a new project, you should be assured that your mortgage lender has the financial strength or committed institutional warehousing to guarantee its obligation to you. Your best assurance of the mortgage lender's capability to deliver is its time and business, total assets, reputation, and record of service in your locality.

Most long-term financing is provided by mutual savings banks, savings and loan associations, REITs, pension funds, and life insurance companies.

SEE ALSO: COMMITTED TECHNICAL WAREHOUSING.

COMMITTED TECHNICAL WAREHOUSING

Funds provided to a mortgage banker to cover the time delay between closing a mortgage loan and its acceptance by a permanent lender is termed committed technical warehousing. Commercial mortgage permanent financing normally is obtained from life insurance companies, mutual savings banks, REITs, or pension funds.

INVESTOR ADVICE

The most common need for warehousing is due to the delay between closing the loan and its acceptance by the permanent lender. At this point in the process, the mortgage banker risks an interest rate rise which may make permanent lenders reluctant to make advanced commitment.

If the mortgage banker is unable to obtain a permanent loan, he/she must rely on standby commitment from a commercial bank. This may cause the mortgage banker to lose in one of two ways:

1. Pay a forfeiture price for failure to perform; or
2. Be forced to close the loan at a price below par value.

SEE ALSO: COMMITTED INSTITUTIONAL WAREHOUSING.

COMMUNITY DEVELOPMENT BLOCK GRANT

Community development block grants are federal and/or state funds awarded to a community to assist in the procurement of land or the rehabilitation of older structures. These projects are usually considered "slum clearance" projects or are initiated in old and depressed commercial areas.

INVESTOR ADVICE

Before becoming involved in a community development project you should examine the tax consequences and requirements for accelerated depreciation. Minor deviations in planning may result in a denial of block funds.

When block funds are available to a community for the purchase of land and its preparation for development, an excellent opportunity often exists for real estate investment. It is not unusual for the community to offer incentives to a developer who form of partial tax relief for a period of time, outright gift of the land to the developer, or preferential financing through Municipal-backed Bonds.

SEE ALSO: ACCELERATED COST RECOVERY.

COMMUNITY PROPERTY

That property acquired by a married couple from funds earned by their labors is termed community property. Those states which recognize community property also recognize separate property—property owned prior to marriage, or inherited or received as a gift after marriage. The concept of separate and community property has its roots in old Spanish law.

INVESTOR ADVICE

Care must be exercised in the management of properties and businesses which have their beginnings as separate properties, if the owner desires to maintain the separate classification.

EXAMPLE

An unincorporated business or partnership will gradually lose its separate classification if earnings are commingled with the business or property. Earnings from labor or from jointly held investments are normally classified as community property funds.

If maintenance of a separate classification is desired, a business can be incorporated and only those earnings removed from the corporation as dividends will become community property.

At the death of a separate property owner, the property is disposed of in accordance with his/her will. One-half of all community property belongs to the surviving spouse and only the other half may be distributed in accordance with the deceased's wishes.

Where property is allowed to shift from separate to community status, the deceased loses control of one-half of the property.

SEE ALSO: OLD SPANISH LAW, and SEPARATE PROPERTY.

COMPARABLE MARKET VALUE

Comparable market value is an appraisal technique in which the value of similar properties sold, adjusted for the differences between those properties and the property being appraised, is used to estimate fair market value.

INVESTOR ADVICE

When reviewing appraisals of real property, you should carefully examine the appraiser's adjustments for differences in the subject property and the market comparables. Although such appraisal adjustments are based on the professional opinion of the appraiser, insufficient justification of such adjustments can result in a poor evaluation.

Adjustments are made for one or more of the following types of differences:

* Size of the land parcel;

* Shape of the land parcel;

* Location;

* Zoning;

- Access to the property;

- Age of improvements on the property;

- Size of improvements (buildings);

- Quality of improvements;

- Ratio of rentable space to total space;

- Type of financing of the sale; and

- Time of sale.

SEE ALSO: MARKET APPROACH TO VALUE, and RENTABLE SQUARE FOOTAGE.

COMPARATIVE SALES APPROACH

The comparitive sales approach is the preferred method of evaluating land parcels where reliable sales data is available. The approach compares actual recent sales of similar parcels, after adjusting for differences in physical and economic factors affecting value.

INVESTOR ADVICE

The appraisal of land is one of the most difficult tasks which a real estate appraiser is required to perform. The reason for this difficulty is the large amount of personal judgement required to make appropriate adjustments in observed sales data. While the sales price and terms of the sale can be verified, the effect of other physical and economic differences on the agreed sales price can only be gauged by the appraiser's past experience.

Differences between comparable sales and the subject property may include any or all of the following:

- Size and shape of the parcels;

- Front-footage versus lot size;

- Location;

- Zoning;

- Access to streets and right-of-ways;

- Terms of the sale;

- Time of the sale;

- Availability of utilities and sanitary sewers; and

- Lot improvements, such as curbs, gutters, paved streets, sidewalks, and street lighting.

In reviewing a land appraisal, you should examine the range of the adjusted values of the comparable sales, to determine if the appraiser has selected a logical value for the subject property. After the adjustments to all comparable sales have been made, it is reasonable to expect the adjusted values to fall into a "shot group" or fairly narrow range.

If a wide variation in adjusted values is observed, it is probably due to a poor selection of comparable sales, or incorrect or inappropriate adjustments. An appraised value, based on an average of the adjusted sales, is probably less accurate than a mean value selected from the list. This is especially true when extreme highs and lows have resulted from the adjustment process.

Your best assurance of a good evaluation is based upon the qualifications, experience, and recommended competence of the appraiser.

SEE ALSO: DEPTH TABLES, and FRONT-FOOT.

COMPASS CALL

Compass call is a surveyor's term indicating direction in degrees, minutes, and seconds, by which a property line extends from a point of beginning or turning. In the metes and bounds method of property identification, each side of the property is defined by a compass call and length of side. The complete description begins at a clearly defined point, travels around the property and returns the reader to the original point of beginning.

EXAMPLE

Beginning at a point 110.05 feet South and 56.87 feet East of the NW corner of Section 25, T 1 South, Range 5 West Salt Lake Base and Meridian and continuing South 38°15'45" East 189.50 feet, thence . . .

SEE ALSO: METES AND BOUNDS, and SURVEY.

COMPETENT PARTY

A competent party is a person or legal entity fully capable by age, position, and mental capacity to enter into a legal contract with others.

INVESTOR ADVICE
See *Investor Advice* under "Capacity to Contract."
SEE ALSO: CAPACITY TO CONTACT, and CONTRACT.

COMPLETION BOND

A completion bond is posted by a property owner in lieu of compliance with certain building codes to assure the required work will be completed at the appropriate time. Completion bonds are also posted by contractors to assure timely completion of projects for which they have contracted to build.

EXAMPLE

Current building codes require curbs, gutters, and sidewalks to be installed for all new buildings or major renovations authorized after a certain date. There are currently no curbs, gutters, or sidewalks on the block on which Mr. Jones is building a new warehouse. Mr. Jones posts a completion bond to assure that he will comply with the new regulation at some time in the future, after a specified percentage of other property owners on the block add these improvements.

The small cost of the bond is less than the present value of the delayed cost of adding the improvements. Thus, funds required for the project can be freed for other investments.

INVESTOR ADVICE
Where possible it will be more economical to post a bond than complete the required items. A bond can usually be acquired for less than the interest earned on the cost of the improvement which is delayed. Please note the applicable term is "delayed" not "avoided." Eventually, the improvements must be made.

SEE ALSO: BUILDING CODES, and CONSTRUCTION PERMIT.

COMPONENT DEPRECIATION
Component depreciation is a method of achieving a larger depreciation than possible by depreciation of a building as a unit. In component depreciation each component—electrical system, plumbing system, roof, etc.—is depreciated on the basis of its useful life. Since many of the components of a building have a shorter life than the building as a whole, a larger dollar depreciation per year is achieved than is possible by depreciating the unit as a whole.

INVESTOR ADVICE
The Tax Reform Act of 1981 and its ACRS rules eliminated component depreciation. This prohibition was continued in the Tax Reform Act of 1986. All properties, both residential and nonresidential, acquired after December 31, 1986, must be depreciated using the straight-line method. The recovery period, however, was extended to 27 1/2 years for residential and 31 1/2 years for nonresidential properties.

SEE ALSO: ACCELERATED COST RECOVERY, and DEPRECIATION.

COMPOUND INTEREST
Compound interest is interest on previous interest earned.

INVESTOR ADVICE
In times when interest rates were very low, compound interest was of little significance. As the value of money has increased, compound interest became more and more important in business decisions.

This expanded use produced a proliferation of compound interest tables, which were later supplemented or replaced by the hand-held financial computer.

Today, business students and practitioners of the various financial arts are eminently familiar with present value and future value techniques, which are practical uses of compound interest.

SEE ALSO: FUTURE VALUE OF ONE, and PRESENT VALUE OF ONE PER PERIOD.

CONDEMNATION
The taking of private property by a government entity, or its authorization, under the power of eminent domain is called condemnation. The taking is authorized where the land is needed for public purposes, such as widening a road, construction of a new road, or redevelopment of a blighted area. It can also be used by a public utility in order to modernize or provide better service.

INVESTOR ADVICE

If your land is to be taken for a public project, the condemning agency will have it appraised and make an offer based upon that appraisal. Having done so, the government agency may proceed with their project even if you do not accept the offer. The agency must deposit the proffered amount in an escrow account, where it remains until the courts have determined the correct compensation.

If you feel an offer for your taken property is unjust, you may seek relief in the courts. The law provides for you to receive compensation for the value of the land taken, plus compensation of any damages to the remainder which was caused by the taking.

The apraisal of real estate under condemnation is a very special art. Following is a list of common errors committed by appraisers in this situation:

- It is not unusual for an inexperienced appraiser to calculate the value of "the taking" but fail to consider the damages to the property remaining.

- The appraiser will accurately determine the value per square foot of the total property, but fail to realize that a strip along the front may be more valuable per square foot.

- The appraiser may accurately determine the value of land to be taken but fail to add compensation for fences, landscaping, or other improvements which are destroyed by the taking.

- The appraiser may fail to realize that the taking may destroy the current utility of the remaining land. In other words, it may prevent easy customer access to or visibility of commercial property.

- The appraiser may not realize that "the taking" will reduce the remaining property size to a point where it is no longer eligible for Greenbelt Tax Classification, and future taxes will be based on a higher value assessment.

> **CAUTION !** All attorneys are not proficient in condemnation work. Choose only an attorney who specializes in this field.

If you feel an offer is unjust, you should consult an attorney who specializes in condemnation actions. Not every attorney will be capable of handling your case, which involves many complex aspects not encountered in the normal practice of law.

SEE ALSO: APPRAISER, BUNDLE OF RIGHTS, and GREENBELT TAX CLASSIFICATION.

CONDITIONAL SALE

In a conditional sale, the buyer receives the property but the seller retains title until all monys due have been paid. This is sometimes referred to as a "land contract sale" or simply a "contract sale."

INVESTOR ADVICE

In some states it is legal to record a contract sale thereby putting the public on notice that the contract buyer has a claim on the property. Unfortunately, it also gives all the details of the sale—interest rate, sales price, etc.

The same protection can be achieved by recording a "notice of contract" without revealing any of the details of the transaction. The buyer can prepare a "notice of interest in real property" form, have it notarized and then record it to accomplish the same results as the recordig of the contract itself.

Figure 14 is a typical form used for this purpose. It should be noted that the seller has no action to perform, as the notice has no effect on the propety title. It is purely a public notice which, if challenged, must be supported by other documentation—the contract between seller and buyer.

SEE ALSO: NOTICE OF CONTRACT.

CONDOMINIUM

A condominium is a common ownership arrangement, dating from Roman times, in which an individual buys an apartment, town house, or commercial unit in a multi-unit project and receives title to it. In addition he/she is a joint owner in the surrounding land, lobby, swimming pool, and other common facilities.

The condominium owner is free to decorate or change the interior of his or her unit at any time. The condominium owner may also sell his/her unit at the going market rate, but may be required to have association approval of the proposed buyer.

The condominium owner is charged a monthly maintenance fee set by the condominium association, of which he/she is a member. Maintenance fees are collected to insure that the project as a whole is properly maintained. This maintenance fee covers the common facilities and the exterior of all buildings and shared amenities, such as swimming pools, exercise rooms, meeting facilities, and parking lots. Each unit owner, however, is responsible for his/her own mortgage and taxes and interior maintenance/decoration.

The cooperative apartment is another type of common ownership but is far more restrictive than the condominium, and differs in manner of title, financing, and other aspects. See the discussion on Cooperative Apartments for details.

INVESTOR ADVICE

You should be very careful in buying a new condominium from the develper, who is often inclined to underestimate the required monthly maintenance fees in order to make the units more saleable. Also, if only a few units have been sold, there is no owner's association. The by-laws of the project provide for the establishment of an owner's association and election of officers after a specified percentage of the units have been sold. Until that time, the developer is, in effect, the association.

??????? Are the quoted condo fees accurate? Check the records of older units. Compare fees on new units with older existing projects.

Until the majority of the units are sold, it is possible you may be associating yourself with a bank, which will foreclose on the unsold units if the developer goes into bankruptcy or otherwise abandons the project. You should be particularly careful in buying into a project in which the develper has not finished all construction.

Where the developer is in financial trouble, he/she may fail to pay his/her share of the maintenance cost on unsold units, thereby leaving that burden to be shared among the sold unit owners.

In buying a condominium unit, you should determine what common facilities are shared by the units being sold and who holds title to them. It is not unusual for developers to point out all of the amenities without saying who owns the facilities which you are allowed to use—temporarily.

After all units have been sold, you may find that titles to swimming pools, tennis courts, golf course, and other amenities have been retained by the developer, who then offers to sell them to the association.

NOTICE OF INTEREST IN REAL PROPERTY

STATE OF UTAH   )
)
COUNTY OF   Salt Lake   )

TO WHOM IT MAY CONCERN:

      Notice is hereby given that the undersigned has an interest in that certain real property situate in Salt Lake   County, State of Utah, described as follows:

    Lots 51,52,53 & 54 Block 23, Big Field Survey, Plat A

      Said interest is evidenced by a certain Uniform Real Estate Contract dated 23rd February, 1989 by and between __Roger P. Rabbit_____ _____ as seller, and the undersigned __Elbert H. Griffith_ _____, as buyers.

_____
_____
_____
_____

Elbert H. Griffith

_____

      Subscribed and sworn to before me this_23rd___ day of _February_ A. D., 19_89_.

Mary Den Thorell
/Notary Public

Residing at _Salt Lake City, Ut._

My Commission Expires:

    June 13th, 1991

Figure 14

While the discussion and emphasis so far has been focused on residential units, offices, shopping centers, and other real estate projects can also be developed and sold as condominiums. Keep in mind, however, that a real estate investor or developer who becomes involved in a condominium project, faces several problems which are different than normal project development. Among these are:

- Inability to effectively sell the product until the project is nearly completed. Buyers/users are not interested in buying the "pie in the sky." They want to see what they will be getting.

- Considerable television, radio, and newspaper advertising is usually required to get project sales going.

- One of each of the unit types must be fully furnished and decorated to provide the sales staff with something to show the customer.

- A resident sales staff will be required for the first few months of the selling period.

- It may be necessary to offer cost-reduction incentives to key personalities to favorably influence potential buyers. For instance, a golf course project might try to entice a well-known professional golfer to move into the project.

SEE ALSO: COOPERATIVE APARTMENTS, and TIME SHARING OWNERSHIPS.

CONSISTENT USE THEORY

Consistent use theory is a real estate appraisal guideline that directs the appraiser to value land as in one use. This theory is usually applied to land which is in transition from one usage to another.

INVESTOR ADVICE

Lesser experienced appraisers may make the mistake of appraising land for one use and the improvements (buildings) at another. Just because a building appears to have a considerable physical life, it does not necessarily improve the value of the land which may have a higher and better use. As a matter of fact, the building may have a negative value based upon the cost of removal to facilitate a higher use.

The experienced appraiser will apply the theory of consistent use by appraising the property in two ways: (1) as a building/land package zoned for that purpose; and (2) as vacant land zoned at the highest and best utilization. The higher of the two values obtained by the two approaches will indicate the current highest and best use of the building/land package.

SEE ALSO: CAPITALIZATION OF INCOME.

CONSTRUCTION DRAW

A construction draw is a partial advance of a construction loan based on work actually accomplished as of the date of the draw. Builders normally construct new projects with borrowed funds. The provisions of the loan provide for periodic payments to be made by the lender in accordance with work accomplished. The construction loan is repaid at the time permanent financing is provided for the completed project.

INVESTOR ADVICE

Payments to contractors and sub-contractors are made only after signing lien wavers, which assure the lender that future claims for the same work will not be submitted. Payments to subcontractors normally require approval of the contractor who arranged the construction loan.

Figure 15 shows a typical lien waver signed by both the contractor and the homeowner, who certifies that the work was actually performed.

If you have control of a construction loan, never authorize a payment unless you have inspected the project and assured yourself that the work claimed has been completed. If you sign a certificate stating the work has been completed and it is later found that it was not, you will be personally liable for the cost to perform the uncompleted work.

> **WHOA!** Don't sign that lien waiver until you or your appointed representative have inspected the property and verified completion of the work.

SEE ALSO: LIEN WAIVER and CONSTRUCTION LOAN.

WAIVER OF LIEN

TO ......Big..National..Bank..of..Salt..Lake..City,..Utah

    I, the undersigned....George..I...Contractor,..D.B.A...Utah..Heating..Co.............,

in consideration of the sum of $.2,.250,.00.... paid to me, the receipt of which is hereby acknowledged, hereby waive and release all lien or right of lien now existing or that may hereafter arise for work or labor

performed, or materials furnished on or before the....10th...day of....October..................., 19..88.,

for the improvement of the following described property situated in.....Salt..Lake.................**County,**

State of......Utah........................., to-wit:

.Residence..on..Lot..27,..Hardwood..Subdivision,..Section..1.........................

....

....

And I further agree to furnish a good and sufficient waiver of lien on said premises from every person or persons or corporation furnishing labor or materials for said premises, who may be acting under any contract with me.

....October..10,......, 19..88   *George I. Contractor*...................................

    I hereby certify that the labor or material, or both, receipted for above was actually performed, or used, at the above described property.

    T. B. Homeowner.......................................

Figure 15

CONSTRUCTION LOAN

A construction loan is a temporary loan made to a contractor or property owner to provide funds for construction. The construction loan is paid off at the time the permanent financing is closed. Funds from a construction loan are normally advanced as portions of the work are completed. Payments are made as authorized by the loan provisions and upon receipt of lien waivers.

INVESTOR ADVICE

Construction loans normally bear significantly higher interest rates than permanent long-term financing.

When beginning a new project, it is imperative that a firm's time schedule be established with all contractors and that they be bonded for timely completion. Where contractor bonding is specified, the bond normally assures proper performance as well as timeliness. Items covered in the bond might include:

- Timely completion of entire project;
- Completion to allow partial occupancy by a specified date;
- Quality of the work to include certain standards and specifications;
- Contractor and sub-contractor responsibility for injuries to workmen or others during the construction period;
- Condition of the property at the time of the contractor's withdrawal from the project; and
- Security protection during the construction period.

SEE ALSO: CONSTRUCTION DRAW, and LIEN WAIVER.

CONSTRUCTION PERMIT

A construction permit is issued by appropriate municipal authorities signifying that the cited plans and specifications conform with all building regulations and zoning requirements. Building permits are posted on the construction site and provide a positive notice of satisfactory completion of each component or phase of the project. This is indicated by the inspector's initials or signature on each of the covered construction phases such as:

- Building footings;
- Building foundation;
- Building framing;
- Rough plumbing and electrical;
- Finished plumbing and electrical; and
- Final inspection and approval for occupancy.

Fees charged for building permits pay for the work of the inspetors charged with checking each phase of the building program. Permit fees are usually based on the estimated cost of the project.

A builder is forbidden to proceed with work phases that will hide or obscure other work until the prior work has been inspected and approved.

Building inspectors must assure that all work is in accordance with the building plans and specifications and that all materials utilized are those meeting plan requirements. The inspector does not assure that the design is good. This is the responsibility of the engineering section that approves the building permit.

SEE ALSO: COMPLETION BOND, RESTRICTIVE COVENANTS, and ZONING.

CONSTRUCTIVE EVICTION

Constructive eviction is an act by a landlord that renders a property uninhabitable.

INVESTOR ADVICE

When remodeling or construction of additions to property is required, you must take into consideration the effect of such actions upon your tenants. Excessive noise, dust, or other inconveniences may constitute constructive eviction. When this occurs, you as landlord may be liable for the expenses of the tenants who were evicted.

Good planning can avoid many problems of this type. For instance, individual units can be refurbished after an old tenant vacates, prior to occupancy by a new one. Hallways and common areas can be refinished in peicemeal fashion, which will allow access to some of these areas while the work is continuing on the remainder.

SEE ALSO: LEASE RIGHTS and TENANT.

CONSTRUCTIVE NOTICE

Constructive notice is one provided in such a manner that a prudent person should have become aware of it. When public notice of a situation or event has been given, all persons are assumed by the law to have been informed.

INVESTOR ADVICE

Most notices to the public which concern real property are made by the recording of appropriate documentation. Notices in the legal section of newspapers are also used to give constructive notice.

EXAMPLE

The recording of a mortgage, notice of contract sale, or lien in the county clerk's official record books (in the county in which a property is situated) constitutes constructive notice to the public of the existence of clouds on the title of that property.

Any prudent person who desired to determine the status of a deed to the property should order a title search which will reveal any such notices.

SEE ALSO: ACKNOWLEDGMENT, NOTARY, and RECORDING.

CONSTRUCTIVE POSSESSION

When title to property is transferred, the owner is said to have constructive possession. Constructive possession differs from actual possession in that the property ownership has changed but actual possession may or may not have occurred.

INVESTOR ADVICE

If actual possession is not possible at the time of deed transfer, the new owner is entitled to a consideration. However, to avoid future problems, the time of actual possession must be clearly indicated in the earnest money receipt and offer to purchase as well as what consideration is to be paid for any anticipated delay in assuming actual possession concurrent with ownership.

This situation often occurs when a residential property is sold. The seller may be reluctant to vacate the premises until he has the money in his pockets, an event that only occurs at closing. The minute the property is closed, the new owner has constructive possession.

When the earnest money receipt provides for a few days to vacate, a consideration to the buyer is in order. Generally this consideratin is an amount equal to or slightly greater than the buyer's mortgage payments including taxes and insurance.

It is not unusual for the same events to occur in the sale of apartments, when the owner is occupying one of the units.

SEE ALSO: ACTUAL POSSESSION, EARNEST MONEY RECEIPT, and OFFER TO PURCHASE.

CONSTRUCTIVE RECEIPT

A constructive receipt is one performed in the eyes of the law but not necessarily in fact. Thus funds delivered to an authorized agent of a principal constitutes constructive receipt by the principal.

INVESTOR ADVICE

Constructive receipt is often accomplished by payments to escrow agents, attorneys, or land title companies.

EXAMPLE

Mr. Carpenter purchases two lots in a new subdivision, which has been sold to the developer on a lot release basis. The XYZ Title Company has been designated as escrow agent for all sales.

Mr. Carpenter makes a full cash payment to XYZ in accordance with an earnest money contract signed by the developer. XYZ then remits the designated amount to the land owner, the balance to the developer, and provides Mr. Carpenter with a warranty deed to the two lots.

SEE ALSO: CONSTRUCTIVE NOTICE, and LOT RELEASE SYSTEM.

CONSTRUCTIVE VALUE

Constructive value is a hypothetical value developed by an appraiser. This is in lieu of a fair market value deduced from actual market data in which idealized conditions of competition were present.

INVESTOR ADVICE

Fair market value, as opposed to hypothetical value, assumes four basic conditions:

1. There exists many buyers and sellers, so that a decision to buy or sell does not materially affect the selling price.
2. All buyers and sellers are reasonably knowledgable of market conditions.
3. The property is not unique.
4. Buyers and sellers are free to enter and leave the market at will.

In certain situations this definition of fair market value will force the appraiser to think in terms of constructive value—a hypothetical value based on idealized conditions in a purely competitive market.

In real life there is no such thing as a "purely competitive market," particularly for the single family residence. There is not an unlimited source of buyers and sellers and, additionally, neither has a perfect knowledge of the market as a whole. Too, residences are so different in size, amenities, and locality that buyers and sellers are unable to make perfect comparisons. Lastly, the fourth criteria for a fair market is seldom achievable. Buyers and sellers more often buy because of a necessity than on a more rational basis.

Where a fair market value is impossible to determine, the appraisor must think in terms of "most probable sales price."

SEE ALSO: APPRAISOR, and FAIR MARKET VALUE.

CONTINGENCY FUND

A contingency fund is set aside to provide for payment of unexpected liabilities.

INVESTOR ADVICE

If your cash flow is very tight, and an unexpected loss or liability would be disasterous to your operation, a contingency fund would be advisable. In start-up situations it is not unusual for rentals to fall short of mortgage and other out-of-pocket payments. A minimum of a two-month cash contingency fund is recommended. The following example illustrates the need for a contingency fund.

EXAMPLE

Dr. Cash recently constructed a twelve-unit apartment complex on a property he owned. Since the land was valued at about 20% of the total value of the proposed project, Dr. Cash was able to borrow enough to completely finance the construction. His investment outlook was very bright.

By the time construction was completed, however, the local economy was in a recession and it became necessary to reduce the anticipated rental price in order to lease the property. Even with these reductions, complete occupancy was not achieved for a full year.

A further problem developed shortly after construction was completed. It was discovered that improper grading was diverting water run-off to a neighbor to the south. Correction of this problem required construction of a concrete retaining wall, considerable fill, and regrading and re-landscaping of the affected area. Total cost of the project was in excess of $15,000.

In spite of the optimistic long-range outlook for the project, Dr. Cash found himself in a cash bind. Cash flow from rentals showed a negative $1,000 per month and the water problem added an additional $15,000 deficit. Dr. Cash was required to borrow on his own residence in order to meet his mortgage obligations.

SEE ALSO: CASH FLOW, DEBT SERVICE, PRO FORMA ANALYSIS, and RESERVES FOR REPLACEMENT.

CONTINGENT FEE BASIS

A contingent fee is an attorney fee for services, based on the amount of a negotiated settlement or court award to his/her client. Contingent fees can be as high as 50% since the outcome of a settlement or litigation is uncertain.

INVESTOR ADVICE

When a dispute arises with another party that cannot be settled amicably, the services of attorneys may be necessary. These professionals working as third parties in a dispute may be able to negotiate a settlement without going to court.

A lawsuit should be considered as a last resort, since the cost of this process is frequently high. When the decision is made to take this path of last resort, be sure that your attorney is the very best available. A poor attorney or one working out of his/her field of expertise is worthless.

However, good trial attorneys are very expensive. They will demand a cash retainer to accept your case, or they may possibly agree to work on a contingency basis. Normally the contingency fee basis will be higher than payment for time involved. If your chances of success are great, it is preferable to pay your attorney directly. If your chances of success are low, a contingency basis may be your best bet.

WARNING Few legal firms will refuse a case, whether experienced in your problem area or not. For real estate matters, select only an attorney who is a real estate specialist.

In litigating real estate problems, you must be aware that *all attorneys are not experts in real estate matters*. Also, all attorneys are *not skilled trial lawyers*. Select your attorney after careful examination of his/her trial record and on the recommendation of others who have used him/her successfully.

Don't expect a quick resolution of your problem. It is not unusual for a case to take one to two years to reach the trial process, which is another good reason to try an out of court settlement.

SEE ALSO: LITIGATION.

CONTINUITY OF OPERATION

The smooth transition of ownership and continued operation of a business after death of one or more owners is termed continuity of operation.

INVESTOR ADVICE

If an owner-partner of a business (proprietorship or partnership) dies, that proprietorship or partnership also dies unless provisions have been made for its continuation. A man and wife constitute a partnership, unless the property is in a state which recognizes separate property. Thus, rental property in joint ownership is in limbo until the deceased's estate can be probated.

If the property is jointly owned with a right of survivor provision, the property can be transferred to the survivor by the simple payment of estate taxes and filing of a proof of death. It may take several months to clear the deed, but the survivor can usually continue the operation without difficulty.

A partnership between persons other than man and wife or without a right of survivorship results in a dissolution of the business upon the death of a partner. To avoid this problem partners should have, during their lifetime, established a funded buy-sell agreement. This agreement must:

• Establish a price for the survivor to buy out the deceased's interest or a formula for calculating the price.

- Be funded through partnership insurance, payable to the surviving partner, to guarantee availability of funds for the buy-out. An agreement allowing the purchase but without the necessary funds is valueless.

If the same property is in a trust, the trustees (surviving spouse and others) may continue to operate the business in spite of the loss of one of the trustees (deceased).

If the property is owned by a family corporation, the officers can continue the business without interruption, even though the stock ownership will not be determined until the estate has been settled.

It is wise to consult your attorney and/or estate planning counselor prior to taking ownership to real property. It may be that a properly worded deed can prevent many future legal problems.

SEE ALSO: CORPORATION, DECEDENT, INTESTATE, JOINT TENANCY, TRUST, PARTNER-SHIP, and WILL.

CONTRACT

A legally binding agreement between two or more parties to do or not to do something is termed a contract. Under the statute of fraud in the various states, contracts involving real estate transactions must be in writing.

INVESTOR ADVICE

The most common types of contracts encountered by the real estate investor are:

- The earnest money receipt and offer to purchase;

- The earnest money receipt and exchange agreement;

- The earnest money receipt and offer to lease;

- The lease;

- The option agreement;

- Uniform real estate contract (land contract);

- Assignment of contract; and

- The sales agency contract—property listing for sale.

Read all contracts carefully. If you do not understand the legal language in the instrument, seek legal advice before signing.

Very often you will be asked to sign certain legal documents at a time when it is impossible to read all of the fine print. This is certainly true at a closing, where many papers must be signed by buyers and sellers. Ask the closing officer to explain any documents about which you have questions.

Most closings involve the signing of standard, state-approved forms. The state has protected you by assuring that the forms are legal and fair. Your responsibility is to carefully review all typed additions and changes to these forms. While this inspection does not completely substitute for the full and careful reading, it usually assures that your specific intentions are properly incorporated into the standard agreement.

SEE ALSO: ASSIGNMENT OF CONTRACT, EARNEST MONEY RECEIPT AND OFFER TO PURCHASE, EARNEST MONEY RECEIPT AND OFFER TO LEASE, EARNEST MONEY RECEIPT AND EXCHANGE AGREEMENT, LEASE, OPTION, and UNIFORM REAL ESTATE CONTRACT.

CONTRACT PRICE

The contract price is the selling price as defined by a land contract sale. This is not necessarily the same as Fair Market Value.

INVESTOR ADVICE

NOTICE Contract price and fair market value are seldom the same.

You should carefully consider any contract sale in its entirety rather than the quoted contract price. When the seller accepts payment at interest rates below the going rate, the contract price has undoubtedly overstated the fair market value by the amount of interest lost to the seller by acceptance of this lower-than-going rate.

The contract price may also have included an amount to compensate for the risk involved in lending to a particular buyer of for instance, less than perfect character. Compensation may also have been included for risks caused by less than a normal downpayment.

Appraisal reports based on contract sales price, without appropriate adjustments, are subject to substantial error. You should make sure that the appraiser has considered the terms of the sale in adjusting his/her market comparables.

Remember that fair market value is based upon a cash sale. If you do not receive all cash for your property, you are entitled to normal interest on all moneys not received and for additional risks taken in agreeing to such a transaction.

SEE ALSO: CREATIVE FINANCING, PURCHASE MONEY MORTGAGE, and CONTRACT RATE.

CONTRACT RATE

Contract rate is the interest rate specified by terms of a contract sale.

INVESTOR ADVICE

If you can purchase property for its fair market value by assuming an existing contract or mortgage or a new contract from the seller which bears a lower rate than available through normal mortgage sources, you will have purchased the property at discount.

The discount is equal to the present value of the monthly savings due to the lower interest rate. To calculate this discount, you would need to know the savings in monthly payments due to the advantageous interest rate, the going value of money, and the holding period in which the savings is applicable. Where the holding period is unknown, an assumed five year period can be used.

EXAMPLE

You have an opportunity to buy an income-producing property for $200,000 and assume an existing contract with a balance of $150,000 at 7.5% interest. The contract payments are calculated on a twenty-year amortization rate with the balance due in five years. Mortgage rates on similar properties are going for 9.0%. The value of money to investors like yourself is 10%.

What is the discount offered?

Monthly payments @ 9.0% = $1,349.59
Monthly payments @ 7.5% =   1,208.39
              Difference $ 141.20
PV of 1 @ 10% for 5 yrs = 47.0654
Discount = $141.20 x 47.0654 = $6,646

SEE ALSO: CONTRACT PRICE, and PRESENT VALUE OF ONE PERIOD.

CONTRACT RENT

Contract rent is that rental price agreed upon between lessor and lessee.

INVESTOR ADVICE

When a leased property is sold, the selling price is often the sum of two values:

1. The leasehold interest; and
2. The owner's interest.

A leasehold interest occurs when a long term lease calls for contract rent less than the economic or market rent. The leaseholder's interest is the present value of the difference between these values. The owner's interest is the fair market value less the leasehold interest.

EXAMPLE

A property owner is considering a sale of his office building, which is currently leased to the United States Government for ten more years, at the rate of $8.00 per square foot/yr. Similar properties are currently leasing for $10.00 per square foot/year.
The building contains 30,000 s.f. of leasable space.
A current appraisal indicates a fair market value of $3,300,000. What is the owner's interest? Does the leaseholder have an interest? If so, what is its value?
Based upon the given definition, a lessor's interest exists since the lessor is required to pay less than the current economic rent.
Lessor's Interest = PV for ten years of the difference between economic rent and contract rent. If the current prime rate of interest is 8.0%, we find that the Present Value Factor for one payment/year for ten years at 8.0% is:

6.7101

Lessor's Interest = 6.7101 x ($10 -$8) x 30,000 s.f.
                  = $402,605
Owner's Equity = $3,300,000 – $402,605 = $2,897,395

SEE ALSO: ECONOMIC RENT, and PRESENT VALUE OF ONE PERIOD.

CONTRACTOR'S LIEN

A contractor's lien is recorded against a property for unpaid services rendered by a contractor. No action by the courts is required for a filing to be effective, provided the filing is accomplished within the number of days specified by state law.

INVESTOR ADVICE

Figure 16 shows a typical form used by contractors to give official notice of their claim for services rendered.

When payments are made to a contractor or sub-contractor, you should have him/her sign a lien waver which can be filed with the invoice of services rendered. If the contractor has recorded a lien, it will be necessary to obtain a release of lien from the contractor and have it recorded to clear the property title. Figure 17 shows the type of form that you should obtain from your contractor at the time of payment on a recorded lien.

SEE ALSO: CLOUD ON THE TITLE, CONSTRUCTION DRAW, LIEN, and LIEN WAIVER.

CONTROLLABLE EXPENSE

Controllable expenses are those expenses which are made at the discretion of the manager. Controllable expenses are in direct contrast to fixed expenses in which little or no control is possible.

INVESTOR ADVICE

As a prudent manager of investment property you are unlikely to expend funds which are not necessary. However, you may be tempted to defer some expenses in order to increase profits for a current accounting period. Before delaying repairs and replacements, the following questions must be answered:

• Will the deferred expense result in an ultimate higher cost due to the delay?

• Will the deferred expense affect the appearance and/or rentability of the property?

• Is the vacancy factor likely to increase as a result of the deferred expense?

If the answer to any of these questions is "yes," you must determine if the use of funds which are deferred are equal to or greater than the cost of the deferral.

SEE ALSO: CASH FLOW, FIXED EXPENSE, and RESERVES FOR REPLACEMENT.

CONVENTIONAL LOAN

A conventional loan is a mortgage loan made by a lending institution without government insurance such as that provided by FHA and VA.

INVESTOR ADVICE

While FHA, non-owner occupancy loans can be obtained on small rental properties, most mortgage loans for investment real estate is of the conventional type.

VA-backed loans are only available on small rental properties where the owner is an occupant of one of the units.

Conventional loans usually command a slightly higher interest rate, since the lender or his/her mortgage buyers are assuming all of the risk of loss.

SEE ALSO: ASSUMPTION AGREEMENT, FHA LOAN, and VA LOAN.

CONVERSION

Conversion is the change from one type of usage or occupancy to another. An example would be the conversion of a single family residence to a duplex (where local zoning will permit).

NOTICE OF LIEN

TO WHOM IT MAY CONCERN:

Notice is hereby given that the undersigned_____

_____

doing business as_____and residing at

_____County of_____State of Utah, hereby claim___

and intend___ to hold and claim a lien upon that certain land and premises, owned and reputed to be

owned by_____ and

situate, lying and being in_____, County of_____

State of Utah, described as follows, to wit:_____

_____

_____

_____

_____

_____

_____

_____

_____

to secure the payment of the sum of_____ Dollars,

owing to the undersigned for_____

_____

as a_____

in, on and about the_____on said land.

That the said indebtedness accrued and the undersigned furnished said materials to (or was em-
                                            (Erase according to the fact)
ployed by) _____

_____who was the

_____

_____owner and the reputed owner of said premises as

aforesaid, under a_____contract made between the said_____

_____and the undersigned

on the_____day of_____, 19_____, by the terms of which the undersigned did agree

to _____

and the said_____

did agree to pay the undersigned therefor as follows, to wit:_____

_____

_____

_____and under which said contract the under-

signed did_____the first_____on the_____day of

_____and did_____the last_____on the

_____day of_____and on and between said last mentioned

days, did _____ amounting

to the sum of_____ Dollars,

which was the reasonable value thereof, and on which the following payments have been made to wit:

_____

leaving a balance owing to the undersigned of_____

_____Dollars after deducting all just credits and offsets, and for which

demand the undersigned hold___ and claim___ a lien by virtue of the provisions of Chapter 1, of Title

38, of the Utah Code Annotated 1953.

Figure 16

RELEASE OF LIEN

(Individual)

KNOW ALL MEN BY THESE PRESENTS:

That the undersigned, for and in consideration of the sum of_____Two-Thousnad_____

_____five hundred and 25/100 ------------------------_____Dollars,

the receipt of which is hereby acknowledged, does hereby certify that that certain claim of lien

heretofore filed by the undersigned in the Office of the County Recorder of__Salt Lake____

County, State of_____Utah_____, in Book___105____, Page___498_____, as

Instrument No.__1567__and dated the__15th__day of____June_____19_88_, is hereby

fully paid, satisfied, discharged and released.

IN WITNESS WHEREOF, the undersigned___Alfred P. Sloan_____

hereunto set__his__hand__, this_23rd_day of__February_____, 19_89.

Alfred P. Sloan *(signature)*

Alfred P. Sloan

_____

State of_____Utah_____ ⎤
                                              ⎬ ss.
County of_____Salt Lake_____ ⎦

On the__23rd__day of___February_____19_89_, personally appeared before me

_Alfred P. Sloan_____

_____,

the signer__ of the foregoing instrument, who duly acknowledged to me that_____He_____

executed the same.

Mary Southworth *(signature)*

Notary Public

Residing at:

Salt Lake City, Utah

My Commission Expires:

__May 15, 1990__

Figure 17

INVESTOR ADVICE

Before planning a conversion it is wise to verify the zoning of the land to determine if a building permit for the conversion will be granted. It is also wise to obtain a builder's estimate of the cost of conversion. It is not unusual to find that the initial cost of the property plus conversion cost will exceed the cost of new construction to satisfy the same need.

Property-use conversion represents one of the best real estate investment opportunities. Numerous examples of investor conversions of property can be cited. Two of the most outstanding examples might be the Fisherman's Wharf project in San Francisco and the Trolley Square conversion in Salt Lake City, Utah.

In each of these successful conversions, a developer saw an opportunity to utilize an abandoned or sparsely utilized property for a higher and better use. Shopping centers are not the only use of existing structures. A most unusual and successful conversion was that of a large church property—the High Bay Sanctuary in San Francisco became a dance studio, the recreation hall was converted to a fitness center, and the classroom and offices were converted to apartments.

In this latter case, it was necessary to apply for and receive a zoning change. This application was approved when it was shown that the tax base increase to the city and the creation of some new jobs would justify the zoning change. It was also necessary to show that the new businesses would be less objectional to nearby residents than the existence of an abandoned property, which had become an eyesore.

> **OLD BUILDING OR GOLDMINE?** Everytime you see an old building, ask yourself, "Is this a good prospect for conversion? What would be a better use?"

As a real estate investor, you should constantly be on the alert for buildings and properties which can be purchased at low cost and converted to a higher use.
SEE ALSO: BUILDING PERMIT, and ZONING.

CONVERTIBLE DEBENTURE

A convertible debenture is a bond or certificate of indebtedness which can, at the owner's will, be converted to common stock in the corporation which issued the debenture. Convertible debentures may be callable or non-callable.

INVESTOR ADVICE

If you are planning to set up a real estate corporation, you may wish to raise some of the capital through debt issues. If all capital is raised through the sale of stock, it is possible that you will loose management control to others, who bind together as a block to oppose your limited holding position.

> **SEEK PROFESSIONAL HELP** State and federal laws regarding stock and bond issuance are very complex. You will need the assistance of a local stock brokerage to assist you to avoid the potholes.

Convertible debentures are more appealing to the investor than straight debt. If the corporation succeeds, the value of its common stock will soon be greater than bonds.

At this point the holder can be expected to convert to take advantage of the appreciated stock and capital gains.

When a convertible debenture is designed, its conversion provisions are established. If you wish to lower your interest payments in the future, you will set the conversion at a level you expect to reach at a given time in the future.

EXAMPLE

You are organizing a real estate corporation to invest in the development of shopping centers. You decide to raise the necessary capital by two-thirds stock sale and one-third convertible bond issuance. The bonds will sell at par for $1,000.

You would prefer to avoid interest payments after the third year, at which time you estimate the common stock will be selling for $30 per share on the open market.

You set the conversion at one bond equaling 400 common shares. Bond holders will then be attracted to covert at the point that their bond can be converted to shares worth $25 ($1,000/400) or more.

You may also wish to make the bonds callable. This provision of the issue states that you may call your bonds payable at certain dates at certain prices. The callable price is always greater than $1,000, to compensate the owner for early call before normal maturity.

SEE ALSO: REAL ESTATE INVESTMENT TRUST (REIT).

COOPERATIVE APARTMENT

A cooperative apartment is a type of joint ownership in which the participant owns a share of a corporate multi-unit property. This ownership allows him to occupy a given unit in the complex. However, unlike the condominium arrangement, the owner of a co-op does not own his/her unit and cannot sell his/her interest except to the apartment association or a person approved by them. Such an owner does not have a deed to his/her portion of the project and cannot obtain a mortgage on his/her assigned unit.

INVESTOR ADVICE

Cooperative apartments are not considered good investments, even if ownership is permitted by non-occupants. The principal reason for the purchase of a cooperative unit should be for your personal use. On the other ahnd, the actual development of a cooperative apartment project can be a profitable investment, where the market assures a sale of the project at a reasonable price and in a reasonable time period.

A developer can mortgage the entire project and pledge the receivables (payments of apartment buyers) of those who buy from the corporation on a time-payment basis.

Until all apartments are sold and the developer's profit paid, he/she remains as a shareholder in the corporation. This situation can create a problem if inexperienced or unscrupulous individuals are involved in the project. Before buying a cooperative apartment, it is wise to consider the past history and reputation of the developer.

There are certain tax advantages to cooperative apartment ownership. Monthly payments cover a proportionate share of the blanket loan amortization and the remainder is interest which is passed to each owner as a tax deduction. Taxes paid on the property are similarly divided pro-rata among the owners. Most cooperative arrangements provide for any operating profit of the cooperative to be returned to the shareholders, thus avoiding corporate taxes.

SEE ALSO: CONDOMINIUM, and CORPORATION.

CO-OWNERSHIP
Property owned by more than one person is termed co-ownership.

INVESTOR ADVICE
When property is owned by more than one person there is said to be a co-ownership with the owners being co-tenants. Regardless of the type of co-ownership, the owners share four unities:

1. Have the same interests;
2. Have the same title;
3. Have the same right of possession; and
4. Took title at the same time.

Co-ownership creates one of four types of estates:

1. *Joint Tenancy*—In which all owners have a right of equal occupancy, even though that right may not always be exercised. Inherent in joint tenancy is the right of survivors to acquire the interest of a deceased owner.

During an owner's lifetime, a tenant, in this type of ownership, has the right to bind his individual interest but cannot bind the interest of others. This right would indicate that his/her interest can be taken to satisfy debts, satisfy judgment against him/her, or permit the creation of easements. Since a tenant's ownership ceases upon his death, *all* of the interest passes to the survivors.

2. *Tenancy by the Entirety*—In which a husband and wife hold title to the property acquired by them jointly after marriage. As a general rule, most states require both the consent of the husband and wife to transfer or encumber property so held.

3. *Tenancy in Common*—In which two or more persons hold separate interests in property, without the right of survivorship. Where unmarried persons take title to property with no mention as to their type of tenancy, most states assume the title to be held as tenancy in common.

4. *Community Property*—In which property is acquired in a state which follows old Spanish law. Community property applies to married persons who hold community property in equality. There is no right of survivorship. The surviving spouse receives one-half interest upon death of the other and the remaining half passes as directed by the deceased's will or by state statute, if the deceased dies intestate.

SEE ALSO: INTESTATE, SEPARATE PROPERTY, OLD SPANISH LAW, and WILL.

CORPORATE DEED FORM
A corporate deed form is a warranty deed form used to transfer real estate ownership, where the grantor is a corporation—also known as a special warranty deed.

INVESTOR ADVICE
Many small business owners and officers of a small corporation may not be aware of the certificate contained in the corporate deed form. When you purchase property owned by a small corporation, it is suggested that you question the corporate principals to ascertain if the required board approval can be obtained prior to the closing date specified in the earnest money agreement.

Figure 18 shows a special warranty deed with the required corporate certificate.
SEE ALSO: CORPORATION, and WARRANTY DEED.

Recorded at Request of___Utah Title Inc._____

at_____, M. Fee Paid $___$3.00_____

by _J. Smith_____ Dep. Book __202__ Page ___107___ Ref.: _9876_____

Mail tax notice to___George M. Brown___ Address _2244 N. Chambers St., SLC, Ut._

SPECIAL WARRANTY DEED

[CORPORATE FORM]

       United Steel Fabricating Inc.   , a corporation
organized and existing under the laws of the State of Utah, with its principal office at
   Salt Lake City   , of County of   Salt Lake   , State of Utah,
grantor, hereby CONVEYS AND WARRANTS against all claiming by, through or under it to

        Browning Industries Inc.   grantee
of   Provo, Utah   for the sum of
                    Ten Dollars   DOLLARS
the following described tract   of land in   County,
State of Utah:

       All of lots 101, 102, 103 & 104 Greenbelt Industrial
       Park Subdivision

    The officers who sign this deed hereby certify that this deed and the transfer represented
thereby was duly authorized under a resolution duly adopted by the board of directors of the
grantor at a lawful meeting duly held and attended by a quorum.
    In witness whereof, the grantor has caused its corporate name and seal to be hereunto affixed
by its duly authorized officers this 22nd   day of   February   , A. D. 19 89

Attest:

_Joan P. Probst_____
   Joan P. Probst
                Secretary.

[CORPORATE SEAL]

       United Steel Fabricating Inc.____

By_James L. Longworth_____
   James L. Longworth
                 President.

STATE OF UTAH,

County of   Salt Lake   } ss.

    On the   22nd   day of   February   , A. D. 1989
personally appeared before me Joan P. Probst and James L. Longworth
who being by me duly sworn did say, each for himself, that he, the said James L. Longworth
is the   president, and he, the said Joan P. Probst   is the secretary
of United Steel Fabricating Inc.   , and that the within and foregoing
instrument was signed in behalf of said corporation by authority of a resolution of its board of
directors and said James L.Longworth   and Joan P. Probst
each duly acknowledged to me that said corporation executed the same and that the seal affixed
is the seal of said corporation.

                      _Elinor M. Moore_____
                               Notary Public.

My commission expires___June 31, 1990 My residence is__Salt Lake City, Ut.__

BLANK No. 104C— © GEM PTG. CO. — 3215 SO. 2600 EAST — SALT LAKE CITY

Figure 18

CORPORATION

A corporation is a type of business organization whose owners are called "stockholders." The stockholders elect a board of directors who in turn elect officers and the chairman of the board. The officers of the corporation operate the business as authorized by the corporate charter and under the direction of the board of directors.

INVESTOR ADVICE

Many business owners do not elect to form a corporation under the mistaken assumption that they will have higher tax liability. Corporations with less than twenty stockholders may elect to be taxed as individuals under Sub-Chapter "S," and may still enjoy the limited liability and other advantages of the corporate form. In some cases, the corporate form may result in a lower tax than individual tax. This depends upon the amount of dividends, if any, which are paid and the need of the corporation to keep profits working in the business.

If you are operating a real estate investment business, it is strongly advised that you seriously consider the advantages of the corporate form to limit your personal liability.

A creditor or holder of a judgment is forbidden to go beyond the corporate veil to collect moneys owed, except when illegal actions by the officers can be shown. When the organization is a proprietorship or a partnership, the creditor may collect from the business and/or you as an individual.

The corporate form also has an advantage in the ease in which ownership gifts can be made, using the annual tax exclusion, or the manner in which the ownership can be transferred in accordance with a will or trust agreement. An appropriate number of shares of stock can be transferred far easier than a percentage interest in a partnership.

The corporate form may also be a convenient way of maintaining separate ownership, for those married persons who reside in states which follow old Spanish law.

SEE ALSO: OLD SPANISH LAW, PARTNERSHIP, PROPRIETORSHIP, TRUST, and WILL.

CORRECTION DEED

A correction deed is executed to correct an error in a prior deed of record.

INVESTOR ADVICE

It is not unusual for one or more errors to be incorporated in a deed. Such errors often occur in the spelling of names or, more often, in the legal description which contains many numbers, compass calls, and other detailed information.

When an error has been identified in a deed, a correction deed should be executed without delay. The normal deed form is utilized with an addition such as:

This deed is made for the purpose of correction of a deed dated _____, between the grantor _____ and grantee _____ and recorded in deed book _____, page _____ , _____ County in the State of _____.

The correction deed is signed by the grantor, then notarized and recorded.

SEE ALSO: ACKNOWLEDGMENT, RECORDING, SPECIAL PURPOSE DEED, and WARRANTY DEED.

CORRELATION

The relationship between two sets of data is the correlation.

INVESTOR ADVICE

As an investor in real estate, you will have the opportunity to review the work of several real estate appraisers. Appraisers primarily use three approaches to value; (1) the cost or replacement approach, (2) the market approach, and (3) the income approach.

All of these approaches are not applicable in all situations. However, the appraiser will use all of them that are applicable. Even though several approaches to value are used, they may not be of equal value in all situations.

When the various data is assembled, the appraiser has the task of correlating the values obtained to determine *the* value, known as the fair market value. This correlation involves assigning weighting values to each set of data and the selecting the final value decision.

While two appraisers may use the same data, they may not interpret it equally or agree that any one number represents the fair market value. In reviewing any appraisal, you should examine the logic of these professional opinions to judge the accuracy of the value opinion. When the logic appears to be faulty, the ultimate value decision will probably be faulty also.

SEE ALSO: COST APPROACH TO VALUE, INCOME APPROACH TO VALUE, and MARKET APPROACH TO VALUE.

CO-SIGNER

A co-signer is a second party who signs a legal payment commitment to support or augment the financial strength of a primary signer.

Mortgage and other loans that would have been impossible without the support and financial backing of a second party are often obtainable with a co-signer.

INVESTOR ADVICE

If you find it impossible to obtain a required loan based upon your own signature, you should examine the possibility of securing a co-signer, such as a parent, or other relative or friend.

As your financial status improves, you may be asked to become a co-signer on a loan being requested by another. Before signing, be sure to determine the financial risks involved and the consequences of a possible call on your resources, in the event of the primary signer's inability to perform.

If you are the principal owner of a real estate corporation, a lender may ask you to sign a loan agreement twice, first as a principal officer of the corporation and second as a co-signing individual. The loan will, therefore, be secured by the assets of the corporation and your own personal assets. Most equipment suppliers, selling on time, will require this type of security.

A personal signature allows the lender to go beyond the corporate veil in seeking redress in the event of a default on the loan.

SEE ALSO: CONTRACT, CORPORATE VEIL, and MORTGAGE NOTE.

COST APPROACH TO VALUE

The cost approach to value is an appraisal approach in which the appraiser builds the subject structure on paper using current building costs, and then depreciates it to reflect its current physical and economic condition thereby arriving at a value.

INVESTOR ADVICE

The cost approach is applicable in most situations. It is particularly appropriate in the case of one-of-a-kind buildings, of which there is no market data, and in the case of new or proposed construction.

Where recent sales of comparable properties are available, the market data is a more important indicator of value. Where the property is income-producing, the income approach is a valuable consideration, but does not necessarily override other approaches or considerations. A good appraiser will utilize all applicable approaches to value, even though he/she may assign little or no weight to some.

SEE ALSO: CORRELATION, INCOME APPROACH, and MARKET APPROACH

CO-TENANT

Property owned by more than one person creates a co-ownership with the owners said to be co-tenants.

INVESTOR ADVICE

In order to understand the philosophy of laws pertaining to co-ownership, it is necessary to understand the four unities that constitute this ownership. These are:

1. Same interest;
2. Same title;
3. Same right of possession; and
4. Same time of taking title.

Co-tenants share in one of the following four types of titles:

1. Joint tenancy;
2. Tenancy by the entireties;
3. Tenancy in common; and
4. Community property.

Before taking title to any property as a co-tenant, you should thoroughly understand the consequences of that action. The four types of titles are discussed in considerable detail under their separate headings.

SEE ALSO: COMMUNITY PROPERTY, JOINT TENANCY, TENANCY BY THE ENTIRETIES, and TENANCY IN COMMON.

COUNTER OFFER

A counter offer is one made by one of the parties to a proposed purchase after the rejection of a prior offer. Counter offers may be the original offer with minor changes or a completely different offer.

INVESTOR ADVICE

In law, a counter offer has the effect of rejection of the prior offer and replacement of that offer with another. Prior offers, although rejected, can serve as a reference point for counter offers in those circumstances in which the offer is *accepted with changes* as listed in the counter proposal.

EXAMPLE

"The above offer is acceptable with the following changes:

1. The price to be $125,000 (offer was for $120,000)
2. Balance due at closing to bear 10.5% interest (offer was for 10%)."

The counter offer is then signed by the party making the counter offer, but it is not a contract until it is accepted by the other party and all parties have been notified of that acceptance.

SEE ALSO: EARNEST MONEY RECEIPT, OFFER TO PURCHASE, and OFFER.

COVENANT

A convenant is a guarantee made by one party to another. In law, it is a written agreement under seal, in which the parties agree to do or refrain from doing something.

INVESTOR ADVICE

A covenant is no better than the party or parties making the covenant. A promise to do something without the financial ability to perform is valueless. Thus a covenant, implied by a warranty deed, that states a title is free and clear but is later found to have a defect, will not provide the buyer with a clear title.

Where title insurance has been provided to the buyer, such problems are quickly resolved. If title insurance was not provided, the buyer's only recourse is through the seller.

SEE ALSO: EASEMENT, JUDGMENT, LIEN, RESTRICTIVE COVENANTS, and TITLE INSURANCE.

CREATIVE FINANCING

Creative financing is a method of financing a real estate purchase by other than standard mortgage arrangements.

INVESTOR ADVICE

Creative financing methods usually involve one of the following:

1. Assumption of existing loan(s);
2. Assumption of the existing first mortgage with the seller carrying a second mortgage for the balance not covered by the downpayment;
3. Use of a piggy-back loan where a lender assumes the first mortgage, advances additional funds at his/her current rate of interest and takes back a second mortgage from the buyer for the additional funds advanced. The new mortgage indebtedness carries a blended interest rate, which is less than the new lender's current rate but more than the original first mortgage rate which was assumed by the new lender; or
4. A contract sale in which the seller finances the sale at an agreeable interest rate. Contract sales typically carry payments based on a long term pay-off but with a balloon payment in five to ten years.

Methods one through three require the basic mortgage to be assumable without the lender's consent or assumable with his/her consent and possible interest rate bump. Most conventional loans made after 1970 have a non-assumable (acceleration) clause.

The exceptions being certain VA and FHA loans in which the original mortgagor agrees to accept responsibility for payment or qualifies you to assume.

Method four presents little problem to you, the buyer, other than a potential balloon call at a time when mortgage rates are high. If an existing mortgage exists, you must take special care to assure that your payments to the contract holder are used to keep the mortgage current.

If you are the seller, you must have the ability to maintain the mortgage payments current, even though the contract buyer is tardy with his/her payments to you. In case of default by the buyer, you may need considerable cash to keep up the payments until foreclosure is completed and the property resold.

Creative financing (particularly in those instances involving land contracts) presents potential title problems to the buyer. For instance, what happens if the seller dies, his estate is undergoing probate and you decide to pay off the contract? Who can provide a title?

This problem can be avoided if the contract is placed in escrow with a signed deed. The escrow agent is instructed to give the deed to the buyer upon payment of the contract in full. This escrow arrangement can also be used to assure that contract payments are used to keep the underlying mortgage current. The buyer makes all payments to the escrow agent, who pays the mortgage and gives the balance to the contract holder.

SEE ALSO: ASSUMABLE MORTGAGE, CONTRACT, PIGGY-BACK LOAN, and PURCHASE MONEY MORTGAGE.

CUBIC FOOT METHOD OF ESTIMATING COST

This is a method of estimating cost by the cost or replacement method in which the cost per cubic foot of space enclosed is used in lieu of the more common method of cost per square foot. This method is particularly applicable to high-bay structures such as warehouses.

INVESTOR ADVICE

When you review an appraisal using the cost approach in which the square foot method is employed, check to determine if the building is above standard height, and if so, that the appraiser has used a factor to compensate for the difference between actual and standard height. A failure to consider building height can produce considerable error in the final results.

EXAMPLE

An appraisal of a warehouse utilized the cost approach to value. The building, used for the storage and distribution of household paper products, contained 100,000 square feet and had a height of fifty feet. The appraiser calculated its value as follows:

Class "A" Average Distribution Warehouse

100,000 s.f. x $33.36/s.f. = $3,336,000

The appraiser had failed to indicate that his appraisal service had provided a height adjustment chart, which indicated that the square foot costs were for a *standard* height of fourteen feet. A fifty-foot high building would require application of a correction factor of 1.930. The above figure of $3,336,000 should have been:

$$\$3,336,000 \times 1.930 = \$6,438,480$$

The appraiser could have avoided the problem and simplified his calculations by simply using the cubic foot values provided by the service. This would have resulted in:

$$100,000 \text{ s.f.} \times 50ft \times \$1.29/\text{cubic foot} = \$6,400,000$$

or basically the same figure obtained by using the height correction.
      SEE ALSO: COST APPROACH TO VALUE.

CUL DE SAC

A cul de sac is a short dead end street ending in a circle for vehicular turn around.

INVESTOR ADVICE

The cul de sac is a very useful design for residential housing where it is useful to eliminate fast auto traffic and limit the number of cars using the street.

Building lots on a cul de sac are usually "pie" shaped with a minimum frontage on the circle. Homes located on this type of street are frequently desired by those families having small children.
      SEE ALSO: DEVELOPMENT COSTS, and RESTRICTIVE COVENANTS.

CULINARY WATER

Culinary water is pure water furnished for household use. The source can be for a private system or a municipal service.

INVESTOR ADVICE

If you are contemplating buying land for development purposes or building a new project in any of the arid areas of the United States, you must assure the availability of culinary water. In these areas all water, both above and below the ground, belongs to someone. A permit is required to dig a well.

The fact that a municipal system is provided to the property is no assurance of water availability. Connection to a municipal system may require the surrender of water right shares, which must be purchased from a current owner. In some areas water rights are not available at any price.

Commercial operations requiring substantial quantities of water, often find that they must buy land and its associated water rights in order to obtain the required water. Land in arid parts of the west is considered useless without water.
      SEE ALSO: IRRIGATION WATER, and WATER RIGHTS.

CURABLE PHYSICAL DETERIORATION

Curable physical deterioration or depreciation is due to wear and tear or lack of preventive maintenance on property, which can be corrected by the expenditure of time and funds.

INVESTOR ADVICE

Where you determine that physical deterioration has occurred, the cost of curing this deficiency should be checked against the cost of new construction. It is not unusual to find the initial cost plus cure expense may exceed new construction cost. Even where this situation exists, you may wish to undertake remedial action. Frequently, the uniqueness of the building or its historical significance may justify the extra expense to preserve the structure and return it to full usefulness.

> **HIRE AN EXPERT** When buying older buildings, it is wise to employ a professional building inspector to ascertain the current condition. A hidden problem, not easily found, can be very expensive to correct.

Physical deterioration can only be determined by a person trained in the inspection field. If you are not fully qualified to make the required inspection, it is highly advisable that a professional inspection service be employed and that your offer to purchase be predicated on acceptance of this inspection. Deterioration is most prevalent in the following areas:

• Roof and associated drainage systems;

• Exterior walls;

• Foundations;

• Windows and trim;

• Heating systems;

• Plumbing systems including fixtures;

• Electrical systems including fixtures;

• Interior decoration and finish which includes carpeting, paint, and wall coverings;

• Lawns, walks, and landscaping; and

• Garages, carports, and other parking facilities.

SEE ALSO: DEPRECIATION, ECONOMIC DEPRECIATION, and INCURABLE DEPRECIATION.

CURTSEY RIGHTS

Curtsey rights are the interest a husband has in his deceased wife's property as defined by some state laws. Like dower rights (wife's interest in husband's property), curtsey rights generally involve a life estate. Curtsey rights have been eliminated in most states.

INVESTOR ADVICE

Curtsey rights can result in a cloud on the title of property. In those states in which the right is preserved, title insurance on acquired property becomes even more necessary.

If the title search reveals the existence of a life estate by virtue of curtsey right, it may be necessary to buy that right as well as the remaining property rights. Please note that the value of the property is not affected by the existence of curtsey right. That value is divided between the living spouse and the ultimate recipient of the property.

SEE ALSO: DOWER RIGHTS.

D

Date of Possession
Debenture
Debt Service
Declaration of Complaint
Declaration of No Set-Off
Declining Balance Method of Depreciation
Dedication of Land
Deed
Deed of Reconveyance
Deed of Restriction
Deep Lot Evaluation
Default
Defeasance
Defeasance Clause
Defeasible
Defendant
Deferred Maintenance
Deficiency Judgment
De Minimis PUD
Demographics

Depreciation
Depreciation Recapture
Depth Tables
Deterioration
Development Costs
Disclosure
Discounted Paper
Disintermediation
Dispossess
Distinct Possession
Distraint
Distressed Property
District
Double Declining Balance
Double Scoop
Dower Rights
Down Payment Float
Due on Sale Clause
Duplex
Duress
Dutch Roof

D

DATE OF POSSESSION

Date of possession is the effective date of transfer of ownership of property. Possession may be actual or constructive.

INVESTOR ADVICE

Where property is purchased or sold, the date of possession is normally indicated as an on/about date in the earnest money receipt and offer to purchase. If actual possession is not possible on the closing date, you must clearly indicate within that earnest money agreement any proposal for rent or other compensation to the buyer until actual possession is achieved.

This language, within the earnest money contract, will authorize the closing agent to prepare a short-term rental agreement for signature by both parties at the time of the closing.

> **SUGGESTED WORDING:** "Actual possession of the property by the buyer is scheduled seven days after closing. Seller agrees to pay buyer $15/day as rental. Additional days of possession after the seventh day will be charged at the rate of $30/day. Possession beyond ten days is prohibited."

If rental property is involved, the disposition of rents and the transfers of tenant escrows must also be clearly indicated in the earnest money contract.

Normally, there will be no problem with actual possession of rented property, unless the owner is actually occupying one or more of the rental units. It is not unusual, however, for a problem to exist in actual possession of single family residences. Owners are sometimes reluctant to move until the sales money is in hand. Even then, a move cannot be accomplished overnight.

SEE ALSO: ACTUAL POSSESSION, CONSTRUCTIVE POSSESSION, EARNEST MONEY RECEIPT AND OFFER TO PURCHASE, and ESCROW.

DEBENTURE

A debenture is a debt instrument, offered for sale to the public to raise funds for the use of the issuing agency (REIT or corporation). Real estate debentures are often backed by a mortgage on the issuing agency's real property.

INVESTOR ADVICE

A debenture, underwritten by an aggressive brokerage house, is one way to raise investment capital in times of high mortgage rates. The cost of this fundraising method depends upon the strength of the issuing organization and the size of the bonding program.

Bonding is more complicated than a simple mortgage. State and federal regulations must be carefully followed when the securities are to be sold interstate. If the sale is small enough to be handled within the state, the problem is less complicated.

Some states allow intra-state sales to twenty or fewer investors with minimum registration requirements. Your local investment house can advise you as to the possibilities of a successful bond offering.

SEE ALSO: CONVERTIBLE DEBENTURE, MORTGAGE, PROSPECTUS, RED HERRING, and SECURITIES EXCHANGE COMMISSION.

DEBT SERVICE

Debt service is the cash required each month to cover mortgage or contract debt payments, taxes, and insurance.

INVESTOR ADVICE

While a portion of the debt service is used to amortize the loan and is an unrealized portion of the income of the rental operation, it is not available to the owner until the property is sold.

Debt service is a cash expense of which all but the part going for debt amortization is tax deductible. It is also a fixed obligation, over which the owner has little or no control. Debt amortization funds are non-income producing, although their payment does reduce interest payments for future periods.

SEE ALSO: CASH FLOW, FIXED EXPENSES, NON-CASH EXPENSE, and VARIABLE EXPENSES.

DECLARATION OF COMPLAINT

This term refers to a legal document (law suit) filed by a person, known as the plaintiff, to describe an action of wrongdoing by another (defendant), where said wrongdoing is alleged to have caused the plaintiff to suffer a physical or financial injury.

INVESTOR ADVICE

Declarations of complaint are normally filed by an attorney on behalf of the plaintiff. If the defendant does not reply to the complaint within a specified time, a judgment of default is entered into the official public record. About 95% of all complaints are settled between parties, without a trial.

As a property owner, you are subject to complaints of others who may feel injured as a result of actions taken or not taken by you. Regardless of the validity of a complaint, it must be answered appropriately to avoid unnecessary financial liability.

If your insurance package provides coverage for damages covered in the complaint, your insurer can handle the problem on your behalf. If you are unsure as to your potential liability, consult your insurance agent and an attorney.

SEE ALSO: INSURANCE.

DECLARATION OF NO SET-OFF

This declaration is a written statement, made by a mortgagor, indicating the balance due on a mortgage to be sold or transferred. This is also known as a certificate of no defense or estoppel certificate.

INVESTOR ADVICE

The purchaser of a mortgage should obtain a certificate from the mortgagor acknowledging the amount due. This assures the buyer that the amount quoted by the mortgagee seller is accurate. It also serves notice on the mortgagor that his/her mortgage has been sold and that future payments should be made to the new owner or his/her designated representative.

Most real estate investors find it advantageous to purchase seasoned mortgages for their investment portfolio. These instruments, when purchased at a discount, can provide very attractive yields with little risk or few administrative problems. You may wish to consider this type of investment for a percentage of your total real estate investment.

SEE ALSO: CERTIFICATE OF ESTOPPEL, CERTIFICATE OF NO DEFENSE, DISCOUNTED PAPER, SEASONED MORTGAGE, TITLE INSURANCE, and TITLE REPORT.

DECLINING BALANCE METHOD OF DEPRECIATION

This term refers to an accelerated depreciation method by which a property is amortized after the first year at 150% or 200% of the normal straight line amount, but on an ever-decreasing balance.

INVESTOR ADVICE

Under the Tax Reform Act of 1986, three-, five-, seven-, and ten-year properties may be depreciated on a 200% basis. Fifteen- and twenty-year properties may be depreciated on a 150% basis.

EXAMPLE

You purchase a piece of business equipment which cost $2,500, and has a seven-year life expectancy. You choose the 200% declining balance method of depreciation. Allowable depreciation for the seven years will be:

Straight line $=$ $2,500/7 $=$ $357.14

Using the 200% declining balance method:

Year	Amt. Dep.	Book Balance
1	$357.14	$2,142.86
2	612.25	1,530.61
3	437.32	1,101.29
4	357.14*	786.64
5	357.14	429.50
6	357.14	72.36
7	72.36	—

*Depreciation this year would have been $314.65 but the IRS will allow the higher of D.D.B value or straight line.

SEE ALSO: ACCELERATED DEPRECIATION, ACRS

DEDICATION OF LAND

Dedication of land involves the transfer of real property to a government entity for public use. The dedication must be accepted by an authorized official of that government.

INVESTOR ADVICE

Local regulations may require a developer to dedicate streets in a new subdivision or sufficient land to widen a street in an existing subdivision. This is often a prerequisite for the approval of a new development, or issuance of building permits where major modification to existing improvements are planned.

While these requirements may seem, on the surface, unfair to the developer, it is in the public interest. The widening of an existing street will enhance the property abutting it, which somewhat compensates for the loss of land. Too, the dedication of subdivision streets relieves the developer and property buyers of all future maintenance costs.

The requirement for street-widening and the addition of curbs, gutters, and sidewalks may be delayed, where the work has not been completed on adjoining properties. In this case the property owner will be required to post a performance bond to assure that the requirements are completed at some designated time in the future.

Where property owners are not willing to dedicate a portion of their property to provide for widening of streets and other improvements, the land can be acquired by the governments by condemnation.

SEE ALSO: EASEMENTS, and EMINENT DOMAIN.

DEED

A deed is an official written document which transfers property ownership from one owner to another. A deed is also known as a conveyance.

INVESTOR ADVICE
In preparing and signing a deed you should be careful to check:

• The legal description of the property being conveyed to assure that it *exactly* corresponds to the official deed of record;

• That the deed is prepared on the proper form—there are several;

• That the deed is signed by a person having authority to deed the property and that his signature is the exact legal signature shown on the deed of record—property owned by a corporation may require action by the board of directors to convey title (see Corporate Deed Form); and

• That the deed is recorded without delay, to give public notice of the transfer.

If an error is made in the legal description or the spelling of names of grantors and grantees, a correction deed must be prepared and recorded to set the record straight.

SEE ALSO: CORPORATE DEED FORM, CORRECTION DEED, DEED OF RECONVEYANCE, QUIT CLAIM DEED, TRUST DEED, and WARRANTY DEED.

DEED OF RECONVEYANCE

A deed of reconveyance reconveys property from a trustee (mortgagee) back to the owner (mortgagor), after full payment of a mortgage note—also known as a deed of release.

INVESTOR ADVICE
When a mortgage loan is made by a mortgagee (lender), the property owner (mortgagor) signs a trust deed, which transfers the property to a trustee selected by the lender. In case of default on the loan agreement, the trustee proceeds to foreclose in accordance with the trust agreement.

Where that trust deed has been recorded (which is the normal case), a deed of reconveyance is required to clear the cloud from the official record at the point the loan has been paid in full.

Figure 19 shows a typical reconveyance form used by an attorney serving as trustee.

In some states, the trust deed is held by the trustee and recorded only after default. In those states, the mortgage note is recorded and a satisfaction piece is required to clear the title.

A common mistake, made by many property owners, is to fail to record the satisfaction piece or deed of reconveyance after its receipt from the lender or his/her trustee. This failure can cause serious problems in the future, when the property is sold or transferred and the old loan appears during the title search.

RECORD THAT MORTGAGE RELEASE PROMPTLY!

This becomes particularly awkward if the lender has merged with another, is no longer in business, or the release document is lost by the mortgagor.

SEE ALSO: MORTGAGE NOTE, SATISFACTION PIECE, and TRUST DEED.

DEED OF RESTRICTION

A deed of restriction is a limitation in a deed of conveyance in which future owners of the property are denied full ownership. For the restriction to prevail, the deed must clearly indicate the intent of the grantor to transfer less than a full estate.

INVESTOR ADVICE

A transfer of less than a full estate is an easement issuing out of the item(s) granted. It may be something which did not exist as an independent and identifiable right prior to the grant. An exception or restriction is normally a separate clause in the deed, which clearly defines the reservation that results in the transfer of less than a full estate—that reservation which withdraws something which would ordinarily have passed to the grantee.

Deed restrictions are often identified by the term *less* followed by a description of the reservation. For example:

Less: a 20.0 ft. right of way along the East boundary of the property from the State road to the adjoining property at the North.

Certain deed restrictions can render a property unmarketable in the future. In accepting a deed to property with restrictions imposed, you must assure that these restrictions do not affect the value of the property or its subsequent marketability.

SEE ALSO: EASEMENTS, GRANTOR, GRANTEE, RESTRICTIVE COVENANTS, and RIGHT-OF-WAY.

DEEP LOT EVALUATION

These are appraisal techniques used to evaluate portions of deep lots.

INVESTOR ADVICE

When evaluating deep lots, appraisers use the "Cleveland Standard Table" which indicates the value for lots of varying depths. The table is based on a standard lot 100

Deed of Reconveyance
(Attorney as Trustee)

J. Stanley Persons   , a member of the

Utah State Bar, as Trustee under a Trust Deed dated   June 24th   , 19 70,

executed by   Mary J & Joseph L. Martin   , as Trustor,

and recorded   June 25th , 19 70, as Entry No.   2876   in Book 101   , Page(s)   23

of the records of the County Recorder of SAlt Lake   County, Utah, pursuant to a written request

of the Beneficiary thereunder, does herby reconvey, without warranty, to the person or persons

entitled thereto, the trust property now held by said Trustee under said Trust Deed, which Trust

Deed covers real property situated in   Salt Lake County   County, State of Utah,

described as follows:

     All of lots 24 & 25 and the South one-half of lot 26

     Ellsion Downs Subdivision

Dated this   23rd **day of** February   , 19 89

_____
Trustee

STATE OF UTAH } ss.

COUNTY OF Salt Lake

On the   23rd day of   February   , 19 89   , personally appeared before me

J. Stanley Persons   , the signer....

of the foregoing instrument, who duly acknowledged to me that ....he.... executed the same.

_____
Notary Public

My Commission Expires: April 20, 1992 Residing at: Salt Lake City, Utah

Figure 19

TO VALUE DEEP LOTS

This table, known as the Cleveland Standard, in which a number of existing methods are adapted, may be used to determine the percentage of value in lots of varying depth. Assuming the land to be worth $100 per front foot, 100 feet deep, it may be seen that a lot 200 feet in depth is worth $122 per front foot for that depth. Any value and depth may be secured. 100 feet depth = 100%.

PERCENTAGE OF UNIT VALUE FOR LOTS FROM 1 TO 700 FEET DEEP

ft.	%	ft.	%	ft.	%	ft.	%	ft.	%
1 ft.	3.10%	51	73.25	101	100.41	151	115.19	201	122.10
2	6.10	2	74.00	2	100.85	2	115.38	2	122.20
3	9.00	3	74.75	3	101.27	3	115.57	3	122.30
4	11.75	4	75.50	4	101.70	4	115.76	4	122.40
5	14.35	5	76.20	5	102.08	5	115.95	5	122.50
6	16.75	6	76.90	6	102.48	6	116.12	210	122.95
7	19.05	7	77.55	7	102.88	7	116.29	15	123.38
8	21.20	8	78.20	8	103.25	8	116.46	20	123.80
9	23.20	9	78.85	9	103.62	9	116.62	30	124.60
10	25.00	60	79.50	110	104.00	160	116.80	240	125.35
1	26.70	1	80.11	1	104.36	1	116.96	50	126.05
2	28.36	2	80.77	2	104.72	2	117.13	60	126.75
3	29.99	3	81.38	3	105.08	3	117.30	70	127.40
4	31.61	4	82.00	4	105.43	4	117.47	80	128.05
5	33.22	5	82.61	5	105.78	5	117.64	90	128.65
6	34.92	6	83.21	6	106.13	6	117.79	300	129.25
7	36.41	7	83.82	7	106.47	7	117.94	10	129.80
8	37.97	8	84.42	8	106.81	8	118.09	20	130.35
9	39.50	9	85.01	9	107.15	9	118.24	30	130.90
20	41.00	70	85.60	120	107.50	170	118.40	340	131.40
1	42.50	1	86.15	1	107.80	1	118.54	50	131.90
2	43.96	2	86.70	2	108.11	2	118.70	60	132.40
3	45.30	3	87.24	3	108.43	3	118.85	70	132.85
4	46.61	4	87.78	4	108.75	4	119.00	80	133.30
5	47.90	5	88.30	5	109.05	5	119.14	90	133.75
6	49.17	6	88.82	6	109.35	6	119.28	400	134.20
7	50.40	7	89.35	7	109.65	7	119.41	10	134.60
8	51.61	8	89.87	8	109.93	8	119.54	20	135.00
9	52.81	9	90.39	9	110.21	9	119.67	30	135.40
30	54.00	80	90.90	130	110.50	180	119.80	440	135.80
1	55.05	1	91.39	1	110.76	1	119.92	50	136.15
2	56.10	2	91.89	2	111.02	2	120.05	60	136.50
3	57.15	3	92.38	3	111.28	3	120.18	70	136.85
4	58.20	4	92.86	4	111.55	4	120.31	80	137.20
5	59.20	5	93.33	5	111.80	5	120.43	90	137.55
6	60.30	6	93.80	6	112.05	6	120.55	500	137.85
7	61.25	7	94.27	7	112.28	7	120.66	10	138.15
8	62.20	8	94.73	8	112.52	8	120.77	20	138.45
9	63.10	9	95.17	9	112.76	9	120.88	30	138.75
40	64.00	90	95.60	140	113.00	190	121.00	540	139.05
1	64.95	1	96.04	1	113.20	1	121.10	50	139.30
2	65.90	2	96.50	2	113.43	2	121.21	60	139.55
3	66.75	3	96.95	3	113.64	3	121.32	70	139.80
4	67.60	4	97.40	4	113.85	4	121.43	80	140.05
5	68.45	5	97.85	5	114.05	5	121.53	600	140.55
6	69.30	6	98.30	6	114.25	6	121.62	20	140.95
7	70.10	7	98.74	7	114.45	7	121.71	40	141.35
8	70.90	8	99.17	8	114.64	8	121.80	60	141.75
9	71.70	9	99.58	9	114.82	9	121.90	80	142.05
50	72.50	100	100.00	150	115.00	200	122.00	700	142.35

Figure 20

feet wide and 100-feet deep. This table is primarily useful where the front-foot is the prime consideration of value. Figure 20 shows a Cleveland Deep Lot Table for lots up to 700 feet deep.[1]

If front footage is not the overriding consideration, total size in square feet becomes more important and the Cleveland table is no longer applicable.

Very often an appraiser is asked to evaluate a small strip of land being condemned under the right of eminent domain or purchased for an easement. In this case the 4-3-2-1 rule of evaluation is employed. In this method, a lot of known value is divided from front to back into four equal parts The front part is said to be valued at 40% of the total value, the second part 30% of total value, the third at 20% of total value and the part in the rear at 10% of the total value.

EXAMPLE

You have an apartment house on Green Street and have been informed that the city wishes to widen the street to the new standard 50 ft. width. To do so, they will require 8 feet from the front of your lot. The lot is 85 ft. wide x 100 ft. deep. The property has been appraised at $8.50/s.f. and the city is offering you 85 x 8 x $8.50/s.f. = $5,780 for the required condemnation taking.

You discuss this offer with your appraiser, who agrees with the $8.50/s.f. evaluation but notes that the city is taking land from the front without consideration for its increased value over the property as a whole.

He suggests the use of the 4-3-2-1 approach which indicates the following:

Land Total Value = 85' x 100' x $8.50/s.f. = $72,250
Value Front 1/4 (25 ft) = $72,250 x 40% = $28,900
Value/s.f. = $28,900 / (85' x 25)) = $13.60
Value of Taking = 85' x 8' x $13.60 = $9,248

Some appraisers will argue that the taking of 8 feet from the front leaves the remainder of the lot still fronting on the street as before. If the lot is vacant, their point might be well taken. However, where the property is developed and landscaped, there is no doubt that the frontage taken is much more valuable than the average price per square foot.

SEE ALSO: APPRAISER, CONDEMNATION, and EMINENT DOMAIN.

DEFAULT

The failure to perform a duty prescribed in a verbal or written contract is called default.

INVESTOR ADVICE

When you buy real estate you must always consider the consequences of your failure to perform on the mortgage or contract. The cost of such failure (risk) must be commensurate with the expected return on your investment.

When you sell property while furnishing all or part of the financing, you must consider the consequences of the buyer's default and its effect on your own financial situation. If such default will produce an untenable situation, you must explore other financing arrangements.

There was a time, just a few years back, when the default on a mortgage resulted in only the loss of the property, which had been mortgaged, and your equity. During the past few years, we have seen many properties decline in value to the point where the mortgage holder cannot recover all of the loan upon default. Consequently, the mortgage holder is forced to obtain a deficiency judgment against the mortgagor to recover the remainder. This means that you can:

- Lose all of your equity in the property;
- Lose the property itself;
- Lose an additional amount equal to the amount not recovered on the foreclosure sale plus costs; and/or
- Lose your good credit rating.

SEE ALSO: ACCELERATION CLAUSE, DEFICIENCY JUDGMENT, and FORECLOSURE.

DEFEASANCE

A defeasance is a clause in a legal instrument, which specifies that under certain conditions that instrument is null and void.

INVESTOR ADVICE
This type of clause is often found in mortgages. It assures the mortgagor that the mortgage instrument is null and void at the point all payments have been made in full.
SEE ALSO: DEFEASANCE CLAUSE, and DEFEASIBLE.

DEFEASANCE CLAUSE

In a mortgage, a defeasance clause gives the borrower (mortgagor) the right to redeem his property when his obligation is paid in full.

INVESTOR ADVICE
In those states in which the mortgage is considered as a legal transfer of title to the mortgagee, it is absolutely essential that the mortgage contain a defeasance clause to terminate all rights of the mortgagee upon payment in full. Only those few Western states which are known as "title theory states" consider a mortgage as a transfer of ownership.
SEE ALSO: DEFEASANCE, and DEFEASIBLE.

DEFEASIBLE

This term refers to property ownership (defeasible fee) which restricts the new ownership. The restrictions may be of time or conditions which will cause a forfeiture of the property to the grantor. If the stipulated conditions are not met, or a specified time period draws to a close, the estate is terminated.

INVESTOR ADVICE

EXAMPLE

Mr. Golden's youngest son has shown little ability to manage his money. He is now married and has two children. Mr. Golden transfers the family farm and residence to the son, under a Defeasible Fee Title with the following restrictions:

- Ownership reverts to the grantor (father) at the death of his son.

• Ownership reverts to the grantor if the son moves from the property or fails to actively pursue farming as his principal occupation.

Property purchased with restrictions imposed by the grantor can produce an unmarketable situation in the future. It is seldom advisable to buy any property in which clear title cannot be obtained.

SEE ALSO: BUNDLE OF RIGHTS, RESTRICTIONS, and RESTRICTIVE COVENANTS.

DEFENDANT

The one accused or called to defend him- or herself in court against charges brought against him or her by a plaintiff is called the defendant.

INVESTOR ADVICE

Any complaint brought against you in court should be considered serious. It also does not mean that the dispute cannot be settled out of court. However, at the point official complaints are filed, the two parties in the dispute are usually too emotionally involved to be able to settle the dispute themselves.

There are two alternatives to going to court. These are:

1. Negotiations between attorneys appointed by the two would-be litigants; or
2. Referral to one of the newly organized arbitration groups with both parties agreeing to settle their difference in accordance with the arbitrator's recommendations.

SEE ALSO: PLAINTIFF.

DEFERRED MAINTENANCE

Deferred maintenance involves the requirements for maintenance which have not been performed in a timely manner.

INVESTOR ADVICE

Maintenance requirements should be performed on schedule to prevent more costly repairs and to maintain the property in a manner which will assure a high occupancy rate at maximum rent.

More often than not the reason for deferred maintenance is a failure to recognize the need. If you are not able to personally inspect your properties on a regular basis, you must assign this task to your on-site manager.

The manager must be given the authority to have necessary repairs accomplished when required or else should be instructed to notify you of the needs as they occur.

Most investors have instructed their on-site managers to take care of immediate needs such as leaky pipes, electrical problems, and/or other items which make the property untenable. However, many investors fail to authorize work on non-emergency problems. This can sometimes lead to serious problems, as a small leak in the roof over a hallway or a plugged gutter drain can cause many dollars of damage if not quickly serviced.

Appearance items are the most likely candidates for deferral. It is difficult for a person living on the site to recognize gradual deterioration. If you cannot make at least a semi-annual inspection of your properties, you should hire an inspection service to perform this task for you. High vacancy rates can often be traced to poor maintenance of property and its resultant loss in eye appeal.

SEE ALSO: RESERVES FOR REPLACEMENT, and PHYSICAL DEPRECIATION.

DEFICIENCY JUDGMENT

A deficiency judgment is a court order against a borrower, whose repossessed property caused by default on a mortgage failed to sell for enough to pay the amount due plus costs of repossession.

INVESTOR ADVICE

At the time you borrow money, you must consider the consequences of a downturn in the real estate market. This is especially true where the property is being purchased with a minimum down payment, and the cash flow with good occupancy is barely capable of covering out-of-pocket expenses and debt service.

In the event of default on the mortgage, the lender may seek a deficiency judgment against your other assets in order to satisfy the loan, and pay court and legal costs, realtor fees, and other expenses incidental to foreclosure.

Mortgage instruments used in the various states to secure the lender normally bind the borrower to payment in full. A decade ago (more or less), in periods of inflation, repossession was no problem. Upon foreclosure, the property was sold and was expected to bring a price sufficient to pay the mortgage obligation and all associated foreclosure expense. The owner, in default, walked away from the situation with only the loss of his/her equity, if any.

During the past five to ten years, we have seen a period of stagnant real estate markets in many parts of the country. Repossession during a recession usually means a poor sales price. In these situations, lenders are increasingly turning to deficiency judgments to recoup their losses.

SEE ALSO: DEFAULT, DISTRESSED PROPERTY, and FORECLOSURE.

DE MINIMIS PUD

A De Minimis PUD is a unit in a planned-unit development, in which the value of commonly owned facilities and amenities is incidental to the total value of the unit itself.

INVESTOR ADVICE

This term will often be found in government appraisal forms and reports. It is important in that it informs you as to the true value of a unit in which you are interested. Where there are a number of amenities such as swimming pools, streets, common areas, etc., which are held collectively by the individual unit owners, the value may be significant and thus detract from the value assigned to the specific unit under consideration.

Planned unit developments vary in ownership type and purpose of construction. Where the PUD is planned for sale to individuals and contains significant common assets, it is more likely to be sold as condominiums, with the condominium association controlling the use of these facilities. If the commonly owned assets and amenities are insignificant or dedicated to the municipality, units are more often sold in fee.

SEE ALSO: CONDOMINIUM, and PUD.

DEMOGRAPHICS

Demographics are the statistical data obtained through the science of demography. Demographics applicable to real estate investing are concerned with the examination of population density, traffic patterns, and other people-related factors which affect the economics of planned and existing real estate developments.

INVESTOR ADVICE

A demographic study is a necessary preliminary step in the consideration of proposed construction projects. Apartment complexes, shopping centers, and other commercial type real estate is largely dependent upon the population which is logically expected to utilize the facilities.

While the current status is easy to determine, predicting the future is more difficult. When you review a demographic study which supports a proposed project, you must decide for yourself if the projections of future growth are reasonable and likely.

You must also consider other construction, which is already announced or proposed, which will compete with your project. Even though your project may be superior to others, it can be expected that those other projects will have some success which will detract from your own.

Where a demographic study is required, you should seek a professional who specializes in this type of work. Most real estate appraisers are not capable of performing these studies; however, those with designations such as "Counselor" may be qualified. Large accounting firms, colleges and universities, and banks are good sources for referrals to qualified professionals.

SEE ALSO: MARKET SURVEY, and PRO-FORMA ANALYSES.

DEPRECIATION

Depreciation is a loss in value of a property which is due to physical deterioration, or economic or functional obsolescence.

INVESTOR ADVICE

The actual physical depreciation rate of a property is a controllable factor, which largely depends upon timely repairs and maintenance. You will have little control of the economic and functional rates of depreciation. However, proper selection of the area can minimize this latter loss.

Tax laws strictly control the amount of depreciation, which may be claimed as an expense of doing business. The various methods used in the calculation of these deductions bear little relationship to actual depreciation, especially accelerated methods.

Depreciation provides an increase in cash flow, since it is a non-cash expense, which reduces income taxes payable.

SEE ALSO: ACCELERATED DEPRECIATION, CASH FLOW, DEPRECIATION RECAPTURE, and RESERVES FOR REPLACEMENT.

DEPRECIATION RECAPTURE

Depreciation recapture is the increase of base cost by an amount of depreciation taken for tax purposes, which exceeds the straight-line depreciation value. Recapture is required when an asset is sold prior to being fully depreciated.

INVESTOR ADVICE

If a property is expected to be sold prior to full depreciation, accelerated depreciation may not be the most cost-effective alternative even though it temporarily increases your cash flow. Your accountant can suggest the best method to select, based upon your future intentions.

The following example illustrates the principle of depreciation recapture.

EXAMPLE

Mr. Smith purchased an apartment house for $130,000. The land value is $30,000. The expected lifetime of the property is estimated to be twenty years. Straight line depreciation would allow:

$$\$100,000/20 = \$5,000/year$$

If a method known as double declining balance is used, the following depreciation schedule would apply:

Year	Value at Beg. Year	Dec. Bal. Factor	Dep. Allow.
1	$100,000	1/20 x 2 = 10%	$10,000
2	90,000	1/20 x 2 = 10%	9,000
3	81,000	1/20 x 2 = 10%	8,100
4	72,000	1/20 x 2 = 10%	7,200
	Total Depreciation Taken		$34,300

Should Mr. Smith sell the property at the end of the fourth year, his base cost would be $130,000 less depreciation taken of $34,300, or $95,700. Straight-line depreciation for the same period would have been $20,000; therefore, the difference between straight line and the accelerated depreciation ($34,300 — $20,000 = $14,300) taken must be recaptured. His base cost would be recalculated at:

$$\$130,000 - \$20,000 = \$110,000$$

SEE ALSO: ACCELERATED DEPRECIATION, BASIS COST, and DEPRECIATION RATE.

DEPTH TABLES
Depth tables are prepared for appraiser-use in certain localities. These tables indicate lot values for those lots which are not of standard depth.

INVESTOR ADVICE
Depth tables are only useful in the locality for which they were prepared and only for those properties where the front footage is the primary consideration.

Current development practices in most localities do not emphasize the frontage as much as overall square footage and shape of the property. In the past all commercial buildings were constructed so as to face on the street(s). Today, many new structures are situated endwise to the street in order to provide adequate customer parking. Hence, an adequate frontage is required but it is not the paramount cost factor.

SEE ALSO: DEEP LOT EVALUATION, and FRONT FOOT.

DETERIORATION
Deterioration is the loss in real estate improvement value due to weather elements, lack of timely maintenance, or normal usage.

INVESTOR ADVICE

Prompt and timely maintenance will prevent deterioration and physical depreciation. You should inspect your properties on a regular basis to determine what repairs are required to maintain the property in a good rentable condition.

Where extensive repairs are required to return a property to its useful condition, the cost of repairs must be carefully compared to the market value after restoration. If the value will not be increased an amount equal to the cost of repair, the work is obviously not economical.

It is often found that the loss in value is due to factors other than physical wear and tear. Economic obsolescence is a good example of a condition which renders physical restoration uneconomical. Sometimes, new construction is found to be less expensive than repair of the old. The same is true of additions to older structures.

For example, the cost of constructing an average brick residence might be about $40.00/s.f., whereas an addition to an existing structure might cost 50% more. The reason for this is that new construction allows the contractor to proceed at his own speed, with little delay or need for unusual care to the lot and surrounding land.

Additions often require considerable site preparation prior to beginning construction, lawns and shrubs may need special protection and special precautions may be required to minimize noise, dust, and allow normal use of the original structure during the construction phase.

SEE ALSO: DEPRECIATION, and RESERVES FOR REPLACEMENT.

DEVELOPMENT COSTS

Developments costs are:

(1) Those additional costs of getting a building or subdivision project to the income production stage which are not part of the direct cost of the construction;

(2) Those costs directly associated with the improvement of raw land for sale as individual improved lots; and/or

(3) Those costs directly associated with the recovery of natural resources such as coal, gas, and oil.

INVESTOR ADVICE

In general development costs must be capitalized and depreciated over the life of the project or added to other direct costs in computing basis costs. Special projects, specified by IRS regulations, may be partially or fully expensed during the first year of operation. Check with your CPA for this latter possibility.

Development expenses associated with new building construction might include such items as:

- Cost of building permits;
- Utility connection fees;
- Excavating and repair of streets during utility connection;
- Architect services;
- Construction loan expenses;
- Liability and natural hazard insurance; and
- Night security expenses.

Development expenses associated with subdivision projects might include:

- Cost of sanitary sewers and connecting trunk lines;

- Grading and drainage work;

- Inspection fees;

- Cost of curbs, gutters, sidewalks, and streets;

- Land costs of streets dedicated to the municipality

- Land cost of property set aside for parks, churches, or other community facilities;

- Interim loan expenses; and

- Title and escrow expenses associated with lot sales and/or lot release payments.

SEE ALSO: AMORTIZATION, BASIS COST, DEDICATION OF LAND, and ZONING.

DISCLOSURE

Disclosure is defined as a detailed revelation of facts.

INVESTOR ADVICE

A seller is required to give full disclosure of any problems or deficiencies in property he/she offers for sale, other than those obvious to a prudent buyer which would be excepted under the rule of caveat emptor.

If you are involved in the sale of real estate securities, such as in the establishment of a limited partnership or a REIT, the various states have specific regulations regarding full disclosure of fact and restrictions on who may be offered or sold those securities. In addition, most states have specific laws and rules regarding the sale of undeveloped or partially developed real estate tracts. These have been enacted as a result of countless acts of unscrupulous developers of useless lands and their high-pressure selling techniques.

It is advisable to seek competent legal advice before securities are offered for sale which involve any of the aforementioned activities.

Federal disclosure laws apply to the mortgage and finance industry. These assure the public that interest rates and loan security arrangements are just, reasonable, and fully understood.

SEE ALSO: ANNUAL PERCENTAGE RATE (APR), CAVEAT EMPTOR, PROSPECTUS, RED HERRING, and SECURITIES COMMISSION.

DISCOUNTED PAPER

Notes, mortgages, and other written evidences of indebtedness which are sold for less than face value are termed discounted paper.

INVESTOR ADVICE

Discounted mortgages offer an excellent opportunity for real estate investment without the problems associated with rentals and rental management.

Property sellers and others holding contracts and mortgages will often offer those instruments for sale at discount prices in order to raise needed cash. These offerings typically provide a higher yield to the investor than new mortgages. Where payment records prove them to be well-seasoned, their risk is less than new paper of the same quality.

EXAMPLE

Mr. Jones holds a first mortgage on an apartment house which he sold five years ago. He took back a purchase money mortgage covering the difference in down payment and selling price. The buyer has paid his mortgage payments faithfully for the past five years.

The mortgage has a current balance due of $89,000 and bears interest at the rate of 9.0%. The mortgage has fifteen years to run with payments of $9,859/yr. What amount could you offer Mr. Jones in order to achieve a 12% return on your investment?

Referring to Figure 50, shown in the discussion of "Present Value of $1 Per Period," we find that the factor for a one dollar payment per year for fifteen years at 12% interest is 6.811. Based upon the current annual payment of $9,859, a 12% yield could be obtained if the mortgage could be purchased for:

$$6.811 \times \$9,859 = \$67,150$$

In this example, annual payments have been used to avoid the need for a financial calculator. In actual practice most mortgage payments are monthly, requiring much larger tables or a calculator; however, the principle is the same.

SEE ALSO: AMORTIZATION, SEASONED MORTGAGE, and YIELD.

DISINTERMEDIATION

Disintermediation is a phenomenon which occurs during high-interest periods in which individual investors do not use an intermediary organization (savings and loans, banks, etc.), but prefer to place their funds directly in higher-paying bonds and other available investments.

INVESTOR ADVICE

Direct investment in municipal (tax-free) and corporate bonds can often offer a higher rate of return than your local bank or savings and loan, but at a higher risk. All federally chartered banks, many state banks, and most savings and loan organizations offer government (FSLIC or FDIC) insurance on your investment up to $100,000. You must decide if the extra yield is worth the extra risk of the principal.

SEE ALSO: BANK, and SAVINGS AND LOAN.

DISPOSSESS

The act of removing a tenant from a property by legal process is called dispossession.

INVESTOR ADVICE

It may be necessary to legally remove a tenant who fails to pay his/her agreed rental or fails to abide by the rules and regulations outlined in his/her lease. The procedures for dispossession vary from state to state. Before proceeding, it is advisable to obtain legal advice from your attorney.

WARNING! Do not attempt to evict a tenant yourself without your attorney's approval.

In most states it is necessary to officially advise the tenant that he/she is legally required to quit the premises and for what reason. Figure 21 shows a typical "Landlord's Notice to Pay Rent or Quit," which is served on the tenant three days prior

𝔏𝔞𝔫𝔡𝔩𝔬𝔯𝔡'𝔰 𝔑𝔬𝔱𝔦𝔠𝔢 𝔱𝔬 𝔓𝔞𝔶 ℜ𝔢𝔫𝔱 𝔬𝔯 𝔔𝔲𝔦𝔱

To   Elmond G. North and Jean L. North

You are hereby notified and required within three days from service of this notice to pay the rent of the premises hereinafter described, and of which you now hold possession, amounting to the sum of   Five hundred and 00/100   DOLLARS, being the amount now due and owing to   Allied Realty   by you for   2   months' rent from the   1st   day of   December   , 1988 , to the   31st   day of   January   , 19 89 , or in the alternative to deliver up possession of the same to   me   or   Eldon T. Turner   agent, or   I   shall institute legal proceedings against you to recover possession of said premises, with treble rents.

Said premises are situate in   Salt Lake City   , county of   Salt Lake   State of Utah, and described as follows, to wit: Apartment 4B, Big Arms Apartments   2930 S. Broadway, Salt Lake City, Ut.

designated and known as No.   ,   Street,
Dated   Feb 22,   , 19 89

James M. Morris

James M. Morris, President
Allied Realty

Figure 21

Eviction Notice

FIVE-DAY NOTICE TO VACATE

(NUISANCE)

To: Mary L. Renter
    George M. Renter

_____
Tenant in Possession

    1456 S. Dagor Dr., Apartment #2
_____
Address

_____

WITHIN FIVE DAYS after service of this notice upon you, you are required to vacate the premises at the above address, which premises you now occupy as a tenant of the undersigned for the reason that you have suffered, permitted or maintained a nuisance on or about the said premises, to-wit:_____

_____Housing 2 dogs and 1 cat prohibited by lease signed 4-15-88_____

_____

_____

_____

_____

_____

_____

_____

_____

In the event of your failure to vacate the said premises within such period of FIVE DAYS you will be deemed guilty of an unlawful detainer and legal action will be initiated against you for restitution of the premises and for three times the damages assessed against you in accordance with the provision of Section 78-36-10, Utah Code Annotated, 1953.

This Notice is given and served in accordance with the provisions of Section 78-36-3(4) and Section 78-36-6, Utah Code Annotated, 1953.

Dated this __22nd__ day of __February__, 19_89_ .

                    Jasper T. Swagart
                    Owner

Figure 22

to his/her expected departure. Figure 22 shows an "Eviction Notice" to be served to a tenant who has failed to abide by the terms of his/her lease and who "suffered or maintained a nuisance." The actual process of serving these legal notices varies from state to state. In some states the notice can be delivered by the landlord or tacked to the tenant's door. In other states the document must be served to the tenant by an officer of the court.

SEE ALSO: RESTRAINT.

DISTINCT POSSESSION

Distinct possession is a requirement of a claim of adverse possession in which the property claimed must be sharply defined and controlled.

INVESTOR ADVICE

Adverse possession is to be avoided at all cost. Where any party is using or controlling your property without legal authorization, a notice to quit the premises should be given and a record of such action maintained in your files for future reference.

If the notice is not served by an officer of the court and thereby officially noted, you should have a witness attest to the fact that notice was given or keep a signed receipt if the notice was delivered by registered mail.

SEE ALSO: ADVERSE POSSESSION, and NOTORIOUS POSSESSION.

DISTRAINT

The act of holding another's personal property for security on a debt is termed distraint.

INVESTOR ADVICE

From time to time, it may be necessary to hold a tenant's personal property in order to collect past rents due. Before taking such actions, you should check with your attorney as to the exact method(s) to be employed.

Personal property can be seized and removed from the rental unit or locks may be changed to prevent the tenant from gaining access to remove his possessions. It is the same principle used by hotels when they keep a guest's bag until their bill is paid.

SEE ALSO: DISPOSSESS.

DISTRESSED PROPERTY

Distressed property is property whose market value has diminished and is therefore difficult to sell.

INVESTOR ADVICE

Distressed property offers an excellent opportunity for the real estate investor to purchase below the normal market price. A property may become distressed for several reasons, such as:

- High interest rates;

- Poor general economic conditions;

- Mortgage foreclosure imminent;

- Death of owner and need to raise cash for estate taxes;

- Tax sales;

- Inability of current owner to properly maintain the property, due to lack of funds or advanced age;
- Functional obsolescence in current form;
- Divorce settlement;
- Business reversal requiring owner to liquidate assets;
- Poor or inadequate management; and/or
- Requirement to pay balloon note or refinance at a time of high interest rates.

During a buyer's market you will find many properties advertised by the VA, FHA, banks and REALTORS®. Single-family residential property may be in poor to very poor condition as a home is the last thing that a debtor will relinquish. Often he/she leaves in a very foul mood and takes appliances, electrical and plumbing fixtures, and anything not nailed down. Never buy a repossessed single family residence without a thorough and professional inspection.

Apartments and other rental properties are usually left in reasonable condition, as the landlord's income was dependent upon keeping the property in a rentable condition. The property may, however, have suffered from deferred maintenance. Carefully inspect all distressed property before you buy or commit to buy.

SEE ALSO: BUYER'S MARKET, DEFICIENCY JUDGMENT, and FORECLOSURE.

DISTRICT

A district is a municipal entity established under state law to perform certain services for the public. Districts are operated by elected commissioners, who are authorized to establish tax (mill) rates sufficient to perform their assigned function.

INVESTOR ADVICE

When you review your various tax statements (which levy taxes on owned real estate), you will note that the tax bill is the total of several levies based on the assessed value of the property.

These levies will provide for such districts as schools, mosquito abatement, hospitals, sewer systems, and similar services.

You have no control of the mill rate levied by each district; however, if you do not agree with the assessed evaluation of the property, upon which these assessments are based, there are established appeal procedures available to you. Before going before the board of equalization or other appeal panels, make sure that you have adequate factual data to support your opinion. This should include a current property appraisal and sales data of comparable properties recently sold.

SEE ALSO: AD VALOREM, ASSESSMENT, and MILL RATE.

DOUBLE DECLINING BALANCE

SEE: DECLINING BALANCE METHOD OF DEPRECIATION.

DOUBLE SCOOP

Double scoop is a technique by which a buyer is able to finance a desired property purchase and put some extra cash in his/her pocket at the same time.

INVESTOR ADVICE

The "double scoop" is a method described by Jack Cummings[2] in his book, *$1,000 Down Can Make You Rich*. The technique requires a very motivated seller and a buyer who can profitably utilize a property in such a way that first mortgage financing is available at good rates.

Here is the technique. An offer is made on a property, which has been exposed to the market for an extended period and you hear that the seller is very anxious to sell. You have a good tenant for the property and make a reasonable offer with a provision that a specified large cash payment will be made from the proceeds of a first mortgage loan.

The balance of the selling price is to be carried by the seller without placing a second mortgage on the property—this would hinder your ability to get a mortgage on the property. The balance of the first mortgage loan over the agreed cash payment is pocketed by you.

For this idea to work, you must convince the seller that your personal note is sufficient security for the balance owed to him, or you might provide him with a mortgage on another of your properties.

The deal will work only if:

- Your financial status is good enough to assure the seller that a second mortgage is not necessary to assure payment of the balance due or that the other mortgage security offered is good enough;

- The seller is truly motivated to sell;

- You have a tenant already committed to a long-term lease, which assures the bank's security on the large first mortgage required;

- The proposed tenant is dependable and financially reliable;

- Rents are sufficient to support the required mortgage loan; and

- There is no language in the mortgage application prohibiting this type of arrangement.

This latter point is the bug-in-the-ointment, so to speak. *Most lenders require the buyer to note the source of his down payment.* Many banks will refuse to make such a loan, knowing the method employed or at best will only loan an amount equal to the cash payment to the seller. This problem can be overcome with a statement that the down payment is from a second mortgage on another property.

Unfortunately, there are too many "get rich quick" schemes which may work, but place the buyer in a very awkward situation. Most of these systems work only in times of inflation, when property values are rising at double-digit rates. Time is the agent that pulls the buyer out of the hole.

If you are willing to consider the risks involved, you must realize that you are building a "house of cards," which may fall if:

- Inflations levels off;

- Vacancy rates begin to increase; and/or

- An economic recession takes over.

A wise investor only commits those funds which he/she can afford to loose. He/she recognizes the risks taken and is willing to proceed in order to get a higher rate of return on his/her investment than is possible through more secure methods. A wise investor knows that there is no such thing as a "free lunch."

SEE ALSO: CREATIVE FINANCING.

DOWER RIGHTS

Dower rights are the rights a wife has to her deceased husband's property.

INVESTOR ADVICE

When you purchase property in which dower rights are applicable, care must be exercised to assure that the transfer of title is proper and leaves no clouds on the deed.

Dower rights are an inchoate or potential right, not a real right as such, because the wife only has such a right at the death of her husband. By common law, in those states which recognize dower and curtsey rights, the surviving spouse has a life estate right to property owned by their spouse at the time of death.

When purchasing property from a man who is married and is the sole title holder, it is wise to require that his wife also sign the agreement of sale and the deed. Thus, she has waived her potential dower right to that property. The courts have held that a wife who signs the agreement of sale but fails to sign the deed retains her dower right.

A dower interest is an encumbrance on the property. If the wife is unwilling to release her dower rights, the buyer must either abandon the sale or accept the husband's deed with the understanding he/she (the buyer) may, in the future, find a cloud on the title by virtue of the seller's death.

Most states have abandoned the principle of dower and curtsey rights.

SEE ALSO: CURTSEY RIGHTS.

DOWN PAYMENT FLOAT

A down payment float is a method used to obtain down payment money by deferring payment to various creditors for a short period of time.

INVESTOR ADVICE

Using this technique is a questionable practice. If your cash flow is so thin that you cannot make a minimum down payment or delay the closing, it is doubtful that the purchase is wise. Any cash flow shortage in the future or delay in the receipt of anticipated collections could place all of your assets in jeopardy.

There are some circumstances which could make the risk worthwhile. For instance, the opportunity to buy a desired property at a very attractive price but only if you act immediately; or where the cash needed to pay your creditors is virtually guaranteed (for example, a balloon payment due from a reliable party) might be worth the chance.

SEE ALSO: CREATIVE FINANCING.

DUE ON SALE CLAUSE

A due on sale clause, in most modern mortgages, requires payment in full at the time a property is sold or transferred to another. Some lenders will permit the new buyer to apply to assume the loan, but nothing is guaranteed as to approval or interest rate.

INVESTOR ADVICE

It is very unwise to attempt to hide a sale of property in order to maintain a current mortgage, even where the buyer and seller are willing to accept the potential problems.

The mortgage holder usually becomes aware of the sale one way or the other. Very often the holder is alerted to the sale by receipt of a new insurance policy with a strange name included as second beneficiary.

The buyer is the one left holding the bag, even when the seller has agreed in writing to refinance the property if the mortgage is called. If he/she is unable to refinance the property or pay off the existing loan due to unforseen financial problems, the buyer has only one alternative to refinance the property him or herself and hope that he/she can collect damages—from the seller at a later date.

SEE ALSO: ACCELERATION CLAUSE, NON-ASSUMPTION AGREEMENT, FHA LOAN, and VA LOAN.

DUPLEX

A duplex is a residential building containing two separate living units. A duplex may contain side-by-side units or an up and down arrangement.

INVESTOR ADVICE

The side-by-side arrangement is preferred to the up-and- down set up as it provides the best privacy to tenants and assures that the upper tenant doesn't benefit from the lower tenant's heat.

In many older neighborhoods, apartments have been created by modification of former single family buildings. The most common are basement units or second-floor apartments.

Converted single family homes, although adequate in size and arrangement, usually are less satisfactory to the landlord than buildings originally built as duplexes. Electrical and plumbing systems are usually common. Heat may also be provided from a single source. In these cases, the landlord must either raise the rents sufficient to provide these services himself or lease with an agreement of tenants to split the bills.

SEE ALSO: APARTMENT BUILDING, and FOUR-PLEX.

DURESS

Duress is the unlawful use of force or other pressure to compel a person to do something against his/her will.

INVESTOR ADVICE

Contracts and other legal instruments are unenforceable if signed under duress. Some states, such as Texas, require a husband and wife to be in separate rooms when signing a deed or mortgage. The notary or other person acknowledging the signature of the wife is required to ask the question, "Are you signing this of your own free will and accord?" This procedure assures a lack of duress on the part of the husband (or vice versa).

SEE ALSO: ACKNOWLEDGMENT, and CONTRACT.

DUTCH ROOF

A Dutch roof design incorporates two slopes, the last one being the steeper.

INVESTOR ADVICE

Figure 23 shows a typical Dutch roof as used on a residence. It will be noted that the gable-end view appears much like a barn.

SEE ALSO: GABLE, HIP ROOF, and MANSARD ROOF.

ONE AND ONE HALF STORY

Figure 23. Dutch Roof

Reprinted by permission of Marshall-Swift Appraisal Service.

ENDNOTES

[1] NATIONAL ASSOCIATION OF REALTORS®, REALTOR NATIONAL MARKETING INSTITUTE®, *Real Estate Salesman's Handbook,* 6th Ed., 1972, Chicago, Ill., p. 139.

[2] Jack Cummings, *$1,000 Down Can Make You Rich* (Englewood Cliffs, N.J.: Prentice Hall Inc.), pp. 123-28.

E

Earnest Money
Earnest Money Contract
Earnest Money Deposit
Earnest Money Receipt and Exchange
   Agreement
Earnest Money Receipt and Offer to
   Lease
Earnest Money Receipt and Offer to Pur-
   chase (Sales Agreement)
Easement
Economic Depreciation
Economic Life
Economic Obsolescence
Economic Rent
Economic Value
Effective Age
Effective Gross Income
Egress
Electrical Equipment
Ellwood Premise
Emblements
Eminent Domain
Encroachment
Encumbrances
Engineering Breakdown Method in Ap-
   praising

Equitable Title
Equity Buildup
Equity Trust
Escalation Clause
Escalator Loan
Escheat
Escrow
ESOPs
Estate at Sufferance
Estate at Will
Estate Planning
Estate Taxes
Estate Tax Lien
Estoppel Certificate
Eviction
Excess Rent
Exchange
Exclusive Agency
Exclusive Right to Sell
Exculpatory Clause
Executor(ix)
Executor's Deed
Extender Clause
Extrapolation

E

EARNEST MONEY

Earnest money is deposited with a broker as a token of good faith and intent to fulfill the obligations of a written offer. The earnest money is normally forfeited in the event the offer is willfully not completed.

INVESTOR ADVICE

Forfeiture of earnest money does not excuse the offerer from his/her obligation. The selling agent has fulfilled his/her obligation to the property owner in bringing a willing buyer and seller together and obtaining a signed agreement to purchase—the agent is still entitled to a commission.

The seller, meanwhile, has agreed to the terms of the earnest money agreement and has the right to sue the buyer for specific performance on the contract. Thus, while you may get off the hook by a forfeiture of earnest money, litigation to settle the matter is a real possibility.

Read the written offer carefully before signing. If there are any possible reasons or situations that could occur to prevent your fulfilling your obligation, make the offer subject to those contingencies.

EXAMPLES

"This offer is contingent upon the successful completion of the sale of the buyer's four-plex, located at 212 E. Hartford Avenue. This sale is scheduled to close on February 12th, 1988."

* * * * * *

"This offer is contingent upon the buyer obtaining long-term financing at an interest rate no higher than 9.5%."

* * * * * *

"This offer is contingent upon a satisfactory inspection by a professional property inspector. The cost of the inspection will be paid by the buyer."

* * * * * *

"This offer is subject to a land survey indicating that the property contains a minimum of 2.5 acres. Cost of the survey will be shared on a 50/50 basis by buyer and seller."

* * * * * *

SEE ALSO: EARNEST MONEY RECEIPT AND OFFER TO PURCHASE, RELEASE OF EARNEST MONEY, and SPECIFIC PERFORMANCE.

EARNEST MONEY CONTRACT

An earnest money deposit and offer to purchase signed by the buyer and seller without change or changed in some details with both parties having signed the amended offer constitutes an earnest money contract. In either case, all parties to the contract must have been notified that the offer has been accepted before it is binding.

INVESTOR ADVICE

The earnest money contract must meet the criteria of any contract; in other words, competence of parties, offer, acceptance, legality of purpose and consideration.

All states require offers for real estate to be in writing. Under the statute of frauds, no verbal agreements are binding and no additional terms can be added during the closing unless fully agreeable to both parties.

The earnest money contract is quite specific as to what is to be purchased, at what price, and by what terms. It is less specific with regard to the date of closing and date of possession.

While these two dates are *included* in the earnest money contract, the closing date is legally *a date that both parties will attempt* to meet. Unless the phrase "time is of the essence" is included in the contract by either party, the date indicated for closing is a "target date."

SEE ALSO: CONTRACT, and STATUTE OF FRAUD.

EARNEST MONEY DEPOSIT

The earnest money deposit is the consideration proffered by a buyer as a part of the earnest money agreement and offer to purchase. The consideration can be cash, check, or anything of value capable of being held in trust until the contract is closed.

INVESTOR ADVICE

When you accept an offer, you should check to determine the amount and type of earnest money deposited with the selling broker. If this is other than cash, the broker must state the form of the consideration so that there can be no misunderstanding of what is held in escrow (trust).

In the event that the earnest money is a check which fails to clear, the selling broker must inform you of that fact as soon as it is known by him or her. The buyer must make the check good or forfeit the deal and be subject to a suit by the seller to recover damages, if any.

At closing, the earnest money funds become a part of the buyer's closing assets and are credited to him/her at the closing. These funds cannot be removed from the trust until the deal is closed. If the earnest money exceeds the commission to be paid the listing/selling brokers, the amount of excess is deposited to the credit of the buyer during closing.

If the earnest money deposit is not sufficient to cover the brokerage fee, the addition fee due is paid to the broker and he/she is authorized to retain the escrowed funds as the balance due.

From a legal viewpoint, the amount of the earnest money deposit is "something of value." In real life, the actual amount depends upon the custom in the area and the degree to which the buyer wishes to impress the seller with his eagerness and ability to perform on the contract.

SEE ALSO: TRUST ACCOUNT.

EARNEST MONEY RECEIPT AND EXCHANGE AGREEMENT

An earnest money receipt and exchange agreement is a state-approved form used by real estate brokers to present offers for exchange of properties between two owners. This form is abrogated at the time the official transfer of properties is accomplished by the property owners.

INVESTOR ADVICE

Figure 24 shows a typical state-approved form for use by real estate brokers. This form, although similar to the offer-to-purchase form, includes spaces to identify both

"THIS IS A LEGALLY BINDING CONTRACT. IF NOT UNDERSTOOD, SEEK COMPETENT ADVICE."

EARNEST MONEY RECEIPT AND EXCHANGE AGREEMENT

1. TO __Big Deal Inc.__ , Broker   Date __Nov 2__ , 19__88__
2. THE UNDERSIGNED, __James A. Investor__ of __Orem__ city, State of __Utah__
3. hereinafter called the first party offers to exchange the following described property owned by the undersigned and situated in __Provo, Utah__ city,
4. __Utah__ County, State of __Utah__ to wit: __Residence and lot, located__
5. __at 2345 S. Big Canyon Drive, legally described as Lot 26, Big Canyon__
7. __Subdivision No 3.__
8. Subject to a (mortgage/contract) balance of approximately $ __None__ held by _____ and
9. payable $ _____ (monthly/yearly) including interest at _____ % per annum (including/not including) taxes and insurance.
10. The following items are included if presently attached to the premises: Plumbing and heating fixtures and equipment, including, water heaters, water softners, t.v.
11. antenna, electric light fixtures, bathroom fixtures, curtain and drape rods and fixtures, venetian blinds, window and door screens, storm indows, storm
12. doors linoleum, all trees and shrubs, and all other fixtures except __None__
13. The following personal property shall be included by first party: __All kitchen Appliances as installed, all__
14. __floor coverings and window treatments.__
15. This property and $ __100,000.00__ to be paid as follows: __$100,000 from the proceeds of a new__
16. __1st mortgage to be obtained on the newly acquired property listed below.__
17.

IS OFFERED IN EXCHANGE FOR

18. The property owned by __Uintah Investors Inc__ of __Provo__ city,
19. State of __Utah__ , hereinafter called the second party, situated in __Provo__ city, __utah__ ,
20. county, State of __Utah__ , to-wit: __A 12 unit apartment house, located at 1200 S.__
21. __University Ave. and legally described as Lot 286, 287 & 288, University__
22. __Heights Commercial Subdivision.__
23. Subject to a (mortgage/contract) balance of approximately $ __56,000.00__ held by __Utah Bank & Trust Co.__ and
24. payable $ __868.25__ (monthly/yearly) including interest rate of __8.5__ % per annum (including/not including) taxes and insurance.
25. The following are included if presently attached to the premises: Plumbing and heating fixtures and equipment, including water heaters, water softeners, t.v.
26. antenna, electric light fixtures, bathroom fixtures, curtain and drape rods and fixtures, venetian blinds, window and door screens, storm windows, storm doors,
27. linoleum, all trees and shrubs, and all other fixtures except __None__
28. The following personal property shall be included by second party: __All built in appliances, window coverings__
29. __and floor coverings as installed.__
30. together with $ _____ to be paid as follows: _____
31.
32. __None__
33. in consideration of the efforts of __Big Deals Inc.__ , Broker to present this offer to the above named second party,
34. the first party hereby deposits with said Broker as earnest money, the sum of $ __5,000.00__ in the form of __Check__ and agrees to deposit an
35. additional $ __5,000.00__ when Second Party accepts this offer. This deposit is made subject to written acceptance by Second Party endorsed hereon within
36. __2__ days from date hereof, and unless so accepted, the return of the money herein receipted shall cancel this offer and agreement without liability against
37. said Broker. Upon acceptance of this offer by Second Party, the First Party agrees to pay said Broker a commission of $ __18,000.00__ for services rendered,
38. said commission to become due and payable upon execution of this agreement by all parties hereto. Upon acceptance by Second Party, the earnest money above
39. referred to may be used to cover necessary closing costs incurred in this transaction.

TERMS AND CONDITIONS OF EXCHANGE

40. Upon acceptance by Second Party within the time limit hereinabove specified, this document shall thereupon become a binding agreement upon each of the
41. parties hereto and enforceable as provided by law. This agreement shall be binding upon and inure to the benefit of the parties hereto, their heirs, executors,
42. administrators, successors and assigns.
43. Each party agrees to furnish to the other, a good and marketable title, with abstract to date on their respective properties, or, at the option of each seller,
44. a policy of title insurance in the name of the purchaser. The Broker, as agent, is authorized to procure and deliver to the respective parties for examination, the
45. abstracts of title, or, at the option of each seller, a preliminary report for title insurance, to the properties covered hereby and a reasonable time be allowed for
46. examination of titles. In the event defects appear in the titles to any of the properties, this agreement shall be extended for a reasonable time until said defects
47. shall have been corrected. In the event any defect cannot be corrected within a reasonable time, this agreement shall be null and void, except as to the payment of
48. commission to the Broker, plus costs by the party unable to convey clear title ,unless the party receiving the property in exchange shall agree to accept the title
49. to said property subject to said defects.
50. Each party hereto shall execute and deliver within __5__ days from the date of acceptance of this offer, all instruments necessary to complete this exchange.
51. Each party shall make final conveyance to the other by warranty deed or __N/A__ . In the event this exchange includes other than real
52. property, the seller shall provide evidence of title or right to sell or lease. Contracts of sale or instruments of conveyance shall be on forms approved by the Utah
53. State Securities Commission, in the name of __James A. Investor__ First Party,
54. and __Uintah Investors Inc.__ Second Party.
55. Closing shall be on or before __Dec 1,__ 19__88__. Possession shall be on or before __Dec 2,__ 19__88__.
56. All property taxes, insurance, rents, interest and other items of income and expense affecting each of said properties shall be prorated as of date of possession.
57. All other taxes and assessments, mortgages, chattel liens and other liens, encumbrances and charges against the property of either party shall be paid by the re-
58. spective sellers or grantors except __None__
59. In the event of default by either party, the party at fault shall pay all costs and expenses of enforcing this agreement, including a reasonable attorney's fee.
60. By mutual agreement of the parties hereto, __Big Deal Inc.__ , Broker is authorized to act as agent and may accept com-
61. missions from all parties hereto. It is presumed and understood that all parties to this agreement have investigated the respective properties, and the agent is hereby
62. released from all responsibility regarding valuation of same.
63. In the foregoing agreement, the use of the singular shall include the plural, and the use of the plural shall include the singular.
64. The undersigned First Party acknowledges that he has read this entire agreement and understands the terms and conditions contained therein

65. Date __November 3,__ 19__88__   First Party *James A. Investor*
66. Witness _____   First Party _____

Figure 24

ACCEPTANCE

67.   The undersigned, Second Party, acknowledges that he has read the entire foregoing Exchange Agreement and understands the terms and conditions con-
68. tained therein and does hereby accept this agreement and agrees to the exchange therein.

69. _____

70. _____

71. _____

72. _____

73. _____

74. _____

75. _____

76. _____

77. _____

78. As earnest money and evidence of good faith and to cover the expenses incurred therein, Second Party hereby deposits with ___Big Deal Inc.___

79. Broker, the sum of $__5,000.00__ in the form of __Co. Check__ and agrees to pay to said Broker the sum of $__10,000.00__ for services
80. rendered in connection with this exchange, such commission to become payable upon execution of this agreement by all parties hereto.

81. Date _____November 4,_____ , 19 __88__   Second Party _George A. Investor_

82. Witness _____   Second Party _CEO, Untoh Inv Inc_

83.   Received from the above named Second Party the sum of $__5,000.00__ to be held, used, and disbursed in accordance with the foregoing instructions.

84. Date _____Nov 4,_____ , 19 __88__   Broker _Big Deal Inc._

85.   By Agent _Eldon P. Agent_

86. The undersigned, hereby acknowledges receipt of a signed copy of the foregoing Exchange Agreement, duly accepted bearing all signatures.

87. Date _____Nov 4,_____ , 19 __88__   First Party _James A. Investor_

88. Date _____Nov 4,_____ , 19 __88__   Second Party _George P. President_
                                                                        C.E.O., Untoh Inv. Inc.

Figure 24 continued

properties involved in the exchange and a detailed statement as to what commissions are to be paid by the two parties.

You will also notice that the broker handling the transaction *may* collect a commission on each property. Normally, the first property mentioned will be a listed property on which the owner has signed a listing contract and commission agreement. The second property may also be listed but more than likely not; hence, the reason for the commission agreement on Line 79, which is payable by the second party.

There is also a very important difference between this agreement and the sales agreement. The sales agreement is a contract between two parties, the buyer and the seller. The exchange agreement is a contract between three parties—party one, party two, and the broker who handles the transaction. In the sales agreement, the broker serves as recipient of the earnest money only. His/her commission contract is a separate document. In the exchange agreement, the broker often becomes a party to the transaction in order to have a legal claim to a commission on the property acquired by the first party.

SEE ALSO: CONTRACT, and EARNEST MONEY DEPOSIT.

EARNEST MONEY RECEIPT AND OFFER TO LEASE

The earnest money receipt and offer to release is a state-approved form used by real estate brokers to present an offer to lease to a property owner and obtain his/her approval. This form is abrogated at the time the official lease is executed by the lessor and lessee.

INVESTOR ADVICE

This form is normally used by a broker who is acting as the leasing agent for a property owner. While this form is not absolutely necessary, it does form a clear and concise agreement between the parties, from which the official lease can be prepared. Figure 25 shows a form approved by the state of Utah for use by real estate brokers. Similar forms are used in other states.

You will note that the form contains no language bearing on commissions to be paid. Any commissions due the real estate broker for his/her services will be contained in a listing contract between the broker and the property owner.

One other interesting point regarding this form is a reference to an "option to purchase." Renters often lease a property with the right to purchase the property at some future date. Terms of the purchase often allow prior rent payments to be applied to the purchase.

If you consider allowing a tenant the right to purchase at some future date, it is wise to hedge on the price to be paid, particularly if the purchase option extends for a considerable period. Rather than fix the price at the time of the lease, it would be wiser to use language similar to the following:

"The purchase price will be established when the lessor decides to exercise his option to purchase" OR "The purchase price of the property shall be established by a competent appraisal of the property, at the point the lessor indicates an intent to exercise his option. The appraiser shall be mutually acceptable to the landlord and tenant. The appraisal fee will be paid by the landlord, if the deal is consummated. If not, the tenant shall pay the appraisal cost."

SEE ALSO: CONTRACT, EARNEST MONEY DEPOSIT, and LEASE.

EARNEST MONEY RECEIPT AND OFFER TO LEASE

1   <u>Nov 2,</u>   19 <u>88</u>

2 I/we <u>James A. & Shirley Renter</u> hereby deposit with you

3 as earnest money the sum of (\$ <u>500.00</u>) <u>five hundred and 00/100 dollars</u> to secure and apply

4 on the lease of the real property and/or fixtures and equipment situated at: <u>Apartment #5, Shadow Apartments,</u>

5 <u>3255 N. Fairway Drive, Big City</u> City <u>Davis</u> County, State of Utah.

6 including the following fixtures and equipment: <u>Kitchen appliances as installed, carpets and</u>

7 <u>window drapes.</u>

8 _____

9 _____

10 _____

11 The base rental shall be (\$<u>500.00</u>) per month for a leasehold term of

12 <u>1</u> years <u>0</u> months, commencing <u>November 10,</u> 19 <u>88</u>, and payable as follows: <u>10th of each</u>

13 <u>month in advance.</u>

14 with a renewal option as follows: <u>None</u>

15 _____

16 _____

17 _____

18 Option to purchase as follows: <u>None</u>

19 _____

20 _____

21 _____

22 MAINTENANCE: Tenant responsible for (T), Landlord responsible for (L)

23 Roof <u>L</u>, Exterior Walls <u>L</u>, Interior Walls <u>T</u>, Structural Repair <u>L</u>, Interior Decorating <u>T</u>, Exterior Painting <u>L</u>, Yard Surfacing <u>L</u>,

24 Plumbing Equipment <u>L</u>, Heating and Air Conditioning Equipment <u>L</u>, Electrical Equipment <u>L</u>, Light Globes and Tubes <u>T</u>, Glass Breakage <u>T</u>,

25 Trash Removal <u>L</u>, Snow Removal <u>L</u>, Janitor <u>L</u>, Others <u>None</u>

26 UTILITIES, TAXES AND INSURANCE: Tenant pays (T) Landlord pays (L)

27 Power <u>T</u>, Heat <u>L</u>, Water <u>L</u>, Sewer <u>L</u>, Telephone <u>T</u>, Real Property Tax <u>L</u>, Increase above 19 <u>88</u> in Real Property Tax <u>N/A</u>, Per-

28 sonal Property Tax <u>T</u>, Fire Insurance on Building <u>L</u>, Fire Insurance of Personal Property <u>T</u>, Glass Insurance <u>N/A</u> Other <u>None</u>

29 _____

30 Each party shall be responsible for losses from negligence or misconduct of himself, his employees, or invitees.

31 Furniture, fixtures and personal property of tenant may not be removed from the premises until rent and other charges are fully paid.

32 Property is leased in its present condition except: <u>None</u>

33 _____

34 _____

35 This payment is received and offer is made subject to the written acceptance of the landlord endorsed hereon with <u>1</u> days from date hereof, and

36 unless so approved the return of the money herein receipted shall cancel this offer without damage to the undersigned agent. Within <u>5</u> days after

37 tender of a firm lease prepared by landlord in a form consistent with the above provisions and containing other customary and reasonable general provisions,

38 the parties agree to execute a written lease which will supersede and abrogate this agreement.

39 In the event the tenant fails to execute said lease as herein provided, the amounts paid hereon shall, at the option of the landlord, be retained as

40 liquidated and agreed damages, or landlord may elect to retain said sum and to require specific performance.

41 It is understood and agreed that the terms written in this receipt constitute the entire Preliminary Contract between the tenant and landlord, and that

42 no verbal statement made by anyone relative to this transaction shall be construed to be a part of this transaction unless incorporated in writing herein.

43 <u>Big Deal Inc.</u>   Agent By <u>Joe Salesman</u>
     Broker Company

44 We do hereby agree to carry out and fulfill the terms and conditions specified above, and the landlord warrants that he has good and sufficient

45 right to lease and/or sell the subject property in accordance herewith and to provide reasonable evidence of such right on demand of tenant. If either

46 party fails to do so, he agrees to pay all expenses of enforcing this agreement, or of any right arising out of the breach thereof, including a reasonable

47 attorney's fee.

<u>Nov 3,88</u>   <u>Geo C. Rich</u>   <u>James A. Renter</u>   <u>Nov 3,88</u>
Date   Landlord   Tenant   Date

                         <u>Shirley Renter</u>
Date   Landlord   Tenant   <u>Nov 3,88</u>
                                    Date

(State law requires brokers to furnish copies of this contract bearing all signatures to tenant and landlord. Dependent upon the methods used, one of the follow-ing forms must be completed.)

I acknowledge receipt of a final copy of the foregoing agreement bearing all signatures:

<u>11-3-88</u>   <u>Geo C. Rich</u>   <u>James A. Renter</u>   <u>11-3-88</u>
Date   Landlord   Tenant   Date

I personally caused a final copy of the foregoing agreement bearing all signatures to be mailed to the _____ Landlord _____ tenant on _____

_____ 19___. Registered mail and return receipt is attached hereto.

Broker <u>Big Deal Inc</u>   By <u>Joe Salesman</u>

Figure 25

EARNEST MONEY RECEIPT AND OFFER TO PURCHASE (SALES AGREEMENT)

The sales agreement is a state-approved form used by real estate brokers to present an offer to purchase to a property owner and obtain his/her approval. This form is abrogated at the time transfer of the property is closed.

INVESTOR ADVICE

This lengthy form, shown as Figure 26, is the source of more disputes and legal actions than any other form used by the general public. It is extremely important to assure that the real estate broker who prepares the offer, does it in strict accordance with the wishes of the buyer. In particular, the broker must assure that the buyer's wishes are correctly translated into the required legal language to accomplish the buyer's desires.

There can be no agreement outside of this document. All agreements and understandings must be in writing. This preliminary contract forms the basis of the final property transfer papers and the preparer of these final papers (closing agent) cannot add or subtract from the provisions listed herein.

This document is so important that it is strongly suggested that the real estate broker earns the majority of his/her commission when he/she advises his/her principal as to the accuracy and completeness of this paper's content. Competent advice prior to signature can save thousands of dollars in future legal fees.

SEE ALSO: CONTRACT, and EARNEST MONEY DEPOSIT.

EASEMENT

An easement is an agreement by a landowner for another to use a portion or all of his/her property for a specific purpose.

INVESTOR ADVICE

Easements are created by one or more of the following property owner actions or lack of action:

- Express grant, reservation, or agreement;

- By implication where the easement is necessary and has been in prior obvious and continued use; and

- By prescription.

Easements are normally established to provide a service to the property or to adjacent property. The following list of easements are typical:

- Right-of-way;

- Utility installation and maintenance; and

- Party walls or fences.

Any granting of an easement is a loss of rights to the property and should be carefully considered in light of present as well as future use of the land. The granting of utility rights are obviously to the advantage of the property owner, but other grants may detract from the value of the property or render it useless for other uses in the future.

EARNEST MONEY SALES AGREEMENT

Legend   Yes (X)   No (O)

This is a legally binding contract. Read the entire document carefully before signing.

GENERAL PROVISIONS
(Sections)

A. **INCLUDED ITEMS.** Unless excluded herein, this sale shall *include* all fixtures and any of the following items if presently attached to the property, plumbing, heating, air-conditioning and ventilating fixtures and equipment, water heater, built-in appliances, light fixtures and bulbs, bathroom fixtures, curtains and draperies and rods, window and door screens, storm doors, window blinds, awnings, installed television antenna, wall-to-wall carpets, water softener, automatic garage door opener and transmitter(s), fencing, trees and shrubs.

B. **INSPECTION.** Unless otherwise indicated, Buyer agrees that Buyer is purchasing said property upon Buyer's own examination and judgment and not by reason of any representation made to Buyer by Seller or the Listing or Selling Brokerage as to its condition, size, location, present value, future value, income herefrom or as to its production. Buyer accepts the property in "as is" condition subject to Seller's warranties as outlined in Section 6. In the event Buyer desires any additional inspection, said inspection shall be allowed by Seller but arranged for and paid by Buyer.

C. **SELLER WARRANTIES.** Seller warrants that: (a) Seller has received no claim nor notice of any building or zoning violation concerning the property which has not or will not be remedied prior to closing; (b) all obligations against the property including taxes, assessments, mortgages, liens or other encumbrances of any nature shall be brought current on or before closing; and (c) the plumbing, heating, air conditioning and ventilating systems, electrical system, and appliances shall be sound or in satisfactory working condition at closing.

D. **CONDITION OF WELL.** Seller warrants that any private well serving the property has, to the best of Seller's knowledge, provided an adquate supply of water and continued use of the well or wells is authorized by a state permit or other legal water right.

E. **CONDITION OF SEPTIC TANK.** Seller warrants that any septic tank serving the property is, to the best of Seller's knowledge. in good working order and Seller has no knowledge of any needed repairs and it meets all applicable government health and construction standards.

F. **ACCELERATION CLAUSE.** Not less than five (5) days prior to closing, Seller shall provide to Buyer written verification as to whether or not any notes, mortgages, deeds of trust or real estate contracts against the property require the consent of the holder of such instrument(s) to the sale of the property or permit the holder to raise the interest rate and/or declare the entire balance due in the event of sale. If any such document so provides and holder does not waive the same or unconditionally approve the sale, Buyer shall have the option to declare this Agreement null and void by giving written notice to Seller or Seller's agent prior to closing. In such case, all earnest money received under this Agreement shall be returned to Buyer. It is understood and agreed that if provisions for said "Due on Sale" clause are set forth in Section 7 herein, alternatives allowed herein shall become null and void.

G. **TITLE INSPECTION.** Not less than five (5) days prior to closing, Seller shall provide to Buyer either an abstract of title brought current with an attorney's opinion or a preliminary title report on the subject property. Prior to closing, Buyer shall give written notice to Seller or Seller's agent, specifying reasonable objections to title. Thereafter, Seller shall be required, through escrow at closing, to cure the defect(s) to which Buyer has objected. If said defect(s) is not curable through an escrow agreement at closing, this Agreement shall be null and void at the option of the Buyer, and all monies received herewith shall be returned to the respective parties.

H. **TITLE INSURANCE.** If title insurance is elected, Seller authorizes the Listing Brokerage to order a preliminary commitment for a policy of title insurance to be issued by such title insurance company as Seller shall designate. Title policy to be issued shall contain no exceptions other than those provided for in said standard form, and the encumbrances or defects excepted under the final contract of sale. If title cannot be made so insurable through an escrow agreement at closing, the earnest money shall, unless Buyer elects to waive such defects or encumbrances, be refunded to Buyer, and this Agreement shall thereupon be terminated. Seller agrees to pay any cancellation charge.

I. **EXISTING TENANT LEASES.** If Buyer is to take title subject to an existing lease or leases, Seller agrees to provide to Buyer not less than five (5) days prior to closing a copy of all existing leases (and any amendments thereto) affecting the property. Unless reasonable written objection is given by Buyer to Seller or Seller's agent prior to closing, Buyer shall take title subject to such leases. If the objection(s) is not remedied at or prior to closing, this Agreement shall be null and void.

J. **CHANGES DURING TRANSACTION.** During the pendency of this Agreement, Seller agrees that no changes in any existing leases shall be made, nor new leases entered into, nor shall any substantial alterations or improvements be made or undertaken without the written consent of the Buyer.

PAGE ONE OF A FOUR PAGE FORM

Figure 26

EARNEST MONEY SALES AGREEMENT

Legend   Yes(X)   No(O)

EARNEST MONEY RECEIPT

DATE: November 2, 1988

The undersigned Buyer(s) James A. & Shirlep P. Homebuyer _____ hereby deposits with Brokerage as EARNEST MONEY, the amount of Five hundred and 00/100 ------------------- Dollars ($ 500.00), in the form of Personal Check on Utah Bank & Trust, Wasatch Branch _____
which shall be deposited in accordance with applicable State Law.

Big Deals Inc.   487-9871 _____   Received by _____
Brokerage   Phone Number

OFFER TO PURCHASE

1. PROPERTY DESCRIPTION The above stated EARNEST MONEY is given to secure and apply on the purchase of the property situated at 130 S. Clover Lane _____ in the City of Salt Lake _____ County of Salt Lake _____ , Utah, subject to any restrictive covenants, zoning regulations, utility or other easements or rights of way, government patents or state deeds of record approved by Buyer in accordance with Section G. Said property is owned by James A. Investor _____ as sellers, and is more particularly described as: All of lots 10,11 & 12, Plat "A", Big Field Survey _____

CHECK APPLICABLE BOXES:

☐ **UNIMPROVED REAL PROPERTY**   ☐ Vacant Lot   ☐ Vacant Acreage   ☐ Other _____
☒ **IMPROVED REAL PROPERTY**   ☐ Commercial   ☐ Residential   ☐ Condo   ☐ Other _____

(a) **Included items.** Unless excluded below, this sale shall *include* all fixtures and any of the items shown in Section A if presently attached to the property. The following personal property shall also be included in this sale and conveyed under separate Bill of Sale with warranties as to title: Floor coverings and mini-blinds as installed. _____

(b) **Excluded items.** The following items are specifically *excluded* from this sale: None _____

(c) **CONNECTIONS, UTILITIES AND OTHER RIGHTS.** Seller represents that the property includes the following improvements in the purchase price:

☒ public sewer ☒ connected   ☐ well ☐ connected ☐ other   ☒ electricity ☒ connected
☐ septic tank ☐ connected   ☐ irrigation water / secondary system   ☐ ingress & egress by private easement
☐ other sanitary system _____   # of shares _____ Company _____   ☐ dedicated road ☐ paved
☒ public water ☒ connected   ☒ TV antenna ☐ master antenna ☐ prewired   ☒ curb and gutter
☐ private water ☐ connected   ☒ natural gas ☒ connected   ☐ other rights _____ None

(d) **Survey.** A certified survey ☐ shall be furnished at the expense of _____ prior to closing, ☒ shall not be furnished.

(e) **Buyer Inspection.** Buyer has made a visual inspection of the property and subject to Section 1 (c) above and 6 below, accepts it in its present physical condition, except: Buyer reserves the right to inspect the property prior to transfer of deed and closing.

2. PURCHASE PRICE AND FINANCING. The total purchase price for the property is Seventy-eight thousand and 00/100 dollars _____ Dollars ($ 78,000.00) which shall be paid as follows:

$ 500.00   which represents the aforedescribed EARNEST MONEY DEPOSIT:

$ 8,000.00   representing the approximate balance of CASH DOWN PAYMENT at closing.

$ _____   representing the approximate balance of an existing mortgage, trust deed note, real estate contract or other encumbrance to be assumed by buyer, which obligation bears interest at _____ % per annum with monthly payments of $ _____
which include: ☐ principal; ☐ interest; ☐ taxes; ☐ insurance; ☐ condo fees; ☐ other _____ .

$ _____   representing the approximate balance of an additional existing mortgage, trust deed note, real estate contract or other encumbrances to be assumed by Buyer, which obligation bears interest at _____ % per annum with monthly payments of $ _____
which include: ☐ principal; ☐ interest; ☐ taxes; ☐ insurance; ☐ condo fees; ☐ other _____ .

$ 69,500.00   representing balance, if any, including proceeds from a new mortgage loan, or seller financing, to be paid as follows: from proceeds of a new 1st mortgage to be applied for upon acceptance of this offer. This sale is contingent upon approval and granting of this loan.

$ _____   Other _____

| $78,000.00 | TOTAL PURCHASE PRICE |

If Buyer is required to assume an underlying obligation (in which case Section F shall also apply) and/or obtain outside financing, Buyer agrees to use best efforts to assume and/or procure same and this offer is made subject to Buyer qualifying for and lending institution granting said assumption and/or financing. Buyer agrees to make application within 2 days after Seller's acceptance of this Agreement to assume the underlying obligation and/or obtain the new financing at an interest rate not to exceed 10.5 %. If Buyer does not qualify for the assumption and/or financing within 30 days after Seller's acceptance of this Agreement, this Agreement shall be voidable at the option of the Seller upon written notice. Seller agrees to pay up to 2 mortgage loan discount points, not to exceed $ 1,500.00 . In addition, seller agrees to pay $ None to be used for Buyer's other loan costs.

Page two of a four page form   Seller's Initials (_____)   Date 11-3-88   Buyer's Initials _____   Date 11-3-88

Figure 26 continued

3. **CONDITION AND CONVEYANCE OF TITLE.** Seller represents that Seller ☒ holds title to the property in fee simple ☐ is purchasing the property under a real estate contract. Transfer of Seller's ownership interest shall be made as set forth in Section S. Seller agrees to furnish good and marketable title to the property, subject to encumbrances and exceptions noted herein, evidenced by ☒ a current policy of title insurance in the amount of purchase price ☐ an abstract of title brought current, with an attorney's opinion (See Section H).

4. **INSPECTION OF TITLE.** In accordance with Section G, Buyer shall have the opportunity to inspect the title to the subject property prior to closing. Buyer shall take title subject to any existing restrictive covenants, including condominium restrictions (CC & R's). Buyer ☐ has ☐ has not reviewed any condominium CC & R's prior to signing this Agreement.

5. **VESTING OF TITLE.** Title shall vest in Buyer as follows: <u>James A. & Shirley P. Homebuyer, JTWROS</u>

6. **SELLERS WARRANTIES.** In addition to warranties contained in Section C, the following items are also warranted: <u>All electrical, Heating and plumbing to be in good working order at time of possession.</u>

Exceptions to the above and Section C shall be limited to the following: <u>None</u>

7. **SPECIAL CONSIDERATIONS AND CONTINGENCIES.** This offer is made subject to the following special conditions and/or contingencies which must be satisfied prior to closing: <u>This offer is contingent upon the successful closing of a sale on the buyers present home at 422 N. Jemeni St., Salt Lake City, Utah. This sale is scheduled to close on/about Dec 1, 1988.</u>

8. **CLOSING OF SALE.** This Agreement shall be closed on or before <u>Dec 5,</u> 19<u>88</u> at a reasonable location to be designated by Seller, subject to Section Q. Upon demand, Buyer shall deposit with the escrow closing office all documents necessary to complete the purchase in accordance with this Agreement. Prorations set forth in Section R shall be made as of ☒ date of possession ☐ date of closing ☐ other

9. **POSSESSION.** Seller shall deliver possession to Buyer on <u>Dec 6, 1988</u> unless extended by written agreement of parties.

10. **AGENCY DISCLOSURE.** At the signing of this Agreement the listing agent <u>James P. Salesman</u> represents (X) Seller ( ) Buyer, and the selling agent <u>George A. Pusher</u> represents ( ) Seller (X) Buyer. Buyer and Seller confirm that prior to signing this Agreement written disclosure of the agency relationship(s) was provided to him/her. ( )( ) Buyer's initials ( )( ) Seller's initials.

11. **GENERAL PROVISIONS.** UNLESS OTHERWISE INDICATED ABOVE, THE GENERAL PROVISION SECTIONS ON THE REVERSE SIDE HEREOF HAVE BEEN ACCEPTED BY THE BUYER AND SELLER AND ARE INCORPORATED INTO THIS AGREEMENT BY REFERENCE.

12. **AGREEMENT TO PURCHASE AND TIME LIMIT FOR ACCEPTANCE.** Buyer offers to purchase the property on the above terms and conditions. Seller shall have until <u>12 PM</u> (AM/PM) <u>Nov 4,</u> 19<u>88</u>, to accept this offer. Unless accepted, this offer shall lapse and the Agent shall return the EARNEST MONEY to the Buyer.

(Buyer's Signature)	(Date)	(Address)	(Phone)	(SSN/TAX ID)
James A. Homebuyer 11-2-88		422 N. Jemeni St, SLC	272-9872	402-55-9864
Shirley P. Homebuyer 11-2-88		422 N. Jemeni St SLC	272-9872	365-24-8872

CHECK ONE
☒ ACCEPTANCE OF OFFER TO PURCHASE: Seller hereby ACCEPTS the foregoing offer on the terms and conditions specified above.
☐ REJECTION. Seller hereby REJECTS the foregoing offer. _____ (Seller's initials)
☐ COUNTER OFFER. Seller hereby ACCEPTS the foregoing offer SUBJECT TO the exceptions or modifications as specified below or in the attached Addendum, and presents said COUNTER OFFER for Buyer's acceptance. Buyer shall have until _____ (AM/PM) _____, 19 ___ to accept the terms specified below.

James R. Investor 11-3-88 1:30P 421 Arlington 272-6060 466-16-1820
(Seller's Signature) (Date) (Time) (Address) (Phone) (SSN/TAX ID)

(Seller's Signature) (Date) (Time) (Address) (Phone) (SSN/TAX ID)

CHECK ONE:
☐ ACCEPTANCE OF COUNTER OFFER. Buyer hereby ACCEPTS the COUNTER OFFER
☐ REJECTION. Buyer hereby REJECTS the COUNTER OFFER. _____ (Buyer's Initials)
☐ COUNTER OFFER. Buyer hereby ACCEPTS the COUNTER OFFER with modifications on attached Addendum.

(Buyer's Signature) (Date) (Time) (Buyer's Signature) (Date) (Time)

DOCUMENT RECEIPT

State Law requires Broker to furnish Buyer and Seller with copies of this Agreement bearing all signatures. (One of the following alternatives must therefore be completed).

A. ☒ I acknowledge receipt of a final copy of the foregoing Agreement bearing all signatures:
SIGNATURE OF SELLER   SIGNATURE OF BUYER
James A. Investor 11-3-88   *James A. Homebuyer* 11-3-88

B. ☐ I personally caused a final copy of the foregoing Agreement bearing all signatures to be mailed on _____, 19 ___ by Certified Mail and return receipt attached hereto to the ☐ Seller ☐ Buyer. Sent by _____

Page three of a four page form

Figure 26 continued

K. **AUTHORITY OF SIGNATORS.** If Buyer or Seller is a corporation, partnership, trust, estate, or other entity, the person executing this Agreement on its behalf warrants his or her authority to do so and to bind Buyer or Seller.

L. **COMPLETE AGREEMENT — NO ORAL AGREEMENTS.** This instrument constitutes the entire agreement between the parties and supersedes and cancels any and all prior negotiations, representations, warranties, understandings or agreements between the parties. There are no oral agreements which modify or affect this agreement. This Agreement cannot be changed except by mutual written agreement of the parties.

M. **COUNTER OFFERS.** Any counter offer made by Seller or Buyer shall be in writing and, if attached hereto, shall incorporate all the provisions of this Agreement not expressly modified or excluded therein.

N. **DEFAULT/INTERPLEADER AND ATTORNEY'S FEES.** In the event of default by Buyer, Seller may elect to either retain the earnest money as liquidated damages or to institute suit to enforce any rights of Seller. In the event of default by Seller, or if this sale fails to close because of the nonsatisfaction of any express condition or contingency to which the sale is subject pursuant to this Agreement (other than by virtue of any default by Buyer), the earnest money deposit shall be returned to Buyer. Both parties agree that should either party default in any of the covenants or agreements herein contained, the defaulting party shall pay all costs and expenses, including a reasonable attorney's fee, which may arise or accrue from enforcing or terminating this Agreement or in pursuing any remedy provided hereunder or by applicable law, whether such remedy is pursued by filing suit or otherwise. In the event the principal broker holding the earnest money deposit is required to file an interpleader action in court to resolve a dispute over the earnest money deposit referred to herein, the Buyer and Seller authorize the principal broker to draw from the earnest money deposit an amount necessary to advance the costs of bringing the interpleader action. The amount of deposit remaining after advancing those costs shall be interpleaded into court in accordance with state law. The Buyer and Seller further agree that the defaulting party shall pay the court costs and reasonable attorney's fees incurred by the principal broker in bringing such action.

O. **ABROGATION.** Except for express warranties made in this Agreement, execution and delivery of final closing documents shall abrogate this Agreement.

P. **RISK OF LOSS.** All risk of loss or damage to the property shall be borne by the Seller until closing. In the event there is loss or damage to the property between the date hereof and the date of closing, by reason of fire, vandalism, flood, earthquake, or acts of God, and the cost to repair such damage shall exceed ten percent (10%) of the purchase price of the property, Buyer may at his option either proceed with this transaction if Seller agrees in writing to repair or replace damaged property prior to closing or declare this Agreement null and void. If damage to property is less than ten percent (10%) of the purchase price and Seller agrees in writing to repair or replace and does actually repair and replace damaged property prior to closing, this transaction shall proceed as agreed.

Q. **TIME IS OF ESSENCE—UNAVOIDABLE DELAY.** In the event that this sale cannot be closed by the date provided herein due to interruption of transport, strikes, fire, flood, extreme weather, governmental regulations, delays caused by lender, acts of God, or similar occurrences beyond the control of Buyer or Seller, then the closing date shall be extended seven (7) days beyond cessation of such condition, but in no event more than fifteen (15) days beyond the closing date provided herein. Thereafter, time is of the essence. This provision relates only to the extension of closing dates. "Closing" shall mean the date on which all necessary instruments are signed and delivered by all parties to the transaction.

R. **CLOSING COSTS.** Seller and Buyer shall each pay one-half (½) of the escrow closing fee, unless otherwise required by the lending institution. Costs of providing title insurance or an abstract brought current shall be paid by Seller. Taxes and assessments for the current year, insurance, if acceptable to the Buyer, rents, and interest on assumed obligations shall be prorated as set forth in Section 8. Unearned deposits on tenancies and remaining mortgage or other reserves shall be assigned to Buyer at closing.

S. **REAL PROPERTY CONVEYANCING.** If this agreement is for conveyance of fee title, title shall be conveyed by warranty deed free of defects other than those excepted herein. If this Agreement is for sale or transfer of a Seller's interest under an existing real estate contract, Seller may transfer by either (a) special warranty deed, containing Seller's assignment of said contract in form sufficient to convey after acquired title or (b) by a new real estate contract incorporating the said existing real estate contract therein.

T. **NOTICE.** Unless otherwise provided in this Agreement, any notice expressly required by it must be given no later than two days after the occurrence or non-occurrence of the event with respect to which notice is required. If any such timely required notice is not given, the contingency with respect to which the notice was to be given is automatically terminated and this Agreement is in full force and effect. If a person other than the Buyer or the Seller is designated to receive notice on behalf of the Buyer or the Seller, notice to the person so designated shall be considered notice to the party designating that person for receipt of notice.

U. **BROKERAGE.** For purposes of this Agreement, any references to the term, "Brokerage" shall mean the respective listing or selling real estate office.

V. **DAYS.** For the purposes of this Agreement, any references to the term, "days" shall mean business or working days exclusive of legal holidays.

PAGE FOUR OF A FOUR PAGE FORM.

THIS FORM HAS BEEN APPROVED BY THE UTAH REAL ESTATE COMMISSION AND THE OFFICE OF THE UTAH ATTORNEY GENERAL — JULY 1, 1987

Figure 26 continued

It should be noted that the granting of an easement to another does not constitute a transfer of ownership. It merely authorizes another to pass over or utilize a portion of the total property for a specific purpose.

SEE ALSO: ECONOMIC VALUE, and ENCUMBRANCES.

ECONOMIC DEPRECIATION

Economic depreciation occurs when property loses value due to economic conditions in the surrounding area where the property is located.

INVESTOR ADVICE

The purchase of property in an area subject to an economic downturn is inadvisable. Economic depreciation is a factor beyond the owner's control.

On the other hand, areas which have suffered a prior economic recession may present an excellent opportunity for rapid capital appreciation. The key to success here is to buy at the point of minimum value and just prior to an economic upturn.

An example of such opportunities would be the many vacant mill properties in the Boston area in the late 1960's, just prior to the introduction of the electronics industry in that area. Similar opportunities may exist in those areas of a city targeted for urban renewal projects.

Capitalizing on projected economic upturns is not a short-term project, but rather one in which substantial capital may be committed for a period of time.

If you are considering this type of investment, be prepared for the required wait and a period of little or no return on investment. These investments will also require a larger than normal downpayment and enough cash for debt service, taxes, and insurance. The gains to be achieved must also be substantial. A quick look at present value tables will show the following five-year capital gains requirements, just to break even, with no additional cash outlay:

Value of Money	Gain Required
10%	60%
12%	76%
14%	93%
16%	110%
18%	129%
20%	149%

SEE ALSO: ECONOMIC OBSOLESCENCE.

ECONOMIC LIFE

Economic life is the period in which a property improvement will continue to produce a return on the investment greater than the value of rent on the land itself.

INVESTOR ADVICE

The economic life of a property can be greatly extended by timely maintenance and modernization. These actions can also increase revenue and decrease vacancy factors.

The economic life of a property is largely determined by the quality of property management. Figure 27 indicates how the income on a property can be extended with timely modernization.

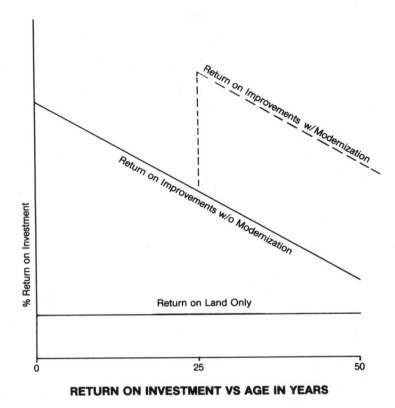

RETURN ON INVESTMENT VS AGE IN YEARS

Figure 27

While modernization will require an additional investment, it is more than offset by the increased economic life of the improvements, and the increased income over the remaining life. In this example it is assumed that the return on the land investment is level. In most real cases, the value of land will gradually increase in value, requiring a corresponding increase in income to maintain a level return.

SEE ALSO: CURABLE DEPRECIATION, and CERTIFIED PROPERTY MANAGER.

ECONOMIC OBSOLESCENCE

This term refers to the uncontrollable loss of property value due to changes in the community and economic conditions which decrease the desirability of the property.

INVESTOR ADVICE

> **KNOWLEDGE:** The key to success in real estate investment. Buy properties in areas that you know well.

Economic obsolescence is seldom a sudden event. It occurs over a period of time and is generally predictable for the short term, but less predictable for an extended period. The best protection against unwise purchases, in an area which may be subject to economic obsolescence, is personal knowledge. Your best and safest buy is in areas in which you live or are personally acquainted with.

Growth patterns are readily discernable by local residents, who have seen their community expand and change. Most communities tend to grow in only one or two directions—toward available land or in or around recreation areas. Existing built-up areas usually do one of two things: (1) continue to increase in value as land becomes less available; or (2) deteriorate rapidly.

SEE ALSO: DEMOGRAPHICS, and ECONOMIC DEPRECIATION.

ECONOMIC RENT

Economic rent is the rent a property will command on an open market at the time of evaluation. Economic rent may be equal to, less than, or greater than contract rent.

INVESTOR ADVICE

When purchasing property with existing long-term leases, the value of the leasehold interests must be considered. In these cases, the selling price may be less than the fair market value of the property. Where the property is encumbered with leases at less than economic rental values, the fair market value has been divided between the landlord and the lessees.

EXAMPLE

A certain office building has been recently appraised for $350,000. It contains 10,000 square feet and is leased to the federal government for an additional ten years at $8.50/s.f., triple-net basis. The owner desires to sell. What is his interest in the property at this time, when the economic rent is $10.00/s.f.?

By definition the lessee interest is the present value of the difference between economic and contract rent. In other words, the tenant is denying the landlord full economic rent due to the terms of his contract. Looking at it from the owner's standpoint, the terms of the lease force him to loose $1.50 per square foot per year. Where money is worth 10%, the leasehold interest is:

$$\text{PV-1/period}_{\text{10yrs.}} @ \text{ 10\%} \times (\$10.00 - \$8.50) \times 10,000 \text{ s.f.} = \$92,169$$

Rounded to: 92,200

The owner's interest is therefore:

$$\$350,000 - \$92,200 = \$257,800$$

SEE ALSO: CONTRACT RENT, and LEASEHOLD INTEREST.

ECONOMIC VALUE

Economic value is the value of a property based upon the monetary return to the owner during the holding period. The return may be based upon the income from the property, capital gains upon its sale, or a combination of the two.

INVESTOR ADVICE

When calculating the economic value of a proposed acquisition, you should not confuse the return produced by the property and the total return realized. Total return is often a combination of a return from the property investment and work (management) performed by the owner.

An accurate calculation of economic value must deduct the value of management effort supplied by the owner. To estimate this value, ask your self the question, "What would it cost me to have that service provided by another?"

The economic value of a property is the sum of the present value of the income stream during the holding period, and the present value of the anticipated sales price, which includes capital gains, that are realized upon the sale of the property.

EXAMPLE

The proposed purchase of an office building is expected to produce a net income of $20,000 per year. Based upon economic projections, it is expected that the property will have a value of about $275,000 at the end of an eight-year proposed holding period. The purchaser considers money to be worth 10%. What is the present economic value to this purchaser?

$$V = PV\text{-}1/period_{8yrs\,@10\%} \times \$20,000 + PV\text{-}1_{8yrs\,@10\%} \times \$275,000 = \$234,988$$

Rounded to: 235,000

Please note that the present value factor is dependent upon the value of money to the purchaser. The economic value of a property therefore may not be the same for all persons.

Appraisers, who calculate fair market value, might utilize the same approach with one exception. The value of money is determined from the market place.

SEE ALSO: RETURN ON INVESTMENT, and ON-SITE MANAGER.

EFFECTIVE AGE

The estimated age of a structure, based upon its physical condition and current economic value is called its effective age.

INVESTOR ADVICE

We have all seen homes that are one or two years old in actual age but because of abuse look ten years old. We have also seen homes twenty years old that have had such tender loving care that they look almost new. Effective age is a personal judgment and may not be viewed the same by everyone.

Appraisers utilize effective age in adjusting comparable sales versus the property being appraised and in applying a depreciation factor, where the cost approach is used.

In judging the effective age of a property, you should not forget to consider the possibility of functional obsolescence, as well as economic and physical depreciation.

SEE ALSO: CHRONOLOGICAL AGE, ECONOMIC DEPRECIATION, FUNCTIONAL OBSOLESCENCE, AND PHYSICAL DEPRECIATION.

EFFECTIVE GROSS INCOME

Effective gross income is the total income actually received from a property based on 100% occupancy, less an allowance for vacancies and lost collections, plus additional income from other than rentals—laundry, parking, etc.

INVESTOR ADVICE

When you review the income projections for a proposed acquisition, be sure that a reasonable vacancy factor and bad debt allowance has been included. Do not accept seller statements such as, "We never have a vacancy—when one tenant leaves, another moves right in."

The fact remains that one tenant does not move out at midnight with a replacement moving in at 12:01 A.M. Even in well-managed properties, some loss should be expected. If nothing else, a vacancy loss will occur between tenants, while redecoration is accomplished. A good financial statement or projection should appear somewhat as follows:

GROSS SCHEDULED INCOME	
5, 3-bedroom apts @ $400/mo.	$24,000
2, 2-bedroom apts @ $300/mo.	7,200
8, 1-bedroom apts @ $250/mo.	12,000
Total scheduled income	$43,200
Less: Vacancy Factor @ 3%	(1,296)
Plus: Laundry Income (est.)	1,200
GROSS EFFECTIVE INCOME	$43,104

In the example given, the owner has estimated his vacancy factor as 3%. To consider the reasonableness of this estimate, it is helpful to calculate the total unit months available and then see what 3% really means. In the example, we have fifteen apartments available for twelve months or:

$$12 \text{ mo. x } 15 \text{ units} = 180 \text{ unit-months}$$

$$3\% \text{ vacancy factor} = 180 \text{ unit-months x } 3\% = 5.4 \text{ unit-months}$$

This figure could be rounded up to six unit-months. A 3% vacancy factor means six units of the fifteen available will be vacant for one month. Is this good or bad? You will have to compare this with the record of other projects in the area to decide.

SEE ALSO: NET INCOME, and NET INCOME AFTER TAXES.

EGRESS

Egress is a way of leaving a property without trespassing on a neighbor's property. One of the sticks in the bundle of rights, ingress (entering a property) and egress are the same, except for the direction of travel.

INVESTOR ADVICE

Care must be exercised when selling a portion of an existing parcel of land to guarantee the right of ingress and egress for the remaining portion. You need not reserve ownership in a right of way but should reserve an easement across the sold portion for that purpose.

Figure 28 shows a property which has been subdivided into two building lots, with a right-of-way reserved for the rear-lot owner.

SEE ALSO: BUNDLE OF RIGHTS, EASEMENT, INGRESS, and RIGHT-OF-WAY.

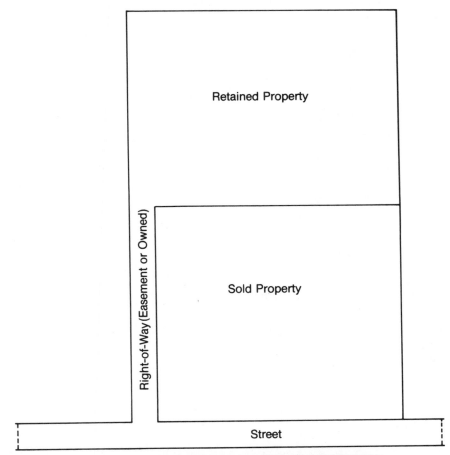

MAINTAINING EGRESS/INGRESS
After Property Sale

Figure 28

ELECTRICAL EQUIPMENT

Electrical equipment encompasses all entrance cables, interior wiring, switches, outlets, meters, motors, and other equipment required to provide a building with electrical service.

INVESTOR ADVICE

Before purchasing a building of any type, a thorough inspection should be made of the electrical equipment. If you do not feel qualified to inspect the property, a qualified inspector should be employed.

In older buildings, it is quite likely that the entire system is inadequate for present-day heavy electrical use and may not meet electrical codes. In older single and multiple residences, it is also not unusual to find a lack of 220-volt service to the residence and an inadequate number of circuits to meet today's heavy electrical usage.

In commercial buildings, it is often found that prior tenants have modified the electrical system in a haphazard manner which will require some expensive overhauling to meet existing commercial codes.

Know what you are buying. Don't take the seller's word that, "Everything is in good shape." A properly wired house will be indicated by the following:

- A three-wire entrance cable indicating availability of 220-volt service;
- Metallic or plastic covered service mains from a breaker-box. A fuse box will indicate a electrical system over twenty years old and very possibly inadequate;
- Wall plugs should accommodate three-prong plugs (protective ground);
- Electrical circuit breakers on wall plug and light circuits not over twenty amp. Larger than twenty-amp breakers will indicate a possible overloading of circuits. Breakers for electrical dryers and stoves will, of course, have higher ratings—thirty to fifty amps.

Commercial property electrical systems will have many of the attributes of residential systems, but with some important differences:

- Electrical circuits will probably be in rigid conduit;
- Circuit amperages will be larger, as larger-size wiring will have been used;
- Several special circuits (some 220 V) may be provided for special equipment such as computers, large copy machines, etc.; and
- In-house cable may be provided for flexible telephone use by various tenants. Access to this type of telephone system is via hand-holds in the floor covered by brass plates and terminals in each office suite.

SEE ALSO: PLUMBING EQUIPMENT.

ELLWOOD PREMISE

Ellwood premise means, "An extension of basic mortgage-equity analysis involving certain additional assumptions, concerning income flows and the nature of claims against those income flows."[1] The assumptions in using this technique include:

1. The purchaser-investor is typically interested in the cash income that the property will produce to support his/her equity investment.
2. The typical purchaser-investor is sensitive to income taxes and will behave in a manner allowing maximum tax avoidance.
3. The purchaser-investor typically seeks to take maximum possible advantage of leverage to enhance his/her equity return.
4. The purchaser-investor will typically retain the investment only so long as there is a cash income advantage in doing so.
5. The purchaser-investor typically will anticipate a level income flow over the income projection period, since it is relatively short.
6. The purchaser-investor will have discoverable expectations about the reversion (the most probable resale price of the property) at the end of the income projection period.

INVESTOR ADVICE

The Ellwood premise is considered a big improvement over other methods for deriving capitalization rates. However, this method is still no more accurate than the values utilized, two of which, estimated appreciation/depreciation and estimated holding period, are estimates.

First, consider the holding period. Few buyers are able to accurately predict the exact time that they will decide to sell a real estate investment. Secondly, the estimate of the value of the property at the time of sale is even more difficult to predict. Significant errors in either or both of the above can result in significant errors in calculation of yield rates. In mathematics we are taught that facts multiplied by guesses result in guesses.

By using several projections of time, and appreciation and depreciation, very accurate curves of overall return can be drawn to provide the investor with an accurate picture of, "What if?" At least you can consider the range of possibilities. The various Ellwood tables have significantly reduced the work in preparing overall return curves for the investor's consideration.

SEE ALSO: CAPITALIZATION RATES, INCOME APPROACH TO VALUE, and MORTGAGE EQUITY TECHNIQUE.

EMBLEMENTS

Emblements are that which is planted and reaped from the land.

INVESTOR ADVICE

When preparing an earnest money receipt and offer to purchase for land upon which crops may be sown or growing, it is essential that the ownership of the emblements be clearly established in the offer.

You may assume that when you take title, all that is upon the land is yours, but the seller may think otherwise. Do prevent any misunderstanding. The ownership of these items must be clearly delineated in the offer.

SEE ALSO: EARNEST MONEY RECEIPT AND OFFER TO PURCHASE, PERSONAL PROPERTY, and REAL ESTATE.

EMINENT DOMAIN

Eminent domain is the power reserved by governments to condemn and take private property for public use, with due compensation to the owner.

INVESTOR ADVICE

See discussion and advice under "Condemnation."
SEE ALSO: CONDEMNATION.

ENCROACHMENT

Encroachment refers to a form of trespassing in which an improvement is constructed on or partially on the property of another.

INVESTOR ADVICE

Prior to developing a property which has not been surveyed recently, it is recommended that a survey be ordered to establish all property lines and provide markers for contractors.

Old surveys, which began from different starting points, frequently produced legal descriptions which now overlap. If overlapping of property legal descriptions are known prior to development, boundary lines can often be settled by mutual consent of owners and quitclaim deeds, thus avoiding costly legal problems.

Figure 29 shows a typical boundary problem identified by a new survey. In this case the problem was solved by owners "A" and "B" just swapping property by way of quitclaim deeds.

The worst problems occur when a building or other improvements are found to partially lie on another's land, requiring the purchase of a strip of land in order to cure the encroachment. If the land cannot be purchased, the encroaching party has no alternative other than to remove the improvement from the other's property.

An open and uncontested encroachment may result in a claim of implied easement and loss of property without compensation.

SEE ALSO: EASEMENT, and IMPLIED EASEMENT.

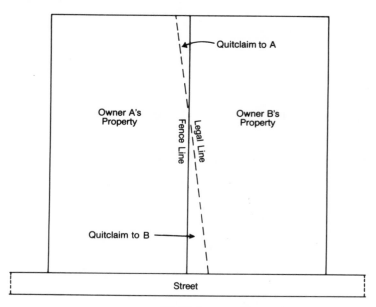

SOLVING BOUNDARY LINE PROBLEMS
with Quitclaim Deeds

Figure 29

ENCUMBRANCES

Claims against a property by other than the owner are encumbrances.

INVESTOR ADVICE

The following are a few of the different types of claims against a property which are considered as encumbrances:

• Mortgages;

• Easements;

• Restrictive covenants;

- Conditional Sales Agreements;

- Leases;

- Options to Purchase;

- Life estates including dower and curtsey rights;

- Tax liens;

- Contractor's liens; and

- Judgments against the owner.

SEE ALSO: ABSTRACT OF TITLE, CLOUD ON TITLE, LIEN, and TITLE INSURANCE.

ENGINEERING BREAKDOWN METHOD IN APPRAISING

This is a method of determining remaining value, in which each major component of a building is examined to determine remaining economic life and its present value.[2]

INVESTOR ADVICE
A breakdown analysis might appear similar to the following:

Component	Replacement Cost New	Life Expectancy in Years	% Good Re- maining	Re- Dept. Cost
Foundation	$16,380	60	.87	$14,251
Floor System	31,200	50	.84	26,208
Floor Cover	31,720	12	.33	10,468
Exterior Walls	111,800	50	.84	93,912
*	*	*	*	*
Elevator	24,000	20	.60	14,400
	$548,000			$400,230

Weighted Average:
$400,230 divided by $548,000 = .73
      * All items not shown

This method of determining the remaining value in a building can be more accurate than methods where the entire building is estimated as a whole. The method does, however, require the ability to accurately estimate life expectancy of each component.
SEE ALSO: COST APPROACH TO VALUE, and EFFECTIVE AGE.

EQUITABLE TITLE

An equitable title is a beneficial title to property as a result of court action or signing of a contract to sell. Equitable title remains with the buyer until such time as legal title is transferred by the seller/grantor.

INVESTOR ADVICE
When a earnest money receipt and offer to purchase has been signed by both parties beneficial title transfers to the buyer, while legal title will not be transferred until the closing of the transaction.

Problems with equitable title can develop during the intervening period between signing and closing. This usually occurs as a result of a loss due to casualty losses or acts of God. Who is responsible for the loss?

Most states have solved this problem by inserting certain language within the earnest money agreements authorized for use by real estate brokers. The following excerpt, taken from the approved Utah Earnest Money Receipt and Offer to Purchase, is a good example:

P. Risk of Loss. All risk of loss or damage to the property, shall be borne by the Seller until closing. In the event there is a loss or damage to the property between the date hereof and the date of closing, by reason of fire, vandalism, flood, earthquake, or acts of God, and the cost to repair such damage shall exceed 10% of the purchase price of the property, Buyer may at his option either proceed with this transaction if Seller agrees in writing to repair or replace damaged property prior to closing or declare this Agreement null and void. If damage to property is less than 10% of the purchase price and Seller agrees in writing to repair or replace and does actually repair and replace damaged property prior to closing, this transaction shall proceed as agreed.

Losses can also occur as a result of zoning changes in the intervening period. Here, the solution is not as clear as the various states have not established a firm ruling through the courts.

It is recommended that when you purchase property for commercial or other uses where the zoning is critical to your operation, appropriate language should be inserted in the offer agreement.

EXAMPLE

"This agreement is subject to the property being zoned (rezoned) commercial prior to closing." or "Buyer assumes this property is zoned for commercial use and that a building permit for the construction of an automobile agency will be issued. This offer is subject to a permit for construction being approved."

SEE ALSO: EARNEST MONEY RECEIPT, and OFFER TO PURCHASE.

EQUITY BUILDUP

Equity buildup is the systematic increase in owner equity as a result of periodic mortgage payments of interest and principal amortization. The equity buildup is represented by the difference between the balance due on the mortgage and the original mortgage amount.

INVESTOR ADVICE

The portion of periodic payments which amortize a mortgage loan constitute an increase in equity; however, that money is not available to you until such time as the property is sold or refinanced. Its present value as a return on investment is less than face value, as it is the value of a sum received in the future.

EXAMPLE

An owner of a warehouse is reviewing his mortgage amortization schedule and notes that the balance due as of the last payment is $42,500. The original mortgage was for $125,000. His equity buildup is:

$$\$125,000 - \$42,500 = \$82,500$$

What is the present value of this buildup if the property is sold five years from now and the value of money at present is 10%?

$$\text{Value} = \text{PV-1/Future}^{5\text{yrs @10\%}} \times \$82,500$$
$$\text{Value} = 0.6209 \times \$82,500 = \$52,226$$
$$\text{Round down to: } \$52,200$$

SEE ALSO: PRESENT VALUE OF $1 (RECEIVED IN THE FUTURE).

EQUITY TRUST

An equity trust is a type of Real Estate Investment Trust (REIT) which invests directly in real estate in the same manner as an individual investor.

INVESTOR ADVICE

Investment in a REIT is one way of diversifying your investment portfolio and limiting your risk. Where a small amount is to be invested or where you desire to avoid the problems of management, an equity trust is a real alternative, even though the tax advantages of such investments are not as great as they were prior to enactment of the Tax Reform Act of 1986 (TRA).

Some of the significant changes to the tax law, as they affect REITs are as follows:

- The depreciation period was increased from nineteen years to twenty-seven and one-half years for residential property and thirty-one and one-half years for commercial. All depreciation, for both types, must be straight line.

- The TRA limits real estate losses to the amount of money at risk—cash plus debt for which the investor is personally liable.

- Losses from "passive activities" cannot be used to offset active income. If no passive income is available, losses can be carried forward as an offset against future passive income.

SEE ALSO: REAL ESTATE INVESTMENT TRUST (REIT), and TAX REFORM ACT OF 1986 (TRA).

ESCALATION CLAUSE

An escalation a clause in a rental agreement increases the rental amount upon occurrence of certain events, such as increases in the cost of living, increases in taxes, etc.

INVESTOR ADVICE

Escalation clauses are advised in all long-term lease agreements as a protection against revenue losses. In times of increasing taxes and inflation, investment yield can be significantly eroded when escalation clauses have not been included in the lease. In the case of long-term leases, it is even possible to loose a significant interest in the property if sold. (See discussion on "Contract Rent.")

> **PROTECT YOURSELF!** Insert an escalation clause in all long-term leases.

To protect yourself against inflation, rentals can be based on some appropriate economic indicator with provisions for increase at periodic intervals, say every January 1.

EXAMPLE

"The Landlord reserves the right to review the rental rate each year on the anniversary date of this lease. Where the government-published Cost of Living index has increased more than 2% since the last rental review and/or initial lease date, the current rental shall be increased by the amount of that cost of living increase, but not to exceed 10% in any one lease-year."

To protect against increases in taxes and/or insurance, the property can be leased on a triple-net basis or you can provide for a rental adjustment equal to any increase in those specified types of expenses.

SEE ALSO: CONTRACT RENT, NET LEASE, and TRIPLE-NET LEASE.

ESCALATOR LOAN

An escalator loan is a type of variable rate loan in which the lender may raise the interest rate *at any time*, based on a change in economic conditions. The only justification for the increase is a lender's belief that the increase is necessary.

INVESTOR ADVICE

This type of variable rate loan should be avoided. There are other variable interest loans which are more advantageous than this type. Most variable loans are adjustable upwards only at specified times, say once each year, and are based on specified economic benchmarks. Even more important is the inclusion of some type of ceiling on each periodic adjustment and on the total adjustment possible during the term of the loan.

With the more conventional variable rate mortgage, you can at least evaluate your risk on a worst case scenario. With an escalator loan, it will be next to impossible to evaluate the possible return versus risk of a project. This situation can be best be appreciated when you realize that the largest cash flow item in most projects is debt service. Why take a chance?

SEE ALSO: VARIABLE RATE MORTGAGE.

ESCHEAT

This term refers to the reversion of property to the state, where the owner dies without a will or legal heirs.

INVESTOR ADVICE

It is inconceivable that anyone intelligent enough to acquire a real estate investment would neglect to have a will and thus die intestate. Anyone with assets of any type should have a will which designates the recipient of those assets, at the time of his/her death. Where there are no relatives, he/she could designate a church, charity, friend, or worthwhile organization to receive the property, rather than have it go to the state at his/her death.

Where there is a spouse, children or legal relatives, all states provide for the disposition of assets, even if no will exists. Thus, anyone with relatives will avoid escheat when state laws of succession are applied at probate.

SEE ALSO: HOLOGRAPHIC WILL, INTESTATE, PROBATE, and WILL

ESCROW

Escrow is the process of closing a real estate transaction, in which the earnest money agreement funds and allied papers are deposited with a neutral third party, with instructions for completion of the transfer of property title(s).

INVESTOR ADVICE

The escrow process is handled in accordance with state law and varies considerably from state to state. In some states the escrow must be handled only through an attorney. In others, the escrow may be handled through a land title company or even a real estate broker.

In some states escrow closing must be delayed for a specific minimum time period. In others, the time to close is only a function of the time required to obtain a mortgage and the escrow agent to prepare the necessary paper work.

Escrow delays may be an important consideration in date of possession, and may affect lessees and transfer of lessee escrow funds. You are advised to carefully explore escrow requirements and timing prior to signing the earnest money receipt and offer to purchase to avoid unnecessary delays in gaining possession of the new property.

EXAMPLE

Mr. Investor had signed an Earnest Money Agreement to acquire a strip shopping center, where he planned to open a franchise restaurant. The franchise agreement stated, "This agreement is null and void if the business is not opened prior to December 1, 1988."

Since possession was absolutely necessary fifteen days prior to the December 1st deadline, and to assure an expedited escrow, Mr. Investor inserted a "time is of the essence" phrase in the earnest money agreement regarding time of possession.

SEE ALSO: AMERICAN LAND TITLE ASSOCIATION (ALTA), EARNEST MONEY RECEIPT, and OFFER TO PURCHASE.

ESOPS

An ESOP is an employee stock ownership plan.

INVESTOR ADVICE

Employee stock ownership plans are provided by many corporations as a method of both rewarding employees for good service and for reducing cash flow.

A pension or profit-sharing plan usually requires the purchase of securities or other types of investments. The ESOP, however, takes advantage of existing capital stock that is paid into the employee's retirement account on a specified basis, which may be:

• Based upon profitability; and/or

• Based upon salary and/or time of service.

In either of the cases mentioned, no cash flow is required even at the point of retirement. Upon retirement, the employee is given his/her accumulated stock in the company and he/she may do with it as he/she wishes.

Employee retirement plans are often used as secondary mortgage markets. Cash set aside for these plans is used to purchase blocks of mortgages from mortgage companies and other lenders. Since an ESOP does *not* involve cash flows, it is not a candidate for the secondary mortgage market.

SEE ALSO: PENSION PLANS, PROFIT SHARING PLANS, and SECONDARY MORTGAGE MARKET.

ESTATE AT SUFFERANCE

Property possessed by a tenant after expiration of a lease and without the consent of the landlord is termed estate at sufferance.

INVESTOR ADVICE

This is a problem which confronts almost all real estate investors at one time or the other. The solution must be handled correctly and within the confines of local law. A landlord who moves in a manner outside of his/her legal rights is subject to legal actions and possible financial damages.

Consult your attorney prior to taking any action to dispossess a tenant who refuses to move. If you suspect a tenant will fail to vacate your property at the end of the lease, timely action prior to the lease expiration may be in order. It is better to pay a small legal fee before a problem exists than a large one after proceeding in the wrong direction.

You should maintain a "tickler file" to alert you, in advance, of all lease terminations. This will allow time to inquire of the tenant's intentions to release or to give timely notice to a tenant you do not desire to keep.

SEE ALSO: LANDLORD, LEASE, and TENANT.

ESTATE AT WILL

An estate at will is a landlord-tenant relationship in which the tenant is in possession of the landlord's property without a lease.

INVESTOR ADVICE

An estate at will can be the result of a verbal agreement for possession in which no formal lease is signed, or after the termination of a lease in which the landlord willingly accepts rent establishing a periodic lease estate or an estate at will.

Informal leasing arrangements should be discouraged. All tenants deserve to know what their rights are and what is expected of them. Similarly, the landlord should be assured of what the tenant is required to do in return for use of the property.

SEE ALSO: HOLDOVER TENANT, and PERIODIC ESTATE.

ESTATE PLANNING

Estate planning is the orderly process of listing one's assets and planning for their distribution after death. The process includes the preparation or revision of wills, establishment of trusts, orderly giving over of property/assets or a period of years, and the selection of trustees, executors, and guardians of minor children. Estate planning should also include the planning for payment of estate taxes.

INVESTOR ADVICE

Proper and timely estate planning in concert with your CPA and attorney can do much to conserve your estate by elimination of unnecessary taxes and will assure that your assets are distributed and managed as you wish them to be.

The following check list will assist you in determination of the status of your estate planning:

- Does your planning include the latest real estate acquisitions or cancel distribution plans for property recently sold?

- Do you know how much money will be required to meet your final expenses and pay estate taxes? Will it be necessary to quickly dispose of some of your assets in order to meet these obligations? Have you considered life insurance as a means of providing the required cash when needed?

- Since life insurance proceeds are taxable in the estate of the policy owner, have you considered transfer of ownership of you current policies?

- Do you and your spouse have separate wills? Do they both stipulate how the estates are to be handled in the event of both deaths by a common disaster?

- Have you provided for an alternate executor in the event the first named is not able to or is unwilling to serve?

- Have you specified who is to become the guardian(s) of your minor children?

- Are you a part-owner in a partnership? If so have you provided for your partner to buy out your interest at your death? Is this agreement funded?

- Have you provided for perpetual management of your minor children's assets until they come of age?

SEE ALSO: CODICIL, EXECUTOR(IX), TRUSTEE, and WILL.

ESTATE TAXES

Estate taxes are federal taxes paid by the executor(ix) or administrator(ix) of an estate before passing assets to the beneficiaries of the estate.

INVESTOR ADVICE

While most astute real estate investors have a will, it is not uncommon for these wills to be outdated by the acquisition or sale of real estate or the change of tax laws.

Careful and current planning is required to minimize estate taxes and probate administration costs. Even where married couples have arranged for their assets to flow to the surviving spouse at death of one of the parties (right of survivorship), the passing may produce excessive taxes and administration costs if the estate is not properly planned.

The most common problem involving estate taxes is the lack of ready cash. Often this requirement requires a quick sale of one or more properties, at distressed prices, in order to make timely payments. Insurance is often used as a method of delivering the correct amount of dollars at the correct time.

Proper estate planning and use of trusts and other planning tools can significantly reduce taxes and administration expenses, prevent distressed sales of real estate assets, as well as provide better successor management.

It is recommended that each sale or acquisition of investment real estate automatically trigger a requirement for estate planning review.

SEE ALSO: ESTATE PLANNING, INHERITANCE TAXES, PROBATE, and TRUST.

ESTATE TAX LIEN

An estate tax lien is a lien on estate-owned property filed by the federal government for the amount of estate taxes due and unpaid.

INVESTOR ADVICE

Current tax law requires prompt payment of estate taxes due on an estate. All taxes due, both income and estate, must be paid by the executor/administrator prior to distribution as directed by will or law.

When the tax is not paid on time, a federal tax lien may be filed in the county clerk's office of the county in which the estate property is located. The tax lien is valid after the notice is filed and remains valid for ten years. Tax liens are subordinate to existing mortgages at the time of filing, but are superior to subsequent mortgages.

SEE ALSO: ADMINISTRATOR(IX), ESTATE TAXES, and EXECUTOR(IX).

ESTOPPEL CERTIFICATE

An estoppel certificate is a document or portion of a mortgage assignment form in which the owner of the mortgage certifies that the mortgage is a lien upon which there is no litigation pending.

INVESTOR ADVICE

The estoppel certificate in a mortgage assignment is often referred to as "the have and to hold" clause.

EXAMPLE

"And the assignor(s) hereby covenant with the assignee(s) that the said deed and note hereby assigned is good and valid security and that the sum of _____ _____ Dollars remains unpaid on the said note, and that the assignor(s) has/have not done or permitted any act, matter or thing whereby the said deed and note has been discharged or released, either in part or in its entirety and has/have the right to assign said deed and note and will upon request, do perform and execute every act necessary to enforce the full performance of the covenants and agreements therein contained and that these covenants shall inure to the benefit of and are extended to and be binding upon the heirs, executors, administrators, successors and assigns of the respective parties hereto."

SEE ALSO: ASSIGNMENT OF MORTGAGE.

EVICTION

Eviction is a legal process by which a landlord recovers possession of his/her property. The actual eviction occurs when the tenant is removed from the premises by force or legal process.

INVESTOR ADVICE

You are advised to become acquainted with local laws and rights of tenants and landlords before an eviction action is necessary. This knowledge will prevent inadvertent actions which may subject you to legal harassment and expense.

The following general provisions of real estate law are representative of those found in most states:

TENANT'S ESTATES

1. An estate at sufferance arises when a tenant remains in possession *without* the landlord's consent after expiration of a lease.

2. An estate at will arises when a tenant takes possession with the landlord's consent but without a lease agreement. It can be terminated with a five-day notice.
3. A periodic estate arises when the parties create a lease but do not identify the ending date for the lease. It can be terminated with a fifteen-day notice.
4. An estate of years arises when the parties identify the ending date for the lease. The lease automatically terminates on that date.
5. The lessee of an estate of years is liable for the rent for the whole period even if he/she vacates early. However, the lessor must use reasonable efforts to rerent before he/she can hold the tenant liable for unpaid rent accruing while the property is vacant.

COVENANTS AND CONDITIONS IN LEASES
1. Utah landlords can evict tenants for breach of either covenants or conditions. If a tenant violates a covenant or condition and fails to remedy the breach *within five days*, he/she may be evicted.
2. If the covenant or condition is remediable, and the tenant ceases breaching *within three days* after receipt of the lessor's Notice to Perform or Surrender, the tenant cannot be evicted.
3. In the absence of a contrary provision in the lease, the tenant has the duty to repair the premises.
4. If the landlord's conduct injures the leased premises, the landlord must make the repairs.
5. If the landlord has a duty to repair the premises and does not do so, and the premises become unfit for habitation, the tenant may treat the lease as terminated and move out. This is called constructive eviction.
6. The lessee is generally liable for injuries caused to the leased premises.
7. The lessor is generally liable for injuries caused by the common areas.

GENERAL REMEDIES
1. Surrender and particularly acceptance will extinguish all lease obligations.
2. Constructive eviction will extinguish the tenant's duties once the tenant moves out.
3. To dispossess a lessee whose lease is terminated, the *lessor must file suit for unlawful detainer.*
4. If the lessor breaches the lease by failing to deliver possession, the lessee can recover damages.
5. If the tenant is unlawfully evicted, he/she may recover possession and collect damages.
6. If the lessor breaches a condition, the lessee may treat the lease as ended. If a covenant is violated, the lessee may recover damages.
7. If a tenant holds over, he/she becomes liable for *treble rent* for the holdover period.
8. If a tenant commits waste, the landlord can collect *treble damages*.

SEE ALSO: CONSTRUCTIVE EVICTION, ESTATE AT SUFFERANCE, LANDLORD, LEASE, and TENANT.

EXCESS RENT
Excess rent is the amount of rent payable over and beyond economic rent.

INVESTOR ADVICE

Excess rent is a rare phenomenon and occurs primarily during periods of economic decline, where existing long-term leases are still in effect.

While excess rents are beneficial to the landlord, they operate against the interests of the tenant. As a landlord you must consider the benefits of excess rent versus tenant goodwill. It may be to your long-term benefit to voluntarily negotiate new rates with your tenants in order to avoid large vacancies in the future.

If the economy suffers a downturn and you find yourself in a situation in which one or more tenants are paying excess rents, you must evaluate all leases which will be expiring in the next year. You may also wish to evaluate those leases of longer-term tenants who appear to be having economic problems. The following actions are recommended:

Short-Term Tenant. Will he/she be in business after the lease term? If yes, a immediate voluntary reduction in rental and renegotiation of a new lease at an economic rent level will retain his/her good will and assure continued occupancy. If no, action not is required.

Long-Term Tenant. What is his/her financial condition? If weak or weakening, a volunteer renegotiation at economic rent levels will assist his/her stability and create goodwill for you. If the tenant's condition is strong, you may be able to renegotiate a new lease with a base rental at the economic rent level plus an override based on gross sales. Thus, the tenant will feel that he/she will pay a higher rent only if justified by his/her economic condition.

While each of the suggested actions will result in less income in the immediate future, it may very well maximize your rentals over the long term. Vacant units produce no income and give rise to the old adage, "Something beats 100% of nothing."

SEE ALSO: CONTRACT RENT, ECONOMIC RENT, and INCOME APPROACH TO VALUE.

EXCHANGE

An exchange is the trading of one property for another, with or without additional monetary consideration.

INVESTOR ADVICE

Exchange of real estate is the most tax-beneficial way of disposing of unwanted properties with capital gains. This is particularly true after the Tax Reform Act of 1986, when capital gains lost their preferential treatment.

In an exchange, the tax is not avoided but delayed until such time as the newly acquired property is sold. Gains in the property traded offset the basis cost of the property being acquired. Eventually a tax will be paid on the gains, but the delay creates additional investment funds or reduces your requirement for borrowing.

To avoid immediate tax payment, the exchange must be like for like, but here the IRS has a rather liberal definition—investment property can be traded for any other investment property. It is not necessary to trade land for land or apartment for apartment.

One often-overlooked possibility is a direct sale of property with the seller allowing the received funds to be placed in escrow until a replacement property can be identified and purchased to complete the trade.

When boot (see definition) is given or taken as a part of the exchange, the basis cost of the acquired property is adjusted by that amount. Boot given adjusts the basis upwards, whereas boot taken adjusts the basis downward.

EXAMPLES

An investor trades an investment property for another and receives $50,000 boot. The investor had originally paid $300,000 for the property and had taken $125,000 in straight line depreciation during his holding period. What is the basis cost of the property for which he traded?

Basis Cost Before Trade = $300,000 - $125,000 = $175,000
Basis Cost After Trade = $300,000 -($125,000+$50,000) or $125,000

Investor No. 2 trades his property for another and gives $25,000 boot. He had originally paid $200,000 for the property and had taken $50,000 in straight line depreciation. What is the basis cost of the acquired property?

Basis Cost Before Trade = $200,000 - $50,000 = $150,000
Basis Cost After Trade = $200,000 - $50,000 + $25,000 or $175,000

In the examples given, it will be noted that "straight line" depreciation was used. This was to simplify the example. If other than straight line (accelerated) depreciation had been use, an adjustment for recapture of depreciation would have been required.
SEE ALSO: BOOT, CAPITAL GAINS TAXES, DEPRECIATION RECAPTURE, and TAX FREE TRADES.

EXCLUSIVE AGENCY
An exclusive agency is a listing agreement giving a broker the exclusive right to sell a property for a given duration and reserving the right by you, the owner, to sell the property yourself without having to pay a commission.

INVESTOR ADVICE
On the surface, the exclusive agency agreement appears to be a great benefit for the listing agency as it gives them a free run at selling the property. It also appears to be to the owner's advantage, if he/she can find his/her own buyer. But, consider the following:

- As a listing broker, would you work as hard on this type of listing and advertise as much as one which was an exclusive listing?

- As the listing owner, would you prefer only one broker trying to sell your property or all members of a real estate board? The exclusive agency would produce many more attempts to sell if listed on the multiple listing system. Even though your agreement is with one broker, to whom you will pay a commission upon sale, a multiple listing agreement with your broker's fellow REALTORS® will allow them to show your property and receive a proportionate share of that commission.

Before listing a property for sale, be sure that you understand what type of listing you are signing and your rights as a property owner.

Before agreeing to an exclusive agency agreement, you should also examine the advantages of an exclusive right to sell listing which is exposed to the entire real estate community through the REALTOR® multi-list system.

Quite often, a broker trying to obtain an exclusive agency listing will justify his/her request by saying, "I have a buyer for your property." Your reply should be, "Good! I'll give you a one party listing for ten days to protect you, in case that buyer buys the property."

SEE ALSO: EXCLUSIVE RIGHT TO SELL, and ONE-PARTY LISTING.

EXCLUSIVE RIGHT TO SELL

An exclusive right to sell is a real estate listing which pays the listing agent a commission regardless of who sells the property.

INVESTOR ADVICE

Don't be upset over the title of this listing. It is more or less the standard in the industry and undoubtedly the best type of listing for both seller and broker. An exclusive right to sell listing with a REALTOR® guarantees that this listing will be placed in the multi-list catalogue of the real estate board and that all REALTOR® members of the board will have an opportunity to show and sell the property.

Although your listing states that only your listing agent will receive a commission, all REALTORS® share with other REALTORS® on a set percentage basis. All board members will have an opportunity to earn a share of the commission you pay to your listing brokerage. Figure 30, the standard form used by members of the Salt Lake City, Utah, Board of Realtors, is typical of those used throughout the United States.

Not all brokers are REALTORS®. Only those brokers who are members of their local, state, and National Board of Realtors is a REALTOR®. It is difficult to understand why any good investor would want to do business with a broker, who doesn't belong to his/her professional organization, but they do obtain some business.

If your listing is with a broker who is not a member of the REALTOR® board, he/she will probably be the only person aware of the listing and your chances of a sale are seriously diminished. If you are a professional investor, you will want to deal only with professionals. Insist on an agent who is a REALTOR®.

SEE ALSO: MULTIPLE LISTING SERVICE, and REALTOR®.

EXCULPATORY CLAUSE

An exculpatory clause is a lease provision which relieves the landlord of liability for personal injury to occupants or damage to their personal property.

INVESTOR ADVICE

In the past, this clause was included in most leases. In recent times it is often omitted and landlord protection against liability for personal and property damage is covered by landlord insurance. Even with the exculpatory clause, many landlords have been found by the courts of some states to be partially or fully responsible for tenant losses. Accordingly, the wise landlord now includes protection for this exposure in his/her casualty insurance package. Generally, the cost is minimal.

SEE ALSO: LANDLORD, LEASE, and TENANT.

EXECUTOR(IX)

An executor(ix) is an institution or person appointed by a will to administer the estate of a deceased person and carry out the provisions of the will and other instructions.

INVESTOR ADVICE

The naming of a desired executor in a will is fundamental. It is just as important to designate an alternate executor to serve if the first named is unwilling or unable to

UTAH BANK NOTE COMPANY (801) 322-1071

FORM A   **SALES AGENCY CONTRACT**
                              (Exclusive Right to Sell)
            This is intended to be a legally binding agreement. Read it carefully.
                       If not understood, seek other advice.

............................**Bowser Realty Associates**............................
              Member of Multiple Listing Service of Salt Lake Board of REALTORS®

1.   In consideration of your agreement to list the property described on Form B and to use reasonable efforts to find a purchaser or tenant therefor, I hereby grant you for the period stated herein, from the date hereof, the Exclusive right to sell, lease or exchange said property or any part thereof, at the price and terms stated herein or at such other price and terms to which I may agree in writing.

2.   During the life of this contract, if you find a party who is ready, able and willing to buy, lease or exchange said property or any part thereof, at said price and terms, or any other price or terms to which I may agree in writing, I agree to pay the Principal Broker listed below a commission of $_____ or __6.0__% of such sale, lease or exchange price which commission unless otherwise agreed in writing, shall be due and payable the date of closing the sale, lease or exchange.

3.   Should said property be sold, leased or exchanged within __3__ months after expiration of this contract to any party to whom the property was offered or shown by me or you or any other party during the term of this listing, I agree to pay you the commission above stated if I am not obligated to pay a commission on such sale, lease or exchange to another Principal Broker pursuant to another valid sales agency contract entered into after the expiration date of this contract.

4.   You are hereby authorized to accept a deposit as earnest money from any potential buyer on the property as described on the property description and informational form (Form B). Said deposit to be held in a trust account.

5.   I hereby warrant the information contained on the property description and informational form (Form B) to be correct and that I have marketable title or an otherwise established right to sell, lease or exchange said property, except as stated. I agree to execute the necessary documents of conveyance or lease and to prorate general taxes, insurance, rents, interest and other expenses affecting said property to agreed date of possession and to furnish a good and marketable title with abstract to date or at my option, a policy of title insurance in the amount of the purchase price and in the name of the purchaser. In the event of sale or lease of other than real property, I agree to provide proper conveyance and acceptable evidence of title or right to sell, lease or exchange.

6.   In case of the employment of an attorney to enforce any of the terms of this agreement, I agree to pay a reasonable attorney's fee and all costs of collection.

7.   You are hereby authorized to obtain financial information from any mortgagee or other party holding a lien or interest on this property.

8.   You are hereby authorized and instructed to offer this property through the Multiple Listing Service of the Salt Lake Board of REALTORS®.

9.   You are hereby authorized to share the commission listed above (paragraph 2) with another (cooperating) Principal Broker, whether that Principal Broker represents the buyer(s) or the seller(s).

10. You are hereby authorized to place an appropriate sign on said property.

11. This Sales Agency Contract may not be changed, modified or altered, except by prior written consent executed by the Principal Broker and the owner(s) shown below, except that the listing price shall be changed by written request received from the owner(s).

> The parties hereto agree not to discriminate against any person or persons based on race, color, sex or national origin in connection with the sale, lease or exchange of properties under this agreement.

LISTED PROPERTY ___9567 So. Manyard Ave., Sandy, Utah___
                                          (Address)

                    (City)   (State)
LISTED PRICE ___$95,000___
This contract is entered into this __23rd__ day of __February__, 19_89_.
This contract expires on the __23rd__ day of __May__, 19_89_.

___Bowser Realty Associates___   *Aston J. Smith*
            Listing Company   Owner (Signature)
___Harry P. Altmont___   *Molly R. Smith*
      Principal Broker (insert name)   Owner (Signature)
BY *George M Baker*
      Authorized Agent (Signature)

   I hereby acknowledge receipt of completed copies of this document (Form A) and the property description and information form (Form B).

                              Aston J. Smith
                                    Owner

Complete both Form A and Form B.
1 copy to owner — 1 copy to listing office.

Figure 30

BRD AUD N ☐ NO   ☐ YES
SUBMIT TOP COPY TO BOARD OFFICE
FORM B (Complete both form A and B)

SALT LAKE BOARD OF REALTORS
RESIDENTIAL/CONDOMINIUM FORM

PLEASE PRINT NEATLY IN INK.
ANY CORRECTIONS MUST BE
MADE ON ALL COPIES.

TYPE DWELLING (✓ One)
RES ☒ Residential   CND ☐ Condominium
MOB ☐ Mobile Home   TWIN ☐ Twin Home
PUD ☐ Planned Unit   COOP ☐ Cooperative
        Development

ADDRESS # 2138   **AD DIR** (N-S-E-W)   **STREET NAME** ROSEMONT DR   **UNIT #** (Enter Unit #)

LOC DIR (✓ One)
N NORTH   E ☒ EAST
S ☒ SOUTH   W WEST

PRICE (Enter Dollar amount) $ 89,500

AREA (✓ One)

RESIDENTIAL		CONDOMINIUM	
R1 ☐	R9 ☐	C1 ☐	C9 ☐
R2 ☒	R10 ☐	C2 ☐	C10 ☐
R3 ☐	R11 ☐	C3 ☐	C11 ☐
R4 ☐	R12 ☐	C4 ☐	C12 ☐
R5 ☐	R13 ☐	C5 ☐	C13 ☐
R6 ☐	OMR ☐	C6 ☐	OMC ☐
R7 ☐	OSR ☐	C7 ☐	OSC ☐
R8 ☐	ODR ☐	C8 ☐	ODC ☐

NS COORD 2138   **EW COORD** 700
(In Salt Lake county enter county coordinate)

PROJ NM/SUB

CITY SALT LAKE

SQUARE FEET (Enter Estimated # For Each Level)
SQ FT MAIN 1500
SQ FT UP
SQ FT DOWN 800
SQ FT TOT 2300

BEDROOMS (Enter # For Each Level)
BDRM MAIN 2
BDRM UP
BDRM DOWN 1
BEDRM TOT 3

BATHS (F = Full, T = ¾, H = ½)
(2FH = 2 Full, 1 Half)
BTHS MAIN 1
BTHS UP
BTHS DOWN
BATHS TOT (Each Fraction Equals One) (2FH = 3)

OTHER RMS (✓ One)
D ☒ Den
L ☐ Library
O ☐ Other

FIREPLACES (Enter # For Each Level)
FPL MAIN 1
FPL UP
FPL DOWN
FIREPLACE TOT 1

EXTERIOR (No More Than 2)
BR ☒ Brick   CD ☐ Cedar
FR ☐ Frame   AS ☐ Asbestos
AL ☐ Aluminum   VY ☐ Vinyl
ST ☐ Stucco   SN ☐ Stone
SH ☐ Shingle   OT ☐ Other
BL ☐ Block

STYLE (✓ One)
RAM ☒ Rambler   CON ☐ Contemporary
SPE ☐ Split Entry TRI ☐ Tri-level
BNG ☐ Bungalow   MUL ☐ Multi-level
2ST ☐ Two Story   HI ☐ High Rise
3ST ☐ Three Story OTH ☐ Other

LIVING ROOM (Enter Dimensions)
___ X ___ (i.e.: 12'6"x11'3" = 13x11)

DINING (✓ No More Than 2)
F ☐ Formal   S ☐ Semi-Formal
K ☒ Kitchen   B ☒ Breakfast Bar

GARAGE/CARPORT (✓ No More Than 2)
1 G ☐ 1 Car Garage   1 C ☐ 1 Car Carport
2 G ☒ 2 Car Garage   2 C ☐ 2 Car Carport
3 G ☐ 3 Car Garage   3 C ☐ 3 Car Carport
4 G ☐ 4 Car Garage   4 C ☐ 4 Car Carport
    ☐ No

REC ROOM (✓ No More Than 2)
M ☐ Main
U ☐ Up
D ☒ Down
2 ☐ Two
3 ☐ Three
  ☐ No

LAUNDRY (✓ No More Than 2)
M ☐ Main
U ☐ Up
D ☐ Down
  ☐ No

LOT

DESC LOT (✓ No More Than 2)
C ☐ Corner   ☐ Irregular
S ☐ Sloping   L ☒ Level

ACRES .25
ZONING R-2

AGE (Enter # Of Years Old, New = 0, Old = 888, Remodeled = 999)

HEAT (✓ No More Than 2)
G ☒ Gas
E ☐ Electric
S ☐ Solar
H ☐ Hot Water
O ☐ Other

AIR COND (✓ No More Than 2)
C ☐ Central
V ☒ Evaporative
W ☐ Window/Wall
G ☐ Gas
E ☐ Electric
  ☐ No

PATIO (✓ No More Than 2)
1 ☒ One
2 ☐ Two
D ☐ Deck
  ☐ No

FENCE (✓ One)
F ☒ Full
P ☐ Partial
  ☐ No

LANDSCAPING (✓ One)
F ☒ Full
P ☐ Partial
  ☐ No

SPRINKLER (✓ One)
F ☐ Full
P ☒ Partial
FA ☐ Full Automatic
PA ☐ Partial Automatic

CARPETS (✓ One)
F ☐ Full
P ☒ Partial
  ☐ No

WINDOW COVERINGs (✓ One) (Drapes, Levelors, etc.)
F ☒ Full
P ☐ Partial
  ☐ No

SEWER (✓ No More Than 2)
Y ☒ Yes
S ☐ Septic
C ☒ Connected
  ☐ No

WATER (✓ As Many As Apply)
M ☒ Municipal
I ☐ Irrigation
W ☐ Well

ROOF (✓ One)
A ☒ Asphalt Shingle
F ☐ Flat
S ☐ Shake
T ☐ Tile

ELEMENTARY 1135
ELEM TRANS (✓ One)
B ☐ Bus   W ☒ Walk

JR HS 121
JRHS TRANS (✓ One)
B ☐ Bus   W ☒ Walk

BASEMENT (✓ One)
F ☐ Full
P ☒ Partial
  ☐ No

FINISHED % (Basement) 75

HIGH SCHOOL 172
HS TRANS (✓ One)
B ☒ Bus   W ☐ Walk

TERMS (✓ No More Than 5)
CV ☐ Conventional
FH ☐ FHA
AS ☐ Assume
UH ☐ Utah Housing
VA ☒ VA
WR ☐ Wrap Around
CS ☐ Cash
EX ☐ Exchange
LO ☐ Lease Option
CT ☐ Contract
AE ☐ Assume Existing
A2 ☐ Assume Second

OTHER TERMS (Enter Other Financial Information Not Shown Elsewhere — Up To 22 Characters)
CASH ONLY TO OWNER

1BAL (Enter Dollar Amount) $ 50,000
1INT % .0615
1PMT (Enter Dollar Amount) $ 458

2BAL (Enter Dollar Amount) $
2INT %
2PMT (Enter Dollar Amount) $

LOAN TYPE (✓ One Primary Loan)
VA ☐ VA   CV ☒ Conventional
FH ☐ FHA   CT ☐ Contract
F23 ☐ FHA-235   UH ☐ Utah Housing
F24 ☐ FHA-245   O ☐ Other
                     ☐ None

MORTGAGEE(S) FIRST FED SAV

TAXES (Enter Dollar Amount) $ 850

DOWN PAYMENT (Enter $ Amount Other Than Refinance) $

PMT TYPE (✓ One)
FIX ☒ Fixed
VAR ☐ Variable
ADJ ☐ Adjustable

PMT INC (Circle Which Apply)
(P)(I)(T) M (MMI)

CONDO FEE (Monthly Assn. Or Maint.) (Enter Dollar Amount) $

INCL (✓ Up To 11)
ALM ☐ Alarm System   DW ☒ Dishwasher   IC ☐ Intercom   SAU ☐ Sauna   WSF ☒ Water Softener
APT ☐ Apartment   EAC ☐ Elect. Air Cleaner MCO ☐ Microwave Oven   SEC ☐ Secluded
BAR ☒ Wet Bar   GDO ☐ Gar. Door Opener OV ☒ Oven   STO ☒ Storage   **(CONDO RESTRICTIONS)**
CLB ☐ Clubhouse   GRD ☒ Garden   PL ☐ Pool   TEN ☐ Tennis   R/A ☐ Age
COM ☐ Compactor   HND ☐ Handicapped (suit. for) REF ☒ Refrigerator   TRE ☒ Trees   R/C ☐ Children
CTV ☒ Cable TV   HOR ☐ Horse Property RNG ☒ Range   VAC ☐ Central Vacuum R/P ☐ Pets
DP ☐ Double Pane Windows HTB ☐ Hot Tub/Whirlpool RVP ☐ R-V Parking   VW ☒ View   R/L ☐ Leasing
DSP ☒ Disposer   HUM ☐ Humidifier   SAT ☐ Satellite Dish   WBS ☒ Wood Burn Stove R/R ☐ R-V's

REMARKS (For New Construction Or Conversion, List Type, Thickness, And R-Value Of Insulation In All Areas Of The Property.)
WELL MAINTAINED. NEW EXT PAINT NEW CPTS UP. EASY WALK TO SHOPPING

CONTRACT TYPE ☐ ERS   ☐ EAL

APPT THRU (✓ One)
O ☐ Owner
T ☐ Tenant
L ☒ List Agt

APPT NAME J. SMITH   **PH** 266-7041   **POSSESSION** ARR

SHOW (✓ As Many As Apply)
KLO ☐ Key In List Off
APP ☐ Appointment
KB ☒ Key Box

LIST AGT J. SMITH   **PH** 227-4095   **SOC** 3.0
OFFICE BROWN REALTY   **PH** 266-7041   **ID** 211

Board will take a Photo unless otherwise indicated below:
O ☐ Outside Photo Taking Boundaries — (See Map in Catalog)
P ☐ Photo, Map or Diagram furnished by REALTOR (If Photo diagram, map or sketch is submitted, it should be 2 7/8" x 1 3/8" in size.)
N ☐ No Photo Desired by REALTOR
U ☐ Under Construction

FOR MLS USE ONLY
(Form 1-Res-1/86)
LIST TYPE ☐ PSC   ☐ CLC

THE UNDERSIGNED HEREBY WARRANTS THE INFORMATION CONTAINED HEREON TO BE CORRECT AND ACKNOWLEDGES RECEIPT OF COMPLETED COPIES OF THIS DOCUMENT (FORM B) AND THE SALES AGENCY CONTRACT (FORM A).

OWNER'S SIGNATURE Jasper L. Smith   **LIST DATE** (01-JAN-86) 02-30-89   **EXP DATE** (01-JAN-86) 4-30-89

Figure 30 continued

serve. To assure that the designated executor will serve, many people designate a perpetual institution, such as a bank, as executor.

The only problem with this latter type of appointment is that institutions merge, are sold, or change key personnel. A good institution today may not be as good when called upon to serve as executor at some time in the future. Too, institutions charge for their service and are prone to work very slowly, since there is no real incentive to get the job done in a hurry. Actually, there is more of an incentive to drag feet and receive a larger fee.

Most investors, of modest means, will have a surviving spouse, child or other relative who is capable of serving as executor(ix). When appointing these types of persons to serve on your behalf, it is wise that you include the following clause or similar wording in the will:

I hereby appoint my husband, _____, to serve as my executor and to serve without bond and compensation, except for any actual expenses required in the administration of my estate. In the event he is deceased or unable to serve for any reason whatsoever, I then direct that my son, _____, serve in his place. In performance of their duties as executor of my estate, it is my desire that they not be held responsible and/or liable for any omissions or errors they may commit as a result of inexperience or lack of training.

SEE ALSO: ADMINISTRATOR(IX), ESTATE TAXES, and INHERITANCE TAXES.

EXECUTOR'S DEED

An executor's deed is one in which the grantor is the executor of an estate in probate. The deed, given under the direction of the probate court, warrants nothing more than acts of the executor.

INVESTOR ADVICE

The executor's deed provides limited warranty as to various aspects of the property being deeded. Therefore, you are stuck with any errors found at a later date. For this reason, it is paramount that any such sale be covered by title insurance.

SEE ALSO: SHERIFF'S DEED, and WARRANTY DEED.

EXTENDER CLAUSE

An extender clause is a standard clause in most exclusive right to sell listings forms, which provides protection to the listing agency for a designated period beyond the listing termination date. The protection applies only to those prospects shown the property during the listing agreement term. If the property is sold to one of these prospects during the designated extended term, the listing broker is entitled to his/her agreed commission.

INVESTOR ADVICE

This clause is fair to both parties. It prevents the seller from postponing a sale or closing until the listing has expired to avoid the payment of a commission.

Where the broker is the procuring cause of the sale, even though delayed, he/she is entitled to a commission. Of course some cut-off date to this entitlement is necessary, hence a definite time period should be specified in the extender clause.

The typical wording in the extender clause is shown as follows:

Should said property be sold, leased or exchanged during the _____ *months after expiration of this contract to any party to whom the property was offered or shown by me or you or any other party during the term of the listing, I agree to pay you the commission above stated, if I am not obligated to pay a commission on such sale, lease or exchange to another broker pursuant to another valid sales agency contract entered into after the expiration date of this contract.*

It should be noted that the extender clause does not subject the property owner to *two* commissions. The owner pays only if sold to a prospect who saw the property during the term of the listing, and then only if not relisted with another broker.

Questions often arise as to what constitutes "offered or shown." It is generally understood that this means a client was taken *to and through* the property by an agent. Just driving by with a client in the car doesn't satisfy the requirement.

SEE ALSO: EXCLUSIVE RIGHT TO SELL.

EXTRAPOLATION

Extrapolation is a statistical method of estimating or inferring a value beyond the range for which real data is available. The estimated value is based upon certain variables within the known range and the assumption that these variables are applicable to the extended range.

INVESTOR ADVICE

Extrapolations are very useful in many investing situations. For instance, in calculating the overall yield on an investment it is necessary to predict the value of the property at the time it will be sold. Market values over the past period of years can be extrapolated to provide a market value at the desired time in the future.

The availability of small hand-held calculators and more powerful personal computers have made the job of extrapolation quite easy for the sophisticated investor, even where the data results in other than straight line projections.

You must realize that extrapolations *are* estimates and based on assumptions that past data can predict the future. This may or may not be true, if economic trends are subject to significant changes, significant errors in the extrapolated values can occur, particularly in the extended time periods of the extrapolation.

Figure 31 shows the income from a rental project projected for an additional five years beyond the availability. To simplify the illustration, it has been assumed that growth in earnings is a straight line function, in which income increases at a uniform rate, hence a straight line.

SEE ALSO: ELLWOOD PREMISE, and INCOME APPROACH TO VALUE.

ENDNOTES

[1]Society of Real Estate Appraisers, *Real Estate Appraisal Terminology,* Rev. Ed. (Ballinger Publications Co., Cambridge Ma.), p. 89.

[2]National Association of Independent Fee Appraisers, *Income Property Appraising,* 1st Ed. (St. Louis, Mo.), pp. 246-47.

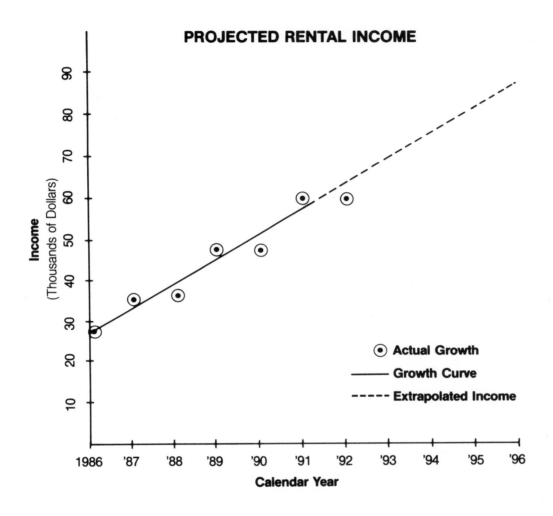

Figure 31

F

Fair Market Value
Farmer's Home Administration
Feasibility Study
Federal Home Loan Mortgage Corpora-
    tion (Freddie Mac)
Federal Housing Administration (FHA)
Federal National Mortgage Association
    (FNMA)
Federal Savings and Loan Insurance
    Corporation (FSLIC)
Fee Simple Title
Fee Tail Estate
Fenestration
FHA-Insured Loan
Fiduciary
Finder's Fee
Fire Insurance
First Right of Refusal
Fixed Expense

Fixtures, Electrical
Fixtures, Plumbing
Flat
Floating Rate Loan
Floor Load
Forces Affecting Value
Foreclosure
Fourplex
Fraud
Freehold Estate
Free Lease
Free Piece
Front Foot
Functional Obsolescence
Future Estate
Future Event Down Payment
Future Sweat
Future Value of One
Future Value of One per Period

F

FAIR MARKET VALUE

Fair market value is the most probable price a property will bring in a competitive and open market under all conditions requisite to a fair sale. This would include the buyer and seller each acting prudently, knowledgeably, and the assumption that the price is not affected by undue stimulus. Implicit in this definition is the consummation of a sale as of a specified date and the passing of title from seller to buyer under conditions whereby:

a. buyer and seller are typically motivated;

b. both parties are well informed or well advised, and each acting in what he/she considers his/her best interest;

c. a reasonable time is allowed for exposure in the open market;

d. payment is made in terms of cash in U.S. dollars or in terms of financial arrangements comparable thereto; and

e. the price represents the normal consideration for the property sold unaffected by special or creative financing or sales concessions granted by anyone associated with the sale.

INVESTOR ADVICE

Few people, other than real estate appraisers, fully understand the term fair market value. It is the concept of "sold for cash" that is the problem.

Listed below are a few of the conditions of sale that prevents the "selling price" from being the same as "fair market value":

- The buyer obtains an FHA or VA loan with points paid by the seller, thereby reducing the amount received for the property by the amount of the points paid.

- The seller agrees to a contract with terms more beneficial to the buyer than those obtainable in the mortgage market place. The seller obviously does not receive full sales price value for his/her property due to the lost interest provided by the contract terms.

- The seller has a low-interest assumable loan that is assumed by the buyer. Note that in this case the seller has sold two items; (1) the property; and (2) an advantageous financing package which allows him/her to charge more for the property than he/she normally could have expected to receive.

- The seller agrees to defer some payments for a period of time without interest charge on the amount deferred. It is assumed, in this case, that the seller will recoup his/her lost interest by a higher selling price.

- The seller agrees to make certain repairs and/or modifications to the property prior to closing. The selling price has included the fair market value of the property plus an amount required to make the required repairs.

Unless adjustments are made to the selling price to reflect money lost by the seller in providing special incentives, it would be impossible to compare sales in the marketplace. The adjustments, normally made by appraisers to the comparable sales, have the effect of reducing all prices to a common denominator.

SEE ALSO: CONTRACT, PRESENT VALUE OF ONE RECEIVED IN THE FUTURE, PRESENT VALUE OF ONE PER PERIOD RECEIVED IN THE FUTURE, and SELLING PRICE.

FARMER'S HOME ADMINISTRATION

The Farmer's Home Administration is an agency of the U.S. Department of Agriculture that grants loans for the purpose of providing rural housing.

INVESTOR ADVICE

> **DON'T BE CONFUSED!** The Farmers Home Administration is *not* the FHA or Federal Housing Administration.

In many cases a farm home loan can be assumed by a buyer. As a potential investor in rural housing, you should be aware of the fact that the interest rates on these loans are adjustable, based on periodic reviews of the buyer's income level. You can assume that if you take over an existing loan the interest rate will be adjusted to the highest allowable rate.

To qualify for a farm home loan, the buyer must be without a current residence that is "safe, decent and sanitary." The home to be purchased must be modest in size (1300 s.f. or less) and located on a minimal but adequate lot.

Farm home loans are restricted to rural areas and towns with less than 20,000 population. Qualifying income need not be from farming. Loans may be made for as long as thirty-three years. Loan to value can be as high as 100%. There are also restrictions on the commission amount, if any, that can be paid by the builder/developer. For this reason, most sales on a farm home loan basis are made directly by the builder/developer.

SEE ALSO: FHA, and GNMA.

FEASIBILITY STUDY

A feasibility study is a pro-forma analysis of expected income, expense, and profitability of a proposed real estate development, which takes into account the marketplace, property location and size, and economic conditions expected in the future.

INVESTOR ADVICE

A feasibility study is required documentation in support of a loan request on a proposed investment property or an existing one in which major changes or additions are proposed.

In reviewing the loan requests of which the feasibility study is a part, the lender will examine the study and other documentation to ascertain the reasonableness of the assumptions used and accuracy of other data quoted in the study. His/her primary concern is the safety of the funds to be loaned. Thus, the conclusions reached by the author of the study must be reasonable and logically follow the factual data presented.

As a minimum requirement, the study should provide answers to the following:

• Gross expected rental income;

• Vacancy factors, based on similar properties in the same or adjacent market areas;

• Other income from such items as parking fees, power and other utilities, furnished tenants, overage rents, and protection fees;

- Expected expenses to include liability insurance, hazard insurance, snow removal, landscaping service, water and electrical service to common areas, management fees, and maintenance expenses.

- It should also take into account reserves for maintenance and replacement, based on reasonable and actual wear-out of equipment, and the requirement to maintain the property in top condition at all times;

- Cash flow, as a multiple of debt service and assuming some logical increase in taxes and other expenses;

- Economic conditions expected in the future as projected by a reliable local sources, such as a bank or university;

- Competition within the served area and vacancy rates of existing comparable projects;

- Gross income and spendable income of the families in the served area; and

- Annual average sales per square foot of retail space in existing stores in comparable areas.

SEE ALSO: CASH FLOW, DEBT SERVICE, and OVERALL RETURN.

FEDERAL HOME LOAN MORTGAGE CORPORATION (FREDDIE MAC)

The Federal Home Loan Mortgage Corporation (Freddie Mac) is a government-sponsored corporation, whose stock is 100% owned by the thrift industry. Its purpose is to expand the source of funds by purchasing mortgage loans in the secondary market and then repackaging them as securities (bonds). The corporation also swaps their securities for pools of loans assembled by individual lenders.

INVESTOR ADVICE

In the past Freddie Mac purchased conventional fixed-interest rate mortgages only. Beginning in October 1987, it also began buying Adjustable Rate Mortgages (ARMs) as well.

It is through the action of GNMA and Freddie Mac that small mortgage loan companies are able to function. Although they may lend their own money on a temporary basis, they are assured that the loans can be resold in the secondary market.

This secondary market for mortgage paper provides money to small communities that would otherwise be unable to finance property purchase, where local institutions were dependent solely upon local funds.

SEE ALSO: Government National Mortgage Association (GNMA).

FEDERAL HOUSING ADMINISTRATION (FHA)

The Federal Housing Administration (FHA) is an organization that approves and insures loans for designated types of residential housing. The FHA makes direct loans for home purchases only on repossessed properties.

INVESTOR ADVICE

The FHA does not normally make direct loans to buyers, except in poor market conditions and then only on repossessed properties that cannot otherwise be sold. FHA loans are made by lending institutions, who process the applications and send them to the FHA for insurance approval.

FHA insurance premiums are paid by the buyer at closing or financed as a part of the loan commitment. In the event of default, the lender is reimbursed and the property transferred to the FHA for disposal.

Interest rates on FHA-insured loans are periodically set by the FHA. Lenders, who are unable to lend funds at the prescribed rate, charge the seller "points" to make the loan. A "point" is defined as 1% of the mortgage amount.

Points are calculated to provide a cash payment to the lender at closing, sufficient to increase the yield on the loan to the lender's acceptable rate. Competition among lenders tends to keep the points to a minimum.

FHA loans are generally assumable by a new buyer, but the original borrower remains responsible unless the assuming buyer qualifies on his/her own and thereby releases the seller from that responsibility.

While FHA loans are primarily made on single-family residences, they are available to purchase certain non-owner occupied properties, such as a duplex.

The buyer often feels he/she has made a good purchase, since the seller pays the discount points. However, the buyer frequently fails to realize that the seller would just as soon sell at a lower price (listed price less points paid) on a conventional loan basis. Thus, the buyer has, in effect, paid the points. It may be worth the difference in price to obtain an assumable loan, qualify with a lower down payment, or have lower monthly payments than are possible on a conventional loan basis.

There is no restriction on the amount of points that a seller may pay, as long as the selling price does not exceed the appraised value of the property. In tough economic times it is not unusual for a builder to pay up to twenty points in order to reduce the interest rate to an acceptable value for the limited number of buyers available. In general, five or six points paid by the seller, will reduce the mortgage rate for a buyer a full percent.

The FHA does more than approve and insure loans. The organization is also responsible for setting industry standards for construction and is responsible for the following items becoming standard equipment:

- Double-pane windows;

- Dead-bolt locks on outer doors;

- Outside air intakes for furnaces;

- 220 lb./square asphalt roofing shingles;

- Minimum density carpeting; and

- Raised water heaters to prevent flame extinguishing by flood waters.

SEE ALSO: CONVENTIONAL LOAN.

FEDERAL NATIONAL MORTGAGE ASSOCIATION (FNMA)

The Federal National Mortgage Association (FNMA) or Fannie Mae, as it is normally referred to, is a private corporation sponsored by the United States Government, which provides secondary mortgage funds to primary lenders. The association is authorized to issue and guarantee securities backed by a portion of its mortgage portfolio.

INVESTOR ADVICE

As a private investor in real estate you will probably be completely unaware of the existence of Fannie Mae, although the funds provided to you by your mortgage lender may have originated in that secondary market.

In 1968 Fannie Mae was reorganized as a private corporation, which operates under the supervision of the federal government. At that same time Fannie Mae was authorized to accept conventional (non-government insured) loans. Under the reorganization plan, the FNMA purchases mortgages from lenders who qualify. It is the largest purchaser of residential mortgages.

An organization that participates in the FNMA program must meet three criteria:

1. It must be experienced in making real estate loans.
2. It must have a minimum net worth of $100,000 in approved assets.
3. It must hire appraisers, attorneys, and underwriters who meet FNMA standards.

Fannie Mae serves a very important monetary policy through its operations. In times of tight money, it provides necessary funds to compensate for shortages of mortgage credit. In credit-easy times, Fannie Mae sells a portion of its portfolio to absorb surplus funds. Most importantly, the FNMA provides funds in areas of need from funds extracted from areas of surplus.

SEE ALSO: CONVENTIONAL MORTGAGE, and GOVERNMENT NATIONAL MORTGAGE ASSOCIATION (GNMA).

FEDERAL SAVINGS AND LOAN INSURANCE CORPORATION (FSLIC)

The Federal Savings and Loan Insurance Corporation (FSLIC) is a federal agency that insures customer accounts in member institutions of the Federal Home Loan Bank System. Federally chartered savings and loans must be insured by the FSLIC. State chartered institutions may be insured if they apply and are acceptable to the Federal Home Loan Bank Board, which is charged with supervision of FSLIC-insured institutions.

INVESTOR ADVICE

The large number of failures of savings and loans in the late 1980s has made it even more important that your funds be invested in a federal government insured account. Real estate investors typically utilize savings and loan institutions as an interim depository for their surplus cash and prefer to make their long-term commitments in real property.

In the past, many made the mistake of putting their funds in state chartered institutions, which offered more favorable yields. Many of these were not government insured, but insured by some type of state insurance corporation. When these institutions failed, the depositors found the state insurance companies inadequately funded or completely broke.

SEE ALSO: SAFE RATE.

FEE SIMPLE TITLE

A fee simple title is the ownership of real estate without limitation or end. This is also referred to as fee, fee estate, or fee simple absolute.

INVESTOR ADVICE

This type of title is the ultimate and provides all of the "sticks" in the bundle of rights. The owner "in fee simple" can do anything with his/her property that does not conflict with the rights of others. It is the source of all lesser estates, such as:

- Life estate;

- Fee tail estates; and

- Leasehold estates.

The term fee simple estate takes its name from old English law which conveyed the ownership over the life of the owner and provided for inheritance without restrictions. The term "simple" was used to indicate that the title was without restriction.

However, while the rights of property owners are recognized as predominant, these rights are subordinate to the restrictions of police power, right of eminent domain, right of taxation, and right of escheat. These limitations are enforced for the public welfare.

Ownership under fee simple authorizes that owner of record to sell or otherwise assign the rights to use a portion of the property (easements), use the airspace over the surface (air rights), or mine the subsurface (mineral rights). His/her ownership extends from the center of the earth to the earth's surface, an area which is explicitly defined, and then upwards to the altitude, designated as public airspace.

SEE ALSO: BUNDLE OF RIGHTS.

FEE TAIL ESTATE

A fee tail estate is the same type of estate as fee simple with a restriction as to the right of inheritance, which limits inheritance only to blood relatives of the owner. In the absence of such designated descendants, the land reverts to the original grantor of the estate.

INVESTOR ADVICE

In general, it can be said that the fee tail estate is a type of life estate, since at the holder's death the property passes automatically to the holder's children regardless of the holder's wishes. The fee tail estate is only extinguished when one of the descendent owners dies without children. At this point the property returns to the original grantor.

Most states have abolished the principal of fee tail estates.

In those states in which it is recognized, your title protection on purchased property will rely on an insistence that title insurance be provided.

SEE ALSO: FEE SIMPLE TITLE, LIFE ESTATE, and TITLE INSURANCE.

FENESTRATION

Fenestration is the number and arrangement of windows in a building.

INVESTOR ADVICE

This is a term often used in appraisal reports which refer to type, quality, and amount of windows in buildings and their affect on value. Fenestration is an important consideration in the purchase of:

- Buildings utilizing solar heating and cooling; and

- Buildings which have too much exposure to the annual solar radiation patterns, without adequate protection by trees, shades, or other blocking systems.

SEE ALSO: APPRAISAL REPORT.

FHA-INSURED LOAN

An FHA-insured loan is a loan granted by any lender and guaranteed to by the Federal Housing Administration.

INVESTOR ADVICE

These loans are primarily for single-family housing, however some FHA loans are available for non-occupant ownership. Non-owner loans are usually limited to 85% of the value of the property.

One might question the advisability of acquiring property with an FHA loan, since it is usually necessary for the seller to pay points in order for you to obtain the loan. Who really pays the points? If the seller is willing to take $50,000 for his property and pay $1000 in points, thereby netting only $49,000, wouldn't an offer for $49,000 with conventional financing succeed?

The lower selling price and conventional financing would:

- Reduce the amount of loan required or allow a larger downpayment with the same down;

- Produce a higher capital gain when the property is sold; and

- Undoubtedly take less time to close than if FHA procedures must be followed.

On the other hand, an FHA loan will:

- Probably require a lower down payment;

- Bear a slightly lower interest rate; and

- Most likely be assumable on resale.

Before buying a property and committing yourself to finance in any particular way, you should review the listed advantages and disadvantages, together with your future plans for the property and decide which is the best investment decision.

SEE ALSO: FEDERAL HOUSING ADMINISTRATION (FHA).

FIDUCIARY

A fiduciary is a person or organization, in a position of trust, who performs a financial service for another. For instance, a real estate broker is said to have a fiduciary responsibility to his principal. Under the rule of agency, this responsibility cannot be violated.

INVESTOR ADVICE

As a buyer, your broker is responsible to you for escrow funds deposited with him/her as a part of the offer process. As a landlord, you have a fiduciary responsibility in regards to advanced rents and deposits which are held on behalf of your tenants. Know your rights as a landlord as well as your responsibilities.

An agent's fiduciary responsibility to his/her principal is more than monetary. For instance, a real estate broker who lists a property and does a poor job of showing it or overstates the listed price would give his/her principal good grounds for cancellation of the listing agreement.

In all states, an agent who breeches his/her fiduciary responsibilities and thereby causes financial injury to his/her principal is held liable for that injury.

SEE ALSO: AGENCY, LANDLORD, TENANT, and TRUST ACCOUNT.

FINDER'S FEE

A finder's fee is paid to a person who assists in the sale or purchase of real estate. Finder's fees are legal only in regards to those activities not requiring a real estate license.

INVESTOR ADVICE

Before promising anyone a finder's or consulting fee, you should be aware of state laws regarding such activities. There should be no doubt as to who expects to be paid for services rendered and what that amount is to be.

In most states a broker cannot pay a finder's fee or any fee to anyone other than his/her own agents or another licensed broker.

Recent changes in realtor operations require written notification by real estate agents to buyers, prior to showing properties for sale. The agent must indicate whether he/she is representing the buyer or seller and who will pay the fee.

Figure 13 (see Commission) shows a realtor notification to client form used by the Salt Lake City, Utah Board. This clearly establishes the agency relationship between listing agent, selling agent, and buyer.

SEE ALSO: COMMISSION.

FIRE INSURANCE

Fire insurance is a policy which insures the owner against loss of property by fire. Fire insurance is usually sold in conjunction with protection for other risks, such as windstorms.

INVESTOR ADVICE

Mortgage lenders require certain insurance coverage as provisions for making the loan. Non-owner occupied properties are normally insured for most "acts of God" and certain other liabilities of the owner.

Owner-occupied residences usually are required to be insured by a homeowner policy which covers fire and other hazard protection, loss protection of contents, and personal liability for injury to others. Liability coverage may even extend beyond the property to say, the golf course.

When purchasing investment property, the lender insurance requirement can be met in one of two ways:

1. A new policy can be applied for and a binder certificate, indicating coverage purchased, presented to the closing officer; or
2. Where existing insurance is adequate, the remaining paid insured period can be reassigned to the new buyer and the seller compensated on a pro-rata basis. This method will normally reduce the closing costs over the first method.

In either case, the lender will probably insist on one or two months premium be held in escrow to assure adequate funds for policy renewal. If an existing policy is transferred, the required escrow will also be transferred.

SEE ALSO: HOME OWNER'S INSURANCE, and LIABILITY INSURANCE.

FIRST RIGHT OF REFUSAL

A first right of refusal is an agreement between a property owner and another which gives a prospective buyer the right to make the first offer on a designated property, prior to it being offered to others.

INVESTOR ADVICE

First right of refusal is not a rigidly binding document, since it only gives the opportunity to make and offer to a tenant or other party interested in the ownership of a property.

To be valid, the right should be placed in writing. Note that this is not an option. Any offer made can be refused, thereby giving the owner the right to immediately offer the property for sale to others.

When such a right is given by you, one caution is advised. It should limit the time available for the offer to be made, thus avoiding any undue delays in getting a sales effort under way.

First rights of refusal are difficult to enforce as they do not normally constitute a contract, especially where no consideration (a contract essential) is received by the grantor of the right.

If you are earnest in your desire to acquire a particular property, it is better to obtain an option to purchase. The option requires a consideration, is an agreement between competent parties, and meets all other contractual requirements. Sellers are often reluctant to sign an option extending into the future because they are reluctant to set a price for a future sale. This problem can be avoided by specifying a selling price based on an appraisal at the time the option is exercised.

SEE ALSO: OFFER, and OPTION.

FIXED EXPENSE

A fixed expense of a business remains at a constant value regardless of the amount of business conducted.

INVESTOR ADVICE

Fixed expenses can be categorized into two types; (1) cash or out-of-pocket expenses; and (2) non-cash expenses. For instance, a debt service payment is a fixed cash expense. Although the amount of interest per period is slowly reduced over the term of the loan, the amount to be paid to the bank each period is constant.

Non-cash expenses would include depreciation, which is a tax deductible expense but requires no cash outlay. Reserves for maintenance and replacement are considered by many investors to be a non-cash expense since they are not tax deductible until actually spent, at which time they are withdrawn from an interest-bearing account maintained for that purpose. However many investors consider maintenance and replacement reserves a necessary cash outlay, and make it a point to set aside an amount each month, for this purpose.

Fixed expenses, one the other hand, would include such items as:

• Debt service payments;

- Telephone service;

- Utility bills;

- Insurance;

- Taxes;

- On-site management fees;

- Snow removal; and

- Landscaping service.

SEE ALSO: RESERVES FOR REPLACEMENT, and VARIABLE EXPENSE.

FIXTURES, ELECTRICAL

Electrical fixtures are those units of the electrical system which provide receptacles for light bulbs of various types. Fixture types vary from a simple porcelain socket for one bulb to a very expensive crystal chandelier containing a number of special lighting accessories.

INVESTOR ADVICE

The selection of electrical fixtures for an income property can have a large effect on the electrical bills for service to common areas. For instance a few, more expensive mercury vapor exterior flood lights with automatic on-off controls will save enough electricity, in a very short time, to pay for their extra cost. Fluorescent light fixtures in hallways will also use less electricity for a given light output and save in bulb replacement costs.

SEE ALSO: COMPONENT DEPRECIATION, and RESERVES FOR REPLACEMENT.

FIXTURES, PLUMBING

Plumbing fixtures are those units of the plumbing system which utilize water for some useful purpose. Typical of this type of fixture are sinks, tubs, lavatories, commodes, and shower stalls.

INVESTOR ADVICE

The number of plumbing fixtures in a residence can have an important effect on appraised value. A residence of a certain quality is expected to contain a prescribed number of fixtures. If the residence has less than expected, the value is decreased by 500-1000 dollars per missing fixture. Similarly, if the residence contains more fixtures than expected, the value is increased.

Appraisers, using the cost or replacement approach to value or making adjustments of comparable sales in the market approach, will carefully note the number of plumbing fixtures in a home or apartment.

Baths are normally classified by type and contain the following number of fixtures:

- Full Bath—tub, lavatory and commode;

- 3/4 Bath—shower, lavatory and commode; and

- 1/2 Bath—lavatory and commode.

When constructing new units, consideration should be given to the selection of plumbing fixtures particularly if you plan to keep the property for a long period. Premium fixtures, such as stainless sinks in kitchens, reduced-flow commodes in baths, and water-saving shower heads can produce a short-term payback in water bills and a potentially longer functional life span.

SEE ALSO: COST APPROACH TO VALUE, and MARKET DATA APPROACH TO VALUE.

FLAT

A flat is an apartment or set of rooms all on one floor. The term is more commonly used in the eastern portion of the United States.

INVESTOR ADVICE

The term "flat" is seldom used today. Investors are more likely to refer to rental properties with names based on the number of units in the complex. Terms such as "duplex," "triplex," "fourplex," and "apartment house" for multiple-unit structures are more common.

SEE ALSO: APARTMENT BUILDING, DUPLEX, FOURPLEX, and TRIPLEX.

FLOATING RATE LOAN

A floating rate loan's interest rate varies in accordance with some designated economic bench mark, such as the prime lending rate.

INVESTOR ADVICE

Normally floating rate loans are made for a short-term need, such as construction or modernization projects. Obviously a fixed-rate loan would provide better planning; however, a bank will often offer a better rate when it can adjust the interest rate as the value of money varies.

You may be offered two rates; (1) a fixed rate at say, 12%, or (2) a floating rate of say, 10%. If you feel that there is little likelihood of an interest increase during the term of the loan, the floating rate is best. If you feel an increase is likely, the fixed rate might be the better deal.

SEE ALSO: CONSTRUCTION DRAW, and VARIABLE RATE MORTGAGE.

FLOOR LOAD

Floor load is an architect's designation of the permissible weight, in pounds per square foot, which a floor is designed to support in continuous use. Short-term overloads may be permissible where design safety factors permit.

INVESTOR ADVICE

When renting warehouse or industrial space above ground, it is recommended that the tenant be informed of the designed floor load. If heavy equipment is to be installed, the lease should specify that equipment installation and use is at the lessee's risk. Furthermore, the tenant should be held accountable for any damage due to installation and use of heavy equipment.

Where heavy manufacturing is to be conducted in the building, concrete ground floor specifications may be a serious consideration. If the concrete floor is not stressed sufficiently to support some items of installed equipment, it may be necessary to replace that existing floor space with a heavy-duty foundation/floor.

These latter requirements are normally handled quite simply by making the lease a triple-net lease, in which the lessor is responsible for all taxes, insurance and maintenance.

SEE ALSO: NET LEASE, and TRIPLE-NET LEASE.

FORCES AFFECTING VALUE

Property value is created by certain economic forces and can be affected by other economic and non-economic forces afterwards.

INVESTOR ADVICE

There are four basic economic forces which create value. These are:

1. Demand supported by purchasing power (money availability);
2. Utility of the property in use;
3. Scarcity of that type of property; and
4. Transferability or ability to exchange for other things of value.

Once property value has been created, it is affected by forces, frequently other than those strictly economic. These forces are identified as:

1. Political;
2. Economic;
3. Social; and
4. Physical.

It is these four latter forces that must be assessed when buying property, particularly for long-term retention. Please note that you, the buyer, can expect to exert little or no control over the first three forces, although you may minimize their deleterious affect by careful selection of the property to be purchased. The latter factor is a function of construction type and maintenance quality. Here, only, can you achieve any significant control.

SEE ALSO: ECONOMIC VALUE, VALUE, and VALUE IN USE.

FORECLOSURE

Foreclosure is the legal process by which property, pledged as security on a mortgage loan which is in default, is repossessed and sold.

INVESTOR ADVICE

Each state has specific laws protecting the borrower and lender. In the event of notification of default on one of your loans, you should immediately determine how much time is available before foreclosure. You should also determine the time available to you to redeem the property after foreclosure.

In trust deed states, such as Utah, the mortgagor signs a deed of trust when the loan is closed. This deed of trust is held by a trustee for benefit of the lender. As long as the mortgagor carries out the terms of that instrument, the trustee retains the trust deed.

Upon default, the lender can have the trustee foreclose on the deed of trust without court action, although it is difficult for the lender to obtain a deficiency judgment if he/she does so. The time required to complete this action is usually less than three months.

The lender may prefer to foreclose on the mortgage even though it requires a court hearing, the issuance of a foreclosure action and finally a sheriff's sale of the property. The redemption period for this procedure is about six months, but the lender retains his/her ability to attempt to procure a deficiency judgment.

SEE ALSO: DEFICIENCY JUDGMENT, SHERIFF'S DEED, and TRUST DEED.

FOURPLEX

A fourplex is a building designed to house four families. Fourplex buildings may be of any style but the most common types are the side-by-side (row house), two units on two floors, or basement plus one floor.

INVESTOR ADVICE

Many localities have specific zoning for fourplex structures, designated as R-4 or some similar notation. This zoning may permit one or more buildings per lot. The number of buildings authorized is usually based on the size of the land parcel and available building space after deduction for setbacks, landscaping, and other plot plan requirements.

Renters frequently prefer duplex and fourplex buildings over multi-unit apartments, due to the reduction of noise and traffic in the project. These types of buildings are, however, more expensive to construct than multi-unit apartments and other more dense residential types.

Your choice of building type for purchase will depend more upon the income potential, vacancy record, and comparable maintenance expenses than style. Where a choice of available units is offered in the marketplace, your best selection can probably be made by asking yourself the question, "Would I want to live here?"

SEE ALSO: APARTMENT, DUPLEX, and FLAT.

FRAUD

Fraud is the intentional use of deception or deceit to cheat another. An essential element of the crime of fraud is that the act succeeded.

INVESTOR ADVICE

The real estate industry is very susceptible to fraud. It is so prevalent that all fifty states have included real estate transactions in their statute of fraud, and require offers and acceptances to be in writing.

Although the majority of real estate agents and sellers are honest, it is important that you always be on your guard when investing in real estate. The following points will minimize the risk of fraud in your real estate investments:

- Deal with a realtor who is a professional member of the National Association of Realtors, and has sworn to uphold the standards of that organization.

- Your choice of realtors should be based on experience and reputation. Honest realtors with limited experience are apt to make mistakes that a more experienced and knowledgeable one would not.

- You should be wary of buying property in an area with which you are not personally familiar. Your best insurance against a purchase in a problem area or one subject to downward economic conditions is personal knowledge.

- Unaudited financial statements are always suspect—most residential business records are unaudited. Read them carefully and make a spot check to verify some of the key items, such as rental rates and vacancy factors. These can be verified by questioning tenants. Be particularly careful to check for missing expense items such as reserves for replacement, management costs, repairs, and maintenance. Costs should reflect "hired costs" not owner do-it-yourself costs which understate the real expense.

- Physically check the facilities for problems and inadequacies. Question the tenants regarding satisfaction or lack thereof. Try the lights, check the plumbing. Better still, hire a professional inspector to go over the property in minute detail. When making an offer, the right to inspect the property just prior to closing should be included in the offer. The offer should state that it is subject to your approval of that inspection.

- If an existing loan is to be assumed, request the documents which list the terms and conditions of the loan and make your offer subject to your approval of those conditions.

- Beware of high pressure salesmen or sellers.

- Check the schedule of rents against rental data, spot checks of tenants, and data available through your realtor and the local apartment house association.

Protecting yourself against fraud in the purchase of office buildings and shopping centers require similar measures as in apartment purchasing. The purchase of warehousing and manufacturing facilities require some additional safeguards. These would include:

- Dun and Bradstreet checks of long-term lease tenants, or in the case of smaller businesses, a check with the local credit bureau;

- Reviewing existing leases to determine if any of the tenants are incorporated. If so, did the officers sign the lease as an officer and as an individual or just as an officer? Small incorporated businesses have a way of going out of business without any warning; and

- Have your REALTOR® provide you with a list of rental rates of comparable properties in the same or comparable areas.

SEE ALSO: CONTRACT, EARNEST MONEY RECEIPT AND OFFER TO BUY, LEASE, OPTION, and STATUTE OF FRAUDS.

FREEHOLD ESTATE

A freehold estate is an estate of unknown duration. This could be either an estate of inheritance or an estate not of inheritance.

INVESTOR ADVICE

Under term "estate of inheritance," there are three classifications:

1. The fee simple, which has the highest classification of all;
2. The fee tail estate, which is inherited only by blood decedents; and
3. The defeasible fee estate, which expires automatically upon the occurrence of some stated event such as when someone marries.

Under the term "estate not of inheritance," there are also three classifications:

1. The normal and very common life estate, wherein the property reverts to another at the death of the holder;

2. The life estate conferred by law such as "dower" and "curtsey"; and
3. The life estate provided by homestead laws, which prevent seizure of a residence to satisfy debts.

SEE ALSO: FEE SIMPLE TITLE, and LIFE ESTATE.

FREE LEASE

A free lease is a syndication technique in which the syndicator leases a property from investors for a sum less than he/she expects the property to return in cash flow. The difference in income and lease payments provides a profit to the syndicator—a free lease.

INVESTOR ADVICE

When acting as a syndicator in a free lease situation, you must attempt to minimize personal financial exposure. This can be handled in two ways:

(1) Provide an exculpatory (escape) clause in the lease which allows you to sell or abandon your interest in the lease at some point in the future, say five years or after the investors have recouped their investment. A term, which is too short, may be objectionable to the investors.

(2) Operate the syndicate as a corporation, thus limiting your exposure to the assets of the corporation only.

SEE ALSO: EXCULPATORY CLAUSE, FREE PIECE, and SYNDICATION.

FREE PIECE

Free piece is a syndication technique in which the syndicator takes a portion of the ownership as a fee for putting the deal together.

INVESTOR ADVICE

As in the case of the free lease, we assume that the selected property to be syndicated will produce more cash flow than necessary to justify the investors requirements. The additional funds available will support additional ownership—the syndicator's share or free piece.

EXAMPLE

You, as a syndicator, have an option on a real estate property which will provide $60,000 in cashflow after all expenses. The property can be purchased for $500,000. Investors, interested in this type of project, demand a 10% cash return on their investment or $50,000. The additional $10,000 available will support an additional $100,000 of ownership @ a 10% cash return rate.

You, as the syndicator, take 16.7% of the equity ($100,000/$600,000) as your fee for putting the deal together. If you are a licensed realtor or professional property manager, you may be able to make some additional money by:

• Acting as the listing or selling agent or both;

• Providing property management for a fee; and/or

• Listing and selling the property at a future date.

Syndication is one of the most popular ways of investing in real estate using other people's money. Most projects can provide up to a 20% free piece and still return an adequate amount to entice the required number of investors.

The free piece is often divided between the syndicator and mortgage holder. Pension funds and insurance companies, which provide multi-million dollar funding for large projects, usually demand a part of "the action" as a concession for providing necessary funds.

SEE ALSO: CERTIFIED PROPERTY MANAGER (CPM), FREE LEASE, REITS, and SYNDICATION.

FRONT FOOT

A front foot is a property measurement utilized for evaluation of standard depth lots. A front foot represents a parcel of land one foot wide and extending from the front to the rear of the lot.

INVESTOR ADVICE

The front foot designation is still used in areas of standard lot depth and high value. Its use as a valuation measurement is based on the need for street exposure in an urban environment.

With the advent of the strip-type shopping center and its requirement for abundant auto parking, building design and plot planning has drastically changed. Front exposure is not the paramount consideration. Primary consideration is a design which locates most stores in proximity to the anchor stores—those drawing the largest customer traffic count.

Development exposure and access to primary traffic arteries are also important, frontage is not. The size and shape of the parcel, which dictates plot flexibility, are more important than front footage in suburban properties.

In those areas in which front footage is significant, it is important to know that comparison of property values by that measurement are of the same depth. To compare front footage prices of two lots, one with 100 foot depth and another with 150 foot depth, is virtually impossible.

SEE ALSO: ANCHOR TENANT, DEEP LOT EVALUATION, EGRESS, INGRESS, and PLOT PLAN.

FUNCTIONAL OBSOLESCENCE

Functional obsolescence is a loss of value due to diminished usefulness of the property improvement.

INVESTOR ADVICE

Functional obsolescence is the one depreciation factor most difficult to assess. While direct inspection of a property will reveal its structural integrity, state of maintenance, and physical condition, the usefulness of the property to a prospective buyer is less obvious.

Apartments with older-style kitchens, small closets, or bedrooms inadequate to accommodate queen- or king-size beds are good examples of functional obsolescence. This depreciation may be curable, partially curable, or incurable. Even if curable, the cost to cure may not provide a return on investment adequate to justify the expense.

When considering acquisition of older properties, functional obsolescence probabilities must be carefully analyzed versus the inherent reduced revenue per square foot versus more modern facilities. Where functional obsolescence is detected, a study of the cost to cure versus revenue enhancement will indicate the desirability for investing.

This is not to say that older properties should not be purchased. All properties are a good buy at *some price*. It is often possible to buy functionally obsolescent properties for slightly more than land value. In this case, the available revenue from older units may provide sufficient income to justify a holding period before beginning new construction. The buy or no-buy decision ultimately rests on *the return on investment projected for the intended holding period.*

SEE ALSO: COST APPROACH TO VALUE, DEPRECIATION, HOLDING PERIOD, INCOME APPROACH TO VALUE, and MARKET APPROACH TO VALUE.

FUTURE ESTATE

Future estates are those estates that come into being at some time in the future. The time is most often designated as the occurrence of a designated event.

INVESTOR ADVICE

Future estates are the result of the termination of some other type of estate. For example:

- At the end of a dower or curtsey life estate;
- At the conclusion of a trust period, when the property is transferred to the designated remainderman;
- When a homestead is no longer in effect; and/or
- At the death of a life tenant.

The numerous ways in which future estates may come into existence emphasizes the need for all real estate investors to ascertain the full status of the property and to insure that apparent status with appropriate title insurance.

SEE ALSO: CURTSEY RIGHT, DOWER RIGHT, and LEASEHOLD INTEREST.

FUTURE EVENT DOWN PAYMENT

A future event down payment is due at the conclusion of a designated future event or time.

INVESTOR ADVICE

In selling property you should beware of the illusive promises of payment in the future, especially those which are predicated upon stipulated events which may or may not occur when expected or may not occur at all. When the offer to purchase is dependent upon such events, acceptance of these conditions may result in pulling your property off the market for an extended period, only to find that the sale has failed.

When the situation justifies a future event consideration, it is recommended that you reserve the right to continue to offer the property for sale. This contingency clause can accept the offer of the buyer to perform in a designated time or after a designated event or lose his/her right to buy. It should also provide that the buyer relinquish his/her right to purchase if; (1) a second acceptable offer is received and (2) he/she fails to remove the contingent condition in a given period.

EXAMPLE

Mr. Homeowner has his home listed for sale and receives a full price offer, subject to the sale and closing of the buyer's current residence. To accept this offer as written would mean taking it off the market for an indefinite period, with no assurance the buyer would ever perform. Mr. Homeowner's realtor suggested the following counter offer.

"This offer is accepted with the following change. It is understood that the seller will continue to offer his property for sale. Buyer has thirty days to remove the contingency of the sale and closing of his current residence or twenty-four (24) hours after notification that seller proposes to accept a second offer, whichever time is the lesser."

This alternative keeps the first buyer on the hook without forfeiting the right to keep trying for a better offer.

SEE ALSO: CONTINGENCY CLAUSE, and EARNEST MONEY RECEIPT AND OFFER TO PURCHASE.

FUTURE SWEAT

Future sweat is a payment on a property purchase by trade of buyer's work for cash value thereof—sometimes referred to as "sweat equity."

INVESTOR ADVICE

Future sweat provides a method of acquiring property with a low down payment or a reduced cash expenditure. Lower-income, single family homes are often purchased in this manner by buyers having sufficient skills to provide acceptable sub-contract efforts. For instance, a licensed plumber or electrician may agree to provide plumbing or electrical work in exchange for a stipulated dollar credit on the down payment.

Even those buyers with minimal skills may be able to provide clean-up work, interior painting, or similar labor. Most lending institutions will agree to these arrangements, since municipal inspections will assure that the work is performed in an acceptable manner.

Your start in real estate investing may be initiated by this method. Regardless of your present employment or skills, it may be possible to trade your work and abilities for a down payment on a modest investment. Everyone has something worthwhile that someone else may need.

SEE ALSO: SWEAT EQUITY.

FUTURE VALUE OF ONE

This term refers to the value to which one dollar will grow in a designated time period at a specified interest rate.

INVESTOR ADVICE

Figure 32 indicates the future values of one dollar which has been allowed to grow for designated periods and interest rates. You will note that one dollar will double in value in about seven years at a 10% interest rate. At a 12% interest rate the value will double in only six years. The value grows, with compound interest, proportionately with time and interest rate.

This concept is most useful to investors who need to estimate the value of a property at some time in the future and at designated inflation rates.

FUTURE VALUE OF $1
Received at the End of the Period
FV1p-%

PERIOD	2%	4%	6%	8%	10%	12%	14%	16%	18%	20%	24%	28%
1	1.020	1.040	1.060	1.080	1.100	1.120	1.140	1.160	1.180	1.200	1.240	1.280
2	1.040	1.082	1.124	1.166	1.210	1.254	1.300	1.346	1.392	1.440	1.538	1.638
3	1.061	1.125	1.191	1.260	1.331	1.405	1.482	1.561	1.643	1.728	1.907	2.097
4	1.082	1.170	1.263	1.361	1.464	1.574	1.689	1.811	1.939	2.074	2.364	2.684
5	1.104	1.217	1.338	1.469	1.611	1.762	1.925	2.100	2.288	2.488	2.932	3.436
6	1.126	1.265	1.419	1.587	1.772	1.974	2.195	2.436	2.700	2.986	3.635	4.398
7	1.149	1.316	1.504	1.714	1.949	2.211	2.502	2.826	3.186	3.583	4.508	5.630
8	1.172	1.369	1.594	1.851	2.144	2.476	2.853	3.278	3.759	4.300	5.590	7.206
9	1.195	1.423	1.690	2.000	2.358	2.773	3.252	3.803	4.436	5.160	6.931	9.223
10	1.219	1.480	1.791	2.159	2.594	3.106	3.707	4.411	5.234	6.192	8.594	11.805
11	1.243	1.540	1.898	2.332	2.853	3.479	4.226	5.117	6.176	7.430	10.657	15.111
12	1.268	1.601	2.012	2.518	3.138	3.896	4.818	5.936	7.288	8.916	13.214	19.342
13	1.294	1.665	2.133	2.720	3.452	4.364	5.492	6.886	8.599	10.699	16.386	24.758
14	1.320	1.732	2.261	2.937	3.798	4.887	6.261	7.988	10.147	12.839	20.319	31.691
15	1.346	1.801	2.397	3.172	4.177	5.474	7.138	9.266	11.973	15.407	25.195	40.564
16	1.373	1.873	2.540	3.426	4.595	6.130	8.137	10.748	14.129	18.488	31.242	51.923
17	1.400	1.948	2.693	3.700	5.055	6.866	9.277	12.467	16.672	22.186	38.740	66.461
18	1.428	2.026	2.854	3.996	5.560	7.690	10.575	14.462	19.673	26.623	48.038	85.071
19	1.457	2.107	3.026	4.316	6.116	8.613	12.055	16.776	23.214	31.948	59.567	108.89
20	1.486	2.191	3.207	4.661	6.728	9.646	13.743	19.460	27.393	38.337	73.864	139.37
25	1.641	2.666	4.292	6.849	10.834	17.000	26.461	40.874	62.668	95.396	216.54	478.90
30	1.811	3.243	5.744	10.062	17.449	29.959	50.950	85.849	143.37	237.37	634.81	1645.5
35	2.000	3.946	7.686	14.785	28.102	52.800	98.100	180.31	328.00	590.67	1861.1	5653.9
40	2.208	4.801	10.285	21.724	45.259	93.050	188.88	378.72	750.37	1469.7	5455.9	19246.
45	2.438	5.841	13.765	31.920	72.890	163.99	363.68	795.44	1715.7	3657.3	15995.	66750.

Last decimal number rounded up if next number was 5 or more.
Table prepared utilizing Hewlett-Packard 38-C calculator.

Figure 32

EXAMPLES

You have just purchased an apartment house for $100,000 and plan to keep it for five years. You estimate that inflation will average 4% per year during that time. What will the value of the apartment be at the end of five years?

Factor from Fig 32 for 5 yrs @ 4% = 1.217

Property value = 1.217 x $100,000 = $121,700

*   *   *   *   *   *   *   *   *

You deposit $1000 in a savings account for the anticipated purchase of three new refrigerators at the end of seven years. The savings account will earn 6% compound interest. How much money will you have in the reserves for replacement account at the end of the period?

Factor from Fig. 31 for 7 yrs. @ 6% = 1.504

Value at end of 7yrs. = $1000 x 1.504 = $1504

The examples given have used a table to simply explain the concept of compound interest growth. Tables, such as that shown in Figure 32, are limited in the interest rates and number of periods shown. To provide factors for all useful interest rates and periods would require a large book of tables.

Most present day real estate investors use economical hand-held calculators which can calculate values for any number of periods and any interest rate, even those to a fraction of a percentage. Most calculators are accurate to at least eight decimal places and some, such as the Hewlett-Packard® units are accurate to sixteen or more decimal places.

SEE ALSO: COMPOUND INTEREST, and FUTURE VALUE OF ONE PER PERIOD.

FUTURE VALUE OF ONE PER PERIOD

This term refers to the value to which a deposit of one dollar per period will grow in a designated time and at a stipulated interest rate.

INVESTOR ADVICE

Figure 33 shows the power of compound interest and periodic payments to make your savings grow. You will note that a one dollar deposit each period for ten periods at an interest rate of 10% will reach a value of $15.937 or almost $16. This growth is larger than that shown in the previous table, and is the result of not only compound interest but the constant periodic addition of principal which also earns compound interest.

This table is useful in calculating the amount of the deposit required each period to achieve a certain goal in the future.

EXAMPLES

You have decided that all of the dishwashers in your twelve unit apartment house will require replacing at the end of fifteen years. You estimate that they will cost $500

FUTURE VALUE OF $1 PER PERIOD
Received at the End of Various Periods
$FV1/P_{p-\%}$

PERIOD	2%	4%	6%	8%	10%	12%	14%	16%	18%	20%	24%	28%
1	1.000	1.000	1.000	1.000	1.000	1.000	1.000	1.000	1.000	1.000	1.000	1.000
2	2.020	2.040	2.060	2.080	2.010	2.012	2.014	2.016	2.018	2.020	2.024	2.028
3	3.060	3.122	3.184	3.246	3.310	3.374	3.440	3.506	3.572	3.640	3.778	3.918
4	4.122	4.247	4.375	4.506	4.641	4.779	4.921	5.067	5.215	5.368	5.684	6.016
5	5.204	5.416	5.637	5.867	6.105	6.353	6.610	6.877	7.154	7.442	8.048	8.700
6	6.308	6.633	6.975	7.336	7.716	8.115	8.536	8.978	9.442	9.930	10.980	12.135
7	7.434	7.898	8.394	8.923	9.487	10.089	10.730	11.413	12.141	12.915	14.615	16.553
8	8.583	9.214	9.898	10.636	11.435	12.299	13.232	14.240	15.327	16.499	19.122	22.163
9	9.369	10.582	11.491	12.487	13.579	14.775	16.085	17.518	19.085	20.798	24.712	29.369
10	10.462	11.463	13.180	14.486	15.937	17.548	19.377	21.321	23.521	25.958	31.643	38.592
11	12.168	13.486	14.971	16.645	18.531	20.654	23.044	25.732	28.755	32.150	40.237	50.398
12	13.412	15.025	16.868	18.977	21.384	24.133	27.270	30.850	34.931	39.580	50.894	65.510
13	14.680	16.626	18.882	21.495	24.522	28.029	32.088	36.786	42.218	48.496	64.109	84.852
14	15.973	18.291	21.015	24.214	27.975	32.292	37.581	43.672	50.818	59.195	80.496	109.61
15	17.293	20.023	23.276	27.152	31.772	37.279	43.842	51.659	60.965	72.035	100.81	141.30
16	18.639	21.824	25.672	30.324	35.949	42.753	50.980	60.925	72.939	87.442	126.01	181.86
17	20.012	23.697	28.212	33.750	40.544	48.883	59.117	71.673	87.068	105.93	157.25	233.79
18	21.412	25.645	30.905	37.450	45.599	55.749	68.394	84.140	103.74	128.11	195.99	300.25
19	22.840	27.671	33.760	41.446	51.159	63.439	78.969	98.603	123.41	154.74	244.03	385.32
20	24.297	29.778	36.785	45.762	57.275	72.052	91.024	115.37	146.62	186.68	303.60	494.21
25	32.030	41.645	54.864	73.105	98.347	133.33	181.87	249.21	342.60	471.98	898.09	1706.8
30	40.568	56.084	79.058	113.28	164.49	241.33	356.78	530.31	790.94	1181.8	2640.9	5873.2
35	49.994	73.652	111.44	172.32	271.02	431.66	693.57	1120.7	1816.7	2948.3	7750.2	20189.
40	60.402	95.025	154.76	259.05	442.59	767.09	1342.0	2360.7	4163.2	7343.8	22728.	69377.
45	71.893	121.03	212.74	386.51	718.91	1358.2	2590.6	4965.3	9531.6	18281.	-	-

(-) number too large for table

Figure 33

per unit. Your bank is now paying 8% on its savings accounts. What annual deposit will be required to achieve your goal?

> Amount Required = 12 X $500 = $6,000
> Factor from Fig 32 for 15 yrs. @ 8% interest = 27.152
> X = Amount of annual deposit required
> 27.152X = $6,000
> X = $6,000/27.152 = $220.98
> Round to: $221

* * * * * * * * * *

You are the president of a real estate investment corporation, which has raised $2,000,000 through issuance of corporate bonds. These bonds are to be redeemed at the end of twenty years. You are currently earning 16% on your investments, but feel that a conservative estimate for the next twenty years should be only 12%. How much must you invest each year for the next twenty years, at 12% average yield to be able to redeem the $2,000,000 in bonds at their maturity?

> Factor from Table 32 for 20 yrs. @ 12% = 72.052
> X = amount of annual investment
> 72.052X = $2,000,000
> X = $27,757.73
> Round to: $28,000

The example given is commonly referred to as a "sinking fund" problem.
SEE ALSO: COMPOUND INTEREST, and FUTURE VALUE OF ONE.

G

Gable
General Mortgage
General Partner
Gift Taxes
Glue Deal
Government National Mortgage Association (GNMA)
Graduated Lease
Graduated Payment Mortgages
Grandfather Clause
Grant Deed

Grantee
Grantor
Gray Water Waste
Grazing Lease
Greenbelt Tax Classification
Gross Income
Gross National Product (GNP)
Gross Potential Income
Gross Rent Multiplier
Ground Rent
Guardian

G

GABLE

A gable is the end of a home having a pitched roof forming a "V"-shaped section above the first story ceiling height.

INVESTOR ADVICE
This, one of the most common roof-types for residences, is illustrated in Figure 34.[1]

SEE ALSO: HIP ROOF, and MANSARD ROOF.

Figure 34. Residential Gable Roof

GENERAL MORTGAGE

A general mortgage pledges all properties owned by the mortgagor as security for a new loan—sometimes called a blanket mortgage.

INVESTOR ADVICE
You would be advised to avoid general mortgages if at all possible. The big problem with this type of mortgage is the difficulty of selling or transferring any of the property covered.

To sell a property covered by a general mortgage, permission from the mortgage-holder must be obtained in order to remove that property from the blanket coverage. When a property has a regular mortgage on it, this poses no problem. When it is sold, a regular mortgage is paid off at closing and transfer of the deed. No prior permission of the mortgage holder is required.

A general mortgage may be helpful if additional funds are required to purchase a new property on which the bank is reluctant or unwilling to make a loan, thereby using that property as the only security. This method should be considered as a last-ditch effort to obtain the required funds.

SEE ALSO: BLANKET MORTGAGE, and LOT RELEASE BASIS.

GENERAL PARTNER

A general partner is the managing partner of a limited partnership organization.

INVESTOR ADVICE

The general partner is usually the one who establishes a real estate investment limited partnership. He/she will usually take a portion (20% or so) of the ownership as his/her fee for getting the partnership established. Most, if not all, of the money invested will come from the limited partners.

When considering an investment in a limited partnership, you should check to determine how much of the "business" was given away to the general partner. Often this will be inordinately high and more than justified for the effort expended by the general partner in putting the "deal" together.

You should also consider the tax changes of the 1986 Tax Reform Act which deals with losses and gains from passive activities. Losses from these partnerships can only be offset against passive income. Thus in the beginning, you may not have that big tax write-off that was available in the past.

Before 1986, most investors were in the 50% tax bracket. A loss of one dollar was worth fifty cents of tax relief or the same return as one dollar of profit. Limited partnerships were established knowing that little or no profit would be available, except through tax losses to the partners.

Under the 1986 regulations, a real estate investment must rise and fall upon its own merits. You should invest in these projects only if the projections of profit and other gains, less taxes at your current rate, fully justify the risks involved.

SEE ALSO: LIMITED PARTNERSHIPS, and MASTER LIMITED PARTNERSHIPS.

GIFT TAXES

A gift tax is federal excise tax payable by the donor on gifts made to others during his/her lifetime.

INVESTOR ADVICE

IRS regulations classify all transfers of cash or property (assets) without adequate or full compensation as gifts. Most gifts, with the exception of charitable gifts, are taxable in the year the gift is made. All gifts in excess of $10,000 to one person per year (annual exclusion) must be reported and are taxed on a cumulative basis. The excess over $10,000 per year given to any one person is taxed on a cumulative basis—the more given in a lifetime, the higher the tax rate becomes. Gifts from married persons are considered as one-half given by each, therefore only $10,000 per person can be given tax-free without reporting the gift.

Gifts to others is one way of reducing estate taxes, although any gifts in contemplation of death are included in the estate. Gifts made three years or less before death are automatically considered to have been made in contemplation of death.

When an estate is larger than needed for foreseeable personal use, good estate planning should include systematic giving. If a gift is also made to a recipient's spouse, the tax free gift to the family can be raised to $20,000 per year. If gifts are also made to grandchildren the total annual gifts can be substantial.

Many people try to avoid the gift tax problem by simply quitclaiming an interest in a property, with the giver and recipient becoming joint owners with a right of survivorship. Thus, when the giver dies, ownership of the property automatically transfers to the other owner. If this procedure is discovered by the IRS, it will trigger an investigation, which involves the filing of a gift tax return for the year of the gift, on behalf of the deceased giver. If taxes were payable at that time, they must be paid plus penalties.

Good records of all gifts, taxable and non-taxable, should be kept to facilitate the executor(ix) job in probating the estate after the death of the donor.

SEE ALSO: ANNUAL EXCLUSION, and ESTATE TAXES.

GLUE DEAL

"A glue deal is a transaction in which the status of the buyer is the main ingredient of the deal. In this kind of deal, the position, reputation, or influence of the buyer is generally more important than cash."[2]

INVESTOR ADVICE

In a glue deal you must not be so overly impressed with the buyer's reputation and standing in the realty community that you fail to take due caution. A person who seems infallible today may suddenly become financially destitute if there is a abrubt change in the real estate economy.

You should be particularly careful of deals in which the buyer appears to have built a house of cards, in which income from his/her properties are financing additional acquisitions. A sudden downturn in the rental market may reduce his/her cash flow below the point needed to meet his/her debt service load, thereby triggering a series of defaults that can bring down the "house."

An audited financial statement showing assets and, more particularly, liabilities is a better indicator of financial stability than reputation alone.

SEE ALSO: CASH FLOW, and LEVERAGE.

GOVERNMENT NATIONAL MORTGAGE ASSOCIATION (GNMA)

The Government National Mortgage Association (GNMA) is a government-owned corporation of the department of Housing and Urban Development (HUD), which assists federally-aided housing projects, guarantees securities issued by private lenders, and backs FHA, VA, and Farm Home Administration loans.

INVESTOR ADVICE

GNMA- or Ginnie Mae-backed loans, as they are commonly referred to, made by mortgage companies are generally assumable by future buyers of the property. For this reason, you would be advised to seek out this type of loan rather than the conventional type, which is seldom assumable.

Ginnie Mae is one of this country's largest secondary mortgage organizations. Its purchases of mortgages are accomplished with funds derived from the sale of GNMA bonds. These bonds, in large denominations, are purchased by various institutions; (1) for their own portfolios; or (2) to back their own issues of Collateralized Mortgage Obligations (CMO).

CMOs are small denomination bonds ($1000) issued and backed by the large GNMA-held bonds. Interest is passed directly to the CMO holders. The CMO issuing agency, such as the Ryan Acceptance Corporation, receives its fee through purchase of the original GNMA bonds at discount.

SEE ALSO: COLLATERALIZED MORTGAGE OBLIGATION, FHA LOAN, and VA LOAN.

GRADUATED LEASE

A graduated lease calls for an initial rental rate for a few months, with graduated increases at stipulated times in the future.

INVESTOR ADVICE

The graduated lease is a good way to acquire small business tenants who would otherwise not be able to afford to lease your property during the initial stages of their business development.

In agreeing to such a lease, you must consider the tenant's possibilities of success in the same manner that a bank would in making a new business loan. This means examination of proforma income, balance sheets, and cash flow statements with particular attention to assumptions used in making those estimates.

The graduated lease approach is also a good method of quickly filling a new shopping center, where the traffic count is only an assumption. Prospective tenants know that as the center matures, the traffic count will improve. The graduated lease allows them to survive during the lean period of their business's development.

SEE ALSO: PRO-FORMA ANALYSIS.

GRADUATED PAYMENT MORTGAGES

A graduated payment mortgage has payments beginning at a lower than normal rate and increasing in steps over a stipulated period of time.

INVESTOR ADVICE

Graduated mortgages are provided by the FHA and some private lenders. They are useful in providing an ability to buy a more expensive property than would otherwise be possible, but should be restricted to those individuals who are very confident of increasing income concurrent with the change in mortgage payments. Typical of this group of mortgagors are young professionals, who are just beginning their careers. Even those individuals should beware of loans with negative amortization features— initial payments which do not cover interest. A property purchased on a negative amortization basis in a stagnant or declining economy may not be marketable at a break-even price in the future. The mortgage payable, under those conditions, may exceed the fair market value of the property.

Those individuals, working for large companies, who are subject to transfer should also be very careful of this type of commitment. Even though you might feel that there is little likelihood of transfer in the next three to five years, a job promotion may change the picture.

COMPARING THE ALTERNATIVES

If you are considering a home purchase with an $80,000 mortgage, you will find that the graduated loan payment will be reduced from the conventional loan rate of 12% to a beginning 10.5%. This will reduce your payments about $100 per month over that of the conventional loan. This might bring you within the qualification range, but you incur a negative amortization situation, which means you increase your mortgage debt each month.

An alternative would be to buy with a conventional 12% loan without negative amortization. To keep within your qualification range, you would need to buy a home with a selling price about $10,000 less. On a new house this might be accomplished by leaving off some finish work in the basement, having one less bath in the beginning or possibly one less fireplace. If you stay in the same location, these amenities can be added later on. If transferred, your mortgage payable is a little less than at the beginning and you have a saleable property at the price you originally paid.

SEE ALSO: AMORTIZATION SCHEDULE.

GRANDFATHER CLAUSE

A grandfather clause in a new rule or regulation exempts prior actions from the effects of the new rule. For instance, a zoning change from business to another category would not require the closing of a business in existence when the new rule was promulgated.

INVESTOR ADVICE

A careful inspection of recent zoning changes or restrictive covenants may reveal a property which is exempt from the change and therefore more valuable than most buyers assume. This is often true with regard to size limitation requirements to develop or the nature of the business that can be conducted.

A word of caution is required. Most grandfather clauses allow continuation of the activity in existence at the time the law was passed, but does not apply if that activity ceases for a period of time. When a new business is established after a break in time, it must usually conform to the new zoning. Be very careful in buying a property which is currently operating under a grandfather clause or so called "non-conforming use."

SEE ALSO: RESTRICTIVE COVENANTS, and ZONING.

GRANT DEED

The grant deed is most common type of deed used in most states. It is also referred to in some jurisdictions as a warranty deed. The grant deed implies certain warranties.

INVESTOR ADVICE

A grant deed guarantees the title, but only in terms of defects which occurred after the grantor received title.

You must remember that the warranties implied or promised in a deed are no better than the person making the warranty. It is not possible to recover compensation for errors not covered by title insurance and found at some time in the future, where the grantor is insolvent at that time.

Figure 35 shows a typical warranty or grant deed. You will note that the deed is divided into several sections; (1) The grantor section, which identifies the grantor; (2) The grantee section, which identifies the grantee; and (3) The property description section, which clearly identifies the property being transferred. The warranties are provided in the first section by the words "convey and warrant to."

SEE ALSO: TITLE INSURANCE, and WARRANTY DEED.

GRANTEE

The person and/or organization that receives a property transferred by a grant deed is the grantee.

Recorded at Request of __Utah Title Company, SLC, Ut.__ _____

at_____. M. Fee Paid $_3.00__. _____

by __J. Smith_____ Dep. Book _201_ Page _196_ Ref.: __2978_____

Mail tax notice to _James P. Smith_ Address _121 So. Orchard Drive____

WARRANTY DEED

        Gerald G. Browning   **grantor**
of Salt Lake City   , County of Salt Lake   , State of Utah, hereby
CONVEY and **WARRANT** to

    James P. Smith and Sarah K. Smith as joint owners with
    rights of survivorship

                                       grantee
of   Salt Lake City   **for the sum of**
                      Ten   **DOLLARS,**

the following described tract of land in
State of Utah: Salt Lake   County,

        All of Lot 26, Orchard Groves Subdivision

WITNESS, the hand of said grantor , this   22nd   **day of**
    February   , A. D. 19 89

       Signed in the Presence of   _Gerald G Browning_

   _____   _____

   _____   _____

   _____   _____

STATE OF UTAH,   ss.

County of Salt Lake

   On the 22nd   **day of**   February   , A. D. 19 89
personally appeared before me Gerald G. Browning

the signer of the within instrument, who duly acknowledged to me that he executed the
same.

                          Mary Tyler Brown
                          Mary Tyler Brown
                              Notary Public.

My commission expires__ Mar 31, 1991 ___ Residing in ___ Salt Lake City _____

BLANK #101—WARRANTY DEED—© GEM PRINTING CO. — SALT LAKE CITY

Figure 35. Warranty Deed.

INVESTOR ADVICE
See GRANT DEED.
SEE ALSO: DEED, GRANTOR, SPECIAL WARRANTY DEED, and WARRANTY DEED.

GRANTOR

The person and/or organization which transfers property by deed to a grantee is the grantor.

INVESTOR ADVICE
See GRANT DEED.
SEE ALSO: DEED, GRANTEE, SPECIAL WARRANTY DEED, and WARRANTY DEED.

GRAY WATER WASTE

Gray water waste is waste water from toilets and other noxious activities which are considered hazardous to watershed areas, particularly those collecting water for human consumption.

INVESTOR ADVICE
When purchasing or proposing to purchase property for development in areas designated as watershed lands, it is advisable to consider the extraordinary cost involved with waste water disposal. This would include both grey and white water disposal.

In most watershed areas, usually hilly or mountainous terrain, it is often impossible to develop successful septic systems due to the inability of the land to absorb the effluent. Where this is the case, the grey water must be collected in holding tanks for transportation to a sewage facility. A good example of this is in the ski resorts near Salt Lake City. Grey water is pumped into tank trucks and moved about fifteen miles to the valley sewage facility at a cost of about five cents per gallon.

SEE ALSO: CULINARY WATER, PERCOLATION TEST, and WHITE WATER WASTE.

GRAZING LEASE

A grazing lease permits a lessee to graze animals upon another's property. The Bureau of Land Management is a prolific lessor of government land to cattlemen in the West.

INVESTOR ADVICE
In considering the purchase of land in the West, one often finds that long-term grazing rights are transferred with the title to the land. Advertisements for land sales often read:

5,000 acres good grazing land, including 1,000 deeded acres.

This means that the offerer proposes to sell his/her own 1,000 acres and transfer a long-term lease to the additional 4,000 acres.
SEE ALSO: LEASE, and LEASEHOLD.

GREENBELT TAX CLASSIFICATION

The Greenbelt Tax Classification authorizes valuable development property adjacent to metropolitan areas to be taxed as farmland as long as it meets certain criteria.

INVESTOR ADVICE

The criteria for Greenbelt Classification are usually as follows:

• Parcel contains a minimum of 5.0 acres;

• Parcel has been in continuous use as farm land for a number of preceding years; and

• Parcel contains no more than one residence.

The purpose of this classification is to allow farmers to continue to farm their land and pay minimum taxes, even though the encroaching metropolis has made the land far more valuable for other purposes.

If the land is subdivided to a point below the minimum acreage, it automatically becomes taxable based on its current assessed value at highest and best use.

SEE ALSO: ASSESSED VALUE, HIGHEST AND BEST USE, and ZONING.

GROSS INCOME

Gross income is the total income credited to a property before expenses have been deducted. Based upon the accounting method employed, the money may or may not have been actually received.

INVESTOR ADVICE

In reviewing the income from a property, you must determine if cash or accrual accounting figures have been employed. A receivable item in the asset column is a tip-off that accrual accounting is being employed. Large receivables are an indication of collection problems.

Gross potential income (gross possible) indicates the maximum income possible with zero vacancies. The gross income of a property is usually somewhat less that the total possible, due to vacancies. A financial statement showing no vacancies is suspect, especially if there are several units available for lease.

SEE ALSO: GROSS RENT MULTIPLIER, RECEIVABLES, and VACANCY FACTOR.

GROSS NATIONAL PRODUCT (GNP)

The Gross National Product (GNP) is the total value of all goods and services produced in a country during a given year. The GNP is a measure of economic activity.

INVESTOR ADVICE

GNP figures are often used as the reference for calculating increases in rents or mortgage interest rates. This would apply to those leases and mortgages that contain an escalation clause based on that published figure. The cost of living or prime interest rate is similarly used for rent and interest adjustments.

SEE ALSO: ESCALATION CLAUSE, FLOATING RATE LOAN, and PRIME RATE.

GROSS POTENTIAL INCOME

The gross potential income is the maximum income possible when all units are rented 100% of the time at scheduled rental rates—sometimes referred to as "gross expected income."

INVESTOR ADVICE

When reviewing income statements from a prospective acquisition, this item is useful as a projection of the maximum situation. The statement should then reflect a deduction for vacancies, even though these may be relatively small. It may also include items such as "rent reductions," "adjustments," or "rebates." The often heard statement, "We never have any vacancies," is unrealistic and unacceptable. One tenant does not move out at midnight and a replacement move in at one minute past midnight. Units will be vacant for a short period to allow redecoration. Some tenants will move in a few days after signing a lease. There may even be some losses in rental collection.

Where vacancy factors are shown, they should be checked against the record of receipts to assure their accuracy. Owners of rental property for sale often conveniently forget certain facts and are particularly prone to omit expenses. It is not unusual to find two sets of books, the actual figures and those prepared for prospective buyers.

This situation is not confined to purchases by the small investor, but is often found in large corporation books, which have been audited. A review of the auditors notes, accompanying the financial statements, may be most revealing regarding missing information.

SEE ALSO: GROSS INCOME, ON-SITE MANAGER, and VACANCY FACTOR.

GROSS RENT MULTIPLIER

The gross rent multiplier is a number used by real estate appraisers to provide a rough estimate of value. The gross rent multiplier is the selling price divided by the gross annual income.

INVESTOR ADVICE

While the gross rent multiplier (GRM) is a good check against other valuation procedures, it is subject to error since the expense of operation is not considered. Two properties with the same GRM could have drastically different values when one is modern and operating with minimum expense and the other is older and operating at a higher expense ratio.

In appraising income-producing property, appraisers will use as many of the evaluation techniques as possible before determining the fair market value. These techniques might include:

- The income approach to value;

- The cost or replacement approach to value; and/or

- The market data approach, which might include any or all of the following:

    ° Gross rent multiplier;

    ° Net income multiple; and/or

    ° Income per unit and size.

EXAMPLE

An appraiser finds the following information is the real estate multiple listing catalogue of past sales:

Sales Price: $240,000
Gross Rent Income: $24,000

What is the GRM for this property?

$$GRM = \text{Sales Price} / \text{Gross Income}$$
$$GRM = \$240,000 / \$24,000 = 10.0$$

If the appraiser finds several other sales with the same or similar GRM's, he/she might conclude that the property he/she is appraising, with a gross rent income of $33,000 is worth:

$$\text{Value} = \$33,000 \times 10.0 = \$330,000$$

SEE ALSO: COST OR REPLACEMENT APPROACH TO VALUE, INCOME APPROACH TO VALUE, MARKET DATA APPROACH TO VALUE, and NET INCOME MULTIPLIER.

GROUND RENT

Ground rent is the total rental received on an improved property less that income attributable to the improvements.

INVESTOR ADVICE

It is not uncommon for an appraiser compare improved property incomes, without consideration for excess land of one or the other properties. Where income from the properties are capitalized, an adjustment in income must be made for the income attributable to the excess land, whether rented or not.

EXAMPLE

Appraiser Jones is comparing a recent $500,000 sale of an office building to a similar property he is appraising. Both properties have the same net income of $50,000. The sold property contains 1.0 acres of land, whereas the property being appraised contained 0.5 acres, which was deemed adequate for its use. On the surface and based on income only, it would appear that both properties are of equal value. The yield rate of the sold property was apparently:

$$\$50,000 / \$500,000 = .10 \text{ or } 10\%$$

But what about the excess 0.5 acres of land? Is it not worth something? Let us assume that a market check shows that 0.5 acres, if rented or utilized effectively, could produce additional income of $5,000 per year. The comparable sold property income must therefore be adjusted upwards $5,000 to $55,000.
The true yield on this property was:

$$\$55,000 / \$500,000 = .11 \text{ or } 11\%$$

The value of the appraised property would be:

$$\$50,000 / .11 = \$454,545$$

This is an easy concept to comprehend as it is obvious the sold property is more valuable than the appraised property. If the excess land of the sold property was useless due to shape, topography, or other reasons no adjustment would have been required.

In this example, we have assumed the land to be of value and the assumed income (ground rent) of $5,000 is based on land value capable of earning income.

SEE ALSO: MARKET DATA APPROACH TO VALUE, and LAND RESIDUAL.

GUARDIAN

A guardian is:

(1) A person legally charged with the responsibility of the care and protection of a minor—guardian of the person.

(2) A person or organization charged with the management of the estate of a minor—guardian of the estate.

INVESTOR ADVICE

Any investor of real estate should have a will that is kept up to date to reflect the total current property holdings. This requires that the will be revised each and every time a property is sold or a general provision which will cover all properties. Many persons with large real estate portfolios prefer to take title to these properties in the name of a living trust.

The two biggest mistakes made by attorneys preparing wills are:

(1) Failure to name a perpetual institution, such as a bank or trust, as manager of the estate. They should at least indicate an alternate guardian or co-guardian to serve in the event the first named is unable or unwilling to serve.

(2) Failure to provide for the personal care of minor children. Since the estate appears to be of prime importance, one often forget that both parents can die at the same time and that someone will be needed to care for the children's personal welfare. If the will is mute to this point, the probate judge will appoint a guardian for the children (usually a close relative). This appointee may not be the decedents' first or even second choice.

SEE ALSO: ESTATE, INTESTATE, PROBATE, TRUST, and WILL.

ENDNOTES

[1]Picture by permission of Marshall-Swift Appraisal Service.

[2]Jack Cummings. *$1000 Down Can Make You Rich* (Prentice Hall Inc., Englewood Cliffs, N.J., 1985), p. 38.

H

Habendum Clause
Hangout
Hazard Insurance
Heating, Ventilating and Air Conditioning (HVAC)
Hereditaments
Highest and Best Use
Hip Roof
Holding Cost
Holding Period

Holdover Tenant
Holographic Will
Homeowner's Association
Homeowner's Insurance
Homestead
Homestead Tax Exemption
Hoskold Method
Hostile Possession
Housing and Urban Development (HUD)

H

HABENDUM CLAUSE

A habendum clause is found in deeds and other legal instruments and defines the quantity of the estate or asset transferred. This clause is often referred to as "the have and to hold clause."

INVESTOR ADVICE

Figure 3, Assignment of Mortgage, contains a habendum clause which states, "To have and to hold the same unto the assignee and to his successors, legal representatives and assigns of the assignee for ever." This wordage is also found in deeds of various types.

In a deed, a habendum clause is often included, in which the grantor identifies any encumbrances which may affect the grantee's estate. In the Warranty Deed, shown in Figure 35, the grantor promises that there are no encumbrances other than those shown in the deed.

Real estate investors should not be concerned with the wording of state-approved forms, but only with those additions or deletions thereto. The style and type of forms used in the various states will vary somewhat, but all are designed to accomplish a certain purpose with due regard for that particular state's laws.

SEE ALSO: ASSIGNMENT OF MORTGAGE, and DEED.

HANGOUT

The mortgage time period that exceeds the major tenant lease period is called the hangout.

INVESTOR ADVICE

The term hangout describes the lender's position when leases of major tenants are less than the period of the mortgage. Without guaranteed tenant income, the lending institution feels it may be hung out on the line to dry, so to speak.

When signing on major tenants for a commercial development, it is advisable to set the lease periods as close to that of the proposed mortgage as possible. This is not always possible as the majority of major tenants will not desire to commit themselves beyond a twenty-year period, and most will not even be willing to go beyond ten years.

A ten- or twenty-year mortgage will require such large payments that most projects will not be viable. Accordingly, some hangout is necessary. Most lending institutions have a set limit on the amount of "hangout" that is acceptable. Before converting your letters of intent to leases, check with your lending institution regarding its hangout policy.

In recent years construction of new buildings designed for specific tenants has become very popular. When special designs and amenities are provided, the usefulness of the structure for future tenants will be in doubt. Your lender will undoubtedly require a full-term lease to match the term of the mortgage.

SEE ALSO: ANCHOR TENANT, LEASE, and LETTER OF INTENT.

HAZARD INSURANCE

Hazard insurance protects property owners in the event of a loss by designated hazards—fire, windstorm, falling aircraft, etc.

INVESTOR ADVICE

All lenders require the mortgagor to provide sufficient hazard coverage in a minimum amount to cover the mortgage payable. Often these requirements go beyond a requirement for coverage against physical loss. They also require liability coverage as well.

Where a mortgagor is subject to lawsuits for injuries to the public while on his/her property, it is conceivable that a major judgment could impair his/her ability to meet mortgage payments.

Mortgages on commercial properties also require certain hazard coverage, which is detailed in the mortgage note or similar instrument. Commercial insurance packages usually provide some liability coverage, in an amount similar to that contained in the Homeowner II package for resident owners.

Residential mortgage requirements normally specify "homeowner" insurance, HO-II or better. This policy covers losses to the building itself, and also provides protection for owner's liability and loss of furnishings and other personal property.

At the closing, you will be required to name the mortgagee as beneficiary to the extent of its interest in the property in the event of loss, and to furnish the lender with a copy of the policy or binder, to assure the lender of adequate and continued coverage from that day forward. Most lenders will require that they be furnished a copy of the policy itself and will collect each month an amount sufficient to renew the policy just prior to expiration.

SEE ALSO: CLOSING COSTS, HOME OWNER'S INSURANCE, and JUDGMENT.

HEATING, VENTILATING AND AIR CONDITIONING (HVAC)

Heating, ventilating, and air conditioning (HVAC) is an essential system of every residential or commercial building.

INVESTOR ADVICE

The HVAC system is one of the most expensive systems in a building and one that must be given strict attention, whether part of a new building or an older one. A poor system installed in a new building can result in excessive cost to you or your tenants and result in the creation of an unprofitable project.

If an inadequate system is inherited in the purchase of an older building, the cost to repair or replace can ruin the most optimistic income projections.

The following considerations must be examined before finalizing your decision on the HVAC system for a new project:

- What environmental control will be required to meet tenant expectations—heat only, heat and cooling, dehumidification, etc.?

- Who will be paying the utility costs, tenant or landlord?

- Who will manage the system operation—turn off, turn on, control temperature, etc.?

- What are the costs of various fuels in the local area? Are any of these expected to change significantly in the near future?

- How long do you expect to own the property?

- Will the addition of high-grade insulation, low emissivity windows, and /or high efficiency heating and cooling units be cost effective over the expected holding period?

When considering the purchase of existing structures, it is mandatory that the current condition of the HVAC system be accurately determined by a professional inspection service. These inspections can reveal hidden problems not even known to the current owners. Problems often found include such items as:

- Holes in the heat exchanger (hot air systems);

- Malfunctioning valves (hot/cold water systems);

- Poorly maintained blower units, obstructed or clogged duct systems, and inadequate filtering systems;

- Incorrectly sized cooling or heating units;

- Functional units but at an age that will require replacement in the near future;

- Poorly insulated buildings, part or all of which cannot be economically corrected;

- Lack of low emissivity windows or storm sashes;

- Duct heat loss and/or moisture condensation due to poor insulation; and/or

- Evidence of condensation damage to the structure.

The importance of the problems listed and considerations thereof can be appreciated when you realize what percent of total costs are attributable to HVAC systems. Marshall & Swift[1] indicate the following percentages for a median-cost, multi-family residence:

Heating	4.0%
Cooling	8.5
Total	12.5%

SEE ALSO: INDIVIDUAL METERING, and MASTER METERING.

HEREDITAMENTS
Hereditaments are the largest classification of property and include land, tenements, and other rights, such as right-of-ways.

INVESTOR ADVICE
See REAL PROPERTY.
SEE ALSO: TENEMENTS, and RIGHT-OF-WAY (ROW).

HIGHEST AND BEST USE
"Highest and best use" is the fundamental concept of value which implies maximum profitability by best utilization of an asset.

INVESTOR ADVICE
Most appraisal texts and appraisal instructors generally define highest and best use as the highest and best use of the land, or the most profitable likely utilization of the parcel at the time the appraisal was made. It may also be defined as the available use and program of future utilization that produces the highest land value. It is generally acknowledged that this concept of highest and best use may be extended to improved real estate for various decision-making situations, but such applications should not be confused with the underlying concept of highest and best use of land only.

When you review property appraisals, you should determine whether the appraisal has been made in conformance with the well-established principle of highest and best use.

It should also be noted that in the appraisal of property for condemnation, the law provides for a much wider interpretation of fair market value to include potential use which is not authorized by the property's current zoning.

SEE ALSO: APPRAISAL REPORT, CONDEMNATION, VALUE, and ZONING.

HIP ROOF

A hip roof is a pitched roof style with sloping sides and ends resulting in the elimination of gables.

INVESTOR ADVICE

Figure 36 show a typical hip roof for a residential property. While very attractive, this type of roof is more expensive than the gable roof and requires gutters on all sides of the building.

SEE ALSO: GABLE, and MANSARD ROOF.

Figure 36. Residential Hip Roof

HOLDING COST

The holding cost is the total cost of acquisition, development, promotion, and interest charges incurred by a developer prior to receipt of initial sales or leasing income from the project. Holding costs might also include non-cash expenses such as lost interest on the capital invested.

INVESTOR ADVICE

The key to minimizing holding costs is proper planning which will eliminate unnecessary time delays. The actual cost of development will increase with time when a property remains unproductive.

COST-SAVING EXAMPLES

Holding costs result in residential development when land is purchased in the fall or winter and held until construction begins in the spring. This requires four to six months of interest charges or, in the case of a cash purchase, loss of income while waiting for the project's start. If possible, take an option and conclude the purchase just prior to starting development work.

In another situation, road, curb, gutter, sidewalk, and utility construction for the entire project may be more economical than a piecemeal approach, even though some carrying charges result. Proper planning can minimize this expense.

Lot sales at slight discounts, prior to starting construction, can provide funds at no interest to finance part of the construction and will probably more than compensate for the reduction in sales price.

Purchase of undeveloped land on a lot release or option basis rather than outright purchase can also reduce holding costs, since only a token down payment is required to get started on the project.

When property is acquired for future development, try to select land with existing income from older structures, rental as a parking lot, etc. Even though this income is less than market rate, it will defray some interest costs during the holding period.

SEE ALSO: LOT RELEASE SYSTEM, and OPTION.

HOLDING PERIOD

The holding period is:

(1) The period of time between acquisition of an undeveloped property and beginning of development; and/or

(2) The period of time between acquisition of an investment property and the sale of that property.

INVESTOR ADVICE

Under Definition No. (1), maximum return on investment is primarily determined by proper timing. This is achieved by minimizing holding costs and selecting the proper period of economic activity.

Under Definition No. (2), maximizing the return on investment is a function of the timing of the sale, judicial use of improvement funds to optimize property marketability, and good management and accurate estimation of future economic conditions.

SEE ALSO: DEMOGRAPHICS, HOLDING COSTS, and RETURN ON INVESTMENT.

HOLDOVER TENANT

A holdover tenant is one who remains in possession of property after the expiration of a lease.

INVESTOR ADVICE

In periods of a stable economy, it may be advantageous to provide for holdover tenancy from month-to-month in lieu of a new lease. This provision should be avoided, however, where rental rates are rising as a results of inflation and vacancy factors are very low or non-existent. Good management techniques will provide you with the correct option.

You should maintain a computer database or manual system which will alert you to approaching lease terminations. Thus, you will be able to take appropriate action prior to the expiration of all leases.

SEE ALSO: TENANT, TENANCY AT WILL, TENANCY FROM MONTH-TO-MONTH, TENANCY FROM YEAR-TO-YEAR, and TENANT SELECTION CRITERIA.

HOLOGRAPHIC WILL

A holographic will is a last will and testament written by hand. Holographic wills are acceptable in most states. The author's signature must be proven, however, before the instrument can be entered into probate.

INVESTOR ADVICE

The property offered for sale by an executor who has been appointed by a holographic will should be carefully considered. Whereas holographic wills are legal in most states, the handwriting must be proven authentic by testimony of one or more persons who knew the deceased and his/her handwriting. In most cases settlement of the estate will present few problems. However, large and valuable estates are sometimes subject to challenge by those who feel they were not adequately provided for by the terms of the will.

Most states protect a surviving spouse from being disinherited. If unhappy with the terms, he/she can usually dissent from the will and receive that which is designated for a spouse whose husband/wife died intestate.

Holographic wills, prepared by laymen, are often deficient in many important aspects. They usually designate an executor but often are mute to the point of who is to settle the estate if the person designated is unable or unwilling to serve. In such cases, the probate judge will appoint an administrator for the estate.

While holographic wills may clearly indicate the desires of the decedent, the procedures outlined may not be the most efficient from an estate tax viewpoint. It is recommended that professional advice be utilized in the preparation of your will, particularly if your estate contains investment real estate.

When considering the purchase of estate property, be sure to ask if the executor or administrator conducting the sale is authorized, at that time, to make a deal or whether the offer must be court-approved. You should also determine:

- If the property has been appraised for estate purposes; and

- Who did the appraisal, the value determined, and date of that value. Tax laws allow a choice of two dates; (1) the date of death; or (2) six months after death.

SEE ALSO: ADMINISTRATOR(IX), EXECUTOR(IX), LETTERS TESTAMENTARY, PROBATE, and WILL OF DECENT.

HOMEOWNER'S ASSOCIATION

A homeowner's association is the administrative body charged with the management of a condominium project. The association manages the common resources and assets of the project, sets maintenance fees which are charged to the unit owners, establishes policies and procedures regarding use of common amenities, and authorizes expenditure of association funds.

INVESTOR ADVICE

One of the most common problems of condominium ownership is the relationship with the owner's association. Those persons elected to conduct the day-to-day business do not always please everyone. Your particular desires may have to be subordinated to the will and direction of the majority.

> **BEWARE** Purchase of a condominium in which the developer is, in effect, the Homeowner's Association can result in many problems.

New projects are particularly vulnerable to problems. In the beginning, the developer *is the association,* until such time as the majority of the units are sold. The developer typically sets a low unrealistic maintenance rate in order to sell units. When the elected association takes over, they invariably find that rates must be increased to meet projected budget needs.

Developers sometimes drag their heels in finishing the project, completing the tennis courts, swimming pools, and other facilities. This produces friction between the association and developer, and too often between owners as well.

An existing project can be much more thoroughly evaluated than a new one. Before buying a condominium, you should determine the following:

* Has the project existed long enough to validate the size of the maintenance fees?

* Does the association work in reasonable harmony with the elected day-to-day managers?

* What does the association own? A golf course adjacent to the project with a free membership means nothing if the developer has retained title to the property. One day you may find that the golf course has been sold and your free membership worth exactly what you paid for it—nothing. Even more upsetting is an offer by the developer to sell the golf course to the membership which will require each to contribute a proportionate share of the purchase price.

SEE ALSO: CONDOMINIUM.

HOMEOWNER'S INSURANCE

Homeowner's insurance is an insurance package sold by most casualty insurance companies to homeowners only. The package includes protection against loss to the structure, household and personal effects, and limited personal liability.

INVESTOR ADVICE

Homeowner's insurance is only available for owner-occupied property. Rental property can be similarly covered, but under different policy types and rates.

If the property is vacant, fire and other physical hazard insurance is almost prohibitive in cost. You may want to consider offering a discount or even free rent to a tenant in order to procure coverage at reasonable rates.

> **WARNING** Homeowner policies assumed from a former owner are not valid for rental properties. Consult your insurance agent.

If you should vacate your residence, make sure that your insurance company is so advised, within the time limit set by your policy. Failure to do so may cancel your policy.

All mortgage lenders will insist on insurance coverage, with an endorsement which will cover their loan commitment in the event of a loss. Most mortgage companies will require a coverage similar to HO-II or equivalent. When closing on a residential purchase, you will be required to prove insurance coverage by submitting a policy or insurance binder, with appropriate endorsement, to the closing officer.

SEE ALSO: CLOSING COSTS, HAZARD INSURANCE, and MORTGAGE.

HOMESTEAD

A homestead is a residence on which the owner has filed an official homestead declaration. This act protects the owner against judgments up to a specific amount set by the state. In some cases this exemption may also reduce your property tax.

INVESTOR ADVICE

When considering the purchase of residence, determine if the tax rate can be reduced by a homestead exemption. If so, inquire whether this exemption will apply to you after the property is purchased.

A homestead declaration is a claim against realty belonging to the owner. In most states, the homestead declaration protects a stipulated amount of the equity from claims of judgment and mechanic's lien-holders. When a property is required to be sold to satisfy a lien-holder, the homestead exempt amount will be paid to the owner before payments are made to lien-holders.

SEE ALSO: HOMESTEAD TAX EXEMPTION, JUDGMENT, and LIEN.

HOMESTEAD TAX EXEMPTION

A homestead tax exemption covers all or part of the normal property tax due on a property which has been officially designated as a homestead.

INVESTOR ADVICE

Investment property, other than one's residence, is not eligible for a homestead exemption. If you are contemplating buying or now own property in a state in which homestead exemption is authorized, you should file for that tax relief.

The tax relief available to a homeowner varies from a token amount in some states to as much as 50% in states such as Florida.

SEE ALSO: ASSESSMENTS, HOMESTEAD, and PROPERTY RIGHTS.

HOSKOLD METHOD

The Hoskold method is a capitalization method which provides for a return *on* investment plus a return *of* the investment. The return of the investment is calculated on a periodic payment (annuity) basis where the annuity is reinvested at a safe rate and returned at the end of the holding period.

INVESTOR ADVICE

The Hoskold method can best be understood by examination of an illustration of a typical investment situation.

EXAMPLE

Mr. Gold is contemplating the purchase of a warehouse building which provides a triple-net income of $40,000 per year.

The risk would indicate a need for a return of 9.0% per annum. The safe rate of return, at local banks, is 6.0%. The land is valued at $30,000. The expected lifetime of the warehouse is estimated to be thirty-five years. What is the value of the property, using the Hoskold capitalization technique?

Total Annual Income	$40,000
Income attributable to	
Land @ 9% return	(3,600)
Building Income	$36,400
Recapture Rate @ 6% for	
35 years	0.0090*
Add: Required Return	0.0900
Capitalization Rate	0.0990 or 9.9%
Building Value = $36,400/.0990 =	$367,677
Add Back: Land Value	30,000
Total Value	$397,677

*Assumes annual annuity which is invested at 6% for 35 years to return the investment at the end of the period.

The Hoskold technique contains several potential errors:

(1) Recapture is based on payment received and immediately reinvested at the assumed rate. In reality, this situation is seldom true.

(2) The safe rate is assumed to be uniform for the entire recapture period.

(3) The improvement (building) is assumed to have no value at the end of the holding period. An examination of depreciation tables will indicate that some value usually remains at the end of the projected lifetime. For instance, the Marshall Appraisal Service shows that a Class "A" warehouse will have a projected life of fifty-five years.[2] The remaining value at that time is still about 25%.

(4) No allowance is made for potential inflation/deflation during the holding period.

SEE ALSO: SAFE RATE, RETURN OF INVESTMENT, and RETURN ON INVESTMENT.

HOSTILE POSSESSION

Hostile possession of a property occurs when an owner's consent is not given.

INVESTOR ADVICE

Hostile possession of property can occur in two situations:

(1) Property is seized or possessed without the owner's permission. Such possession, if left unchallenged, may result in a claim of adverse possession.

(2) Continued possession of rented property after expiration of the lease or rental agreement. In this case, you should reject any proffered rental payments or it will be deemed that the tenant is on a month-to-month or similar basis.

Each state has prescribed methods for dispossession of tenants or others in hostile possession. Consult your legal council for advise on actions to be taken to protect your property rights.

Utah law provides for the forcible eviction of tenants at the end of their lease. The landlord is also due reasonable rent for the holdover period. When a landlord accepts rental payments after the expiration of the lease, the lease is transformed into a periodic estate for the length of the payment period. Other states have different but similar laws.

SEE ALSO: ADVERSE POSSESSION, EVICTION, LANDLORD, PROPERTY RIGHTS, and TENANT.

HOUSING AND URBAN DEVELOPMENT (HUD)

The Housing and Urban Development (HUD) agency is a federal agency formed by an act of Congress in 1968 to assist in urban redevelopment and provide funds for low-income housing. The Federal Housing Administration (FHA) and Government National Mortgage Association (GNMA) are a part of HUD.

INVESTOR ADVICE

The national policy of assisting low-income citizens to obtain adequate housing was further modified by the acts of 1974, which added eight titles or programs. These were:

TITLE NO.	TOPIC
I	Community Development
II	Assisted Housing
III	Mortgage Credit Assistance
IV	Comprehensive Planning
V	Rural Housing
VI	Mobile Home Construction, Safety, and Standards
VII	Consumer Home Mortgage Association
VIII	Miscellaneous

SEE ALSO: FEDERAL HOUSING ADMINISTRATION (FHA), and GOVERNMENT NATIONAL MORTGAGE ASSOCIATION (GNMA).

HYPOTHECATE

A hypothecate pledge is made to a creditor as security for a debt or other demand, without the transfer of title or loss of possession.

INVESTOR ADVICE

A mortgage given in return for a loan is a prime example of hypothecation. You continue to be the owner of record and in possession of the property.

Hypothecation also occurs when an owner of a mortgage sells or pledges as security an instrument in which he/she has an interest.

SEE ALSO: DISCOUNTED PAPER, LIEN, MORTGAGE, and TRUST DEED.

ENDNOTES

[1]Marshall & Swift Publication Company, *Residential Cost Handbook* (Los Angleles, Calif., 12-87 Ed.), p. D-11.

[2] Marshall & Swift Publication Company, *Marshall Evaluation Service* (Los Angeles, Calif., 1988), Sections 15 and 97.

I

IFA Appraiser
IFAC Appraiser
IFAS Appraiser
Implied Easement
Implied Warranty Doctrine
Impounds
Improvements
Imputed Interest
Inchoate
Income Approach to Value
Income Multiplier
Income Stream
Income Tax
Incurable Depreciation
Individual Metering
Industrial Building
Industrial Park
Industrial Property
Inflation

Ingress
Inheritance Taxes
Installment Land Contract
Installment Payment
Insulation
Insulation "R" Value
Insurable Interest
Insurance
Insurance Value
Interest Computing
Interest-Only Loan
Internal Rate of Return (IRR)
Interpolation
Inter Vivoce Trust
Intestate
Investment Income
Inwood Method
Irrigation Water

I

IFA APPRAISER

An IFA appraiser is a member of the National Association of Independent Fee Appraisers (NAIFA), who is certified to appraise residential properties.

INVESTOR ADVICE

An NAIFA member who indicates a designation of IFA has achieved the following[1]:

- Completed an acceptable membership application;
- Completed a narrative appraisal report/single-family residence; and
- Met appraisal/education experience—requirement currently in effect at the time the designation was awarded.

The IFA designation indicates that the appraiser is considered fully competent to perform residential appraisals: while he/she is not restricted to this type of appraisal, the member is limited by the Association's code of ethics from accepting any assignment which he/she is not fully competent to perform.

You would not normally expect an appraiser with the IFA designation to be able to perform commercial, income property, or land appraisals. However, if he/she has completed the additional courses required for the IFA'S designation and has considerable experience in these more difficult assignments, he/she may then be considered.

SEE ALSO: IFAC APPRAISER, and IFAS APPRAISER.

IFAC APPRAISER

An IFAC appraiser is a member of the National Association of Independent Fee Appraisers, who has achieved that association's highest designation of Counselor Member.

INVESTOR ADVICE

A member of NAIFA who indicates a designation of IFAC has achieved the following[2]:

- Has been a senior member for a minimum of three (3) years at the time application for the designation was made; and
- Has submitted a thesis of an actual counselling experience, which has been approved by the National Education Committee and the Board of Directors of the NAIFA.

A member with the IFAC designation is considered fully capable of appraising all types of property or conducting counselling studies related to real estate development, value or feasibility.

A member of NAIFA with the designation IFAS would also be able to perform studies and conduct counselling, provided he had sufficient experience. Your best indication of this capability would be a check of his/her references with former clients.

SEE ALSO: IFA APPRAISER, and IFAS APPRAISER.

IFAS APPRAISER

A senior member of the National Association of Independent Fee Appraisers with the IFAS designation has achieved that association's second highest designation.

INVESTOR ADVICE

The IFAS designation indicates the following achievements[3]:

- Has completed an acceptable membership application;
- Has successfully passed the IFAS senior examination;
- Has submitted a narrative demonstration appraisal report, conforming with the prescribed guidelines, of an improved income producing property, which was approved by the Educational Committee of the NAIFA. The property may have been commercial, industrial, institutional, special purpose, farm or ranch income property, or a multi-family residential consisting of eight or more units; and
- Has met the appraisal/education experience requirements in effect at the time the senior member designation was awarded.

This member has completed all of the required course work for NAIFA's highest earned designation. The next highest designation is primarily based on demonstrated experience and a membership time requirement.

SEE ALSO: IFA APPRAISER, and IFAC APPRAISER.

IMPLIED EASEMENT

An implied easement is apparent by past and continued use, but is not officially recorded.

INVESTOR ADVICE

State laws regarding implied easements vary in small detail but generally follow the same concept. An easement is created by *implication* at the time an owner conveys a realty parcel and with that parcel whatever is necessary for the grantee to use and enjoy, while at the same time the grantor retains whatever is necessary for the grantor to enjoy the property that remains after the conveyance.

Although most states require easements to be in writing, they may be created by other means, such as:

- Implication;
- Estoppel;
- Necessity;
- Prescription;
- Encroachment; and
- Extended use and enjoyment.

When buying or proposing to buy any property, your personal inspection should discover any possible implied easements or public usage which could result in a claim of adverse possession. Such usage can prevent the planned development or redevelopment of the property, thereby greatly reducing its market value. Where unauthorized usage has continued for a number of years or is suspected, you must determine the legal status of that use prior to making an offer to purchase.

These possibilities emphasize the need for personal on-site inspection prior to purchase. If the property has been appraised by a competent appraiser, implied easements or potential claims of adverse possession will undoubtedly be noted in the report.

But what if the appraiser has missed this problem? Would you have a claim against the appraiser? Probably not, if it was a problem considered evident to the average buyer and excused under the rule of caveat emptor. Listed here are some obvious indicators that an easement may exist:

- No evidence of fences to delineate the boundaries of the parcel to be purchased;

- A roadway along one or more boundaries, which indicates constant or continuous use;

- Buildings or other improvements located very close or adjacent to the indicated boundary lines;

- An official plat of the property showing different ownership of property to the rear with no obvious means of ingress and egress; and

- Property in use by other than the owner, with no indication of an existing and valid lease.

SEE ALSO: ADVERSE POSSESSION, CAVEAT EMPTOR, EASEMENT, ENCROACHMENT, ESTOPPEL, and PRESCRIPTION.

IMPLIED WARRANTY DOCTRINE

An implied warranty doctrine is:

1. A modern court determination, in many states, which rules that a lease of an apartment or dwelling to a tenant implies that the landlord will maintain the property in a habitable condition.
2. A common law assumption that a legal instrument, such as a grant deed, implies certain warranties, even though not specifically mentioned in that instrument.

INVESTOR ADVICE

When preparing and signing leases of real property, make sure that you are fully cognizant of your rights and obligations as a landlord. Many legal instruments have implied obligations not specifically mentioned in the instrument being signed.

Most deeds, other than the quit claim deeds, have implied warranties as to title. The use of title search (preliminary reports) and title insurance will minimize problems resulting from property transfers which later prove deficient.

Implications are also applicable to contracts, such as those established by a duly signed earnest money receipt and offer to purchase. It is implied that both parties will cooperate in concluding the transaction in a timely and efficient manner.

SEE ALSO: LANDLORD, LEASE, TENANT, TITLE INSURANCE, TITLE REPORT, and WARRANTY DEED.

IMPOUNDS

Impounds are trust accounts established by a lender to collect and hold periodic payments to assure payment of taxes, insurance, and mortgage insurance fees (FHA, PMI, etc.).

INVESTOR ADVICE

Recent government regulations provide that lenders cannot hold impounds on an interest-free basis, except with the approval of the mortgagor. Most lenders will not pay interest on impounds since they consider the cost of administration of funds more or less equal to interest due. Therefore, it is their policy to inform you that you may have a choice:

(1) Receive interest on impounds and no service; or
(2) Receive no interest on impounds but receive the service of tax and other payments made on a timely basis.

As a mortgagor, you must choose one or the other alternative listed. Your decision will undoubtedly rest on the size of interest payments lost versus your ability and desire to handle the various insurance and tax bills in a timely manner.

At closing your lender will require one or two months of taxes and one or two months of insurance be deposited in the impound account. This will ensure that sufficient funds are available in the account to pay the bills as received. The actual amounts to be impounded will depend upon the dates when payments must be made and the time allowed from the billing to the last permissible payment date.

SEE ALSO: CLOSING COSTS, HAZARD INSURANCE, and PROPERTY MANAGEMENT.

IMPROVEMENTS

Improvements are additions or modification to a land parcel which become part of the property and increase its market value.

INVESTOR ADVICE

One normally thinks of improvements in terms of fences, buildings, roads, and similar additions, but there are other additions which are also considered improvements. These would include:

• Topographic grading;

• Drainage systems;

• Sidewalks, curbs, and gutters;

• Landscaping;

• Landfill;

• Sanitary sewer installations; and

• Additions of improved access to the property by purchase or granted easement.

SEE ALSO: APPURTENANCES, EASEMENT, and RIGHT-OF-WAY.

IMPUTED INTEREST

Imputed interest is taxable interest deemed received by a taxpayer as a result of a contract sale or purchase of a debt obligation, even though that interest was not actually received.

INVESTOR ADVICE

Deferred payment contracts entered into prior to July 23, 1975, often contained provisions for very low interest or no interest at all. This procedure eliminated the requirement for tax payments on all or a portion of interest received. The interest not received was added to the contract selling price. Thus the actual interest was taxable as a capital gain (lower rate).

All deferred payment sales after the 1975 date required a minimum interest of 6%, and sales prior to that date 4%, to avoid the imputed interest procedure. Of course the 1986 tax law changes, which basically eliminated the capital gains tax advantage, also virtually eliminated the advantage of no and/or low interest contacts, since all gains from then on were now taxed as regular income.

Similarly, short-term sales of certain non-government and governmental obligations are now subject to the imputed interest provisions. The Tax Reform Act of 1986 made some clarifications to this portion of the law, but no basic changes.

You should be aware of the imputed interest provisions when setting terms of sales with less than the going rates of interest. There continues to be constant pressure for tax law changes, which would give some preference for long-term capital gains over normal income. Most advisors expect a change in the near future. Based upon this expectation, it may still be wise to accept minimum interest and an increased sales price in lieu of normal interest. Consult your CPA or other tax advisor *prior* to signing any agreement of sale.

SEE ALSO: CAPITAL GAINS, CONTRACT, and INVESTMENT INCOME.

INCHOATE

"Inchoate" is a legal term meaning started but not completed.

INVESTOR ADVICE

An example of the inchoate term as applied to real estate is in those states which recognize a dower right. The inchoate dower refers to the anticipated interest of her husband's land. An interest that, in those states, cannot be overthrown by the husband or by his will. Therefore, the wife holds a contingent or inchoate interest in the husband's property during his lifetime. Some states permit the wife to take a portion of the husbands personal and real estate holdings in place of the dower interest[4].

SEE ALSO: DOWER, and LIS PENDENS.

INCOME APPROACH TO VALUE

The income approach to value is an appraisal technique in which the income produced by a property is capitalized to produce an estimate of value of that property.

INVESTOR ADVICE

Whereas the three basic approaches to determining property value, cost or replacement, market, and income, are applicable in various situations, the income approach is mandatory and the most applicable method in the evaluation of income-producing property. A buyer of income property is interested in three things:

(1) The annual income produced, after payment of expenses;
(2) Potential capital gains at the time the property is sold; and
(3) The cash flow from the operation.

An investment buyer cares little about the reproduction cost. He/she *is* interested in what the market is saying about the value, as he/she does not want to pay more than absolutely necessary, even though a certain asking price may meet his/her investment objectives.

The income derived from the investment is most critical in an investor's decision to buy, hence the importance of the income approach to value. In the income approach, it is normal for the appraiser to use the net income plus the increase in equity through mortgage payments in his/her calculations.

It is not unusual for the appraiser to refrain from deducting taxes payable from these figures, as various individuals are taxed at different rates. With the passage of the 1986 tax laws, which reduce the tax rate to a maximum (after the transition period) rate of 28% for most real estate investors, appraisers will undoubtedly begin to include the tax deduction.

When you review an appraisal of a prospective purchase, you must pay particular attention to the following aspects of the appraiser's income analysis:

- Has the appraiser included all expenses, cash and non-cash, when computing the net income or net income after taxes?

- Are the appraiser's estimates of unknown or estimated expenses logical?

- Are the appraiser's projections of future gross income and vacancy factors reasonable?

- Has the appraiser developed his/her capitalization rate accurately and logically.

- Is that capitalization rate supported by current market data? It is not uncommon to find an appraisal which does an excellent job of determining projected income, but fails to indicate how the capitalization rate was obtained. The reader is often left with the impression that the rate was chosen to give a predetermined value, rather than by some logical method. You should reject any appraisal which fails in this respect.

SEE ALSO: COST APPROACH TO VALUE, ELLWOOD PREMISE, EQUITY BUILD UP, HOSKOLD METHOD OF CAPITALIZATION, MARKET APPROACH TO VALUE, and NET INCOME AFTER TAXES.

INCOME MULTIPLIER

An income multiplier is a factor equal to the selling price (of a property) divided by the income from an investment property. Income multipliers may be expressed as annual or monthly factors of either gross or net income.

INVESTOR ADVICE

The income multiplier is a very useful tool of the market approach, as it gives a quick evaluation of a property in comparison with other properties recently sold. The multiplier (factor) is derived by dividing the true sales price by the income (net or gross) produced by that property.

EXAMPLE

A certain apartment house was recently sold for $250,000 cash. The net income from the property was $22,500 per year. What is the net income multiplier?

$$Monthly\ Income\ Multiple\ =\ \frac{Cash\ Sales\ Price}{Year\ Income/12}$$

$$MIM\ =\ \$250,000/\ \frac{\$22,500}{12}\ =\ 133.33$$

If the appraiser determines that the above multiplier represents the market, he might conclude that the property he is appraising, with a net income of $2,000/mo. was valued at:

$$\$2,000 \times 133.33\ =\ \$266,667 \qquad Rounded\ to:\ \$267,000$$

Income multipliers developed by appraisers should always be carefully examined, particularly net income multipliers. Appraisers often overlook some expenses conveniently forgotten by sellers in order to provide a more favorable picture. Too, non-cash expenses such as reserves for redecoration and replacement of equipment are often not shown on financial statements, unless actually expensed during the accounting period being examined

Due to the difficulty of obtaining good and accurate net income figures, many appraisers prefer to use gross income figures which can be more easily verified.

SEE ALSO: GROSS RENT MULTIPLIER, MARKET APPROACH TO VALUE, and NET RENT MULTIPLIER.

INCOME STREAM

The income flow expected from a property during the projected holding period is called the income stream. The income is usually, but not always, expressed in cash flow terms (net income less debt service).

INVESTOR ADVICE

When examining income flow, you must consider the fact that money received at some time in the future is not the same as cash in hand:

EXAMPLE

Mr. Smith has estimated that his office building will be valued at $500,000 by the end of his projected holding period in ten years. Mr. Smith considers that his investments should earn at least 12% per year. What is the present value of the office building sale at the end of the ten-year holding period?

$$PV\text{-}1^{10\ Yrs.,12\%}\ =\ 0.3220*$$

Building Sale Present Value = $500,000 x 0.3220 = $160,987
Rounded to: $161,000

* See table, Present Value of One.

The Hoskold Method consideration of this present worth factor has been made. You should become familiar with the concept of present worth and learn to use one of the many available financial calculators, which make it easy to compute the present values of income flows or present value of lump sums received in the future.

SEE ALSO: PRESENT VALUE OF ONE, HOSKOLD METHOD, and PRESENT VALUE OF ONE PER PERIOD.

INCOME TAX

Income tax is levied by the federal, state, or local government on taxable income. Income taxes are payable by corporations, trusts, and individuals. Income taxes due from limited partnerships, ordinary partnerships, proprietorships, and Subchapter "S" corporations are paid by the individual owners or participants in those organizations.

INVESTOR ADVICE

When you become a real estate investor, you must do one of two things: (1) Become personally knowledgeable of income tax laws which will affect your investment; or (2) Consult a tax specialist before agreeing to buy or sell property.

Even if you become well-informed on tax matters, the selling or buying of properties involving large dollar amounts should prompt you to check with your tax advisor prior to making a commitment. Often subtle changes in tax laws may go unnoticed to the casual observer. Your tax advisor will be aware of any changes which will affect your proposed transaction and will advise you accordingly.

The Tax Reform Act (TRA) of 1986 has complicated the income tax structure, while effectively reducing the rate of payment. Prior to 1986, we were concerned with: (1) income; and (2) capital gains—long and short. Now everything is income, but income has been subdivided into three classes:

(1) Earned income, from labor and services rendered;

(2) Investment income, received in the form of dividends and interest on investments; and

(3) Passive income, received from ownership in any real estate or business in which the participant is not materially active.

It is no longer possible to deduct passive losses against other income. Passive losses are only deductible against passive gains, or they can be carried forward to be deducted in future years. The principal effect of this tax change is to make each property stand on its own in profitability. This has had a depressing effect on the sale of limited partnerships, which considered losses to their participants as good as income.

SEE ALSO: ACTIVE INCOME, INVESTMENT INCOME, and TAX REFORM ACT OF 1986 (TRA).

INCURABLE DEPRECIATION

Incurable depreciation is a reduction in value due to a defect which cannot be or is not economical to cure.

INVESTOR ADVICE

Incurable depreciation can be one of three types:

(1) Physical, due to wear and tear above that corrected by normal maintenance;

(2) Economic, usually due to factors beyond your control. This can be the result of economic conditions in the area or a change in the desirability of that area; and

(3) Functional, largely resulting from the changes in more modern building design, which then reduces the usefulness of older property to the average user/buyer.

A close personal inspection or an inspection by a qualified specialist may reveal foundation instability, cracks, or other structural depreciation which would be more costly to correct than to buy a new building. This incurable depreciation is usually sufficient to change your intentions to buy.

When the earnest money receipt and offer to purchase has been properly prepared, it will state that the buyer has the right to personally inspect the property and that the offer is contingent upon his/her approval of that inspection.

Owners placing property on the market for sale are prone to plaster, paint, or paper over cracks which reveal settlement or other structural problems. When the proposed property is in an area subject to subsidence, earthquake disturbances, known ground instability, or termite infestation, it is advisable to hire a competent building inspector who can discover hidden defects, not visible to the untrained eye.

Your personal knowledge of the area and its future desirability is the best bet against unanticipated economic depreciation. Your personal experience in renting to others will avoid a purchase where functional depreciation is likely to become a significant factor during your projected holding period.

SEE ALSO: ECONOMIC DEPRECIATION, DEPRECIATION, FUNCTIONAL DEPRECIATION, and PHYSICAL DEPRECIATION.

INDIVIDUAL METERING

Individual metering refers to separate gas, electric, and/or water systems with individual meters for each tenant of a commercial or residential complex designed to be occupied by more than one tenant.

INVESTOR ADVICE

Older properties seldom have individual metering for utility use. These systems can be converted to separate metering systems if utility entrances and distribution is in an unfinished attic or basement space. If contained within the ceilings or walls, the cost will probably be very large. Where an inspection of the facilities shows that it will be prohibitive to install separate meters, a substitute method can be employed.

As leases are negotiated, the matter of utility bills can be specified as a proportional billing, by the landlord, based on the total bill for the building/complex and the percentage of total building/complex occupied by each tenant. For example, in a building with four equal-sized apartments, each tenant would pay one-quarter of each utility, electric, water, etc., bill.

Even though this method is a reasonable alternative, it can be subject to abuse by one or more tenants who make no attempt to conserve. It can also be unfair if various tenants have unusual needs which dictate greater than or less than average use of a particular utility.

A second alternative would be to price the rentals to include all utility services. This method will require a research of utility bills for prior years in order to establish the average cost of these services.

Most utility companies can provide these historical figures from their computer banks. The seller's accounting records may also be adequate for the purpose. *WARNING:* Where this alternative is selected, don't forget to provide an escalator clause in the lease to provide for utility rate increases. This is extremely important in long-term leases.

SEE ALSO: SEPARATE METERING, and UTILITIES.

INDUSTRIAL BUILDING

An industrial building is designed and built to be used for industrial purposes.

INVESTOR ADVICE

> **CONSIDER** Industrial buildings for ease of management.

Industrial buildings should be seriously considered for your real estate portfolio. Management of these properties is much simpler than residential projects for the following reasons:

* Leases are generally longer than those for residential units;

* Leases are most often on a net[4] basis (lessor responsible for maintenance, taxes, and insurance);

* On-site management is seldom required;

* It is easier to obtain credit data on a company than on an individual;

* Major company tenants are usually able to pay their bills, even if they decide to abandon the property during the lease period; and

* Industrial buildings are inherently more ruggedly built and subject to fewer maintenance problems.

SEE ALSO: NET LEASE.

INDUSTRIAL PARK

An industrial park is a land parcel developed for multi-tenant use and zoned for industrial occupants. Industrial parks are normally subdivided into half- to-five-acre lots which are used for light industrial purposes.

INVESTOR ADVICE

Industrial parks are not restricted to light industrial purposes by small- to medium-sized businesses, but are more likely to be so occupied as heavy industrial needs require more land.

Industrial parks are typically characterized by open spaces which have been attractively landscaped. Outside storage and other objectionable uses are usually restricted to walled-in enclosures.

Such a park is not restricted to industrial users only but may also include banks, restaurants, and other facilities required to serve the employees and businesses located within the park. While rail facilities may be provided, most parks depend upon truck traffic to deliver supplies and carry out finished goods.

The development of an industrial park is quite different than a residential project. Local zoning requirements will probably dictate wider streets, and installation of electric, gas, water and telephone facilities which are designed for much heavier use than residential. Water, for instance, must be adequate for industrial users but may also have to accommodate the sudden demands of fire sprinkling systems as well. Telephone facilities must be adequate for business use, which may mean 100 or more lines per facility, all of which are data grade.

If you are planning an industrial park, good estimates of the time to sell the developed lots are very important. It may be necessary to invest large sums in land, utilities, roads, and other improvements before any income is forthcoming.

It is suggested that land acquisition be made on a lot release basis, wherever possible, to minimize your initial cash outlay. Construction of roads, curbs, gutters, and utility lines should be in incremental phases and in a quantity that minimizes cost. Obviously the cost will be excessive if the increments are too small. On the other hand an optimum size can be cost efficient when holding costs are considered.

SEE ALSO: HOLDING COSTS, LOT RELEASE SYSTEM, RESTRICTIVE COVENANTS, and ZONING.

INDUSTRIAL PROPERTY

Industrial property is land or improved property zoned for industrial use. Zoning of industrial property is normally subdivided into light and heavy industrial categories having designations such as M-1 for light and M-2 for heavy.

INVESTOR ADVICE

In selecting land for future development for heavy industrial use, the availability of rail facilities should be a strong consideration. Most buyers of industrial sites will have a requirement for raw material receipt by rail as well as the eventual shipment of their finished products.

The installation of rail spurs is a different process than the provision of other facilities. Rail lines are usually provided by the railroad company having the nearest roadbed. However, the developer is expected to pay for the installation, but will be reimbursed over a period of years on the basis of freight shipped. It is the usual practice for the ownership of the track and track equipment to remain with the railroad company to ensure adequate safety and maintenance. Land ownership is subject to negotiation.

Your initial planning should include a discussion with any and all railroad companies capable of providing service to the project. They will be able to assist in site planning as well as provide accurate cost estimates.

SEE ALSO: INDUSTRIAL BUILDING, and INDUSTRIAL PARK.

INFLATION

Inflation is an increase in the cost (price level) of goods and services, due to a fall in the value of currency and/or a rise in the cost of labor. Inflation is primarily caused by an increase in the amount of currency available in a country due to federal expenditures in excess of income, the over-printing of money, or the lack of sufficient goods to meet demand. It can also be caused by "too much money chasing too few goods."

INVESTOR ADVICE

An accurate estimation of future inflation/deflation is critical to the investment decision. A return on investment can be from two sources; (1) Property income; or (2) Capital gains the time the property is sold.

INFLATION A good bet against inflation is the ownership of real estate. Land is especially good if income is not required.

If little or no increase in value is anticipated during the holding period, an adequate return from property income only will be required to support the investment objective. If an increase in fair market value can be anticipated, the requirement for income can be correspondingly less, since a portion of the return on investment will be provided by capital gains when the property is sold. This later condition, of course, assumes that the increase in property value is real—that is, in excess of the monetary inflation rate during the same period.

SEE ALSO: CAPITAL GAINS, and RETURN ON INVESTMENT.

INGRESS

Ingress is an entrance into a property without trespassing on another. This is one of the sticks in the bundle of rights of property ownership.

INVESTOR ADVICE

Property without freedom of access is of little or no value.

Most properties will have a natural access from roads or streets. Where a parcel, formerly a part of a larger tract, is contemplated for purchase, you must be assured that access will be provided by one or more of the following:

- An adjoining public road or street;

- A right-of-way which is clearly indicated in the deed; and/or

- A perpetual easement over another's property, said easement being transferred with the property at the time of purchase.

SEE ALSO: BUNDLE OF RIGHTS, EASEMENT, and RIGHT-OF-WAY.

INHERITANCE TAXES

Inheritance taxes are state taxes levied on assets inherited and paid by the person receiving a legacy or inherited assets.

INVESTOR ADVICE

While inheritance taxes are officially paid by the person receiving the legacy, most states require the administrator(ix) or executor(ix) to collect the tax prior to making his/her payment to the recipient.

State inheritance taxes, unlike federal estate taxes, have rates which are usually based on the amount received by each individual. The tax rate is usually a sliding scale, which increases with the amount received. Each beneficiary of an estate is taxed on the amount he/she inherited, not the total value of the estate being divided.

The value of properties inherited is usually that set by federal tax laws in effect at the time of the decedent's death or six months thereafter, whichever is most advantageous to the estate and beneficiaries.

To minimize federal estate taxes and state inheritance taxes and thus maximize the amount passed on, it is necessary to constantly revise your estate planning to include or eliminate property which is acquired or sold. Changes in inheritance and estate taxes laws will also require corresponding changes in estate planning.

Only those attorneys and CPAs *versed in estate planning* are competent to advise you on these matters. The use of living and testamentary trusts, planned giving, and other tax reduction techniques are essential to estate conservation.

SEE ALSO: ESTATE PLANNING, ESTATE TAXES, GIFT TAXES, TRUST, and WILL.

INSTALLMENT LAND CONTRACT

An installment land contract is a legal contract for the sale of property in which the deed is not transferred to the buyer until the contract is paid in full. This is sometimes referred to as a conditional sales contract, land contract, or simply, contract.

INVESTOR ADVICE

Prior to the passage of the Tax Reform Act of 1986, installment sales were often used primarily to spread the gains over a number of years and thereby achieve a lower tax on the total gains. With the elimination of the numerous tax brackets and the establishment of a top level of 28% (high-income taxpayers have a surtax applied, which raises the rate to as much as 33%), the tax rate reduction will be less of an advantage.

Although there will be some advantage gained by higher-income people, there will continue to be other good reasons for all to use the contract sale. Some of these are:

- To make a sale by offering lower than the going rates of interest;

- The ability to tailor the payment schedule to the buyer's ability or desire to pay; and

- The use of payment schedules with balloon payments, not normally available through lending institutions.

When property is to be sold on a contractual basis, certain safeguards are recommended to protect the buyers and sellers.

Buyer Protection

When the purchased property is covered by a mortgage, the buyer must be assured that a portion of his/her payments are being used to make the required mortgage payments. This can be accomplished by a contract requiring the establishment of an escrow account, into which all payments are made, rather than paying the seller directly. The escrow agent is instructed to make mortgage payments first, and then pass the balance to the contract holder.

The suggested escrow agreement can also provide for timely transfer of the deed to the buyer. When all payments have been made, the escrow instructions provide for the previously signed deed to be passed to the buyer.

Without this provision getting clear title after full payment can be a problem. Suppose the buyer makes his/her final payment a short time after the seller's death and before the estate is settled. Who is empowered to sign the deed? If the escrow agreement contains this provision, the escrow agent transfers the deed upon satisfaction of the contractual terms.

Where legal, it is also wise to record a notice of contract. This will put the public on notice that a party, other than the seller, has an interest in the property. However this type of notice will not reveal the specifics of that transaction. Simply recording the contract will accomplish the same notification, but will reveal all details of the transaction.

Seller Protection

Payment to an escrow agent will assure the seller that the mortgage, taxes, and insurance payments are kept current. It will also provide for prompt notification in the event of default by the buyer. It will also eliminate any seller propensity to use the cash payments, frequently by putting off mortgage payments with the idea of catching up later.

WHEN RECORDED MAIL TO:
Elvis P. Stone
2245 S. Hastings St.
Salt LAke City, Ut.

_____
SPACE ABOVE THIS LINE FOR RECORDER

CAUTION: READ BEFORE YOU SIGN

- *This is a legally binding contract; if you do not understand it, seek legal advice before you sign.*
- *This contract is intended to be filled in by lawyers or by real estate brokers. All others seek professional advice.*
- *To assure protection of certain priority rights in the property, it is recommended that this contract and any assignments, or addenda, be recorded in the office of the applicable County Recorder.*

UNIFORM REAL ESTATE CONTRACT

1. **Parties.** This contract, made and entered into this __24th__ day of __February__ , 19 __89__ is by and between __Mary K. Smith and Bufford L. Smith__
(hereafter collectively called "Seller"), whose address is __190 N. Marion St. Salt Lake City, Ut.__

and __Broadway Investment Company, 222 S. Main Street, Salt Lake City, Ut.__
(hereafter collectively called "Buyer"), whose address is _____

2. **Property.** Seller agrees to sell and Buyer agrees to buy the real property (the "Property") located at __444 Ea.__ __Elmwood Drive,__
_____ (street address), in the City of __Sandy City__
County of __Salt Lake__ , State of Utah, described as: _____

__All of lots 26 & 27 Elmwood Estates__

3. **Date of Possession.** Seller agrees to deliver possession and Buyer agrees to enter into possession of the Property on the __1st__ day of __March__ , 19 __89__ .

4. **Price and Payment.**

   A. Buyer agrees to pay for the Property the purchase price of __One Hundred Thousand and 00/100__
   _____ Dollars ($__100,000.00__) payable at Seller's address above given,
   or to Seller's order on the following terms: __Cash at closing $25,000 (Twenty-Fife Thousand__ __dollars)__
   _____ **Dollars**
   ($__5,000.00__) down payment, receipt of which is hereby acknowledged, and the balance of __Seventy Thousnad__ __and 00/100 --__ **Dollars**
   ($__70,000.00__) to be paid as follows:

   $639.00 each 1st of month after closing, with the balance due
   payable in full March 1, 1994.

   B. Payments shall include interest at the rate of __Ten__ percent (__10.0__%) per annum on the unpaid principal balance from the date of __March 1, 1989.__ Any payment not made within __Ten__ (__10__) days of its due date shall subject Buyer to a late payment charge of __Five__ percent (__5__%) of such overdue payment, which charge must be paid before receiving credit for the late payment. The foregoing payments include a reserve for payment of [ ] taxes [ ] insurance [ ] condo fees [ ] other (explain) __None Buyer is responsible for taxes and insurance when due.__
   Initially, the reserve amount per payment is __None__ . In the event reserve payments on underlying obligations for the Property change, Seller shall give Buyer thirty (30) days written notice of change, and reserve payments herein shall be adjusted accordingly.

This form is approved by the Utah Real Estate Commission and the Office of the Attorney General. January 1, 1987.

Figure 37

C.   All payments made by Buyer shall be applied first to payment of late charges, next to Seller's payments under Section 12, with interest as provided therein, next to the payment of reserves if any, next to the payment of interest, and then to the reduction of principal. Buyer may, at Buyer's option, pay amounts in excess of the periodic payments herein provided, and such excess shall be applied to unpaid principal unless Buyer elects in writing at the time of such payment that it shall be applied as prepayment of future installments. In the event of any prepayment by Buyer, Buyer shall assume and pay all penalties incurred by Seller in making accelerated payments on any underlying obligations.

D.   When the unpaid principal balance owing under this contract is equal to or less than the total balance outstanding on the underlying obligation(s) shown in Section 8 below, then:

(1)   Upon (i) assumption by Buyer of the underlying obligation(s) and (ii) release of Seller from all liabilities and obligations thereunder, Buyer may request and Seller shall execute and deliver a Warranty Deed subject to the then existing underlying obligation(s) shown in Section 8 below; or

(2)   Provided there is no "due-on-sale" provision contained in any underlying obligation(s) shown in Section 8 below, Seller may execute and deliver to Buyer a Warranty Deed subject to the then existing underlying obligation(s) shown in Section 8 below, which Buyer agrees to assume and pay; or

(3)   In the event neither Buyer nor Seller exercises the options provided in (1) and (2) of this sub-section, and this contract therefore remains in effect, then the payments and interest rate shown in this Section, to the extent they differ from the underlying obligations, shall immediately and automatically be adjusted to equal the payments and interest rate then required under the underlying obligations, and Buyer, in addition to such adjusted payments, shall also pay a monthly servicing fee to Seller in the amount of $_____.

5.   **No Waiver.**   If Seller accepts payments from Buyer on this contract in an amount less than or at a time later than herein provided, such acceptance will not constitute a modification of this contract or a waiver of Seller's rights to full and timely performance by Buyer.

6.   **Risk of Loss.**   All risk of loss and destruction of the Property shall be borne by Seller until the agreed date of possession.

7.   **Evidence of Title.**   Buyer has received a Commitment for Title Insurance (Commitment) on the Property at the time of or prior to execution of this contract. Seller shall, at his expense, furnish Buyer evidence of marketable title in the form of an Owner's Title Insurance Policy (Title Policy) insuring Buyer's interest in the Property under this contract for the amount of the purchase price. The Title Policy will be based on Commitment No. __1928__ issued by: __Utah Title Co__. The Title Policy issued to Buyer will contain the following numbered exceptions shown on the Commitment: _____None_____

8.   **Underlying Obligations.**

A.   Seller warrants that the only underlying obligations against the Property are:
(1)   Obligation in favor of __None__

with an unpaid principal balance of _____ Dollars
($_____) as of _____, 19____ with monthly payments of $_____, with interest at _____ percent (_____%) per annum and balloon payments as follows: _____

(2)   Obligation in favor of _____

with an unpaid principal balance of _____ Dollars
($_____) as of _____, 19____ with monthly payments of $_____, with interest at _____ percent (_____%) per annum and balloon payments as follows: _____

(3)   Obligation in favor of _____

with an unpaid principal balance of _____ Dollars
($_____) as of _____, 19____ with monthly payments of $_____, with interest at _____ percent (_____%) per annum and balloon payments as follows: _____

B.   COPIES OF SUCH UNDERLYING OBLIGATIONS [ ] HAVE [ ] HAVE NOT BEEN DELIVERED TO BUYER AT OR PRIOR TO CLOSING. SUCH UNDERLYING OBLIGATIONS [ ] CONTAIN [ ] DO NOT CONTAIN DUE ON SALE OR DUE ON ENCUMBRANCE PROVISIONS.

C.   IN THE EVENT THE HOLDER OF ANY UNDERLYING OBLIGATION(S) REFERRED TO IN SUB-SECTION A. CAUSES TO BE ISSUED A WRITTEN NOTICE OF ITS INTENT TO EXERCISE ANY OF THE DUE ON SALE REMEDIES, THEN BUYER AGREES TO EITHER PAY, ASSUME OR REFINANCE SUCH UNDERLYING OBLIGATION(S) IN THE MANNER PROVIDED BELOW, AND BUYER AGREES TO PAY ALL COSTS, FEES AND CHARGES INCURRED IN CONNECTION WITH SUCH PAYMENT, ASSUMPTION OR REFINANCING (INCLUDING, BUT NOT LIMITED TO, PREPAYMENT PENALTIES, LOAN POINTS, INCREASED INTEREST RATE, APPRAISAL AND CREDIT REPORT FEES, ESCROW AND TITLE CHARGES, TITLE INSURANCE PREMIUMS, AND RECORDING FEES). BUYER'S INABILITY OR FAILURE TO PAY, ASSUME, OR REFINANCE SUCH UNDERLYING OBLIGATION(S) WITHIN FORTY-FIVE (45) DAYS FROM THE DATE OF NOTICE TO BUYER OF SUCH WRITTEN NOTICE FROM THE HOLDER, SHALL CONSTITUTE A DEFAULT BY BUYER UNDER THIS CONTRACT.

(1)   **Assumption.**   In the event buyer elects to assume such underlying obligation(s), Buyer shall be entitled to the delivery of a Warranty Deed executed by the Seller wherein the Buyer is the Grantee upon the satisfaction of the following conditions precedent: (i) Buyer is not then in default under the terms of this contract; (ii) Buyer has deposited with Seller written evidence from the holder of the underlying obligation(s) being assumed that such holder has approved Buyer's assumption; and (iii) if any portion of the Seller's equity under this contract remains unpaid, Buyer shall execute and deliver to Seller, Buyer's Trust Deed Note in a principal amount equal to the unpaid balance of Seller's equity under this contract, which shall include any accrued unpaid interest. Said note shall bear interest from the date thereof at the same rate at which interest accrues on the Seller's equity under this contract. Installments shall be made over the term then remaining and at the same time as provided for in this contract with the exact amount of the installments being calculated by re-amortizing the aforesaid

Figure 37 continued

amount of the Trust Deed Note utilizing the interest rate at which interest accrues on Seller's equity under this contract, the schedule of payments, and term specified herein. Such note shall be secured by a Deed of Trust encumbering the property which shall be subordinate only to the Deed or Deeds of Trust securing the underlying obligation(s) and any obligations refinanced as provided in sub-section C.(2).

(2) **Refinancing/Pay-Out.** In the event Buyer pays or obtains a new loan refinancing one or more of the underlying obligations, then buyer shall be entitled to the delivery of a Warranty Deed executed by the Seller wherein the Buyer is Grantee; provided, however, if any portion of the seller's equity remains unpaid, then the following conditions precedent shall have been satisfied: (i) Buyer is not then in default under any of the terms of this Contract; (ii) the principal amount of the new loan may exceed the unpaid balance of the underlying obligation(s) being refinanced only if all loan proceeds which exceed the unpaid balance of the underlying obligation(s) are paid to the Seller as a credit against the unpaid balance of Seller's equity in this Contract; and (iii) Buyer shall have executed and delivered to Seller, Buyer's Trust Deed Note in the form, the amount, and with the terms of the Trust Deed Note described in Section C(1)(iii). Such note shall be subordinate only to the Deed(s) of Trust securing the new loan(s) and any remaining Deed(s) of Trust securing the underlying obligation(s) which have not been reconveyed.

9. **Taxes and Assessments.** Buyer agrees to pay all taxes and assessments of every kind which become due on the Property during the life of this contract. Seller covenants that there are no taxes, assessments, or liens against the Property not mentioned in Section 8 except: Current taxes due for portion of 1989 which are reimbursed to buyer by closing statements this date

which will be paid by: [ ] Seller [ ]Buyer [ ] Other (explain) _____

10. **Covenant Against Liens.** Except for the liens and encumbrances listed in Sections 8 and 9, Seller covenants to keep the Property free and clear of all liens and encumbrances resulting from acts of Seller. So long as Buyer is current hereunder, Seller agrees to keep current the payments on all obligations to which Buyer's interest is subordinate. Should Seller default on the foregoing covenants on any one or more occasions, Buyer may, at Buyer's option, in whole or in part, make good Seller's default to Seller's obligee and deduct all expenditures so paid from future payments to Seller and Seller shall credit all Buyer's sums so expended to the indebtedness herein created just as if payment had been made directly to Seller under provisions of Section 4 above.

11. **Insurance.** On and after the agreed date of possession, Buyer shall maintain at Buyer's expense, the following insurance policies naming the Seller as an additional insured and with a certificate of insurance provided to Seller that includes a ten (10) day notice of cancellation in favor of Seller: (i) insurance against loss by fire and other risks customarily covered by "All Risk" insurance on insurable buildings and improvements at 80% of replacement value; and (ii) general liability insurance having coverage of not less than $_____. All such insurance policies shall be in companies which are duly licensed by the State of Utah and are acceptable to Seller. Acceptance of such companies by Seller may not be unreasonably withheld.

12. **Seller's Option To Discharge Obligations.** In the event Buyer shall default in the payment of taxes, assessments, insurance premiums or other expenses of the Property, Seller may, at Seller's option, pay said taxes, assessments, insurance premiums or other expenses, and if Seller elects so to do, Buyer agrees to repay Seller upon demand all such sums so advanced and paid by Seller together with interest thereon from date of payment of said sums at the rate of the greater of one (1%) or _Fifteen_ percent (_15_%) per month until paid, and when the principal sum provided in this contract is paid, if Buyer fails to also repay Seller such advances, Seller may refuse to convey title to the Property until such repayment is made.

13. **Conveyance of Title.** Seller on receiving the payments herein reserved to be paid at the time and in the manner specified herein, agrees to execute and deliver to Buyer or assigns, a good and sufficient warranty deed conveying the title to the above described premises free and clear of all encumbrances except those which have accrued by or through the acts or neglect of Buyer and those which Buyer has specifically agreed to pay or assume under the terms of this contract, and subject to the following numbered exceptions to title that are contained in the commitment for title insurance described in Section 7 hereof: _None_

14. **No Waste.** Buyer agrees that Buyer will neither commit nor suffer to be committed any waste, spoil or destruction in or upon the Property which would impair Seller's security, and that Buyer will maintain the Property in good condition.

15. **Attorney's Fees.** Both parties agree that, should either party default in any of the covenants or agreements herein contained, the non-defaulting party or, should litigation be commenced, the prevailing party in litigation, shall be entitled to all costs and expenses, including a reasonable attorney's fee, which may arise or accrue from enforcing or terminating this contract, or in obtaining possession of the Property, or in pursuing any remedy provided hereunder or by applicable law.

16. **Buyer's Default.** Should buyer fail to comply with any of the terms hereof, Seller may, in addition to any other remedies afforded the Seller in this contract or by law, elect any of the following remedies:

A. Seller shall give Buyer written notice specifically stating: (1) The Buyer's default(s); (2) that buyer shall have thirty (30) days from his receipt of such written notice within which to cure the default(s), which cure shall include payment of Seller's costs and reasonable attorney's fees; and (3) Seller's intent to elect this remedy if the Buyer does not cure the default(s) within the thirty (30) days. Should Buyer fail to cure such default(s) within the thirty (30) days, then Seller shall give to Buyer another written notice informing Buyer of his failure to cure the default(s) and of Seller's election of this remedy. Immediately upon Buyer's receipt of this second written notice, Seller shall be released from all obligations at law and equity to convey the Property to Buyer, and Buyer shall become at once a tenant-at-will of Seller. All payments which have been made by Buyer prior thereto under this contract shall, subject to then existing law and equity, be retained by Seller as liquidated and agreed damages for breach of this contract; or

B. Seller may bring suit and recover judgment for all delinquent installments and all reasonable costs and attorneys' fees, and the use of this remedy on one or more occasions shall not prevent Seller, at Seller's option, from resorting to this or any other available remedy in the case of subsequent default; or

C. Seller shall give Buyer written notice specifically stating: (1) The Buyer's default(s); (2) that Buyer shall have thirty (30) days from his receipt of such written notice within which to cure the default(s), which cure shall include payment of Seller's costs and reasonable attorney's fees; and (3) Seller's intent to elect this remedy if the Buyer does not cure the default(s) with the thirty (30) days. Should Buyer fail to

Figure 37 continued

cure such default(s) within the thirty (30) days, then Seller shall give to Buyer another written notice informing Buyer of his failure to cure the default(s), Seller's election of this remedy, and that the entire unpaid balance hereunder is at once due and payable. Thereupon, Seller may treat this contract as a note and mortgage, pass or tender title to Buyer subject thereto, and proceed immediately with a mortgage foreclosure in accordance with the laws of the State of Utah. Upon filing the foreclosure complaint in court, Seller shall be entitled to the immediate appointment of a receiver. The receiver may take possession of the premises, collect the rents, issue and profits therefrom and apply them to the payment of the obligation hereunder, or hold them pursuant to the order of the court. Upon entry of a judgment of foreclosure, Seller shall be entitled to possession of the premises during the period of redemption.

17. **Time of Essence.**   It is expressly agreed that time is of the essence in this contract.

18. **Warranties of Physical Condition.**   With respect to the physical condition of the Property, Seller warrants the following: —— All plumbinf, electrical and mechanical equipment to be in good working order on date of possession.

19. **Other Provisions.**   Buyer shall have the right to inspect the property prior to closing.

20. **Captions.**   Section captions shall not in any way limit, modify, or alter the provisions in the Section.

21. **Notices.**   Except as otherwise provided herein, all notices required under this contract will be effective when: (a) **personally** delivered or; (b) mailed certified or registered, addressed to the applicable party at the address shown in Section 1, or at such other address as may be hereinafter designated by such party by written notice to the other party.

22. **Binding Effect.**   This contract is binding on the heirs, personal representatives, successors and assigns of the respective parties hereto.

23. **Entire Agreement.**   This contract contains the entire agreement between the parties hereto. Any provisions hereof not enforceable under the laws of the State of Utah shall not affect the validity of any other provisions hereof. No supplement modification or amendment of this contract shall be binding on the parties hereto unless signed in writing by both parties hereto.

IN WITNESS WHEREOF, the parties have set their signatures on the day and year first above written.

BUYER: SELLER:

James L. Tafford, President
Broadway Investment Company

STATE OF UTAH
                                        ss.
COUNTY OF _____ Salt Lake _____

On the _1st_ day of _March_ , 19 _89_ personally appeared before me
Mary K & Bufford L. Smith , Seller and signer of the above instrument, who duly acknowledged to
me that _they_ executed the same.

NOTARY PUBLIC

My Commission Expires:
June 15, 1992   Residing at: Salt Lake City, Utah

STATE OF UTAH
                                        ss.
COUNTY OF _____ Salt Lake _____

On the _1st_ day of _March_ , 19 _89_ personally appeared before me
James L. Tafford, Pres. Broadway Inv Buyer and signer of the above instrument, who duly acknowledged to
me that _he_ executed the same.

NOTARY PUBLIC

My Commission Expires:
June 15, 1992   Residing at: Salt Lake City

Figure 37 continued

While a contract may be prepared to satisfy any provisions required by the seller or buyer, most contracts are completed on a standard form, such as the Utah-approved form shown in Figure 37.

These forms can be completed by REALTORS® and closing officers, without referral to attorneys.

When signing uniform contract forms, you need not be wary of any language of the form as it has been reviewed and shown to protect both the buyer's and seller's interest. You *should* pay very close attention to any additions or deletions to ensure that they are in accordance with your understanding and the terms and provisions of the earnest money receipt and offer to purchase agreement.

SEE ALSO: EARNEST MONEY RECEIPT AND OFFER TO PURCHASE, ESCROW, NOTICE OF CONTRACT, and TAX REFORM ACT OF 1986 (TRA).

INSTALLMENT PAYMENT

A periodic payment of principal and interest on a contractual agreement is an installment payment.

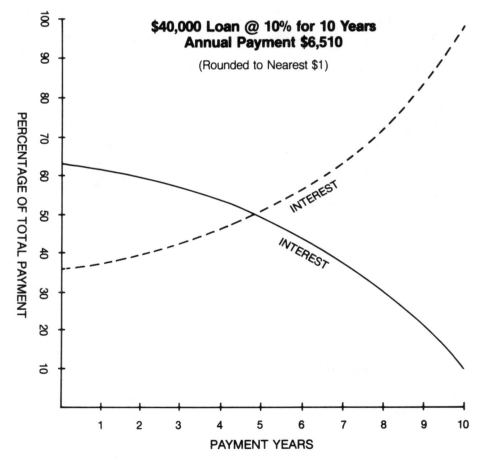

Figure 38

INVESTOR ADVICE

Installment payments are calculated to amortize a debt in a specific time period, thirty years for instance. In the early days of the payback period, a large percentage of the payment goes to pay the interest due and the small amount remaining is applied to principal. As time advances and the debt is reduced, less of the payment is applied to interest, leaving more to go towards debt reduction. The last few payments are almost all debt reduction.

Figure 38 shows a typical amortization schedule with interest and principal payments indicated as a percent of the overall payment.

A little known fact is that a thirty-year debt can be fully paid in about fifteen years, provided one additional payment is made each year. This extra payment is 100% debt reduction and results in lower interest for the remainder of the time and thus greater debt reduction with each succeeding payment. This procedure can save thousands of dollars, with little cash flow affect.

Another method of reducing the loan time period, which is rapidly gaining favor in the mortgage industry, is the twice-monthly mortgage payment. This method divides the normal monthly payment and escrows by two and requires them to be paid on the 1st and 15th of the month.

On the surface, it would appear that this would have little affect on the loan payment period, but it actually does. The twice monthly payment reduces the interest payments, since part of the principal payment is paid on the 15th of the month instead of all of it at the end of the month. The loan period reduction depends upon the interest rate, but generally this technique can reduce a normal thirty-year mortgage to the middle twenties or less.

SEE ALSO: AMORTIZATION SCHEDULE.

INSULATION

Insulation is:

1. A material applied in such a way as to reduce the flow of heat into or out of a building; and/or
2. A material used to prevent the unwanted passage of sound, light, or electricity.

INVESTOR ADVICE

When designing a new structure, the amount and type of insulation to be used must be carefully considered. The better the insulation, the lower the heating and cooling costs are, not to mention increased comfort. There are many trade-offs to be considered, such as:

- The better the insulation, the lower the heating and cooling costs but the higher the installation cost;

- The better the insulation, the lower the cost for heating and cooling equipment; and

- The higher the installation cost, the longer it takes to recoup the extra expense (payback period).

Insulation priorities, based on cost payback, are applied first to ceilings, then walls, and finally to windows and doors. Your architect can best advise you on the correct planning.

When buying existing structures, the quality and type of insulation should be carefully considered and determined. You should answer the following questions?

- What is the amount and type of installation installed?

- If found to be inadequate, what will be the cost of upgrading the insulation?

- Have any materials been previously used, which are now considered as a health hazard? (This may include foam insulation, fiberglass, asbestos, etc.)

Depending upon the severity of the climate, an optimum insulation is recommended. Figure 39 shows the recommended minimum insulation for various portions of the United States.

SEE ALSO: INSULATION "R" VALUE.

INSULATION "R" VALUE

Insulation "R" value is a quantitative measure of insulation effectiveness. The higher the number, the better the insulation.

INVESTOR ADVICE

Figure 39 shows the various climatic regions in the U.S. and the recommended insulation "R" value for average construction. Many materials can be used for insulation purposes. Insulation can be air space, the building material itself, or air space which is filled with insulating material. The following materials are the ones most often used in U.S. construction:

- Rockwool—bats and loose fill;

- Fiberglass

- Foam—put into the cavity, or applied in sheets;

- Storm windows and doors;

- Double and triple glass with air spaces;

- Special low-emissivity glass;

- Glass reflective coatings; and

- Chemically treated shredded paper.

This latter material is more economical than others but can cause problems with roof leaks carrying the chemical into the home.

Some types of foam are also not recommended due to out-gassing of harmful chemicals. Your local architect is the best advisor of what to use for maximum results at minimum cost.

SEE ALSO: INSULATION.

INSURABLE INTEREST

Insurable interest is a financial interest in the property insured. For instance an insurance policy on a property, sold on contract, would find two parties with an insurable interest—buyer and seller.

CLIMATE CLASSIFICATION KEY

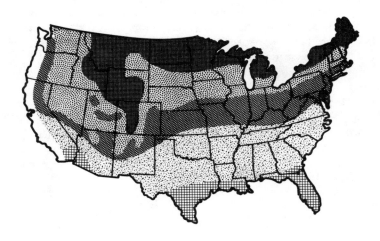

CLIMATE CLASSIFICATION:	MILD		MODERATE		EXTREME	
TYPICAL CEILING:	R-19	R-26	R-26	R-30	R-33	R-38
INSULATION WALL:	R-11	R-13	R-19	R-19	R-19	R-19
(R-VALUE) FLOOR:	R-11	R-11	R-13	R-19	R-22	R-22

FLOOR NOT INCLUDED IN SECTION A SQUARE FOOT COSTS

INSULATION REQUIREMENTS

The following table lists the typical thickness required $\pm 1/2''$ at a designated R-value for fiberglass or mineral wool insulation which is used in residential construction for the ceiling, wall, and floor areas. Rockwool is typically 1/2'' thinner than fiberglass at the same R-value. R-values are averages of unfaced, foil-faced, and kraft paper faced insulation when available.

CEILINGS

Fiberglass batt or blanket insulation
R-13 One 3-5/8'' batt
R-19 One 6-1/2'' batt
R-26 Two 3-5/8'' batt
R-30 One 6-1/2'' batt & one 3-1/2'' batt
R-35 One 7'' batt & one 3-5/8'' batt
R-38 Two 6-1/2'' batts
Loose fill wool & fiberglass batts
or blankets:
R-19 7-1/2'' wool fill or 6-1/2'' batt
R-26 2-1/2'' wool fill and 6-1/2'' batt
R-30 4-1/2'' wool fill and 6-1/2'' batt
R-38 7-1/2'' wool fill and 6-1/2'' batt

12/87
page D-10

WALLS

R-5.5 5/8'' rigid insulation board
R-7   2-1/2'' fiberglass batt
R-11 3-1/2'' fiberglass batt
R-19 3-5/8'' fiberglass batt and
      1'' polystyrene sheathing, or
      One 6-1/2'' batt

FLOORS

(Not included in Section A costs)
R-11 3-1/2'' fiberglass batt or blanket
R-13 3-5/8'' fiberglass batt or blanket
R-19 6-1/2'' fiberglass batt or blanket
R-22 7'' fiberglass batt or blanket

Figure 39

INVESTOR ADVICE

Mortgagees or contract holders will demand that a property, upon which money is owed, is adequately insured against fire, windstorm, and other hazards. Most debt instruments will also require that the parties having an insurable interest be furnished copies of the policies. If you, as the contracting party or mortgagor, fail to keep your insurance policy current, the contract or mortgage holder reserves the right to provide the required coverage at your expense.

The following is a typical clause, found in mortgages and contract forms:

Insurance: *On and after the agreed date of possession, buyer shall maintain, at buyer's expense, the following insurance policies, naming the seller/mortgagor as an additional insured and with a certificate of insurance provided to the seller/mortgagor that includes a ten (10) day notice of cancellation in favor of the seller/mortgagor: (1) insurance against fire and other risks customarily covered by "All Risk" insurance on all insurable buildings and improvements at 80% of replacement value; and (2) general liability insurance having coverage of not less than $____ * _____. All such insurance policies shall be in companies which are duly licensed in the state in which the property is located and are acceptable to the seller/mortgagor. Acceptance of such companies by seller/mortgagor may not be unreasonably withheld."*

*Usually the amount of the mortgage owed.

If your insurance is not paid as a part of monthly payments, you must provide a foolproof means of knowing when to renew the policy. Don't depend upon the agent. If he/she misses a date, he/she only misses or postpones a commission. If you miss the date and a loss occurs, you would not only suffer the property loss but the responsibility for paying the debt as well.

SEE ALSO: HAZARD INSURANCE.

INSURANCE

Insurance is a contact for protection against a loss, which the insured is unable to protect him or herself.

INVESTOR ADVICE

Owners of real property will find the need for several types of insurance. These are:

- *Title Insurance*—This protects a buyer from any unknown defects in title, which are discovered at a later date.

- *Hazard Insurance*—These may be combination or separate policies and usually cover protection from real and personal property losses due to acts of God. Flood insurance is available in some areas, but is always sold as a separate policy.

- *Liability Insurance*—These may be combination or separate policies. Liability coverage protects the owner against judgments for the injury to others on the insured's property.

- *Theft Insurance*—This protects the owner from losses due to theft or mysterious disappearances.

- *Partnership Life Insurance*—These are two or more policies made payable to partners, other than the insured. The purpose of these policies is to provide ready cash to exercise a buy/sell agreement executed by the partners.

> **NOTE** A buy/sell agreement is of no value if the buyer has no means of purchasing. Fund all buy/sell agreements with insurance or provide other means to facilitate payment.

EXAMPLE

Mr. "A" and Mr. "B" are equal partners in a shopping center. They have executed a buy/sell agreement, which authorizes a surviving partner to buy the deceased partner's share of the property. This may be at a price stated, a price established by appraisal, or a price established by a given formula.

The right to buy is a fine agreement, but of little value if the survivor has no money. Accordingly "A's" policy is made payable to "B" and "B's" policy is made payable to "A." Funds for the buyout are thus insured if either partner dies. The policies can be purchased by each of the partners or be the property of the partnership.

SEE ALSO: HAZARD INSURANCE, INSURANCE VALUE, INSURABLE INTEREST, and LIABILITY INSURANCE.

INSURANCE VALUE

Insurance value is the appraised value of a property for insurance purposes. The value is normally the improvement value less:

- Architect fees;

- Foundation below ground costs;

- Basement excavation costs;

- Landscaping and other exterior improvements including underground piping; and

- Utility connection fees.

INVESTOR ADVICE

The listed exclusions assume that, in event of loss, the structure(s) being insured would be replaced by an identical improvement and that those items will not have to be duplicated. In the case of older structures, the same identical building would normally not replace the old one; however, the maximum insurance coverage obtainable will make that assumption.

If you require an appraisal of your property for insurance purposes, it is necessary that the real estate appraiser be informed of this purpose.

SEE ALSO: CO-INSURANCE, HAZARD INSURANCE, INSURABLE INTEREST, and LIABILITY INSURANCE.

INTEREST COMPUTING

This term refers to the method for calculating the interest due on a loan or other indebtedness.

INVESTOR ADVICE

Real estate interest is quoted as "Annual Percentage Rate" (APR), which is simple interest payable at the end of the payment period for which the interest was calculated.

When closing a mortgage loan, you may be surprised to see an APR shown which is slightly higher than the quoted mortgage rate. This does not represent an increase in the mortgage rate but represents the fact that certain fees were collected up front, which adjusts the true simple interest rates slightly upwards. Federal truth in lending laws require that this be indicated to the borrower.

You will note that the amortization statement indicates the quoted mortgage interest rate for each period in the future. You will also note that when a payment is made and interest deducted, the interest was calculated on the loan balance after the last payment and for the period since that last payment.

EXAMPLE

Payment No.	Payment Amt.	Interest Due*	Principal Paid	Balance After Payment
X				$49,500.00
X + 1	$600.00	$412.50	$187.50	$49,312.50

*APR rate = 10%, monthly rate = .0083

SEE ALSO: ANNUAL PERCENTAGE RATE (APR).

INTEREST-ONLY LOAN

A interest-only loan payment requirements are for interest due only. Normally this is a short-term loan, calling for a balloon payment in the near future.

INVESTOR ADVICE

Current tax laws permit interest-only loans but will impute a minimum interest of 6% APR deduction for interest paid by the borrower and the same amount as interest income received by the lender.

There is little advantage to a short-term interest-only loan, other than it avoids the need for an amortization schedule and considerable calculations when the note is paid. In a short period of time, little principal would have been paid anyway.

Interest-only loans are normally granted to borrowers pending the receipt of moneys due, but not in time for a closing transaction.

EXAMPLE

You have recently sold a property to a buyer who is borrowing the money. His loan has been approved and a closing is scheduled in thirty days.

You are buying another property, which will be closed tomorrow. Your bank grants an interest-only loan in the amount needed to close at that time. The bank may grant the loan on your signature only or may require you to assign a portion of your interest in the earnest money receipt and offer to purchase contract which is scheduled to close in thirty days.

SEE ALSO: IMPUTED INTEREST, and TAX REFORM ACT OF 1986 (TRA).

INTERNAL RATE OF RETURN (IRR)

The internal rate of return (IRR) is the interest rate at which the present value of all periodic payments during the holding period, plus the present value of the estimated future selling price exactly equals the original investment.

INVESTOR ADVICE

In Figures 49 and 50, we can see that a payment of one dollar, received at some point in the future is not worth one dollar today (present value). The exact value is dependent upon the rate of interest with which the payment has been discounted. Similarly, a series of payments in the future is not as valuable as the sum of those payments.

Internal rate of return discounts each payment received based upon the amount received, the time of receipt, and the assumed interest rate. The internal rate of return is the assumed percentage rate which produces a sum of present values, which exactly equals the original investment. Inherent in this definition is the assumption that all payments are immediately reinvested when received, and at the internal rate.

NOTE In reality, money received is seldom invested immediately upon receipt.

In its use to calculate the IRR of a real estate investment, the payments consist of the periodic payments (yearly income) plus the estimated sales price of the investment (property) at the end of the holding period. This sales price at the end can be less, more, or the same as the initial investment. It is the original value multiplied by an inflation/deflation factor less depreciation.

Business calculators, such as the Hewlett-Packard 12-C® can easily calculate the internal rate of return of a series of payments for a given holding period. Without such calculators, it is necessary to assume an interest rate, use present value tables such as "X" and "Y", and calculate the present value sum which is then compared to the investment value.

An interest assumption which is too high will yield a sum lower than the investment and require a new try at a lower rate. An interest assumption which is too low will yield a sum higher than the investment, thus indicating the need for another try. Through trial and error, the exact internal rate of return can be found.

EXAMPLES

An investor is considering the purchase of a strip shopping center, which is currently listed for $2,000,000. The audited books indicate that the property is currently returning a net profit of $220,500 per year.

If the investor buys the property, he will probably retain it until his retirement in ten years. He estimates that the property, well maintained, will increase in value to about $2,700,000 at the time of sale.

What is the IRR indicated?

Try No. 1, est. rate = 12.5%
  PV-1/pd.12.5%,10yrs. x $220,500 = $1,220,783.00
  PV-112.5%,10yrs. x $2,700,000   =   831,454.60
                      Total   = $2,052,237.60

Since this total is too high, our interest rate assumption is apparently too low.

Try No. 2, est. rate = 13.0%
  PV-1/pd.13.0%, 10yrs. x $220,500 = $1,196,486.69
  PV-113.0%, 10yrs. x $2,700,000   =   795,388.54
                      Total   = $1,991,875.23

Our value is now slightly too low.

Try No. 3, est. rate = 12.9%

PV-1/pd.12.9%, 10yrs. x $220,000	=	$1,201,283.90
PV-112.9%, 10yrs. x $2,700,000	=	802,461.76
Total	=	$2,003,745.66

We can continue to refine our answer by moving a fraction of a percent in the right direction; however, the results from the third try appear to be reasonably correct. We can assume that the IRR for this problem is just a little less than 12.9%.

Note: The values given were obtained by the use of a book of tables, which provide factors for each 1/10%. Tables "X" and "Y" could have been used, but the results would have been less accurate and indicated a value somewhere between 12 and 14%.

SEE ALSO: PRESENT VALUE OF ONE, and PRESENT VALUE OF ONE PER PERIOD.

INTERPOLATION

Interpolation is a mathematical method of estimating a value which falls between two values of a given table of data.

INVESTOR ADVICE

Appraisers are often required to interpolate cost data given in commercial appraisal service data sheets. For example, let us suppose we need the cost of a basement containing 1,300 square feet. The appraisal data sheet shows the following:

Unfinished Basement Size	200	400	800	1200	1600
Cost/square foot	$16.93	12.64	9.56	8.11	7.22

We can see that a 1,300 square foot basement will be somewhere between the 1,200 square foot value of $8.11 and the 1,600 square foot value of $7.22. We interpolate the value by considering the fact that 1,300 lies one-fourth of the way between 1,200 and 1,600. Each quarter of the distance is:

$$(\$8.11-7.22)/4 = \$.28$$

The value interpolated for 1300 square foot is therefore:

$$\$8.11 - .28 = \$7.83$$

SEE ALSO: AVERAGE, and MEAN.

INTER VIVOCE TRUST

An inter vivoce trust is established during the lifetime of the trustor. The trust can be revocable or non-revocable, depending upon the desires and objectives of the trustor.

INVESTOR ADVICE

Prior to passage of the 1986 Tax Reform Act, living trusts were used to spread income among family members and thereby reduce the total family income tax. This ability was largely negated by the 1986 act, which requires the income of minors to be taxed at the parent's rate. Living trusts still have many useful purposes, however.

For instance, a proprietorship which is placed in a living trust and continues to be operated by the trustor (who is then designated as a trustee) will ensure the continuation of the business after the trustor's death. Otherwise, the proprietorship would cease upon the death of any partner. The business cannot be continued until the decedent's will is probated, the assets passed to the heirs, and a new partnership formed.

A partnership placed in a living trust can provide for the orderly continuation of a business when one partner dies, and/or the orderly sale of the business to the survivor(s), in accordance with a buy-sell agreement.

A living trust can also serve as a vehicle to bypass the probate system. Where the trust is revocable, the assets of the living trust are taxable in the estate of the decedent. If the trust is non-revocable, the estate will have been previously taxed as gifts or exempted therefrom.

SEE ALSO: GIFT TAXES, TRUST, and TRUSTEE.

INTESTATE

The term *intestate* refers to a legal situation resulting from a person dying without having made a will.

INVESTOR ADVICE

A real estate investor or any other person who dies without a valid will has been grossly negligent. As a result, his/her estate will suffer from excess taxation, higher administrative charges, and an estate distributed in accordance with law, rather than his/her own wishes.

A will is the basis of all estate planning. Without it, the estate must be distributed in accordance with the will provided by the state, referred to as the laws of descent and distribution. When the deceased was married, state laws generally provide for the spouse and children to share equally in the estate's assets, or possibly on an equal basis with the spouse receiving the remaining half. When the deceased was not married, the estate is distributed to the nearest relatives in some prescribed manner.

The manner of distribution is usually based on the nearness of those relatives to the deceased. Ranked in priority, these would be indicated as follows:

1st Priority—Parents and children of the deceased
2nd Priority—Grandchildren and grandparents
3rd Priority—Great grandparents

When any of the above are deceased, the estate flows to their relatives in a similar manner. For instance, if the parents are the recipients of the estate but are deceased, the estate flows to the children of the parents (decendent's brothers and sisters).

The problems no will presents are often more concerned with the cost of administration and settlement, than who gets the assets. When a will exists, the estate is generally managed by an appointee (usually a close relative), who serves without significant cost. If there is no will, it will be administered by a court appointee, who is paid for his/her time, effort, and expenses.

If the estate contains real properties, it may be necessary to sell them to raise funds for payment of the deceased's debts. Often these forced sales are conducted at an inopportune time, which produces a minimum sales price.

As an informed real estate investor, you should have a will prepared by an attorney. In lieu of this, at least prepare a holographic will to serve until a better one can be prepared.

SEE ALSO: HOLOGRAPHIC WILL, and WILL.

INVESTMENT INCOME

Investment income is:
1. As defined by the Tax Reform Act of 1986, "portfolio income" or income from bonds, certificates of deposits, savings accounts, stock dividends, and similar instruments; and/or
2. Any income, not capital gains, received from any investment.

INVESTOR ADVICE

In estimating taxes, you must be careful to separate income of the various types—Active, Passive, and Investment. This is especially true where losses have occurred during the taxable year.

SEE ALSO: ACTIVE INCOME, and PASSIVE INCOME.

INWOOD METHOD

The inwood method reduces future income projections to present worth.

INVESTOR ADVICE

The Inwood factors, or tables as they were formerly known, are nothing more than the present worth tables and/or calculations shown in Figures 49 and 50. A method of reducing future payments to present value was first outlined by William Inwood in a book of tables, published in 1811.

At a time when money earned 1-2% per annum, the true value of a payment received one or two years in the future was not significantly different than a current payment. As interest rates began to rise and the value of a future payment became far less valuable than cash in hand, investors and financial personnel were forced to consider time and value factors.

The concept, introduced by Inwood in 1811, was little known or used until the middle of the 1950's. The prestigious Harvard Graduate School of Business introduced the concept of present worth for the first time then in 1955.

With today's interest rates often in double digits, all money managers and investors are fully cognizant of present worth's affect on decision-making.

SEE ALSO: PRESENT VALUE OF ONE, and PRESENT VALUE OF ONE PER PERIOD.

IRRIGATION WATER

Irrigation water is specifically provided for agricultural use.

INVESTOR ADVICE

Investors who are unfamiliar with the problems of water collection and distribution in arid regions of the U.S. have been known to make serious errors in property acquisition.

In most of the western United States there is no such thing as *free water*. All water, whether it is underground, in running steams, or collected in reservoirs belongs to someone. Even though you have legal title to property, you are not permitted to dig a well or use water flowing through that property unless you also own the water.

Land in the western U.S. is therefore valueless or effectively so, unless water rights are provided with the land. Public utilities that wish to build a facility requiring large amounts of water are often forced to buy large tracts of land just to acquire the water that goes with it.

If you are contemplating buying land for development for any purpose, prime consideration must be given to water needs of the development. Water rights must be acquired to allow development of water distribution systems or provisions for needed water arranged with an appropriate utility having excess capacity. Such arrangements may require annexation to an adjacent municipality and appropriate zoning for the intended use.

Water rights are generally transferred by the secretary of the water company, upon instructions from a current owner. It is wise to obtain a water certificate, when purchasing land, even though the deed may state:

"… together with 400 shares of Big Ditch water."

This statement may well show the intent of the grantor, but does not transfer ownership. It does little good to determine at some future date that you don't own the water shown in the deed. You may have cause for a law suit to recover the value of the water at the time of closing, but you can't buy water if it is not for sale.

Water shares may be indicated in second- or acre-feet for unpressurized systems, or gallons per period for pressurized systems and well authorizations.

Most irrigation water is delivered to the owner by open ditch. The owner of rights obtains his/her water by opening the ditch at a time specified by the water master. Times are rotated so that the inconvenient night hours are equally shared by all. Water for lawn and landscaping use is often collected in wells during the permitted times and then pumped out at a later time when it is needed.

Well permits and pressurized water systems are regulated as to the amount per period that is permissible for use. Even municipal systems are limited in the amount of water that can be pumped from their wells. This often limits the number of customers that can be served.

Any purchase of western development land must be made subject to the resolution of any existing water problems.

SEE ALSO: ACRE-FEET, CULINARY WATER, SECOND-FEET, and WATER RIGHTS.

ENDNOTES

[1] National Association of Independent Fee Appraisers, *Requirements & Procedures for Upgrading,* revised 1/87 (St. Louis, Mo.).

[2] *Op. cit.,* pp. 5–6.

[3] *Op. cit.,* p. 5.

[4] William M. Shenkel, *Modern Real Estate Principals* (Business Publications Inc., Dallas, Texas, 1977), p. 101.

J

Joint Tenancy
Joint Ventures
Judgment

Junior Lien
Junior Mortgage

J

JOINT TENANCY

Joint tenancy is an ownership title in which all parties enjoy joint use of the property, and after the death of one or more of the parties the ownership vests to the remaining owners.

INVESTOR ADVICE

Joint ownership with the right of survivorship is a very popular title choice for married couples. When one party dies, the other automatically becomes the owner. Thus, the property is transferred by means of the original deed, which avoids probate and other delays. The transfer of ownership is accomplished by the simple proof of death and payment of inheritance taxes due, if any.

However, where the estate is very large and subject to large federal estate taxes, this method of ownership may not be the most desirable. Therefore, before taking title to newly acquired property, you should consult your tax advisor as to the best method of doing so.

Once title has been taken jointly, a transfer of one-half interest to the other party may be considered a gift requiring payment of gift taxes. When property is purchased or acquired, care must be exercised in the completion of the earnest money agreement to indicate the method in which title is to be transferred.

The following widely used methods of taking title to property are available to purchasers:

- Title held by one as separate property;

- Joint tenancy, with right of survivorship;

- Tenants in common, each holding a designated percentage share in the overall ownership and without the right of survivorship;

- Partnership interest, each holding a designated percentage of ownership;

- Limited partnership participation, in which the limited partner's liability is limited to his participation (dollar) investment;

- Real Estate Investment Trust (REIT), in which ownership is evidenced by the number of shares purchased;

- Trust ownership, in which the trust may be a living trust which is revocable or non-revocable;

- Trust ownership, in which the trust was established at the time of a death, in accordance with the decedent's will;

- Real estate corporation, in which the percentage of ownership is primarily determined by the shares owned;

- Cooperative ownership, in which an owner purchases the use of a specific unit (apartment) of a project, which is jointly owned by a non-profit corporation or other legal entity;

- Condominium ownership, in which the purchaser owns a specific unit (apartment) of a condominium complex plus a proportionate share of the common lands and facilities.

277

The selection of the method of title is generally based on:

1. What the owner desires to happen to the ownership upon his/her death;
2. Method of managing the property;
3. The value of the owner's current and future estate;
4. The number, age and relationship of the beneficiaries of the owner's estate;
5. Current tax laws which set the rate for inheritance and gift taxes and exemptions allowable therefrom;
6. Marital status of the owner;
7. Availability of a trusted relative or other who can and is capable of managing the property after the death of the owner; and
8. Age of the property owner.

SEE ALSO: COOPERATIVE APARTMENT, CONDOMINIUM, FEE SIMPLE TITLE, LIMITED PARTNERSHIP, PARTNERSHIP, and REAL ESTATE INVESTMENT TRUST (REIT).

JOINT VENTURES

Joint ventures are real estate projects undertaken by a number of investors acting through a common organization.

INVESTOR ADVICE

Joint ventures are usually organized as Real Estate Investment Trusts (REITs), limited partnerships, real estate corporations, or simple partnerships. The differences in these methods are dictated by:

- How the investment money is to be raised;
- How specific ownership is designated;
- Investors' desire to limit liability;
- Organizational management and control;
- Method of taxation, under current tax laws; and
- Transferability of ownership.

Joint ventures often result from the joining of a land owner with a skilled developer or organizer, each of which contributes to the project. The landowner contributes his/her land and the organizer contributes his/her ability to raise additional needed funds and the ability to develop the project.

Joint ventures are often dictated by the major financier's desire to share in the profits of the development as well as achieve a fair return on his/her money, used to finance the project. Almost all insurance companies, pension funds and similar money sources will demand a percentage ownership as a reward for furnishing mortgage money for the project.

Insurance companies often do not use their own money, but borrow it from others, using their good name and assets as security. Thus an insurance company may borrow $100 million @ 8.5% interest, loan it to the joint venture at 9.0% interest, and also obtain a 20% ownership in the project. Since none of the insurance company's own funds are invested, the yield is astronomical. They are at risk, however, for the borrowed funds.

SEE ALSO: LIMITED PARTNERSHIP, REAL ESTATE INVESTMENT TRUSTS, REAL ESTATE CORPORATIONS.

JUDGMENT

A judgment is:
1. The final determination of a court; and/or
2. A levy of debt placed upon an organization or person by a competent court. The judgment becomes a lien against all present and/or future assets of the organization or person until paid in full. Judgments are automatically made a matter of public record.

INVESTOR ADVICE

Real estate investors are often involved with matters of court judgments. These occur when:

- Purchasing property which reveals a judgment against the current owner.

- Selling property after a judgment debt has been made against you and your assets.

- Becoming a judgment creditor as a result of a judgment of debt against another who refused to pay money owed to you.

Judgments are obtained against another as a result of complicated court actions involving judges, juries, attorneys and considerable time or, in the case of small dollar amounts, the simplified actions of a small claim court.

A judgment differs from a lien in that it is against *all* assets present and future until paid. Judgments are matters of official record and remain on the books until the claim is satisfied. It is important to remember that when you pay a judgment in full you should obtain *a notarized release of judgment*. This release can then be recorded to clear the official record.

SEE ALSO: ABSTRACT OF TITLE, SATISFACTION PIECE, and TITLE REPORT.

JUNIOR LIEN

A junior lien is a recorded encumbrance against a property which is subordinate to another indebtedness.

INVESTOR ADVICE

A title search will often turn up junior liens and mortgages which are unknown or not reported by a seller. These may prove to be real or errors, due to failure of the owner to record a release when an obligation was paid. This is a very common occurrence with those less astute in legal and financial matters.

Regardless of the status of any encumbrances revealed by the title search, they must be cleared or paid before clear title to you, the new owner, can be transferred.

Although title searches will reveal all liens of record, a search is not a substitute for title insurance which *guarantees* a clear title regardless of any future revelations. Too, in the case of new construction, there may be some outstanding contractor and sub-contractor liens at the time of closing which have not been filed. These liens can be filed as late as 60-120 days after *the last* work is performed. Some states permit title insurance against contractor and sub-contractor liens. Others do not.

SEE ALSO: ABSTRACT OF TITLE, JUNIOR MORTGAGE, SPECIAL WARRANTY DEED, TITLE INSURANCE, and WARRANTY DEED.

JUNIOR MORTGAGE

A junior mortgage is a mortgage recorded against a property subsequent to another mortgage being filed. The junior mortgage takes secondary priority to payment of the first recorded.

INVESTOR ADVICE

Junior mortgages are often revealed by title searches and sometimes prove to be unknown to the property owner. This occurs due to one or more of the following:

- An unauthorized member of a corporation obtains a loan on corporate property, without knowledge of the principal officers.

- Lending institutions lose or misplace records of a second lien, or nonpayment on a lien, and the institution is then unaware of the default; and

- Former sale of a property without a title search or title insurance, which leaves a junior mortgage (lien) outstanding on the property. The current owner may be unaware of the encumbrance until it is revealed by the new title search.

The situations described, all of which seem ridiculous and almost impossible, have been encountered by the author. These instances serve to emphasize the necessity of an accurate title search and issuance of title insurance on each and every real estate transaction. This is to the advantage of both the buyer and the seller.

Without title insurance, in the event of a future revelation of an unknown lien the seller would be required to clear the title, as his/her signature is on the warranty deed. In the event the seller is unable to make good on said warranty due to lack of assets, the title company will pay the buyer. Title insurance, therefore, protects the buyer and seller.

Although the definition of a junior mortgage indicates that it is "filed subsequent to another mortgage," it may also result from a subordination agreement.

EXAMPLES

A property owner desires to obtain a large percentage of his equity from a property by placing a mortgage on it. He currently has a small first mortgage, which he would prefer to keep rather than pay off. The owner asks the current first mortgage holder to subordinate his position in order to permit a new mortgage to be placed on the property. The old lender agrees, since its second position is adequately secured by the remaining equity in the property.

*   *   *   *   *   *   *   *   *   *

A landowner sells his property and takes a mortgage for the balance due. The new owner wishes to build a new office building on the property, which will require a substantial mortgage. The mortgage-lender demands a first position. The land-seller agrees to subordinate his claim for the balance due on the land sale. He feels that his position is secured by the new building and the new owner's cash which has been invested in the project.

SEE ALSO: ABSTRACT OF TITLE, JUNIOR LIEN, TITLE INSURANCE, and WARRANTY DEED.

K

Kicker

K

KICKER
A kicker is a gift of interest in a project to a lender as a bonus for granting a mortgage loan.

INVESTOR ADVICE
Kickers are often used by Real Estate Investment Trusts (REITs) or limited partnerships as a means of obtaining necessary mortgage commitments. There is nothing illegal about this transaction if revealed in the prospectus, but it does warrant that investors be well aware of the situation and the resultant diminishing of their equity position.

In a limited partnership, funds for the proposed project usually comes primarily from a mortgage lender and the down payment from limited partners. Ownership, on the other hand, may constitute lenders, general partners, and limited partners. It may well be that the limited partners will own only 60–75% of the project, yet are the only ones really at risk. The lender assumes some risk, but that risk is largely covered by the mortgage on the property. The general partner's only risk is the loss of an idea or opportunity.

These comments are not to suggest that a limited partnership or REIT is a bad deal. They merely suggest that the investor should be fully aware of his/her risks and potential rewards before he/she invests.

As a potential investor, here are the questions you should ask as you read the prospectus:

- If the limited partners are putting up all of the cash and assuming the greatest risk, what percent of the project do we own?

- What percent of the project is held by the General Partners? Did they put up any equity or just the idea?

- Are the assumptions in the prospectus reasonable?

- What percent of the project must be rented to break even and keep the debt properly serviced? Is this reasonable to expect in the time period estimated?

- Who is scheduled to manage the project? Are their fees competitive with other management firms in the same business?

- What about the liquidity of my investment? Is the partnership widely held or closely held?

SEE ALSO: GENERAL PARTNER, JOINT VENTURE, LIMITED PARTNERSHIP, and REAL ESTATE INVESTMENT TRUST.

L

Laches
Land Identification Methods
Landlord
Land Residual
Land Rights Reserved by Government
Late Payment Charge
Law of Contracts
Law of Principal and Agent
Lease
Leaseback
Lease Guarantee Insurance
Leasehold Insurance
Lease Rights
Legal Description
Legality of Object
Letter of Intent
Letters Testamentary
Leverage
Liabilities
Liability Insurance
License
Lien
Lien Waiver
Life Estate

Life Pour Autre Vie
Life Tenant
Limited Liability
Limited Partnership
Line of Credit
Link
Liquid Assets
Liquidated Damages
Lis Pendens
Listing Contract
Listing Price
Litigation
Living Trust
Loan Assumption
Loan Broker
Loan Ratio
Loan Window
Lock-in Period
Locus Sigilli
Loft Building
Long-Term Gains
Lot Improvements
Lot Release System

L

LACHES

Laches are legal doctrines in which neglect of action for an unreasonable time is a bar in a court of equity.

INVESTOR ADVICE

You will be barred from pursuing an otherwise equitable claim if the defendant can show that you were not diligent in pursuing your claim or used unreasonable or unexplained time in seeking redress.

It is always wise to avoid the courts, whenever possible. Courts are expensive and time consuming. If you suffer a loss due to the actions or lack of actions of others, your first approach to the problem should be a frank discussion with the other party.

When this party is unreasonable or unwilling to negotiate a settlement, your next approach should be negotiation through a third and disinterested party. Your own attorney may be a logical choice; however, one of the new arbitration organizations may be able to do the job faster and at a lower cost.

Settlement by arbitration requires the consent of both parties. Explore this avenue and others before you commit to a particular line of action.

SEE ALSO: DEFENDANT, and PLAINTIFF.

LAND IDENTIFICATION METHODS

Land identification methods or systems are used to identify real estate property (legal descriptions) in the United States.

INVESTOR ADVICE

Legal descriptions of land parcels must identify the property in such a way that it cannot be misconstrued with any other parcel. The following systems are used in the United States:

GOVERNMENT SURVEY SYSTEM

This system was adopted by Congress in 1785 from the work of a special committee headed by Thomas Jefferson. The system, referred to as the Rectangular Survey System, divides land into rectangles called townships which are six miles square. In 1796 congress directed that townships be further divided into thirty-six sections. Further divisions into half-sections were authorized in 1800; quarter-sections in 1805; half-quarter sections in 1820; and finally, quarter-quarter sections of forty acres each in 1832.

Townships are a part of a twenty-four-square mile area designated by north-south lines with named meridians and east-west lines designated as named base lines. Vertical rows of townships are referred to as ranges. Horizontal rows of townships are known as tiers.

There are thirty-six numbered sections in each township, each one mile square and containing 640 acres. Section numbering begins in the northeast corner; proceeds to the western boundary; then south to the next row; thence east, and finally ends with section number thirty-six in the southeast corner.

A legal description of a quarter section might read:

The NE quarter of Section 22, Township 2 South, Range 3 East, Salt Lake Base and Meridian.

This description states that the subject Section 22 is located in the second township south of the Salt Lake base line and the third range line east of the Salt Lake Meridian. See Figure 7 for an illustration of this concept.

METES AND BOUNDS

This system, which had its beginnings in the thirteen original colonies, is still used in the eastern and southern parts of the United States. In this method of identification, property is identified by a series of directions and distances from some designated point of beginning. The point of beginning can be any easily recognizable terrain feature, or if combined with the Government Survey System, a section or part-section corner. The following is a typical legal description, combining both methods:

Beginning at a point in the center of a 4.0 rod street, which point is North 20.0 rods and East 4.0 rods and North 286.2 feet from the Southeast corner of the Southwest Quarter of the Northwest Quarter of Section 1, Township 2 South, Range 1 West, Salt Lake Base and Meridian: and running thence Westerly 200.0 feet, more or less, to a point which is North 17.42 feet and West 200.0 feet from the point of beginning; thence North 108.0 feet; thence Easterly to a point which is 108.0 feet North of the point of beginning; thence South 108.0 feet to the point of beginning.

LOT AND BLOCK SYSTEM

In this system, developments are divided into rectangular numbered blocks comprised of rectangular numbered lots. The complete survey is recorded for permanent reference. Future references to properties in the developments can be accurately described by lot and block number. A typical description, using this method, is as follows:

Lots 25,26 and the Eastern half of Lot 27, Block 5, Plat "A," Big Field Survey.

SUBDIVISION SYSTEM

The subdivision system is similar to the lot and block system, but property is not necessarily partitioned into rectangular blocks and lots. Lots in a subdivision may be of any size and shape and are shown on the official plat, which is recorded for future reference. Legal reference to these properties can, therefore, be simplified to the lot number and subdivision name.

A typical description, using this system, would read:

All of Lot 23, Broadhurst Subdivision, Number 1.

All land measurements are recorded as if the land was perfectly flat and the observer (map-maker) was overhead, looking down. Topography is not considered. A property located on a steep hill will therefore contain more surface area than one of the same size, but located on flat terrain.

SEE ALSO: BASE LINE, COMPASS CALL, MERIDIAN, METES AND BOUNDS, and RECTANGULAR SURVEY.

LANDLORD

A landlord is an owner of real property which is leased to others.

INVESTOR ADVICE

When investing in real estate to be leased to others, it is most important that you become eminently familiar with your rights as a landlord and the rights of your tenants. This knowledge will avoid future problems and legal expenses. Landlord concerns are many but knowledge and skill in the following is of particular importance:

- Landlord/tenant rights;

- Preparation of the lease;

- Tenant selection criteria;

- Legal repossession;

- Property management.

SEE ALSO: EVICTION, LEASE, TENANT, and TENANT SELECTION CRITERIA.

LAND RESIDUAL

This term refers to an appraisal technique for determining land value, where the improvement value is known and income from the improved property is capitalized.

INVESTOR ADVICE

A simple illustration of the land residual technique can be shown by the following:

EXAMPLE

Property: 4-unit apartment located on 1 acre lot
Net Income: $9600/year
Market Cap Rate: 10.3% (derived from market data)
Building Value: $70,000
Total Property Value = Income/cap rate
Value = $9600/.103 = $93,204
Land Value = Total Value — Building Value
Land Value = $93,204 — $70,000 = $23,204
       Round to: $23,200

The given illustration is a reasonably accurate method of determining land value, provided the inherent assumptions of the method apply. These assumptions are as follows:

- The land value is nominal versus total property value;

- The land is adequate for the improvement needs, but not excessive in size;

- The current use of the land represents its highest and best use;

- Income capitalization rate is determined by one of three acceptable techniques:
    1. Straight Line Method;
    2. Sinking Fund Method (Hoskold); or
    3. Annuity Method (Ellwood).

- The appraiser considers the income curve shape—level or declining; and

- The future reversion value of the land at the end of the economic life of the improvements is considered.

In this simplified illustration, it has been assumed that the income stream is level and that the present value of the land reversion is insignificant.

SEE ALSO: COST APPROACH TO VALUE, ELLWOOD PREMISE, and HOSKOLD METHOD.

LAND RIGHTS RESERVED BY GOVERNMENT

Land rights reserved by the government are fee simple ownership limitations, which limit the unrestricted exercise of the bundle of rights.

INVESTOR ADVICE

Although fee simple title to real estate implies complete and full utilization of the land by the owner, these rights are restricted by the following rights reserved by government:

1. Power of taxation;
2. Police power, or the power to regulate the use of land for public safety, health, general welfare, and morals. These powers are usually exercised through zoning, restrictive ordinances, building codes, etc.;
3. Power of eminent domain or the right to take private land for the public good, provided the owner is reimbursed for the taking and any damages due because of that taking; and
4. Power of escheat or right to take ownership if the owner dies without a will or known heir.

Fee title ownership is also restricted by the understanding that an owner cannot do anything with his/her land which interferes with the rights of others.

Further restrictions have been imposed on land owners, during the past few years. These restrictions have to do with air rights, or that area above the surface of the land. The government has declared that the area above normal surface usage be declared as "public air rights" for the use of aircraft—the exact height has not been defined. Above that area of public air rights is another area designated internationally as "international air rights" which authorizes the overflight of spacecraft and other high-flying objects.

SEE ALSO: EMINENT DOMAIN, ESCHEAT, and ZONING.

LATE PAYMENT CHARGE

A late payment charge is a penalty charge payable on late periodic payments of contracts and mortgages.

INVESTOR ADVICE

The terms of most mortgage notes will specify the due date of periodic payments and another date by which payments must be received. This clause will often call for a penalty or surcharge on any payments not made by the specified *last date*.

When selling property by contract, it is wise to include a significant late payment charge to ensure timely payment, particularly where part of the payment is required to pay an underlying mortgage.

The following late payment clause has been extracted from the Utah-approved Uniform Real Estate Contract and represents typical provisions:

Payments shall include interest at the rate of 10% (Agreed in Contract) per annum on the unpaid balance from the date of (date of contract). Any payment not made within five (5) working days of its due date shall subject Buyer to a late payment charge of five percent (5%) of such overdue payment, which charge must be paid before receiving credit for the late payment.

The above wording would indicate, for instance, that where the periodic payment was specified as $600.00, payment after five days would subject the Buyer to a $30.00 penalty.

SEE ALSO: CONTRACT, and ESCROW.

LAW OF CONTRACTS

There are five essential elements (laws) required for a valid contract between parties. These are:

1. All parties are competent to contract;
2. The object of the contract is legal;
3. There is an offer;
4. There is an acceptance; and
5. There is a consideration.

INVESTOR ADVICE

Contract law in the United States has slowly evolved through the case law process, appellate decisions, and regulations promulgated by the various states. Over time, contract laws of the states began to vary and made it difficult to conduct state to state business. With the passage of the Uniform Commercial Code (UCC), these problems were eased. UCC does not apply to all real estate transactions, most of which continue to be covered by the real estate laws of the various states.

However, all states, under the statute of frauds, require real estate contracts to be in writing and signed by all parties thereto. In addition, these contracts must be consistent with four additional requirements. These are:

1. The contract must be signed by all parties, and in the case of the seller some states require the spouse to sign also, even though the property may be classified as separate property.
2. There must be a consideration to bind the agreement. This consideration does not have to be any set amount but only that which will satisfy the seller that the buyer is earnest and has the ability to buy.
3. The contract must contain an offer and an acceptance. In other words, there must have been a meeting of the minds and each of the parties must be informed of the other's acceptance. This requirement often comes into play when a counter-offer is made. The deal is not a deal until both parties are informed.
4. All of the states require real estate contracts to be in writing per their statute of frauds.

All contractual laws are devised to assist a party with purported contracts, particularly when one party does not keep its promise.

Restitution to the damaged party is made by one of two remedies: (1) directed specific performance or (2) damages to compensate.

SEE ALSO: SPECIFIC PERFORMANCE, and STATUTE OF FRAUDS.

LAW OF PRINCIPAL AND AGENT

This term refers to that body of written law and court decisions which establishes the legality of the relationship between a principal and his/her appointed agent.

INVESTOR ADVICE

The law of principal and agent, as it applies to real estate, is quite basic and has been defined by the hundreds of suits brought by both buyers and sellers.

Basically, the laws have indicated that a person (principal) can contract with another (agent) to perform certain acts, such as leasing, selling, and managing real estate property. As an agent, certain duties and requirements exist. Among these are:

- The agent is licensed by the state in which the property is located to perform real estate services.

- The agent broker is a fiduciary and as such must perform his/her services in accordance with fiduciary law, carefully accounting for all funds belonging to his/her principal.

- The agent is only authorized to follow the instructions of the principal.

- The agent is authorized to collect a commission for those services rendered to the principal, but only in accordance with his/her contract with that principal.

- The agent is forbidden to perform his/her functions in a negligent manner.

- The agent cannot delegate his/her responsibilities, but must preform his/her acts in person.

- The agent must keep the principal fully informed and report all negotiations.

- In most states the broker agent is prevented, by law, from paying commissions or fees to anyone other than his/her licensed agents or another licensed broker.

The principal has certain responsibilities to the agent. These are:

- To clearly specify what duties are to be performed by the agent; and

- To establish a fee for services to be rendered and to promptly pay those fees on completion of services rendered. The broker-agent is said to have earned his/her fee at the point he/she has obtained a willing buyer and has negotiated a meeting of the mind between the principal and that buyer. The agent is entitled to his/her fee, even if the principal fails to conclude the transaction.

Many problems between agent and principal can be avoided by a complete and clear understanding of both the contract between the two and the contract prepared by the agent and agreed to by principal (seller) and buyer.

Contracts between principal and agent are usually made on standard real estate forms, such as those shown in Figures 13 and 30. Before you sign a listing contract or a notice to prospective purchaser, be sure that you fully understand the document. If you don't understand it, have your broker explain the terms in detail.

When you sign an earnest money receipt and offer to purchase, you must remember that this document is the guide for the final closing document preparation. Nothing may be added or subtracted at the closing, unless both parties, buyer and seller, are in full agreement.

Before signing, make sure the agreement is complete, covers all possible contingencies and represents your exact understanding of the contract. Be especially careful to consider all possible contingencies which might keep you from performing on the contract. Make this contractual document contingent upon those things which must occur or not occur before you perform as contracted. These contingencies might include such items as:

- Mortgage approved and granted;
- Current-owned property sold and closed; and/or
- Closing and possession made by a certain date.

SEE ALSO: EARNEST MONEY RECEIPT AND OFFER TO PURCHASE, LISTING CONTRACT, and NOTICE TO PROSPECTIVE PURCHASER.

LEASE

A lease is a contract between the property-owner and a tenant which relinquishes possession and use of certain property for a specified length of time, under specified conditions, and for specified compensation.

INVESTOR ADVICE

You must understand that a lease becomes an encumbrance on the title of the property. By virtue of the lease, the lessee has obtained certain property rights (a leasehold interest) which are binding upon the lessor, his/her heirs and assigns. Future sales or assigns of the property by the lessor owner have no effect upon the rights of the lessee for the term of his/her lease.

If you are considering a long-term lease or a lease with options, provisions must be made for unknown economic changes such as inflation, increases in taxes, etc. Provisions for increases to cover these contingencies must be specific, if not in dollar amounts, then in the method used to compute the required increase.

Typical methods for covering the contingencies of inflation usually require a recalculation of the lease payment at the end of specified periods, say the first of each year. The following year's rents are then calculated on a basis of some well-published indicator, such as the cost of living.

A lease may be a simple one-page form like that shown in Figure 40, or a lengthy document prepared by your attorney. Leases generally fall into one of the following general forms:

- Simple 1-page form with or without escalation clauses;
- Triple net commercial lease, in which the tenant is responsible for most maintenance, taxes, and insurance;
- Percentage commercial lease, which sets the rental rate at a minimum base price plus a percentage of the gross sales of the lessee's business; and/or
- Part of a sale and leaseback agreement.

All of the types may have options for renewal with or without the rental specified or formulized. There is no limit to the provisions or prohibitions that can be included in a lease agreement, as long as the terms are legal and agreeable to all parties.

SEE ALSO: EARNEST MONEY RECEIPT AND OFFER TO LEASE, and NET LEASE.

"This is a legally binding form, if not understood, seek competent advice."

LEASE

........Big Deals Incorporated..
of ...., County of ....Salt Lake.................., State of Utah, hereinafter referred to as landlord, hereby remise, release and let to....Janie.R..&.Robert.B..Browning.............
of .....Salt.Lake.City................................. County of .....Salt.Lake................. State of Utah,
hereinafter referred to as tenant, all those premises situate, lying and being in the ......City.of.Salt.Lake.....
.... of .... County of ..Salt.Lake.........
and State of Utah, commonly known as .....Apartment.27F,.Greenbrier.Apartments...........................
and more particularly described as follows, to wit: ....

........Lot.98,.Greenbrier.Subdivision...
....

(Legal Description)

TO HAVE AND TO HOLD the said premises, together with the appurtenances, unto the tenant, from the ...1st...
day of ..March......... A.D. 19.89, for and during and until the ....28th. day of ..February...... A.D. 19.90, a term
of ....One.Year......

And tenant covenants and agrees to pay to landlord as rental for said premises, the sum of ...$650....
Dollars, payable as follows: One.month.in.advance.and.$650.each.1st.day.of.month..................
thereafter.through..January.1,.1990.

And tenant further agrees to deliver up said premises to landlord at the expiration of said term in as good order and condition as when the same were entered upon by tenant, reasonable use and wear thereof and damage by the elements excepted, and the tenant will not let or underlet said premises, or any part thereof without the written consent of landlord first had and obtained, which consent will not be unreasonably withheld.

And tenant further covenants and agrees that if said rent above reserved or any part thereof shall be unpaid for ...10...... days after the same shall become due; or if default in any of the covenants herein contained to be kept by tenant is not cured within ......5.......... days from written notice, or if tenant shall vacate such premises, landlord may elect, without notice or legal process, to re-enter and take possession of said premises and every and any part thereof and re-let the same and apply the net proceeds so received upon the amount due or to become due under this lease, and tenant agrees to pay any deficiency.

Responsibility for the maintenance shall be as indicated: Tenant responsible for (T), Landlord responsible for (L). Roof....L..., Exterior Walls......L..., Interior Walls....T...., Structural Repair.....L..., Interior Decorating....T..., Exterior Painting....L..., Yard Surfacing........L, Plumbing Equipment......L..., Heating and Air Conditioning Equipment....L...., Electrical Equipment....L..., Light Globes and Tubes......T..., Glass Breakage........T..., Trash Removal....L......, Snow Removal....L..., Janitor.....L..., Others .....None.................

Responsibility for utilities, taxes and insurance shall be as indicated: Tenant responsible for (T), Landlord responsible for (L).
Power....T..., Heat....T..., Water....L..., Sewer....L..., Telephone.......T., Real Property tax....L..., Increase above 19.88 in Real Property Tax...T......, Personal Property Tax...T...., Fire Insurance on Building....L...., Fire Insurance on Personal Property.....T..., Glass Insurance....T..., Other ....None..................

Each party shall be responsible for losses resulting from negligence or misconduct of himself, his employees or invitees.

Furniture, fixtures and personal property of tenant may not be removed from the premises until rent and other charges are fully paid.

In case of failure to faithfully perform the terms and covenants herein set forth, the defaulting party shall pay all costs, expenses, and reasonable attorneys fees resulting from the enforcement of this agreement or any right arising out of such breach.

....
....
....

Witness the hands and seals of said landlord............ and said tenant............ at ....Salt.Lake.City.............
this ...23rd... day of ....February............ A.D. 19..89.

Signed in presence of

Nartha R. Goldman, Resident Manager

Janie R. Browning (Seal)

Robert B. Browning (Seal)

Narth R. Goldman

Wilbur C. Realtor (Seal)
agent for Big Deals Inc.

.... (Seal)

Figure 40

LEASEBACK

A leaseback is a contractual agreement for the purchase of a real property with a provision for leasing it back to the seller.

INVESTOR ADVICE

Leaseback agreements are excellent real estate investments, which combine the known factors of selling price and terms of lease (usually long-term). These factors guarantee a known rate of return on the investment.

Leasebacks are often used by corporations as a means of financial restructuring by simultaneously: (1) reducing debt; and (2) obtaining much needed cash. The procedure may also prove to be a tax advantage to the seller, as the larger lease fees are an increased expense of doing business versus the smaller deduction of mortgage interest, maintenance, and depreciation.

When considering a purchase-leaseback situation, you should also consider the cost of lease guarantee insurance and leasehold insurance to further secure the potential return on investment. Although the seller may be a very large and strong company now, the fact that financial restructuring is required can cast some doubt about their ability to perform on a long-term lease.

SEE ALSO: LEASE, LEASE GUARANTEE INSURANCE, LEASEHOLD INSURANCE, and NET LEASE.

LEASE GUARANTEE INSURANCE

Lease guarantee insurance is obtained by the owner/lessor to guarantee that a certain rental amount will be paid over the term of the lease.

INVESTOR ADVICE

Lease insurance can be obtained on a financially stable tenant at a modest cost. Insurance on lesser-qualified tenants will be more expensive.

Lease insurance can be beneficial in several ways:

- It can increase the property value due to the reduced risk of lower income.

- Mortgage loans can be easier to obtain and even then are usually at a lower interest rate.

- Rental rates can be higher than if only high-quality tenants were considered. Anchor type tenants usually demand discounted rental rates.

SEE ALSO: INSURANCE.

LEASEHOLD INSURANCE

Leasehold insurance compensates a landlord for losses resulting from a lease cancellation occasioned by fire or other natural peril.

INVESTOR ADVICE

Leasehold insurance will compensate the lessor-owner for his/her losses in rentals, as well as the lessee, who may lose advanced payments and his/her improvements to the property.

Insurers normally issue separate policies for the two losses and will demand a copy of the lease agreement to determine the ease of tenant cancellation.

SEE ALSO: INSURANCE, HAZARD INSURANCE, and LEASE INSURANCE.

LEASE RIGHTS

Lease rights are those property rights specifically assigned to a lessee by the owner of property and listed in the lease agreement.

INVESTOR ADVICE

Figure 40 is a standard lease agreement form used by most landlords for apartment and small office rentals. Lease agreement for larger properties are usually much more complicated and contain many more provisions.

The simple lease covers the following points of consideration between the parties:

- Names the landlord and tenants;
- Clearly identifies the property concerned;
- Stipulates the rent to be paid, when, and how;
- States the length of the lease term and provision for return of the property to the landlord to include condition of the property at that time;
- Contains provision or prohibition for subleasing;
- Describes responsibilities of tenant;
- Describes responsibilities of the landlord;
- Contains provisions for enforcement of lease provisions; and
- Witness and/or acknowledgments.

SEE ALSO: LEASE.

LEGAL DESCRIPTION

A legal description is a unique description which unequivocally identifies a property from all other properties.

INVESTOR ADVICE

A legal description can be short or long, depending upon the method of describing the property. The length of the description is more dependent upon the method of description than size. For instance, a property containing 640 acres could be simply described as:

Section 27, Range 1 East, Tier 2 South, Salt Lake Base and Meridian

On the other hand a half-acre lot with several sides might require a half-page, single-spaced description which indicates the various lengths of sides, their compass calls, and the directions to the point of beginning.

SEE ALSO: BASE LINE, COMPASS CALL, DEED, and LAND IDENTIFICATION METHODS.

LEGALITY OF OBJECT

A legality of object is one of the five essential elements of a legal contract.

INVESTOR ADVICE

Under the statute of frauds of the various states and the federally recognized Uniform Commercial Code (UCC), it is illegal to contract for a service or act which is in itself illegal. For instance, a contract with a hit man to murder your rich uncle would not be enforceable in court.

SEE ALSO: CONTRACT.

LETTER OF INTENT

A letter of intent indicates intent to perform a certain act at some time in the future. Such letters are not legally binding but are useful for planning purposes and the preliminary search for mortgage money. In indicating interest in buying, renting, etc. the letter writer does not formally bind him or herself to do anything.

INVESTOR ADVICE

Letters of intent are often solicited from potential renters and buyers of proposed projects. These letters serve as an indicator of the possible success of the proposed project, but fall short of being legally binding documents.

When a new project is proposed, it is often impossible to set rental rates, selling prices, etc., sufficient to obtain firm contractual commitments. Letters of intent can do the next best thing—show a positive indication of potential success.

Lenders, particularly those who provide construction funds, may be positively impressed with letters of intent provided by reliable persons and organizations.

Figure 41 shows a typical letter of intent to lease which would be included in the developer's portfolio of data as he/she applies for the required financing.

SEE ALSO: CONSTRUCTION LOAN.

LETTERS TESTAMENTARY

Letters testamentary are issued on authority of a probate court and authorize an executor(ix) or administrator(ix) to collect debts, pay bills, and perform other necessary tasks in the settlement of a decedent's estate.

INVESTOR ADVICE

Letters testamentary are used to officially advise the public that the person named therein is authorized to collect debts owed to the deceased, pay bills incurred by the deceased and perform any or all tasks to settle the estate that the deceased would do him or herself if still living.

A letter testamentary, a copy of the death certificate and a receipt for any inheritance taxes due are required to remove the decedent's name from joint titled with right of survivorship.

SEE ALSO: ADMINISTRATOR(IX), CODICIL, EXECUTOR(IX), PROBATE, and WILL.

LEVERAGE

Leverage is the return on investment less than or greater than the cost of borrowed funds. Leverage may be negative or positive.

INVESTOR ADVICE

All real estate investors strive for positive leverage in the operation of their income properties. This occurs when the net income, after taxes but before debt service, is a greater percentage of the total investment than that paid for borrowed (mortgage) money.

A good example of positive leverage would be a situation where rental income, less maintenance and other costs, produces a net income of 14% on property cost. If 80% of the funds were provided by a mortgage at 12% interest, the extra 2% earned will

ALL POINTS
Appraisal Service

3538 S. SUNILAND DRIVE
SALT LAKE CITY, UTAH 84109
TELEPHONE: 801 - 487-9871

Frank J. Blankenship

IFA

Senior Member

December 5, 1988

SUBJECT: Letter of Intent to Lease

TO: Green River Limited
      4930 S. Ellington Blvd.
      Orem, Utah   84228

Gentlemen:

This letter will confirm our interest in leasing, on a five (5) year basis, administrative office space in your proposed building, to be build at 4980 S. State Street, Salt Lake City, Utah.

It is our understanding that our required office space of approximately 6,000 s.f. can be furnished on a full service basis for approximately $12.00 per square foot per year.

In addition to the above indicated square foot requirement, we will also require the following:

1.   Dedicated parking space for 10 automobiles.
2.   Customer parking in undedicated parking spaces.
3.   Office space located on or above the 5th floor.
4.   Sub-Floor ducts for telephone and data cables to locations to be later determined.
5.   Special non-interference power service for our computer needs.

This letter does not constitute a contract or guarantee, in any way, that a contract and/or lease will be negotiated with your organization. It is furnished, at your request, for planning purposes only.

Yours truly,

FRANK J. BLANKENSHIP
President

Figure 41

vest to the investor to provide him or her with a substantially greater return than that on the total value.

EXAMPLE

The following facts apply to the subject property:

Cost of Property	$100,000
Net Return on Value @ 12%	12,000
Borrowed Money 80% of Inv.	80,000
Cost of Borrowed Money @ 10%	8,000*
Owner Equity @ 20%	20,000
Income to Owner	
$12,000 – $8,000	4,000
% Return on Equity	
$4,000/$20,000	20%

The equity return of 20% is due to positive leverage. You will note that a 2% leverage in earnings produces an 8% greater overall return.

Failure to earn the mortgage rate, say 8%, would produce a negative leverage and result in a near disaster for the investor. Using the data given but changing the net return to 8% would indicate the following situation:

Cost of Property	$100,000
Net Return on Value @ 8%	8,000
Borrowed Money 80% of Inv.	80,000
Cost of Borrowed Money @ 10%	8,000*
Owner's Equity @ 20%	20,000
Income to Owner	
$8,000 - $8,000	None
% Return on Equity	None

*Based on first year mortgage balance due.

Had the owner earned less than 8%, he would not have been able to cover his mortgage obligations.

SEE ALSO: NET INCOME AFTER TAXES, and RETURN ON INVESTMENT.

LIABILITIES

"Liabilities" is an accounting term for a list of debts owed to others. In accounting parlance the assets of a company exactly equal the liabilities of the company plus the ownership.

INVESTOR ADVICE

When reviewing the financial statements of a business, you must first determine the method of accounting—cash or accrual.

Where cash accounting is being used, most liabilities of the business will not be shown. Similarly, moneys due (receivables) will be missing. Undoubtedly, you won't mind missing these latter items but will regret not knowing about the missing debts.

When purchasing a real estate operation which was managed as a proprietorship or partnership, you will not be liable for debts incurred by the previous owner(s). If the operation was a corporation, however, the debts go with the package. Even though you may not be liable for debts, the very fact that they were incurred should be made known to you for your consideration of the potential profitability of the business

SEE ALSO: BALANCE SHEET, CASH VERSUS ACCRUAL ACCOUNTING, PAYABLES, and RECEIVABLES.

LIABILITY INSURANCE

Liability is insurance the property owner's protection against suits for injuries to others or their property which are deemed the responsibility of the property owner.

INVESTOR ADVICE

Property owners are viewed by many as rich. They often become the targets of persons who are hurt or alleged to have been hurt on the premises. To protect against possible losses, it is advisable to carry liability insurance.

Reasonable coverage for potential liability awards is available as a separate policy or in combination with hazard insurance policy, which is carried by all prudent property owners. The provisions of most mortgage loans specify a minimum coverage requirement. The purpose of this requirement is to prevent a serious financial loss to the property owner which might reduce his/her ability to repay the mortgage.

SEE ALSO: FIRE INSURANCE, HOMEOWNER'S INSURANCE, and HAZARD INSURANCE.

LICENSE

A license is:
1. A legal authorization to perform some specific act(s) for a specified period; and/or
2. A personal authorization to enter upon the land of another for a specific purpose. Such authorization is revocable by the licensing authority.

INVESTOR ADVICE

When contemplating the purchase of a real estate income-producing investment, it is advisable to determine the need for an operating license. You should also inquire as to whether the existing license is transferable to a new owner and the annual cost of the permit.

Many municipalities and other government entities require apartment houses and other quasi-business ventures to be licensed. Such licenses are usually for purposes of regulation rather than income production, therefore their fees are nominal.

It is not unusual for small apartments, such as duplex and triplex units, to operate without a license even though one is required. The owners just haven't been caught. It is wise to determine the need and the ability to obtain a license for the required rental operation. Even though current zoning prohibits the rental operation, it may be possible to continue it under a grandfather clause.

Although one normally thinks of "license" as a permit to be displayed on the wall, it means "permission." Thus, a lease is a license to a tenant to use a certain specified property for the lease term. Another example is an easement granted for use of a right-of-way.

SEE ALSO: GRANDFATHER CLAUSE, RIGHT-OF-WAY, EGRESS, INGRESS, and ZONING.

LIEN

A lien is a legal encumbrance on a property which effectively pledges the property as security for specified debts of the property owner.

INVESTOR ADVICE

Liens may often be routinely filed by contractors or subcontractors without the knowledge of the property owner, since no court action is required to file. Liens for other types of debts are generally well-known to the property owner as they result from a prolonged failure to pay a legitimate debt.

It is wise to require lien waiver receipts for all contractor and sub-contractor invoices that are paid. In the event a lien has been previously filed against the property, it can then be cleared by filing the waiver.

In some states, such as Utah, property owners contracting for over $2,000 of improvements are responsible to insure that contractors are bonded to insure payment for all mechanic's labor and materials furnished. The bond must "run to the owner and all subcontractors, laborers and materialmen." Failure to obtain this required bond from a contractor will make the property owner liable for any unpaid bills.

Where available, it is wise to obtain lien-waiver insurance on all new construction property purchased. This will insure that any unknown liens or those filed after the closing will be covered.

SEE ALSO: ABSTRACT OF TITLE, LIEN WAIVER, and TITLE INSURANCE.

LIEN WAIVER

A lien waiver is a voluntary release of claim for work performed by a contractor or subcontractor as a prerequisite for payment for the work performed.

INVESTOR ADVICE

Most lending institutions who advance money for construction purposes will require that a lien waiver be signed for each cash advance made on the project. When the work is performed by a contractor and his/her subcontractors, signatures from all parties may be required.

Most lending institutions and contractors have specially prepared payment checks with an endorsement on the back similar to the following:

In consideration of the payment of this check, the payee, by endorsement hereon, hereby waives and releases all lien or right of lien, now existing or that may arise hereafter for work, labor, or materials furnished for the improvement of the following property:

> *3538 S. Suniland Dr.*
> *Salt Lake City, Ut.*
> *Reference: Loan #25-5689*

A more formal type of lien waiver is shown as Figure 15, under the discussion of Construction Loans.

To protect yourself from unscrupulous contractors, it is advisable to require the lender to obtain both the *contractor's and your signatures* on each lien waiver. It is also your responsibility to inspect the project to determine that work has actually been performed before signing the waiver. When large sums of money are involved, the lender may also want to inspect the construction site to verify completion or partial completion of the work for which reimbursement is requested.

SEE ALSO: CONSTRUCTION LOAN, LIEN, and RELEASE OF LIEN.

LIFE ESTATE

A life estate is an interest in a property granted to a person for their lifetime, at which time the property reverts to another. While the life estate is in effect, it represents a dilution of the bundle of rights and an encumbrance on the property.

INVESTOR ADVICE

Abstracts of title will reveal any current life estate encumbrances on the property. If one exists, the title can be cleared by a purchase of this interest or other compensation.

Life estates are generally created at the death of a property-owner who desires that a particular person (a spouse or child) have the use of a property during their lifetime, but who wants the final disposition of the asset to go to another. This would be the case of a husband with children by his first wife and now living with a second wife. The second wife could retain the property for her lifetime, after which the property would go to the children.

The value of a life estate can only be determined by actuarial methods, based on the age of the life tenant. Regardless of the appraised value of the property and the application of actuarial data, the life estate may be far more valuable to a particular buyer. For instance, a life estate in a small residence which blocks a major commercial development could be very valuable.

SEE ALSO: CLOUD ON TITLE, ENCUMBRANCE, and FEE SIMPLE TITLE.

LIFE ESTATE POUR AUTRE VIE

A special type of life estate in which the property is granted to "B" for the life of "C."

INVESTOR ADVICE

In this special title situation, at the death of "C" the property reverts to the grantor or his/her assigns. An example would be a divorced father who grants the title for a residence to a daughter "B," for the life of her mother "C," at which time the property would be returned to the father, the grantor.

SEE ALSO: LIFE ESTATE.

LIFE TENANT

A life tenant is the grantee of a life estate in a property.

INVESTOR ADVICE

While the person who possesses the life estate is known as the life tenant, the person who receives the property at the life tenant's death is known as:

- The revisioner if he/she is the grantor; or

- The remainderman if he/she has all rights of ownership except possession.

The life tenant has certain restrictions placed upon him/her during tenancy. These are:

- He/she cannot permanently damage the property.

- He/she cannot change the nature of the land, its uses or its improvements without the permission of the revisioner or remainderman.

- He/she can only lease the property subject to the provisions of the life estate.
- He/she can receive the income from mineral and oil rights but only if he/she compensates the revisioner/remainderman for its depletion.

The life tenant also has certain duties imposed upon him or her. These are:

- Pay taxes due and a proportionate share of any special assessments; and
- Pay the interest on any mortgage outstanding. The principal portion of the debt service payments is the responsibility of the revisioner/remainderman, as this amount accrues to his or her account.

A tenant possessing a property by virtue of a homestead declaration is also said to hold a legal life tenancy.
SEE ALSO: HOMESTEAD, LIFE ESTATE, REMAINDERMAN, and REVISIONER.

LIMITED LIABILITY

A limited liability is less than full liability. This situation is usually the result of legal limitations imposed by contractual agreement, such as in a limited partnership.

INVESTOR ADVICE
You should consult your legal representative before investing in any operation which purports to limit your liability. You should also be very careful in your investing to ensure that your liabilities are as limited as possible.

It is recommended that whenever possible your investment properties be held in other than a proprietorship or partnership. In either of these two organizations, you, as a participant, are fully responsible and accountable for all actions. A partnership is even worse. You, as a partner, are fully liable for your own actions as well as those of your partner.

Investment property can be held in one of the following three types of organizations, which will limit your potential liabilities:

1. Limited Partnership;
2. Corporation; or
3. Trust.

SEE ALSO: CORPORATION, INTER VIVOCE TRUST, LIABILITY, LIMITED PARTNERSHIP, SUBCHAPTER "S" CORPORATION, and PARTNERSHIP.

LIMITED PARTNERSHIP

A limited partnership is a special kind of partnership in which the participants (limited partners) share in the profits and losses of the business which is operated and managed by general partners.

INVESTOR ADVICE
Before investing in a limited partnership, it is wise to review the financial structure to determine what percent of the ownership is claimed by the general partners, lenders, and so on.

It is not unusual to find a limited partnership in which all of the required investment is provided by the limited partners. A close examination of the prospectus may reveal that 10-20% of the equity is claimed by the general partners as their share of putting the deal together. An additional 5-10% of the action may be claimed by the organization which lends the funds. This ownership was provided as a "kicker" or as a partner in the "joint venture."

> **CAREFULLY CHECK** ownership by others than the investors who provide the capital. Is it excessive?

However, just because a portion of the participation is claimed by people or organizations other than those putting up the venture capital (limited partners), does not necessarily mean that is a bad deal. It is merely a flag waving and signaling, "Very carefully examine the income projections and the assumptions underlying those assumptions."

Some protection is provided the investor if the venture is widely marketed and subject to Security and Exchange Commission (SEC) regulations. When the financing is undertaken in accordance with state security regulations only, there is always a potential opportunity for a less than honest operation.

SEE ALSO: JOINT VENTURE, KICKER, PROSPECTUS, RED HERRING, SECURITIES COMMISSION, and SECURITIES AND EXCHANGE COMMISSION (SEC).

LINE OF CREDIT

A line of credit is an arrangement which allows the borrower credit, as his/her needs require, up to a set limit.

INVESTOR ADVICE

In planning your new real estate operation, it is recommended that a proforma cash flow analysis be performed. From this analysis, you can project what your maximum cash needs will be and arrange a line of credit to provide those funds. This type of analysis can be further refined as actual expense data is gathered.

By anticipating your needs in advance, you will eliminate last minute requests for funds in addition to showing your ability to operate the business in an effective manner.

A line of credit, based upon equity in the property and secured by a mortgage, will probably provide needed funds at the lowest possible interest rate. A personal note or commercial short-term loan will be much more expensive.

SEE ALSO: PRO-FORMA ANALYSES, and TAX REFORM ACT OF 1986 (TRA).

LINK

A link is a unit of land measure which is equal to 1/100th part of a chain of sixty-six feet.

INVESTOR ADVICE

A link is 7.92 inches in length. There are twenty-five links in a rod and four rods per chain.

Link, rod, and chain are seldom found on modern surveys; however, you will find them on many legal descriptions which are based on older surveys.

SEE ALSO: CHAIN, and ROD.

LIQUID ASSETS

Lqiuid assets are cash or instruments readily converted to cash. These would include such items as short-term certificates of deposit, treasury notes, demand deposits, and checking accounts.

INVESTOR ADVICE

Good investment techniques provide a balance between "fully invested" and "excess cash." It is obvious that sufficient liquid assets are required to meet current and other obligations, but excess liquidity usually results in reduced earnings.

Few investments offering high liquidity can approach the higher returns expected from real estate investments, which are far less than liquid and offer considerable risks.

A pro forma cash flow analysis will indicate the level of liquid assets needed to effectively operate the real estate project. With this guidance, a minimum amount of assets can be tied up in lower return investments and more kept working in projects offering higher returns.

SEE ALSO: ASSETS, and RISK VERSUS RETURN.

LIQUIDATED DAMAGES

Liquidated damages are the amount of compensation agreed upon in the event of default on a contractual commitment, such as a mortgage.

INVESTOR ADVICE

In the past, real estate investors were not too concerned about the potential for mortgage or contract default. They assumed that the result would be loss of their small investment in the property and a possible black mark on their credit rating.

As inflation has cooled and the real estate market changed, default on a mortgage or land contract can result in a deficiency judgment against the buyer to recover indebtedness not recovered in the resale of the foreclosed property. In areas where property prices have seriously receded, it is not uncommon for a property to fail to cover the entire mortgage and other legal costs. When the investor has other assets, lenders are quick to seek relief through court actions and deficiency judgments.

SEE ALSO: FORECLOSURE, JUDGMENTS, NOTE, MORTGAGE, and TRUST DEED.

LIS PENDENS

Lis pendens is a legal term meaning legal action has begun or is now in progress.

INVESTOR ADVICE

If you should have a dispute with another over a property matter, it is important that the public be advised through the filing of a lis pendens notice. This will assure that anyone planning to buy the property will be advised of the potential claim against that property.

The lis pendens recording has the same effect as a "notice of interest" document. Nothing of a private nature is revealed, yet the public has been constructively notified of a potential claim.

SEE ALSO: ABSTRACT OF TITLE, INCHOATE, and NOTICE OF INTEREST IN PROPERTY.

LISTING CONTRACT

A listing contract is a legal contract between a property owner and a real estate brokerage, which authorizes that brokerage to offer for sale a designated property.

INVESTOR ADVICE

Figure 30 (under discussion on Exclusive Listing) shows a typical listing contract for a residential property. The main form, "B," provides all of the details concerning the property in a format readily reduced for computer input to the multiple listing system. Form "A" provides legal terms of the contact between the parties.

The important aspect of this contract is that it is legally binding upon the parties and must be carefully read prior to being signed. When you list your property, care must be exercised to ensure that the information is accurate as future revelations of errors after a sale can result in litigation.

It should be noted that the property owner *warrants* that the information contained in the listing contract is correct. This warranty does not relieve the listing broker from his/her responsibilities for checking the data to determine its accuracy.

For instance, a listing showing 2.0 acres of land where a professional REALTOR® should know that the size appears less would indicate negligence on the part of the listing agent/agency. Similarly, errors made by the property owner in providing facts, which an ordinary person should know, will not relieve that property owner from liabilities resulting from an error in listing.

SEE ALSO: EXCLUSIVE AGENCY, and EXCLUSIVE RIGHT TO SELL.

LISTING PRICE

A listing price is the price shown on the listing contract and often referred to as the "asking price."

INVESTOR ADVICE

The listing or asking price is the price which the listing agent is bound by his/her agent/principal to quote to prospective buyers. It is unethical for any agent to suggest that the property owner will take a lesser amount, although it is generally recognized by buyers and sellers that a property seldom sells for the listed price.

Experience has shown that a listing price that is too high will delay the sale of the property and might even result in a no-sale situation. No property owner wants to leave money lying on the table, therefore he/she is prone to setting the listing price a little higher than he/she really expects to receive.

The problem then becomes a question of what that price should be—high enough to achieve his/her objective of a sale at a reasonable price, yet not so high as to preclude interest by most buyers.

The buyer, on the other hand, doesn't want to pay more than absolutely necessary, yet he/she doesn't want to offer so little as to insult the seller or fail to get the property he/she desires.

Often the buyer will approach the dilemma by offering just enough to avoid an insult and then depend upon a higher counter-offer by the seller. The buyer hopes that this counter-offer will represent the seller's lowest acceptable figure. The reasoning here is that the seller, knowing the buyer to be a fully qualified and interested party, will be reluctant to lose a sale. Accordingly, it is assumed that he/she will counter with his/her very best offer.

SEE ALSO: EARNEST MONEY RECEIPT AND OFFER TO PURCHASE, LAW OF PRINCIPAL AND AGENT, and LISTING CONTRACT.

LITIGATION

Litigation is the legal procedure for seeking redress through the courts .

INVESTOR ADVICE

The biggest mistake an investor can make when faced with litigation is to hire an attorney who is not a specialist in real estate law. Few attorneys will turn down an opportunity to represent a client. Most will jump at the chance to represent anyone who appears to have some money.

Not all attorneys are qualified in the very specialized field of real estate, nor are all attorneys excellent trial lawyers. The best advice that can be given to anyone facing litigation is to hire the best attorney available who is a specialist in your problem area.

Don't economize. If your case is important enough to fight in court, it justifies hiring the very best, even if such a lawyer is a bit more expensive. The reason he/she is expensive is probably because he/she is the best in the field.

Next, be prepared to spend a lot of time in waiting for your case to appear in court. In most areas of the United States, you will be lucky to have your case heard in twelve to eighteen months. The success you will have in court will depend upon your ability to furnish your attorney with good information. For this reason, it is imperative that your income property records be complete and accurate.

Here is a checklist of records and files that will be helpful, if you ever go to court:

- Keep a copy of all leases and correspondence with the lessee, including his/her initial application to lease your property;

- If a credit check was made on the tenant prior to leasing, it should also be in the file. If the telephone was your source of credit information, make a memo for the record indicating what you found out, from who, and on what date.

- Keep accurate records of all lease payments, showing when they were due and when the money was received.

- Maintain a copy of all bulletins or tenant advisories which have been sent to the tenants or posted on a bulletin board for their information. Show the date of posting and date of removal.

- Maintain a rental-unit file indicating all repairs and maintenance, date of work and cost.

- Prepare some type of alerting system, which will advise you in advance of lease terminations, rental revision dates, and options to renew. Advise your tenants of these coming events in order to provide them with ample time to react.

- Keep all tenant deposits in a separate trust account and make sure that any other funds are not commingled with this account. If funds are withdrawn as a result of a forfeit, be sure that your check voucher indicates the tenant name and reason for the forfeiture.

SEE ALSO: LANDLORD, LEASE, and TENANT SELECTION CRITERIA.

LIVING TRUST

SEE: INTER VIVOCE TRUST.

LOAN ASSUMPTION

This term refers to the concurrent transfer of a property and its existing encumbrance. The loan assumed by the buyer is credited toward the selling price.

INVESTOR ADVICE

Currently only a few lenders permit assumption of existing loans. Government backed VA and FHA loans are the major exceptions. Assumption of a loan, if permitted, means that the person assuming the loan is bound by the same terms and conditions as the original mortgagor.

Unless specifically relieved of responsibility by the lender, that original mortgagor remains liable for payment in the event the assuming party defaults. Specific means are provided for relief of liability in the case of VA and FHA loans.

A variation on outright assumption is, "assumption with permission of the lender." Some loan provisions provide for assumption, where the lender has the opportunity to adjust the interest rate and/or qualify the borrower. Generally this means the assuming party pays the going rate of interest.

The only advantages in assuming a loan are a saving of time, a possible lower assumption fee than a new origination fee, and a possible omission of the qualification procedure. The required deposits for escrow are essentially the same—on assumption the buyer "buys" the seller's escrow account.

If the assumption of a loan is specifically not permitted, many parties attempt to subvert the terms of the loan by not informing the lender of the property transfer. However, eventually the lender becomes aware of the transfer and calls the note due and payable. This forces the original borrower or the assuming party to refinance the indebtedness, depending upon the agreement between those parties at the time of property transfer.

When considering the purchase of a property upon which an existing loan is outstanding, it is advised that the loan agreement be carefully reviewed by a competent authority. Many sellers are unaware of the non-assumption restriction which they agreed to in the distant past. Generally speaking, any loan made after 1970 most probably contains a non-assumption (acceleration) clause.

SEE ALSO: ACCELERATION CLAUSE, CONTRACT, and MORTGAGE REFINANCING.

LOAN BROKER

A loan broker is an organization or person who specializes in arranging loans from his/her client-lenders to qualified borrowers. Broker fees are generally paid by the borrower. Loan brokers may or may not service the loan on behalf of the lender.

INVESTOR ADVICE

Residential loans are often handled by mortgage bankers or brokers, who have access to funds of insurance companies and pension plans. Mortgage bankers very often utilize their own funds for the loan and then sell them in large packages to appropriate lenders. After the sale, the banker may or may not provide loan servicing.

Loan brokers usually act as agents for lenders. Their fees (say 1% of the loan amount) are paid by the borrower when the application is made. That fee is earned at the point the broker provides a firm mortgage commitment from the actual lender. Most often the broker also handles the paperwork involved in processing the mortgage and property transfer.

SEE ALSO: MORTGAGE COMPANY.

LOAN RATIO

A loan ratio is the loan amount divided by the appraised value of a property. This is also known as the loan to value ratio.

INVESTOR ADVICE

All lending organizations have maximum loan ratios, which are set by appropriate government regulations or company policy. These ratios determine the maximum loans permissible and vary by:

- Lender;
- Property type;
- Property use; and
- Loan priority claim on property.

In order to achieve the maximum return on investment, most real estate investors are interested in maximum borrowing, which in turn provides maximum leverage.
SEE ALSO: LEVERAGE.

LOAN WINDOW

A loan window is a long-term loan with provisions for interest renegotiation at the end of specific periods or windows, such as every five years.

INVESTOR ADVICE

During high interest periods, borrowers are reluctant to borrow at existing rates—rates which are primarily based on risk and length of loan. Often a lower rate can be negotiated, if the borrower is willing to allow interest rate negotiation at each window period.

The loan usually provides for a mutual agreement on the interest to be charged during each window period. When no mutual agreement can be reached, the loan must be refinanced.

Interest rates can also be reduced by accepting a shorter amortization period; however, this is usually unsatisfactory to the investor as it increases the periodic payments beyond his/her acceptable level.
SEE ALSO: ADJUSTABLE RATE MORTGAGE, and REFINANCE.

LOCK-IN PERIOD

The lock-in period is the time allowed from application or mortgage commitment until a loan must be finalized at a stated guaranteed interest rate.

INVESTOR ADVICE

When seeking a mortgage loan during times of rising interest rates, it is essential to know the exact interest rate which will apply when the loan is finalized.

Some lenders will make a commitment on the interest rate at the time the application is taken. Others will not guarantee the interest rate until such time as the loan application has successfully progressed through the loan processing procedure and been approved.

A firm commitment on interest rates is often necessary in order to justify proceeding with a planned project. Where leverage is required to produce a required return on investment, a small upward move in the interest rate can reduce a profitable project to an unprofitable one.

When seeking a loan commitment, a good question to ask is, "Is this interest rate guaranteed . . . and for what term?"
SEE ALSO: LEVERAGE.

LOCUS SIGILLI

This legal term means, "Place of the seal."

INVESTOR ADVICE

The term *locus sigilli* is often found on legal documents to indicate the place where the person who acknowledges the document (notary or other officer of the court) is to place their seal.

Documents to be officially recorded into the public record must be acknowledged. As an investor, you will find many instances in which acknowledgments are required, such as:

* Deeds;

* Trust instruments;

* Lien waiver releases;

* Mortgage notes;

* Notices of contractual interest;

* Wills and codicils to wills.

SEE ALSO: ACKNOWLEDGMENTS, NOTARY, and RECORDING.

LOFT BUILDING

A loft building contains more than one floor.

INVESTOR ADVICE

Loft buildings are normally found in urban areas and are frequently occupied by tenants who conduct light manufacturing operations, such as the needle trade.

In some areas, loft buildings have been successfully converted to residential condominiums, cooperative apartments, and artist studios. A good solid building may be an excellent investment for a recycling project. Before you buy, however, carefully check the current zoning or potential for rezoning.
SEE ALSO: INDUSTRIAL BUILDING, and RECYCLED REAL ESTATE.

LONG-TERM GAINS

Long-term gains are profits made from holding real estate for certain periods of time.

INVESTOR ADVICE

The tax reform laws of 1986 virtually eliminated long-term capital gains, except for certain properties purchased prior to the change of law. Prior laws had provided for a reduced tax rate on property gains which were held for a minimum of six months. This was later change to a one-year holding period.
SEE ALSO: SHORT-TERM GAINS.

LOT IMPROVEMENTS

Lot improvements are any improvements to the land which make it more valuable for its highest and best use.

INVESTOR ADVICE
Lot improvements usually consist of:

- Curbs and gutters;
- Sidewalks;
- Sanitary sewers;
- Storm sewers;
- Electrical service;
- Telephone service;
- Culinary water; and
- Paved streets.

When buying building or development lots, it is important to determine what lot improvements exist on the property at that time.

If the property is not improved, you should determine the local development requirements and their projected costs. If culinary water and sanitary sewers are not already present, how far from the property are these facilities? Will you be able to connect to these nearest facilities and at what cost?

SEE ALSO: COMPLETION BOND, RESTRICTIVE COVENANTS, and ZONING.

LOT RELEASE SYSTEM

The lot release system is a method of acquiring development property for resale with minimum down payment.

INVESTOR ADVICE
When you acquire property to be developed and resold in smaller parcels or lots, the standard mortgage or contractual indebtedness will preclude your ability to sell these parcels and provide clear title.

The lot release system is an answer to this problem. If the property is purchased from an owner who is willing to carry a purchase money mortgage, or even where a new mortgage is obtained from a lending organization, you should negotiate a lot release arrangement. Such provisions can be inserted into the loan agreement.

EXAMPLE

Mr. D. Veloper has found a thirty-acre parcel of land, which appears to be an excellent prospect for building lot development. The land can be purchased for $20,000 per acre on a contract, with $100,000 down.

Mr. Veloper has surveyed the property and determined that 120 building lots can be provided on the property. He has two alternatives:

1 Buy a part of the land with available funds; or
2. Buy the entire property on contract and negotiate a lot release payment arrangement.

Here is what he proposes to the current land owner. He will purchase the entire property on contract to allow immediate construction of utilities, streets, curbs and gutters, etc. As he finds buyers for the lots, the local title company will provide the buyer with a clear title for his purchased lot and pay the land owner 120th of the original contract amount.

The difference between the lot selling price and the contract payment will be paid to Mr. Veloper. Mr. Veloper estimates he must sell about eighty lots in order to pay for the land and all development costs. The remaining forty lots will constitute his profit.

The lot release system is beneficial to all parties as follows:

1. Land sellers can dispose of land parcels at a time when mortgage money is expensive or unavailable;
2. Developers can gain full control of the land at minimum interest rates and with lower down payments; and
3. Buyers are assured of good and equitable title to parcels or lots purchased.

SEE ALSO: BLANKET MORTGAGE.

M

Mack Truck Factor
MAI Appraiser
Mansard Roof
Manufactured Housing
Market Data Approach to Value
Market Rent
Market Survey
Market Value
Master Limited Partnership
Master Metering
Master Plan
Mean
Mechanical Equipment
Mechanic's Lien
Medical Office Building
Meridian
Metes and Bounds
Mill Rate
Mineral Lease

Mini-Warehouse
Mixed-Use Property
Mobile Home
Mobile Home Park
Modular Housing
Month-to-Month
Monument
Mortgage
Mortgage Commitment
Mortgage Company
Mortgage Constant
Mortgage Equity Technique
Mortgage Note
Mortgage Package
Mortgage Refinancing
Multiple Listing Service
Muniments
Mutual Savings Bank

M

MACK TRUCK FACTOR

"Mack truck factor" is money lender parlance for a test of borrower management strength. A passing mark indicates the borrowing company management has sufficient strength and depth to survive the loss of a key member—"hit by a Mack truck."

INVESTOR ADVICE

One of the critical considerations of a lender to a real estate development company is the company's ability to succeed if a key member of the management team should die or leave the organization.

The application for loan, containing all of the pertinent facts of the proposed project, will also provide the lender with a thorough revelation of management strengths. The supporting data should contain a resumé of each of the management personnel, showing their proposed contribution to the project, education, and past experience which is expected to assure the success of the project.

Since the lender will review all of the data in its worst possible scenario, it is important to show that the death or defection of any one member of the management team will not adversely affect the success of the planned project.

SEE ALSO: LIMITED PARTNERSHIP, PARTNERSHIP, and REAL ESTATE INVESTMENT TRUST (REIT).

MAI APPRAISER

An MAI appraiser is a member of the American Institute of Real Estate Appraisers (AIREA). The MAI is AIREA's highest designation and indicates that the appraiser is fully qualified, through education and experience, to appraise all types of real property.

INVESTOR ADVICE

The AIREA (founded in 1928) is the oldest appraisal organization in the United States and the only one that is a part of the National Association of Realtors. Because of its age, relationship to the National Association of Realtors, and its comprehensive requirements for membership, the MAI appraiser is well known to all lending institutions and other financial organizations. Because of this, these members like to think that their designations are superior to those offered by other professional appraisal organizations.

The actual fact is that there are good and bad appraisers in all organizations. A particular appraiser's competence is determined first by his designation, which indicates his formal training and experience; and second by the success of his past work experience. This latter qualification can only be determined by a review of his references and the testimony of his former clients.

When selecting an appraiser, you should demand the following:

- A membership in one of several professional organizations, which trains and certifies its members as competent;

- A designation which indicates the appraiser is trained to perform appraisals of the type you require;

- Minimum experience of not less than 3 years—more is preferable;

- Favorable recommendations from lending institutions and others for which he/she has worked on similar projects; and

- Evidence that the appraiser has been recertified by his organization through continued education in the field.

SEE ALSO: RM APPRAISER.

MANSARD ROOF

A mansard roof has two slopes on each side, the second or lower slope usually being steeper than the first. In recent years, a flat roof such as this, with a short sloping roof screen around the perimeter which hides the main roof, has been referred to as a mansard.

INVESTOR ADVICE

When buying a building with a mansard roof, an inspection by a competent roofing contractor is advised. Most flat roofs have a limited life, although new materials are extending this lifetime beyond the old ten to fifteen year average. Still, flat roofs tend to collect and hold water which causes the roofing materials to deteriorate.

Some indication of the roof condition can be determined from ground level by a careful inspection of the interior ceilings and by viewing the metal drip strip at the lower edge of the roof. Freshly painted ceilings or those indicating recent drywall work may indicate recent roof leaks. These will undoubtedly have been fixed before the property was listed for sale, but may have been repaired by patching an old and generally unserviceable roof.

Figure 42. Mansard Roof (Reprinted by permission of Marshall Swift).

A discolored or rusting metal drip strip will also indicate an old roof subject to problems. A new and shiny drip strip usually indicates a new roof installation. When in doubt, have the roof inspected by an expert.

Figure 42 shows a mansard roof used in residential construction.

SEE ALSO: GABLE, and HIP ROOF.

MANUFACTURED HOUSING

Manufactured housing units are built in a factory for transportation in either a knocked-down or completed condition—also known as pre-fab housing.

INVESTOR ADVICE

The term *manufactured housing* should not be confused with mobile home or trailer home. Manufactured housing is generally classified into two types:

1. A home which is shipped to the construction site as panels and modules. Wall, roof, and floor sections are generally manufactured in 4–8 foot widths in much the same way as a stick-built home. The modules are then joined at the construction site to form the finished framework, which is then completed in a conventional manner. This type of construction is actually stronger than conventional construction in that there is a double stud, or rafter or floor support in spots where two modules are joined.
2. Prefabricated homes which are completed in the factory and shipped to the site as one or more units. These homes only require utility connections and minor trim work at the site, as everything else is completed in the factory.

Although many manufactured homes are of as good or better quality than on-site stick-built homes, some localities will not allow their construction. Before planning such construction, it would be wise to determine the building codes in the area proposed.

SEE ALSO: BUILDING CODES, and RESTRICTIVE COVENANTS.

MARKET DATA APPROACH TO VALUE

This term refers to an appraisal technique in which the subject property is compared to recent sales of similar properties in comparable locations.

INVESTOR ADVICE

Market data is always essential in the appraisal of land and improved property. Even though the "market data approach" is not always the primary consideration, market data is used in most of the other approaches.

Market sales data can be utilized for the direct comparison of land parcels or structures with appropriate adjustments for their differences. Rental and sales data can be used to project market values of income property being appraised. Market income data can be analyzed to establish capitalization rates.

The use of rental/sales data is known as the gross or net income multiplier method, and the use of market data to establish income capitalization rates is known as the income approach.

Normally the market data approach to value indicates *the direct comparison of sold properties with the subject.*

EXAMPLE

An appraiser is evaluating a home in a subdivision in which all homes are similar and were constructed by the same builder about twenty years ago. The appraiser's inspection of the property indicates some remodeling and additions, since the property was first built.

The appraisal inspection notes the following differences from a nearby home, which recently sold for $65,000 on an FHA sales basis:

SUBJECT HOME

• Contains 240 square feet more floor space

- Has a newly remodeled kitchen

- Original 2-car carport has been converted to a 2-car garage.

COMPARABLE SALE

- Has one additional bath

- Has new roof

The appraiser makes the following adjustments between the comparable sale and the subject home. Plus and minus figures are used to "make the comparable look like the subject—on paper":

Size up, 240 sq. ft.	+ 7,200
Gar. versus cpt.	+ 3,000
New kitchen	+ 3,500
1 less bath	− 2,200
New roof versus old	− 1,500
Points paid for FHA financing	− 1,900
Total Adjustments	+ 8,100

The adjusted value is the sales price +/- the adjustments for differences, or

$$\$65,000 + \$8,100 = \$73,100$$

The same adjustment work would be performed with at least two other sales for comparison and the final appraised value determined from the adjusted values of all three comparables.

Please note that the adjustments are not the cost of the improvement or lack thereof, but the difference in *buyer perceived value difference*. It may cost $5,000 to remodel the kitchen, but the adjustment says, "An average buyer would be willing to pay $3,500 more for a home with a modern kitchen versus an older kitchen." Adjustment values are determined by the appraiser's experience in the marketplace.

SEE ALSO: CAPITALIZATION RATE, GROSS RENT MULTIPLIER, and INCOME APPROACH TO VALUE.

MARKET RENT

Market rent is the most probable rent which would be received from a property, based on similar rentals of comparable properties in the same or comparable area.

INVESTOR ADVICE

When purchasing a rental property or proposing to build such a property, a market survey to determine market rent is advisable. This data is useful in estimating gross income and in determining market value by the gross or net rent multiplier method.

Accurate market rent data is also required in the calculation of leasehold interests, which results from a situation, in which contract rent is less than market rent. If a proposed property is rented for less than market rent, this leasehold interest must be considered in determining what to offer for the property. In all cases this will be something less than the appraised value.

SEE ALSO: GROSS RENT MULTIPLIER, LEASEHOLD INTEREST, and NET RENT MULTI-PLIER.

MARKET SURVEY

A market survey is a factual study of the real estate market for the purpose of determining a need for additional rental units, average rentals being charged, and market price for real estate based on current or projected income and occupancy rates.

INVESTOR ADVICE

Most real estate investors prefer to deal in properties in areas which are personally well known to them. Occasionally, an investment opportunity will surface in an unfamiliar area. Before investing, a competent market survey should be conducted.

Market data can be obtained from real estate agencies, apartment house associations, local banks and newspapers, and educational institutions. The required data for analysis can be personally gathered or obtained through a professional marketing survey source.

A good excuse can be made for failure of a project due to erroneous future economic projections, however there is no excuse for lack of current knowledge. You wouldn't buy a stock from your broker without knowing its past, current and projected income. A real estate investment is generally a much larger investment than a stock purchase, yet many buy before determining the facts. Know what you are buying before agreeing to purchase. Some of the factors affecting income property marketing are:

COMMERCIAL RETAIL SPACE

- Size of the market area from which trade will be drawn

- Spendable income of that market area

- Existing commercial space and yearly sales per square foot of space available

- Projected growth of the market area

- Accessibility and convenience of the project to the market population

RESIDENTIAL UNITS

- Existing availability of comparable rental units.

- Proximity to major job sources

- Proximity to public transportation

- Vacancy factors of comparable properties

- Economic growth projections

- Eye appeal of the proposed project

- Amenities offered in the proposed project

SEE ALSO: MARKET RENT, and MARKET VALUE.

MARKET VALUE

Market value is the most likely price that a willing buyer and a willing seller would agree upon for the sale of a property exposed to the open market for a reasonable period of time.

INVESTOR ADVICE

In the appraisal of real property, the appraiser attempts to determine the "market value" which is his or her estimation of what that property will bring if placed on the market for a reasonable time. It is, in effect, an educated guess based on currently available sales data, which is analyzed by the appraiser.

Two appraisers, of equal experience and competence, will not necessarily arrive at the exact same figure. However, their two values will usually be very close. Employee relocation companies, who buy their transferred employee's homes, normally expect two independent appraisals to vary by no more than 5%.

SEE ALSO: FAIR MARKET VALUE, and MARKET DATA APPROACH TO VALUE

MASTER LIMITED PARTNERSHIP

A master limited partnership looks like a corporation, operates like a corporation, and trades on a major stock exchange.

INVESTOR ADVICE

The master limited partnership is a relatively new business structure, spawned by the 1986 tax change which reduced personal taxes below the corporate rate. For businesses that produce large amounts of income which is distributed to its owners, this operating method avoids the double taxation of the corporate form, and lowers the overall tax rate to the investor.

As of June 30, 1987, there were 99 master limited partnerships trading on the major stock exchanges.[1] Growth of these are expected to continue, unless Congress changes the existing tax laws. Already, the projected tax loss is causing many to advocate a change which would treat all income from publicly traded organizations as if it were from a corporation.

Until such changes are passed, the master limited partnership is an excellent way to invest in real estate. It offers all of the advantages of the older type limited partnerships plus the liquidity of trading on the major exchanges. Even if the law is changed, there will undoubtedly be a transition period for existing investors.

SEE ALSO: LIMITED PARTNERSHIP.

MASTER METERING

Master metering is a method of measuring utility use from one single point of a multiple user facility—sometimes referred to as "single point metering."

INVESTOR ADVICE

Master metering is not a preferred method, but often must be used in facilities in which individual metering is not economically feasible. Many developers will not even consider the purchase of a complex if utilities are not or cannot be economically separated.

Since the early 1960s utility bills have become a significant expense and one which, if not controlled, will wipe out all profits from the rental operation. If you have a property with single point or master metering, you should consider the possibility of conversion. If this proves infeasible, action must be taken to provide for an equitable utility payment method for all tenants. This can be accomplished as each new lease is signed.

Utility bills in commercial buildings can be prorated to tenants on a unit basis. It might be done according to square footage utilized provided all tenants have similar utility requirements. In residential buildings, proration is usually based on apartment size or may be included with the rent. This latter arrangement is not the best, since the tenant has no incentive to conserve.

If utility usage is not prorated between tenants, some additional means must be incorporated in the leases to provide for periodic increases in utility rates, especially if the lease terms tend to be for extended periods.

SEE ALSO: INDIVIDUAL METERING.

MASTER PLAN

A "master plan" in real estate is the guideline established for the orderly zoning and development of an area.

INVESTOR ADVICE

Years ago, areas developed in accordance with the needs and desires of its citizens and with little interference of the governmental agencies. As development in areas accelerates, however, especially in recent years, governmental authorities have begun to exercise their police power to regulate all development to assure that it meets the goals and common good of the community.

One of the first steps in regulation is the development of a master plan for the community. This designates areas for particular types of growth—recreational, residential, business and commercial, manufacturing, and so on. All future rezoning generally follows this master plan.

If you are planning to acquire property for a particular type of development, it is imperative that you select property already zoned for that type of operation or property which fits the master plan and is capable of being rezoned.

WARNING Make all purchase offers subject to required rezoning approval if not currently zoned for your needs.

SEE ALSO: RESTRICTIVE COVENANTS, SPOT ZONING, and ZONING.

MEAN

The mean is the value of a number within a series of numbers, which lies halfway between the smallest and largest numbers of the series.

INVESTOR ADVICE

The mean value is often used by appraisers, market analysts, and others who do not want to utilize an average value. Averages can be grossly affected by very low or very high numbers in a series, which distort the results. A mean, on the other hand, eliminates the low and high extremes and produces a value which is more useful for determination of middle-of-the-road value.

A good example of the use of the mean follows:

EXAMPLE

Mr. K, a real estate appraiser, has compared a property to seven others recently sold. He has made appropriate addition and subtraction adjustments for the differences between the comparable sales, properties, and the subject property. He arrives at the following "Adjusted Values" per square foot.

COMPARABLE NUMBER

1	2	3	4	5	6	7
$2.00	$5.00	$1.82	$0.75	$2.01	$2.10	$1.75

Common sense tells him that the value of the appraised property is probably around $2.00 per square foot. However, the average of the seven values is $2.20. He realizes that this value has been affected by the highest number, which is out of the "ball park" so to speak. He decides that a mean value is probably more accurate. He finds the mean by first listing the values in ascending order, according to value. This produces the following list:

$0.75 $1.75 $1.82 $2.00 $2.01 $2.10 $5.00

He begins the process by striking out the lowest and the highest number, and repeats this process until only one mean figure, $2.00, remains.

Often, in the appraisal process, numbers resulting from a particular analysis won't make sense. A low number could be due to a sale by a person who is forced to sell and a high number by a person very anxious to buy—facts unknown to the appraiser. Thus, the mean value is often employed.

SEE ALSO: AVERAGE, and MARKET DATA APPROACH TO VALUE.

MECHANICAL EQUIPMENT

Mechanical equipment is installed in a building for heating, ventilating, and air conditioning.

INVESTOR ADVICE

Repair and replacement of mechanical equipment is a major expense of operating a rental facility and often represents up to 10% of the total value. When buying an older building it is advisable to hire an expert inspector to survey all mechanical equipment to determine its condition and life expectancy.

When that economic or useful life figure is determined, you should begin to set aside sufficient funds as reserves for replacement. If air conditioning is not provided, it may be necessary to add this convenience to the existing equipment or install new equipment which incorporates this feature. Except in the most moderate climates, most tenants now insist on air conditioning. Your vacancy rate will certainly be improved by this addition.

SEE ALSO: INDIVIDUAL METERING, ELECTRICAL EQUIPMENT, MASTER METERING, and PLUMBING EQUIPMENT.

MECHANIC'S LIEN

A mechanic's lien is filed against a property for work performed or materials furnished by a contractor or subcontractor.

INVESTOR ADVICE

You should be advised that a title search may or may not reveal all mechanic claims on a property. A title search is conducted on a certain date and reveals liens of records filed up to that date. Most states provide for the filing of mechanic liens sixty or more days after the last work is performed, which means they may not appear until well after the deal is closed.

A title search made just prior to the closing of the sale would also not reveal these possible claims. Thus, when buying a new property which has just been constructed or an older one recently remodeled, you have two possible ways of protecting yourself against these future claims:

1. Require the contractor to be bonded.
2. Acquire title insurance, where possible, with protection against mechanic's liens.

Often an income property is purchased and later remodeled by the new owner. In this case you should be aware that you may be subject to double payment of sub-contractors and suppliers if the contractor accepts your full payment and then fails to pay his/her own subcontractors and suppliers.

Many states do not relieve the property owner of the responsibility to pay sub-contractors unless the contractor has been bonded. To avoid liability, Utah and other states require the property owner to insist that contractors doing work in excess of $2,000 furnish a bond to guarantee sub-contractor and supplier payment.

SEE ALSO: CONTRACTOR'S LIEN, LIENS, and SUBCONTRACTOR.

MEDICAL OFFICE BUILDING

A medical office building is specifically designed and built to house members of the medical profession. Medical buildings are more expensive than regular office buildings, due to requirements for extensive electrical, plumbing, and sanitary facilities.

INVESTOR ADVICE

When proposing to buy or build a medical office building, particular care must be exercised in site selection. Successful medical or professional buildings should be located in easily accessible areas to the population. They are designed to serve. Ideally, facilities should be near or adjacent to a large medical facility, such as a hospital. It is very important that medical buildings also provide adequate parking, with particular attention given to handicapped access.

In addition, materials selection for a medical office is more important than a regular office. The requirement for super cleanliness may very well dictate the use of stainless steel, high grade vinyl floor coverings, tile walls, highest grade plumbing fixtures, and extra-high-quality paint. While initially more expensive, these features will prove more economical in the long run through reduced replacement, repairs, and redecoration.

It is often possible for a developer to obtain financing from the prospective tenants, either through the sale of condominium office space, formation of a limited partnership, or development of the property as a joint venture. Use of any of these three methods can be very lucrative.

You can undoubtedly acquire partial ownership by accepting some of the units in the condominium complex for rent to other physicians or allied businesses, such as a pharmacy. If the joint venture or limited partnership approach is taken, you can be assured of a good percentage of the ownership. In addition, it may be possible to obtain the management contract and, if you are also a REALTOR®, the eventual sale of the facility can produce a good commission.

SEE ALSO: CONDOMINIUM, JOINT VENTURE, LIMITED PARTNERSHIP, and OFFICE BUILDING.

MERIDIAN

A meridian is the principal north-south line of the government survey system.

INVESTOR ADVICE

The distance from a designated meridian is called a "range." A legal description showing "Range 3 East" would indicate that the property is located in the third range to the east of the named meridian. Figure 7 (shown in the discussion of base lines) indicates the use of base lines and meridians in government surveys.

SEE ALSO: BASE LINE, and LAND IDENTIFICATION METHODS.

METES AND BOUNDS

This term refers to a method of land identification which begins at a designated point and continues with a series of distances and compass calls to identify the various boundaries. The description ends with a final return to the point of beginning.

INVESTOR ADVICE

This system is employed in many parts of the world as well as many areas of the United States. It had its beginning in the original thirteen colonies and in the Southern states. This system was widely used prior to the introduction of the government survey system.

Metes and bounds can be used alone to identify a specific property or in conjunction with a lot and block or the government survey system. When the systems are combined it usually is for convenience in locating the point of beginning (POB).

EXAMPLE

Beginning at the SE corner of Section 29, T 1E, R 2S, Salt Lake Base and Meridian and continuing South 14.5 rods to the point of beginning, etc.

or

Beginning at the SW corner of Lot 25, Block 16, Big Field Survey and continuing West 4.5 chains to a point of beginning, etc.

SEE ALSO: CHAINS, LAND IDENTIFICATION METHODS, and RODS.

MILL RATE

A mill rate is the tax rate expressed in mills per dollar of assessed value. A mill is equal to 1/10th of a cent or 1/1000th of a dollar.

INVESTOR ADVICE

A tax rate of 78 mills expressed as a decimal would be:

$0.0078/dollar of assessed evaluation

A property assessed at $100,000 would be taxed an amount per year equal to:

$$\$100,000 \times 0.0078 = \$780.00$$

The tax rates in most parts of the United States are based on antiquated methods and techniques. Most agree that taxes should be based on current market value with the tax rate set to provide the required revenue for the various authorities.

In some areas, such as Boston, Massachusetts, property is frequently taxed on assessments made years previously. This encourages renovation in lieu of razing and new construction, which is taxed on its value when built. A tax rate based on a percentage of fair market value is much easier to understand than an assessment based on a percent of fair market value multiplied by a mill rate.

SEE ALSO: ASSESSED VALUE, AD VALOREM, and FAIR MARKET VALUE.

MINERAL LEASE

A mineral lease permits the lessee to explore for and remove certain materials from under the surface of the property.

INVESTOR ADVICE

Mineral leases generally provide for token payments during the period up to actual discovery and extraction. When extraction of the mineral begins, royalty payments per ton, barrel, or other measure of the natural resource actually removed, is made to the owner.

Where the mining or extraction of the mineral will disturb the surface, such as in strip-mining, the land is generally purchased rather than leased. State laws are very strict in regard to mineral mining and set certain requirements for rehabilitation of the land after the minerals have been removed.

Drilling operations for gas, oil, or other subterranean products require special lease agreements to provide access to and from the sites for construction of collection pipelines and/or roads for transportation of the product produced. In certain areas, environmental restrictions are imposed by the state to ensure that the surrounding land or environment is not unduly harmed.

Before signing a mineral lease, you should review it very carefully with regard to potential damages to the property which may result from extraction of the natural resource.

Some materials can be removed with minimum damage to the land. However, strip-mining and other extraction methods often leave the land useless for a considerable time to come.

SEE ALSO: BUNDLE OF RIGHTS, and LEASE.

MINI-WAREHOUSE

A mini-warehouse project contains many individual rental storage facilities. Storage compartment sizes vary from small 6 x 10 foot lockers to double car-size drive-ins. These facilities are largely self operated, with each renter entering and leaving at will. Renters are provided with computer codes for electronic gate access.

INVESTOR ADVICE

Mini-warehousing is an excellent investment program for retirement. It requires a minimum effort to advertise, lease, and collect rentals. With the exception of occasional inspection and minimum maintenance, the facility can be largely self-supporting.

Most mini-warehouses are built of concrete block or other durable material. Roofs are of steel or similar long-lasting covering. Driveways are typically asphalt. Each locker is provided with a steel door which can be locked by the occupant. The entire compound is secured by heavy chain-link or other acceptable type security fencing to prevent unauthorized entrance and exit.

Once constructed, the primary operating expenses are taxes, insurance, security lighting, and reserves for future fence and asphalt-paving repairs. In areas of heavy snowfall, it may also be necessary to provide snow removal from the driveways.

As in the case of all proposed rental projects, a market survey is recommended, before construction begins. The location selected should be convenient to apartment complexes and small retail businesses which often utilize such storage facilities for off-season merchandise. Renters of miniwarehousing facilities come from all walks of life and procure facilities for various reasons. The following is a list of typical customers:

- Apartment dwellers who store excess furniture and other personal effects;

- Antique car buffs, who rent facilities to repair and rework their prized acquisitions;

- Small business distributors and wholesalers, who require additional temporary storage space;

- Landscapers and other journeymen who need winter storage facilities for their equipment;

- Auto tire retailers, who prefer to buy in very large quantities, but do not have sufficient on-site storage.

Rental fees are dependent upon economic conditions in the area and the availability of competitive properties. If properly sited and constructed, it can be expected that vacancy factors will be very low—in the neighborhood of 5–10%.

SEE ALSO: MARKET SURVEY, and ZONING.

MIXED-USE PROPERTY

Mixed-use property is zoned for more than one type of use. An example would be apartments and small retail stores.

INVESTOR ADVICE

Mixed-use properties are usually more carefully protected by zoning authorities than single use. This is to assure that the various authorized uses are fully compatible.

Before buying or making a commitment for construction on mixed-use property, you should check to determine what additional requirements must be satisfied before construction is authorized and/or what restrictions are imposed on the property use.

Development of mixed-use properties can be more expensive than other types. Local restrictive covenants and zoning regulations require specified open landscaping areas, ample parking, limited street access, and screened fencing between commercial and residential portions of the project.

If your interest is primarily in residential housing, however, mixed-use property can be beneficial. A large property can be subdivided into commercial and residential sections, with the commercial portion resold at a price which can pay for close to the entire plot.

SEE ALSO: PLOTTAGE, RESTRICTIVE COVENANTS, and ZONING.

MOBILE HOME

A mobile home is a single-family housing unit, constructed of aluminum or other lightweight materials, which is designed to be pulled from site to site or semi-permanently installed on a mobile home pad.

Mobile homes may be self-contained, or require connection to utilities and sanitary sewer.

INVESTOR ADVICE

The original mobile home was designed for intermittent use, was light enough to be towed by an automobile, and was self-contained, at least for a short period.

Modern mobile homes are typically much larger and approach the size of manufactured homes. Most are expandable on site or designed to be connected to additional units. These large heavy units require special towing facilities and are usually semi-permanently installed on site. They require considerable effort to connect to utilities and sanitary facilities, install porches, carports, underpinnings and other improvements. Most modern units are at least 20 x 50 feet in size. Most contain two baths and as many as four bedrooms.

Smaller units are easily moved and connected to facilities for short term use, usually in seasonal recreational vehicle parks. Larger units are most commonly installed in mobile home parks.

SEE ALSO: MOBILE HOME PARK, RESTRICTIVE COVENANTS, and ZONING.

MOBILE HOME PARK

A mobile home park is a development designed and built for rental to mobile or manufactured home owners. Rental units are known as "pads" which contain all utility hook-up connections, sanitary sewers, and paved access.

INVESTOR ADVICE

Due to the high density use, mobile home parks are very strictly controlled as to location, type of facilities, security fencing, and access roads. Land authorized for this use is usually at a premium, particularly if located close to a city center.

Turnover is very low in this type of facility. The favorite size of home now approaches twelve to fifteen feet wide and fifty or more feet long. The expense of moving, setting, installing skirting, utilities, and other amenities such as patios and porches makes a move most uneconomical. The tendency is to sell the unit on the pad rather than to move it. This largely assures the park owner of 100% occupancy once the park is established. A good pad will rent for as much as $200-300 per month and each tenant pays his own utility bills. Pad sizes may vary but generally tend to be of uniform size —large enough for the largest units with no more than six-foot clearance on either side and a very small backyard, which depends upon the home length.

While individual pads are maintained by the tenant, the park owner is responsible for common areas, interior roads, swimming pools, tennis courts, party rooms, and, of course, internal security. This latter requirement can often be the largest problem, unless prospective tenants are carefully screened.

While most homeowners consider the mobile home park a low-cost housing project, this characterization is not necessarily correct. Some Arizona, California, and Florida parks are restricted to luxury homes costing $200,000 and up. The Lawrence Welk facility in Escondido, California, is a good example.

Mobile home parks are not restricted to rental facilities only. Many parks have been developed specifically for lot sales to owners of mobile homes. These facilities are characterized by their larger size compared to the typical rental facilities, which are designed for maximum income production.

SEE ALSO: MANUFACTURED HOUSING, and MOBILE HOME.

MODULAR HOUSING

Modular housing is manufactured housing delivered to the site as complete units or large components.

INVESTOR ADVICE

Several manufacturers of modular housing can provide components for construction of custom-designed homes. These components are equal in quality to stick-built homes and provide for rapid construction on site. They are particularly popular in areas subject to inclement weather conditions.

When the foundation or basement is ready, a modular home can be completely constructed to the "dried-in" point by one small crew, in one working day. The exterior finish and interior work then proceeds as in conventional housing. A modular home can often save up to 20% of the cost of a comparable stick-built home.

Smaller homes, up to 1,400 square feet for instance, can be delivered to the site in one or more units, which are complete in all details.

These units are ready for occupancy in as little as one day.

Several commercial projects have been constructed from modular units. One of the best examples of this was a hotel constructed for the San Antonio Exposition in the late 1960s. In this project, complete rooms, constructed of prefabricated concrete and ready for use, were delivered to the site and stacked by crane. Each unit was then connected to pre-installed utilities and occupied the following day.

SEE ALSO: STICK-BUILT HOME.

MONTH-TO-MONTH

This term refers to:
1. A real property lease for the term of one month which is renewable at the will of both the lessor and lessee.
2. A tenant who remains in possession of property after expiration of a lease with the approval of the landlord (said to be a "Tenant at Will").

INVESTOR ADVICE

For convenience of the landlord and tenant, a clause is often inserted into a fixed-term lease which allows a month-to-month tenancy at the end of the lease period. Neither party is required to give notice and acceptance of rent by the landlord, extends the lease from month to month.

In times of inflation, this arrangement is not recommended, as the landlord may miss an opportunity to increase the rental rate. Where there is no provision for month-to-month continuance, acceptance of rental moneys, when due, can be construed as establishing a month-to-month tenancy.

Laws in the various states vary somewhat. Utah law recognizes only four tenant estates:

1. *Estate at Sufferance*—A tenant takes possession of property as a lessee but then remains in possession after the termination date of the lease. A court order is required to dispossess this tenant.

2. *Estate at Will*—A tenant takes possession of a property, with the owner's permission but without entering into a verbal or written lease. Five days notice must be given by the owner to terminate this tenant.

3. *Periodic Estate*—A tenant takes possession under a legal lease with no specified termination date. Fifteen days notice is required to terminate this tenant.

4. *Estate for Years*—A tenant takes possession for an agreed period, one week, one month, one year, etc. No notice is required to terminate this lease as all of the parties are aware of the termination date.

You can avoid problems of expired leases by maintaining a record of lease periods for monthly inspection. A horizontal bar chart, indicating each tenant's lease period, can serve as an excellent alerting device.

SEE ALSO: HOLDOVER TENANT, LEASE, TENANCY AT SUFFERANCE, and TENANCY AT WILL.

MONUMENT

A monument is a fixed object installed by surveyors from which land descriptions can be measured. Monuments can be brass tacks in concrete, buried blocks or stones with reference points carved thereon or any other device which is expected to remain for a long period of time.

INVESTOR ADVICE

In the Western United States and those other parts which have been government surveyed, permanently installed section monuments are the basis for most surveys. These provide the location of section corners and often elevation data as well.

If you require a land survey, it is advisable to have the surveyor install permanent monuments at all reference points. This will avoid a future requirement for a new survey when building on or fencing the property at some future time. If not specifically advised to install permanent monuments, the surveyor will probably indicate his/her reference points by temporary wooden stakes.

When developing raw land into building lots, it is customary in most areas to provide brass tacks in the sidewalks to indicate lot boundaries. Rear boundaries may be marked in a number of ways, the most popular methods being stakes and/or concrete monuments.

SEE ALSO: COMPASS CALL, and LAND IDENTIFICATION METHODS.

MORTGAGE

A mortgage is an official acknowledgment of indebtedness given to a lender by a borrower as security for a loan on his/her real property.

INVESTOR ADVICE

There are several mortgage types in use in the United States:

- The ordinary or common mortgage;

- The deed of trust;

- The equitable mortgage;

- The deed absolute.

The Common Mortgage
This is the ordinary printed form used in many states, which provides for the following:

- Must be in writing

- Must be signed (executed);

- Must contain a mortgaging clause such as "grants and conveys" or "conveys and warrants" or some similar language;

- The mortgagor must have an interest in the property and only that interest can be mortgaged.

- There must be a debt, which is described. The debt can be pre-existing, or created by a loan at the same time as the mortgage;

- The mortgaged property must be clearly identified in a similar manner as a deed;

- The mortgage instrument must clearly specify what recourse is available to the mortgagee, in the event of payment default; and

- It must be signed, accepted, and acknowledged. This latter requirement is to permit recording for public notice.

The Deed of Trust
This type of deed brings a third party, the trustee, into the mortgage transaction. In the deed of trust, the borrower conveys the mortgaged property to the trustee to be held for the benefit of the lender, who holds a note of indebtedness. Upon failure to comply with the terms of the note, the trustee can exercise the "power of sale" clause to attempt to satisfy the debt.
The advantage of the trust deed, used in about one-third of all the states, is that it allows the property to be foreclosed without court proceedings. The note held by the lender can also be used to obtain a deficiency judgment in instances where the sale of the property failed to liquidate the debt due.

The Equitable Mortgage
Any mortgage which clearly indicates the intention of the parties to hold the property as security for the loan is an equitable mortgage and can be foreclosed in a court of equity.
In addition, any mortgage which contains defects can operate as an equitable mortgage.

The Deed Absolute
This type of mortgage is one which is used far less than the other types. The deed absolute uses a quit claim or warranty deed to convey the mortgaged property to the lender, as security for a loan. Many times this instrument is just held by the lender and not recorded until such time as foreclosure is necessary.
For the deed to be considered a mortgage, the court requires substantial and convincing evidence that it was intended to be a mortgage and not a sale. Evidence of this fact can be shown by:

- Prior negotiations, loan applications, etc.;

- Size and adequacy of the consideration received by the mortgagor (assignor);

- Conduct of both parties subsequent to the signing of the deed; and

- Possession of the property—buyers normally possess the property upon sale, lenders do not.

While this outlines the general requirements of the various mortgage types, most mortgage instruments contain many additional provisions. These generally provide for:

- Mortgagee refinancing protection;

- Prepayment fees;

- Requirement for insurance coverage;

- Prohibitions against alterations and destruction;

- Provisions for tax payments; and

- "Due on sale" or payment acceleration in event of transfer of property or interest to another.

SEE ALSO: TRUST DEED, TRUSTEE, QUIT CLAIM DEED, and WARRANTY DEED.

MORTGAGE COMMITMENT

A mortgage commitment is a notification, usually in writing, that a mortgage institution is willing to grant a mortgage on a property with conditions listed.

INVESTOR ADVICE

Before construction begins, you will want to apply for a long-term loan with a mortgage banker or other intermediary, who will obtain permanent financing from a money source. Such sources are usually large insurance companies, pension funds, and trusts which deal in large loans through mortgage bankers.

Once the loan is approved, your banker will then be able to arrange interim financing through a commercial bank, based on the take-out letter furnished by the committed lender, which details:

- Loan amount committed;

- Fees to be paid; and

- Date the loan is to be finalized.

If your mortgage banker is unable to find a permanent lender quickly, he/she may arrange an interim loan with a commercial banker, with the understanding that:

- Your mortgage banker will continue to try to find permanent financing.

- If unsuccessful, the commercial banker will provide the long-term funds in return for a mortgage. If the mortgage banker continues to be unable to find permanent financing, he/she agrees to take the mortgage from the commercial banker after a specified time has elapsed. The mortgage banker will continue to try to sell the mortgage and will probably find a lender at a later date.

It should be realized that this procedure applies to large projects requiring substantial mortgage money. Smaller projects are less involved, as they can usually be satisfied through local lenders or other clients of the mortgage banker.

SEE ALSO: TAKE-OUT LETTER, COMMITTED INSTITUTIONAL WAREHOUSING, and COMMITTED TECHNICAL WAREHOUSING.

MORTGAGE COMPANY

A mortgage company processes loan applications and closing loans, all or a majority of which are sold on the secondary mortgage market.

INVESTOR ADVICE

When considering applying for a loan with a mortgage company, you should determine the following:

- Can the loan be granted with that company's own funds or will a loan-sale commitment on the secondary market be required before closing?

- When the loan is sold to a secondary buyer, who will service the loan?

- Will government (FHA, VA) or quasi-government (FNMAE, GNMA) approval be required to close? What is the time delay for this action?

Your selection of a mortgage company or other lending institution will probably hinge on the answer to these questions. Most investors consider the following, in their order of importance:

- Interest rate;

- Time required to approval and close;

- Loan service ease; and

- Familiarity with and perceived professional competence of loan staff.

SEE ALSO: MORTGAGE PACKAGE.

MORTGAGE CONSTANT

A mortgage constant is the periodic payment required to pay off a debt and includes interest on the constantly declining balance over the lifetime of the payments.

INVESTOR ADVICE

The mortgage constant is differentiated from the annual constant, in that mortgages are normally payable on a monthly or other basis than annual. Tables of mortgage constants can be found in amortization books, which provide constants for various periods and interest rates. The constant, when multiplied by the amount to be borrowed, equals the periodic payment or debt service requirement.

The annual constant is really no more than the periodic payment required to amortize a loan over the stated period or the interest rate plus the sinking fund at the same interest rate. Referring to Figure 50, the present value of $1/period for ten years at 10%, we find that the factor is 6.145. How much must be deposited each year, for ten years at 10% interest to equal $1.00?

$$\$1.00/6.145 \ = \ 0.162 \text{ or annual constant}$$

In other words, a deposit of 16.2¢ per year will buy $1.00 of present value mortgage. Analyzing this constant further, we see that of the total annual constant of 0.162, 0.10 is interest and 0.062 is repayment of debt (sinking fund).

Amortization books and mortgage constants are gradually becoming obsolete, due to the availability of low cost financial calculators capable of computing payments directly. These can instantaneously calculate the payment amount for any mortgage, at any rate, for any periods to an accuracy of sixteen decimal places.

SEE ALSO: AMORTIZATION SCHEDULE, and ANNUAL CONSTANT.

MORTGAGE EQUITY TECHNIQUE

This refers to an appraisal technique which blends six investment considerations to obtain an Overall Rate (OAR), which is used to capitalize the income stream.

INVESTOR ADVICE
The six considerations utilized in the mortgage equity technique are:

1. Loan ratio;
2. Loan term;
3. Loan interest rate;
4. Equity yield rate;
5. Expected holding period; and
6. Projected appreciation/depreciation expected during the above holding period.

As an investor, you will be primarily concerned with the yield on equity. If you invest $400,000 of your own money and obtain a loan of $1,600,000, you are not too concerned about the yield on the entire $2,000,000 purchase price. Your prime concern is, "What is the return on my $400,000 investment?"

The OAR obtained by this technique is "yield to maturity." It combines the current yield (cash income/down payment) with the deferred income (equity build up + capital gains) received at the end of the holding period, where the deferred income is compounded at the equity yield rate.

The mortgage equity technique is quite sophisticated and appears to take in all of the major considerations. *It is subject to error, where the holding period is incorrectly assumed, and more importantly, where the assumed inflation/deflation at the end of the holding period is missed a few percentage points high or low.*

The overall rate obtained by this technique is therefore no better than the assumptions used in the calculations. An even greater problem is how to explain the calculations to the layman investor.

EXAMPLE

Mr. Investor proposes to buy a certain property. He plans to put 25% down and borrow the remainder at 12% interest for twenty-five years. He will probably keep the property for ten years during which time he expects a 15% return on his equity. He does not wish to consider any possible inflation/deflation gain/loss. What is the overall rate required to obtain the required 15% return on equity?

	Value Ratio		Rate	Weighted Average
Mortgage	.75	x	0.1275*	0.09562
Equity	.25	x	0.1500	0.03750
Weighted Average	1.00			0.13312

*Annual Constant for 25 yrs @ 12%

Weighted Average from above	0.13312
Less: .1924 ** X .75 X .04925***	(0.00711)
Basic Rate = OAR =	0.12601#
Say: 12.6%	

** Amt. of loan amortized in 10 Yrs.
*** 10-yr Sinking Fund Factor @ 15%
# The Basic Rate = OAR where holding period gain/loss is estimated to be zero.

If the above property had a net income of $100,000/year, then Mr. Investor could afford to pay:

$$V = I/R = \$100,000/.126 = \$793,650$$

and achieve his desired 15% return on equity.

The author has long believed that a lesser complicated technique, that is also understood by the client investor, is preferable. The "Short Form Approach to Rate Determination" was developed for this specific task.[2]

SEE ALSO: ELLWOOD RATE, EQUITY BUILDUP, and OVERALL RATE OF RETURN (OAR).

MORTGAGE NOTE

A mortgage note is the legal instrument which requires the borrower to pay the debt, regardless of what is offered as security.

INVESTOR ADVICE

The note is what prevents the borrower from walking away from the property. Upon default and sale, if the property sale does not satisfy the note, the lender can ask the courts for a deficiency judgment for the balance owed.

In trust deed states, the mortgage holder may also require a note. In the event of default, the lender can foreclose on the trust deed for quick action but may have difficulty in obtaining a deficiency judgment. By taking the slower course of action and closing on the note, the borrower can obtain a deficiency judgment if required to satisfy the note.

SEE ALSO: DEFICIENCY JUDGMENT, FORECLOSURE, and TRUST DEED.

MORTGAGE PACKAGE

A mortgage package is all of the documents required for submission with the mortgage application for approval by the lender.

INVESTOR ADVICE

The mortgage package contains many items. The following list is typical:

• The mortgage application listing the amount of loan requested, personal financial data of the borrowers, borrower's job history, real estate to be purchased, and agreed sales price;

• Verification of employment(s) and salary(ies);

• Credit checks;

• Property appraisal;

• Verification of bank deposits and/or loan amounts;

- Verification of charge accounts due, including auto loans, if any;

- Copy of the authenticated earnest money deposit and offer to purchase;

- Where applicable, request for government or other mortgage insurance; and

- Preliminary title search report

Mortgage applications for an investment property may require additional data to indicate the probable success of the purchase.

If the purchase is of an existing building or complex, the lender will probably want to review the financial statements for the past 3–5 years and review existing leases.

If the property is new construction, the lender will probably require the following additional documentation:

- Pro-forma income statement and balance sheet for 1–3 years into the future;

- Leases or letters of intent, showing potential lessees;

- Feasibility studies; and

- Resumé of principals who are proposed as managers of the project.

SEE ALSO: PRO-FORMA ANALYSIS, FEASIBILITY STUDY, LETTERS OF INTENT, and TITLE REPORT

MORTGAGE REFINANCING

This term refers to the act of paying off an old loan with funds obtained from a new loan.

INVESTOR ADVICE

Refinancing may be accomplished by personal choice or by necessity. You will be required to refinance a loan when:

- A balloon payment is due on a contractor mortgage;

- You purchase a property upon which a non-assumable loan exists;

- You purchase a property upon which a VA or FHA loan exists and the seller will not permit it to be assumed; and

- The interest rate on the existing loan makes it non-economical in relation to current interest rates.

When considering the possibilities of refinancing to obtain a lower rate of interest, you must carefully evaluate the present value of the interest saved during the expected holding period versus the cost of refinancing (points plus appraisal plus mortgage fees plus title insurance plus other closing fees etc.). Refinancing costs normally run to about 3% of the mortgage amount, depending upon local area fees.

In the case of a contract balloon payment, it is suggested that you attempt to negotiate an extension of the contract terms, before refinancing. It is entirely possible that the contract holder will be willing to extend the balloon payment at the same or possibly a slightly higher interest rate. Even if an increase in interest is demanded, this may be much more economical than the refinancing alternative. An increase in interest rate will mean an increase in the payment rate, but over a period of time. You must consider the *present value* of this increase versus the cash needed to refinance.

EXAMPLE

You have a five-year balloon payment of $80,038 due on an old $85,000 contract, payable @ 10% interest, on a 25-year payout basis. The contract holder agrees to extend the balloon for another five years, but insists on an interest rate of 11.0%—the going rate at the bank.

You estimate that refinancing cost will be about 2.5% of the mortgage, or $2,000. What should you do?

New Pmt. @ 11.0%, 25 yrs., $80,038	$784.46
Old Payment @ 10%, 25 yrs., $85,000	772.40
Difference/mo.	$ 12.06

PV-1/period 11%, 5yrs. x $12.06 = $554.68

If the extra five years will suffice and take you to the point that you plan to dispose of the property, the contract holder's offer should be accepted at a present value savings of $1400+. If you plan to keep the property for a longer time, the extension must be extended or refinancing considered.

SEE ALSO: BALLOON PAYMENT, NONASSUMABLE MORTGAGE, and PRESENT VALUE OF $1 PER PERIOD.

MULTIPLE LISTING SERVICE

This is a service provided by local boards of REALTORS® to their members. The service lists all properties for sale by member brokers and data on all sales made by member brokers. Statistical data regarding listings and sales are also provided, in many cases.

INVESTOR ADVICE

Multiple listing data is essential for the professional real estate salesman and appraiser who want to offer their clients a wide variety of available properties and current market data. Multiple listings, in most areas, represent the vast majority of properties offered for sale. Others may be available through real estate agents, who are not REALTORS® and from sellers who are attempting to sell their own property.

Multiple listing sales data and statistics are essential for the professional appraiser. Having access to the multiple listing computer data bank assures him of a huge bank of comparable sales data. He/she is then able to determine quickly what properties have been sold, for what price, when, and on what terms.

The computer data bank does an efficient job of quickly selecting specific types of sales in a specific area from the hundreds and thousands of recorded sales. It provides all data contained on the original listing plus an additional data line, relative to the sale to include:

• Selling agency;

• Time on the market;

• Selling price; and

• Terms of the sale.

Figure 43 shows a sample computer sales report in which the member asked for sales in a particular area of the city. The member further specified the style of the house (Rambler), price range ($60,000-$80,000), and exterior (Brick). The bottom line of this report indicates the home sold for $73,500 on an FHA loan basis and was on the market for 110 days. The sale was through cooperative agency # 210.

```
................Copyright, 1988, Any City Board of Realtors ...........
#59345  AD:  1927 E. Broadway        Pt: Res  ST:S  Vol: 28     $74,500
Area: R4  Loc: SE 2200,1927   City:  Anytown       Pg. 289   Proj:
EST Sq FT  BR  BATHS  FP  EXT: BR  HT: Gas  FNC: F  AGE: 25
M:   960    2    1    1             AC: Cent LAN: P  SEWER:Y  TYPE: Res
U:     0    0    0    0   G/C: 2G   RC: D    SPK: FA
D:   960    1    1    0   STY: RAM  LN: D    ZN : R-1          WATER: M
T:  1920    3    2    1   DIN: F,K  PT: 1    WC : F  LOT: 0.12AC BSMT:90%F
INCL:  AP,GD,HF,MO,RF,RG,TR
REMARKS:  SHARP HOME.  OAK FLOORS REFINISHED, NEW PAINT INSIDE AND OUT.
          NEW ROOF ON GAR, STORM WINDOWS, NEW FURNACE. COVERED PATIO
          CARPETED.
APPL: L. KEYBOX     PH:           SHOW: APT, KEYBOX      ELEM: 805
L. AGT. SARAH JONES PH: 755-4083  POSS: ARRANGE          JRHS: 853
OFFICE: CENTURY 21  PH: 755-9080  ID: 917  SOC: 3.5%     HS  : 856
TERMS: FH,AS,CSH, CNT
DN$         MTG: $45,000 @ 8.5%  PMT: $548  PITI
            AM. SAVINGS                     TAXES: $831
LOT: 64 X 138

SOLD INFO:   DOM 110  TERMS: FHA  DATE: 07-OCT-88  $73,500  ID: 210
```

Figure 43. Computer search of comparable sale.

You should be wary of any appraiser, who is not a member of the local Realtor Board and privy to the very latest sales data. If not a member, he/she probably operates with limited sales data and hearsay information, which is next to impossible to verify.

SEE ALSO: APPRAISER, LISTING CONTRACT, LISTING PRICE, and NATIONAL ASSOCIATION OF REALTORS.

MUNIMENTS

Muniments are written or other evidence of title.

INVESTOR ADVICE

A muniment may exist as part of an agreement of the past. For instance, if Mr. Jones deeded a land parcel to Mr. Smith with a limitation on the use of the land or time of that use, the deed would infer a potential reverter interest. A later deed granting fee title to Brown would not extinguish Jones' interest. In the original deed, Jones to Smith would be a "muniment."

SEE ALSO: ABSTRACT OF TITLE, GRANTEE, GRANTOR, REMAINDERMAN, and TITLE INSURANCE.

MUTUAL SAVINGS BANK

Mutual savings banks are institutions mutually owned by their depositors. Mutual savings banks are primarily chartered in the eastern states, with 75% of their assets in New York and Massachusetts.

INVESTOR ADVICE

Mutual savings banks are thrift organizations quite similar to savings and loan associations. They are permitted to be members of the FSLIC, and most of them are.

The principal difference between a mutual savings bank and a savings and loan association is its ability to invest in a broader type of investment, such as bonds and consumer loans. Mutual savings banks are often able to offer construction loans, wraparound mortgages, junior mortgages, land, joint ventures, and commercial mortgage loans as well. If your project falls into a category that is acceptable to your local mutual savings bank, you should examine this potential source of funds. Undoubtedly arrangements can be made available at very competitive rates.

SEE ALSO: FEDERAL SAVINGS & LOAN INSURANCE CORPORATION (FSLIC), and SAVINGS AND LOAN INSTITUTIONS.

ENDNOTES

[1]*Wall Street Journal,* June 30, 1987, p. 1 col. 6.

[2]Frank J. Blankenship, *The Prentice Hall Real Estate Appraiser's Handbook* (Englewood Cliffs, NJ: Prentice Hall Inc., 1986), pp. 93-95.

N

National Association of Independent Fee
    Appraisers (NAIFA)
National Association of Realtors® (NAR)
Necessity Easement
Net Income
Net Income after Taxes
Net Lease
Net Rent Multiplier
Neutron Bomb Analysis
Nonapparent Easement
Nonassumable Loan
Noncash Expense

Nonconforming Use
Normal Maintenance
No Springing Interest
Notary
Note
Notice of Contract
Notice of Default
Notice of Lien
Notorious Possession
Novation
Nuisance Rent Raise

N

NATIONAL ASSOCIATION OF INDEPENDENT FEE APPRAISERS (NAIFA)

A nonprofit professional society of real estate appraisers, founded in 1961. Members of the Association are comprised of full-time professional real estate appraisers and others in related fields, such as real estate, banking, building and construction, agencies, and savings and loans.

INVESTOR ADVICE

NAIFA appraisers are awarded one of three designations, based on examination, experience, and other requirements. These are:

IFA: A designated member who has passed all required examinations, submitted an acceptable demonstration appraisal on a residential property, and attained the required experience. This appraiser is fully qualified to perform residential appraisals.

IFAS: A designated senior member of NAIFA, who has passed the required examinations, submitted an acceptable demonstration appraisal on an income property, and attained the required experience. This appraiser is qualified to perform appraisals on any real property.

IFAC: A designated real estate councillor, who has been a senior member for a minimum of three years and has at least five years experience in counseling real estate investors and/or other buyers and sellers of real estate.

The applicant for the IFAC designation must submit an acceptable thesis of an actual counseling experience, which must be approved by the NAIFA National Education Council.

All NAIFA members are required to perform their work in strict conformance with standard appraisal practices and must adhere to a rigid code of ethics in their dealings with clients and other appraisers.

NAIFA is a charter member and contributor to The Appraisal Foundation. The foundation, established in 1988, has as its goal the eventual federal or mandatory state licensing of real estate appraisers and the establishment of designated standards of performance. The foundation is composed of seven member organizations, which include:

APPRAISAL FOUNDATION MEMBERS

- National Association of Independent Fee Appraisers

- American Institute of Real Estate Appraisers

- Society of Real Estate Appraisers

- International Association of Assessing Officers

- American Society of Farm Managers and Rural Appraisers

- International Right of Way Association

- American Society of Appraisers

SEE ALSO: IFA, IFAC, IFAS.

NATIONAL ASSOCIATION OF REALTORS® (NAR)

A professional organization of real estate agents and brokers, organized in 1908. Members are known as *realtors* or *realtor associates*. The term *REALTOR*® is a registered trademark of the association. All members are sworn to uphold a strict code of ethics and must be a member, in good standing, of their local and state boards.

INVESTOR ADVICE

The term *REALTOR*® should not be confused with the terms *real estate agent* and *real estate broker*, who are not members of NAR, but are merely licensed to do business in the state in which they operate.

Local REALTOR® board members are constantly undergoing additional professional training. They have access to the multiple listing service and are the only sales personnel able to provide your property with the broadest exposure to prospective buyers.

Professional real estate appraisers are associated with the local board as REALTORS® or associate members. Access to the multiple listing service is the only way to obtain verified current sales data, required to perform accurate appraisals.

SEE ALSO: MULTIPLE LISTING SERVICE, REAL ESTATE AGENT, and REAL ESTATE BOARD, REALTOR®.

NECESSITY EASEMENT

An implied easement, where the intent is clear and strictly necessary to provide access to dominant land, to support adjoining buildings, partition walls, or party driveways.

INVESTOR ADVICE

You should be extremely careful when buying property where a necessity easement appears to exist. Most easements are only enforceable where they are in writing. Although most courts will uphold the existence of necessity easements, conflict with adjacent property owners should be avoided by acquiring written permission for use.

Two requirements must be met in a claim of easement by necessity. These are:

1. There must be a unity of title shown; that is, the parcel owned by the party seeking an easement must have been a part of the property over which an easement of necessity is sought.
2. The easement must be shown to have been reasonably necessary for the enjoyment of the dominant estate at the time of its conveyance.

SEE ALSO: EASEMENTS, and RIGHT OF WAYS.

NET INCOME

Total revenues less all expenses chargeable to the operation. Also known as net profit.

INVESTOR ADVICE

When reviewing the income statement of various operations, it should be remembered that sole proprietorships and partnerships do not include wages of the owners as an expense. To obtain a true picture of the net income, a deduction equal to the value of labor furnished, by the owners, should be made. Thus, the resulting net income figure will represent the true return of the operation and the investment.

WARNING! Don't confuse net profit with spendable cash!

SEE ALSO: CAPITALIZATION OF INCOME, NET INCOME AFTER TAXES, OVERALL RATE OF RETURN, and RETURN ON INVESTMENT.

NET INCOME AFTER TAXES

Net income less income taxes payable by the owner(s).

INVESTOR ADVICE

You are primarily interested in the total income that you are able to keep—net income after taxes. When comparing potential investments in several operations, income taxes payable can become an important consideration. Some operations, due to tax credits available, may return a higher after-tax net income than others with the same net income. The depreciation available on one property versus another can increase the net income after taxes substantially.

WATCH OUT! Accelerated depreciation may subject you to the recapture rules, if the property is sold before fully depreciated.

SEE ALSO: DEPRECIATION, NET SPENDABLE INCOME, and TAX REFORM ACT OF 1986 (TRA).

NET LEASE

A lease that requires the tenant to pay certain.

INVESTOR ADVICE

Net income leases are most prevalent in the operation of commercial property leases. The rental agreement can specify that the tenant is responsible for taxes, insurance, maintenance, or other landlord expenses. Where all three are payable by the tenant, the lease is said to be a triple-net lease or net to the third power.

Net leases return to the landlord no more than any other type of lease for comparable property. The net feature is usually just one of convenience. It is normal for the lease terms to specify that during the lease term any future increases in taxes and insurance will be added to the lease price. The net feature automatically removes these potential increases from consideration since the lessee is responsible.

In the case of interior maintenance, it is usually easier for the tenant to repair any inoperative electrical, plumbing, or mechanical equipment than to call the landlord, who in turn calls a repairperson, which usually delays the needed repair. Exterior problems are usually not included in the net lease arrangement.

SEE ALSO: LEASE.

NET RENT MULTIPLIER

Fair market value divided by net rental income.

INVESTOR ADVICE

Net rent multiplier is only useful where there is no additional income from other sources, such as laundry facilities, extra parking, rental of party rooms, and so forth. The use of net *income* multiples is more common.

Appraisers often determine market value by using the average Net Income Multiplier (NIM) applied to the net income from the subject property. The formula is:

$$NIM \ x \ Net \ Income = Value$$

More often than not, accurate net income figures are not available to appraisers. Sellers conveniently forget certain expenses and reserves for replacements in order to increase the advertised net income figure. Where this type of book manipulation is suspected or very apparent, appraisers will utilize gross income figures, which are more easily verified.

Unfortunately, this procedure may not take into account increases in net income due to various tax savings. The gross income multiplier will consider the subject property as an average property.

SEE ALSO: GROSS RENT MULTIPLIERS, and INCOME APPROACH TO VALUE.

NEUTRON BOMB ANALYSIS

A lender's "worst-case" scenario of a borrower's pro-forma income statement, which assumes a situation in which everything bad that can happen does happen, and the lender is forced to take the property back on default of the loan.

INVESTOR ADVICE

Too often developers and investors assume a rosy picture of a property's potential. They are willing to risk their 20–25% equity. Lenders, on the other hand, must take the opposite view to assure that their mortgage investment (a 75–80% investment) is safe and the risks commensurate with the interest to be received.

You would be wise also to review the income possibility, under a worst-case scenario. This review will determine if survival is possible in the event of unforeseen circumstances, such as an economic turndown, delays in construction, or failure to obtain full rental in the anticipated time.

SEE ALSO: DEBT SERVICE, INCOME AFTER TAXES, MACK TRUCK FACTOR, and SPENDABLE CASH.

NONAPPARENT EASEMENT

Intangible easements, such as scenic rights.

INVESTOR ADVICE

Nonapparent easements, such as scenic rights and right-of-ways that do not include paths or the right to post advertisements or signs and that have not been brought in to visible existence by the exercise of those rights, are subject to loss if not recorded.

Loss will occur when the servient tenement is sold or transferred. Should you acquire such rights, you must take immediate action to have the rights made a matter of public record. Thus, if the land is sold or transferred, your rights will be retained.

SEE ALSO: EASEMENTS.

NONASSUMABLE LOAN

A mortgage loan which contains a provision of nonassumption.

Most mortgages made after 1970 contain a nonassumption provision. Check before you buy.

INVESTOR ADVICE

A nonassumable loan is one which cannot be assumed at all or at the very least is not assumable as originally written. This provision became common in the early 1970s, at a time when interest rates began to creep upward and forecasts of future rates were becoming difficult.

The nonassumption agreement is inserted in the loan agreement to prevent assumption at a time when money is being lent at a higher interest rate or to prevent unqualified buyers from gaining control of the property. It also is based on the assumption that the original mortgagor will utilize the property only in a way consistent with his or her application.

Even though an assumption of the loan does not relieve the original mortgagor of responsibility for payment, the risk is considered greater than where the original mortgagor continues to occupy the property. The actual wording of the nonassumption clause may prohibit assumption or achieve the same effect by an acceleration clause, which makes the loan due and payable upon transfer of any or all interests in the property. Most lenders prefer this latter approach, which clearly prohibits a sale of the property on contract.

Some so-called nonassumable loans can be assumed with the lender's approval, which usually adds the following qualifications:

- The assuming party (or parties) must, from a financial and credit standpoint, qualify to assume the loan.

- The interest rate is normally adjusted to reflect the going rates, but is often set at somewhat less than the existing rate.

- An assumption fee must be paid to compensate the lender for administrative costs associated with the change of mortgagor.

If you should contemplate the purchase of a property on which *any* loan exists, check with the lending agency to see if they will agree to your assumption and under what conditions. This assumption may be more advantageous than obtaining a new loan, for the following reasons:

- The interest rate may be somewhat less.

- Closing costs, including assumption fee, may be far less than the closing costs on a new loan.

- Less time will be required to close than if a new loan is sought.

SEE ALSO: ASSIGNMENT OF MORTGAGE, ACCELERATION CLAUSE, and ASSUMPTION AGREEMENT, CONTRACT.

NONCASH EXPENSE

An expense of operating an investment property, which does not require a cash outlay.

INVESTOR ADVICE

The largest noncash expense attributable to all real estate operations is that of depreciation. Noncash expenses reduce the taxable income but require no cash outlays.

Many investors include reserves for replacement under this category, but the wise manager will establish a sinking fund account for this purpose and deposit the amount, each period, required to grow at interest to meet anticipated cash outlays.

SEE ALSO: DEPRECIATION, RESERVES FOR REPLACEMENT, and SINKING FUND.

NONCONFORMING USE

A use which is permitted for a building or land, by special permission, but which does not conform to the current use regulations of the zone in which it is located.

INVESTOR ADVICE

A good example of nonconforming use would be permission to operate a beauty salon in one's home, where it can be shown that this commercial enterprise will not affect other resident owners and where neighbors voice no objection to the operation. In granting nonconforming use permission, zoning authorities must be very cognizant of the following factors:

• Amount of traffic to be generated by the operation;

• Adequacy of parking for clients and customers; and

• Noise, odors, or other objectionable emanations.

> **BUYER BEWARE!** Businesses and properties operated counter to current zoning may become a Pandora's box.

It is strongly advised that property or a business operating under nonconforming use *not* be purchased. It should not even be considered without a thorough understanding of the implications of its current and intended use.

Property operating under a "Grandfather" clause is subject to continuous and exacting scrutiny of the zoning authorities. Any change in your operation, even though minor, could revoke your right to operate.

SEE ALSO: GRANDFATHER CLAUSE, RESTRICTIVE COVENANTS, and ZONING.

NORMAL MAINTENANCE

The preventive procedures and correction of normal wear and tear required to maintain a property in a good operating condition.

INVESTOR ADVICE

Failure to provide constant and necessary maintenance, including periodic redecoration, can result in a serious devaluation of a property through physical depreciation. The estimated useful life of a property improvement assumes that normal maintenance will be performed as required.

When analyzing the income potential from a property, it is necessary to include funds for normal maintenance at contractor cost. An estimate which includes owner provided labor will overstate the actual income by the amount of the labor furnished. Where labor is owner furnished, the cash flow can be increased; however, it is erroneous to conclude that the increased cash flow is income from the property—it is income earned by the owner, not his or her investment.

The establishment of reserves for periodic replacement and redecoration is highly recommended. These reserves should be funded by periodic deposits in a sinking fund account to assure availability when required. Failure to provide such reserve funds for future work will result in maintenance delays and the inevitable increased cost of those delays.

SEE ALSO: PRO FORMA ANALYSIS, RESERVES FOR REPLACEMENT, and SINKING FUND.

NO SPRINGING INTEREST

An attempt to transfer property in the future, without a current conveyance.

INVESTOR ADVICE

It is illegal to attempt to transfer property at some time in the future or after the occurrence of some event, while maintaining full-fee ownership for the present. For instance, you cannot transfer, by deed, property "as of my death."

The same transaction could be legally accomplished by immediate transfer of the property to a living trust, with the intended future owner designated as the remainderman. It would also be possible to make the intended transfer by provisions of the grantor's will.

SEE ALSO: INTER VIVOCE TRUST, and WILL.

NOTARY

A person authorized by law to take acknowledgments and oaths or to certify legal documents. A notary is appointed by the state in which he or she operates.

INVESTOR ADVICE

A notary is forbidden to acknowledge an instrument in which he or she has a financial interest. A rotary may not authenticate a document unless he or she has personally witnessed the signature thereon, regardless of his or her familiarity with the signor.

All documents to be officially recorded must be notarized. The various states have specific laws and procedures regarding notary performance. Some demand a log showing document title, number of pages, and the signor's name. Other states only require minimal records. All states require a notary to post a fidelity bond.

> **WARNING!** The notary's signature and seal certifies only that he or she witnessed the signing of the document and that the signor was the person whose signature is on the document. No guarantee is implied as to the accuracy of the data within the document.

SEE ALSO: ACKNOWLEDGMENT, and LOCUS SIGILLI.

NOTE

A signed document acknowledging a debt to another, together with the agreed terms for repayment and interest rate payable.

INVESTOR ADVICE

The mortgage note is the official document evidencing the agreement to pay. Although the mortgage is pledged as security for the loan, the note binds the individual to the agreement. The mortgage is only a pledge of property to secure the note.

When a mortgage note is signed, it is no longer possible for the signer to walk away from the property unscathed. If the sale of the foreclosed property does not produce enough cash to pay off the note, you can be held accountable for the balance.

Notes are also used as evidence of debt, which requires only the borrower's acknowledgement of that debt. Short-term loans for working capital and other short-term needs are often made on the financial strength of the borrower and his reputation.

A note may be a simple acknowledgement of a debt: the amount owed, the interest rate, and the payment date. It may also add ownership restrictions regarding a purchase which initiated the note. In this case, it becomes a chattel mortgage.

SEE ALSO: CHATTEL MORTGAGE, COMMERCIAL LOAN, DEFAULT, and DEFICIENCY JUDGMENT.

NOTICE OF CONTRACT

An official document giving public notice of a contractual interest in the property described therein. Details of the loan agreement are usually not disclosed, since the document is a constructive notice to the public.

INVESTOR ADVICE

Figure 14 (see CONDITIONAL SALE) shows a typical form used to give public notice of a contractual interest. Note that only the following information is provided:

- property affected by the transaction;
- parties to the transaction; and
- notary acknowledgment.

This arrangement allows the parties to maintain their business relationship on a private basis but still advise the public that a possible encumbrance on the described property exists. This arrangement is in contrast to the recording of the mortgage or trust note, in which all details are spelled out for public scrutiny. The only fact not revealed is the current status of the loan.

Remember that when property is sold on contract, the deed remains with the seller or designated escrow agent until such time as the amount due is paid in full. Without official notice of interest in the property, a title researcher would conclude that the property is still owned by the seller, and since no mortgage is recorded, that the property is free and clear.

SEE ALSO: CONSTRUCTIVE NOTICE, and CONTRACT.

NOTICE OF DEFAULT

A notice, filed in the official county records by the owner of a trust deed, that a borrower has defaulted on his or her agreement and that foreclosure proceedings may begin.

INVESTOR ADVICE

The notice of default is the first step, taken by the lender, to collect on a loan in default. Each state sets the time required between default notice and actual sale of the property, as well as the redemption period in which the owner can pay his or her debt and reacquire the property.

In Utah, a mortgage holder, who elects to obtain a court decree of default is required to wait until the six-month redemption period has expired before a sheriff's sale can be made. If the holder elects to foreclose on the trust deed, minimum delay is required; however, the holder may not be able to obtain a deficiency judgment where the sales proceeds do not cover the amount due.

Most trust deeds contain a provision which empowers the trustee to sell the property on default, without court action—this procedure is often referred to as the shortcut foreclosure.

SEE ALSO: DEFICIENCY JUDGMENT, FORECLOSURE, and TRUST DEED.

NOTICE OF LIEN

A form recorded by a business to give official notice of a debt due for labor and/or materials furnished for a cited property. This is commonly referred to as a mechanic's lien.

> NOTICE! Title insurance does not normally insure the property owner against mechanic's liens.

INVESTOR ADVICE

Figure 44 shows a standard form used in the state of Utah for public notice of debts due for materials and workmanship. No court action is required for filing mechanic's liens. Most other debts require a court ordered judgment before a lien can be filed.

SEE ALSO: MECHANIC'S LIEN.

NOTORIOUS POSSESSION

The open holding or possession of real property in direct opposition to one or more additional claimants. This is a first step in a claim of adverse possession.

INVESTOR ADVICE

As a rental property owner, you must be familiar with your landlord rights in order to remove a tenant legally who remains in notorious possession of your property. If in doubt, consult your legal counsel before taking any action.

As a landowner, you must be ever vigilant regarding unauthorized use of any part of your property. This is particularly necessary regarding road- and walkways which are often used by others as a means of avoiding a roundabout passage. Failure to attempt to stop unauthorized use of your property can result in an inability to close the passageway legally.

SEE ALSO: ADVERSE POSSESSION, LICENSE, and TENANT.

NOVATION

1. The substitution of an older obligation on a property for a new one.
2. The substitution of one obligor for another, in which the first obligor is released from all responsibility.

INVESTOR ADVICE

It is often possible to renegotiate a contract or a mortgage loan commitment for a better one. Through the process of novation, the old obligation can be canceled and a new and more satisfactory one substituted. Clearly, novation is only possible where the new obligation is of benefit to both the borrower and the lender or the seller and the buyer.

Novation occurs when an mortgage or other obligation is assumed by another and the original mortgagor is released of all responsibility. FHA and VA loans are normally

NOTICE OF LIEN

TO WHOM IT MAY CONCERN:

Notice is hereby given that the undersigned _Kool King Heating & Ventilating_ of Salt Lake City, Utah

doing business as _McDuffy H & V Corp._ and residing at
Salt Lake City County of _Salt Lake_ State of Utah, hereby claim__
and intend__ to hold and claim a lien upon that certain land and premises, owned and reputed to be
owned by _Big Stick Developers & Builders_ and
situate, lying and being in _SAlt Lake City_, County of _Salt Lake_
State of Utah, described as follows, to wit: _____
_____Lot 101, Greengrass Subdivision_

to secure the payment of the sum of _Two-Thousand Fifty and 00/100_ **Dollars,**
owing to the undersigned for _Gas heating and ventilating system installation_
at 413 E. Bloodhound Dr. (Lot 101, Greengrass Subdivision)
as a _Contractor_
in, on and about the _5th of January 1989_ on said land.

That the said indebtedness accrued and the undersigned ~~furnished said materials to (or was em-~~
(Erase according to the fact)
~~ployed by)~~ _did install and complete_ per instructions of _____
Allen L. Ludwig, President of Big Stick Developers & Builders ~~who was the~~

~~owner and the reputed owner of said premises as~~ x x
~~aforesaid under XXXXXXXXXXXX contract made between the said~~
_____ and the undersigned
on the _6th_ day of _January,_ 19_89_, by the terms of which the undersigned did agree
to _Install said system_
and the said _owner, Big Stick Development and Builders_
did agree to pay the undersigned therefor as follows, to wit: _Two-Thousand Fifty and 00/100_
Dollars

_____ and under which ~~said contract~~ the undersigned did _begin_ the first _work_ on the _28th December_ day of
_____ and did _continue until_ the last _Finish Work_ on the
_3rd_ day of _February 1989_ ~~and on and between said last mentioned~~ x x
~~days, did~~ x x x x _____ amounting
to the sum of _Two-Thousand and Fifty and 00/100 --------------_ **Dollars,**
which was the reasonable value thereof, and on which the following payments have been made to wit:
_____ _None_

leaving a balance owing to the undersigned of _Two Thousnad Fifty and 00/100 --_
_____ Dollars after deducting all just credits and offsets, and for which
demand the undersigned hold__ and claim__ a lien by virtue of the provisions of Chapter 1, of Title
38, of the Utah Code Annotated 1953.

[signature]
Pres., McDuffy H & V Corp

Figure 44

assumable; however, the original borrower remains liable for the debt unless specifically released through processes established by those agencies.

SEE ALSO: ASSUMABLE MORTGAGE, CONTRACT, and REFINANCE.

NUISANCE RENT RAISE

An artificially high rent increase imposed on a tenant at the end of a lease period
for the purpose of causing the tenant to move voluntarily.

INVESTOR ADVICE

Certain landlord actions can be construed as an attempt to evict, this is particularly
true in low-income designated housing. The key to avoiding problems in these cases is
equal treatment of all tenants. Consult your legal counsel when in doubt of your rights.

SEE ALSO: EVICTION.

O

Obsolescence
Offer
Offeree
Office Building
Old Spanish Law
One-Party Listing
On-Site Manager
Open-End Mortgage
Open Listing

Operating Expenses
Operating Statement
Option
Other Income
Overage Rent
Overall Rate of Return (OAR)
Overimprovement
Owner's Equity

O

OBSOLESCENCE

Obsolescence is a reduction in the value of real property due to loss of desirability or usefulness. Obsolescence can be physical or economic.

INVESTOR ADVICE

Property improvements which have been well maintained will often become less valuable if their design no longer is useful to the average person. This is particularly true of multifamily housing units, which depend on renter appeal. Few people want to rent an apartment that is difficult to heat, has an outmoded kitchen, or has a bedroom with inadequate closet space or that is too small to accommodate a queen-size bed.

Those units which fail to provide desired amenities, such as swimming pools, meeting rooms, and health spa facilities or have inadequate parking for more than one car per unit are said to be obsolete. This does not mean that they are not rentable, but that they will no longer command the top price, which represents the highest and best use of the investment.

Economic obsolescence is more subtle. The property can be of good design, provide all desired amenities, and be quite competitive in rental, yet suffer from economic obsolescence. This loss in value is more often caused by uncontrollable factors, such as a decline in the general economic condition of the rental area or specific problems of the local area in which the units are located. Economic obsolescence is the principal cause of commercial property value loss.

Physical obsolescence can be correctable, but sometimes the cost is such that the project is not economical. There is little the owner can do to correct economic obsolescence.

> **AVOID ECONOMIC OBSOLESCENCE.** Personal knowledge of the area is your best guard against an unwise purchase of real property.

When inspecting property for purchase, be sure to check these important items:

- past vacancy factors;
- rental rates; and
- amenities provided to tenants.

These factors are often indicators of obsolescence. An inability to stay fully rented, or unusually low rentals, is the tip-off.

SEE ALSO: DEPRECIATION, and HIGHEST AND BEST USE.

OFFER

An offer is one essential ingredient of a contract. The contract consists of three principal parts: offer, acceptance, and consideration. The offer is the start of bargaining. Negotiations between the parties begin when a buyer makes an offer for the seller's consideration.

INVESTOR ADVICE

When an offer is made together with a consideration, the seller has three options:

1. Accept the offer as made.
2. Reject the offer.
3. Accept the offer with changes—a counteroffer.

When you list a property for sale, you should know what you are willing to accept and on what terms. Even though the listing price is somewhat higher than you expect to receive, you should know that the buyer has anticipated this fact.

It is easy to accept an offer which fully meets your expectations. This seldom occurs. An intelligent buyer is aware that the asking price is probably a bit higher than the minimum the seller is willing to accept. His or her first offer, therefore, is probably a "trial balloon" sent up to test the market. It is high enough to avoid an insult, but probably not as high as the buyer is willing to go.

What the buyer's offer is really saying is, "I'm interested in buying. Tell me what your lowest acceptable price and terms are." The buyer knows that you, the seller, will do your best to:

- Keep the buyer on the hook until a mutually acceptable agreement is reached.

- Counteroffer at a price to keep the buyer interested, but one within your acceptable range.

You should realize that most deals are consummated on at least one counteroffer basis. Few buyers will continue to negotiate if they feel the seller is unreasonable. If a basic agreement can be reached, minor sale provisions can be negotiated in the second or third counteroffer, but most sale prices become quite firm with the first counter.

Consider any offer carefully and make your best price offer on the first go-around. Other terms can be negotiated once you have set the hook and have the buyer on the line. The following is a list of the major considerations of any offer.

- true value to be received, which considers the selling price, terms of payment, time required to receive payment in full, and the closing costs to you;

- downpayment, which tends to secure the transaction;

- financial strength of the buyer(s);

- tax consequences of the sale as proposed;

- earnest money deposit size; and

- time required to close the transaction.

DON'T BE FOOLED! The quoted selling price is not always the real value received. Time is money.

SEE ALSO: EARNEST MONEY RECEIPT AND OFFER TO LEASE, EARNEST MONEY RECEIPT AND OFFER TO PURCHASE, POINTS, PRESENT VALUE OF $1, and PRESENT VALUE OF $1/PERIOD.

OFFEREE

The offeree is the party or parties that makes an offer to purchase or lease.

INVESTOR ADVICE

In order to acquire investment real estate, you must become the offeree. Remember that a deal can be made or lost by the tone of the initial offer, regardless of your ultimate intentions. The following checklist is a good guide in the preparation of your offer:

- What is the property worth to *you*?

- What is the fair market value of the property?

- Has the property been appraised recently—by whom?

- What do you know about the seller's desire to sell?

- What is the maximum cash you are willing to commit to this purchase?

- Is the listing price reasonable versus its fair market value?

- How do you propose to finance the property?

- How badly do you wish to acquire the property?

- How well does this property fit your current portfolio?

If you are really serious about buying the property, avoid the following mistakes made by the inexperienced buyer.

- Make sure your earnest money deposit is commensurate with the proposed purchase price.

- Don't insult the seller by making a ridiculous offer.

- Make sure your REALTOR® communicates your desire and ability to buy.

- Don't ask for an unreasonable closing period.

- Don't expect the seller to wait for you to sell something or get your financial house in order before closing.

SEE ALSO: COUNTEROFFER, EARNEST MONEY DEPOSIT AND OFFER TO PURCHASE, FAIR MARKET VALUE, FIDUCIARY, LISTING PRICE, and OFFER.

OFFICE BUILDING

A building specifically designed and built to provide office space for the owner and/or his or her tenants is an office building. Space may also be provided for commercial operations required to service the tenants.

INVESTOR ADVICE

Office buildings consist of rentable office space, common space, and commercial space for tenant services. The ratio of the rentable to the total is critical to the return on investment. A certain amount of common space—halls, baths, elevators, and utility room—is required for maximum functional utility, but an excess can reduce maximum revenue and add to the owner's expense for heat, lights, and utilities.

Before you build or buy, compare the gross potential rental space to the total building size. Avoid purchasing existing buildings with unfavorable ratios. Insist on new building designs with this ratio of paramount importance.

The addition of first-floor or basement space that can be utilized by commercial tenants is advisable. These operations for cafeterias, restaurants, secretarial bureaus, or other businesses that can serve your tenants will probably rent for a premium over standard office space. Consider percentage leases for these businesses to maximize your income.

SEE ALSO: PERCENTAGE LEASE, PROFESSIONAL OFFICE BUILDINGS, and RENTABLE SQUARE FOOTAGE.

OLD SPANISH LAW

Old Spanish law is a property law practiced in some of the western states. It recognizes property obtained by inheritance or prenuptial acquisitions as separate property.

> **IMPORTANT!** Title of property acquired in old Spanish law states must consider the owner's financial and martial status. Avoid unecessary estate and inheritance taxes.

INVESTOR ADVICE

Those states that operate under provisions of old Spanish law recognize two types of property ownership by married property owners: (a) separate property—that property owned by the marital partner at the time of the marriage or subsequently acquired by inheritance or procured with funds generated by separate property, and (b) *community property*—that property purchased by income of either or both marital partners, during the term of their marriage.

Estate planning, wills, and trusts established by married partners must take local law into consideration in order to reduce inheritance and estate taxes. If it is the desire of the property owner to maintain a separate property designation, all operations of that property must be conducted in such a way as to prevent any commingling of income between separate and community property.

When acquiring property, you must be extremely careful in designating how title is to be recorded. Once the title is finalized, a change may be construed as a gift subject to gift taxes. Check with your accountant and/or attorney before taking title to property.

SEE ALSO: CURTSEY RIGHTS, DOWER RIGHTS, ESTATE TAXES, GIFT TAXES, INHERITANCE TAXES, INTER VIVOCE TRUSTS, TESTAMENTARY TRUSTS, and WILLS.

ONE-PARTY LISTING

A one-party listing is any contract with a real estate broker which limits his or her right to sell and receive a commission to one potential and designated buyer.

INVESTOR ADVICE

The property owner is constantly being hounded to list his or her property for sale with one or more local brokers. The request is often prefaced with the statement, "I have a buyer interested in purchasing your property." This statement may be true or only a ploy to obtain a listing and the right to advertise the property for sale.

A good answer to such a request is, "Who is your buyer?" If the agent is unable or unwilling to divulge this information, you can offer him or her three alternatives:

1. a one-party listing, in which the agent must designate the potential buyer;
2. a verbal agreement (not contractually binding) that you will pay a commission if the agent brings you an acceptable offer; or

3. an invitation to get lost and quit bothering you.
SEE ALSO: EXCLUSIVE LISTING TO SELL, and OPEN LISTING.

ON-SITE MANAGER

The on-site manager is the person designated to show property to prospective renters, take tenant complaints, perform minor maintenance, supervise major maintenance tasks, and assure the orderly operation of the rented property.

INVESTOR ADVICE

Although you may desire to perform most of the management functions to reduce out-of-pocket expenses, an on-site manager is essential to:

- keep you advised of tenants about to vacate;

- collect rents;

- show prospective tenants available units, accept applications, and check references;

- maintain the common areas in a clean, sanitary, and acceptable manner;

- perform minor maintenance tasks and supervise major tasks performed by contractors;

- act as a point of contact between you and tenants; and

- avoid vandalism by tenants as well as outsiders.

In small to medium apartment and office buildings, the on-site management function can be performed by a designated tenant. This tenant can be given a reduced rental rate or, where the task is larger, a free unit in exchange for services rendered.

When reviewing the rental list of a prospective purchase, make sure to ask, "Who acts as on-site manager? What is his or her compensation?" Sellers often conveniently forget to mention that one apartment produces no rental or at best reduced rental in order to provide this function. Don't forget that management services performed by the owner are not free. They may reduce out-of-pocket expenses but represent valuable labor donations, which must be taken into account when calculating return on investment.

SEE ALSO: CASH FLOW, NET INCOME, NORMAL MAINTENANCE, and TENANT SELECTION CRITERIA.

OPEN-END MORTGAGE

A mortgage with provision for the mortgagor to borrow additional funds after reduction of the original balance without change to the original agreement terms and conditions is an open-end mortgage.

INVESTOR ADVICE

This type of mortgage is seldom found in today's market. The one exception is short-term loans, in which the mortgage acts as security for a line of credit.
SEE ALSO: ADD-ON MORTGAGE and LINE OF CREDIT.

OPEN LISTING

An open listing is a listing contract with a broker which guarantees a commission to that broker if he or she is the *first* to provide a willing buyer on the seller's terms.

INVESTOR ADVICE

Although it would appear that the open listing is to the seller's benefit, this is not necessarily so. Under this listing, the seller can give several brokers a chance to sell; therefore, this theoretically produces more prospects in a given time. In actuality, this is not always true. In fact, an exclusive listing with a multilist REALTOR®-broker may produce more action.

The open listing is subject to potential problems, since it is sometimes difficult to determine which of the several brokers produced the seller. In addition, the better brokers, who are members of the local REALTOR® board and its multilist service, may be unable to accept an open listing due to board restrictions.

A REALTOR®-broker, assured of a commission regardless of who sells the property, is more likely to work harder on a listing than one who is not guaranteed a commission unless he or she is the selling agency. All REALTOR® members of the multilist service have an agreed commission split with their fellow members.

SEE ALSO: EXCLUSIVE AGENCY LISTING, EXCLUSIVE RIGHT TO SELL, and MULTIPLE LISTING SERVICE.

OPERATING EXPENSES

Operating expenses are those necessary tax-deductible expenses required to conduct a business operation.

INVESTOR ADVICE

You should not confuse operating expenses with other cash flow requirements. Basically, a rental property has four types of outward cash flow. These are:

1. Operating expenses, which are paid periodically in order to keep the business operating efficiently.
2. Debt service, which is not a tax deductible expense but a necessary outward cash flow. Debt service payments may also include some operating expenses, such as taxes and insurance.
3. Depreciation expense, which is a noncash item but is deductible for income tax purposes.
4. Reserves for redecoration and equipment replacement, which normally involves a deposit of a certain amount set aside at interest, to provide for future large expenses and equipment replacements. These large cash outlays could not easily be provided from the normal cash flow available.

SEE ALSO: CASH FLOW, FIXED EXPENSE, RESERVES FOR REPLACEMENT, and VARIABLE EXPENSE.

OPERATING STATEMENT

An operating statement is one of two or more periodic accounting statements prepared for tax and other operation assessments.

INVESTOR ADVICE

A complete accounting statement is suggested on at least a quarterly basis, in order for you, the owner, to determine the success or failure of your operation. Financial statements, prepared by accountants, consists of one required item and possibly two additional items. These are:

1. The profit and loss (P&L) operating statement, which details all operating income and other revenues received, expenses incurred, and the resulting profit (or loss) for the accounting period. Reserves for future expenses, net income before taxes, debt service payments, and cash flow available to the owner may also be shown. In addition, the accountant will provide additional useful data, such as occupancy percentage, vacancy rates, expense as a percent of total expense, and totals of reserves held for future expenditures.
2. Possibly, a balance sheet indicating the total assets and liabilities, receivables, payables, accumulated depreciation, and owner's equity.
3. In large operations, a third statement is usually included to indicate the source and use of funds generated by the operation during the accounting period.

Figure 45 shows a typical P&L statement for an apartment complex. Figure 46 shows the Balance Sheet for the same operation.

SEE ALSO: ASSETS, BALANCE SHEET, LIABILITIES, and OWNER'S EQUITY.

PROFIT AND LOSS STATEMENT
Blue Moon Apartments
1st Qtr. 1988

INCOME:				
Rental Income			$14,400.00	96.0%
Other Income			600.00	4.0%
	Total Income		$15,000.00	100.0%
FIXED EXPENSES:				
Taxes	$1,500.00	12.2%		
Insurance	400.00	3.2%		
On-site management	900.00	7.3%		
Interest	9,562.00	77.3%		
Total	$12,362.00	100.0%		
VARIABLE EXPENSE				
Water	$225.00	47.3%		
Electricity	150.00	31.6%		
Snow Removal	100.00	21.1%		
Total	$475.00	100.0%		
TOTAL ALL EXPENSES			($12,837.00)	85.6%
NET OPERATING INCOME			($ 2,163.00)	14.4%
EQUITY DEBT SERVICE			($ 152.00)	
CASH FLOW			$ 2,011.00	
LESS: Reserves for Replacement and Repair			$ 150.00	
SPENDABLE CASH			$ 1,861.00	

Figure 45

BALANCE SHEET
Blue Moon Apartments
End 1st Qtr. 1988

CURRENT ASSETS:		
Cash in Bank	$ 3,152.00	
Reserves for Repl. & Rpr.	150.00	
Rents Receivable	300.00	
Tenant Deposits	2,400.00	
Total Current Assets		$ 6,002.00
LAND AT COST		60,000.00
IMPROVEMENTS		540,000.00
Less: Accumulated Depreciation		(2,000.00)
TOTAL ASSETS		$604,002.00
LIABILITIES & NET WORTH		
Current Liabilities	$ 2,400.00	
Tenant Deposits	210.00	
Utility Bills		$ 2,610.00
Total Current Liabilities		427,000.00
Long-term Liabilities		174,392.00
Mortgage Payable		
NET WORTH		
TOTAL LIABILITIES AND NET WORTH		$604,002.00

Figure 46

OPTION

An option is a written agreement between buyer and seller which, for a consideration, gives the buyer the right to purchase a property at any time during the option period on the terms indicated.

INVESTOR ADVICE

Figure 47 shows a typical option form used to obtain an option to purchase a property. Although somewhat similar to an earnest money deposit and offer to purchase, there are two distinct differences worthy of note:

• An option payment replaces the deposit in an offer. This payment is kept by the seller, regardless of the outcome. In effect, the payment is compensation to the seller for taking his or her property off of the market for a period of time.

• The option states that the buyer *may* purchase the property, not that he or she agrees to purchase. The final action taken is at the will and pleasure of the buyer.

A FEW DOLLARS CAN control millions of dollars of property with little risk.

"This is a legally binding form, if not understood, seek competent advice."

OPTION

KNOW ALL MEN BY THESE PRESENTS:

That ....Elvis..J..Purvis..
of ..Salt..Lake..City,..Utah.., hereinafter referred to as "Seller, hereby agrees for and in consideration of ....One Thousand and 00/100 -------------------- ($1,000.00.......) Dollars,
paid by ......American Investors Inc., a Limited Partnership...
of ...Salt Lake City, Utah..., hereinafter referred to as "Buyer", as follows:

1. PROPERTY: Seller hereby gives and grants to Buyer and to his heirs and assigns for a period of ..12.. months from
the date hereof, hereinafter referred to as "First Option Period", the exclusive right and privilege of purchasing the following described real property located at ......Salt..Lake..City.......... ...., County of
...Salt..Lake..., State of ....Utah.................................., **and more particularly described**
as follows:

       Lot 299, Homewood Hills Subdivision

Together with all water rights appurtenant thereto or used in connection therewith.
(Said real property and improvements, if any, shall hereinafter be referred to as "The Property").

2. PRICE. The total purchase price for said property is ...One..Hundred..Fifty..Thousand..and..00/100
($150,000.00......) Dollars, payable in lawful money of the United States, strictly within the following times, to-wit. All
sums paid for this option and any extension thereof as herein provided, shall be first applied on the purchase price, and the
balance shall be paid as follows:

       Cash

3. EXTENSION OF OPTION. Upon payment by Buyer to Seller of an additional sum of One..Thousand..and....
00/100 Dollars... ($1,000.00......) Dollars, cash or by cashier's
check, prior to the expiration of the first option period, this option shall be extended for ....12.................... months, hereinafter referred to as "Second Option Period". Upon Buyer's payment to Seller of a further sum of ....
.... $.............................) Dollars, prior to the expira-
tion of the second option period, this option shall be extended for a third period of .... additional months,
hereinafter referred to as "Third Option Period".

4. EXERCISE OF OPTION. This option shall be exercised by written notice to Seller on or before the expiration of
the first option period, or if extended, the expiration of the second or third option periods as the case may be. Notice to
exercise this option or to extend the option for a second or third option period, whether personally delivered or mailed to
Seller at his address as indicated after Seller's signature hereto, by registered or certified mail, postage prepaid, and post-
marked on or before such date of expiration, shall be timely and shall be deemed actual notice to Seller.

5. EVIDENCE OF TITLE.

(a) Promptly after the execution of this option, Seller shall deliver to Buyer for examination such abstracts of title,
title policies, and other evidences of title as the Seller may have. In the event this option is not exercised by Buyer, all
such evidences of title shall be immediately returned without expense to Seller.

(b) In the event this option is exercised as herein provided, Seller agrees to pay all abstracting expense or at Seller's
option to furnish a policy of title insurance in the name of the Buyer.

(c) If an examination of the title should reveal defects in the title, Buyer shall notify Seller in writing thereof,
and Seller agrees to forthwith take all reasonable action to clear the title. If the Seller does not clear title within a reasonable time, Buyer may do so at Seller's expense. Seller agrees to make final conveyance by Warranty Deed or ....
.... in the event of sale of other than real property. If either party fails to perform
the provisions of this agreement, the party at fault agrees to pay all costs of enforcing this agreement, or any right arising
out of the breach thereof, including a reasonable Attorney's fee.

Figure 47. Option form (front).

6. CLOSING ADJUSTMENTS. All risk of loss and destruction of property and expenses of insurance shall be borne by Seller until date of possession. At time of closing of sale, property taxes, rents, insurance, interest and other expenses of property shall be prorated as of date of possession. All other taxes, including documentary taxes, and all assessments, mortgage liens and other liens, encumbrances or charges against the property of any nature, shall be paid by Seller except ....None...

7. POSSESSION. Seller agrees to surrender possession of the property on or before ...Thirty............... days following written notice of the exercising of this option by Buyer.

8. The Seller recognizes ......Big..Deals..Realtors... Real Estate Company (Broker and Agent) through its salesman ....Alfred..S...Brown.., as the Real Estate Broker with whom Seller listed this property for sale, and Seller agrees to pay a commission to said Broker of ......6.....% of the gross sale price. Seller hereby authorizes the agent to withhold such commission from the proceeds of sale at time of closing.

9. If this option be not exercised on or before the dates specified herein for exercise of same, the option shall expire of its own force and effect and the Seller may retain such option monies as have been paid to the Seller as full consideration for the granting of this option.

IN WITNESS WHEREOF, the Seller hereunto has set his name this ......24th........ day of ....March....................., 19...89...

SIGNED IN PRESENCE OF:

Elvis J. Pernis
....
Seller

Alfred S. Brown, agent
Big Deals Realtors
....

Address of Seller: ...150..S...Green..St..................
                         Salt Lake City, Ut.
....

Figure 47 continued

The option is a useful tool to the real estate investor. For a minimum payment, you are able to tie up a property and assure its availability for a period of time—time required to assure yourself that you can obtain financing and that a proposed project will be viable when and if initiated.

The option tool is also very useful in plottage attempts. If all of the required property is not acquired, you will loose only your option fees—no leftover property to sell when the project doesn't succeed.

One additional item of difference should be noted. The option agreement has a provision for automatic extension of time, which can be obtained by the agreed additional option payment.

Last of all, note that the option contract involves a third party, the selling broker. In the earnest money agreement, which may or may not mention a REALTOR® fee, the selling agency's legal right to a commission is by a separate contract—the listing agreement.

In the option agreement, the seller contracts with the optionee and his or her REALTOR®. The seller agrees to pay a stipulated commission *if* the option is exercised. There is good reason for this difference. The option agreement may extend for a long period of time, even years. The normal listing agreement is not expected to be in effect for that extended period.

SEE ALSO: EARNEST MONEY RECEIPT AND OFFER TO PURCHASE, EXCLUSIVE LISTING, and PLOTTAGE.

OTHER INCOME

Other income is a classification of income which indicates that it is other than the principal income from the operation. Rental income produced by a rental property would be the primary source, where as additional income from parking rentals, laundry operations, and so forth would be classified as other income.

INVESTOR ADVICE

Income other than rental is often produced by an investment property. Apartments often provide coin-operated laundry equipment for the tenants. Switchboard service may be available, and extra parking facilities and meeting room rentals will enhance the overall income to the owner.

In commercial projects, additional income may be provided by percentage rents over and above the base rentals, hallway space may be rented for seasonal promotions and commissions received from vendors, who are authorized to sell their products within the buildings. They may also provide for food service and other concessions, which produce additional revenue.

In shopping centers, additional income is often derived from parking space rentals to truckload sales promoters. Large shopping malls may also obtain considerable income from attached multistory parking garages.

Warehouse and other manufacturing properties may provide rental equipment to the tenants and rent vacant land for temporary storage.

SEE ALSO: OPERATING STATEMENT.

OVERAGE RENT

Overage rent is rental payments over and above the minimum rental specified in the lease. Overage rents occur in commercial leases which specify minimum rents plus a percentage of gross sales or other sweeteners.

INVESTOR ADVICE

Overage rent should not be anticipated in the early years of a new project. Your pro forma income analysis should anticipate that minimum rent will be the standard for the first year or so. Anticipation of overage rents is justified only in mature projects, where a significant rental history is available for examination and verification.

Lease provisions for higher rents if the lessee's business exceeds certain limits are usually easier to sell than a lease that anticipates a high level of business activity. The lessee sees these provisions as a way to reduce his or her expenditures if business is bad. The lessee doesn't mind paying more rent if he or she is making a higher than expected profit.

In negotiating a lease with overage provisions, the problem is how to establish a reasonable and acceptable base. It must be reasonable to the landlord to assure a minimum rental, yet not so high as to prevent the attainment of 100% occupancy. Statistical data to assist in this endeavor can be obtained from:

- local colleges and universities;

- economic departments of major banks in the area;

- government publications;

- data from feasibility studies;

- franchise headquarters; and

- annual reports of publicly held franchisees.

In searching for this type of data, you will be primarily interested in the average sales per square foot for specific retail store types. For instance, in the Salt Lake City area, the average retailer averages about $120 per square foot per year. In other words, a 10,000-square-foot store is expected to produce $1,200,000 in sales during an average year.

SEE ALSO: PERCENTAGE LEASE.

OVERALL RATE OF RETURN (OAR)

The overall rate of return is net income from a property divided by the sales price or fair market value.

INVESTOR ADVICE

The overall rate of return is most often considered in relationship to that required to return a certain percentage on an investment. Thus, many additional factors are involved in the calculation of OAR, such as:

- mortgage ratio;

- mortgage interest rate;

- mortgage term;

- anticipated holding period; and

- anticipated inflation/deflation during the holding period.

The overall rate of return is calculated as the first step in determining return on investment.

EXAMPLE

An office building, which was recently purchased for $300,000, has a net income of $37,000 per year. What is the overall rate of return?

$$OAR = \text{Net Income/Cost}$$
$$OAR = \$37,000/\$300,000 = 0.123 \text{ or } 12.3\%$$

OAR may also be the final figure in determination of the required income to produce a given return on investment.

EXAMPLE

An investor is considering the purchase of a warehouse, but feels that he must obtain an overall rate of return of 12% to justify the purchase. The property is listed for $250,000. What net income must the property produce to provide a 12% return?

$$0.12 = \text{Income}/\$250,000 \qquad \text{Income} = \$30,000$$

SEE ALSO: ELLWOOD RATE, HOSKOLD METHOD, and LEVERAGE.

OVERIMPROVEMENT

Overimprovement is property improvement which does not utilize the land at its highest and best. Overimprovement indicates excessive cost or size not justified by the site and its potential income production.

INVESTOR ADVICE

DON'T OVERIMPROVE. An overimprovement is money wasted.

The optimum situation is to have one of the lowest cost improvements in an area of higher cost—for example, own a $60,000 home in a $100,000 neighborhood.

Overimprovement is no unusual in the renovation of older property. It is very easy to spend more than anticipated to bring an older building up to modern standards. Unknown deficiencies, uncovered during remodeling, can greatly increase the cost of modernization.

In appraisal practice the principle of substitution states that when several commodities or services are available to satisfy a need, the market selects the lowest-priced solution. The overpriced structure is no more valuable than any other that satisfies the basic needs for which it was designed.

You should be extremely cautious in undertaking the renovation of an existing structure. Contractors, having a financial interest in a proposed project, are likely to produce estimates which are attractive but unrealistically low. It is recommended that you obtain your estimates of potential cost from an uninterested party, such as an architect. Even then a fund to cover unknown contingencies is advised. The following checklists of potential problems in renovating various types of buildings are suggested for study:

MULTIFAMILY RESIDENCES

- Are existing heat ducts and returns adequate for the addition of air conditioning? Are the ducts insulated to prevent condensation from cool air?

- Are existing utility services, water, gas, and electricity adequate for the expansion?

- What changes, other than modernization, will be required to meet existing building codes?

- If additional rental units are to be added, will you have sufficient parking for the new tenants?

- Will major modifications trigger a requirement for landscaping, curbs, gutters, wheelchair access, and other currently required land improvements?

OFFICE BUILDINGS

- What will the total investment per square foot of rental space be after completing the modernization? What is the expected lifetime of the renovated structure? How does this compare with new construction? Will required rentals be competitive with new buildings?

- What are the economic projections for the subject area? Will the area remain viable during the expected economic life of the renovated structure?

- Can subfloor cable ducts be installed to meet the communication and power requirements of the modern office?

- Will the renovated structure attract tenants in competition with newer facilities in the area?

WAREHOUSE AND MANUFACTURING FACILITIES

- Will the renovated structure and surrounding area compete with new facilities in new industrial parks?

- Are adequate utilities available in the area without expensive renovations?

- Is the available water pressure adequate for fire sprinkler system installation?

- Are floors stressed for anticipated equipment and storage loading?

- Are rail spurs available?

- Is additional land available to increase employee parking facilities?

SEE ALSO: HIGHEST AND BEST USE, and PERFORMANCE BOND.

OWNER'S EQUITY

Owner's equity is:

1. The fair market value of the property less all indebtedness.
2. In accounting, total assets less liabilities.

INVESTOR ADVICE

When reviewing the balance sheet of a real estate operation, you should be aware that it has been prepared in accordance with generally accepted accounting practices and may or may not represent the true value. Errors in value are often the result of:

- real estate recorded at cost, which may not be accurate at the current time;

- improvements carried on the books at cost less depreciation, which may not reflect the true wear and tear;

- unrecorded assets, such as goodwill, which produce more income than justified by the assets employed in the operation; and

- equipment not shown on the books because it is fully depreciated. It may still have value.

When considering the purchase of a business, you should have an appraisal performed by a qualified appraiser. Be aware that a good real estate appraiser is not necessarily a good business appraiser. Select an appraiser with experience and a proven reputation in business appraisal work.

In performing this evaluation, the appraiser will start with the current and latest balance sheet and examine each item thereon. All land values will be corrected to reflect a current appraisal of the property. Similarly, all improvements on the land will be appraised and an appropriate +/— adjustment made to reflect the correct value rather than the book value (cost — depreciation taken).

The next step will be to perform an inventory of all personal equipment used in the business. Any equipment found which is not on the books (fully depreciated) will be appraised and added to the asset list. All equipment on the books will be evaluated and appropriate adjustments made to reflect its true current value. Thus, a true value for all assets is determined.

Next, the latest income statement will be reviewed to determine if any adjustments should be made. The following are typical adjustments required +/—.

- Expenses for the sole benefit of the owner have been charged to the business. These should be removed (-).

- If the business is a proprietorship/partnership, no expense will be shown for owner wages. A value equal to the cost of hiring such labor must be deducted from the indicated earnings in order to determine what the *assets* are earning.

- If company automobiles have been utilized by the owner(s), an appropriate adjustment (+) must be made to reflect this expense erroneously charged to the business.

Lastly, the adjusted income is divided by the adjusted asset value to determine the return on assets. Let's say that this figure indicates a return of 50%, which is higher than the risk of doing that type of business would justify. This indicates that an unknown asset is at work. This unknown is usually referred to as *goodwill*. A finding of goodwill is a rare event. Usually the return is barely sufficient to support the investment at a value commensurate with the risk involved. If goodwill does exist, a value must be assigned to this asset so that the return on total investment is the correct percentage.

EXAMPLE

A certain operation is found to employ total assets of $500,000, including a mortgage due of $400,000. The adjusted net income is $50,000, after payment of mortgage interest. A normal return on equity for this type of operation is 25%. What is the value of the goodwill? What is the owner's equity?

Book Equity = Assets – Liabilities
Book Equity = $500,000 – $400,000 = $100,000
Income/Book Equity = Return on Equity
$50,000/Total Equity = 25%
Total Equity = $200,000*
* Assumes no leverage —/+ due mortgage loan.

Based on the average return on equity of 25%, we find that there is actually $200,000 at work. Since the assets–liabilities indicate a value of only $100,000, the goodwill value must be the difference, or $100,000.

SEE ALSO: BALANCE SHEET, and INCOME STATEMENT.

P

Parcel
Parole Evidence Rule
Partial Release Clause
Partnership
Party Wall
Passive Income
Patent Claim
Payables
Payback Period
Pension Plans
Percentage Lease
Percolation Test
Performance Bond
Periodic Estate
Personal Property
Physical Depreciation
Physical Life
Piggyback Loan
Plaintiff
Planned Unit Development (PUD)
Pledged Savings
Plot Plan
Plottage
Plumbing Equipment
Point of Beginning (POB)
Points
Police Power
Policy Binder
Possession Before Closing
Power of Attorney
Power of Eminent Domain

Prepayment Penalty
Prepayment Provision
Prescription
Prescriptive Easements
Present Value of One
Present Value of One Per Period
Prime Rate
Principle of Anticipation
Principle of Balance
Principle of Change
Principle of Competition
Principle of Conformity
Principle of Contribution
Principle of Substitution
Principle of Supply and Demand
Principle of Surplus Productivity
Private Investor
Private Mortgage Insurance (PMI)
Private Offering
Probate
Professional Office Building
Pro-Forma Analysis
Profits à Prendre
Profit-Sharing Plan
Property Improvement
Property Management
Property Rights
Prospectus
Proximate Cause
Purchase Money Mortgage
Pyramiding

P

PARCEL

A parcel is a land tract which is delineated by one legal description.

INVESTOR ADVICE

When purchasing property which is described in terms of "containing XX acres more or less" and with side boundary descriptions such as "in a westerly direction to a point," you should not offer a price for the parcel. Rather, you should require a survey and make your offer based on a unit price, say $5,000/acre.

> **WARNING!** Land parcels which were surveyed more than 50 years ago may be subject to survey errors. Insist on a new survey before buying expensive land.

Properties surveyed many years ago are often subject to substantial errors, both in size and in boundaries. A new survey may indicate two adjacent property owners with a claim on a portion of the property. You make your offer subject to a satisfactory survey, which will give you an opportunity to drop the purchase if problems are found.

If a survey is required, don't forget to indicate in the earnest money agreement who is to pay for the survey. The cost of surveys are dependent on the amount of work required to define accurately the beginning point from a known accurate reference and to resurvey the subject parcel. A modest 1.0 acre parcel survey may cost from $500 to $2,000.

Where errors are found, action must be taken to resolve the dispute between adjacent property owners. This can be amicably settled or taken to court. Before going to court, which is expensive and time-consuming, you should understand that most court decisions are based on long-standing and existing fence lines.

Survey errors usually occur as a result of two former surveys beginning from different reference points. New laser and satellite survey techniques are accurate to a fraction of an inch.

SEE ALSO: ENCROACHMENT, and LEGAL DESCRIPTION.

PAROLE EVIDENCE RULE

The parole evidence rule is a judicial principle which prohibits oral testimony in a court action attempting to explain or clarify a real estate contract which is considered the complete and final agreement between the parties.

INVESTOR ADVICE

The statute of frauds in most states requires that all real estate transactions be in writing to be enforceable. Accordingly, verbal testimony would not be admissable in court if there is evidence that the written instrument represented a complete understanding between the parties. The contract must, therefore, stand on its own merits.

The determination of the finality and completeness of the written agreement is often disputed. The length and complexity of the written agreement is usually cited as evidence that the document was intended to be the final and complete agreement. A statement within the document such as, "It is agreed that the terms herein constitute the entire contract between the parties," leaves no doubt as to the intent.

Parole evidence can be admissable in very few instances. These are:

- It is shown that the written agreement was never intended to be final.

- Fraud is claimed or suspected.

- The contract was never executed.

- The parties agreed on other conditions after the original document was executed.

- Ambiguities are found in the original document.

With the foregoing considerations in mind, it becomes essential that any real estate contract must be complete and accurate. All considerations and provisions must be covered. A good rule of thumb is, "Write the agreement as if you are going to court—you very well may have to at some time in the future."

> **READ ALL LEGAL DOCUMENTS CAREFULLY!** Don't sign any document that you don't fully understand. Don't sign hastily—sleep on it, read it again before you sign.

SEE ALSO: EARNEST MONEY RECEIPT AND OFFER TO PURCHASE, and STATUTE OF FRAUDS.

PARTIAL RELEASE CLAUSE

A partial release clause is a provision of a mortgage or trust deed that permits a lien release on a portion of the total covered property, usually in exchange for a stipulated payment on the amount owed.

INVESTOR ADVICE

A partial release clause will be helpful when developing recreational land, building lots, a condominium, or similar projects. This will allow you to provide your customers with a clear title without the necessity of paying off the mortgage.

Most lenders are willing to provide for the partial release but will probably demand that all transactions be closed through a neutral third party, such as a land title company.

This provision, with appropriate instructions to the land title company, will authorize transfer of portions of the mortgaged property after equity payments of stipulated amounts. Generally, this payment is the same proportion of the debt represented by the property to be transferred.

EXAMPLE

A developer borrows $100,000 to improve a certain property being subdivided into 20 building lots. On payment of one twentieth of the mortgage ($5,000), the title company is authorized to provide clear title to a buyer of a lot.

SEE ALSO: BLANKET MORTGAGE, GENERAL MORTGAGE, and LOT RELEASE SYSTEM.

PARTNERSHIP

A partnership is a type of business organization in which two or more persons participate in the ownership.

INVESTOR ADVICE

Most business attorneys will recommend against the establishment of a partnership, even when shared with close relatives or friends, due to the incurred personal liability to each partner.

The partnership does have some advantages, but it also has many disadvantages which are overriding considerations. The advantages are:

- Easy to organize—little or no paperwork required to get started.

- Simplified tax reporting—each partner reports his or her proportional share of earnings/loss on his or her private tax return.

- Simplified financing—each partner puts in his or her proportionate share of assets required to start the business.

The disadvantages are:

- Each party is fully responsible for what the other does or does not do.

- Unlimited liability—a claim against the partnership, if not satisfied by the partnership's assets, can be paid from the private assets of any or all of the partners.

- The partnership is automatically dissolved at the death of any partner—the business must stop until a new partnership or proprietorship is legally established.

Before establishing your business relationship, consult your attorney about the possibilities of incorporation as a Subchapter S organization.
SEE ALSO: CORPORATION VERSUS PARTNERSHIP and SUBCHAPTER S CORPORATION.

PARTY WALL

A party wall is a wall built, by agreement between two parties, on the property line between two properties for the joint benefit of all.

INVESTOR ADVICE

A party wall can save space and money, which can be important in the construction of adjoining buildings. The agreement for a common wall grants to each party an easement on the other party's property, equal to one-half the wall thickness.

The party wall may be a building wall or a lower wall used to separate the properties. If the party wall is a building wall, your attorney will probably suggest that a provision for transfer of ownership of the wall be included in the agreement, to cover that contingency in which one of the parties decides to remove their building from their property.
SEE ALSO: EASEMENT and PROFITS À PRENDRE.

PASSIVE INCOME

The Tax Reform Act (TRA) of 1986 defines passive income as:

1. income from a business or activity in which the taxpayer does not actively participate; or
2. any rental income, regardless of the taxpayer's participation.

INVESTOR ADVICE

The TRA effectively prevents an investor from using real estate investment losses from offsetting active income, say from regular employment. Prior to the passage of TRA, limited partnerships were often set up in such a way that the investor's return on investment was based partially on contemplated losses in the beginning operation. Losses resulted in tax relief, equal to the same amount of profit. In other words, an investor in the 50% tax category reaped a 50¢ reward for every dollar *earned or lost*. Under TRA passive losses can only be used to offset passive income. This forces the real estate investor to assure that his or her projects can stand on their own merits. Passive losses, in excess of gains in any one year can be carried forward and used to offset passive income in future years. There are minor exceptions to the rule, but these are too involved and complicated to be treated here.

SEE ALSO: TAX REFORM ACT OF 1986 (TRA).

PATENT CLAIM

A patent claim is a claim for an original conveyance of government land in which the claimant seeks title by letter patent. Patent claims on government lands usually arise from mining or homestead activities.

INVESTOR ADVICE

When examining abstracts of land parcels, particularly in the western United States, it is often noted that the original title to a parcel was obtained by patent. This was the beginning of private ownership.

SEE ALSO: ABSTRACT OF TITLE.

PAYABLES

Payables are a class of liabilities used in accounting to denote assets belonging to others.

INVESTOR ADVICE

Payables are only shown on financial statements in which the accrued accounting method is employed. In the accrual method, debts become expenses when the debt is obligated, and income becomes income when goods or services are provided.

Most rental activities operate on a cash basis—income is income when received, and expenses are expenses only when paid. As a prospective purchaser of an operation reviewing the cash basis financial statements, you will be unable to ascertain what bills, if any, are outstanding. This should be carefully reviewed with the current owner to assure that all debts against the operation will be cleared on the closing of the sale.

This is particularly important if the operation is a corporation. The corporation will be liable for any debts incurred in the past. If the operation is a partnership or proprietorship, the debt will fall legally on the prior owner, but it would be wise to ascertain that all of these obligations are cleared at the closing.

SEE ALSO: CASH VERSUS ACCRUAL ACCOUNTING, and RECEIVABLES.

PAYBACK PERIOD

This term refers to the time required for the investor to recoup his or her investment—purchase price divided by annual income.

INVESTOR ADVICE

The payback period is a useful tool for comparing two possible investments. The payback period is the reciprocal of the percent of return. If one has a return of 10%, it indicates a payback period of 1/income percent(10%) or 10 years, whereas one with a 5% return has a payback period of 1/5% or 20 years.

As a real estate investor, you are interested in two things:

1. a return *of* your investment, and
2. a return *on* your investment.

The payback period considers only the first of these interests, although it is often quoted in casual conversations between real estate investors.

SEE ALSO: RETURN OF INVESTMENT and RETURN ON INVESTMENT.

PENSION PLANS

Company plans that provide funds for employee retirement are called pension plans.

INVESTOR ADVICE

Most successful companies have some type of retirement plan for their employees. These are generally one of three types:

1. pension plans;
2. profit-sharing plans;
3. employee stock ownership plans (ESOPS).

The pension plan provides annual payments into each qualified employee's account, which grows through new deposits and the investment of the funds. The amount of each employee's annual deposits is based on the provisions of the plan, which include consideration for age, years of service, and salary.

The pension plan differs from other retirement funds in that a deposit is made by the company each year, regardless of the company's profitability for that year. Because of this fact, many companies prefer a profit-sharing plan or other arrangement to provide for employee retirement.

While annual company contributions are generally required, high investment yields on the pension funds may be sufficient to provide for the anticipated retirement needs without further contributions. Total retirement needs are determined by actuarial means, and if existing funds exceed those needs, the company may not only skip payments but withdraw an excess in the fund. Plan provisions, payments and withdrawals are strictly regulated by the Internal Revenue Service (IRS).

Pension and profit-sharing funds are one of the primary sources of mortgage money. Managers of the pension fund investments may fund large projects directly or purchase smaller mortgages in multimillion dollar bundles. In this latter case, the fund operates as a secondary mortgage market.

SEE ALSO: ESOP, PROFIT SHARING PLANS, and SECONDARY MORTGAGE MARKET.

PERCENTAGE LEASE

A percentage lease specifies a minimum rental period with an additional amount (percentage) due on all gross income over a stipulated figure.

INVESTOR ADVICE

The percentage lease provides a reasonable income to the landlord, with the opportunity to share in the good fortune of the tenant as his or her business increases. This overage rent often becomes the dominant factor in the success of the rental operation. It is not unusual for the overage rent in a successful shopping center to equal or exceed the minimum (base) rents.

The percentage lease is also a good way to fill vacant space at fees that the average tenant can afford. The tenant doesn't mind paying an additional rental *if* he or she is doing better than anticipated. The tenant will object to a mandatory higher rental rate.

SEE ALSO: OVERAGE RENT.

PERCOLATION TEST

A percolation test determines the ability of the soil to absorb water. This is a standard requirement in many areas of clay or rocky soil where permission is requested to install a septic sanitary waste disposal system.

INVESTOR ADVICE

In areas in which sanitary sewers have not been installed, most construction requires the installation of septic tank systems for disposal of wastewater. These systems depend on a distribution of the effluent into the surrounding soil. The amount of the drain field required is determined by the soil's ability to absorb the maximum discharge from the system.

Before buying property for development where sanitary sewers are not available, be sure that all health requirements can be met with low-cost septic systems. The only alternative to the septic system is a holding tank system, requiring periodic pumping.

Even if sanitary sewers are available in the area, it is no assurance that your proposed development can be connected without changes or additions to the existing collection system. Your development may be accommodated, with necessary changes, but only at your considerable expense. In worst-case situations, sanitary sewers are available but are currently running at full capacity. No additional connections will be permitted.

If available sanitary sewers can be utilized, it is wise to determine the connection fee per housing unit. Although your assumption may be that this charge will be negligible, you may be surprised to learn that the fee is $1,000–$2,000.

SEE ALSO: GRAY WATER WASTE, SANITARY SEWER, and WHITE WATER WASTE.

PERFORMANCE BOND

A performance bond is posted by a contractor, property owner, or developer to assure the timely and proficient completion of a contractual commitment and payment of all contractors and subcontractors. This is sometimes referred to as a *completion bond*.

INVESTOR ADVICE

A developer is wise to require a completion bond of his or her contractor. This will assure the completion of the project, in accordance with the contract, even if the contractor should go broke in the process. Where a heavy investment is committed, based on timely rental of a project, a timely completion of the project is essential, particularly if the building season is likely to prohibit delays.

Bonds are often required by municipalities if a portion of a project is to be delayed due to factors not under the developer's control. An example would be the inability to construct curb and gutter and/or sidewalks due to a planned street construction program. Occasionally, revised requirements for improvements such as curbs and gutters and/or sidewalks are not practical in a specific area at a specific time. In this case, the municipality may allow an omission of these improvements until a later date. The bond requirement assures compliance at that designated time.

Some states, such as Utah, require contractors on projects over and above certain values to be bonded to assure payment of their subcontractors and suppliers.

SEE ALSO: LIENS, RESTRICTIVE COVENANTS, and ZONING.

PERIODIC ESTATE

A periodic estate is a tenant–landlord relationship in which the tenant has permission to occupy the landlord's property for a stated time.

INVESTOR ADVICE

A lease is considered an estate for years and has a well-defined ending date. No notice need be given the tenant at the end of the lease, as he or she is knowledgeable of the terms of the lease.

If the landlord accepts additional rental moneys after the termination of a lease, he or she will have established a periodic estate for the period covered by the rental payment. In Utah, a periodic estate may be canceled by either party with 15 days notice. Other states have varying time requirements.

SUGGESTION! Allow tenants to occupy your property *only* by authority of a valid lease.

It is recommended that all tenant occupancy be on the basis of a lease. If a small period of time is required for the tenant to relocate after expiration of the lease, the original termination date can be amended and initialed by both tenant and landlord.

SEE ALSO: EVICTION, HOLDOVER TENANT, and TENANCY AT WILL.

PERSONAL PROPERTY

Property not attached to real estate with the intent to remain with that real estate is called personal property—it is often referred to as *personalty*.

INVESTOR ADVICE

While the law of most states is quite specific in the delineation of real estate and personalty, the owner's intent is often fuzzy when it comes to specific items.

The earnest money receipt and offer to purchase has specific areas to list the personal property to be included with a real estate purchase. The problem arises in those items not specifically listed. A good REALTOR® will insist that any item, likely to be viewed by either of the parties as personal, be listed to avoid difficulty.

The rule of thumb for the transition from personalty to real estate is that it be attached with the intent to remain. Bookshelves, for instance, can be either type of property, depending on the intentions of the owner when installed.

SEE ALSO: EARNEST MONEY RECEIPT AND OFFER TO PURCHASE, and REAL ESTATE.

PHYSICAL DEPRECIATION

This term refers to a loss in value due to the physical deterioration of an improvement. This may be due to natural wear and tear, continuous use, or exposure to the elements.

INVESTOR ADVICE

Often the lack of and/or delay in performance of normal and necessary maintenance is a cause of physical depreciation over and above that expected with age. Most physical depreciation can be prevented by timely and regular maintenance. Timely maintenance assures minimum depreciation and lessens ultimate repair costs. For instance, a leaking roof will require a certain expense to repair. If left unattended, additional damage may occur to the interior, thereby greatly increasing the repair cost.

It is advised that a maintenance reserve be established for all income property. If this is not feasible, an alternative solution would be an established line of credit to assure the prompt availability of funds as required.

SEE ALSO: ECONOMIC DEPRECIATION, and FUNCTIONAL OBSOLESCENCE.

PHYSICAL LIFE

The estimated period over which a building is expected to be capable of use for its intended purpose—sometimes referred to as *structural life* or *estimated life.*

INVESTOR ADVICE

Do not confuse an estimate of physical life with an estimate of economic life. It has often been stated that more buildings are torn down than fall down. It is not unusual for a structure to last well beyond its useful economic life.

The point at which a building no longer represents the highest and best use of the property, regardless of its physical condition, is when it has reached the end of its economic life. In determination of this point, it is necessary to subtract the return on investment attributable to the land from the total return. If little or no return is indicated as attributable to the improvements, the economic life has expired.

SEE ALSO: CHRONOLOGICAL AGE, ECONOMIC DEPRECIATION, EFFECTIVE AGE, and FUNCTIONAL OBSOLESCENCE.

PIGGYBACK LOAN

This term refers to a loan from a conventional lender which is supplemented by a second mortgage, provided by a private lender.

INVESTOR ADVICE

The preceding definition is the original explanation of the term *piggyback loan,* which has now been expanded to include any two loans put together to finance a property.

Piggyback loans are useful in preserving original first mortgage loans at low interest rates, while providing additional funds necessary to finance the property. General Electric Credit Corporation and similar lenders were very active a few years ago in this type of operation. The lender would assume the original loan and advance additional funds, at the going rate, necessary to finance the transaction. The mortgage interest rate then became a blended rate with the added advantage of one payment to only one lender.

EXAMPLE

Mr. N. Vestor is contemplating the purchase of an existing strip shopping center. There is an existing first mortgage loan of $800,000, with 25 years remaining. This loan bears an interest rate of 8.5%. Payments are $6,920 monthly. Mr. Vestor assumes that the property will sell for about $1,500,000. He has $500,000 available as a downpayment.

A check with his commercial bank indicates a willingness to arrange a piggyback loan to provide the additional $200,000 required for the purchase. The rate on this additional amount will be 12% for the 25 years remaining on the first mortgage loan. What will be the total monthly payments? What will be the effective interest rate on the total loan?

```
Payment on $200,000 @ 12% for 25 years  $2,106
Payment on Original Mortgage              6,920
     Total Payment                       $9,026/Monthly
 Old Loan  = $800,000/$1,000,000  =  80%
 New Loan = $200,000/$1,000,000  =  20%
Effective Rate:
     80% ö 8.5%   =  0.068
     20% ö 12.0%  =  0.024
     Effective Rate   0.092 or 9.2%
```

With the virtual demise of the assumable loan, this type of operation is currently out of vogue. Similar financing is possible with the use of first and second mortgages, where a conventional lender provides the largest portion of the financing on a first mortgage basis while another, such as the seller, provides the additional funds on a second mortgage basis. The problem here is that most lenders are reluctant to make a first mortgage loan knowing that the mortgagor will be committing him or herself for an additional mortgage. In addition, there is the inconvenience of two payments to two lenders.

SEE ALSO: BLENDED INTEREST RATE and SECOND MORTGAGE.

PLAINTIFF

A plaintiff is one who initiates a request for redress in the courts.

INVESTOR ADVICE

Court actions are expensive and take a considerable amount of time. You should always seek a satisfactory solution to a problem: (a) through personal negotiation with the offending party, or (b) through negotiations with a third party, such as your attorney.

> **STAY OUT OF COURT!** Wherever possible, avoid the length and expensive court alternative.

It is not unusual for a filed legal action to take a year or more before being placed on the court calendar. In the meantime, you are paying attorney fees and are lacking the funds or other redress you seek in court.

Placing your problem before an arbitration agency is suggested as a possible alternative to court.

SEE ALSO: INCHOATE, LACHES, and LIS PENDENS.

PLANNED UNIT DEVELOPMENT (PUD)

A PUD is a relatively high-density development of single-family residences. Lot sizes may be as small as 2,500 square feet with zero-lot-line type construction authorized.

INVESTOR ADVICE

The planned unit development has the appearance of a condominium project, with many closely spaced buildings of various types, from single standalone units to larger apartment-type structures.

The difference between this type of development and the condominium is that each owner owns his or her own land and building. There are no commonly owned areas or facilities, although the developer may dedicate parks and playgrounds to the municipality in order to make the units more easily saleable.

PUDs are usually approved for construction on a conditional use basis, with the developer held responsible to see that all construction is in accordance with plans and specifications as approved by the local zoning authorities.

The PUD concept is one of the available ways for utilizing high priced land in a manner that will produce moderate priced affordable units. This would appear to be the trend of the future, as land prices continue to escalate.

SEE ALSO: BUILDABLE UNITS, PARTY WALLS, RESTRICTIVE COVENANTS, and ZONING.

PLEDGED SAVINGS

Pledged savings are a method of obtaining a larger loan-to-value mortgage than is justified by the property value and income of the borrower.

INVESTOR ADVICE

Lending institutions have specific maximum loan to value ratio guidelines for mortgage loan approval. Except in the case of government-backed mortgages, this ratio is usually 80%. Ninety percent ratio loans are possible, with the top 10% being insured by a private mortgage insurer.

Where a high-ratio loan is required, pledged savings can be used to support the higher loan request. It works like this:

EXAMPLE

Dr. Jones just graduated from medical school and has assumed his first professional position. He has three children and requires a large home, which will cost around $180,000. The bank is willing to loan 80% on the first 80% of value, but only 50% on the additional value.

This means that Dr. Jones can qualify for only:

$$80\% \ddot{o}\ \$100,000 \qquad = \quad \$\ 80,000$$
$$\text{Plus}$$
$$50\% \times (\$180,000 - 100,000) = \quad \underline{40,000}$$
$$\text{Total} \qquad\qquad\qquad \$120,000$$

Even with all of Dr. Jone's savings of about $20,000 as a downpayment, he will need to borrow an additional $40,000. Dr. Jone's father agrees to deposit $40,000 in a savings account and pledge this as security for the additional loan required. His father will receive the interest on his $40,000 deposit and can withdraw it as soon as the principal balance of the loan has been reduced by that amount. The savings pledged does not have to be from a relative. A friend or associate could have assisted Dr. Jones.

SEE ALSO: LOAN RATIO and PRIVATE MORTGAGE INSURANCE.

PLOT PLAN

A plot plan is a drawing indicating the property boundaries and the location of all improvements existing or proposed.

INVESTOR ADVICE

Special attention is given to the size of backyards, side yards, and the distance from buildings to the lot lines. Most applications for a building permit require the applicant to furnish a proposed plot plan. Title policies often include plot plans as a part of the insurance package. Appraisers routinely provide a plot plan for the property appraised, particularly where more than one building is involved.

In the case of multifamily housing and other commercial developments, most municipalities have strict requirements for the amount of land which can be occupied by buildings, the location, and the type of fences and land devoted to landscaping. The following is a typical requirement for an apartment complex:

1. The minimum lot area shall be 5,000 square feet for each one-family dwelling unit, with 750 square feet additional required for each additional dwelling unit in structures having more than one dwelling unit.
2. The minimum width of any lot shall be 50 feet at a distance of 25 feet from the front lot line.
3. The minimum side yard for any dwelling shall be 8 feet, and the two required side yards shall not total less than 187 feet.
4. The minimum depth of the front yard shall be 25 feet or the average of existing buildings in the block, where 50% or more is developed, but no less than 15 feet.
5. The minimum rear yard for any main building shall be 30 feet and accessory buildings (garages, etc.) 1 foot.
6. No building or group of buildings shall cover more than 60% of the total area of the lot.

SEE ALSO: CONSTRUCTION PERMIT, RESTRICTIVE COVENANTS, TITLE INSURANCE.

PLOTTAGE

Plottage is the combination of several small parcels to make one larger and more valuable parcel.

INVESTOR ADVICE

Plottage is a recognized approach to land acquisition for redevelopment to obtain a higher and better use of land. Older residential areas can often be converted to strip shopping centers, office buildings, or other commercial uses.

It would be nice to have sufficient funds to move into an area and start buying property, but this is not usually advisable unless sufficient property can be obtained on the first attempt to assure success of the project.

Once it is known that a developer needs land in a selected area, the price usually goes up on all of the available property not already sold.

Most developers prefer to tie up required properties on an option basis, with the actual purchase contingent on all needed properties being optioned and/or acquired.

Realtors often list several adjoining properties with the understanding between all owners that all of the properties will be promoted as a one building site. In recognition of the plottage effect, the asking price for each property is usually greater than if each is offered separately.

SEE ALSO: HIGHEST AND BEST USE, PLOT PLAN, and ZONING.

PLUMBING EQUIPMENT

All water meters, supply lines, interior distribution pipes, and fixtures required to provide water service to a building are considered plumbing equipment.

INVESTOR ADVICE

> **BEWARE OF OLD PLUMBING!** In hard-water areas, old plumbing may not be service-able due to clogging by calcium deposits.

The age of plumbing can be determined by its type and the pressure available. Interior plumbing in homes 40 years or older was usually iron pipe. Later installations or remodeling utilize copper pipes, and in some localities, recently, plastic pipe has been authorized.

Iron pipe, when subjected to hard water flow, tends to precipitate hard-water grains (usually calcium or one of its compounds). In time, the interior dimensions will be reduced until the pipe is no longer useful. A good check of plumbing adequacy can be made by turning on two or more faucets in one bathroom and noting the flow rate. If it appears inadequate, a professional inspection should be initiated.

Other plumbing problems to avoid are:

- old-style bathtubs and lavatories, usually with legs and space underneath;

- stained kitchen and/or bathroom sinks and tubs (red iron stains usually cannot be removed);

- leaking or dripping commodes;

- hose bibs without convenient seasonal cut-offs or freeze-proof fittings;

- absence of pressure regulators, in areas where water pressure exceeds 40 pounds per squre foot; and

- old and uninsulated water heaters or those which have a low efficiency rating.

SEE ALSO: ELECTRICAL EQUIPMENT.

POINT OF BEGINNING (POB)

The point of beginning is a recognizable terrain feature or monument used as the starting point for a legal description of a land parcel.

INVESTOR ADVICE

In the metes and bounds method of property identification, the point of beginning is carefully described, since all other measurements and directions are based upon this point and the accuracy of its location.

In areas where rectangular surveys have been made, the POB is usually a section or quarter section point. In the eastern and southern United States, POBs are often described as "an old oak tree," "the point of intersection of Snake Creek and the Mudd River," or in similar language.

In colonial times it was common to use a "witness tree" as a point of beginning. The point got its name from the fact that a young man was paid a fee to be flogged soundly beside that tree and in front of several witnesses. It was believed that during the young man's lifetime, he would never forget that point.

Trees are cut down and other points are often impossible to find at some future date. When property undergoes a modern survey, the engineer usually plants permanent stone monuments, brass tacks in sidewalks, or other nondestructible points of reference.

SEE ALSO: LAND IDENTIFICATION METHODS.

POINTS

Points are bonuses and commissions are often expressed in points—a point being 1% of the selling price. Fees charged by lenders are also designated as points, where a point is equal to 1% of the mortgage loan amount.

INVESTOR ADVICE

All interest rates are quoted as annual percentage rates (APR). Where the lender charges a mortgage initiation fee or additional amounts in lieu of a higher interest rate, the actual interest rate will be somewhat more than quoted.

On closing statements, you may find the interest rate listed at a higher amount than offered by the lender. The reason for this is the truth in lending law, which specifies that lender interest rates must show the true annual percentage rate.

If the mortgage is to bear 9.5% and you pay three points to obtain the mortgage, it is obvious that the APR will be something greater that the 9.5% indicated. You will pay the 9.5% annual rate on each periodic payment and an amount of cash up front representing three points.

FHA and VA rates are set by their respective agencies and are adjusted periodically. A lender is prevented, by regulations, from charging more than the published rate; however, if he or she is unwilling to lend at that rate, points can be *paid by the seller* sufficient to raise the lender's yield to an acceptable level.

In times of high interest rates, builders will often pay points to obtain lower interest rates for their buyers. Generally, five to seven points up front will reduce the interest 1% on a 30-year loan.

SEE ALSO: ANNUAL PERCENTAGE RATE.

POLICE POWER

This term refers to the power reserved by the state to enact and enforce laws for the common good. Zoning, health, and safety laws are some of the regulations enacted under this provision of law.

INVESTOR ADVICE

Whenever you buy property for development purposes, make sure that your proposed operation is in accordance with current and contemplated zoning laws and other restrictions. If an offer must be made prior to a full determination of these facts, your offer should be made subject to your verification that the property is suitable for your intended needs and objectives; for example, "This offer is subject to buyer verification of zoning suitable for construction of a _____."

SEE ALSO: BUILDING CODES, BUNDLE OF RIGHTS, RESTRICTIVE COVENANTS, ZONING.

POLICY BINDER

A policy binder is a certificate of insurance provided the insured prior to issuance of the policy. Binders are required to close on a property in which the mortgage holder has demanded insurance coverage of a specified type.

INVESTOR ADVICE

Insurance rates can vary for identical coverage. Check several agencies and compare prices prior to closing. Payment for the insurance coverage can be made directly by you or the insurance agency can deliver the binder to the closing officer, who will assure payment.

> **COMPARE PRICES.** Identical coverage can vary in price from company to company. Don't forget to ask about potential year-in dividends.

SEE ALSO: HAZARD INSURANCE, INSURABLE INTEREST, and INSURANCE.

POSSESSION BEFORE CLOSING

This term refers to an agreement between buyer and seller that permits the buyer to occupy the purchased property prior to completing the closing.

If your position is as the seller, you will seldom want to agree to possession prior to closing, except under very unusual circumstances. When such agreement is made, it should:

- Provide for adequate rent during the period that you retain title.

- Provide for a definite closing date.

- Provide for an excessive rental rate, if the closing is not on schedule. This excessive rental, at say 10 times the normal rate, will force the prompt closure or rapid evacuation of the property.

- Insert a provision in the earnest money agreement that forces the buyer to forfeit his or her earnest money if the deal is not closed.

- Insist on a larger than normal earnest money deposit.

As a buyer, you will be pleased to be able to occupy the property before spending your money. This arrangement can eliminate a second move, in which case you should be willing to pay the seller some premium for his or her agreement to satisfy your urgent need.

In the case of single-family residence sales, the daily rental specified is usually one thirtieth of the monthly mortgage payment, including taxes and insurance. This rental fee is usually collected at the closing as a debit to the buyer's account.

Early possession agreements can be a part of the earnest money receipt and offer to buy, or a separate rental agreement can be drawn up when it is first known that the closing will be delayed.

This practice of early possession is fraught with problems. What if the buyer moves in and then dies before the closing? Even though his or her mortgage has been approved, it will not be granted under these conditions. How do you morally dispossess a widow or widower under these circumstances? There are countless other circumstances other than outright fraud that can prevent the orderly and timely closing of the sale. Then too, the possibility of fraud on the part of the buyer cannot be completely discounted.

SEE ALSO: EARNEST MONEY RECEIPT AND OFFER TO BUY, EVICTION, and TENANCY AT SUFFERANCE.

POWER OF ATTORNEY

Power of attorney is a legal instrument authorizing a designated person to act for and on behalf of the person who granted it. The power of attorney can be specific and limited to one action, a class of actions, or a general power of attorney, which authorizes any actions deemed necessary.

INVESTOR ADVICE

A power of attorney must be notarized and a copy made part of any transaction in which the authorized person (agent) acted for or on behalf of his or her principal. This authorization may also be recorded to provide constructive notice to the public. The normal signature on such transactions is, for example,

> *George P. Smith, for John A. Jones, his*
> *Attorney-in-fact.*

The attorney need not actually sign his or her own name, the name of the principal is adequate. Most agree, however, that both signatures are better.

Figure 48 shows a typical General Power of Attorney form. Specific authorities are generally prepared by legal counsel to assure proper limitations of authority.

SEE ALSO: ACKNOWLEDGMENT, AGENT, FIDUCIARY, and NOTARY.

POWER OF EMINENT DOMAIN

Authority granted government agencies to take, by condemnation, private property for public use. Fair payment must be offered for the actual taking and compensation provided for any damages caused the owner due to the taking. If the property owner is not satisfied with the amount offered, he or she may go to court to have a price established.

INVESTOR ADVICE

Governmental agencies may authorize condemnation of private property for the use of utility and similar corporations. (See the advice to investors in the discussion of Eminent Domain.)

SEE ALSO: BUNDLE OF RIGHTS, CONDEMNATION, and POLICE POWER.

PREPAYMENT PENALTY

A prepayment penalty is charged a borrower who desires to repay a loan at some period before it is due.

INVESTOR ADVICE

> **WATCH OUT!** A prepayment penalty in a nonassumable loan may prevent an early and otherwise profitable sale during the first five years or so.

𝕶𝖓𝖔𝖜 𝖆𝖑𝖑 𝕸𝖊𝖓 𝖇𝖞 𝕿𝖍𝖊𝖘𝖊 𝕻𝖗𝖊𝖘𝖊𝖓𝖙𝖘

THAT   Marion J. Waterford

      115 S. Main St.

      Salt Lake City, Utah

have made, constituted and appointed, and by these presents do make, constitute and appoint

      Arthur J. Waterford

      29389 S. Sumit Dr.

      Orem, Utah

as true and lawful Attorney for me and in My name, place and stead and for My use and benefit:

to ask, demand, sue for, recover, collect and receive all such sums of money, debts, dues, accounts, legacies, bequests, interests, dividends, annuities and demands whatsoever, as are now or shall hereafter become due, owing, payable, or belonging to Me, and have, use and take, all lawful ways and means in My name or otherwise, for the recovery thereof by attachments, arrests, distress or otherwise, and to compromise and agree for the same, and acquittances or other sufficient discharges for the same, for Me and in My name to make, seal and deliver; to bargain, contract, agree for, purchase, receive and take lands, tenements, hereditaments, and accept the seizing and possession of all lands, and all deeds and other assurances in the law thereof; and to lease, let, demise, bargain, sell, remise, release, convey, mortgage and hypothecate, lands, tenements and hereditaments, upon such terms and conditions and under such covenants as He shall think fit. Also to bargain and agree for, buy, sell, mortgage, hypothecate, and in any and every way and manner deal in and with goods, wares and merchandise, choses in action, and other property in possession or in action, and to make, do and transact all and every kind of business of what nature or kind soever, and also for and in My name and as My act and deed, to sign, seal, execute, deliver and acknowledge such deeds, covenants, indentures, agreements, mortgages, hypothecations, bottomries, charter parties, bills of lading, bills, bonds, notes, receipts, evidences of debt, releases and satisfaction of mortgage, judgment and other debts, and such other instruments in writing of whatever kind and nature as may be necessary or proper in the premises.

GIVING AND GRANTING unto Him said Attorney full power and authority to do and perform all and every act and thing whatsoever requisite and necessary to be done in and about the premises, as fully to all intents and purposes as I might or could do if personally present hereby ratifying and confirming all that My said Attorney Arthur J. Waterford shall lawfully do or cause to be done by virtue of these presents.

IN WITNESS WHEREOF I have hereunto set My hand and seal the 24th day of March, A. D. 19 89

Signed, Sealed and Delivered in the Presence of

      Joseph L. Calella [Seal]

      Atty at Law [Seal]

      [Seal]

Figure 48

Mortgage companies and other lenders seldom make a profit on a loan during the first year or so. This is due to the expense of setting up the accounts and other loan processing costs. To assure a profitable operation, lenders typically include a prepayment penalty clause in the loan agreement.

This specifies the points to be paid during each period in which early payment, over and above a stated minimum, is made. The penalties are usually graduated so that the highest is in the early years of the mortgage and gradually diminish until the end of, say five years, when the penalty no longer applies. Without this provision, borrowers would rush to refinance their loans if the interest rate decreased enough to justify doing so.

SEE ALSO: NOVATION, POINTS, and REFINANCE.

PREPAYMENT PROVISION

A prepayment provision is a clause in a loan agreement which (a) prohibits prepayment of the loan during the first few years without a significant penalty; and/or (b) authorizes early prepayment of certain amounts without penalty.

INVESTOR ADVICE

Prepayment penalties can be avoided, if the agreement specifies that the loan is liquidated with the mortgagor's own funds. Penalties are inserted primarily to prevent refinancing. Where the lender insists on a prepayment penalty, request that this exception be granted.

SEE ALSO: NOVATION, POINTS, and PREPAYMENT PENALTY.

PRESCRIPTION

Prescription is the acquisition of property easement rights by unrestricted use.

INVESTOR ADVICE

Prescription is similar to adverse possession except that it applies to uses generally associated with easements. For a claim of prescription to prevail, property taxes need not have been paid.

Whereas a claim of adverse possession requires a belief of ownership together with payment of taxes on the property, this tax omission may still not prevent a claim of prescriptive easement. This claim, if upheld, would authorize the continued use of your property. You must constantly guard against notorious possession or continued unauthorized use of all or part of your property.

SEE ALSO: ADVERSE POSSESSION.

PRESCRIPTIVE EASEMENTS

This term refers to an easement, allowed by law, due to continuous and uncontested use for a prescribed period of time.

INVESTOR ADVICE

A property owner must be aware of the potential for the establishment of prescriptive use of his or her property. Although you may have no real objection to that use, you must advise the users

that the use is illegal unless specifically granted by you. Failure to restrict the use, prevent the use, or otherwise acknowledge the action of others can eventually result in a loss of some of your rights to the property.

SEE ALSO: ADVERSE POSSESSION.

PRESENT VALUE OF ONE

This term refers to the discounted value of $1 received at a designated time in the future and at specified interest rate.

INVESTOR ADVICE

Figure 49 is a table of values showing the present value of $1 received at various times in the future and at varying interest rates. This table is only representative of the principal and only covers a few interest rates and selected periods of time.

The principle of discounted value for present worth is very useful to you as an investor, as it is obvious that a bird in the hand is worth more than something in the future. Common sense attests that if you had something less than a dollar, say $0.90, and placed it on deposit at 10% interest, it would grow to about a dollar at the end of one year.

Figure 49 indicates that $1 received at the end of one year at a 10% interest rate would be worth about $0.91—proof that the preceding assumption was correct.

In the calculation of overall return (OAR), it is necessary to reduce any capital gains from a future sale to a present value to accurately consider that gain in today's dollars.

Applying the factors in Figure 49, we find that a $50,000 gain to be realized at the end of a 10 year holding period, with money valued at 10% per annum is worth only about one-third of the amount received at that time. Again referring to Figure 49, we find the 10-year factor for 10% to be 0.386. The present value of this gain is therefore:

$$0.386 \times \$50,000 = \$19,300$$

If the same gain would not be realized for 20 years, the value would be:

$$0.149 \times \$50,000 = \$7,450$$

From these two illustrations we can see that the longer we must wait and the higher the interest, the less the present value. Conversely, the shorter the wait and the lower the interest, the higher the present value.

SEE ALSO: PRESENT VALUE OF ONE PER PERIOD.

PRESENT VALUE OF ONE PER PERIOD

This term refers to the amount $1 deposited each period for a number of periods will grow at a designated interest rate.

INVESTOR ADVICE

Figure 50 is a representative table of present values for $1 per period deposited for various periods and at various interest rates. Whereas $1 received in the future was always less than one, due to discounting, this table indicates that most of the factors are positive values. Why is this future receipt more valuable? Two factors are in effect have:

1. periodic deposits which add up over the periods, together with the interest that these deposits earn, and
2. the discounting of that end of period total value, due to the fact that the money will not be received for a period of time.

PRESENT VALUE OF $1
Received at the End of the Period
PV1 p-%

PERIOD	2%	4%	6%	8%	10%	12%	14%	16%	18%	20%	24%	28%
1	0.980	0.962	0.943	0.926	0.909	0.893	0.877	0.862	0.848	0.833	0.807	0.781
2	0.961	0.925	0.890	0.857	0.826	0.797	0.770	0.743	0.718	0.694	0.650	0.610
3	0.942	0.889	0.840	0.794	0.751	0.712	0.675	0.641	0.609	0.579	0.525	0.477
4	0.924	0.855	0.792	0.735	0.683	0.636	0.592	0.552	0.516	0.482	0.423	0.373
5	0.906	0.822	0.747	0.681	0.621	0.567	0.519	0.476	0.437	0.402	0.341	0.291
6	0.888	0.790	0.705	0.630	0.565	0.507	0.456	0.410	0.370	0.335	0.275	0.227
7	0.871	0.760	0.665	0.584	0.513	0.452	0.400	0.354	0.314	0.279	0.222	0.178
8	0.854	0.731	0.627	0.540	0.467	0.404	0.351	0.305	0.266	0.233	0.179	0.139
9	0.837	0.703	0.592	0.500	0.424	0.361	0.308	0.263	0.226	0.194	0.144	0.108
10	0.820	0.676	0.558	0.463	0.386	0.322	0.270	0.227	0.191	0.162	0.116	0.085
11	0.804	0.650	0.527	0.429	0.351	0.288	0.237	0.195	0.162	0.135	0.094	0.066
12	0.789	0.625	0.497	0.397	0.319	0.257	0.208	0.169	0.137	0.112	0.076	0.052
13	0.773	0.601	0.469	0.368	0.290	0.229	0.182	0.145	0.116	0.094	0.061	0.040
14	0.758	0.578	0.442	0.341	0.263	0.205	0.160	0.125	0.099	0.078	0.049	0.032
15	0.743	0.555	0.417	0.315	0.239	0.183	0.140	0.108	0.084	0.065	0.040	0.025
16	0.728	0.534	0.394	0.292	0.218	0.163	0.123	0.093	0.071	0.054	0.032	0.019
17	0.714	0.513	0.371	0.270	0.198	0.146	0.108	0.080	0.060	0.045	0.026	0.015
18	0.700	0.494	0.350	0.250	0.180	0.130	0.095	0.069	0.051	0.038	0.021	0.012
19	0.686	0.475	0.331	0.232	0.164	0.116	0.083	0.060	0.043	0.031	0.017	0.009
20	0.673	0.456	0.312	0.215	0.149	0.104	0.073	0.051	0.036	0.026	0.014	0.007
25	0.610	0.375	0.233	0.146	0.092	0.059	0.038	0.025	0.016	0.011	0.005	0.002
30	0.552	0.308	0.174	0.099	0.057	0.033	0.020	0.012	0.007	0.004	0.002	0.001
35	0.500	0.253	0.130	0.068	0.036	0.019	0.010	0.006	0.003	0.002	0.001	–
40	0.453	0.208	0.097	0.046	0.022	0.011	0.005	0.003	0.001	–	–	–
45	0.410	0.171	0.073	0.031	0.014	0.006	0.003	0.001	–	–	–	–

(–) Number less than 0.001
Where 4th decimal place is 5 or greater, 3rd. decimal rounded up.
Table prepared utilizing Hewlett-Packard 38-C calculator.

Figure 49

PRESENT VALUE OF $1 PER PERIOD
Received at the End of Those Periods

$$PV1/P_{p-\%}$$

PERIOD	2%	4%	6%	8%	10%	12%	14%	16%	18%	20%	24%	28%
1	0.980	0.962	0.943	0.926	0.909	0.893	0.877	0.862	0.848	0.833	0.807	0.781
2	1.942	1.886	1.833	1.783	1.736	1.690	1.647	1.605	1.566	1.528	1.457	1.392
3	2.884	2.775	2.673	2.577	2.487	2.402	2.322	2.246	2.174	2.107	1.981	1.868
4	3.808	3.630	3.466	3.312	3.170	3.038	2.914	2.798	2.690	2.589	2.404	2.241
5	4.714	4.452	4.212	3.993	3.791	3.605	3.433	3.274	3.127	2.991	2.745	2.530
6	5.601	5.242	4.917	4.623	4.355	4.111	3.889	3.685	3.498	3.326	3.021	2.759
7	6.472	6.002	5.582	5.206	4.868	4.564	4.288	4.037	3.812	3.605	3.242	2.937
8	7.326	6.733	6.210	5.747	5.335	4.968	4.639	4.344	4.078	3.837	3.421	3.076
9	8.162	7.435	6.802	6.247	5.759	5.328	4.946	4.772	4.607	4.303	3.566	3.184
10	8.983	8.111	7.360	6.710	6.145	5.650	5.216	4.833	4.494	4.193	3.682	3.269
11	9.787	8.761	7.887	7.139	6.495	5.938	5.453	5.029	4.656	4.327	3.776	3.335
12	10.575	9.385	8.384	7.536	6.814	6.194	5.660	5.197	4.793	4.439	3.851	3.387
13	11.348	9.986	8.853	7.904	7.103	6.424	5.842	5.342	4.910	4.533	3.912	3.427
14	12.106	10.563	9.295	8.244	7.367	6.628	6.002	5.468	5.008	4.611	3.962	3.459
15	12.849	11.118	9.712	8.560	7.606	6.811	6.142	5.576	5.092	4.676	4.001	3.483
16	13.578	11.652	10.106	8.851	7.824	6.974	6.265	5.669	5.162	4.730	4.033	3.503
17	14.292	12.166	10.477	9.122	8.022	7.120	6.373	5.749	5.222	4.775	4.059	3.518
18	14.992	12.659	10.828	9.372	8.201	7.250	6.467	5.818	5.273	4.812	4.080	3.529
19	15.679	13.134	11.158	9.604	8.365	7.366	6.550	5.878	5.316	4.844	4.097	3.539
20	16.351	13.509	11.470	9.818	8.514	7.469	6.623	5.929	5.353	4.870	4.110	3.546
25	19.524	15.622	12.783	10.675	9.077	7.843	6.873	6.097	5.467	4.948	4.147	3.564
30	22.397	17.292	13.765	11.258	9.427	8.055	7.003	6.177	5.517	4.979	4.160	3.569
35	24.999	18.665	14.498	11.655	9.644	8.176	7.070	6.215	5.539	4.992	4.164	3.571
40	27.356	19.793	15.046	11.925	9.779	8.244	7.105	6.234	5.548	4.997	4.166	3.571
45	29.490	20.720	15.456	12.108	9.863	8.283	7.123	6.242	5.552	4.999	4.166	3.571

Where 4th place decimal is 5 or greater, 3rd. place rounded up.
Table prepared utilizing Hewlett-Packard 38-C calculator.

Figure 50

As an investor you will find considerable use for this concept in the calculation of mortgage payments. Consider present value as the amount of the mortgage loan. You know the time period and the interest rate. This allows you to solve for the payment as follows:

EXAMPLE

$50,000 is borrowed for 30 years at 10% interest. What are the annual payments required to amortize the loan? From Figure 50, for 30 years at 10% we find the factor for $1 present value to be 9.427. What this says is that $1 per period deposited has a present value of $9.427—or $1 deposited per period would buy a 30-year loan at 10% of $9.427.

We can now state that payment of $1/period (30 years at 10%) = 9.427

a $50,000 loan requires an annual payment of

$$\$50,000 \times 9.427 = \$5,303.91$$

The preceding illustration used annual payments, since our table is rather limited. In real life we would have used monthly payments, which would have required that the interest rate be adjusted to the rate per period, or

$$10\%/12 = 8.33\%$$

Mortgage payment books and financial calculators provide us with all interest rates and all periods. The values shown are usually annual constants, which can be multiplied by the amount borrowed to find the required payment.

Mortgage books are quickly being replaced by hand-held financial calculators capable of instantaneously calculating various present values, future values, and mortgage payments for any time and interest rate.

SEE ALSO: AMORTIZATION, ANNUAL CONSTANT, and PRESENT VALUE OF ONE.

PRIME RATE

The lowest rate at which a lender will loan funds to his or her very best customers.

INVESTOR ADVICE

You will find that the subject of prime rate will be introduced in many instances other than during your application for a loan. Most investors do not qualify for a prime interest rate loan but will be quoted rates such as, "prime plus 1%" or "prime plus 2%."

Where your loan has a variable rate, it may call for an interest rate adjustment at various periods. The value at that time will be based on the prime rate. For example, the loan may specify that at the end of a five year period and each five year period thereafter, the lender will have the right to adjust the interest rate, up or down, to a value equal to the average prime rate during the past five years plus, say, 1% or 2%.

> **WARNING!** Leases on rental property with variable rate loans should include provisions for rent increases in the event of mortgage rate increases.

SEE ALSO: ADJUSTABLE RATE MORTGAGE.

PRINCIPLE OF ANTICIPATION

This principle affirms that value is created or destroyed by expectations of benefits to be gained or lost in the future.

INVESTOR ADVICE

Whether you are an appraiser or an investor, you must examine the current and past income history of a property in order to predict its future performance. You must weigh your opinion of value against the anticipation of future benefits. Will the income be more, the same, or possibly less in future years?

Value is defined as the present value of all future benefits, tangible and intangible, which add or subtract to the rights of property ownership. Thus, your analysis must weigh the past factual data to estimate the amount, quality, and extent of future benefits.

Your opinion can be compared with the opinions of others who have recently purchased comparable properties. Does your opinion compare favorably with the attitudes of other informed buyers?

SEE ALSO: PRINCIPLE OF BALANCE, PRINCIPLE OF CHANGE, PRINCIPLE OF CONFORMITY, PRINCIPLE OF COMPETITION, PRINCIPLE OF CONTRIBUTION, PRINCIPLE OF SUBSTITUTION, and PRINCIPLE OF SUPPLY AND DEMAND.

PRINCIPLE OF BALANCE

This principle requires the investor and/or appraiser to consider the proper economic balance between types and locations of properties in the subject area to assure that value will be sustained by the population.

INVESTOR ADVICE

A surplus of commercial property in a small community that cannot sustain a large number of commercial establishments would tend to devalue commercially zoned land. Similarly, a balance between the agents producing income is essential if maximum income is to be derived and maximum land value achieved.

Balance consists of three elements:

1. increasing and decreasing returns;
2. contribution; and
3. surplus productivity.

SEE ALSO: PRINCIPLE OF ANTICIPATION, PRINCIPLE OF CHANGE, PRINCIPLE OF COMPETITION, PRINCIPLE OF CONFORMITY, PRINCIPLE OF CONTRIBUTION, PRINCIPLE OF SUBSTITUTION, and PRINCIPLE OF SUPPLY AND DEMAND.

PRINCIPLE OF CHANGE

This principle of property evaluation considers that nothing remains the same and that all things are subject to constant and inevitable change.

INVESTOR ADVICE

As a potential investor, you must be aware of the economic and social forces that tend to affect the value of property. You must recognize those subtle forces of change as well as the obvious big movements and assess their relationship to value today and in the future. The more trends that you can identify, the more accurate your assessment of potential change.

Here are a few changes that should be considered:

- pattern of growth;

- current neighborhood, city, and district growth/decline in desirability; and

- availability of similar properties in the same or nearby area.

SEE ALSO: PRINCIPLE OF ANTICIPATION, PRINCIPLE OF BALANCE, PRINCIPLE OF COMPETITION, PRINCIPLE OF CONFORMITY, PRINCIPLE OF CONTRIBUTION, PRINCIPLE OF SUBSTITUTION, and PRINCIPLE OF SUPPLY AND DEMAND.

PRINCIPLE OF COMPETITION

This principle of appraising requires the evaluator to consider that when net income is greater than the average return on labor, capital, management, and land, the excess tends to breed competition.

INVESTOR ADVICE

If the profit from an operation is too great, it is sure to attract others to the same type of operation. This can have the effect of reducing profits of all similar operations until no one is successful.

Competition is the most easily recognizable force, which affects value. A reasonable amount of competition will enhance value, whereas too much can destroy it.

SEE ALSO: PRINCIPLE OF ANTICIPATION, PRINCIPLE OF BALANCE, PRINCIPLE OF CONFORMITY, PRINCIPLE OF CONTRIBUTION, PRINCIPLE OF SUBSTITUTION, and PRINCIPLE OF SUPPLY AND DEMAND.

PRINCIPLE OF CONFORMITY

The principle of conformity is an appraisal principle which considers how compatible the subject property is with surrounding properties.

INVESTOR ADVICE

Is there a reasonable degree of homogeneity of architectural types, or is the subject unique? Conformity tends to create maximum value and a maximum return on investment. Conformity, on the other hand, should not be confused with monotony; but the differences should not be so great that the property becomes uniquely strange to its surroundings.

Violations of the rule of conformity are often observed in overimprovement and underimprovement. There is a direct relationship between the principles of regression and progression. In regression we observe that the value of a superior property is adversely affected by the mere existence of an inferior property in the same immediate area. In progression, on the other hand, we find that the inferior property is improved by the superior one.

Two old adage of home ownership are, "Give me a modest home in a very expensive neighborhood," and "Avoid having the best home on the block."

SEE ALSO: PRINCIPLE OF ANTICIPATION, PRINCIPLE OF BALANCE, PRINCIPLE OF CHANGE, PRINCIPLE OF COMPETITION, PRINCIPLE OF CONTRIBUTION, PRINCIPLE OF SUBSTITUTION, and PRINCIPLE OF SUPPLY AND DEMAND.

PRINCIPLE OF CONTRIBUTION

This principle of value requires the appraiser to consider the property based on its contribution to income.

INVESTOR ADVICE

The value of any structure or land parcel is directly related to its contribution to income production. Maximum income is produced when all of the four agents of production are in economic balance. If labor, management, capital, or land are excessive to the required balance, a maximized return is not realized.

You must keep this principle in mind when considering the addition, modification, or improvement of any property. The additional capital invested must contribute a corresponding increase in income production. For instance, the addition of a swimming pool to your apartment complex should produce increased rental income or, at the very least, prevent an increase in vacancy rate.

SEE ALSO: PRINCIPLE OF ANTICIPATION, PRINCIPLE OF BALANCE, PRINCIPLE OF CHANGE, PRINCIPLE OF COMPETITION, PRINCIPLE OF CONFORMITY, PRINCIPLE OF SUBSTITUTION, and PRINCIPLE OF SUPPLY AND DEMAND.

PRINCIPLE OF SUBSTITUTION

The principle of substitution is an appraisal principal which states that when several commodities are available to satisfy a need, the one with the lowest price will have the greater demand.

INVESTOR ADVICE

This is a principle often overlooked by the inexperienced investor, who becomes so engrossed in the evaluation of the subject property that he or she fails to note that others, of lesser value, satisfy the same need.

The principle of substitution has its place in each of the three principal means of evaluation.

The Cost Approach. No one will pay more for a property than for another property which satisfies the same need. This assumes, of course, that the availability of the substitute is reasonably the same.

The Market Approach. No one will pay more for a property than the price of another which is considered a good substitute. Appraisers are most cognizant of this principle and strive to determine what the public is paying for comparable property.

The Income Approach. Value of income property is set by the amount of income produced. No one pays more than the price of comparable property which is reasonably available and producing the same or greater income.

Inherent in each of the three preceding evaluations is the assumption that substitute properties of equal utility are available. Thus, we assume that no one would pay more for a look-a-like tract home than the going price of others which are available. Where shortages of properties require long waits, one might be justified in paying more for the privilege of immediate availability.

SEE ALSO: PRINCIPLE OF ANTICIPATION, PRINCIPLE OF BALANCE, PRINCIPLE OF CHANGE, PRINCIPLE OF COMPETITION, PRINCIPLE OF CONFORMITY, PRINCIPLE OF CONTRIBUTION, and PRINCIPLE OF SUPPLY AND DEMAND.

PRINCIPLE OF SUPPLY AND DEMAND

This basic principle of value determination considers the economic factors of supply and demand. A surplus of property will reduce the price that a seller can expect (buyer's market), whereas scarcity can inflate the price expectations of the seller (seller's market).

INVESTOR ADVICE

There is only one case in which market price tends to approach that of the cost of reproduction or replacement. This is the point at which supply and demand are more or less in balance.

The factors which affect supply and demand are population changes, taxation, building codes, governmental controls and the basic economy factors:

- purchasing power,

- wage rates, and

- price levels.

SEE ALSO: PRINCIPLE OF ANTICIPATION, PRINCIPLE OF BALANCE, PRINCIPLE OF CHANGE, PRINCIPLE OF COMPETITION, PRINCIPLE OF CONFORMITY, PRINCIPLE OF CONTRIBUTION, and PRINCIPLE OF SUBSTITUTION.

PRINCIPLE OF SURPLUS PRODUCTIVITY

Surplus productivity is defined as the income remaining after payment of labor, capital, and management—income attributable to the land.

INVESTOR ADVICE

Labor is said to have first claim on the income produced. The cost of capital (interest on and amortization of invested funds) is second, and the cost of management coordination is third. Economic theory assigns the last claim to land.

SEE ALSO: PRINCIPLE OF ANTICIPATION, PRINCIPLE OF BALANCE, PRINCIPLES OF CHANGE, PRINCIPLE OF COMPETITION, PRINCIPLE OF CONFORMITY, PRINCIPLE OF CONTRIBUTION, PRINCIPLE OF SUBSTITUTION, and PRINCIPLE OF SUPPLY AND DEMAND.

PRIVATE INVESTOR

A private investor is an investor not connected with a lending institution, who provides investment funds from his or her own resources.

INVESTOR ADVICE

Private investors are often able to provide funds for a project when conventional lenders are unable or unwilling to participate. Private investors are also a good source of second mortgage money and often purchase seasoned real estate contracts.

You can expect to pay a higher interest rate with the private investor than with a conventional lender, who competes for business with others in the lending business. Of course, you can expect to pay a higher interest rate on any project which has a risk greater than acceptable by traditional lenders.

Private investors, who specialize in buying real estate contracts, also expect a higher yield than the going rate. It is not unusual for an investor to demand 18% return on a contract, when the going rate is 12% for conventional loans.

EXAMPLE

Farmer Brown sold his farm on contract 5 years ago. The contract still has a balance of $75,000 and bears interest at 12% annually. Monthly payments on the contract are $843. The contract runs for another 20 years.

Brown sees an advertisement in the local paper which reads, "We buy contracts." He calls and is told that they would pay him $51,000 in cash for his seasoned contract. What interest rate is the private investor asking? How much is he discounting the contract?

Investor Discount = $75,000 – $51,000 = $24,000
PV — $843/month x % @ 20 years = $51,000
    where x = interest rate = 19.4% *
    *Using Hewlett–Packard 12C financial computer.

If a computer had not been available, we could have determined the factor ($51,000/$843 = 60.498) and then looked under a table for that factor in the (20 x 12 = 240 periods) column to find what percentage was represented by that factor.
SEE ALSO: SEASONED MORTGAGE.

PRIVATE MORTGAGE INSURANCE (PMI)

Priveate mortgage insurance is mortgage insurance, provided by other than a government agency, beyond the legal or usual limit of a conventional lender.

INVESTOR ADVICE

Banks and mortgage companies who make conventional loans are often limited as to the maximum loan that can be made (for example, 80%). By insuring the additional risk with a private mortgage insurer, the lender can sometimes provide up to a 95% loan ratio.

Where mortgage insurance is required, the borrower is required to pay the insurance premium, which adds 0.5% to 1.0% to the interest rate. When the loan principal is reduced to that of a standard loan commitment, the insurance is no longer required.

Private mortgage insurance serves a purpose similar to the FHA and VA insurance programs. In the VA program, the Veterans Administration pays for the insurance. In the FHA program the borrower pays for the insurance program.

> **ASSUMING A PMI- OR FHA-INSURED LOAN?** Check to see if the loan value is down to the 80% ratio point. If so, insurance is no longer required. To delete insurance payments, proof of current value must be furnished.

SEE ALSO: LOAN RATIO.

PRIVATE OFFERING

A private offering is a syndication offering which does not require registration with the Security and Exchange Commission to comply with Regulation D.

INVESTOR ADVICE

Regulation D allows up to 35 nonaccredited investors to be sold syndicated shares. There is no limit to the number of accredited investors that are allowed to participate.

An accredited investor is one with a net worth of $1 million or more, who has an income of at least $200,000 annually, and who buys a syndication unit of $150,000 or more. The purpose of Regulation D is to protect the innocent, nonsophisticated investor.

Syndications and private offerings sold entirely within one state to residents of that state are not required to comply with federal regulations. Check your local securities commission in regard to intra-state selling rules and regulations.

SEE ALSO: LIMITED PARTNERSHIP, RED HERRING, SECURITIES AND EXCHANGE COMMISSION, and SYNDICATION.

PROBATE

Probate is the legal process by which an estate is settled, all debtors satisfied, federal and state taxes paid, and the remainder distributed to the heirs in accordance with the will of the decedent or as directed by state law. The manager of this process is called the executor(ix) if appointed by a will, and the administrator(ix) if appointed by the court.

INVESTOR ADVICE

There have been literally hundreds of books and articles written on the subject of how to avoid probate, indicating the importance of the subject. Federal and state laws require all assets of a decedent to pass through the probate process. The higher the value of the estate, the higher the administrative cost.

Estate planning, including the establishment of trusts (both inter vivoce and testamentary), well-drafted wills, and gift programs during the decedent's lifetime, can reduce taxes and administrative costs.

> **BEWARE!** Many profess to be expert estate planners, but few are properly qualified.

For the investor with considerable assets, proper and timely estate planning is essential.
SEE ALSO: ADMINISTRATOR(IX), ESTATE PLANNING, ESTATE TAXES, EXECUTOR(IX), GIFT TAXES, INHERITANCE TAXES, INTER VIVOCE TRUST, TESTAMENTARY TRUST, TRUST, and WILL.

PROFESSIONAL OFFICE BUILDING

A professional buildiang is a building designed and constructed for doctors, dentists, and similar professionals.

INVESTOR ADVICE

Professional office buildings are usually designed and built specifically for that purpose. It is difficult to convert other types of buildings to professional use, due to the requirements for extensive plumbing, electrical, and compressed air service in each suite.

Ordinary office buildings can be in almost any location, where tenants and their clients can drive to them and park. Professional office buildings, on the other hand, are best located adjacent to similar offices, hospitals, and clinics. Special provisions must also be made for disabled parking and entrances.

Professional office buildings are far more expensive to construct than a standard office building. A class top-quality office building costs about $75 per square foot, whereas the same quality professional building costs about $100 per square foot.

> **OPPORTUNITY KNOCKS!** A good site for a professional building can be converted to a profitable condominium.

SEE ALSO: COST APPROACH TO VALUE.

PRO-FORMA ANALYSIS

Pro-forma analysis is an income or cash flow analysis of a proposed project which is based on as much actual cost and market data as is available. Where facts are not available, reasonable assumptions are substituted.

INVESTOR ADVICE

Applications for loans for a proposed new project should include pro-forma income and cash flow analyses. Where assumptions or guesses are included, they should be based on reasonable estimates which are supportable by further documentation. Figure 9 shows a typical proforma analysis.

The pro-forma analysis has the appearance of actual income or cash flow statements prepared by accountants using factual data. The difference is that many assumptions and guesses are utilized to complete the analysis, since actual data is not available.

Pro-forma income statements project the income that is likely from a proposed operation. This is necessary to support the loan request. The pro-forma cash flow analysis is useful in predicting the possible need for future loans to keep the operation afloat until the operation reaches an acceptable occupancy rate and is profitable or at least self-supporting.

SEE ALSO: BALANCE SHEET, CASH FLOW ANALYSIS, DEBT SERVICE, and INCOME STATEMENT.

PROFITS À PRENDRE

This term refers to easements with a right to take part of the soil or products of the land.

INVESTOR ADVICE

Profits à prendre are usually those for hunting, fishing, or grazing of cattle. They must be created and extinguished in writing. They may be "attached to" or total property. In most states they cannot be transferred or acquired by prescription.

SEE ALSO: EASEMENTS.

PROFIT-SHARING PLAN

A profit-sharing plan is a company plan that allocates a certain percentage of its annual company profits for the benefit of employees.

INVESTOR ADVICE

Profit-sharing plans are gaining in popularity as the preferred way to provide for employee retirement. A profit-sharing plan accomplishes two goals:

1. It encourages employees to work diligently and efficiently in order to feather their own nest.
2. The company only contributes *if* there is a profit, thus relieving it of responsibility in unprofitable years.

Profit-sharing funds, provided by the company, are usually divided among eligible employees on a proportional basis of each employee's annual earnings as a percentage of all employee earnings.

The profit sharing fund may be further increased by employee volunteer contributions and investment earnings.

Employee profit-sharing plans are one of the major sources of mortgage funds. They provide mortgage money to developers or may purchase large bundles of existing mortgages from mortgage companies, savings and loans, and other lenders. When purchasing existing mortgages, the fund acts as a secondary mortgage market.

The provisions for profit-sharing plans, the distribution of available profits, and the investment of funds are strictly regulated by the Internal Revenue Service.

SEE ALSO: PENSION FUNDS, SECONDARY MORTGAGE MARKET.

PROPERTY IMPROVEMENT

Any addition to land to include buildings and appurtenances is a property improvement.

INVESTOR ADVICE

Beware of overimprovement of any land parcel. Make sure that any added improvements will utilize the land at its highest and best and that the added investment will contribute a proportionate share to income production.

Improvements to raw land require extensive planning in order to minimize cash flow consistent with projected sales of the improved property. Cash flow can be reduced through use of lot release arrangements and options to purchase.

SEE ALSO: HIGHEST AND BEST USE, LOT RELEASE SYSTEM, OPTION, PRINCIPLE OF BALANCE, and PRINCIPLE OF CONTRIBUTION.

PROPERTY MANAGEMENT

The effort required to advertise, show, lease, collect rents, maintain, and regulate the use of a property is called property management.

INVESTOR ADVICE

Residential rental property cannot normally be managed by the owner, unless he or she lives on the premises. On-site management assistance is absolutely essential to the profitable operation of residential rental property.

Commercial property can be controlled successfully from off-site with occasional owner visits to ascertain the condition of the property. Warehousing and manufacturing buildings are by far the easiest to manage, particularly where net leases are in force.

Management involves more than interface with tenants and the structures which are rented. Bills must be paid on a regular basis, mortgage payments mailed on schedule, and future replacements and repairs planned. If successfully operated, the property should throw off a cash flow, which must be invested promptly and profitably.

SEE ALSO: CASH FLOW and CERTIFIED PROPERTY MANAGER (CPM).

PROPERTY RIGHTS

The right to enter, leave, enjoy and all other rights associated with property.

INVESTOR ADVICE

All the rights of property ownership must be jealously guarded to assure protection against trespass and prescriptive use by others and potential loss of some of these important assets.

SEE ALSO: ADVERSE POSSESSION and BUNDLE OF RIGHTS.

PROSPECTUS

A prospectus is a printed document that outlines a proposal to raise money through the sale of shares of a corporation or owner participation in a limited partnership. The Securities Exchange Commission requires all offerings to more than 35 investors to include a copy of the prospectus.

INVESTOR ADVICE

Under penalty of law, a prospectus must be factual and complete, but often they do not contain the most important information. When you are considering investing in a new real estate project, you should pay particular attention to the following:

- Who are the principals; who will be the officers or general partners in the proposed operation?

- What is the history of success of these principals in former similar operations?

- Based on your knowledge of the locale in which the project will be constructed, is the proforma income statement reasonable?

- What percentage of the operation will be taken by the promoters and their mortgage lenders?

- Is the projected return on investment large enough to justify the risk taken?

- What other real estate projects are available to you for investment, and what is their return? How does their risk compare?

- What is the multiple of available cash to debt service?

- Is this multiple based on full occupancy or something less?

- What is the estimated date that the partnership can expect to receive income from the project?

- What other *investments* are available to you which offer the same or less risk?

SEE ALSO: CORPORATION, GENERAL PARTNER, LIMITED PARTNERSHIP, and SECURITIES AND EXCHANGE COMMISSION (SEC).

PROXIMATE CAUSE

Proximate cause is that continuous effort in a course of events, unbroken by any other efforts, which produces a certain result and without which that result would not have occurred.

INVESTOR ADVICE

Proximate cause is often discussed in conjunction with a dispute between one group of real estate salespeople and brokers and another. To collect a commission, the listing broker must show that he or she (or the agent) was the proximate cause of the sale. In other words, the sale must have been concluded through his or her efforts and not the efforts of others.

Disputes usually are occasioned when a certain party buys are listed property which was shown by another broker. Realtor boards of arbitration usually award the commission to the agent who took the buyer "to and through" the property and reject the claim of the agent who talked about the property, showed the buyer the listing data, and so forth.

Proximate cause is also used in defense of insurance claims in which a loss was occasioned by more than one peril, one of which was covered by insurance. For a claim to prevail, the owner must show that the insured peril was the proximate cause of the loss.

SEE ALSO: LISTING CONTRACT and HAZARD INSURANCE.

PURCHASE MONEY MORTGAGE

A purchase money mortgage is a mortgage given to the seller in consideration of all or a part of the sales price of the property.

INVESTOR ADVICE

The purchase money mortgage differs from a real estate contract in that the sale is completed and the property is passed to the buyer at the time of closing. The seller then holds a first or second purchase money mortgage for the balance due from the buyer.

In a purchase money mortgage contract, the seller is the financing party but keeps title to the property until the obligation is paid in full. Any existing mortgages in effect when the contract was assigned are paid by the seller from monthly payments. The contract holder keeps the balance as payment against the contract.

Purchase money mortgages are subordinate to any existing mortgages on the property at the time of sale. If assumable, the normal procedure is for the buyer to assume that obligation as part payment on the sales price. A typical sale might appear as follows:

Sales Price	$100,000.00
Payments:	
First Mortgage Assumed	50,000.00
Cash Downpayment	20,000,00
Purchase Money Mortgage (Second Note)	30,000.00
Total Payment	$100,000.00

SEE ALSO: CONTRACT, SUBORDINATE DEBENTURE.

PYRAMIDING

Pyramiding refers to:
1. An illegal operation that pays investors an unusually high return on investment from later sales. This provides an illusion of a successful enterprise, which is actually a scam.
2. A legal commission method which encourages real estate salespeople to obtain other new salespeople and receive an override on those new hires' earnings, and their new hires', and their new hires' and so forth.

INVESTOR ADVICE

Beware of any investment scheme which offers a return on investment out of proportion to the risk or greater than similar operations are paying.

> **SOUND TOO GOOD TO BE TRUE?** If the return is too good to be true, there is probably something wrong with the deal.

Remember, no one pays a higher fee for the use of money than is absolutely necessary. If someone is offering more than the going rate, their is a reason—he or she can't get the money from any other source—probably due to the risk involved.

SEE ALSO: RISK VERSUS RETURN.

Q

Qualifications of the Appraiser   Quit Claim Deed

Q

QUALIFICATIONS OF THE APPRAISER

This term refers to the total of the appraiser's practical experience, education, and designations awarded by various appraisal organizations.

INVESTOR ADVICE

Appraisal organizations, which award designations, require an appraiser qualification sheet to be included as a part of each report. The appraiser's qualification sheet is the key to your evaluation of his or her capabilities. For a residential appraiser, you should expect the following:

- a designated member of American Institute of Real Estate Appraisers, Society of Real Estate Appraisers, or National Association of Independent Fee Appraisers;
- a minimum of three years appraising experience;
- all clients listed indicate satisfaction with his or her work; and
- the appraiser is familiar with the area in which the property is located.

For a land or income property appraiser, you should expect the following:

- a designated member of AIREA, SRA, or NAIFA;
- a minimum of five years appraising experience;
- a bachelor's degree from a recognized college or university and in an applicable discipline;
- all clients listed express satisfaction with his or her work; and
- the appraiser is familiar with businesses and property in the area where the subject property is located.

While formal education and appraisal organization training are important considerations in appraiser selection, by far the most important consideration is the appraiser's reputation for accurate and complete appraisals, as witnessed by his or her clients.

In rural areas it is not unusual to find appraisers with what appear to be minimum designations and training, yet a check with local lenders will indicate that these people are highly regarded.

SEE ALSO: AMERICAN INSTITUTE OF REAL ESTATE APPRAISERS (AIREA), NATIONAL ASSOCIATION OF INDEPENDENT FEE APPRAISERS (NAIFA), and SOCIETY OF REAL ESTATE APPRAISERS (SRA).

QUIT CLAIM DEED

A quit claim deed is an official document used to transfer any interest in real property without warranty.

INVESTOR ADVICE

The quit claim deed is a useful device for transferring interest in property to another person without warranty. Its use is varied, but it is most useful in transferring minor interests such as that required to clear property line disputes and errors, transfer title among family members, grant easements, and so forth.

Figure 51 shows a typical quit claim deed. Please note that the grantor transfers his or her interest (if any) to the grantee, with no reference to a warranty as to the grantor's ownership or rights.

It would be perfectly legal for you to give another person a quit claim deed to the Hotel Astor in New York City. Although possibly misleading, the deed in effect says, "If I have any interest in the Hotel Astor, I grant it to the grantee."

In signing the document you do not profess or warrant to have any interest whatsoever in that property.

SEE ALSO: WARRANTY DEED.

Recorded at Request of........Anthony..G...Smith,..Summit..Realtors..INc..............................

at................ M. Fee Paid $...3..00.......... ....

by.. Dep. Book....108..... Page.........226. Ref.:.........#1978................

Mail tax notice to.....A.G...Smith........................... Address..221..S...Main..St..,..SLC...Ut........

QUIT CLAIM DEED

Martin H. Browning   grantor
of   Salt Lake City   , County of   Salt Lake   , State of Utah, hereby
QUIT CLAIM   to

Christ United Methodist Church
2343 Ea. 3300 So., Salt Lake City, Ut.
                                                       grantee
of   Ten and 00/100   for the sum of
                                                     DOLLARS
                                                     County,
the following described tract   of land in   Salt Lake
State of Utah, to wit:

        All of Lot 95, Shady Acres Subdivision

WITNESS the hand   of said grantor , this 24th day of   March   19 89

    Signed in the presence of

                                            { *Martin H. Browning*
.... {
.... {

STATE OF UTAH,   }
                           } ss.
County of Salt Lake   }
    On the 24th day of   March   19 89
                                       personally appeared before me

        Martin H. Browning
the signer   of the foregoing instrument, who duly acknowledged to me that   he   executed the same.

                                    Mary ....
                                     Notary Public, residing at

My commission expires................May..22,.1991.............. Salt..Lake..City,..Ut.,................

THIS DEED PRINTED ESPECIALLY FOR PHOTO-RECORDING. USE BLACK INK AND TYPE.

Figure 51

R

Range of Values
Real Estate
Real Estate Agent
Real Estate Board (National Associaton of Realtors®)
Real Estate Investment Trust (REIT)
Real Estate Mortgage Investment Conduit (RELIC)
Real Property
REALTOR®
Recapture
Recapture Rate
Receivables
Recital
Reconciliation
Reconveyance Deed
Recording
Rectangular Survey
Recycled Real Estate
Redemption Rights
Red Herring
Redlining
Referee's Deed in Partition
Refinance
Regression Technique
Regulation Z
Release of Earnest Money
Release of Lien
Release or Satisfaction of Mortgage
Reliction
Remainderman
Remaining Economic Life

Rent
Rent Schedule
Rentable Square Footage
Rental Deposit
Rental Income Insurance
Replacement Cost
Repossession Lists
Reproduction Cost
Reserves for Replacement
Residual Techniques
Restrictive Covenants
Return of Investment
Return on Investment
Revenue Stamps
Reverse Mortgage
Reversioner
Review Appraiser
Right of First Refusal
Right of Survivorship
Right-of-Way (ROW)
Rights of Ownership
Riparian Rights
Risk versus Return
RM Appraiser
Rod
Roll-Over Loan
Row House
Rule of 1/4
Rule of 3
Rule of 5
Rule of 78s
Rules of Contractual Construction

R

RANGE OF VALUES

The range of values is the highest to lowest values found by the various appraisal approaches, or those found in one approach but utilizing various comparable sales.

INVESTOR ADVICE

In the simplest appraisal, which is a residential evaluation using three or more comparable sales (market approach), the appraiser invariably arrives at different indicated values after adjusting each sale for its differences with the subject property. For example, let's say that three comparable sales are used and the indicated values of the subject, considering each comparable sale, are:

Sale No.	Selling Price	Adjustment	Indicated Value
1	$75,000	+5,000	$80,000
2	82,500	-2,000	82,500
3	85,000	-3,000	82,000

The appraiser has a range of indicated values from a low of $80,000 to a high of $82,500. Which is the correct fair market value of the subject property?

Considering no aspect other than the range of values, the appraiser would ask him or herself, "Is any one of these comparables more comparable than the others?" If the answer is yes, the appraiser would probably select that value as representing the fair market value. If the answer is no, the appraiser might resort to a median or average value as *the* value.

If there are other important considerations, say a declining market, the appraiser might decide that the lower of the three is more representative. Similarly, in a rising market, the appraiser might select the higher of the three. There is no cut-and-dry way to decide. The answer is based on the appraiser's professional experience, gut feeling, and consideration of all factors, big and small, believed to affect the value.

In the appraisal of income property, several approaches to value may be employed. These approaches—cost, income, and market—will undoubtedly produce a range of values. Here, the appraiser may wish to give higher weighting to one or more of the approaches rather than select a median or average value. In the case of income property, the income approach and the market approach are usually given more weighting than the cost or replacement approach.

SEE ALSO: COST APPROACH TO VALUE, INCOME APPROACH TO VALUE, and MARKET APPROACH TO VALUE.

REAL ESTATE

Real estate is the land and all of its improvements, including tenements, hereditaments, or rights therein and whatever is attached thereto.

INVESTOR ADVICE

The preceding definition refers to the physical land and its improvements. In many states real estate differs from real property in that real property can include more than the land itself. Real property includes all of the bundle of rights inherent in the ownership of real estate. In some states the legal definition of real property is the same as real estate.

Regardless of your state of residence, you are likely to have little difficulty with the definition of real estate/real property, but much difficulty with the difference between real and personal property.

Generally, personal property is characterized by:

* its mobility;

* the manner in which it has been added to the real property;

* the intent of the party who added the property; and

* the purpose or use of the property.

The sale of residential property usually involves the transfer of both real estate and personalty. Here the buyer must be on guard to determine *exactly* what is being sold. If any item is in doubt, it should be clearly spelled out in the earnest money receipt and offer to purchase.

Where the sale involves a business, both the seller and buyer may be in jeopardy if the sale is not correctly consummated. This is especially true where merchandise (personalty) is transferred to a buyer.

In Utah and other states, specific statutes have been enacted to protect creditors. In Utah, the laws are called bulk sale laws, and they require:

* both buyer and seller to list all properties to be transferred;

* all creditors to be advised of the transfer at a specific time prior to the actual transfer; and

* records of the transfer to be maintained for at least six months.

If merchandise is involved in the transaction, make sure you are fully cognizant of bulk law requirements.

SEE ALSO: EARNEST MONEY RECEIPT AND OFFER TO PURCHASE, and PERSONALTY.

REAL ESTATE AGENT

A real estate agent is a person licensed by the state to list, sell, and rent real estate under the direction of a real estate broker.

INVESTOR ADVICE

Do not confuse the term *real estate agent* with that of REALTOR®. A REALTOR® is an agent who is also a member of the local, state, and national association of REALTORS®. While both are licensed to do business, only a REALTOR® is a member of the professional organization.

Why would you choose a REALTOR® in lieu of a real estate agent? Both may be well-qualified; but you must question the fact that the agent did not choose to become a member of his or her professional association, which:

* provides continuous training to its members to assure that they are competent and up to date;

* requires members to perform their services in strict accordance with a code of ethics;

* provides a multiple listing service to its members to assure that their listings are given the widest dissemination;

- provides continuous updating of sales activities in the area to help establish listing prices which maximize sales price while at the same time minimizing the time to sell; and

- lobbies the legislature and the Federal government to pass legislation to protect the public from unscrupulous dealers.

SEE ALSO: BROKER, NATIONAL ASSOCIATION OF REALTORS, and REALTOR®.

REAL ESTATE BOARD (NATIONAL ASSOCIATION OF REALTORS®)

A real estate board is a local organization of brokers, agents, and others interested in the real estate profession. All broker and agent members are also members of the state and NATIONAL ASSOCIATION OF REALTORS®.

INVESTOR ADVICE

In large metropolitan areas, there may be more than one Board of REALTORS®, who have jurisdiction over a prescribed portion of the area. Members of REALTOR® boards cooperate with members of other nearby boards and normally provide access to their multiple listing services, either directly by computer access or by copy of their publications. A REALTOR® may also cooperate with nonmembers.

REALTOR® Boards have various types of memberships, typical of which are:

1. REALTOR® members, who are Principal Brokers or Broker Associates.
2. REALTOR-ASSOCIATE® members, who are agents licensed to a Principal Broker member.
3. Affiliate Members, who are not eligible for REALTOR® membership, but who have an active interest in real estate transactions in their area. These members may be bankers, mortgage firms, appraisers or similar business persons.

Applicants for membership in REALTOR® Boards must possess the required state licenses and pass an indoctrination course, which covers the policies, rules and regulations of the local board, State Association and the National Association including the Code of Ethics of the National Association. A Board of REALTORS® may require an applicant to meet the 8-Point Membership Qualification Criteria of the National Association if the applicant is applying for REALTOR® (principal) Membership. A Board of REALTORS® may require an applicant for membership to meet the 6-Point Membership Qualification Criteria if an applicant is applying for REALTOR® (nonprincipal) Membership or REALTOR-ASSOCIATE® Membership. These are the most rigorous qualifications which may be required by a Board of REALTORS®.

Nonmembers often indicate that the reason they are not members is the fees charged and the small return to them. This is usually an excuse. Any active real estate agent knows that access to the multiple listing service is the life of their business and well worth the fees charged for membership.

Figure 52 indicates the code of Ethics and Standards of Practice to which all REALTORS® subscribe.

SEE ALSO: MULTIPLE LISTING SERVICE and NATIONAL ASSOCIATION OF REALTORS®.

Code of Ethics and Standards of Practice

of the

NATIONAL ASSOCIATION OF REALTORS®

Where the word REALTOR® is used in this Code and Preamble, it shall be deemed to include REALTOR-ASSOCIATE®. Pronouns shall be considered to include REALTORS® and REALTOR-ASSOCIATE®s of both genders.

Preamble...

Under all is the land. Upon its wise utilization and widely allocated ownership depend the survival and growth of free institutions and of our civilization. The REALTOR® should recognize that the interests of the nation and its citizens require the highest and best use of the land and the widest distribution of land ownership. They require the creation of adequate housing, the building of functioning cities, the development of productive industries and farms, and the preservation of a healthful environment.

Such interests impose obligations beyond those of ordinary commerce. They impose grave social responsibility and a patriotic duty to which the REALTOR® should dedicate himself, and for which he should be diligent in preparing himself. The REALTOR®, therefore, is zealous to maintain and improve the standards of his calling and shares with his fellow REALTORS® a common responsibility for its integrity and honor. The term REALTOR® has come to connote competency, fairness, and high integrity resulting from adherence to a lofty ideal of moral conduct in business relations. No inducement of profit and no instruction from clients ever can justify departure from this ideal.

In the interpretation of this obligation, a REALTOR® can take no safer guide than that which has been handed down through the centuries, embodied in the Golden Rule, "Whatsoever ye would that men should do to you, do ye even so to them."

Accepting this standard as his own, every REALTOR® pledges himself to observe its spirit in all of his activities and to conduct his business in accordance with the tenets set forth below.

Articles 1 through 5 are aspirational and establish ideals the REALTOR® should strive to attain.

ARTICLE 1

The REALTOR® should keep himself informed on matters affecting real estate in his community, the state, and nation so that he may be able to contribute responsibly to public thinking on such matters.

ARTICLE 2

In justice to those who place their interests in his care, the REALTOR® should endeavor always to be informed regarding laws, proposed legislation, governmental regulations, public policies, and current market conditions in order to be in a position to advise his clients properly.

ARTICLE 3

The REALTOR® should endeavor to eliminate in his community any practices which could be damaging to the public or bring discredit to the real estate profession. The REALTOR® should assist the governmental agency charged with regulating the practices of brokers and salesmen in his state. (Amended 11/87)

ARTICLE 4

To prevent dissension and misunderstanding and to assure better service to the owner, the REALTOR® should urge the exclusive listing of property unless contrary to the best interest of the owner. (Amended 11/87)

ARTICLE 5

In the best interests of society, of his associates, and his own business, the REALTOR® should willingly share with other REALTORS® the lessons of his experience and study for the benefit of the public, and should be loyal to the Board of REALTORS® of his community and active in its work.

Articles 6 through 23 establish specific obligations. Failure to observe these requirements subjects the REALTOR® to disciplinary action.

ARTICLE 6

The REALTOR® shall seek no unfair advantage over other REALTORS® and shall conduct his business so as to avoid controversies with other REALTORS®. (Amended 11/87)

- **Standard of Practice 6-1**

  "The REALTOR® shall not misrepresent the availability of access to show or inspect a listed property. (Cross-reference Article 22.)" (Amended 11/87)

ARTICLE 7

In accepting employment as an agent, the REALTOR® pledges himself to protect and promote the interests of the client. This obligation of absolute fidelity to the client's interests is primary, but it does not relieve the REALTOR® of the obligation to treat fairly all parties to the transaction.

- **Standard of Practice 7-1**

  "Unless precluded by law, government rule or regulation, or agreed otherwise in writing, the REALTOR® shall submit to the seller all offers until closing. Unless the REALTOR® and the seller agree otherwise, the REALTOR® shall not be obligated to continue to market the property after an offer has been accepted. Unless the subsequent offer is contingent upon the termination of an existing contract, the REALTOR® shall recommend that the seller obtain the advice of legal counsel prior to acceptance. (Cross-reference Article 17.)" (Amended 5/87)

- **Standard of Practice 7-2**

  "The REALTOR®, acting as listing broker, shall submit all offers to the seller as quickly as possible."

- **Standard of Practice 7-3**

  "The REALTOR®, in attempting to secure a listing, shall not deliberately mislead the owner as to market value."

Figure 52

- ## Standard of Practice 7-4
  (Refer to Standard of Practice 22-1, which also relates to Article 7, Code of Ethics.)

- ## Standard of Practice 7-5
  (Refer to Standard of Practice 22-2, which also relates to Article 7, Code of Ethics.)

- ## Standard of Practice 7-6
  "The REALTOR®, when acting as a principal in a real estate transaction, cannot avoid his responsibilities under the Code of Ethics."

ARTICLE 8

The REALTOR® shall not accept compensation from more than one party, even if permitted by law, without the full knowledge of all parties to the transaction.

ARTICLE 9

The REALTOR® shall avoid exaggeration, misrepresentation, or concealment of pertinent facts relating to the property or the transaction. The REALTOR® shall not, however, be obligated to discover latent defects in the property or to advise on matters outside the scope of his real estate license. (Amended 11/86)

- ## Standard of Practice 9-1
  "The REALTOR® shall not be a party to the naming of a false consideration in any document, unless it be the naming of an obviously nominal consideration."

- ## Standard of Practice 9-2
  (Refer to Standard of Practice 21-3, which also relates to Article 9, Code of Ethics.)

- ## Standard of Practice 9-3
  (Refer to Standard of Practice 7-3, which also relates to Article 9, Code of Ethics.)

- ## Standard of Practice 9-4
  "The REALTOR® shall not offer a service described as 'free of charge' when the rendering of a service is contingent on the obtaining of a benefit such as a listing or commission."

- ## Standard of Practice 9-5
  "The REALTOR® shall, with respect to the subagency of another REALTOR®, timely communicate any change of compensation for subagency services to the other REALTOR® prior to the time such REALTOR® produces a prospective buyer who has signed an offer to purchase the property for which the subagency has been offered through MLS or otherwise by the listing agency."

- ## Standard of Practice 9-6
  "REALTORS® shall disclose their REALTOR® status when seeking information from another REALTOR® concerning real property for which the other REALTOR® is an agent or subagent."

- ## Standard of Practice 9-7
  "The offering of premiums, prizes, merchandise discounts or other inducements to list or sell is not, in itself, unethical even if receipt of the benefit is contingent on listing or purchasing through the REALTOR® making the offer. However, the REALTOR® must exercise care and candor in any such advertising or other public or private representations so that any party interested in receiving or otherwise benefiting from the REALTOR®'s offer will have clear, thorough, advance understanding of all the terms and conditions of the offer. The offering of any inducements to do business is subject to the limitations and restrictions of state law and the ethical obligations established by Article 9, as interpreted by any applicable Standard of Practice." (Adopted 11/84)

- ## Standard of Practice 9-8
  "The REALTOR® shall be obligated to discover and disclose adverse factors reasonably apparent to someone with expertise in only those areas required by their real estate licensing authority. Article 9 does not impose upon the REALTOR® the obligation of expertise in other professional or technical disciplines. (Cross-reference Article 11.)" (Amended 11/86)

ARTICLE 10

The REALTOR® shall not deny equal professional services to any person for reasons of race, creed, sex, or country of national origin. The REALTOR® shall not be party to any plan or agreement to discriminate against a person or persons on the basis of race, creed, sex, or country of national origin.

ARTICLE 11

A REALTOR® is expected to provide a level of competent service in keeping with the standards of practice in those fields in which the REALTOR® customarily engages.

The REALTOR® shall not undertake to provide specialized professional services concerning a type of property or service that is outside his field of competence unless he engages the assistance of one who is competent on such types of property or service, or unless the facts are fully disclosed to the client. Any person engaged to provide such assistance shall be so identified to the client and his contribution to the assignment should be set forth.

The REALTOR® shall refer to the Standards of Practice of the National Association as to the degree of competence that a client has a right to expect the REALTOR® to possess, taking into consideration the complexity of the problem, the availability of expert assistance, and the opportunities for experience available to the REALTOR®.

- ## Standard of Practice 11-1
  "Whenever a REALTOR® submits an oral or written opinion of the value of real property for a fee, his opinion shall be supported by a memorandum in his file or an appraisal report, either of which shall include as a minimum the following:

  1. Limiting conditions
  2. Any existing or contemplated interest
  3. Defined value
  4. Date applicable
  5. The estate appraised
  6. A description of the property
  7. The basis of the reasoning including applicable market data and/or capitalization computation

  "This report or memorandum shall be available to the Professional Standards Committee for a period of at least two years (beginning subsequent to final determination of the court if the appraisal is involved in litigation) to ensure compliance with Article 11 of the Code of Ethics of the NATIONAL ASSOCIATION OF REALTORS®."

- ## Standard of Practice 11-2
  "The REALTOR® shall not undertake to make an appraisal when his employment or fee is contingent upon the amount of appraisal."

Figure 52 continued

• Standard of Practice 11-3

"REALTORS® engaged in real estate securities and syndications transactions are engaged in an activity subject to regulations beyond those governing real estate transactions generally, and therefore have the affirmative obligation to be informed of applicable federal and state laws, and rules and regulations regarding these types of transactions."

ARTICLE 12

The REALTOR® shall not undertake to provide professional services concerning a property or its value where he has a present or contemplated interest unless such interest is specifically disclosed to all affected parties.

• Standard of Practice 12-1

(Refer to Standards of Practice 9-4 and 16-1, which also relate to Article 12, Code of Ethics.) (Amended 5/84)

ARTICLE 13

The REALTOR® shall not acquire an interest in or buy for himself, any member of his immediate family, his firm or any member thereof, or any entity in which he has a substantial ownership interest, property listed with him, without making the true position known to the listing owner. In selling property owned by himself, or in which he has any interest, the REALTOR® shall reveal the facts of his ownership or interest to the purchaser.

• Standard of Practice 13-1

"For the protection of all parties, the disclosures required by Article 13 shall be in writing and provided by the REALTOR® prior to the signing of any contract." (Adopted 2/86)

ARTICLE 14

In the event of a controversy between REALTORS® associated with different firms, arising out of their relationship as REALTORS®, the REALTORS® shall submit the dispute to arbitration in accordance with the regulations of their Board or Boards rather than litigate the matter.

• Standard of Practice 14-1

"The filing of litigation and refusal to withdraw from it by a REALTOR® in an arbitrable matter constitutes a refusal to arbitrate." (Adopted 2/86)

• Standard of Practice 14-2

"The obligation to arbitrate mandated by Article 14 includes arbitration requests initiated by the REALTOR®'s client." (Adopted 5/87)

• Standard of Practice 14-3

"Article 14 does not require a REALTOR® to arbitrate in those circumstances when all parties to the dispute advise the Board in writing that they choose not to arbitrate before the Board." (Adopted 5/88)

ARTICLE 15

If a REALTOR® is charged with unethical practice or is asked to present evidence in any disciplinary proceeding or investigation, he shall place all pertinent facts before the proper tribunal of the Member Board or affiliated institute, society, or council of which he is a member.

• Standard of Practice 15-1

"The REALTOR® shall not be subject to disciplinary proceedings in more than one Board of REALTORS® with respect to alleged violations of the Code of Ethics relating to the same transaction."

• Standard of Practice 15-2

"The REALTOR® shall not make any unauthorized disclosure or dissemination of the allegations, findings, or decision developed in connection with an ethics hearing or appeal." (Adopted 5/84)

• Standard of Practice 15-3

"The REALTOR® shall not obstruct the Board's investigative or disciplinary proceedings by instituting or threatening to institute actions for libel, slander or defamation against any party to a professional standards proceeding or their witnesses." (Adopted 11/87).

• Standard of Practice 15-4

"The REALTOR® shall not intentionally impede the Board's investigative or disciplinary proceedings by filing multiple ethics complaints based on the same event or transaction." (Adopted 11/88)

ARTICLE 16

When acting as agent, the REALTOR® shall not accept any commission, rebate, or profit on expenditures made for his principal-owner, without the principal's knowledge and consent.

• Standard of Practice 16-1

"The REALTOR® shall not recommend or suggest to a client or a customer the use of services of another organization or business entity in which he has a direct interest without disclosing such interest at the time of the recommendation or suggestion." (Amended 5/88)

• Standard of Practice 16-2

"When acting as an agent or subagent, the REALTOR® shall disclose to a client or customer if there is any financial benefit or fee the REALTOR® or the REALTOR®'s firm may receive as a direct result of having recommended real estate products or services (e.g., homeowner's insurance, warranty programs, mortgage financing, title insurance, etc.) other than real estate referral fees." (Adopted 5/88)

ARTICLE 17

The REALTOR® shall not engage in activities that constitute the unauthorized practice of law and shall recommend that legal counsel be obtained when the interest of any party to the transaction requires it.

ARTICLE 18

The REALTOR® shall keep in a special account in an appropriate financial institution, separated from his own funds, monies coming into his possession in trust for other persons, such as escrows, trust funds, clients' monies, and other like items.

ARTICLE 19

The REALTOR® shall be careful at all times to present a true picture in his advertising and representations to the public. The REALTOR® shall also ensure that his status as a broker or a REALTOR® is clearly identifiable in any such advertising. (Amended 11/86)

Figure 52 continued

- **Standard of Practice 19-1**

"The REALTOR® shall not submit or advertise property without authority, and in any offering, the price quoted shall not be other than that agreed upon with the owners."

- **Standard of Practice 19-2**

(Refer to Standard of Practice 9-4, which also relates to Article 19, Code of Ethics.)

- **Standard of Practice 19-3**

"The REALTOR®, when advertising unlisted real property for sale in which he has an ownership interest, shall disclose his status as both an owner and as a REALTOR® or real estate licensee." (Adopted 5/85)

- **Standard of Practice 19-4**

"The REALTOR® shall not advertise nor permit any person employed by or affiliated with him to advertise listed property without disclosing the name of the firm." (Adopted 11/86)

- **Standard of Practice 19-5**

"The REALTOR®, when acting as listing broker, has the exclusive right to control the advertising of listed property prior to the closing. The listing broker may delegate the right to post 'For Sale' and 'Sold' signs and to make related advertising representations to a cooperating broker.

After the transaction has been closed, the listing broker may not prohibit the cooperating broker from advertising his 'participation' or 'assistance' in the transaction." (Cross-reference Article 21.)" (Amended 2/89)

ARTICLE 20

The REALTOR®, for the protection of all parties, shall see that financial obligations and commitments regarding real estate transactions are in writing, expressing the exact agreement of the parties. A copy of each agreement shall be furnished to each party upon his signing such agreement.

- **Standard of Practice 20-1**

"At the time of signing or initialing, the REALTOR® shall furnish to the party a copy of any document signed or initialed." (Adopted 5/86)

- **Standard of Practice 20-2**

"For the protection of all parties, the REALTOR® shall use reasonable care to ensure that documents pertaining to the purchase and sale of real estate are kept current through the use of written extensions or amendments." (Adopted 5/86)

ARTICLE 21

The REALTOR® shall not engage in any practice or take any action inconsistent with the agency of another REALTOR®.

- **Standard of Practice 21-1**

"Signs giving notice of property for sale, rent, lease, or exchange shall not be placed on property without the consent of the owner."

- **Standard of Practice 21-2**

"The REALTOR® obtaining information from a listing broker about a specific property shall not convey this information to, nor invite the cooperation of a third party broker without the consent of the listing broker."

- **Standard of Practice 21-3**

"The REALTOR® shall not solicit a listing which is currently listed exclusively with another broker. However, if the listing broker, when asked by the REALTOR®, refuses to disclose the expiration date and nature of such listing; i.e., an exclusive right to sell, an exclusive agency, open listing, or other form of contractual agreement between the listing broker and his client, the REALTOR®, unless precluded by law, may contact the owner to secure such information and may discuss the terms upon which he might take a future listing or, alternatively, may take a listing to become effective upon expiration of any existing exclusive listing." (Amended 11/86)

- **Standard of Practice 21-4**

"The REALTOR® shall not use information obtained by him from the listing broker, through offers to cooperate received through Multiple Listing Services or other sources authorized by the listing broker, for the purpose of creating a referral prospect to a third broker, or for creating a buyer prospect unless such use is authorized by the listing broker."

- **Standard of Practice 21-5**

"The fact that a property has been listed exclusively with a REALTOR® shall not preclude or inhibit any other REALTOR® from soliciting such listing after its expiration."

- **Standard of Practice 21-6**

"The fact that a property owner has retained a REALTOR® as his exclusive agent in respect of one or more past transactions creates no interest or agency which precludes or inhibits other REALTORS® from seeking such owner's future business."

- **Standard of Practice 21-7**

"The REALTOR® shall be free to list property which is 'open listed' at any time, but shall not knowingly obligate the seller to pay more than one commission except with the seller's knowledgeable consent. (Cross-reference Article 7.)" (Amended 5/88)

- **Standard of Practice 21-8**

"When a REALTOR® is contacted by an owner regarding the sale of property that is exclusively listed with another broker, and the REALTOR® has not directly or indirectly initiated the discussion, unless precluded by law, the REALTOR® may discuss the terms upon which he might take a future listing or, alternatively, may take a listing to become effective upon expiration of any existing exclusive listing." (Amended 11/86)

- **Standard of Practice 21-9**

"In cooperative transactions a REALTOR® shall compensate the cooperating REALTOR® (principal broker) and shall not compensate nor offer to compensate, directly or indirectly, any of the sales licensees employed by or affiliated with another REALTOR® without the prior express knowledge and consent of the cooperating broker."

- **Standard of Practice 21-10**

"Article 21 does not preclude REALTORS® from making general announcements to property owners describing their services and the terms of their availability even though some recipients may have exclusively listed their property for sale or lease with another REALTOR®. A general telephone canvass, general mailing or distribution addressed to all property owners in a given geographical area or in a given profession, business, club, or organization, or other classification or group is deemed 'general' for purposes of this standard.

Figure 52 continued

Article 21 is intended to recognize as unethical two basic types of solicitation:

First, telephone or personal solicitations of property owners who have been identified by a real estate sign, multiple listing compilation, or other information service as having exclusively listed their property with another REALTOR®; and

Second, mail or other forms of written solicitations of property owners whose properties are exclusively listed with another REALTOR® when such solicitations are not part of a general mailing but are directed specifically to property owners identified through compilations of current listings, 'for sale' signs, or other sources of information required by Article 22 and Multiple Listing Service rules to be made available to other REALTORS® under offers of subagency or cooperation.'' (Adopted 11/83)

- **Standard of Practice 21-11**
  ''The REALTOR®, prior to accepting a listing, has an affirmative obligation to make reasonable efforts to determine whether the property is subject to a current, valid exclusive listing agreement.'' (Adopted 11/83)

- **Standard of Practice 21-12**
  ''The REALTOR®, acting as the agent of the buyer, shall disclose that relationship to the seller's agent at first contact. (Cross-reference Article 7.)'' (Adopted 5/88)

- **Standard of Practice 21-13**
  ''On unlisted property, the REALTOR®, acting as the agent of a buyer, shall disclose that relationship to the seller at first contact. (Cross-reference Article 7.)'' (Adopted 5/88)

- **Standard of Practice 21-14**
  ''The REALTOR®, acting as agent of the seller or as subagent of the listing broker, shall disclose that relationship to buyers as soon as practicable.'' (Adopted 5/88)

- **Standard of Practice 21-15**
  ''Article 21 does not preclude a REALTOR® from contacting the client of another broker for the purpose of offering to provide, or entering into a contract to provide, a different type of real estate service unrelated to the type of service currently being provided (e.g., property management as opposed to brokerage). However, information received through a Multiple Listing Service or any other offer of cooperation may not be used to target the property owners to whom such offers to provide services are made.'' (Adopted 2/89)

- **Standard of Practice 21-16**
  ''The REALTOR®, acting as subagent or buyer's agent, shall not use the terms of an offer to purchase to attempt to modify the listing broker's offer of compensation to subagents or buyer's agents nor make the submission of an executed offer to purchase contingent on the listing broker's agreement to modify the offer of compensation.'' (Adopted 2/89)

ARTICLE 22

In the sale of property which is exclusively listed with a REALTOR®, the REALTOR® shall utilize the services of other brokers upon mutually agreed upon terms when it is in the best interests of the client.

Negotiations concerning property which is listed exclusively shall be carried on with the listing broker, not with the owner, except with the consent of the listing broker.

Form No. 166-288-1 (2/89)

- **Standard of Practice 22-1**
  ''It is the obligation of the selling broker as subagent of the listing broker to disclose immediately all pertinent facts to the listing broker prior to as well as after the contract is executed.''

- **Standard of Practice 22-2**
  ''The REALTOR®, when submitting offers to the seller, shall present each in an objective and unbiased manner.''

- **Standard of Practice 22-3**
  ''The REALTOR® shall disclose the existence of an accepted offer to any broker seeking cooperation.'' (Adopted 5/86)

- **Standard of Practice 22-4**
  ''The REALTOR®, acting as exclusive agent of the seller, establishes the terms and conditions of offers to cooperate. Unless expressly indicated in offers to cooperate made through MLS or otherwise, a cooperating broker may not assume that the offer of cooperation includes an offer of compensation. Entitlement to compensation in a cooperative transaction must be agreed upon between a listing and cooperating broker prior to the time an offer to purchase the property is produced.'' (Adopted 11/88)

ARTICLE 23

The REALTOR® shall not publicly disparage the business practice of a competitor nor volunteer an opinion of a competitor's transaction. If his opinion is sought and if the REALTOR® deems it appropriate to respond, such opinion shall be rendered with strict professional integrity and courtesy.

The Code of Ethics was adopted in 1913. Amended at the Annual Convention in 1924, 1928, 1950, 1951, 1952, 1955, 1956, 1961, 1962, 1974, 1982, 1986, and 1987.

EXPLANATORY NOTES (Revised 11/88)

The reader should be aware of the following policies which have been approved by the Board of Directors of the National Association:

''In filing a charge of an alleged violation of the Code of Ethics by a REALTOR®, the charge shall read as an alleged violation of one or more Articles of the Code. A Standard of Practice may only be cited in support of the charge.''

The Standards of Practice are not an integral part of the Code but rather serve to clarify the ethical obligations imposed by the various Articles. The Standards of Practice supplement, and do not substitute for, the Case Interpretations in *Interpretations of the Code of Ethics*.

Modifications to existing Standards of Practice and additional new Standards of Practice are approved from time to time. The reader is cautioned to ensure that the most recent publications are utilized.

Articles 1 through 5 are aspirational and establish ideals that a REALTOR® should strive to attain. Recognizing their subjective nature, these Articles shall not be used as the bases for charges of alleged unethical conduct or as the bases for disciplinary action.

Figure 52 continued

REAL ESTATE INVESTMENT TRUST (REIT)

A REIT is real estate investment medium that passes 95% or more of its earnings to its stockholders, thus avoiding trust income taxation.

INVESTOR ADVICE

If you decide that you are interested in real estate investing but don't have the expertise or time to manage your own investments, you will be interested in real estate investment trusts.

The real estate investment trust (REIT) invests its funds in equity positions of various developments or in real estate mortgage activities. A real estate investment trust is a corporation formed for the purpose of investing for capital gains, income, or both. By passing the majority of its earnings directly to the stockholders, it avoids the payment of corporation taxes and thus functions more or less like a limited partnership, as far as income taxes are concerned.

The REIT has one advantage over the limited partnership or other forms of participant investing. The stock of the REIT is usually listed on the major stock exchanges and is very liquid. It is also more widely held and more desirable for that reason.

The 1986 Tax Reform Act has changed the character of these trusts somewhat. Income received is classified as passive, and thus losses incurred in the operation are only deductible against passive income. This change has no effect on the profitable enterprise. It does prevent loss operations and marginal activities from passing losses to the stockholders, where these losses are written off against other types of income.

Now, a REIT must stand on its own merits. No longer will projects be saleable that project losses for a number of years and offer pie-in-the-sky profits in the distant future, as was the case in the past. This is good for the potential investor, since he or she will not be presented with marginal propositions.

A number of REITs are now offering two classes of stock: (a) income, and (b) capital appreciation. In these types of trusts, all of the rents or income from mortgage lending go to the income shares, whereas the capital appreciation on sale of equity investments goes to the capital shares.

Stock in REITs can be purchased through your local stockbroker. If the offering is a new one, you will be provided with a prospectus which has been approved by the Securities and Exchange Commission (SEC). Your broker will also be able to advise you regarding the risk involved. Unless your broker has a vested interest in the corporation, you can expect him or her to offer an unbiased opinion. Your broker has nothing to gain by getting you into a bad investment and has many other worthwhile investments to sell.

Here is a checklist for deciding if you should invest in REITs.

- Above all, do you believe that a real estate investment offers a good opportunity for you?

- Is the amount that you wish to invest too small to provide you with a diversified portfolio?

- Are you limited as to the time that you can afford to apply to the management of your investment?

- Are you less than an expert in real estate investing?

- Is your local area too small or too big for you to be able to know where your money should be invested?

- Do you like the idea of a large, diversified (type and region) portfolio?

- Is liquidity of the investment important?

SEE ALSO: ACTIVE INCOME, CORPORATION, LIMITED PARTNERSHIPS, PASSIVE INCOME, and TAX REFORM ACT OF 1986.

REAL ESTATE MORTGAGE INVESTMENT CONDUIT (RELIC)

A child of the 1986 Tax Reform Act, the RELIC is a mortgage pool placed in trust and then sold to the general public.

INVESTOR ADVICE

The RELIC varies somewhat from other types of mortgage pools, such as Collateralized Mortgage Obligation (CMOs) and the Mae pools (GNMA and FNMA). The RELIC trust is often broken into two or more segments called *tranches* (French for *slices*), listed as *A, B, C,* and so forth, which mature at different times. The last of these tranches, called the *Z* tranche, pays off only after all others. Until then, the income in the *Z* tranche accrues in a manner similar to a zero-coupon bond.

SEE ALSO: COLLATERALIZED MORTGAGE OBLIGATION, FEDERAL NATIONAL MORTGAGE ASSOCIATION (FNMA), and GOVERNMENT NATIONAL MORTGAGE ASSOCIATION (GNMA).

REAL PROPERTY

1. In some states, land and that which is affixed and unmoveable and that which is incidental or appurtenant thereto.
2. In other states, a collective term to include the foregoing plus all other benefits and rights to land ownership.

INVESTOR ADVICE

The first of the foregoing definitions is used in those states that make a distinction between real estate and real property, which includes those things other than the land and appurtenances thereon. The second definition is used in those states that do not legally separate the land and other rights and refer to them collectively as real property.

Do not be concerned about these subtle differences in definition. Your prime concern is with the difference between real property and personalty.

SEE ALSO: HEREDITAMENTS, REAL ESTATE, and PERSONALTY.

REALTOR®

A realtor is a licensed real estate broker who is a member of his or her local, state, and national Association of REALTORS®.

INVESTOR ADVICE

Real estate salespeople who work for REALTOR® brokers are designated as REALTOR® Associates. A salesperson, who is also a state licensed broker may also be a REALTOR® but is usually designated in the books of the local board as *other REALTOR®*. His or her boss is usually known as the broker or principal broker.

SEE ALSO: NATIONAL ASSOCIATION OF REALTORS, REAL ESTATE AGENT, and REAL ESTATE BOARD.

RECAPTURE

This term refers to Internal Revenue Service regulations requiring certain depreciation, allowed as deductions in the past, to be taxed at the time of sale.

INVESTOR ADVICE

When selling or proposing to sell property which has been depreciated on other than a straight-line basis, you should consider the possibility and tax consequences of recapture of previous excess depreciation.

This is particularly true since the Tax Reform Act of 1986, which makes capital gains fully taxable. In some cases, a short delay in selling can make a considerable tax difference.

> **WARNING!** Recaptured depreciation is taxed as ordinary income. Check your timing before selling.

Basically, the recapture provision applies to those properties that are sold before being fully depreciated. In effect, it states that all depreciation in excess of straight-line depreciation must be recaptured on sale to reduce the basis cost and increase the taxable gain.

SEE ALSO: ACCELERATED DEPRECIATION, BASIS COST, and TAX REFORM ACT (TRA) OF 1986.

RECAPTURE RATE

The recapture rate is the rate of return *of* the investment.

INVESTOR ADVICE

All investors are interested in two things:

1. a return *of* their investment, and
2. a return *on* their investment.

When a mortgage payment is made to the lender, it contains two components: (a) a return on the lender's investment, and (b) a return of his or her investment. This return is known as *loan amortization*, or the amount required to extinguish the loan in the agreed time period.

Based on the principle of present value of money, the faster the investment is returned, the greater the value of that return.

SEE ALSO: MORTGAGE CONSTANT, RETURN OF INVESTMENT, and RETURN ON INVESTMENT.

RECEIVABLES

This term is accounting nomenclature for those items of income for which payments have not yet been received.

INVESTOR ADVICE

When proposing to purchase an operation in which receivables are included in the asset list, you should carefully examine their true worth by:

- determining the amount of time that each item has been on the books (aging of accounts);
- determining the potential for actual payment;
- adjusting the total value downward to reflect the actual value versus book value;

- calculating the present value of each item based on the value of money and the estimated time to collect; and

- considering buying the business less receivables with a corresponding reduction in selling price.

Everyone would like to operate on a cash income basis, but that is not always possible. Where competitive pressures indicate the necessity of providing some customer credit, considerable care and experience in credit management is required. There is an old adage in business that states, "A bad credit manager can throw more money out the back door with a spoon than a good sales manager can shovel into the front."
SEE ALSO: CASH VERSUS ACCRUAL ACCOUNTING, and PRESENT VALUE OF ONE.

RECITAL

In law, a recital is that part of a deed which indicates the reasons or arguments supporting the purpose of that document.

INVESTOR ADVICE

The recital is usually a statement of facts for the use of persons examining a title. It may explain why the deed is being prepared or offer some other remark. It becomes an essential part of the deed when it includes contractual matters between the parties to the instrument.

In a warranty deed, the statement may be simply, "for $10 and other considerations." However, the recital in a trust deed may be lengthier, enumerating many contractual terms.
SEE ALSO: DEED, GRANTEE, and GRANTOR.

RECONCILIATION

1. In accounting, the process of checking the books against past events to determine their accuracy.
2. In appraising, the process of assessment and evaluation of all approaches to value and other pertinent facts to arrive at the appraiser's estimate of fair market value.

INVESTOR ADVICE

In the evaluation of a business operation, it is usually necessary to adjust or reconcile the books with other factual data, current property appraisals, and equipment evaluations to determine the true value of the business as compared to the book value.

In accounting, land is carried at cost. It may now be higher or lower in value. Improvements and equipment are carried at cost less depreciation. It may be much more valuable, as actual wear-out and depreciation rates seldom are the same.

It is not unusual to find an unknown or unlisted asset, such as goodwill, which is actually producing income. Where the assets are producing a greater return than justified by the risk, goodwill is probably a factor.

In an appraisal report, the final paragraph is usually entitled "Reconciliation and Final Estimate of Value." Here, the appraiser lists those values which he or she has determined, by various approaches, in the prior pages and indicates his or her professional opinion of what these values mean, their accuracy, and the weighting assigned to each.

EXAMPLE

A certain appraiser concludes his report with the following statements:

The following values were obtained by the various approaches:

Market Approach	*$125,000*
Cost or Replacement Approach	*$150,000*
Income Approach	*$130,000*

The appraiser has rejected the value indicated by the cost or replacement approach, since it has been shown to be in excess of what the market indicates or that is justified by its income production.

The values indicated by the other two approaches are reasonably close and within the realm of reasonable computational error. Since this appraiser feels that both the income and market approaches should be given equal weighting, it is his conclusion that the current fair market value is the average of these two, or:

ONE HUNDRED THIRTY-SEVEN THOUSAND FIVE HUNDRED
$137,500.

SEE ALSO: COST APPROACH TO VALUE, INCOME APPROACH TO VALUE, MARKET APPROACH TO VALUE, and RETURN ON INVESTMENT.

RECONVEYANCE DEED

A reconveyance deed is a deed to reconvey title to the former owner, usually a mortgagor, after satisfaction of a mortgage note. The reconveyance is necessary where a deed of trust has been used as a part of the mortgage package.

INVESTOR ADVICE
Many mortgagors fail to record the reconveyance deed when received after payment of a mortgage. This leaves the official records showing a lien on the property.

CLEAR THE TITLE! Immediately after receipt of your satisfaction piece or reconveyance deed, get it recorded to clear the title officially.

Normally, the mortgage holder will mail a reconveyance deed to the mortgagor a month or so after final payment is received. *It is your responsibility to see that the instrument is recorded.*

The reconveyance deed is no longer widely used. Various states have adopted other means of noting officially the satisfaction of a recorded obligation. These methods may be as simple as the North Carolina system of noting the date paid across the debt document itself and signing it in the presence of a notary; or the substitution of another document, such as a release of mortgage, notice of payment in full, or any other acknowledged notification which can be recorded.

SEE ALSO: DEED OF TRUST, RECORDING, and SATISFACTION PIECE.

RECORDING

Recording is the act of placing a document into the official record of the county or jurisdiction in which the property is located.

INVESTOR ADVICE

All documents to be recorded in the county clerk's office must be acknowledged by a notary or other officer of the court.

Be aware that recording does not assure the accuracy of the recorded document or indicate its authenticity. The acknowledgment thereon merely certifies that the person signing the document was who he or she professed to be and that he or she signed it in the presence of an officer.

When recording real estate documents, the legal description must be carefully checked to assure that it represents the subject property. A minor error in the legal description can be very expensive to correct at a later date, particularly if the grantor is no longer living or a resident in the area.

SEE ALSO: ACKNOWLEDGMENT and NOTARY.

RECTANGULAR SURVEY

A rectangular survey is a government survey system that utilizes base and meridian lines, from which townships and sections are sequentially numbered and referenced.

INVESTOR ADVICE

See Land Identification Methods.

SEE ALSO: BASE LINE, LAND IDENTIFICATION METHODS, MERIDIAN, SECTION, and TOWNSHIP.

RECYCLED REAL ESTATE

Recycled real estate is a building or group of buildings originally designed and built for a different purpose than that currently used or proposed to be used.

INVESTOR ADVICE

Recycled real estate can be a source of significant profits, where the recycled use is prudently established in a changing market area. A miscalculation of the cost to convert the structure(s) or a poor and incorrect economic analysis can result in failure.

The keys to a successful conversion are:

- an established economic need for the type of building space to be derived from the recycled structure(s);

- an accurate estimation of the costs to renovate and convert;

- an accurate estimation of the economics, showing that the uniqueness of the renovated space will produce sufficient income to justify renovation and conversion costs in lieu of rebuilding on the same or equivalent site;

- a determination that adequate parking space can be made available on-site or on additional property;

- an indication that the prospective conversion/renovation will have a positive effect on the value of the general area in which the property is located; and

- a positive indication that the new facility will provide for the customer's safety.

The following property types have been successfully recycled as indicated:

- a fisherman's wharf (San Francisco) to a shopping center;

- a streetcar barn (Salt Lake City) to a shopping center;

- a hotel (Salt Lake City) to a church office and chapel complex;

- a large lodge hall to a restaurant and theater complex;

- a church to an office building and a dance and modeling studio;

- a high school to a radio and TV studio;

- a school to an office building; and

- a warehouse complex to a builder's mart.

The three keys to success in buying real estate are area, area, and area. Obviously, if a candidate for recycling is an excellent buy, something has happened to the area during the recent past. It may be that:

- "undesirables" have moved in;

- surrounding property has been allowed to deteriorate;

- traffic patterns have changed; or

- the general economic condition of the city, town, or general area has degenerated.

These are reasons for the decline in value. Your success in acquiring good properties for conversion will depend on your ability to select those few properties that *can be revitalized.* If you are successful, you can profit from the project itself as well as additional nearby properties obtained on options.

Here are a few of the major factors that can assure your successful recycling:

- The property will soon be located on a major traffic street due to new highway construction, or construction of a major new complex will divert increased traffic past your site.

- The urban growth pattern favors your area and site.

- Street or highway construction will adversely affect existing facilities and thereby force the construction of replacements, which are more favorably located.

You must be aware of the need for strong and complete financing. Recycling cannot be done gradually or piecemeal. It involves a fast and complete character change which achieves your objective before others get the same idea. It means a grand opening with financially stable tenants—anchor tenants committed and located on-site. It means large advertising budgets and lots of promotion. It means large returns on investment, if successful.

SEE ALSO: ANCHOR TENANT, COST APPROACH TO VALUE, DEMOGRAPHICS, and PRINCIPLE OF HIGHEST AND BEST USE.

REDEMPTION RIGHTS

Redemption rights are the right of a mortgagor to redeem (buy back) property which has been foreclosed and sold at a sheriff's sale or sold by a trustee after loan default. The redemption period in each case is prescribed by law.

INVESTOR ADVICE

When buying or considering buying property at a sheriff's sale, you must be aware of the potential for redemption. While a loss of money is not likely, if the property is redeemed a hasty decision to remodel or renovate could present problems. These actions should be avoided until after the redemption period has expired. The redemption period varies from state to state but usually is in the neighborhood of six months.

A similar situation occurs when a mortgagor defaults on a loan protected by a trust deed. In this case, the property is sold by the trustee, not the sheriff, and the redemption period allowed is much less than that allowed for foreclosure. In most states, the redemption period for a trust deed sale is three months or less, usually means that the redemption period has been exceeded by the time the property is sold.

SEE ALSO: FORECLOSURE, SHERIFF'S SALE, and TRUST DEED.

RED HERRING

A red herring is an initial and unapproved prospectus proposing to sell securities in the interstate market. The name comes from the large red warning, on the front page, indicating that as of the printing date the securities described therein have not been approved by the Securities and Exchange Commission (SEC).

INVESTOR ADVICE

All securities do not require the approval of the SEC—only those proposed to be sold interstate and those intrastate securities which are not exempt by applicable state law.

Beware of those investment offerings which require minimum state scrutiny, and those offered by new and unknown syndicators. Protection from bad real estate investments is not absolute, but the possibility of loss can be minimized by:

- using good personal judgment;

- buying through a major (nationwide) securities dealer;

- buying securities from an organization with a proven track record; and

- avoiding speculative issues.

SEE ALSO: PROSPECTUS, and SECURITIES AND EXCHANGE COMMISSION (SEC).

REDLINING

Redlining refers to the reluctance of a lender or lenders to loan money in a specified area (redlined on the map).

INVESTOR ADVICE

Redlining can be construed as a prudent practice of lenders where an area is in economic decline, subject to flooding, or subject to aircraft noise. It is illegal if motivated by racial or national origin of residents.

Properties which are difficult to finance are often good candidates for recycling or redevelopment. Owners may be willing to provide favorable financing to assist in the acquisition of sufficient acreage to make redevelopment feasible.

SEE ALSO: OPTION, PLOTTAGE, RECYCLED PROPERTY.

REFEREE'S DEED IN PARTITION

This term refers to a quit claim deed provided by a court-appointed referee who has sold property formerly owned by two or more persons as tenants in common. The sale is the result of an inability of court-appointed commissioners to achieve a satisfactory partition of the property between the former owners (Tenants in Common).

INVESTOR ADVICE

Any tenant with an interest in property held as tenants in common can request that the court partition the property. This request is usually made after all attempts to partition the property voluntarily have failed. Once the partition action has been filed with the court, the court appoints commissioners to divide the property in accordance with the owner's percentage interests. In many cases, partition is not practical or possible. If so, a referee is appointed to sell the property and make a rateable distribution of the proceeds.

SEE ALSO: JOINT TENANCY.

REFINANCE

Refinancing is the act of repaying one or more loans with the proceeds of a new loan.

INVESTOR ADVICE

When interest rates rise to investor-unacceptable levels, there is a tendency to look for sellers who are willing to take a contract or second mortgage. There is nothing wrong with this if the interest rates are acceptable and you are aware that you are probably paying an excess amount for the property to compensate the seller for lost interest.

You should avoid contracts which call for refinancing at the end of a term of less than five years. Ten years would be preferable. Five or less years allows little time for a significant change in the economic picture. A balloon payment due in a short time may be just delaying the agony.

> **INVESTOR BEWARE!** Never accept financing terms calling for short-term balloon payment unless funds for payment are guaranteed at that point in time.

SEE ALSO: NOVATION.

REGRESSION TECHNIQUE

The regression technique is a mathematical approach to appraising which uses statistical methods and actual sales data to determine the appraised value of the subject property.

INVESTOR ADVICE

Mathematicians continue to develop scientific methods of appraising in an attempt to raise the profession from an art to a science. In spite of the availability of high-powered computers and improved realty sales data bases, the reluctance of appraisers to use these methods has produced little change in appraisal techniques.

This reluctance is due to several factors, among which is the natural hesitance to try something new, the lack of education in higher mathematics, and the nonavailability of economically priced computers capable of handling multiple regression problems required to achieve acceptable results. Too, many areas do not produce sufficient data to provide accurate answers.

Simple linear regression techniques, which compare selling price with usually one aspect, size, are not sufficiently accurate to account for the many variables encountered from property to property. To accurately assess value by mathematical means, the regression methods would be required to accept many variables customarily found in different residences. The bare minimum is at least 15 or 20 variables, such as:

- size of main floor,
- size of other floors above ground,
- size of basements,
- number of baths,
- garage size and type,
- appliances and equipment,
- heating and ventilating systems,
- type of construction,
- effective age of building,
- lot size and shape,
- location, and
- landscaping and sprinkling systems.

As better computers and programs become available and appraisers are trained in their use, it may be possible to appraise simple residences, in more or less uniform areas, by automated means. It is doubtful if unique homes, land, and commercial properties can ever be handled through these impersonal methods, at least in the foreseeable future.

SEE ALSO: MARKET APPROACH TO VALUE.

REGULATION Z

Regulation Z is a government regulation which requires a lender to disclose certain facts to the borrower.

INVESTOR ADVICE

Regulation Z, the so-called truth in lending act, applies to consumer loans to individuals. All real estate mortgages are covered. Business and commercial loans are not covered by the act, since it was assumed that business managers are capable of protecting their own interests.

The lender is required to furnish the borrower a statement which discloses finance charges and annual percentage rate prior to entering into a permanent contractual relationship. The finance charge must include any of the following:

1. interest rate expressed as annual percentage rate,
2. loan fees (points),
3. time–price differential,
4. finder's fees, if any,
5. discount points paid,
6. service fees and carrying charges, and
7. any insurance required to be carried as a condition of the loan.

If you are a sophisticated investor, you are already aware of this regulation. If not, you should have it explained at your first closing. The closing officer will explain the difference in the quoted interest rate, which is charged on each period, based on the unpaid balance and the rate shown on the disclosure statement.

Since the lender will have charged several of the aforementioned fees, you have in effect paid money in advance, which raises the effective rate of the loan by a fraction of a percent. Regulation Z requires this to be brought to your attention.

SEE ALSO: ANNUAL PERCENTAGE RATE, DISCLOSURE, and POINTS.

RELEASE OF EARNEST MONEY

A release of earnest money is a signed document that authorizes the selling broker to release an earnest money deposit from his or her escrow account.

INVESTOR ADVICE

When an offer to purchase or lease is made, together with a consideration known as the earnest money deposit, the money is immediately deposited in the selling broker's escrow account. That broker cannot release those funds until:

- the offer and acceptance contract is closed, or

- the deal is dead.

Four agencies/persons have or may have an interest in the earnest money. These are:

1. the buyer,
2. the seller,
3. the selling brokerage, and
4. the listing brokerage.

The buyer is entitled to a return of his or her earnest money if the deal is not accepted or fails due to reasons made subject to in the original offer. The seller is entitled to keep the earnest money as part compensation if the seller fails to perform. The selling broker is entitled to a commission at the time he or she brings a willing buyer and seller together and an agreement is reached. Where the sale is a REALTOR® board cooperative effort, the listing brokerage is also entitled to an agreed percent of the selling commission.

Many state laws and board directives promulgate strict procedures for the return of earnest money deposits. Even if not a requirement by state law or board regulations, a wise broker should complete a form similar to the one shown in Figure 53. This form contains the signed agreement of all four parties as to the disposition of the earnest money deposit.

Note that paragraph two states that the four parties "hereby release each other from all obligations and from all liability for claims and demands arising out of the Earnest Money Receipt and Offer to Purchase Agreement, dated _____ and concerning the property located at _____."

It is obvious that where any of the parties fails to sign, the earnest money cannot be returned or distributed until the matter is legally resolved. This would occur where the seller plans to sue for specific performance and/or damages; or either broker demanded full selling compensation, which cannot be covered by the deposit.

SEE ALSO: EARNEST MONEY DEPOSIT AND OFFER TO PURCHASE, and SPECIFIC PERFORMANCE.

RELEASE OF EARNEST MONEY DEPOSIT

WE___Mary J. & Buford O. Parrott_____AS SELLERS,

AND____Amy F. & Charles T. Bigbucks_____AS PURCHASERS,

____Big Deals Realtors_____AS LISTING BROKER, AND

____Dark Horse Associates_____AS SELLING BROKER

hereby release each other from all obligations and from all liability for claims and

demands arising out of Earnest Money Receipt and Offer to Purchase Agreement dated

___20 February 1989 concerning the property situated at ___2257 Broadway,_____

__Sandy, Utah_____,

(including any and all amendments to said agreements) on condition that the earnest

money deposit of $500.00_ made in connection with said agreements be disbursed as follows:

$___$250.00_____ to Sellers

$___None_____ to Purchasers

$___100.00_____ to Listing Broker

$___200.00_____ to Selling Broker

and on further condition that all of the above named persons agree to this Release.

PURCHASERS: DATED___March 1, 1989   SELLERS: DATED___March 1, 1989

_Amy F. Bigbucks_____   _Mary J Parrott_____

_Charles T Bigbucks_____   _Buford O. Parrott_____

LISTING BROKER: DATED___March 2, 1989   SELLING BROKER: DATED___March 2, 1989

_Big Deal Realtors_____   _Dark Horse Associates_____

BY _Joseph Lister_____   BY _James L. Jockey_____

Figure 53

RELEASE OF LIEN

A release of lien is an official document which indicates that the stated judgment, mortgage, or claim has been paid in full, thus removing a cloud on the title.

INVESTOR ADVICE

NOTE! The lien is not officially cleared until the release or satisfaction piece is recorded.

There are many types of liens that may be placed against a property. Some may be claims of contractors, subcontractors, and suppliers; some the result of court judgments; and others a result of owner borrowings. Regardless of the original source of the lien, they must be removed legally to clear the title.

The release may take the form as shown in Figure 17 or may be in the form of a satisfaction piece. The requirement is that the document clearly states that the indebtedness has been paid in full, signed by the person authorized to certify that the debt has been cleared, and that his or her signature is acknowledged by a notary or officer of the court. The lien is officially cleared only when this document has been recorded.

SEE ALSO: ACKNOWLEDGMENT, JUDGMENT, LIEN WAIVER, and SATISFACTION PIECE.

RELEASE OR SATISFACTION OF MORTGAGE

An official document that discharges a property from a mortgage obligation is a release or satisfaction of mortgage.

INVESTOR ADVICE
A release of mortgage can be made in several ways:

• by issuance of a deed of reconveyance, where a trust deed has been used;

• by issuance of a standard mortgage release form;

• by issuance of a satisfaction piece; and

• by issuance of a quit claim deed.

In all cases, it becomes the responsibility of the mortgagor to assure that the document, when received, is recorded in the official records of the legal jurisdiction in which the property is located.

Figure 54 shows a typical form used by a mortgage company or bank to release a mortgage officially. Note that this form also includes information in regards to the initial recording of the lien. This is helpful but not absolutely necessary.

SEE ALSO: RECONVEYANCE DEED, SATISFACTION PIECE, and QUIT CLAIM DEED.

RELICTION

This term refers to land created by the gradual and imperceptible withdrawal of water from land. The withdrawal must be permanent in order for the property to be claimed by the adjoining property owner.

INVESTOR ADVICE
Reliction is similar to avulsion, but the land increase is from different causes. When buying land subject to avulsion or reliction, you should attempt to obtain a deed which

Recorded at Request of Low Rate Mortgage Corporation

at_____. M. Fee Paid $ 3.00 . _____

by_____ Dep. Book 202 Page 100 Ref.: #8980

Mail tax notice to Low Rate Mortgage Address 222 S. Brow Ave., SLC Ut.

RELEASE OF MORTGAGE

KNOW ALL MEN BY THESE PRESENTS:
 That

      Low Rate Mortgage Corporation

do hereby certify and declare that a certain Mortgage bearing date the 24th
day of March one thousand nine hundred and Seventy Five
made and executed by Mary J. Bean and Arthur L. Bean
Mortgagor(s) therein, to
 Low Rate Mortgage Corporation **Mortgagee(s) therein**
and recorded 25th March 19 75 , in Book 308 of Mortgages at page 123
in the office of the County Recorder of Salt Lake County, State of Utah
together with the debt thereby secured, is fully paid, satisfied and discharged.

      IN WITNESS WHEREOF, I have hereunto set My hand and seal at Salt Lake City
County of SAlt Lake State of Utah, the 25th day of March
one thousand nine hundred and eighty-nine
Signed, Sealed and Delivered in the Presence of

_____ _____ (Seal)
      V.P. Mortgages, Low Rate Mortgage Inc.
_____ _____ (Seal)
_____ _____ (Seal)
      _____ (Seal)

STATE OF UTAH,
COUNTY OF Salt Lake } ss.

    On the 25th day of March , A. D. one thousand nine hundred
and eighty-nien personally appeared before me Ellwood Suggins, V.P.
Low Rate Mortgage Corporation

the signer of the foregoing instrument, who duly acknowledged to me that he

executed the same.

                          Notary Public.

My residence is Salt Lake City, Ut
My commission expires June 20, 1991

BLANK No. 121— © GEM PTG. CO. — 3215 SO. 2600 EAST — SALT LAKE CITY

Figure 54

specifies the land boundary as to the water or similar terms rather than one specified in metes and bounds.

SEE ALSO: ACCRETION, AVULSION, and LAND IDENTIFICATION METHODS.

REMAINDERMAN

The term *remainderman* refers to a person(s) named in a trust to receive the assets (corpus) at a specified time or date, when the trust is dissolved.

INVESTOR ADVICE

Remaindermen(persons) are named in insurance, inter vivoce or testamentary trusts for the purpose of terminating the life and effect of the instrument at a stipulated date or event. The life of these trusts is depicted in Figures 55, 56, and 57.

The reasons for establishment of trusts vary. Sometimes the idea is avoiding probate, lowering income taxes, reducing estate taxes, or management of assets. Regardless of the reason for the creation, there comes a time at which the trust must, by law or other reason, be terminated and the assets distributed.

SEE ALSO: BENEFICIARY, DECEDENT, PROBATE, TRUSTEE, and WILL.

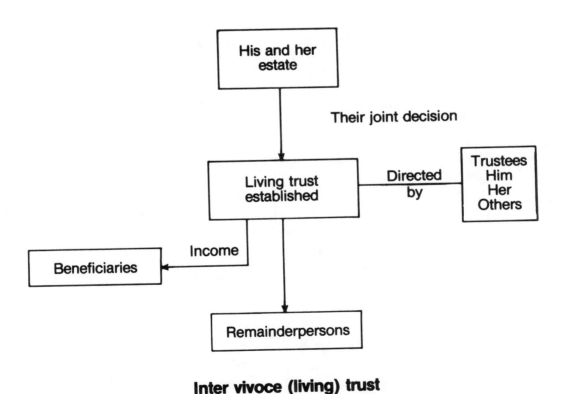

Inter vivoce (living) trust

Figure 55

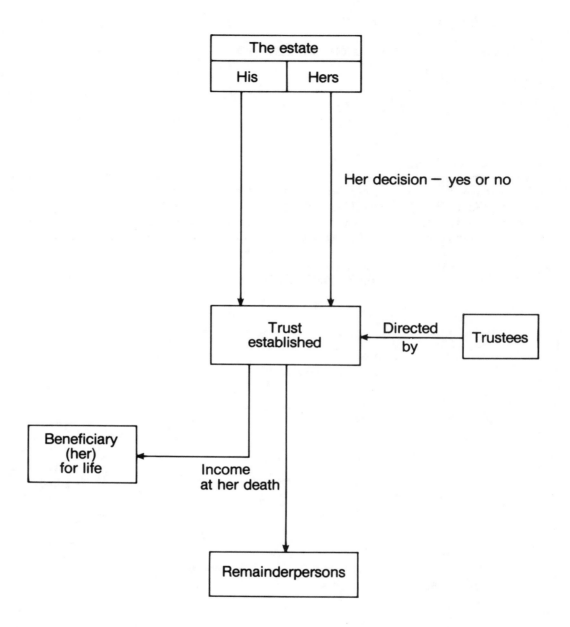

**Testamentary trust life
(he dies first)**

Figure 56

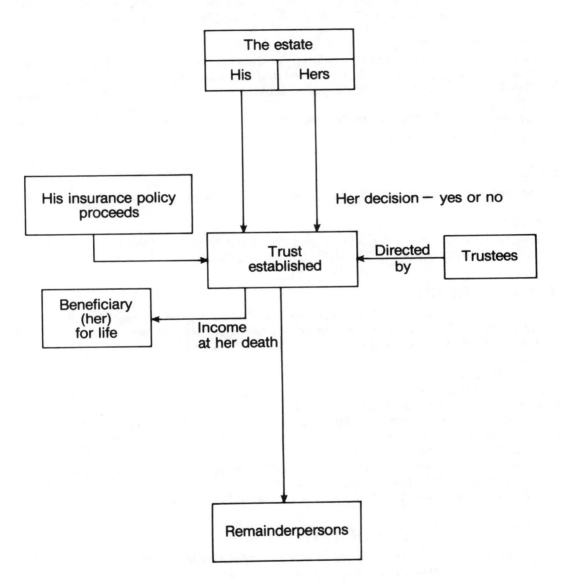

**Life insurance trust life
(he dies first)**

Figure 57

REMAINING ECONOMIC LIFE

Remaining economic life is the time remaining in which a property improvement will continue to produce income and provide for the recapture of the investment.

INVESTOR ADVICE

As an investor, your interest is focused on the remaining economic life. The actual lifetime is of no consequence, as it is assumed that at the time the investment is recovered, it will no longer be capable of producing acceptable income in accordance with the principle of highest and best use.

SEE ALSO: ECONOMIC DEPRECIATION, ECONOMIC LIFE, ECONOMIC OBSOLESCENCE, RE-CAPTURE, and RECAPTURE RATE.

RENT

Rent is a consideration paid for the use and possession of property belonging to another.

INVESTOR ADVICE

Acceptance of rent from a tenant creates a license for the period of the rental agreement.
SEE ALSO: CONTRACT RENT, ECONOMIC RENT, and LEASE.

RENT SCHEDULE

A rent schedule is a list containing the names of renters, property rented, and amount of rent payable. Where leases are employed, the document should also contain the date of the lease and expected termination.

INVESTOR ADVICE

The rent schedule is the basis for determination of gross expected income. It also provides information as to the time remaining on current leases.

In proposing to acquire an existing property, make your offer subject to verification of the rent schedule and approval thereof. The schedule can then be verified by a spot-check of the tenants to determine its accuracy.

The verified rent schedule can be provided to the prospective lender as support for the loan request and your proforma income analysis.

SEE ALSO: LEASE, MONTH TO MONTH, and PRO-FORMA ANALYSIS.

RENTABLE SQUARE FOOTAGE

Rentable square footage is the gross square footage of a building less that space occupied by halls, service facilities, and common areas.

INVESTOR ADVICE

Only the rentable square footage of a building or project is capable of income production. In considering the purchase of or construction of a rentable facility, pay strict attention to:

1. rentable square footage; and
2. rentable efficiency (rentable space/gross space).

While a certain amount of space must be devoted to the common needs of the prospective tenants, a design which includes more than the minimum requirement is dead space. Dead space costs as much as rentable space and returns nothing on the investment.

Wherever possible, it is wise to utilize so-called common space for a dual purpose; for example, newsstands or snack kiosks in the hallways.

The ideal rental space design is a warehouse in which the tenant occupies 100% of the included space and pays an appropriate amount per square foot for the privilege.

SEE ALSO: GROSS POSSIBLE INCOME.

RENTAL DEPOSIT

A deposit of funds with a landlord representing advanced rental for a certain period in the future is a rental deposit. Deposits are usually for one month in advance or sometimes for the first and last month of a lease.

INVESTOR ADVICE

Advanced rental of at least one month is necessary to prevent unacceptable losses in rental income. Where the tenant pays in advance and fails during the term of the lease to continue monthly payments, you have enough time to correct the situation prior to reaching a loss.

Rental deposits should be maintained in a separate account from the operating account. This will assure immediate availability of funds for return to tenants who complete their leases. You must remember that this money is not yours but is merely held in trust for the tenant. There is nothing wrong with getting a little interest on the account, which will increase the net income of the operation.

> **CAUTION!** Most banks are not allowed to pay interest on trust accounts or charge fees for the maintenance thereof. Be careful as to the name you choose for the rental deposit account.

SEE ALSO: CLEANING DEPOSIT.

RENTAL INCOME INSURANCE

This term refers to insurance against the loss of contract rent due to damage to the property which renders it unrentable.

INVESTOR ADVICE

Your banker may require you to carry rental income insurance in addition to hazard insurance. While the hazard insurance would cover the repair of the property which was damaged, the rent lost during the repair period would not be so covered, nor would the vacancy time to replace tenants be considered. Rental policies, depending on the type, usually cover:

- Ordinary losses to the property, whether rented or not. The landlord must prove a loss of rent to unoccupied space—that it was scheduled for occupancy, and so forth.

- Seasonal losses due to damage which occurs and prevents the normal seasonal occupancy. Properties in resort areas are prime candidates for this coverage.

Another type of rental insurance is lease guarantee insurance, which protects the owner from losses due to tenants who breech their contract. This insurance is very expensive and seldom carried except as a requirement of a mortgage lender.

SEE ALSO: HAZARD INSURANCE, and VACANCY FACTOR.

REPLACEMENT COST

Replacement cost is the cost of reproducing a structure or improvement having the same utility as the original before its loss. This approach uses current prices, materials, and methods of workmanship as a basis of the evaluation.

INVESTOR ADVICE

Replacement cost is normally used for insurance purposes, since the original materials, workmanship techniques, and designs are usually unavailable at the time of the insured's loss.

The replacement cost value is usually less than the cost to build a new structure or improvement with the same utility. Many costs can be avoided in a case of physical loss by fire or natural phenomenon. For instance, the foundation usually remains, water and sewer connection fees are not required for reconstruction, and architectural fees are less, since no new plans and specifications will be required. Architect supervision may still be required to oversee the new construction.

The following table indicates the cost savings in replacement versus new construction.

Insurance Exclusions

Basement excavation	2.0%
Foundation below ground	3.4%
Architect's fees	2.4%
Total savings	7.8%

SEE ALSO: COST APPROACH TO VALUE, and REPRODUCTION COST.

REPOSSESSION LISTS

Repossession lists are lists of properties that have been repossessed by a lender, such as a bank, VA, FHA, or FNMA.

INVESTOR ADVICE

In poor economic times, lenders often advertise their repossessions in order to sell them quickly. In better times, there are still a number of repossessed properties available, but they are not widely advertised. Repossessions can represent excellent values for the real estate investor.

Banks and other lenders are not in the business of buying and selling properties. They are only interested in protecting their capital. An inquiry to local lenders may reveal a number of good buys for your investment portfolio.

Often these properties are in poor condition and will require repairs and redecoration. The seller knows this and has probably discounted the price accordingly.

A lender is often satisfied to recover his or her capital, which represents 50%–90% of the current value. The lender's willingness to sell cheaply is based on two factors: (a) a desire to move the property quickly, thereby cutting potential losses, and (b) the lender may have recourse to the mortgagor for any deficiencies suffered in the repossession/resale process.

Many investors have found the purchase of repossessions very profitable, particularly where they can profit from any required rehabilitation prior to resale. Properties thus acquired may be resold after repair or held in the investor's portfolio for income and future capital gains. It is not unusual for the selling lender to offer qualified buyers financing at less than going rates in order to dispose of excess properties.

VA and FHA repossessions are usually offered for sale in two categories: (a) fixed price offerings, and (b) invitations to bid.

While the VA and FHA organizations are normally insurers of mortgages granted by lenders, they often are willing to finance directly their surplus properties. Mortgages provided directly by these agencies may or may not be assumable. Check your local VA and FHA offices or discuss your needs with your realtor.

SEE ALSO: DEFICIENCY JUDGMENT and FORECLOSURE.

REPRODUCTION COST

Reproduction cost is the cost to restore a structure or improvement after loss with the exact same materials, workmanship techniques, and designs as in the original.

INVESTOR ADVICE

It is not always possible to reproduce a structure or improvement with the same workmanship, designs, and materials, many of which may no longer be available. Usually, a replacement cost must be calculated.

A loss to a structure requiring consideration of exact reproduction in lieu of replacement would apply to old historic structures or to those whose uniqueness contributes to a significant percentage of their value.

SEE ALSO: HAZARD INSURANCE, and REPLACEMENT COST.

RESERVES FOR REPLACEMENT

This term refers to an accounting method for allocating or setting aside a portion of earnings for the future expense of periodic equipment replacement.

INVESTOR ADVICE

The accounting procedure which sets up a reserve account for equipment replacement recognizes that these expenses will occur in the future. The reduction of annual earnings by the amount set aside, at interest, will produce the estimated amount of funds required for anticipated future expenses. This accounting procedure does not reduce cash flow, since it is a noncash expense similar to depreciation expense.

A failure to recognize a need for future equipment replacement results in an overstatement of earnings which, if capitalized, produces a higher than justified fair market value of the operation.

EXAMPLE

Mr. Gallagher is the owner of a 12-unit residential dwelling which he recently purchased. In going over his planning for the future, he estimates that the following will be required to keep the units fully occupied and in good repair:

Repair/Replacement Item	Cost	Frequency	Yearly Cost
Kitchen Appliances	$ 800.00	8 years	$ 100.00
Draperies	1,000.00	5 years	200.00
Carpets	2,500.00	5 years	500.00
Redecoration/Painting	1,600.00	4 years	400.00
Total Cost/Unit/Year			$1,200.00

Mr. Gallagher decides that he will require $1,200 x 12 = $14,400 at the approximate end of the sixth year of ownership. He refers to Figure 32 (Future value of $1/period) and finds that the factor for his required annual deposits, at an assumed interest of 8%, is 7.336.

He will need to deposit $14,400/7.336, or $1,963 per year in order to have the necessary money at the end of six years.

SEE ALSO: CAPITALIZATION OF INCOME, FUTURE VALUE OF $1/PERIOD, and SINKING FUND.

RESIDUAL TECHNIQUES

Residual techniques are appraisal methods of determining land or improvement value by capitalization of income and subtraction of the known value of land or improvements. These techniques are known as land residual or building residual.

INVESTOR ADVICE

The residual techniques are useful in determining building value where the land value is known or in determining land value where the building value is known. Both techniques require an accurate capitalization of income produced by the land–building package.

The accuracy of the results obtained by the residual technique depends on an accurate capitalization rate, taken from the market place.

Land Residual Technique

EXAMPLE

A certain income property is found to produce a net income of $75,000 per year. The appraiser has also determined that a capitalization rate of 11.5% is applicable for this type of property. A calculation of the improvements, using the cost or replacement approach, indicates an improvement value of $490,000. What is the value of the land?

    Value = Income/Cap Rate
    Value = $75,000/0.115 = $652,174, rounded to $652,000
    Land Value = Total Value – Improvement Value
    Land Value = $652,000 – 490,000 = $162,000

Building Residual

EXAMPLE

An apartment building located on a one-half-acre lot is currently producing a net income of $62,000 per year. Comparable properties in the area are currently selling at a cap rate of 10.0% and land at $80,000/acre. What is the value of the improvements?

    Value = Income/Cap Rate
    Value = $62,000/0.10 = $620,000
    Improvement Value = Total Value – Land Value
    Improvement Value = $620,000 – (0.5 x $80,000)= $580,000

SEE ALSO: BUILDING RESIDUAL, CAPITALIZATION OF INCOME, COST APPROACH TO VALUE, ELLWOOD RATE, INCOME APPROACH TO VALUE, LAND RESIDUAL, and MORTGAGE EQUITY TECHNIQUE.

RESTRICTIVE COVENANTS

Restrictive covenants are building or improvement restrictions imposed by a developer for protection of other land purchasers. Restrictive covenants are effective for a stated period of years and can, in most states, be renewed at the option of the developer.

INVESTOR ADVICE

Restrictions imposed by developers are intended to provide conformity of construction in a development. They prevent the possibility that a land buyer might construct an eye sore or other structure which would depreciate the value of surrounding property.

Legally, a restrictive covenant is a promise made to the seller by the buyer. The second buyer of the property is also bound by the covenant if the covenant "runs with the land." The principal test to determine if the covenant runs with the land, is that the restriction "touches" or concerns the land. Thus, a restriction on mowing the lawn on Sunday would only apply to the first buyer. A restriction prohibiting fences in front of the house would be binding on all parties. (A restrictive covenant can also be established by the first seller, if the sale transferred a conditional estate.)

Challenges to restrictive covenants are normally upheld by the courts, although unreasonable requirements are occasionally struck down. For instance, a Utah case in which the restrictive covenants required all exteriors to be made of brick was held unreasonable. In this case, the builder was constructing a home of equal or higher value than others in the development and represented no potential harm to surrounding properties.

SEE ALSO: BUILDING CODES, CONDITIONAL SALE, and ZONING CODES.

RETURN OF INVESTMENT

That consideration, in calculating the capitalization rate, which returns the basic investment over the amortization period of the loan is called return of investment.

INVESTOR ADVICE

This is the part of the periodic loan payment which consists of a return *on* the investment plus a return *of* the investment. In most considerations, the investment is assumed to be returned during the term of the loan (recaptured).

SEE ALSO: CAPITALIZATION RATE, ELLWOOD RATE, MORTGAGE CONSTANT, MORTGAGE EQUITY TECHNIQUE, OVERALL RETURN (OAR), RECAPTURE RATE, and RETURN ON INVESTMENT.

RETURN ON INVESTMENT

That consideration, in calculating the capitalization rate, which provides a return on the basic investment during the amortization period of the loan is called return on investment.

INVESTOR ADVICE

The return on the investment is the interest rate received. The mortgage constant consists of two parts: (a) the interest payable on the unpaid balance, and (b) the amount required to amortize (return) the initial investment to the lender during the term of the loan. It is the part of the periodic loan payment which consists of a return *of* the investment and a return *on* the investment.

SEE ALSO: CAPITALIZATION RATE, ELLWOOD RATE, MORTGAGE CONSTANT, MORTGAGE EQUITY TECHNIQUE, OVERALL RATE (OAR), RECAPTURE RATE, and RETURN OF INVESTMENT.

REVENUE STAMPS

State revenue stamps represent taxes paid on a real estate transaction.

INVESTOR ADVICE

Revenue stamps are evidence of a state-imposed tax on the transfer of real estate. Besides raising revenue, real estate transfer taxes provide information to the public as to the approximate selling price of the property.

Where the tax rate is known, an appraiser or other person examining the official record is able to determine the selling price by counting the value of the tax stamps attached to the deed and dividing by the tax rate.

EXAMPLE

A property deed has $50.00 in tax stamps attached to the deed. The state transfer tax at the time of transfer was one mill ($0.001) per dollar of value. For what price did the property sell?

$$\text{Sales Price} = \$50 / 0.001 = \$50,000$$

Because of this revelation of private information, many states have repealed the revenue tax laws.

SEE ALSO: ABSTRACT OF TITLE, CLOSING COSTS, and RECORDING.

REVERSE MORTGAGE

A reverse mortgage is a relatively modern technique of removing equity from a property in the form of an annuity.

INVESTOR ADVICE

Many property owners reach a period in life in which they would like to obtain some of the equity in their property without selling it. An equity loan would be an alternative but would probably require monthly payments, which defeat the purpose of the loan.

A relatively new technique, now being insured by the FHA on a pilot basis through 1991, will provide FHA insurance on reverse mortgage loans. The amount of the monthly payment will be based on a percentage of the appraised value of the property and the going FHA interest rate.

In effect, the loan is an annuity based on the borrower's age and the other factors listed above. Reverse mortgage loans are repaid after the death of the mortgagor or sale of the property, whichever comes first. Some private organizations and local governments are also experimenting with reverse mortgage loans.

SEE ALSO: MORTGAGE and PRESENT VALUE OF $1/PERIOD.

REVERSIONER

A reversioner is the grantor of a life estate who receives the estate after its termination. If the life estate is received by other than the grantor, he or she is known as the remainder man (person).

INVESTOR ADVICE

While the life tenant has the right of possession, use, and enjoyment, the remainder man retains all other rights. For this reason, a life estate is considered the smallest type of freehold estate.

Life estates are of two types: (a) the conventional, as previously discussed; and (b) the legal. A legal life estate is established by law; for example, dower and curtesy rights.

SEE ALSO: DOWER RIGHTS, CURTESY RIGHTS, LIFE ESTATE, and LIFE TENANT.

REVIEW APPRAISER

A review appraiser is one who reviews the work of another appraiser to assess its accuracy and applicability.

INVESTOR ADVICE

Many banks and other lending institutions utilize review appraisers to check the appraisal work being performed by their independent fee appraisers. In most cases, the review is rather cursory and is primarily aimed at checking for completeness and assessing the approaches used by the appraiser, his or her criteria in selection of market data, and the weighting assigned to each of the approaches to value.

When large amounts of money are at stake, it is wise to obtain more than one appraisal on the subject property and to have them reviewed by a competent senior review appraiser. You do not have to be a certified appraiser to do a reasonably good job as a reviewer. Most investors can do a passable job by use of their own common sense and experience. The following is a useful checklist of errors often made in property appraisals:

Income Property

- expenses omitted which increase projected income;

- capitalization rates not correctly developed or supported by facts from the marketplace;

- incorrect assumptions of future economic activity;

- future changes in demographics not considered;

- unverified income schedules; and

- failure to provide reserves for replacements and repairs.

Residential Property

- comparable property sales do not reflect the current market;

- comparisons made on realtor data only—no personal inspection;

- economic trends up/down not considered;

- failure to consider FHA/VA points paid by sellers of comparable properties;

- failure to calculate accurately the enclosed square footage; and

- incorrect assumptions of time required to sell.

Land

- comparable sales used from areas with different zoning and without appropriate adjustments for differences;

- failure to adjust for accessibility;
- failure to consider availability/nonavailability of utilities;
- no consideration for utility value due to shape of the plot;
- failure to adjust for time of sales;
- failure to adjust for size of sales; and
- failure to adjust selling price for seller—provided favorable financing.

SEE ALSO: COST APPROACH TO VALUE, INCOME APPROACH TO VALUE, MARKET APPROACH TO VALUE, RETURN ON INVESTMENT.

RIGHT OF FIRST REFUSAL

A right of first refusal is the right granted by a property owner which provides the grantee the right to consider the purchase of a property if and when it is offered for sale.

INVESTOR ADVICE

The right of first refusal differs from an option in several ways. Whereas an option provides *the right to purchase a property at a given price*, the right of first refusal merely says, "You can have the first chance to make a bid on my property, if I should decide to sell it." Nothing is really promised and no one is bound to make a deal.

Leaseholders often request such rights from their landlords as a method of protecting their location. This is particularly useful where the seller is known to be considering a sale. Rights of first refusal may be in writing or oral. Since they do not include specifics as to selling price, terms, and other considerations they are seldom legally binding.

The right of first refusal is not considered very useful as a selling tool, since realtors, who list a property for sale usually consider tenants as prime buyer prospects. The minute the listing is signed, they contact all tenants and advise them of the listing and its terms.

SEE ALSO: OPTIONS.

RIGHT OF SURVIVORSHIP

This term refers to the legal right of a person(s) who owns property with title as *joint ownership with right of survivorship* to claim ownership of a deceased partner's portion of the property on his/her/their death.

INVESTOR ADVICE

Joint ownership with right of survival is the most common type of ownership by husband and wife, although it is not always wise from an estate tax standpoint. This type of ownership avoids most of the problems of probate, since full title is easily gained by the survivor. The survivor simply submits a death certificate and evidence that all inheritance and estate taxes due from the decedent's estate have been paid.

A joint tenancy requires that the title state the intent to create a joint tenancy, and the four unities must be present:

1. same right of possession,
2. same title,
3. same time of taking title, and
4. same interests.

Even though joint tenants have the same right of possession, they do not have to occupy the property jointly. A joint tenant can bind him or herself or his or her individual interest, but is different from a partnership in that he or she cannot bind the joint tenant. The right of survivorship is extremely strong and is superior to:

- judgments against the deceased,

- easements created solely by the deceased,

- the decedent's will, and

- dower or curtesy of the deceased.

> **WARNING!** A judgment against a deceased person's property, held as joint tenant, is not enforceable unless the judgment is against his or her joint tenant as well.

SEE ALSO: DECEDENT, ESTATE PLANNING, JOINT TENANCY, and WILL.

RIGHT-OF-WAY (ROW)

Right-of-way is an easement or right of access permitting passage over another's property.

INVESTOR ADVICE

A right-of-way is an appurtenant easement, which means that it benefits the nearby land. The most common type of appurtenant easement is a right-of-way for passage over the dominant tenement (nonowned property) to a servient tenement.

Rights-of-way may be subdivided into apparent and nonapparent. An apparent easement would be that represented by a road or pathway; whereas a nonapparent right-of-way might be an intangible, such as scenic rights or other rights not yet exercised.

Appurtenant easements come into existence by several means, such as:

- by prescriptive use over a period of years, required by state law;

- by implication, where a landowner sells a portion of property and, by implication, a right-of-way is implied;

- by dedication of a property owner to a governmental body (for example, a roadway in which all adjacent properties are presumed to have a right of access over that dedicated roadway); and

- by direct grant. This is the most common type of right-of-way, in which the grantor of a property provides for access by deed. Here the detailed use, size, and legal description is included as a part of each property deed requiring use of the right-of-way. Generally, an easement appurtenant (right-of-way) cannot exist except in conjunction with the adjacent property. It cannot, therefore, be separated and must go with the land.

A right-of-way created by direct grant would be evident by the adjacent property deed, which would read something like this:

Beginning at a point etc. . . . and thence back to the point of beginning. Contains 1.0 acres.
Together with a right-of-way, 20 ft. wide extending from Baker Street along and East of the Big Ditch Irrigation Canal, North 89°36'44" East to the Southwest corner of the property.

SEE ALSO: DEED, EASEMENT, GRANTEE, GRANTOR, and LEGAL DESCRIPTION.

RIGHTS OF OWNERSHIP

Rights of ownership are the legal rights of a property owner called the bundle of rights.

INVESTOR ADVICE

See discussion on BUNDLE OF RIGHTS.
SEE ALSO: FEE SIMPLE TITLE.

RIPARIAN RIGHTS

Riparian rights are the rights of a landowner to use the water which is under, on, or adjacent to his or her property.

INVESTOR ADVICE

Because water flows under or across an owner's land, the owner's rights thereto are not as absolute as his or her control of surface and mineral rights. Riparian rights are not recognized in all states, particularly western states in which *all water* belongs to someone, not necessarily the landowner.

When purchasing or proposing to purchase land in the western states, you must ascertain what water rights, if any, go with the property. Water rights may be mentioned on a deed, but this is generally an indication of intent to transfer, not the actual transfer.

In most western areas, irrigation water originates in a water holding project; and all of the water therein is assigned to users in the form of rights or shares, which are official certificates issued by the secretary of the water authority. The certificate holder is the owner of the water rights.

Water rights are indicated in second-feet or acre-feet. Water is delivered to the owners in irrigation ditches. Owners are assigned specific time slots in which they may divert all or part of the flow onto their property. In more urban areas, water is furnished through pressurized water lines. Each owner's share of the water is limited only by the size of his or her approved connecting line.

In certain parts of Arizona, Utah, and Nevada, water is so valuable that users often buy land in order to acquire the water rights that go with it. It is not unusual for the buyer to return the land to the previous owner, free of charge, but without the water necessary to raise crops. The previous owner can utilize the land for dry farming or as a residence.

Underground water is strictly controlled by the states and their bureaus of natural resources. To dig a well on your own property, a permit must be obtained.

You should never buy property in any of the western states without assuring yourself that adequate water is available or can be made available for your intended use of the land. In most cases, land without water is valueless.
SEE ALSO: ACRE-FOOT and SECOND-FEET.

RISK VERSUS RETURN

This term refers to the ratio of the risk of loss of investment versus the expected return on that investment. In general, the higher the risk, the higher the expected return.

INVESTOR ADVICE

A simple economic principle dictates the relationship between risk and return on investment—the higher the risk, the greater the expected return on investment.

This relationship between risk and return provides a check in evaluating various investment opportunities. If an investment is guaranteed, such as government bonds, you can expect a minimum return at more or less "bank rates." If the risk is greater, such as a business venture or real estate investment, you would expect a far greater rate of return to compensate for the

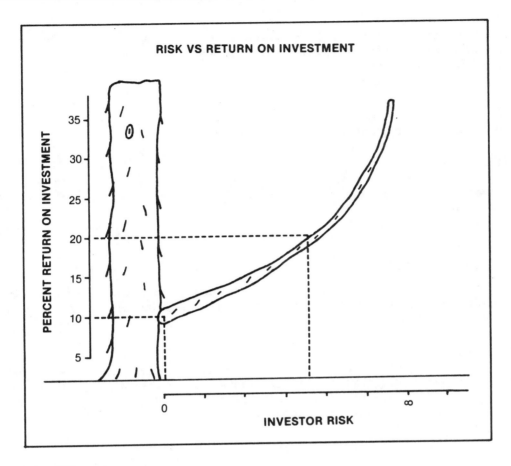

Figure 58

additional risk taken. A high return with a stated low risk is probably a fraudulent operation.

No one pays a higher interest rate than necessary to procure their needed capital. If a high return is offered, it can only mean one thing—the borrower or his or her proposed use of the funds is such that most lenders refuse to loan at a lower rate. Figure 58 indicates the relationship between risk and return. If one stays next to the tree trunk, risk is minimal; but the higher one goes on the limb, the higher the risk of falling.

SEE ALSO: PRIME RATE, RETURN ON INVESTMENT.

RM APPRAISER

An RM appraiser is a certified residential member of the American Institute of Real Estate Appraisers who is qualified to appraise certain residential properties.

INVESTOR ADVICE

When you consider hiring an appraiser with the RM designation, you should be aware that he or she has achieved the first level of certification with the Institute but has not been certified to appraise large residential properties, land, or income-producing properties.

That the appraiser has not attained the MAI designation (member of the Institute) does not preclude his or her ability to do more specialized appraisal work, but before hiring the

appraiser you should check to see if he or she has taken and passed the necessary advance courses and has significant experience in that type of appraising.
SEE ALSO: MAI APPRAISER.

ROD

A rod is equal to one fourth of a chain, or 16.5 feet.

INVESTOR ADVICE
The rod is often mentioned in various legal descriptions which were prepared in the past. Modern appraisers using laser measuring equipment have gradually converted to the foot and fraction-of-a-foot designations.
SEE ALSO: CHAIN and LINK.

ROLL-OVER LOAN

A roll-over loan is a variable rate loan in which the payment rate is over a long-term mortgage period, but the interest rate and loan are renegotiated at specific intervals, usually every 5 or 10 years.

INVESTOR ADVICE
The variable rate loan is useful in times of high interest rates. Often, a loan can be negotiated at 1% or 2% less than the going rate, if you are willing to accept the variable provision.

If your estimate of the economic future is that rates are likely to decline, this type of loan would be acceptable. If you are unable to predict the future, then certain considerations must be taken into account:

• If interest rates rise in the future one, two, or even three percentage points, will the property income be sufficient to carry the loan?

• Would a fixed rate loan on a shorter call basis be preferable at this time?

• Will a penalty payment be required if you refinance the project at some time in the future?

SEE ALSO: FLOATING RATE LOAN, NOVATION, and VARIABLE INTEREST LOAN.

ROW HOUSE

A term used to designate a residential unit which is attached to other units to form a row or block-long number of units.

INVESTOR ADVICE
The row house concept originated in the northeastern United States, principally in the urban areas of Baltimore, Boston, Philadelphia, and New York. These older row houses fell into disrepair but were revived in the 1950s and 1960s as townhouses for the affluent.

The continued appreciation in land prices has revived the concept of high-density housing, which is gaining in popularity as planned unit developments. These developments are superior to the original idea in that more open areas are provided and most contain commonly owned amenities such as clubhouses and swimming pools.
SEE ALSO: CONDOMINIUM, DE MINIMIS PUD, and PLANNED UNIT DEVELOPMENT.

RULE OF 1/4

This rule of thumb in real estate investing states that rental rates should not exceed one fourth of the income of the typical tenant.

INVESTOR ADVICE

This rule makes good sense. Competitive rental rates should allow you to buy, renovate, and maintain the property to achieve a reasonable return on investment. If interest rates and other factors will not allow you to attract the average tenant, maybe you should consider another investment.

Mortgage lenders also use this basic rule in determining if a buyer will qualify for a loan. While some flexibility is possible, the rule is basically sound. Most wage earners require about three quarters of their income to cover expenses other than housing.

SEE ALSO: GROSS SCHEDULED INCOME, RENT SCHEDULE, and VACANCY FACTOR.

RULE OF 3

This basic rule of developers states that improved single-family building lots should sell for at least three times the raw land value (land cost = 33 1/3% of selling price).

INVESTOR ADVICE

In many areas, the Rule of 3 is not applicable. Most developers prefer to use a factor of 5, which indicates a 20% land cost.

SEE ALSO: RULE OF 5

RULE OF 5

This basic rule of developers states that single-family residential improved building lots should sell for at least five times the raw land value (land cost = 20% of selling price).

INVESTOR ADVICE

The Rule of 5 is far preferable to the Rule of 3, which indicates a raw land price of 33 1/3% of the lot selling price. The applicability of such rules depends on land costs in the local area.

SEE ALSO: RULE OF 3.

RULE OF 78s

The Rule of 78s is a quick method of calculating the amount of interest payable each month on a one-year note, where the interest is computed as simple interest on the previous month's balance.

INVESTOR ADVICE

This method is actually a sum of the digits method, in which the sum of the digits of a 12-month loan is 78. The rule is useful for quickly calculating an amortization schedule.

In the 78s method, the interest is amortized over the 12-month period by the sum of the digits method. In the first month, 12/78s of the interest is due, in the second 11/78s, etc.

Figure 59, page 452, shows a $5,000 loan at 12% amortized by the Rule of 78s.

SEE ALSO: ANNUAL PERCENTAGE RATE.

RULES OF CONTRACTUAL CONSTRUCTION

State or other laws that establish owner/contractor relationships and requirements for bonding are considered rules of contractual construction.

INVESTOR ADVICE

Utah, as well as other states, has established requirements for dealing with contractors, subcontractors, and suppliers to assure that all debts are paid. A property owner who contracts for improvements of $2,000 or more must require his or her contractor to furnish a bond to assure payment of subcontractors and suppliers. If the bond is not obtained, the property owner is responsible for any debts not paid by the contractor.

When contracting for any repairs, improvements, or new construction, you would be wise to check local requirements in relation to bonding. You may also want the contractor to be bonded to assure a timely and professional completion of the contracted work.

SEE ALSO: CONTRACTOR, LIEN, MECHANIC'S LIEN, PERFORMANCE BOND, and SUBCONTRACTOR.

Loan Amortization by Rule of 78s

Loan amount: $5,000; Interest rate: 12$APR; Period: 1 year

Using a loan amortization table or a financial calculator such as the HP-12C, we find that a monthly payment of $444.24 is required to amortize the aforementioned loan. The total payments to be made are:

$$\$444.24 \times 12 = \$5,330.99$$

The interest paid will be:

$$\$5,330.99 - \$5,000.00 = \$330.93$$

By the Rule of 78s, 12/78s of the interest is due the first month, 11/78th the second, etc. The amortization schedule then appears as:

Payment No.	Payment Amt. (1)	Interest Payable (2)			Principal Payment (1-2)	Balance Due
0						$5,000.00
1	$444.24	12/78 x 330.93	=	50.91	$393.33	$4606.67
2	"	11/78 x "	=	46.67	397.57	4209.10
3	"	10/78 x "	=	42.43	401.81	3807.29
4	"	9/78 x "	=	38.18	406.06	3401.23
5	"	8/78 x "	=	33.94	410.30	2990.93
6	"	7/78 x "	=	29.70	414.54	2576.39
7	"	6/78 x "	=	25.46	418.78	2157.61
8	"	5/78 x "	=	21.21	423.03	1734.58
9	"	4/78 x "	=	16.97	427.27	1307.31
10	"	3/78 x "	=	12.73	431.51	875.80
11	"	2/78 x "	=	8.49	435.75	440.05*
12	"	1/78 x "	=	4.24	440.00	0*

Figure 59

S

Safe Harbor Rules
Safe Rate
Sale and Buyback
Sale and Leaseback
Sale of Leased Property
Sale Proceeds
Sales Price
Salvage Value
Sandwich Lease
Sanitary Sewer
Satisfaction Piece
Savings and Loan Association
Scrap Value
Seasoned Mortgage Loan
Second-Feet
Second Mortgage
Secondary Mortgage Market
Section
Securities Commission
Securities and Exchange Commission
    (SEC)
Security Deposit
Separate Metering
Separate Property
Septic System
Sheriff's Deed
Short-Term Financing
Short-Term Gains
Sinking Fund
Small Claims Court
Society of Real Estate Appraisers
Special Assessment

Special Warranty Deed
Specific Performance
Spot Zoning
Square Footage
SRA Appraiser
SREA Appraiser
SRPA Appraiser
Statute of Frauds
Stick-Built House
Storm Sewer
Straight-Line Cost Recovery
Straight-Line Depreciation
Subchapter S Corporation
Subcontractor
Subcontractor Lien
Subdividend Land
Subdivision
Subject-To Clause
Sublease
Subordinate Debenture
Subordination
Subpoena Duces Tecum
Subscription Agreement
Sufferance Lease
Sum of the Digits
Super-Six Magic Numbers
Survey
Sweat Equity
Syndicated Equity Pools
Syndication
Syndicate Vehicles

S

SAFE HARBOR RULES

Rules established for limited partnerships where the general partner is a corporation. Internal Revenue Service safe harbor rules must be met if the earnings are to enjoy the tax benefits of a partnership.

INVESTOR ADVICE

There are two rules that must be met when the general partner is the sole general partner. These are:

1. The corporate general partner must have a net worth equal to the smaller of:
   a. $250,000, not considering its asset value in the limited partnership, or
   b. 15% of the amount invested by the limited partners. If the total amount invested by the limited partners exceeds $2.5 million, the corporate general partner must invest 10% of the amount invested by the limited partners.
2. The limited partners, as a group, cannot own directly or indirectly, 20% or more of the general partnership or any corporation affiliated with it.

> **NOTE!** Safe harbor rules apply only in situations in which the sole general partner is a corporation.

If there is an individual general partner as well as a corporate general partner, safe harbor rules do not apply. There is no statutory or regulatory basis for prohibiting the limited partners from owning 20% or more of the general partnership—it is what the Internal Revenue Service has decreed. To be safe, keep the ownership below 20%.

All Internal Revenue Service rulings and decrees are revised constantly in accordance with court decisions and other pressures. Before setting up your limited partnership, seek the advice of competent legal counsel regarding the latest rulings and decrees.

SEE ALSO: GENERAL PARTNER, LIMITED PARTNER, and PARTNERSHIP.

SAFE RATE

The rate of return on investment available through government- or quasi-government insured organizations—the guaranteed rate.

INVESTOR ADVICE

Any return on investment that exceeds the safe rate is said to involve a risk. The higher the return, the higher the risk. The economic principle of supply and demand applies to money as well as other commodities. You cannot get a higher rate of return on your investment without taking a corresponding greater risk of loss of capital.

The key to successful investment is to determine the amount of risk you are willing to take in order to achieve your objectives. Figure 58 clearly indicates the investment tree and its associated risks. If you venture out on the limb and away from the safe trunk, you are subject to a potential disaster. Each investor must decide how far out on the limb he or she is willing to go and should not be surprised if the limb breaks when he or she goes too far.

Expressed in 1989 investment returns, we find the following available investments and expected returns. You will note the return goes up as the risk increases:

Government notes and treasuries	9.50%
Government-backed mortgages	9.75%
High-grade corporate bonds	10.50%
Seasoned second mortgages	15.00%
Corporate junk bonds	17.50%

There is no quantitative measurement of risk except as indicated by the return. Risk is generally expressed as safe, risky, and very risky.

SEE ALSO: RISK VERSUS RETURN.

SALE AND BUYBACK

A provision of a sale which states that the seller can repurchase the property at the end of the lease.

INVESTOR ADVICE

The problem with such an arrangement is the setting of the purchase price at the end of the lease. If the purchase price is less than fair market value, the Internal Revenue Service will probably declare that no actual sale was made. All rents paid will be disallowed as income and considered as interest paid on a loan. Deductions normally incident to ownership, such as taxes and maintenance, will be disallowed.

Sale and buyback became very useful prior to the Tax Reform Act of 1986. A limited partnership would buy a property at a very high price, lose money on its operation for a number of years, and then resell the property to the original owner at a profit. The limited partners enjoyed the tax benefits of the operating losses and of the low-taxed capital gains at the end—all at the expense of other taxpayers.

SEE ALSO: LIMITED PARTNERSHIP, SALE AND LEASEBACK, and TAX REFORM ACT OF 1986 (TRA).

SALE AND LEASEBACK

The sale of a property with the simultaneous leasing back of the facility by the seller.

INVESTOR ADVICE

The sale and leaseback arrangement can be a good deal for both parties. The seller releases capital (tied up as equity in the building), improves the looks of the balance sheet, and still retains possession of the facility. The facility may be an existing one which is sold or a new one built by the seller to his or her specific needs.

The sale is also good for the buyer. Where the tenant-seller is a good risk, the buyer can usually obtain or assume a low interest loan based on the tenant's credit rating and by virtue of the long-term lease which has been executed. There are some risks to the buyer attendant to this type of arrangement.

First of all, the buyer must understand that bankruptcy of the tenant-seller may limit his claim to rental. Second, since the lease is long-term, care must be exercised in setting the lease payments to provide for inflation. Third, the lessee-seller may demand the right to repurchase the property at the end of the lease, in which case you must assure that the contract is fair to all and, more importantly, that the sale is recognized as a sale by the Internal Revenue Service and not as a financing arrangement.

The sale and leaseback arrangement is used by many large chain stores to provide adequate facilities with a minimum cash outlay. Local real estate investors snap up these opportunities as soon as they become available. A typical 20–25 year lease assures a return of the investor's money and a good return on the invested equity. At the end of the lease, the investor is left with an older building of questionable value, but the land is generally expected to have appreciated substantially. A short-term release of the facilities in a successful location is not out of the question.

SEE ALSO: ANCHOR TENANT, SALE AND BUYBACK, and TRIPLE NET LEASE.

SALE OF LEASED PROPERTY

A sale of the owner's interest only. The appraised fair market value may include two interests: the owner's fee interest and the tenant's leasehold interest.

INVESTOR ADVICE

The owner of record may dispose of his or her interest only. The tenant's interest continue under the new ownership and in accordance with the lease.

Since the sale of a leased property does not affect the tenant, you should be careful to access properly the leasehold interest and be sure that your purchase price pays only for the owner interest.

A leasehold interest occurs only where the contract rent (called for in the lease agreement) is less than economic rent (the going rate). If the contract rent is greater than the economic rent, the owner's equity is enhanced. If it is less, which is usually the case, the owner's equity is diminished.

EXAMPLE

A certain retail building has been appraised for $600,000. The building is currently leased on a triple net basis for $60,000 annually. The lease has 10 years to run. A prospective investor has determined that the market rent for comparable structures is $70,000 per year. What is the leasehold interest and the owner's interest?

Leasehold interest is the present value (*pv* in the following equation) of the difference in market rent and contract rent. Money is valued at 10% by the potential buyer.

Rent difference = $70,000 – $60,000 = $10,000/yr.

$$pv - 1/p10\%,10yrs. = 6.145*$$

Leasehold interest = $10,000 x 6.145 = $60,145

Owner's interest = $600,000 – $60,145 = $539,855   Or: $540,000

*See Figure 50.
SEE ALSO: CONTRACT RENT, ECONOMIC RENT, and FAIR MARKET VALUE.

SALE PROCEEDS

Sales proceeds include:
1. Money remaining from a sale after payment of seller closing costs, outstanding debts, and sales commissions.
2. Money obtained from a foreclosure sale which is applied to the mortgage note (gross sale proceeds – [foreclosure expenses + closing costs]).

INVESTOR ADVICE
Sale proceeds, as a percent of gross sales, vary from locality to locality and from sale to sale. Normal seller closing costs include:

- one half title company closing fees;
- title insurance fee;
- recording costs;
- mortgage points, where VA or FHA financing was employed;
- sales commissions; and
- mortgage and other liens paid to clear the title.

The gross sale proceeds would include the agreed selling price plus a return of mortgage escrow funds held for payment of taxes and insurance. If the existing mortgage is assumed by the buyer, these funds are usually purchased from the seller by the buyer.
SEE ALSO: DEFICIENCY JUDGMENT, FORECLOSURE, and TITLE INSURANCE.

SALES PRICE

The sales price is the true price paid by the buyer for the property—not necessarily the amount reported as received by the seller for the property.

INVESTOR ADVICE

> **NOTE!** Terms of the sale must be known to establish the true sales price.

Appraisers who consider comparable sales must be careful to determine that the sales price and the amount received by the seller are one and the same. Often, the seller actually receives a substantial sum less than the reported sales price. This reduction occurs when:

- Points are paid by the seller to allow the buyer to finance the property by a VA or FHA loan.

- The property is sold on contract, or other favorable terms, with the seller receiving an interest rate less than the going rate for commercially available funds.

- The property is leased at the time of sale and only the owner's interest is sold—a substantial leasehold interest was held by the lessee.

- The sale involved a trade for other property. Beware of sales which involve the trade of a "million dollar dog" for a "million dollar cat"—realtor parlance for a trade at artificially high sales prices.

When counting revenue stamps to determine the sales price, the aforementioned factors must also be taken into account.
SEE ALSO: CONTRACT, POINTS, LEASEHOLD INTEREST, REVENUE STAMPS, and TRADE OF PROPERTY.

SALVAGE VALUE

Salvage value is the value of property improvements remaining on the land at the end of the economic life of the property.

INVESTOR ADVICE

Salvage value may be positive or negative. Where the materials, such as used brick, hardwood trim, stained glass windows, and so forth, can be sold for an excess of the razing expense, the salvage value is positive. If the value of materials, if any, which can be sold are less than the razing cost, the salvage value is said to be negative and must be accounted for in the evaluation of the land.

Even very old and fully depreciated property may have some value to some buyers of redevelopment land. Where redevelopment is not planned for the immediate future, it may be possible to obtain some income by rental of the old facilities. Thus, a buyer with a holding period in mind might be willing to pay an amount equal to the present value of this income stream.

SEE ALSO: FAIR MARKET VALUE, and PRESENT VALUE OF $1/PERIOD.

SANDWICH LEASE

A sandwich lease is held by one who subleases the property to another. The original lessee is in the middle (sandwiched) between the property owner interest and the current occupant's interest.

INVESTOR ADVICE

Just as in the case of an ordinary lease, it is possible for the sandwich lessee to have a leasehold interest. This occurs when the lessee subleases at a rate greater than he or she is currently required to pay on the lease contract. That amount can still be less than the economic rent of comparable property in which a second leasehold interest is generated. In the usual case, however, the sublease would reflect current market conditions.

EXAMPLE

Tenant Jones has 20 years remaining on his lease of an industrial building at a monthly rate of $2,000. Current economic rent is $2,500 monthly. Jones subleases the property for the remaining 20 years for $2,500 monthly. Money is currently worth 12%.

Jones, in effect, receives an annual annuity of $500 x 12 = $6,000 for 20 years. Figure 50 indicates that this annuity factor is 7.469. Jones has a sandwich leasehold interest of

$6,000 x 7.469 = $44,814   Or: $44,800*

* Actual value would be $45,400, due to monthly payments (not provided for in Figure 50).

SEE ALSO: LEASEHOLD INTEREST.

SANITARY SEWER

A municipal or development-owned underground pipeline for the collection of wastewater products. Sanitary sewers transport the collected waste material to a holding area or a sewage treatment plant, normally the latter.

INVESTOR ADVICE

Where sanitary sewer facilities are not available, sewage is usually handled by a private septic tank system. Septic systems require soil capable of absorbing the effluent produced by the septic tank system. This capability is determined by a percolation test.

Special attention is required in watershed areas, which are the source of municipal culinary water. In those situations, disposal of wastewater is usually authorized for waste from washing facilities only—"white water." Other sewage is usually held in tanks for transportation to an appropriate sewage treatment facility.

SEE ALSO: CULINARY WATER, GRAY WATER WASTE, PERCOLATION TEST, SEPTIC SYSTEM, and WHITE WATER WASTE.

SATISFACTION PIECE

This term refers to an official document, acknowledged and ready for recording, which indicates payment in full of a recorded mortgage or lien.

INVESTOR ADVICE

The satisfaction piece may be a release of mortgage, lien release, or other type of document. Its requirements are as follows:

- It must be signed by the mortgage or lien holder.

- It must be acknowledged.

- It must contain a clear and exact description of the property on which the lease or mortgage encumbered—it may even include the book and page number of the recorded debt.

- It must be dated to show when the obligation was satisfied.

- It must include a statement to the effect that the obligation has been paid in full.

A satisfaction piece may be a formal document or, as in North Carolina, a statement saying, "Paid in full [date]" and signed diagonally across the debtor document.

SEE ALSO: ACKNOWLEDGMENT, RECONVEYANCE DEED, RELEASE OF LIEN, and RELEASE OF MORTGAGE.

SAVINGS AND LOAN ASSOCIATION

A federally chartered or state-licensed institution whose prime function is to provide mortgage loans for real estate.

INVESTOR ADVICE

Federally chartered institutions are regulated by the Federal Home Loan Bank Board, while state institutions are regulated by the state commissioner overseeing savings and loans.

Federally chartered savings and loans provide insurance for their accounts up to $100,000 through the Federal Savings and Loan Insurance Corporation (FSLIC). State institutions may or may not provide insurance on their accounts. Even when insured, these state institutions are often unable to pay depositors after the institute fails.

> **WARNING!** State-chartered savings and loans, which are not federally insured, can be very risky.

In the past few years we have witnessed the failure of hundreds of savings and loans, many of which were not federally insured. Many weak institutions are still in existence. Before depositing large sums in a state-chartered institution, make sure that the insurance provided is adequate to cover your investment.

SEE ALSO: FEDERAL SAVINGS AND LOAN INSURANCE CORPORATION (FSLIC).

SCRAP VALUE

This term refers to the value assigned to the materials recovered from a building after it is razed; sometimes referred to as *salvage value.*

INVESTOR ADVICE

There is seldom any scrap value after deduction for the cost of razing. Even in areas where secondhand brick and other materials are valuable, the cost of razing can be less than the value of the materials recovered. Generally speaking, it is unwise to count on any value remaining.

One exception is the razing of old or historic structures. Often, exotic woodwork, mantels, doors, and trim can be sold for significant amounts. Some historic structures with sentimental value have resulted in the sale of individual bricks as mementos of the past.

SEE ALSO: COST APPROACH TO VALUE and SALVAGE VALUE.

SEASONED MORTGAGE LOAN

A seasoned loan is a loan which has been in existence for a period of time and which has experienced timely repayments.

INVESTOR ADVICE

Seasoned first and second mortgages are excellent investment vehicles. They are expected to yield four to five percentage points above the loan interest rates. The higher yields are due to the fact that these mortgages are offered at discount by holders requiring cash.

Due to the large discount demanded by buyers of existing mortgages, their sale by investors should be a last resort. Often a loan using the mortgage as security can be arranged to provide the necessary cash at a lower expense than a direct sale.

SEE ALSO: DISCOUNTED PAPER, PRESENT VALUE OF $1/PERIOD, RETURN ON INVESTMENT, and YIELD.

SECOND-FEET

Second-feet is a measure of the quantity of flow of irrigation water equal to 1 cubic foot per second.

INVESTOR ADVICE

Where irrigation water is available to a property through ownership of water rights, your portion of the flow of the ditch is often designated as a number of second-feet. The actual delivery is regulated by the water master, who dictates the size of weir authorized to allow flow to your property. This size, the water height maintained in the ditch, and the flow rate provide an approximate amount equal to your water rights.

A second foot would indicate a weir 1 foot wide, with a water level of 1 foot above the weir and a flow rate of 1 foot per second; that is, 1 ft. x 1 ft. x 1 ft./sec. Flow rates are monitored by the water master by observation of a floating object. An object that moves 1 foot per second down the ditch indicates a flow rate of 1 foot per second.

Standing water (capacity) of an irrigation lake or reservoir is designated in acre-feet or water covering 1 acre of land and 1 foot deep.

Well permits usually authorize a maximum pumping rate in second-feet. There may be a time limit imposed on pumping as well.

SEE ALSO: ACRE-FEET, WATER MASTER, WATER RIGHTS, and WELL PERMIT.

SECOND MORTGAGE

A second mortgage is a mortgage that has a second priority position in the event of failure to pay—a junior mortgage.

INVESTOR ADVICE

When you accept a junior mortgage as security for a loan, you must ascertain that the total debt against the property is substantially less than the fair market value during an economic slowdown. A sudden economic decline can leave you, second mortgage holder, in a very vulnerable position.

Since the risk of a second position is greater than that of a first, the interest rate should be correspondingly greater than the first mortgage interest rate, say two to five points higher. Where first mortgage money is currently going for 10%, a 12%–14% second mortgage is not unreasonable.

SEE ALSO: DISCOUNTED PAPER, JUNIOR MORTGAGE, and SEASONED MORTGAGE LOAN.

SECONDARY MORTGAGE MARKET

The secondary mortgage market is a market for the purchase and sale of existing first mortgage loans.

INVESTOR ADVICE

Mortgage companies, savings and loans, and other institutions who originate mortgage loans are heavily dependent on the secondary market to replenish their supply of available funds and for income from the servicing of mortgages sold to others.

The secondary market is composed of quasi-government agencies and private lenders, such as insurance companies and pension funds. Without these sources of funds, local money would soon be exhausted and mortgage loans unavailable. Fannie Mae and GNMA are the two quasi-government organizations which feed the loan originators.

Mortgage loans made by the local lenders are packaged into large (one million or larger) bundles for resale in the secondary market. Many buyers, such as pension funds and some insurance companies, do not desire to service their loans and thus pay the local lenders a fee to collect payments and maintain records. This service work provides a significant income to the loan originators.

The individual investor seldom enters the secondary mortgage market, except through a syndication. Most syndicators prefer the junior mortgage market to the primary market, since yields are significantly higher.

SEE ALSO: FEDERAL NATIONAL MORTGAGE ASSOCIATION (FNMA), GOVERNMENT NATIONAL MORTGAGE ASSOCIATION (GNMA), LIMITED PARTNERSHIPS, and SYNDICATE EQUITY POOLS.

SECTION

A section is a land parcel designation in the government land survey system equal to one thirty-sixth of a township or one square mile. A section contains 640 acres.

INVESTOR ADVICE

Land, particularly in the West, is most often referred to by section number or part of a section. It is common to see a parcel designated as, for example, "the South 1/2 of the NW 1/4 of the NE 1/4 of section 20."

A quick method of determining the content of a parcel such as that just described is to multiply the denominators of the fractions together to determine what part of a section (640 acres) it contains. In the preceding example, the acreage would be:

$$2 \times 4 \times 4 = 1/32 \text{ of a section} \quad \text{or} \quad 640/32 = 20 \text{ acres}$$

SEE ALSO: LAND IDENTIFICATION METHODS and RECTANGULAR SURVEY.

SECURITIES COMMISSION

A name often applied to the state organization that oversees investment activities within that state is *securities commission.*

INVESTOR ADVICE

Security commissions or divisions, as they are known in some states, vary in their effectiveness from very poor to excellent. Normally, these organizations control all investment activities involving limited partnerships, corporation stock sales, and the sale of large land parcels which have been subdivided for sale to individuals.

In general, it is much easier to clear a syndication or stock sale for intrastate sale than for an interstate sale. In most states, a small offering to a limited number of investors may be totally exempt from control.

Investments in real estate syndicates and corporations, which require limited state examination, are very risky. An exception might be made for such an investment in which the principals and their objectives are personally well-known.

SEE ALSO: PROSPECTUS, RED HERRING, SECURITIES AND EXCHANGE COMMISSION (SEC), and SYNDICATE EQUITY POOL.

SECURITIES AND EXCHANGE COMMISSION (SEC)

The federal agency having regulatory jurisdiction over the issuance, interstate sale, and trade of securities.

INVESTOR ADVICE

The SEC does an excellent job of assuring accuracy in financial reporting and of approving the prospectuses which accompany all offers to sell new corporation stock and limited partnerships. In investing in an operation which has been given SEC approval, you can be virtually assured that the facts provided are accurate. *The SEC does not qualify the risk involved and no such assurance should be assumed.*

Beware of those issues which are sold intrastate and require approval only by the appropriate state agency. These agencies usually do not have the manpower sufficient to investigate investment proposals properly. It is not uncommon to find such intrastate approved offerings seriously deficient in fact and truth.

SEE ALSO: PROSPECTUS, RED HERRING, SECURITIES COMMISSION, and SYNDICATE EQUITY POOL.

SECURITY DEPOSIT

This term refers to a deposit made with a landlord to guarantee that his or her property will be returned at the end of the lease period in acceptable condition.

INVESTOR ADVICE

Most apartment owners require certain deposits from the tenant prior to occupancy. These may include:

- first and last months rent in advance;

- a cleaning deposit to be forfeited if the property is not left in an acceptable condition; and

- a security deposit to cover damage to the property or equipment over and above normal wear and tear.

The kind and size of required deposits are determined by the marketplace. Obviously, property owners would like to have all of the aforementioned deposits and in large amounts, but the public will object to unreasonable or uncustomary requirements. Thus, the requirements are reduced to what the market will bear. Most renters expect to pay at least one month's rent in advance and to make a reasonable cleaning deposit.

All advanced rentals, cleaning deposits, and security deposits are lessee funds to be held in escrow by the landlord. Most prudent landlords maintain such funds in a separate account to assure their immediate availability to departing tenants. Most states place no restrictions on such deposits and do not prevent the collection of interest on bank accounts.

SEE ALSO: CLEANING DEPOSIT, and RENTAL DEPOSIT.

SEPARATE METERING

An arrangement of utilities distribution in apartment houses, office buildings, or other multitenant structures which provides for individual rental unit metering of services and responsibility for payment.

INVESTOR ADVICE

During the construction phase of a new building, it is usually practical to provide separate electrical and gas metering for each tenant. In offices and other commercial buildings subject to flexible partitioning, this method may not be practical. Older buildings can seldom be converted to individual metering, except where major renovation and remodeling is in progress. In these cases, utilities are prorated among tenants based on the floor space occupied. Water usage and common area lighting is usually the responsibility of the landlord.

If proration of utility bills is not advisable and these expenses are included in the rental price, make sure that your leases provide for an automatic rent increase if utility bills are raised by the supplier.

SEE ALSO: MASTER METERING and UTILITIES.

SEPARATE PROPERTY

Property that is owned prior to marriage or is inherited is called separate property. Some states follow the old Spanish law in regard to property rights; thus, a married couple in those states can have her property, his property, and their joint property.

INVESTOR ADVICE

If you are buying property in California, Texas, or one of the other states which follow the old Spanish law, you must be very careful in your determination of how you take title. An error in this respect can be costly in estate taxes.

Your selection as to title method will depend on the size of your estate and the objectives set forth in your estate planning. Before making an offer to purchase, consult your attorney and estate planner. A later change of title may involve gift taxes.

Separate property can become joint property through the inadvertent commingling of income. For instance, a business owned by one marital partner at the time of marriage and continued as a partnership will soon commingle annual income with the original net worth until it is no longer distinguishable as a separately owned asset.

If you desire to maintain a business as separate property, you should incorporate it. Income paid out as dividends will be separate income, and the activity will remain as separate property. However, a salary drawn from the company will be joint income in the eyes of the law.

SEE ALSO: CORPORATION, GIFT TAXES, PARTNERSHIP, and JOINT TENANCY.

SEPTIC SYSTEM

A septic system is a sewage disposal system consisting of an underground tank for bacterial action and an effluent disposal pipe field.

INVESTOR ADVICE
The effectiveness of the system is largely dependent on the absorption capability of the ground surrounding the disposal pipe field. Most localities require sanitary sewer collection systems for new developments. Some rural locations still allow septic systems where the ground is adequate for good disposal. In these areas, percolation tests are generally required.

If you are considering a land purchase for development, the availability of sanitary sewers and adequate culinary water supply is of primary importance.

Even though local government will permit wells and septic sanitary systems, buyers are reluctant to purchase homes and other facilities subject to future mandatory high-cost property improvements.

SEE ALSO: CULINARY WATER, GRAY WATER WASTE, PERCOLATION TEST, SANITARY SEWER, and WHITE WATER WASTE.

SHERIFF'S DEED

A sheriff's deed is a deed to property sold for nonpayment of taxes or foreclosure of mortgage. The deed to the property is subject to the redemption rights of the former owner—also known as a marshall's deed.

INVESTOR ADVICE
Property sold at a sheriff's sale can often be acquired at a substantial savings. When purchasing such property, you must carefully consider the possibility of redemption, although this occurrence is quite rare. Most property owners whose property is sold for nonpayment of debt are unable to recover the lost property in the time allotted by law.

Lenders who foreclose on property in default are interested in recovering their investment as fast as possible. Most go to the sheriff's sale with the purpose of bidding, only if someone else does make a bid large enough to extinguish the debt and foreclosure expenses. They will not bid more than the fair market price, however.

A smart investor desiring to acquire a property will determine the outstanding indebtedness prior to going to the sale. A bid of that exact amount or slightly more will usually take the property at a bargain price.

SEE ALSO: FORECLOSURE, REDEMPTION RIGHTS, and TAX SALE.

SHORT-TERM FINANCING

Short-term financing is a financing arrangement designed to provide funds for immediate use and until long-term permanent financing can be arranged.

INVESTOR ADVICE

Short-term financing is appropriate where long-term financing is assured by a formal loan commitment letter or other guaranteed method. To begin a project with short-term funds and only an assumption that long-term financing will be obtained is foolish. Even though funds are found at a later date, they may be available at interest rates or other terms which will preclude a profitable venture.

Short-term financing, such as construction loans, are acceptable and are the general rule of procedure; however, they should not be taken out without positive knowledge that long-term financing is assured at acceptable interest rates and terms.

SEE ALSO: COMMITTED INSTITUTIONAL WAREHOUSING, COMMITTED TECHNICAL WAREHOUSING, CONSTRUCTION LOAN, and MORTGAGE COMMITMENT.

SHORT-TERM GAINS

Short-term capital gains are capital appreciation realized from the sale of assets held for less than 6 or 12 months, depending on the year applicable.

INVESTOR ADVICE

Prior to the 1986 Tax Reform Act, short-term gains were defined as capital gains from property sold in less than 6 months. For one short period in the late 1970s, the time period was extended to less than 12 months.

The Tax Reform Act of 1986 repealed the tax relief formerly available for long-term and certain short-term gains. Since 1988 most sales, both long- and short-term gains, are taxed as ordinary income.

For noncorporate individual filers, $3,000 of long-term losses can be deducted from taxable income. If the long-term loss exceeds that amount, the balance of the loss can be carried forward and deducted in subsequent years at the $3,000 anual rate.

SEE ALSO: ACTIVE INCOME, LONG-TERM GAINS, and PASSIVE INCOME.

SINKING FUND

A sinking fund is established by periodic payments and invested at interest to provide for a lump sum liquidation of an indebtedness at a specified time in the future.

INVESTOR ADVICE

Sinking funds are used to retire bonds or other long-term debts. The sinking fund is defined as a periodic deposit which will grow at a specified interest rate to the size necessary to retire a known debt at a stipulated time in the future.

EXAMPLE

Corporation Z issues bonds in the amount of $2,000,000 to be redeemed twenty years in the future. The prospectus states that a sinking fund will be established with a financial institution to provide for the bond redemption at maturity. It is estimated that the deposited funds will earn interest at an average rate of 8%. What annual payments will be required?

This problem is easily solved by using tables or a financial calculator, with the following data given:

- time period—20 years;
- payment period—annually;
- interest rate—8%; and
- future amount required—$2,000,000.

The problem is to determine the amount of each annual deposit at 8% interest which will grow to $2,000,000 in 20 years. Using the Hewlett–Packard 12-C hand-held calculator or the table shown in Figure 32, we find that $1 deposited annually will be worth $45.762 at the end of 20 years. Thus, in order to have $2,000,000 available, we would need to deposit

$$\$2,000,000/45.762 = \$43,705/\text{year}$$

If the payments are made monthly, they would be only $3,395.47 or $40,745.62 per year.

This would represent a savings of almost $3,000 per year, since the payments would be working at interest for a longer period. Unfortunately, our tables do not include sufficient data to do a monthly calculation.

SEE ALSO: FUTURE VALUE OF ONE PER PERIOD.

SMALL CLAIMS COURT

A court, available to claimants in most states, which does not require attorney representation by the defendant or plaintiff. Small claims courts provide for collection of debts up to a specified amount, usually less than $1,000.

INVESTOR ADVICE

The small claim court system is an excellent tool for the landlord to collect rents and other claims which are less than the maximum amounts handled by the court. It also is a very economical way to settle disputes legally over security and other deposits.

To place a claim before the court, the plaintiff usually completes a short, self explanatory form, files it with the clerk of the court, and pays a small fee. The court then issues a summons to the defendant, who is required to appear on the date indicated to tell his or her side of the story. Many defendants are sufficiently scared by the receipt of the summons that they settle the debt before the court date.

The decision of the court can be appealed, but more often results in an agreed method of payment and/or a judgment filed against the debtor. You must be prepared to present your case. For instance, if your claim is for damages to your property, have pictures of the damages, a witness to verify when the pictures were made, and a professional estimate of the cost to repair.

If the dispute is for rents due, you should have a copy of the rental agreement and a ledger to indicate all prior payments. A copy of your letter to the defendant requesting payment would also be good. Don't forget to have positive proof that the letter was received by the defendant—use certified mail and receipt.

SEE ALSO: DEFENDANT, JUDGMENT, LIEN.

SOCIETY OF REAL ESTATE APPRAISERS

The largest appraisal organization in the United States. The society was organized in 1935 and places great emphasis on the professional development of the individual member. All members must uphold the standards of professional practices and conduct; all work must be performed under the constraints of this code.

INVESTOR ADVICE
The Society awards three designations to its qualified members. These are:

- Senior Residential Member (SRA);

- Senior Real Property Appraiser (SRPA); and

- Senior Real Property Analyst (SREA).

All designations are awarded only after the candidate has passed a strict examination on all required courses, demonstrated competence by submission of acceptable demonstration reports, and acquired the necessary experience. Professionally designated members must have a college degree or equivalent. To satisfy such degree requirements, substitute college level courses and experience must be acceptable to the Society.
SEE ALSO: QUALIFICATION OF THE APPRAISER, SRA, SREA, and SRPA.

SPECIAL ASSESSMENT
A one-time tax assessment made against property owners for the purpose of providing property improvements, such as paving, curbs and gutters, sidewalks, or street lighting.

INVESTOR ADVICE
When buying raw land or building lots, it is advisable to ascertain if any special assessments are likely in the near future. Most municipalities now require developers to provide all required improvements as a condition of development approval or provide bonding to assure their timely completion at an appropriate time in the future.

Where older properties are acquired and a building permit is required to modernize or rehabilitate the property, you may find that a condition of approval of the building permit is the addition of all currently required property improvements. This can often be very expensive. For instance, a building permit to add 2,000 square feet of education space to a local church resulted in additional expenses to:

- install sidewalks front and rear of the property, which faced on two streets;

- install curbs and gutters on both streets;

- dedicate 8 feet of frontage to widen one of the streets;

- install a new fire plug; and

- remove 4 feet of parking pavement on two sides of the property and replace with landscaping.

The total cost of these special improvements was more than the addition to the church building.
SEE ALSO: RESTRICTIVE COVENANTS and ZONING.

SPECIAL WARRANTY DEED

This term refers to a special form of the standard warranty deed for use when the grantor is a corporation—sometimes referred to as a corporate warranty deed.

INVESTOR ADVICE

Figure 18 is a copy of the special warranty deed. Note that it provides a certification that the sale has been authorized by the appropriate corporate decision and attested to by the treasurer of the corporation.

Other than this small difference and the requirement for two signatures, both of which are acknowledged, the special warranty deed form and the regular form are identical.

SEE ALSO: GRANTOR, GRANTEE, and WARRANTY DEED.

SPECIFIC PERFORMANCE

Specific performance is an order by a court which instructs someone to do what he or she has previously contracted to do.

INVESTOR ADVICE

In your investing actions, you will undoubtedly encounter one or more instances in which the term *specific performance* will come to mind. Most often it occurs when a seller refuses to close on a property that he or she has agreed to sell by signing the earnest money agreement.

When your requests fail to bring about the required closing, you may be required to seek specific performance through the courts. A specific performance order will require the seller to make good on the previous agreement. In some cases, the seller may not absolutely refuse to close but hesitates and delays the action.

You may request specific performance after a reasonable time has past beyond the closing date specified in the earnest money agreement. The courts have not specifically defined reasonable time, but it is generally considered to be thirty days or less.

A court-directed order of specific performance can be issued only when monetary recourse will not compensate the buyer for the seller's failure to perform. A contract to buy a standard product available through two or more sources cannot be cause of specific performance. Only when there is no other item, such as a described parcel of real estate, can this action be invoked.

Where it is important that the deal close on a specific date, the earnest money agreement should state the closing date and add the phrase, "time is of the essence." This is an indication that the on/about date set for the closing is very specific and an essential part of the transaction.

SEE ALSO: EARNEST MONEY RECEIPT AND OFFER TO PURCHASE, and TIME IS OF THE ESSENCE CLAUSE.

SPOT ZONING

This term refers to a unique zoning that applies to only one parcel among a number of parcels, say one lot in the block.

INVESTOR ADVICE

Spot zoning is very difficult to achieve in most localities. Zoning authorities usually take their lead for approval of any zoning change from a master development plan, which designates specific *areas* for specific future uses. It is difficult to persuade the zoning boards that a variance from this master plan is in the community's interest.

Spot zoning occurs in situations in which a business or other activity has operated for a considerable length of time, during which the area has been rezoned for another use. If that activity, now operating under the grandfather clause, appears likely to continue for a long time in the future, zoning authorities will often recognize that de facto zoning by officially spot zoning the land parcel. Another alternative to spot zoning is authorization for continued operation under a variance order.

SEE ALSO: GRANDFATHER CLAUSE, ZONING, ZONING VARIANCES.

SQUARE FOOTAGE

This term refers to:
1. The total size of the space enclosed within a building.
2. The total size of a land parcel.

INVESTOR ADVICE

Real estate appraisers calculate the square footage within a structure by utilizing outside measurements. This square footage is usually slightly more than the useful interior size, due to the wall thickness. Although the interior square footage is usually less than the square footage indicated by outside measurement, it is usually greater than the useful and/or rentable square footage.

Except in parcels which have square corners, it is difficult to calculate the square footage contained within a legal description. Surveyors utilize all side dimensions and the bearing angle of the lines in order to calculate the exact square footage.

A rough estimate of the size of an odd-shaped parcel (for example, pie-shaped) can be calculated by averaging the opposite sides and multiplying them together.

EXAMPLE

A pie-shaped lot, located on a cul-de-sac, has the following dimensions:

Back side	120.0 ft.
Front side	50.8 ft.
Left side	160.8 ft.
Right side	130.0 ft.

Average front and back = (120.0 + 50.8)/2 = 85.4 ft.
Average of sides = (160.8 + 130.0)/2 = 145.4 ft.
Approximate size of lot = 145.4 x 85.4 = 12,417 sq. ft.

If the property shape is more complicated than the preceding illustration, it is sometimes possible to subdivide it into several standard shapes, calculate their size, and add them to get the total.

SEE ALSO: RENTABLE SQUARE FOOTAGE and USEFUL SQUARE FOOTAGE.

SRA APPRAISER

This term refers to a senior member of the Society of Real Estate Appraisers. The SRA designation indicates that the appraiser has been found qualified to appraise most residential properties.

INVESTOR ADVICE

The SRA designation is the lower of three designations awarded by the Society. While it indicates that the member is qualified to appraise only residential property, some SRA members may have passed all of the examinations and completed the requirements for a higher designation. If so, they can be considered for appraisal work other than residential.

Regardless of an appraiser's earned designations, the quality of his or her work as indicated by former clients is the best reflection of his or her ability. In hiring an appraiser, review his or her qualification sheet and personally check with listed former clients to ascertain their assessment of the appraiser's ability.

SEE ALSO: SOCIETY OF REAL ESTATE APPRAISERS, SREA APPRAISER, and SRPA APPRAISER.

SREA APPRAISER

This term refers to a senior member of the Society of Real Estate Appraisers who has been found qualified to appraise all types of real estate and perform market, investment, and feasibility studies. The SREA designation is the highest designation awarded by the Society.

INVESTOR ADVICE

> **NOTICE!** The SREA designation is the highest awarded by the Society of Real Estate Appraisers.

The SREA designation is awarded only to those members who have been designated SRPAs for a number of years and have, in addition, demonstrated their ability to perform market, investment, and feasibility studiesfor their clients.

SREA members must show that at least 20% of their work is devoted to that involving income analysis. Three additional course examinations, beyond that required for the SRPA designation, must be passed successfully to qualify for this prestigious designation.

SEE ALSO: SOCIETY OF REAL ESTATE APPRAISERS, SREA APPRAISER, and SRPA APPRAISER.

SRPA APPRAISER

The SRPA designation is given to advanced members of the Society of Real Estate Appraisers who have been found qualified to appraise all types of real estate. This designation is the second highest awarded by the Society.

INVESTOR ADVICE

The SRPA member must satisfactorily pass four additional examinations above the requirement for senior member (SRA). He or she is also required to demonstrate ability to perform an income analysis of a property and have the necessary experience in income property appraisal.

SEE ALSO: SOCIETY OF REAL ESTATE APPRAISERS, and SREA APPRAISER.

STATUTE OF FRAUDS

This term refers to state laws that require certain enforceable contractual agreements to be made in writing for the protection of all parties.

INVESTOR ADVICE

The most notable implication of the statute of frauds in real estate is the requirement that all agreements and contracts be made in writing. This requirement emphasizes the need for careful review of the earnest money receipt and offer to purchase to assure its accuracy and completeness.

At the closing table, the closing agency is powerless to interject any changes that have not been previously agreed to in writing or subsequently approved by both the buyer and seller. Changes made at the closing table can seriously delay the closing by requiring the retyping of many forms.

SEE ALSO: EARNEST MONEY RECEIPT AND OFFER TO PURCHASE and FRAUD.

STICK-BUILT HOUSE

Stick-built houses are a form of construction that utilizes wooden stud walls, usually placed on 16-inch centers, together with wooden rafters or trusses. The exterior of the home can be of many types.

INVESTOR ADVICE

The stick-built home is a standard in the United States, except in some of the warmer climates where stucco and block are more economical to construct. Stick-built construction carries over into commercial construction as well, although interior walls may require steel studs for fire prevention. Small buildings of no more than three floors usually have stick-built framing with brick or stone exteriors.

If a building is to be constructed of block or other materials and will have a finished interior, it is usually necessary to furr-out the exterior walls in order to apply the conventional drywall or panel finish. The use of a stick-built frame with brick or stone exterior is usually more economical. The one exception is where the walls are required to support unusually heavy loads.

Figure 60 illustrates the typical stick-built construction method.

SEE ALSO: COST APPROACH TO VALUE.

STORM SEWER

A system of inground catch basins, aboveground gutters, and underground pipes designed to provide proper drainage of an area to prevent excessive dampness or flooding.

INVESTOR ADVICE

When purchasing or proposing to purchase land in low-lying areas, you should carefully research all data available regarding water table level and potential for flooding. If data is not available, it may be necessary to perform an engineering study to determine the cost of flood control. A developer must show adequate planning for drainage as a part of the development approval process.

Where drainage is required, it is equally important that the disposal of collected water be considered. Where storm sewers are available in the area, you must determine if you will be allowed to connect your system to the existing collector system. In some cases, it may be necessary to allocate considerable acreage for lakes or other holding facilities. Where this is required, the useful acreage of the parcel (buildable lots) may be seriously diminished.

SEE ALSO: DEDICATION OF LAND and SUBDIVISION.

RESIDENTIAL CONSTRUCTION NOMENCLATURE

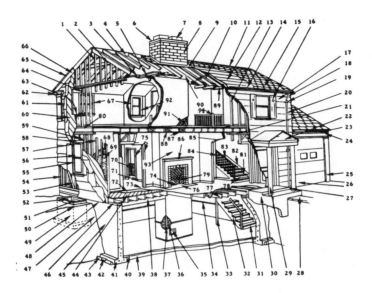

1 Gable stud	31 Basement stair riser	62 Frieze or barge board
2 Collar beam	32 Stair stringer	63 Rough header
3 Ceiling joist	33 Girder post	64 Cripple stud
4 Ridge board	34 Chair rail	65 Cornice moulding
5 Insulation	35 Cleanout door	66 Fascia board
6 Chimney cap	36 Furring strips	67 Window casing
7 Chimney pot	37 Corner stud	68 Lath
8 Chimney	38 Girder	69 Insulation
9 Chimney flashing	39 Cinder or gravel fill	70 Wainscoting
10 Rafters	40 Concrete basement floor	71 Baseboard
11 Ridge	41 Footing for foundation wall	72 Building paper
12 Roof boards	42 Tar paper strip	73 Finish floor
13 Stud	43 Foundation drain tile	74 Ash dump
14 Eave trough or gutter	44 Diagonal subflooring	75 Door trim
15 Roofing	45 Foundation wall	76 Fireplace hearth
16 Blind or shutter	46 Mud sill	77 Floor joists
17 Bevel siding	47 Backfill	78 Stair riser
18 Downspout or leader gooseneck	48 Termite shield	79 Fire brick
19 Downspout or leader strap	49 Areaway wall	80 Sole plate
20 Downspout, leader or conductor	50 Grade line	81 Stair tread
21 Double plate	51 Basement sash	82 Finish stringer
22 Entrance canopy	52 Areaway	83 Stair rail
23 Garage cornice	53 Corner brace	84 Balusters
24 Frieze	54 Corner studs	85 Plaster arch
25 Door jamb	55 Window frame	86 Mantel
26 Garage door	56 Window light	87 Floor joist
27 Downspout or leader shoe	57 Wall studs	88 Bridging
28 Sidewalk	58 Header	89 Lookout
29 Entrance post	59 Window cripple	90 Attic space
30 Entrance platform	60 Wall sheathing	91 Metal lath
	61 Building paper	92 Window sash
		93 Chimney breast
		94 Newel post

Figure 60

STRAIGHT-LINE COST RECOVERY

A method by which costs are recovered in equal amounts over a designated period. Internal Revenue Service regulations will not allow certain cost of a new project to be expensed in the initial year of operation. These items must be capitalized and recovered over a period of years.

INVESTOR ADVICE

Cost recovery is best accomplished as expeditiously as possible. Wherever accelerated recovery methods are authorized, they should be utilized to recover the investment as fast as possible. Expenses such as organizational costs, represent nonincome production assets. The faster they are recovered the better.

SEE ALSO: DOUBLE DECLINING BALANCE and SUM OF THE DIGITS.

STRAIGHT-LINE DEPRECIATION

A method of depreciation in which an equal amount is charged as an expense each year for the depreciation period selected.

INVESTOR ADVICE

An example of straight line depreciation would be a piece of office equipment costing $1,000 and authorized by the Internal Revenue Service to be depreciated on a ten-year basis. In straight-line depreciation the annual charge would be:

$$\$1000/10 = \$100 \text{ per year}$$

Although accelerated depreciation would be preferable in most cases, you must be aware that where the property is sold before being fully depreciated, all excess depreciation over and above straight-line must be recaptured and the basis cost adjusted accordingly.

SEE ALSO: DEPRECIATION RECAPTURE, DOUBLE DECLINING BALANCE, and SUM OF THE DIGITS.

SUBCHAPTER S CORPORATION

A corporation which qualifies under Internal Revenue Service regulations to have corporate profits/losses taxed to the individual shareholder(s) based on percentage of ownership.

INVESTOR ADVICE

To qualify for election as a Subchapter S corporation, the following conditions must be met:

1. It must be a domestic corporation.
2. It must no have more than 15 stockholders, all of whom are individuals or a decedent's estate.
3. No nonresident alien may be a shareholder.
4. The corporation may have only one class of stock.
5. The corporation may not get more than 80% of its gross receipts from sources outside of the United States.
6. The corporation may not get more than 20% of its gross receipts from interest, dividends, royalties, rents, annuities, and gains from sales or exchange of securities.
7. All valid stockholders must consent to the election.

A Subchapter S corporation is preferable to a partnership in that the tax is about the same, but the shareholders have limited liability. Except in cases of fraud, stockholders are isolated by the corporate veil, and are not individually responsible for debts of the corporation.

Subchapter S election is usually preferred in cases of low income or loss, or in those cases in which the stockholders are taking all profits from the corporation each year. If profits are to be plowed back for expansion purposes, a lower tax rate may be achieved through the straight corporation selection.

EXAMPLE

Corporation X has five stockholders, each owning 20% of the stock. Corporate earnings for the next few years are calculated to be $20,000 annually. All stockholders are in the 28% individual tax bracket and do not require dividends. The company is growing and will require additional assets to continue its present pattern.

If Subchapter S is elected, each stockholder will have to pay personal taxes on

$$\$20,000 \times 20\% = \$4,000$$

Each will be taxed 28% x $4000 = $1,120 each, for a total tax of 5 x $1,120 = $5,600.

If they elect to operate as a straight corporation, the total tax will be $20,000 x 15% = $3,000. Of course, the $17,000 remaining in the corporation after taxes is locked in. If the stockholders want those profits at some time in the future, a dividend must be paid, and that will be taxed again at the individual's tax rates.

The guidelines below are useful in deciding the type of corporation that is best for you.

Subchapter S Corporation

• Small size with earnings under $50,000 per year;

• corporate earnings needed by owners in addition to that provided by salaries;

• minimum plans for expansion of the business requiring additional capital;

• all owners directly involved in the company's operation.

Standard Corporation

• Most earnings required for business expansion;

• salaries satisfy most owner cash requirements;

• several owners, some not directly involved in the operation of the company;

• earnings exceed $50,000 per year.

SEE ALSO: CORPORATION VERSUS PARTNERSHIP.

SUBCONTRACTOR
A person who contracts to do a portion of a large task, for which another has contracted.

INVESTOR ADVICE

Regardless of the size of the contractor's business, few are able to perform all tasks economically in-house. Contractors normally employ subcontractor specialists to perform portions of the overall job. For instance, the contractor for a shopping center might do most of the construction in-house but would subcontract such tasks as:

- parking lot grading and pavement;
- roofing;
- glass work;
- heating and ventilating; and
- floor covering installation.

Subcontractors may be paid directly by the contractor or by the agency providing the construction loan. In this case, the lender may require three signatures on the lien waiver payment voucher. (a) the property owner and borrower of construction funds, (b) the contractor; and (c) the subcontractor.

ATTENTION! Don't approve payments to subcontractors until their work has been completed and verified by you or your representative.

Remember, your property secures the payments of subcontractors who are not paid by the contractor. Contractor bonding can prevent losses from contractor nonpayment.
SEE ALSO: CONTRACTOR'S LIEN.

SUBCONTRACTOR LIEN

This term refers to a lien placed on a property by a subcontractor who has not been paid for services or materials furnished.

INVESTOR ADVICE

Most title insurance does not cover items that are not a matter of record on the date of closure. Subcontractors and contractors are allowed a period of time after completion of their last work to file claims. This period is usually 60–90 days.

A contractor or subcontractor doing a minimum task on the day prior to closing has the state-allowable period to file claim for payment. In Utah, the law allows a contractor 100 days for filing, and subcontractors 80 days.

Know your state laws! Best of all, make no payments or authorize your lender to make no payments without signed lien waivers and inspections to assure that the work has actually been accomplished. Even though the contractor waives the right to further payment, it doesn't assure that the work has been accomplished—inspect prior to payment.

SUBDIVIDED LAND

Subdivided land is a parcel of land that has been divided into smaller tracts, lots, or portions.

INVESTOR ADVICE

Most localities have strict rules and regulations regarding subdividing land. It is not just a matter of having a surveyor survey the property and subdivide it on an engineering drawing.

Some localities require subdividers to perform certain tasks other than the physical subdivision procedure. It may be necessary to install streets, curbs and gutters, sidewalks, sanitary sewers, storm sewers, and other required utilities. Each subdivision plan must be approved and periodically inspected by a number of agencies including, flood control, water department, fire department, and so forth.

Subdivision restrictions are often binding on the buyer as well as the seller. The following Salt Lake County, Utah, regulation is typical:

Sec. 19-7-5. **Violation.** *No person shall subdivide any tract or parcel of land located wholly or in part in the county except in compliance with the provisions of this title. No person shall purchase, sell or exchange any parcel of land which is in any part of a subdivision or a proposed subdivision submitted to the planning commission, nor offer for recording in the office of the county recorder, any deed conveying such parcel of land or any fee interest therein, unless such subdivision has been created pursuant to and in accordance with the provisions of this title.*

SEE ALSO: RESTRICTIVE COVENANTS, SUBDIVISION, and ZONING.

SUBDIVISION

A subdivision is a group of lots or parcels of land resulting from the subdividing of a larger tract of land. Subdivisions may be named, numbered, or both.

INVESTOR ADVICE

Before attempting to subdivide land, carefully research the local requirements for subdividing and for the sale of those parcels which result from the action. In most states, securities regulations carefully monitor the sale and all offers to sell lots within subdivisions of certain sizes, typically large subdivisions of one, five, or more acres per lot.

There have been numerous instances of unscrupulous developers who have sold useless land parcels in the western states, Florida, and other areas. Most states have now enacted security regulations to prevent this practice.

The Utah Uniform Land Sales Practices Act was passed in 1973 and is typical of those in other states. This act provides that:

- The sale of subdivisions of 10 or more units be registered.

- A public offering statement must be provided to prospective buyers at least 48 hours prior to signing a contract.

- The offering statement must acknowledge any encumbrances affecting more than one unit, the consequences to the purchaser if the lien is not discharged, and the steps, if any, taken to protect the purchaser.

- The offering statement must indicate what existing provisions have been made for access, sewage disposal, water supply, and other public utilities, or, if they are not presently available but are feasible, the estimated cost to the purchaser of their procurement.

- A copy of all public reports must be made available to the prospective purchaser.

SEE ALSO: CONTRACT, LIEN, and LOT RELEASE SYSTEM.

SUBJECT-TO CLAUSE

This term refers to a modifying clause, contained in an offer to sell or purchase, which preconditions the transaction based on some stated event or situation.

INVESTOR ADVICE

Subject-to clauses are excellent escape hatches. For instance, most offers to buy real estate are subject to the buyer obtaining a mortgage. Your offer might also require that it be subject to your close of another sale to provide the funds. Your offer might even be conditioned on your ability to obtain a mortgage at an interest rate not to exceed a stated amount.

If your purchase cannot be concluded without some other event occurring first, your offer should be made subject to those provisions. The following statements are commonly found in the earnest money receipt and offer to purchase:

"This offer is subject to the buyer qualifying for a loan of at least $_____ and the loan being granted."

*   *   *   *   *   *   *   *   *   *   *

"This offer is subject the close of the sale of the owner's residence at 121 E. Longstreet, which is currently under contract to sell."

*   *   *   *   *   *   *   *   *   *   *

"This offer is subject to the buyer obtaining a mortgage at an interest rate not to exceed 9.5% APR"

*   *   *   *   *   *   *   *   *   *   *

"This offer is subject to buyer obtaining an FHA loan in which the seller is not required to pay over four discount points."

*   *   *   *   *   *   *   *   *   *   *

"This offer is subject to the buyer obtaining a mortgage commitment in writing on/before (date)."

SEE ALSO: EARNEST MONEY RECEIPT AND OFFER TO PURCHASE.

SUBLEASE

A sublease is a lease obtained from a lessee who has control of the property by virtue of a lease from the property owner.

INVESTOR ADVICE

Before signing a sublease, you should ask to read the original lease to assure yourself that your lessee has the right to sublease the property and under what conditions.

It is advisable that leases for residential and commercial property either prohibit subleases or restrict subleasing to those parties approved by the landlord. Without these provisions, you are subject to acquiring tenants who you would otherwise reject for one or more reasons.

SEE ALSO: LEASE, LESSEE, LESSOR, SANDWICH LEASE, and TENANT SELECTION CRITERIA.

SUBORDINATE DEBENTURE

A subordinate debenture is a certificate of indebtedness that has a lower than first claim on the assets of the borrower.

INVESTOR ADVICE

A real estate investment in a trust offering subordinated debentures (bonds) may be perfectly legitimate and a reasonable risk. Before investing, however, you should carefully review the prospectus paying particular attention to cash flow projections and the number of times coverage of interest. For instance, the cash flow from the operation should be at least twice the total of all mortgages, superior positioned bonds, and obligations. This will assure payment of your interest even in the event of an economic downturn.

Convertible debentures are usually a better real estate investment than ordinary debentures. The convertible debenture has a feature allowing the debenture to be traded for a set number of common shares of stock. Where the project is a success, common stock ownership will provide not only income but eventual capital gains as well. If the project is less successful, the bonds can be retained to assure the stated income.

SEE ALSO: CONVERTIBLE DEBENTURE, JUNIOR MORTGAGE, SUBORDINATION.

SUBORDINATION

Subordination is the acceptance of a secondary creditor position to another creditor.

INVESTOR ADVICE

In the sale of land for development, it is often necessary to accept a secondary loan position (subordinate) to allow the buyer to borrow funds for construction and development of the property. Bankers, who advance funds for property development, do so only if they are in the prime (first) position.

A secondary position can be reasonably secure, providing the finished project is valued in excess of the first loan plus the amount which you have subordinated. The real risk, in these situations, is that something will happen to prevent completion of the project, thereby placing your loan position in jeopardy.

Subordination should be accepted only as a last resort. If the buyer is unable to proceed without this approach, it can be considered. Before acceptance, you should determine that the risk involved is worth the gain from the property sale at that time.

Liens or other encumbrances on a property can also be subordinated to induce a lender to make a loan to the property owner.

The following situation is a typical one requiring a seller to accept a second position:

EXAMPLE

A syndicate approached Mr. Farmer with an offer to purchase his 10-acre property for a proposed shopping center. The offering price was $100,000 per acre, which represented a very good offer.

One provision of the sale was that the seller accept 50% down, with the balance of $500,000 to be subordinated to the required construction loan and until completion of the project and long-term financing was arranged.

The completed value of the project was estimated to be $10,000,000. The construction loan would be for $7,000,000 or $3,000,000 less than the total value of the improved property. Mr. Farmer believed that this equity would be ample to protect his $500,000 second mortgage interest. He agreed to the proposed sale.

SEE ALSO: CONTRACT, JUNIOR MORTGAGE, and LOT RELEASE SYSTEM.

SUBPOENA DUCES TECUM

This term refers to a supplemental proceeding following an award of judgment which requires the debtor to submit a record of his or her assets for examination.

INVESTOR ADVICE

After the debtor assets have been made known as a result of the subpoena duces tecum, the creditor must then request the court clerk to issue an order of execution. The sheriff then serves a copy of the execution on the debtor, demanding payment. If payment is not made, the sheriff is empowered to seize and sell all realty and other assets necessary to satisfy the judgment.

Judgments in most states are valid for about 10 years and are against all property located within the state. It is in your best interest to pursue the judgment to assure prompt payment. If the amount due is small, you may want to delay action until a larger debtor forecloses, at which time your claim will be paid in its order of filing.

SEE ALSO: JUDGMENT, LIEN, SMALL CLAIMS COURT.

SUBSCRIPTION AGREEMENT

A subscription agreement is a document signed by a potential investor which acknowledges receipt of all documentation regarding a proposed syndication, and which affirms that the investor is aware of the possible loss of investment position if payment is not made. The signer also acknowledges that the document is not official until countersigned by the partnership.

INVESTOR ADVICE

In completing the subscription agreement, you may also be asked to name your representative responsible for your decision to invest in the project. These representatives are normally compensated for their work by the partnership.

General partners and syndicators may delay the actual implementation of the project until sufficient subscription agreements have been received to assure success of the venture. In this respect, the subscription agreement operates much like the letter of intent, except the signors are bound to purchase *if* the fund-raising effort is a success.

SEE ALSO: GENERAL PARTNER, LIMITED PARTNERSHIP, PROSPECTUS, and SYNDICATION.

SUFFERANCE LEASE

This term refers to retention of property possession after termination of the lease and without the landlords permission—also known as *estate at sufferance.*

INVESTOR ADVICE

An estate at sufferance exists during the period after the expiration of a lease and before the tenant is evicted. In some states, such as Utah, the lessor landlord is forbidden to remove the tenant but is required to obtain a court order of eviction, after which the sheriff will effect the necessary eviction.

Careful property management will prevent this occurrence. As landlord, you should be constantly aware of current lease expirations. At some convenient period prior to the expiration, the intent of the tenant should be ascertained. If the tenant refuses to renew the lease, immediate advertising and other steps should be taken to acquire a replacement tenant. Constant follow up action is required to assure that the tenant is preparing to and will vacate the premises on schedule.

SEE ALSO: ESTATE AT SUFFERANCE.

SUM OF THE DIGITS

This is a method of amortization, depreciation, or cost recovery in which acceleration of the process is achieved.

INVESTOR ADVICE

This method get its name from the mathematical process from which it is computed. The computation is as follows:

1. The numbered periods involved are summed. A 12-year period would yield a sum of 1 + 2 + 3 and so on for a total of 78.
2. The amount to be amortized, depreciated, or recovered is determined by dividing the total by the sum of the digits.
3. For the first period, multiply the amount obtained in item 2 by 12; by 11 for the second period; by 10 for the third period; and so on until the total sum is amortized, depreciated, or recovered.

EXAMPLE

Mr. Smith buys an office copy machine which the Internal Revenue Service allows to be depreciated on a five-year basis. The cost of the machine is $7,200. What is the indicated depreciation for the five-year period?

The sum of the five-year digits is 5 + 4 + 3 + 2 + 1 = 15. The schedule for depreciation is therefore:

Year		Depreciation Allowed
1	5/15 x $7,200 =	$2,400.00
2	4/15 x $7,200 =	$1,920.00
3	3/15 x $7,200 =	$1,440.00
4	2/15 x $7,200 =	$ 960.00
5	1/15 x $7,200 =	$ 480.00
	Total	$7,200.00

Internal Revenue Service regulations allow certain capitalized costs and equipments to be recovered and depreciated by utilization of the sum of the digits method.

SEE ALSO: DOUBLE DECLINING BALANCE, RULE OF 78S, and STRAIGHT-LINE DEPRECIATION/RECOVERY.

SUPER-SIX MAGIC NUMBERS

The six values most often considered by investors who use compound interest tables.

INVESTOR ADVICE

The six most common uses of the compound interest tables are:

1. future value of $1 (see Figure 30),
2. future value of $1/period (see Figure 30),
3. present value of $1 (see Figure 40),
4. present value of $1/period (see Figure 50),
5. periodic payment, and
6. sinking fund.

All of these six values can be obtained directly from the four basic tables shown in Figures 31, 32, 49, and 50 or derived by simple multiplication or division of a factor found in those tables.

All of the modern hand-held financial calculators provide for direct calculation of these numbers for an infinite range of periods and interest values.

SEE ALSO: AMORTIZATION SCHEDULE, FUTURE VALUE OF $1, FUTURE VALUE OF $1/PERIOD, PRESENT VALUE OF $1, PRESENT VALUE OF $1/PERIOD, SINKING FUND.

SURVEY

1. An engineering procedure which defines the boundaries of a parcel of property by bearings and length of sides.
2. A study of a locality or situation to determine facts bearing on a proposed action.

INVESTOR ADVICE

Before buying property which has not been surveyed for a long period of time (say, within the past 50 years), a survey should be ordered to determine the accuracy of the apparent boundaries and to calculate the acreage enclosed.

An offer for such property should be made contingent on your acceptance of the resulting survey. It is also advised that the offer be based on dollars per acre, square foot, front foot, and so forth, rather than for the parcel. Thus, errors found by the survey will adjust the total offering amount in accordance with the amount of land contained.

Proposed developments often require studies (surveys) of the locality to determine the feasibility of the project. Survey results may also affect decisions as to size, type and cost of the proposed development.

Studies may be of one or more of the following types:

- feasibility,
- economic,
- demographic,
- rental rate,
- existing space or units,
- lessee preferences, and
- location decision.

SEE ALSO: DEMOGRAPHICS, LAND IDENTIFICATION METHODS.

SWEAT EQUITY

Work performed in lieu of a cash downpayment.

INVESTOR ADVICE

Sweat equity is a good method of obtaining the required down payment for purchase of property. It is more common in the purchase of low-income housing, but it is also appropriate for larger and more expensive properties which require repair or modernization to qualify for a mortgage loan.

Tasks generally performed as sweat equity are those requiring lower levels of building or contractor skills, but they are actually limited only by the buyer's ability. They include the following:

- exterior and interior painting,

- landscaping,

- paper hanging,

- preoccupancy clean-up,

- floor finishing,

- screen installation,

- lawn sprinkler installation, and

- trash and debris removal.

Currently there are several low-income housing projects under construction throughout the United States in which the owner is required to provide a set number of labor hours as a provision for a home purchase. In these situations, more complicated skilled jobs are accomplished under the direction of knowledgeable supervisors, who employ the future homeowner more or less as apprentice craftsperson.

SEE ALSO: MORTGAGE.

SYNDICATED EQUITY POOLS

Any organization of multiple owners (usually limited partnerships) formed for the purpose of raising equity to invest in real estate.

INVESTOR ADVICE

> **THINK!** Buying into a syndicated pool is like buying without inspection.

The problem of investing in this type of vehicle is the vagueness inherent in the prospectus, since little can be revealed as to contemplated earnings or potential capital gains.

Your only protection when investing in this type of operation is the background and reputation of the general partners who are forming the syndicate.

SEE ALSO: CORPORATION, LIMITED PARTNERSHIP, REAL ESTATE INVESTMENT TRUST, SYNDICATION.

SYNDICATION

A joint venture involving two or more persons who pool their assets for the purpose of investment in real estate.

INVESTOR ADVICE

You should ask yourself the following questions before joining any syndicate:

- How much will it cost me, including all fees and hidden costs?

- What is the return based on the risk? Are there other projects that are better?

- What is the track record of the syndicate organizers?

- Have I carefully read all literature provided on the syndication, and do I understand it?

- If property is to be purchased, have I inspected it?

- How often and how well will I be advised of the progress of the project?

- Have all legal requirements, prospectus, and so forth been approved by the state or federal authorities having jurisdiction over such ventures?

- Is the proposed method of profit distribution beneficial to me?

- What are my safeguards against potential fraud or misrepresentation?

- What happens to my investment if I decide to withdraw?

- What percent of the ownership or profits are allocated to the syndicators?

- Do the objectives and timing of the syndication appear reasonable?

- **VERY IMPORTANT**—How liquid is my investment in the event that I need to repossess my funds?

SEE ALSO: LIMITED PARTNERSHIPS, REAL ESTATE CORPORATION, REAL ESTATE INVEST-MENT TRUST, and SYNDICATED EQUITY POOLS.

SYNDICATE VEHICLES

The form of the business arrangement between joint owners used to finance the project or syndication.

INVESTMENT ADVICE

Vehicles commonly employed in syndication are the limited partnership, real estate investment trust, real estate corporation, or syndicated equity pools.

SEE ALSO: CORPORATION, LIMITED PARTNERSHIP, REAL ESTATE INVESTMENT TRUST, SYNDICATED EQUITY POOLS, SYNDICATION.

T

Take-Out Letter
Tax Deed
Tax-Free Trades
Tax Lien
Tax Reform Act of 1986 (TRA)
Tax Rolls
Tax Sale
Tax Shelter
Tenancy at Sufferance
Tenancy at Will
Tenancy by the Entireties
Tenancy from Month-to-Month
Tenancy from Year-to-Year
Tenancy in Common
Tenant
Tenant Caretakers
Tenant Selection Criteria
Tenements
Terminal Shape

Testamentary Trust
Thin Corporation
Three-Party Blanket
Time Is of the Essence Clause
Time-Sharing Ownership
Title Insurance
Title Report
Torrens System
Town House
Township
Tract Housing
Trading Area Analysis
Triple Net Lease
Trust
Trust Account
Trust Deed
Trustee
Trustor
Twenty-Four Hour Contingency Clause

T

TAKE-OUT LETTER

A take-out letter is an advanced commitment for a long-term loan obtained by a mortgage banker. The letter states the loan amount, fees chargeable, and the loan delivery date.

INVESTOR ADVICE

The receipt of the take-out letter greatly simplifies the financing process. Once your banker has received that letter, he or she will arrange for an interim builder's loan, and the project can get under way. A take-out letter is shown as Figure 61.

If a take-out letter is not received, your mortgage banker must proceed with interim financing and continue the search for long-term money. Since the banker has committed to find financing, you can proceed; however, the interest rate may vary according to the final source of the long-term funds.

SEE ALSO: CONSTRUCTION LOAN, MORTGAGE COMPANY, and POINTS.

TAX DEED

A tax deed is given by a sheriff or marshall when property is sold for delinquent taxes.

INVESTOR ADVICE

Remember that property purchased at a tax sale is subject to redemption by the former owner. An owner who loses property for failure to pay taxes is far more likely to redeem the property than one who loses it due to nonpayment of a mortgage loan.

Nonpayment of a mortgage loan is a strong indication of a serious financial situation, which is unlikely to change. The nonpayment of taxes can signify a temporary financial problem or a deliberate use of county funds, which are often available at a lower rate than bank loans. County governments have become aware of this latter problem and have begun to raise their delinquency interest rates to discourage this practice.

Immediately after the last day that taxes can be paid, the treasurer will file a tax lien on the property for which taxes are delinquent. A tax sale of the property is usually not initiated until the taxes have been due for two to three years. This varies from state to state.

Utah law provides for taxes to become a lien on January 1 of each year after nonpayment. Four years are provided the land holder before the property is sold for taxes. An additional redemption period of four years after the tax sale is provided for the owner to pay the taxes and fees due and redeem the property.

SEE ALSO: SHERIFF'S DEED, TAX LIEN, and TAX SALE.

TAX-FREE TRADES

Tax-free trades are investor trades for like property, which avoid the payment of capital gains on the property that was traded.

INVESTOR ADVICE

Property trades which qualify as tax free trades do not really avoid taxes. They delay the payment of gains. When a property is traded in which a capital gain has been

GOLDEN FLEECE MORTGAGE COMPANY
242 S. Main Street
Anytown, USA

Rocksolid Developers, Inc.
445 N. Green Street
Anytown, USA 99452
Atten: George Smith

Dear Mr. Smith:

It is with great pleasure that we inform you that the
Metropolitan Insurance Corporation has agreed to finance
your new project at the Consolidated Center. The following details are applicable:

Loan Amount	$10,000,000
Interest Rate	Prime Rate + 1% *
Loan Fee	1.5 points
Loan Delivery Date	March 15, 1990

* Prime Rate to be based on rate as of the first
  day of the month in which loan is closed.

The above delivery date is in consideration of an estimated project completion on/before July 15, 1989 and an
estimated selling day of January 15, 1990. If there
should be any delay in your plans, it is imperative that
you contact the undersigned without delay.

The above loan fee is payable to Metropolitan Life
Insurance Company at the time the loan is closed. We will
add an additional 0.5 points as our finder's fee, for a
total cost to you of 2.0 points or $200,000.

Yours truly,

Jasper P. Coinage
V.P., Acquisitions

cc: Metropolitan Ins. Co.

Figure 61

realized, the new property cost basis is adjusted downward for the amount of the gains postponed.

EXAMPLE

Mr. G trades 500 acres of commercial property, held for investment, for a warehouse. Mr. G paid $100,000 for the land 10 years ago. The warehouse was traded at a fair market value of $150,000, the value placed on Mr. G's land. Mr. G had realized a capital gain of

$$150,000 - \$100,000 = \$50,000$$

Mr. G must adjust his records to indicate a cost basis for the warehouse of

$$150,000 - \$50,000 = \$100,000$$

Since Mr. G. is in the 28% tax bracket, he has avoided payment of $14,000 until a later date—money which he can keep invested.

Prior to passage of the Tax Reform Act of 1986, the deferral of taxes was even more advantageous if the seller was in a very high tax bracket and the capital gains in that year might place him or her in an even higher tax bracket. The seller could save even more by spreading the gains over the term of a contract. The seller could avoid the extra high taxes by payment on the principal payment received. Now that there is essentially a top tax bracket of 28%, there is no real savings, just a delay in payment whether by deferring the gains entirely or deferring gains through the contract process.

SEE ALSO: CONTRACT and TAX REFORM ACT OF 1986 (TRA).

TAX LIEN

A lien placed on property in which taxes are delinquent. This becomes a matter of public record and if not cleared in a specified time will result in a sheriff's sale of the property to satisfy the outstanding lien.

INVESTOR ADVICE

Property sold for nonpayment of taxes may be redeemed by the property owner if payment is made in a stipulated time. The time allowed may extend to five or more years, depending on the specific state law.

SEE ALSO: LIEN and SHERIFF'S SALE.

TAX REFORM ACT OF 1986 (TRA)

The Tax Reform Act was a major revision of the tax code, passed by Congress in 1986.

INVESTOR ADVICE

The major changes in the TRA effecting real estate investors are:

- Creation of a new type of income called *passive*, whose losses cannot be deducted against other types of income except in some minor instances.

- A change in the taxability of capital gains. After 1988, both long- and short-term gains are taxable as ordinary income.

- Limited partnerships and similar tax shelter organizations are much more closely examined than before.

- Losses of passive income cannot be written off against active income. Syndications now stand on their own merits.

- Depreciation times on most properties were extended.

- The at-risk provisions, regarding deductibility of losses, were extended to real estate.

- There was a reduction in the number of tax brackets, and there will be a top bracket of 28% when the law is fully implemented.

- Personal tax exemptions are to be adjusted for inflation, beginning in 1990.

SEE ALSO: ACTIVE INCOME and PASSIVE INCOME.

TAX ROLLS

This term refers to the list of property owners and assessed evaluations on their properties which is maintained by the appropriate county official, usually the tax assessor.

INVESTOR ADVICE

The county tax rolls are an excellent source of data for real estate traders. The tax officials maintain an up-to-date record of all property in the county, by official plats and tax identification (serial) numbers.

If you desire to rezone property or to locate the owners of a certain parcel, the official records are available. Rezoning usually requires that the property owner desiring to rezone property notify all other property owners in a specified area.[1] The official tax records are the source of this data.

SEE ALSO: ASSESSMENTS, LEGAL DESCRIPTION, MILL RATE.

TAX SALE

A tax sale is the sale of property in which the owner has failed to pay taxes in the time specified by law.

INVESTOR ADVICE

Check your local laws to determine the time allowed for redemption after the tax sale. Also, the time after the lien is recorded against the property and the property is sold will vary from state to state.

SEE ALSO: SHERIFF'S SALE, TAX DEED, and TAX LIEN.

TAX SHELTER

A tax shelter is a taxable entity that provides a tax loss that can shelter income from another source.

INVESTMENT ADVICE

The provisions of the Tax Reform Act of 1986 virtually eliminate tax shelters through the reclassification of income from these activities as passive income. Passive losses are only deductible against passive gains; however, any additional losses can be carried forward for possible deduction against future gains.

Depreciation allowable may be considered as a type of tax shelter, since the amount allowed as an expense is a noncash deduction. Theoretically, the depreciation allowance is equal to the actual wear-out. This is not true, as the depreciation rates are much greater than the actual wear-out rate.

SEE ALSO: PASSIVE INCOME, TAX REFORM ACT OF 1986.

TENANCY AT SUFFERANCE

Tenancy at sufferance refers to one who comes into possession of land and tenements by lawful title and continues in possession after title has been transferred.

INVESTOR ADVICE

A simple example of tenancy at sufferance is a tenant who remains in possession of leased property after expiration of the lease term. Acceptance of rental payments by the landlord after the expiration of a lease may imply a month-to-month tenancy.

WARNING! Acceptance of rent after the lease expires may create a month-to-month tenancy.

SEE ALSO: TENANCY AT WILL.

TENANCY AT WILL

Tenancy at will refers to permission to occupy and use lands and tenements at the will of the owner.

INVESTOR ADVICE

A situation of tenancy at will is not recommended. It is better to charge a nominal rate of, say, $1 per year and thus make the occupancy a legal lease. Continued tenancy at will may eventually provide a case for tenant ownership by adverse possession.

SEE ALSO: ADVERSE POSSESSION.

TENANCY BY THE ENTIRETIES

Tenancy by the entireties refers to an estate existing between two parties with equal rights of possession and enjoyment during their joint lives and with the right of survivorship—also known as joint ownership with right of survivorship (JTWROS).

INVESTOR ADVICE

This type of ownership is usually taken by husband and wife or two other closely related or friendly individuals. It provides for automatic transfer of ownership to the survivor on the death of one of the individuals. This automatic transfer by deed avoids the need for probate of the decedent's estate in order to transfer title.

The survivor gains sole ownership by presentation of a death certificate and evidence that the decedent's estate has paid any/all state taxes due.

Individuals with large estates may not desire to acquire property in this deed form. You should consult your tax accountant and estate planner prior to closing on any property acquisition to assure that the type of title taken is in your best interest.

Tenancy by the entirety can be terminated by:

- conveyance by both spouses to another;
- conveyance by one spouse to the other;
- divorce; and
- death of both spouses.

Tenancy by the entirety is not recognized in all states, principally those with community property laws.
SEE ALSO: DECEDENT, ESTATE PLANNING, JOINT TENANCY, and PROBATE.

TENANCY FROM MONTH-TO-MONTH

Tenancy from month-to-month refers to a tenant who has a valid lease calling for monthly rent but no specific period of the lease stipulated.

INVESTOR ADVICE

Many leases or oral agreements are of this type. As a landlord, you must recognize that the tenant has the right to continue renting the property until such time as he or she is notified to the contrary.

Similarly, the tenant is liable for rent unless he or she gives due notice to the landlord. The period for notification by tenant and landlord varies from state to state.

In Utah, a lease for a specified period terminates on the date indicated. Where a landlord accepts additional rental money, a periodic estate is established which can be terminated with 15 days' notice. Possession without a signed lease creates an estate at will. An estate at will can be terminated with 5 days' notice.
SEE ALSO: ESTATE AT WILL, HOLDOVER TENANT, and PERIODIC ESTATE.

TENANCY FROM YEAR-TO-YEAR

A tenancy from year-to-year exists at the expiration of a year-to-year lease, with neither the tenant nor the landlord giving notice of termination.

INVESTOR ADVICE

When a tenant has a lease for a year or longer and remains in possession after the term has expired, he or she is said to be a holdover tenant with a year-to-year tenancy.

The tenant cannot force the landlord to accept a year-to-year tenancy, but the landlord may accept this arrangement. A tenant with a year-to-year lease who holds over becomes liable for another year's rent.
SEE ALSO: TENANCY FROM MONTH-TO-MONTH, and PERIODIC ESTATE.

TENANCY IN COMMON

Tenancy in common is the ownership of equal or various other unequal undivided interests in a property by two or more persons and without the right of survivorship—also known as joint tenancy.

INVESTOR ADVICE

Joint tenancy is a very cumbersome method of ownership. Even among children who have inherited the property, it becomes a source of friction and dispute.

If one of the tenants decides that they no longer want to own a part of the property, they effectively have only two alternatives:

1. Sell their portion to one of the other owners who is willing to buy.
2. Sue to have the property partitioned, after which their portion can be sold to anyone.

In preparing a will, it is recommended that the property to be bequeathed:

1. should be left to only one person, with others to receive equal value in other assets;
2. should be subdivided and deeded to the beneficiaries, prior to death, with the benefactor retaining a life estate;
3. should be sold and the proceeds divided; or
4. should be handled as suggested by your attorney and/or estate planner.

Tenancy in common has only one requirement: joint tenancy. When that tenant dies, his or her ownership passes on in accordance with his or her will or in accordance with the law. The new owner also is a joint tenant.

Each joint tenant owner is subject to liens or judgment against ownership. Any tenant can mortgage, lease, convey, or otherwise dispose of his or her portion of the property as desired. A tenancy in common is terminated whenever the unity of possession is terminated; this can occur in two ways—sale or partition.

Any one tenant can force partition. If partition is not possible, a court can appoint a referee who orders its sale and rateable distribution of the proceeds.

SEE ALSO: BENEFICIARY, DECEDENT, and LIFE ESTATE.

TENANT

A tenant is one who is allowed possession of real estate for a fixed period or at the will of the landlord.

INVESTOR ADVICE
A tenancy can be for a period (periodic estate) or at the will of the landlord (estate at will).
SEE ALSO: TENANCY AT SUFFERANCE and TENANCY AT WILL.

TENANT CARETAKERS

Tenant caretakers are given tenancy in exchange for a low or no rental plus specified services to be rendered in maintaining the property—sometimes combined with on-site management.

INVESTOR ADVICE
Large commercial and residential properties require some on-site management as well as continuous maintenance, which is the landlord's responsibility. Both of these tasks can be preformed at minimum expense by a designated tenant as caretaker/manager. Payment for these services is generally made in reduced rental rates to the appointed caretaker.

Where you are not a resident of the leased property, an appointed on-site manager is required. The manager should be given the authority to:

• show prospective tenants units for rent;

• perform minor maintenance tasks or call the required professionals to perform emergency and/or necessary repairs;

- collect rents;

- perform joint inventory of entering or exiting tenants;

- report tenant actions not authorized by the terms of their lease; and

- keep you advised of all necessary information.

Additional tasks may be assigned to the on-site manager but are probably best retained by you. These are:

- deposit of rental funds;

- maintenance of the rental deposit account to include returns to tenants on expiration of their lease;

- prospective tenant reference checking;

- payment of utility and repair bills; and

- bookkeeping.

Regarding this latter task, discounts of rental for services rendered should be recorded as management expenses. The rental should reflect the full rental, not the reduced price due to services rendered.
SEE ALSO: ON-SITE MANAGER.

TENANT SELECTION CRITERIA
The basis by which prospective tenants are screened for approval prior to signing a lease.

INVESTOR ADVICE
Both residential and commercial properties must have established criteria for screening prospective tenants. This is to assure compatibility of tenants in the project and overall satisfaction of all tenants. Screening criteria must not be made on the basis of age, race, or national origin.

Screening is accomplished by means of an application to rent, filed by the prospective tenant with the landlord. These applications should give permission for the landlord to examine the applicant's credit history and provide references from former landlords. A personal interview is often used as a final step in the approval process.

In commercial projects, the applicant's intended use of the property is as important as his or her financial capability. A shopping center, for instance, would like to attract tenants whose business complements other businesses in the project and who's clientele will provide a synergistic effect. The landlord may wish to avoid direct tenant competition in the same or similar business.

In spite of the landlord motivation to rent quickly the entire project, it is in the landlord's and tenant's best interests to obtain good compatible tenants who will succeed in their chosen businesses and remain good tenants for an extended period of time.

NOTICE! Small incorporated business owners should be asked to sign leases as (a) officers of the corporation, and (b) individuals.

Except in the case of fraud or illegal actions, you may not go beyond the corporate veil in search of rents due. Where the tenant also signs as an individual, his or her entire estate can be subject to judgment and liens.

SEE ALSO: LEASE.

TENEMENTS

Tenements include everything of a permanent nature that is attached to the land; that is, buildings, fences, roads, and so forth.

INVESTOR ADVICE

In purchasing real estate, the term *permanent* becomes an important factor in classifying what is personalty and what is real estate. The two criteria which separate personalty and real estate are: (a) permanently attached, and (b) with intent to remain.

In preparing the earnest money receipt and offer to purchase, carefully spell out all items that *you* consider to be personalty to be included in the sale. An acceptance of the offer then binds the seller to that agreement. At the closing, the closing officer should provide you with a bill of sale covering all items of personalty transferred with the sale.

SEE ALSO: HEREDITAMENTS and PERSONALTY.

TERMINAL SHAPE

Terminal shape is one of the four aspects of the income stream analyzed by an appraiser of income property.

INVESTOR ADVICE

The appraiser of income property is required to analyze the income stream regarding four aspects:

1. quantity of income per period;
2. quality of income;
3. duration of that expected income stream; and
4. shape of the income stream.

Income streams usually take one of the following forms:

1. single payment at the end, which is adjusted to present value;
2. level series of payments; or
3. declining level of payments.

SEE ALSO: CAPITALIZATION OF INCOME, CAPITALIZATION RATE, and OVERALL RETURN ON INVESTMENT.

TESTAMENTARY TRUST

A testamentary trust is a trust established in accordance with the instructions of a will which names the trustees to manage the trust, directs the transfer of assets, names the beneficiaries of income from the trust operations, and designates the remainder men, who will receive the corpus of the trust at the time of its demise.

INVESTOR ADVICE

The testamentary trust is an excellent way to assure the continuance of a real estate operation without undue interruption due to the death of the decedent. The trust can provide:

- for continuity of operation;
- appointment of qualified trustees to manage the assets;
- income for the beneficiaries named; and
- eventual disposition of the corpus (assets) in a timely manner and to those the decedent desires to receive them.

Part of the assets allocated to the trust may be the proceeds of insurance policies on the life of the decedent. In this case the trust is usually called an *insurance trust.*

Figure 57 indicates the life of a testamentary trust. Generally, this is established by transfer of the decedent's property to the trust. The decedent's spouse may also elect to have his or her part of the estate also transferred to the trust, in which case he or she is entitled to receive the income from the trust and *any additional amounts of principal required to maintain a normal standard of living.*

Generally, the living spouse is appointed as one of the trustees, along with other family members or institutions necessary to manage the trust funds and carry out the intent of the trustor. Where the trust is sizeable, it is generally recommended that a permanent institution be appointed as one of the trustees, even though a management fee will be required for the services rendered.

You, as the trustor, and your advisors will want to consider the following in preparing the trust instrument details:

- expected value of the trust fund;
- age and competency of the beneficiaries;
- close relatives who are capable and willing to serve as trustees;
- tax laws currently in existence;
- anticipated final expenses and estate taxes to be paid;
- prior gifts made and gift taxes paid;
- number and age of remainder men;
- amount of cash available at your death to liquidate final expenses and estate taxes; and
- types of assets to be included in the trust.

SEE ALSO: BENEFICIARY, DECEDENT, REMAINDER MEN, TRUSTEE, and WILL.

THIN CORPORATION

A thin corporation is considered to be undercapitalized—debt to equity ratio is too high.

INVESTOR ADVICE

Everyone would like to form a real estate corporation with a minimum amount of money, borrow all that is necessary to accomplish the task, and receive a high rate of return on equity by the leveraging effect.

To establish a public syndication in which the general partner is a corporation, the syndicator must meet certain Internal Revenue Service criteria, known as safe harbor rules. This will assure that the syndication will be taxed as a partnership.

The Internal Revenue Service guidelines are as follows:

- The general partner must have a net worth, not considering its investment in the syndication, in an amount which equals the lesser of $250,000 or 15% of the amount invested by the limited partners, where the limited partner's investment is $2.5 million or less. If the limited partners have invested more than $2.5 million, the general partner must invest 10%.

- The limited partners, taken as a group, cannot own, directly or indirectly, 20% or more of the corporate general partner or any company associated with it.

The safe harbor rules only apply to corporate general partners. If the general partner is an individual, the requirement is that the general partner have substantial net worth—the term *substantial* is yet to be defined.

It should be noted that the safe harbor rules need not be approved prior to the syndication offering; however, you will probably want to make sure that your organization will be approved prior to proceeding.

SEE ALSO: LEVERAGE, RETURN ON INVESTMENT, and SAFE HARBOR RULES.

THREE-PARTY BLANKET

A three-party blanket is a deal involving a buyer, a seller, and a third party who furnishes collateral to secure the paper carried back by the seller.

INVESTOR ADVICE

The three-party blanket goes something like this: Mr. B wants to buy Mr. S's property by assuming an existing low-interest mortgage and having Mr. S carry back a second mortgage for the balance due.

Although Mr. S wants to sell the property, he is reluctant to do so where the buyer puts up nothing in cash and leaves him holding the paper. The deal is closed by the seller when the buyer offers additional security in the form of property owned by a third party, who is willing to have his property encumbered for a period of time. This loan of collateral may be for a consideration or as a friendly gesture of a relative or friend.

Usually, the second mortgage provides for a release of the encumbrance on the third party's property when the debt has been reduced a specified amount. In this respect, the three-party blanket resembles the pledged savings arrangement.

The consideration paid to the third party could be the love of a relative or a share of the gains in the property being purchased, to be paid when the property is resold.

SEE ALSO: CONTRACT SALE and PLEDGED SAVINGS.

TIME IS OF THE ESSENCE CLAUSE

This term refers to a clause inserted in an offer to purchase which states that the closing must be on/before a certain date, rather than a general on/about date, which is usually indicated.

INVESTOR ADVICE

This clause is necessary if the deal *must* be closed by a certain time. If not, a failure to meet the date voids the transaction. There are many instances in which a general closing date, usually meaning that both parties will try to meet this date, will not be satisfactory—

for example, the purchase of property in which development must begin before bad weather sets in; or a retail establishment that must be opened to take advantage of the Christmas shopping season.

EXAMPLE

"Time is of the essence. This offer is subject to the close of the sale being accomplished not later than noon, November 15, 1989."

SEE ALSO: DATE OF POSSESSION and EARNEST MONEY RECEIPT AND OFFER TO PURCHASE.

TIME-SHARING OWNERSHIP

This term refers to joint ownership of real estate which permits an owner to possess and occupy the property for a specific time period or number of days during the calendar year.

INVESTOR ADVICE

Time-sharing ownership, usually of apartments or condominiums, is most popular in resort locations. The purchase of a specific unit for a specific period, say the month of December, permits that owner to use the facility every December of each calendar year. The owner may also trade occupancy rights any one year for another similar right in another location.

In some time-sharing arrangements, the ownership is not for a designated unit in a specific location but for a class of unit, say a two-bedroom apartment, for the month specified, in any one of a number of developments several locations. In this type of ownership, you are guaranteed a specific period but not necessarily in a specific development or location.

The price of time-sharing ownership varies in accordance with the location, quality of the unit, and the time of year that occupancy is authorized. Obviously, similar units at a ski resort would vary in price from a low for summer months to a high for ski season. Similarly, locations in Hawaii or other warm climates would bring a premium price for winter months.

The variations on ownership and use are unlimited. Many provide for rental of a unit, not required by the owner. Thus a two-month ownership might allow rental for six weeks and owner occupancy for two weeks. Rental fees collected by management, less a small service charge, may be applied toward the mortgage, taxes, insurance, or maintenance fees.

The expense of ownership and upkeep of time-sharing units is usually allocated on an equitable basis, which is then computed as a monthly service charge. This allows management to maintain the property in a good and acceptable manner and relieves the owners of this responsibility. Interest charges and property taxes are tax deductible in the same manner as 100% ownership. Some restrictions on the sale of a time-sharing unit may be enforceable by the bylaws of the selling/management organization. These regulations are to assure the financial stability and compatibility of prospective new owners.

When considering the purchase of a time-sharing ownership, it is important to ascertain the financial strength and management ability of the selling/management organization. Without good and continuing management, your investment could be seriously impaired.

SEE ALSO: BUNDLE OF RIGHTS.

TITLE INSURANCE

Title insurance is a policy issued by a land title company which guarantees that the ownership of the property is as stated in the title report. A preliminary title report is made available to the buyer at closing.

INVESTOR ADVICE

The title policy guarantees that the title is as stated in the title report, not that it is clear. In most cases, the title at closing will be clear, but often mortgage loans and other encumbrances are assumed by the buyer with full knowledge of those liens against the property.

Carefully read the provisions of the title insurance policy. Most often, these policies do not insure the buyer against encroachments either on the purchased property or of the purchased tenements on adjacent properties. Similarly, unless specifically requested by the buyer and authorized by the state, the policy probably does not protect the buyer against mechanic liens of contractors and subcontractors, which may be filed 80–90 days after the purchase.

Most earnest money receipts and offer to purchase agreements state that the seller will furnish an up-to-date abstract of the title or title insurance. The insurance is preferable to an abstract. Insurance guarantees the title, whereas the abstract cites the status of the title as found by the abstractor—no warranty is provided.

The warranty deed, furnished to a buyer by the former owner, is legally binding on the grantor; however, their is no assurance that the grantor can make good on this warranty at the time a deficiency is found. A title insurance policy is good for both parties. It guarantees the buyer a good title and takes the seller off the hook for any future problems.

SEE ALSO: ABSTRACT OF TITLE, AMERICAN LAND TITLE ASSOCIATION, CONTRACTOR'S LIEN, and WARRANTY DEED.

TITLE REPORT

A title report is provided to a buyer at the time of closing which indicates the status of the title. If the property is not clear, the report lists all encumbrances or other clouds on the title which are a matter of official record. With the exception of boiler-plate additions of insurance language, the report is identical to the title policy issued at a later date.

INVESTOR ADVICE

If you are not familiar with the standard title reports issued in the state in which property is purchased, ask for a sample copy. Each state has minor variations to its title policies. Some offer additional coverage, such as contractor lien insurance, for an additional fee. Know what you are getting before you close the deal. Study the addendum sheet, which lists all clouds on the title. Make sure that these are cleared during the closing process or that you have agreed to accept the property and its encumbrances.

SEE ALSO: AMERICAN LAND TITLE ASSOCIATION and TITLE INSURANCE.

TORRENS SYSTEM

This term refers to a land registration system used in some states which is gradually being supplanted by the simpler land title insurance system.

INVESTOR ADVICE

Under the torrens system, any person with a fee-simple ownership may apply to have a property placed on the register of titles. Henceforth, it is not necessary to examine prior ownerships, as the certificate of title is absolutely conclusive.

The torrens system has been most successfully used in the states of Illinois and Massachusetts. The system gets its name from its originator, Sir Robert Torrens, who introduced it in Australia is 1858. This system has not made any great inroads into the recording systems of this country, primarily due to the opposition of title companies.

SEE ALSO: TITLE INSURANCE and TITLE REPORT.

TOWN HOUSE

A town house is a type of residence which is characterized by being a portion of a row of attached homes. The residence shares common walls and, in some instances, common roofs.

INVESTOR ADVICE

The town house project makes maximum use of available land and is particularly useful in locations with land scarcity or high land costs.

When planning a residential project, examine the potential for town house construction. This approach will provide buyers with maximum space at minimum cost. Where the fronts and rears are designed with a variety of architectural variables, the objection of "sameness" can be largely eliminated.

Town house projects are usually built as a part of planned unit developments (PUDs). Often, significant amenities, such as swimming pools and tennis courts, greatly add to the appeal of the project.

SEE ALSO: DE MINIMIS PUD and ZERO LOT LINE.

TOWNSHIP

A township is a unit of the rectangular survey system consisting of 36 square sections of land.

INVESTOR ADVICE

The township is 6 miles wide by 6 miles deep. Specific properties contained in the township reference that partition as, for example:

"Township 3 South, Range 2 East"

This designation would indicate that the subject township is located in the third tier south of the designated base line and two tiers east of the designated meridian line.

SEE ALSO: LAND IDENTIFICATION METHODS, and RECTANGULAR SURVEY.

TRACT HOUSING

Tract housing is low- to medium-income housing characterized by limitations of floor plans, basic design, and common appearance.

INVESTOR ADVICE

Most tract type developments are constructed to VA, FHA, and state low-income housing standards. Purchase of this type of housing as an investment is not recommended, since renters are able to acquire their own properties with little down and monthly mortgage payments comparable to rents.

Although these projects are reasonably well constructed, they tend to depreciate at a higher than normal rate due to the financial inability of the buyers to maintain them in an acceptable manner. When first constructed, they are attractive and in good condition. Five to ten years afterward these projects tend to be lacking uniform landscaping, need exterior maintenance, and are often cluttered with old broken-down cars, trucks, and other vehicles.

Your investment would be better applied to less units of a higher value, thus assuring a reasonable depreciation and renters in a higher income bracket.

SEE ALSO: FHA LOAN and VA LOAN.

TRADING AREA ANALYSIS

A study performed by an SRPA appraiser or other similarly qualified professional to determine the probable sales potential in an area in which a shopping center development is proposed.

INVESTOR ADVICE

The study may also indicate the need for various types of businesses and the likely amount of shopping space that can be absorbed in a reasonable time span. Undoubtedly, your mortgage banker will require a trading area analysis as support for your request for long-term financing.

The report will also provide you with planning information regarding the ultimate size of the project and the rate at which new units should be introduced to the market.

Individuals having the qualifications to perform the required studies are real estate appraisers with the designations MAI, SRPA, and IFAC; and certain local college and university personnel who are familiar with shopping center economics and the subject area.

Before hiring an individual to perform the study, carefully review his or her history of past work and check with former clients regarding the acceptability of his or her study and predictions.

SEE ALSO: IFAC APPRAISER, MAI APPRAISER, and SRPA APPRAISER.

TRIPLE NET LEASE

A triple net lease is a lease of property in which the tenant is responsible for maintenance, taxes, and insurance—sometimes referred to as a *net lease*.

INVESTOR ADVICE

Most commercial leases of individual structures are best made on a triple net basis. The cost to the lessee is the same, since the landlord must charge enough to cover these costs. Where the tenant is responsible, the lease can be simpler and not require extensive language regarding future increases in taxes and insurance.

In the net lease, maintenance is faster and simpler. If something needs repairing, no communication with a middleman is required—the tenant simply has the work performed as needed. In a net lease, the landlord may still be responsible for exterior and roof maintenance.

SEE ALSO: NET LEASE.

TRUST

A trust is a legal entity that provides trust fund management and has the right to buy and hold property and other assets, as outlined in the trust instrument. A trust is managed by trustees.

INVESTOR ADVICE

Trusts are often established by wills (testamentary trust) or by living persons (inter vivoce) for management purposes. A trust is established by a trustor, who provides the assets to establish the trust by will, by proceeds of insurance, or by transfers of assets during his or her lifetime.

Living trusts can be of two basic types: (a) revocable, or (b) nonrevocable, depending on the purpose of establishment.

The revocable trust is usually established to spread the trust income among family members. This ability to save taxes was largely eliminated by the Tax Reform Act of 1986.

The assets of a revocable trust are taxable as assets in the estate of the trustor. The assets of a nonrevocable trust are not includable in the decedent's estate unless the trust was established in the three years prior to death (assumed to be in contemplation of death).

The lifetime of the trust varies and is indicated by the person who establishes the trust.

The testamentary trust is established by the terms of a will and after the death of the trustor. Assets to establish the trust are enumerated in the decedent's will. Often, the major assets are the proceeds of life insurance. In this case the trust may be known as a life insurance trust. Usually, the terms of a testamentary trust provide for the voluntary addition of the surviving spouse's half of the estate and for that survivor to receive the income from the trust. Internal Revenue Service regulations provide, in this case, for the survivor to be paid additional amounts over and above the trust income to maintain an accustomed standard of living.

Trustees, named to manage the trust, may not be able to serve when the time arrives. It is recommended that alternates be designated to forestall this problem. Also, it is generally regarded as good policy to designate a perpetual institution as one of the trustees, thus assuring some continuity of management. Where the surviving spouse is competent, it is also customary to name that person as one of the trustees.

The trustees of a trust may perform any duties outlined by the provisions of the trust instrument. These would normally include the ability to invest moneys, sell and purchase assets, pay income derived to the beneficiaries designated, and so forth. Where income is retained within the trust, it is subject to income taxes.

The lifetimes of various trusts are shown in Figures 55, 56, and 57. Please note that when the trust is liquidated at the time indicated, all assets are dispersed to persons designated as remaindermen.

SEE ALSO: INTER VIVOCE TRUST and TESTAMENTARY TRUST.

TRUST ACCOUNT

A trust account is a checking or other financial account established for the purpose of holding other people's money. The account is managed by an attorney, broker, or other individual who serves in a fiduciary capacity.

INVESTOR ADVICE

Those persons who control trust accounts are subject to strict supervision by state and other regulatory authorities. They may not commingle their own funds with those belonging to others. Moneys received must be promptly deposited, and those funds cannot be withdrawn except in accordance with appropriate rules and regulations.

EXAMPLE

A certain earnest money receipt and offer to purchase contains a receipt by the realtor for a deposit of $5,000. This money is deposited in the brokerage trust account.

The property is sold for $150,000 and the broker is entitled to a 6% commission ($9,000). The closing statement to the seller will indicate an expense of $9,000 with an additional note:

a. check to broker for $4,000;
b. earnest money deposit of $5,000, held by broker.

After the deal is closed, the broker is authorized to withdraw the $5,000 from the trust and indicate, "Deal closed (Date) and (File Number)."

Real estate brokers' trust files are audited periodically by the state agency having cognizance over real estate activities. Even minor variations of approved procedures can result in significant fines and other penalties.

SEE ALSO: EARNEST MONEY RECEIPT AND OFFER TO PURCHASE and FIDUCIARY.

TRUST DEED

A trust deed is given by a mortgagor to a trustee to be held until such time as a loan is paid in full and in accordance with the trust agreement. When payment is received, the property is reconveyed to the mortgagor by a deed of reconveyance or other type of satisfaction piece.

INVESTOR ADVICE

In some trust deed states, lenders require the borrower to sign a note as well as a trust deed. In the event of default the lender can quickly foreclose on the trust deed or take a more time consuming route of foreclosure on the note. Many states do not allow a lender to seek a deficiency judgment if the foreclosure was on the trust deed, hence the slower alternative action.

Figure 62 shows a typical trust deed and its provisions. Trust deeds vary in size from one page to many pages, depending on the lender's needs and applicable state laws.

SEE ALSO: FORECLOSURE, MORTGAGE, and SHERIFF'S SALE.

TRUSTEE

A trustee is a person or entity appointed to manage a trust.

INVESTOR ADVICE

A trustee may be any competent party or institution named by the trustor. In setting up a trust or preparing a trust instrument, provisions should be made for alternate trustees to serve in the event the first-named are unwilling or cannot serve for one or more reasons.

Generally, an odd number of trustees should be appointed. This will prevent a deadlock when voting on actions to be taken by the trust. Where the assets of the trust are large, it is also recommended that a bank or other perpetual institution be named as one of the trustees, even though their services may involve a considerable fee.

> **WARNING!** All banks and similar institutions may not do acceptable management jobs. It is not unusual for their conservative management to produce less income yield than government securities.

A wise trustor will provide for a change of an institutional trustee in the event that the majority of the other trustees believe that the institution is doing less than a competent job. If this provision is not included, an institution cannot be removed except by court action, and then only if that institution is guilty of negligence or fraud.

SEE ALSO: TRUST, TRUSTOR, and REMAINDERMAN.

TRUSTOR

A trustor is one who establishes a trust.

INVESTOR ADVICE

Trusts are often used during the trustor's lifetime for management purposes or to assure continuity of management in the event of the trustor's untimely demise. A business placed

Recorded   10 March, 1989
Book 405, Page 2

SPACE ABOVE THIS LINE FOR RECORDER'S USE

DEED OF TRUST

THIS DEED OF TRUST ("Security Instrument") is made on ......March..8., ...,
19..89... The grantor is ......LaBell..J...Smart..and..Jason..M...Smart.......................................
.... ("Borrower"). The trustee is ....Utah..Title..Company..Inc...
.... ("Trustee"). The beneficiary is
....Large..Bank..&..Trust..Company.., which is organized and existing
under the laws of ....Utah......................................, and whose address is ..111..S...Main..St...........
....Salt..Lake..City.,..Utah.. ("Lender").
Borrower owes Lender the principal sum of ..Ninety-five..Thousand..and..00/100..............................
.... Dollars (U.S. $..95.,000.,00.......). This debt is evidenced by Borrower's note
dated the same date as this Security Instrument ("Note"), which provides for monthly payments, with the full debt, if not
paid earlier, due and payable on ....March..8.,..2019....................
This Security Instrument secures to Lender: (a) the repayment of the debt evidenced by the Note, with interest, and all
renewals, extensions and modifications; (b) the payment of all other sums, with interest, advanced under paragraph 7 to
protect the security of this Security Instrument; and (c) the performance of Borrower's covenants and agreements under
this Security Instrument and the Note. For this purpose, Borrower irrevocably grants and conveys to Trustee, in trust,
with power of sale, the following described property located in ....Salt..Lake................................ County, Utah:

Lot 15, Big Rock Subdivision

which has the address of ....10267..South..Big..Rock..Lane..............., ...Sandy.................................,
                                                    [Street]   [City]
Utah ....84092.............................. ("Property Address");
                 [Zip Code]

TOGETHER WITH all the improvements now or hereafter erected on the property, and all easements, rights,
appurtenances, rents, royalties, mineral, oil and gas rights and profits, water rights and stock and all fixtures now or
hereafter a part of the property. All replacements and additions shall also be covered by this Security Instrument. All of the
foregoing is referred to in this Security Instrument as the "Property."

BORROWER COVENANTS that Borrower is lawfully seised of the estate hereby conveyed and has the right to grant
and convey the Property and that the Property is unencumbered, except for encumbrances of record. Borrower warrants
and will defend generally the title to the Property against all claims and demands, subject to any encumbrances of record.

THIS SECURITY INSTRUMENT combines uniform covenants for national use and non-uniform covenants with
limited variations by jurisdiction to constitute a uniform security instrument covering real property.

UTAH—Single Family—FNMA/FHLMC UNIFORM INSTRUMENT   Form 3045 12/83

Figure 62

UNIFORM COVENANTS. Borrower and Lender covenant and agree as follows:

1. Payment of Principal and Interest; Prepayment and Late Charges. Borrower shall promptly pay when due the principal of and interest on the debt evidenced by the Note and any prepayment and late charges due under the Note.

2. Funds for Taxes and Insurance. Subject to applicable law or to a written waiver by Lender, Borrower shall pay to Lender on the day monthly payments are due under the Note, until the Note is paid in full, a sum ("Funds") equal to one-twelfth of: (a) yearly taxes and assessments which may attain priority over this Security Instrument; (b) yearly leasehold payments or ground rents on the Property, if any; (c) yearly hazard insurance premiums; and (d) yearly mortgage insurance premiums, if any. These items are called "escrow items." Lender may estimate the Funds due on the basis of current data and reasonable estimates of future escrow items.

The Funds shall be held in an institution the deposits or accounts of which are insured or guaranteed by a federal or state agency (including Lender if Lender is such an institution). Lender shall apply the Funds to pay the escrow items. Lender may not charge for holding and applying the Funds, analyzing the account or verifying the escrow items, unless Lender pays Borrower interest on the Funds and applicable law permits Lender to make such a charge. A charge assessed by Lender in connection with Borrower's entering into this Security Instrument to pay the cost of an independent tax reporting service shall not be a charge for purposes of the preceding sentence. Borrower and Lender may agree in writing that interest shall be paid on the Funds. Unless an agreement is made or applicable law requires interest to be paid, Lender shall not be required to pay Borrower any interest or earnings on the Funds. Lender shall give to Borrower, without charge, an annual accounting of the Funds showing credits and debits to the Funds and the purpose for which each debit to the Funds was made. The Funds are pledged as additional security for the sums secured by this Security Instrument.

If the amount of the Funds held by Lender, together with the future monthly payments of Funds payable prior to the due dates of the escrow items, shall exceed the amount required to pay the escrow items when due, the excess shall be, at Borrower's option, either promptly repaid to Borrower or credited to Borrower on monthly payments of Funds. If the amount of the Funds held by Lender is not sufficient to pay the escrow items when due, Borrower shall pay to Lender any amount necessary to make up the deficiency in one or more payments as required by Lender.

Upon payment in full of all sums secured by this Security Instrument, Lender shall promptly refund to Borrower any Funds held by Lender. If under paragraph 19 the Property is sold or acquired by Lender, Lender shall apply, no later than immediately prior to the sale of the Property or its acquisition by Lender, any Funds held by Lender at the time of application as a credit against the sums secured by this Security Instrument.

3. Application of Payments. Unless applicable law provides otherwise, all payments received by Lender under paragraphs 1 and 2 shall be applied: first, to late charges due under the Note; second, to prepayment charges due under the Note; third, to amounts payable under paragraph 2; fourth, to interest due; and last, to principal due.

4. Charges; Liens. Borrower shall pay all taxes, assessments, charges, fines and impositions attributable to the Property which may attain priority over this Security Instrument, and leasehold payments or ground rents, if any. Borrower shall pay these obligations in the manner provided in paragraph 2, or if not paid in that manner, Borrower shall pay them on time directly to the person owed payment. Borrower shall promptly furnish to Lender all notices of amounts to be paid under this paragraph. If Borrower makes these payments directly, Borrower shall promptly furnish to Lender receipts evidencing the payments.

Borrower shall promptly discharge any lien which has priority over this Security Instrument unless Borrower: (a) agrees in writing to the payment of the obligation secured by the lien in a manner acceptable to Lender; (b) contests in good faith the lien by, or defends against enforcement of the lien in, legal proceedings which in the Lender's opinion operate to prevent the enforcement of the lien or forfeiture of any part of the Property; or (c) secures from the holder of the lien an agreement satisfactory to Lender subordinating the lien to this Security Instrument. If Lender determines that any part of the Property is subject to a lien which may attain priority over this Security Instrument, Lender may give Borrower a notice identifying the lien. Borrower shall satisfy the lien or take one or more of the actions set forth above within 10 days of the giving of notice.

5. Hazard Insurance. Borrower shall keep the improvements now existing or hereafter erected on the Property insured against loss by fire, hazards included within the term "extended coverage" and any other hazards for which Lender requires insurance. This insurance shall be maintained in the amounts and for the periods that Lender requires. The insurance carrier providing the insurance shall be chosen by Borrower subject to Lender's approval which shall not be unreasonably withheld.

All insurance policies and renewals shall be acceptable to Lender and shall include a standard mortgage clause. Lender shall have the right to hold the policies and renewals. If Lender requires, Borrower shall promptly give to Lender all receipts of paid premiums and renewal notices. In the event of loss, Borrower shall give prompt notice to the insurance carrier and Lender. Lender may make proof of loss if not made promptly by Borrower.

Unless Lender and Borrower otherwise agree in writing, insurance proceeds shall be applied to restoration or repair of the Property damaged, if the restoration or repair is economically feasible and Lender's security is not lessened. If the restoration or repair is not economically feasible or Lender's security would be lessened, the insurance proceeds shall be applied to the sums secured by this Security Instrument, whether or not then due, with any excess paid to Borrower. If Borrower abandons the Property, or does not answer within 30 days a notice from Lender that the insurance carrier has offered to settle a claim, then Lender may collect the insurance proceeds. Lender may use the proceeds to repair or restore the Property or to pay sums secured by this Security Instrument, whether or not then due. The 30-day period will begin when the notice is given.

Unless Lender and Borrower otherwise agree in writing, any application of proceeds to principal shall not extend or postpone the due date of the monthly payments referred to in paragraphs 1 and 2 or change the amount of the payments. If under paragraph 19 the Property is acquired by Lender, Borrower's right to any insurance policies and proceeds resulting from damage to the Property prior to the acquisition shall pass to Lender to the extent of the sums secured by this Security Instrument immediately prior to the acquisition.

6. Preservation and Maintenance of Property; Leaseholds. Borrower shall not destroy, damage or substantially change the Property, allow the Property to deteriorate or commit waste. If this Security Instrument is on a leasehold, Borrower shall comply with the provisions of the lease, and if Borrower acquires fee title to the Property, the leasehold and fee title shall not merge unless Lender agrees to the merger in writing.

7. Protection of Lender's Rights in the Property; Mortgage Insurance. If Borrower fails to perform the covenants and agreements contained in this Security Instrument, or there is a legal proceeding that may significantly affect Lender's rights in the Property (such as a proceeding in bankruptcy, probate, for condemnation or to enforce laws or regulations), then Lender may do and pay for whatever is necessary to protect the value of the Property and Lender's rights in the Property. Lender's actions may include paying any sums secured by a lien which has priority over this Security Instrument, appearing in court, paying reasonable attorneys' fees and entering on the Property to make repairs. Although Lender may take action under this paragraph 7, Lender does not have to do so.

Any amounts disbursed by Lender under this paragraph 7 shall become additional debt of Borrower secured by this Security Instrument. Unless Borrower and Lender agree to other terms of payment, these amounts shall bear interest from the date of disbursement at the Note rate and shall be payable, with interest, upon notice from Lender to Borrower requesting payment.

If Lender required mortgage insurance as a condition of making the loan secured by this Security Instrument, Borrower shall pay the premiums required to maintain the insurance in effect until such time as the requirement for the insurance terminates in accordance with Borrower's and Lender's written agreement or applicable law.

8. Inspection. Lender or its agent may make reasonable entries upon and inspections of the Property. Lender shall give Borrower notice at the time of or prior to an inspection specifying reasonable cause for the inspection.

Figure 62 continued

9. Condemnation. The proceeds of any award or claim for damages, direct or consequential, in connection with any condemnation or other taking of any part of the Property, or for conveyance in lieu of condemnation, are hereby assigned and shall be paid to Lender.

In the event of a total taking of the Property, the proceeds shall be applied to the sums secured by this Security Instrument, whether or not then due, with any excess paid to Borrower. In the event of a partial taking of the Property, unless Borrower and Lender otherwise agree in writing, the sums secured by this Security Instrument shall be reduced by the amount of the proceeds multiplied by the following fraction: (a) the total amount of the sums secured immediately before the taking, divided by (b) the fair market value of the Property immediately before the taking. Any balance shall be paid to Borrower.

If the Property is abandoned by Borrower, or if, after notice by Lender to Borrower that the condemnor offers to make an award or settle a claim for damages, Borrower fails to respond to Lender within 30 days after the date the notice is given, Lender is authorized to collect and apply the proceeds, at its option, either to restoration or repair of the Property or to the sums secured by this Security Instrument, whether or not then due.

Unless Lender and Borrower otherwise agree in writing, any application of proceeds to principal shall not extend or postpone the due date of the monthly payments referred to in paragraphs 1 and 2 or change the amount of such payments.

10. Borrower Not Released; Forbearance By Lender Not a Waiver. Extension of the time for payment or modification of amortization of the sums secured by this Security Instrument granted by Lender to any successor in interest of Borrower shall not operate to release the liability of the original Borrower or Borrower's successors in interest. Lender shall not be required to commence proceedings against any successor in interest or refuse to extend time for payment or otherwise modify amortization of the sums secured by this Security Instrument by reason of any demand made by the original Borrower or Borrower's successors in interest. Any forbearance by Lender in exercising any right or remedy shall not be a waiver of or preclude the exercise of any right or remedy.

11. Successors and Assigns Bound; Joint and Several Liability; Co-signers. The covenants and agreements of this Security Instrument shall bind and benefit the successors and assigns of Lender and Borrower, subject to the provisions of paragraph 17. Borrower's covenants and agreements shall be joint and several. Any Borrower who co-signs this Security Instrument but does not execute the Note: (a) is co-signing this Security Instrument only to mortgage, grant and convey that Borrower's interest in the Property under the terms of this Security Instrument; (b) is not personally obligated to pay the sums secured by this Security Instrument; and (c) agrees that Lender and any other Borrower may agree to extend, modify, forbear or make any accommodations with regard to the terms of this Security Instrument or the Note without that Borrower's consent.

12. Loan Charges. If the loan secured by this Security Instrument is subject to a law which sets maximum loan charges, and that law is finally interpreted so that the interest or other loan charges collected or to be collected in connection with the loan exceed the permitted limits, then: (a) any such loan charge shall be reduced by the amount necessary to reduce the charge to the permitted limit; and (b) any sums already collected from Borrower which exceeded permitted limits will be refunded to Borrower. Lender may choose to make this refund by reducing the principal owed under the Note or by making a direct payment to Borrower. If a refund reduces principal, the reduction will be treated as a partial prepayment without any prepayment charge under the Note.

13. Legislation Affecting Lender's Rights. If enactment or expiration of applicable laws has the effect of rendering any provision of the Note or this Security Instrument unenforceable according to its terms, Lender, at its option, may require immediate payment in full of all sums secured by this Security Instrument and may invoke any remedies permitted by paragraph 19. If Lender exercises this option, Lender shall take the steps specified in the second paragraph of paragraph 17.

14. Notices. Any notice to Borrower provided for in this Security Instrument shall be given by delivering it or by mailing it by first class mail unless applicable law requires use of another method. The notice shall be directed to the Property Address or any other address Borrower designates by notice to Lender. Any notice to Lender shall be given by first class mail to Lender's address stated herein or any other address Lender designates by notice to Borrower. Any notice provided for in this Security Instrument shall be deemed to have been given to Borrower or Lender when given as provided in this paragraph.

15. Governing Law; Severability. This Security Instrument shall be governed by federal law and the law of the jurisdiction in which the Property is located. In the event that any provision or clause of this Security Instrument or the Note conflicts with applicable law, such conflict shall not affect other provisions of this Security Instrument or the Note which can be given effect without the conflicting provision. To this end the provisions of this Security Instrument and the Note are declared to be severable.

16. Borrower's Copy. Borrower shall be given one conformed copy of the Note and of this Security Instrument.

17. Transfer of the Property or a Beneficial Interest in Borrower. If all or any part of the Property or any interest in it is sold or transferred (or if a beneficial interest in Borrower is sold or transferred and Borrower is not a natural person) without Lender's prior written consent, Lender may, at its option, require immediate payment in full of all sums secured by this Security Instrument. However, this option shall not be exercised by Lender if exercise is prohibited by federal law as of the date of this Security Instrument.

If Lender exercises this option, Lender shall give Borrower notice of acceleration. The notice shall provide a period of not less than 30 days from the date the notice is delivered or mailed within which Borrower must pay all sums secured by this Security Instrument. If Borrower fails to pay these sums prior to the expiration of this period, Lender may invoke any remedies permitted by this Security Instrument without further notice or demand on Borrower.

18. Borrower's Right to Reinstate. If Borrower meets certain conditions, Borrower shall have the right to have enforcement of this Security Instrument discontinued at any time prior to the earlier of: (a) 5 days (or such other period as applicable law may specify for reinstatement) before sale of the Property pursuant to any power of sale contained in this Security Instrument; or (b) entry of a judgment enforcing this Security Instrument. Those conditions are that Borrower: (a) pays Lender all sums which then would be due under this Security Instrument and the Note had no acceleration occurred; (b) cures any default of any other covenants or agreements; (c) pays all expenses incurred in enforcing this Security Instrument, including, but not limited to, reasonable attorneys' fees; and (d) takes such action as Lender may reasonably require to assure that the lien of this Security Instrument, Lender's rights in the Property and Borrower's obligation to pay the sums secured by this Security Instrument shall continue unchanged. Upon reinstatement by Borrower, this Security Instrument and the obligations secured hereby shall remain fully effective as if no acceleration had occurred. However, this right to reinstate shall not apply in the case of acceleration under paragraphs 13 or 17.

NON-UNIFORM COVENANTS. Borrower and Lender further covenant and agree as follows:

19. Acceleration; Remedies. Lender shall give notice to Borrower prior to acceleration following Borrower's breach of any covenant or agreement in this Security Instrument (but not prior to acceleration under paragraphs 13 and 17 unless applicable law provides otherwise). The notice shall specify: (a) the default; (b) the action required to cure the default; (c) a date, not less than 30 days from the date the notice is given to Borrower, by which the default must be cured; and (d) that failure to cure the default on or before the date specified in the notice may result in acceleration of the sums secured by this Security Instrument and sale of the Property. The notice shall further inform Borrower of the right to reinstate after acceleration and the right to bring a court action to assert the non-existence of a default or any other defense of Borrower to acceleration and sale. If the default is not cured on or before the date specified in the notice, Lender at its option may require immediate payment in full of all sums secured by this Security Instrument without further demand and may invoke the power of sale and any other remedies permitted by applicable law. Lender shall be entitled to collect all expenses incurred in pursuing the remedies provided in this paragraph 19, including, but not limited to, reasonable attorneys' fees and costs of title evidence.

Figure 62 continued

If the power of sale is invoked, Trustee shall execute a written notice of the occurrence of an event of default and of the election to cause the Property to be sold and shall record such notice in each county in which any part of the Property is located. Lender or Trustee shall mail copies of such notice in the manner prescribed by applicable law to Borrower and to the other persons prescribed by applicable law. Trustee shall give public notice of the sale to the persons and in the manner prescribed by applicable law. After the time required by applicable law, Trustee, without demand on Borrower, shall sell the Property at public auction to the highest bidder at the time and place and under the terms designated in the notice of sale in one or more parcels and in any order Trustee determines. Trustee may postpone sale of all or any parcel of the Property by public announcement at the time and place of any previously scheduled sale. Lender or its designee may purchase the Property at any sale.

Trustee shall deliver to the purchaser Trustee's deed conveying the Property without any covenant or warranty, expressed or implied. The recitals in the Trustee's deed shall be prima facie evidence of the truth of the statements made therein. Trustee shall apply the proceeds of the sale in the following order: (a) to all expenses of the sale, including, but not limited to, reasonable Trustee's and attorneys' fees; (b) to all sums secured by this Security Instrument; and (c) any excess to the person or persons legally entitled to it or to the county clerk of the county in which the sale took place.

20. Lender in Possession. Upon acceleration under paragraph 19 or abandonment of the Property, Lender (in person, by agent or by judicially appointed receiver) shall be entitled to enter upon, take possession of and manage the Property and to collect the rents of the Property including those past due. Any rents collected by Lender or the receiver shall be applied first to payment of the costs of management of the Property and collection of rents, including, but not limited to, receiver's fees, premiums on receiver's bonds and reasonable attorneys' fees, and then to the sums secured by this Security Instrument.

21. Reconveyance. Upon payment of all sums secured by this Security Instrument, Lender shall request Trustee to reconvey the Property and shall surrender this Security Instrument and all notes evidencing debt secured by this Security Instrument to Trustee. Trustee shall reconvey the Property without warranty and without charge to the person or persons legally entitled to it. Such person or persons shall pay any recordation costs.

22. Substitute Trustee. Lender, at its option, may from time to time remove Trustee and appoint a successor trustee to any Trustee appointed hereunder. Without conveyance of the Property, the successor trustee shall succeed to all the title, power and duties conferred upon Trustee herein and by applicable law.

23. Request for Notices. Borrower requests that copies of the notices of default and sale be sent to Borrower's address which is the Property Address.

24. Riders to this Security Instrument. If one or more riders are executed by Borrower and recorded together with this Security Instrument, the covenants and agreements of each such rider shall be incorporated into and shall amend and supplement the covenants and agreements of this Security Instrument as if the rider(s) were a part of this Security Instrument. [Check applicable box(es)]

☐ Adjustable Rate Rider   ☐ Condominium Rider   ☐ 2–4 Family Rider

☒ Graduated Payment Rider   ☐ Planned Unit Development Rider

☐ Other(s) [specify]

By Signing Below, Borrower accepts and agrees to the terms and covenants contained in this Security Instrument and in any rider(s) executed by Borrower and recorded with it.

La Bielle J. Smart ....(Seal)
—Borrower

Jason M. Smart ....(Seal)
—Borrower

———————————— [Space Below This Line For Acknowledgment] ————————————

State of Utah   )
) ss.
County of Salt Lake)

On the 8th day of March, 1989, before me Mary Southwell, a Notary Public in and for the County of Salt Lake, State of Utah, personally appeared <u>La Bell J. Smart and Jason M. Smart</u>, personally known to me to be the persons described in and who executed the foregoing instrument, who acknowledge to me that they executed the same, freely and voluntarily, and for the uses and purposes therein mentioned.

WITNESS my hand and notarila seal, this 8th day of March 1989

My Commission Expires:
June 18th 1993

Mary Southwell
Notary Public, residing in
Salt Lake City, Ut.

Figure 62 continued

in a living trust would continue after the trustor's death with only the loss of a trustee (the decedent). If the trust is nonrevocable, the assets will not be included in the decedent's estate.

Prior to enactment of the Tax Reform Act of 1986, living trusts could be used to divide family income and thus reduce the total family income tax. This advantage has been largely eliminated by the TRA.

So called revocable blind trusts are utilized by public officials as managers of their assets to guarantee that their public position will not present an actual or seeming conflict of interest. In a blind trust, the trustor is not a trustee and has no control over the assets until such time as the trust is revoked.

SEE ALSO: BENEFICIARY, REMAINDER MAN, TRUSTEE.

TWENTY-FOUR HOUR CONTINGENCY CLAUSE

A clause contained in an earnest money receipt and offer to purchase which accepts an offer with a contingent condition allowing the seller a 24-hour time period after the occurrence of a stipulated event before a second offer is accepted or rejected.

INVESTOR ADVICE

An example of the use of this vehicle would be a seller who receives an offer for his or her property but is reluctant to accept all of the conditions—say the need for the buyer to obtain financing, sell existing property, and so forth. The seller accepts the offer with the contingency that he will not have to remove his property from the market but will continue to offer it for sale.

If another offer which is fully acceptable to the seller is received, the first party is informed of that fact and has 24 hours to remove the contingency having to do with obtaining financing, selling property, and so forth or else cancel the accepted offer. Language in the agreement might read as follows:

Seller accepts the offer as written with the following contingency—Seller reserves the right to continue offering his property for sale. If an acceptable second offer is received, the buyer shall have 24 hours, after notification, to remove the contingency regarding his arranging necessary financing, or cancel this offer.

SEE ALSO: EARNEST MONEY RECEIPT AND OFFER TO PURCHASE

ENDNOTE

[1]In Utah, the requiremnt is all property owners within 300 feet of the property proposed for rezoning.

U

Unit in Place Method
Units of Comparison
Useful Life
Useful Square Footage

Usufructuary Right
Utilities
Utility Value

U

UNIT IN PLACE METHOD

The unit in place method is an estimation of the cost of construction which computes the expense of putting each component of a building in its place.

INVESTOR ADVICE

The unit in place method is utilized by appraisers in their calculation of the cost approach to value. Usually, these costs supplement commercially available, appraisal which provides the total cost of construction for various building types as dollars per square foot of enclosed space.

The unit in place costs are useful in refining the gross building costs with more detail. Since these costs are for more or less standard buildings, features added to the subject building or omitted must be considered as plus or minus corrections to the gross values.

For example, the commercial data might indicate that an office building of a certain class currently costs $55 per square foot. The appraiser notes that the building also includes 10 refrigerated water fountains. The unit in place cost of these fountains would be added to the basic $55 per square foot building cost, to obtain the cost of the specific building being appraised.

The following calculations would be representative of a cost approach using gross cost figures and modified by unit in place figures:

CLASS A GOOD OFFICE BUILDING	
15,000 s.f. @ $82.47/s.f.	$1,237,050
Warm and cool air vs. std. of chilled and hot	
water, 15,000 s.f. @ 2.25/s.f.	(33,750)*
No elevators, 15,000 s.f. @ $5.20/s.f.	(78,000)*
Stone front vs. std. for brick, 2,000 s.f.	
@ $11.25/s.f.	22,500*
Total book cost	$1,147,800
Adjusted for local area cost factor = 1.06	1,216,668
Less: depreciation based on expected life	
of 60 years and effective age of 10	
years = 3%	(36,500)
Present value by cost approach	$1,180,168

*Unit in place adjustments.

SEE ALSO: COST APPROACH TO VALUE.

UNITS OF COMPARISON

Standard units of measure used to compare real estate and improvements thereon.

INVESTOR ADVICE

In the appraisal of real estate, it is important that sold properties and the subject property be compared in the same units of measure. The following list indicates some of the standards used for various types of property:

LAND
Small parcels—square foot,
larger parcels—acre,
very large parcels—section or partial section,
commercial land—square foot or front foot.

LAND IMPROVEMENTS
Curb and gutter—linear foot,
sidewalks—square foot,
streets—square foot or linear foot and width,
sanitary sewers—linear feet,
landscaping—number of shrubs and trees by type and size, and sod per square foot.

PRIVATE RESIDENCE
Main floors—square foot,
basement—square foot of space and finished space.

APARTMENTS
Number of rental units of each size—one bedroom, two bedrooms, and so forth.

OFFICE BUILDINGS
Rentable space—square foot,
total space—square foot.

MANUFACTURING BUILDINGS
Manufacturing space—square foot,
office space—square foot,
warehouse space—square foot.

SEE ALSO: COST APPROACH TO VALUE and MARKET APPROACH TO VALUE.

USEFUL LIFE

Remaining time that a building is expected to produce an economic return on investment is called *useful life*.

INVESTOR ADVICE
The useful life of a property can be extended by proper and timely maintenance plus occasional remodeling to meet current needs and market. The critical decision point comes when the cost of remodeling and its subsequent return on investment approaches the return from a replacement facility. Key to this decision is a consideration of highest and best use of the land.
SEE ALSO: ECONOMIC LIFE, EFFECTIVE AGE.

USEFUL SQUARE FOOTAGE

Useful square footage is the space contained within a structure which is useful for the production of income—rentable space.

INVESTOR ADVICE
Few if any multitenant buildings are 100% efficient. Most commercial structures contain hallways, entrances, toilet facilities, utility space and other square footage

which cannot be leased. While such space can be considered an amenity and may help to attract desirable tenants, it is nonproductive. One-tenant buildings are often 100% useful, since the tenant enjoys the use of the entire structure.

Architects are often swayed by the esthetics of a proposed building and fail to understand the economics involved. The developer must impress on the selected designer the importance of the rental efficiency of the project, particularly where the facility will be a multitenant operation.

When proposing to buy an existing facility, pay careful attention to rentable space rather than overall size. This is also an important factor for the appraiser, who compares one rental facility with another.

SEE ALSO: RENTABLE SQUARE FOOTAGE.

USUFRUCTUARY RIGHT

This term refers to the right of use and full enjoyment of another's property, with provision that the use and enjoyment be without alteration or damage beyond fair wear and tear.

INVESTOR ADVICE

The usufructuary right is an implied covenant of all lease agreements. Each agreement has numerous promises which flow between the tenant and landlord. In lieu of any written agreement between the parties, each state considers certain covenants and conditions to be implied.

In Utah, the tenant has a duty to repair a rented property if the agreement is mute to this point; however, in actual practice most leases place this responsibility on the landlord. Common law obligations in all states require the tenant to prevent property waste or deterioration through his or her actions or failure to act in a responsible manner.

SEE ALSO: BUNDLE OF RIGHTS and LEASEHOLD ESTATE.

UTILITIES

Those amenities, usually public, which provide required or otherwise desirable services for real estate.

INVESTOR ADVICE

Developers are normally required to provide connection to necessary utilities to serve their developments. The basic service is normally provided by public facilities owned by governmental or quasi-governmental agencies. These developer-furnished connections include:

- streets;
- curbs and gutters;
- sidewalks and street lighting;
- sanitary and storm sewers; and
- culinary water.

Other utilities which are installed during the project's construction may be provided at the expense of the company furnishing the service. These facilities would include:

- electrical service;

- telephone service;

- cable TV service; and

- pressurized irrigation water (western and arid areas).

> **CAUTION!** Service lines to your property may not guarantee their availability to your project. Check before you buy or proceed.

Very often, existing service lines are inadequate for additional connections. It is strongly recommended that you check with each utility supplier to determine if service can be made available to your new development. You may find that new trunk lines must be installed to serve your project—an expense that will be borne, if not fully then at least partially, by you.

Where your property lies just outside of an incorporated area, you may have a choice of how or if the property is to be annexed. Your choice may well depend on that city's ability to provide necessary utility services and/or the cost of those services.

SEE ALSO: ANNEXATION, CONSTRUCTION PERMIT, and EASEMENTS.

UTILITY VALUE

Utility value is something that has the ability to satisfy a human need or desire.

INVESTOR ADVICE

A useful object may not have the same or any utility value to all persons. For instance, food would have a far greater utility value to a hungry person than to one who is not hungry.

Value is the product of utility, desire, and scarcity coupled with the purchasing power to satisfy the desire. The appraiser, who attempts to determine fair market value, must consider all of these factors.

SEE ALSO: PRINCIPLE OF SUBSTITUTION, VALUE, and VALUE IN USE.

V

VA Loan
Vacancy Factor
Valuable Consideration
Valuation
Value
Value in Use
Variable Expense

Variable Rate Mortgage
Vendor's Lien
Vertical Revitalization
Visible Possession
Void Contract
Voidable Contract

V

VA LOAN

A VA loan is a mortgage loan that has been guaranteed or provided by the Veteran's Administration.

INVESTOR ADVICE

The purpose of the VA loan is to provide veterans with the ability to acquire a residence with minimum downpayment. VA loans are normally made by mortgage companies and other lenders and are guaranteed by the Veterans Administration. These loans are similar to FHA loans, made by the same lenders, except the downpayments are minimal or none at all and the insurance is paid by the Veteran's Administration.

Where a number of VA-insured properties have been repossessed and the Administration is anxious to reduce their inventory, the VA may make direct loans to qualified buyers, veterans and nonveterans alike. Normally, the Administration is only in the insurance business, not the loan business.

As in the case of FHA loans, the Administration periodically establishes interest rates. If the lender is unable or unwilling to lend at the established rate, he or she may charge the *seller* a number of points (cash up front) to compensate for the lower interest loan. Buyers are forbidden to pay points, even though the selling price plus points is less than the Certificate of Reasonable Value (CRV).

In appraising, where VA loan sales are used as comparables, the appraiser adjusts the sales price downward for seller points paid in order to arrive at the true selling price.

VA loans are assumable under two conditions:

1. The veteran, who possesses the loan, agrees to allow another party to assume the loan. In allowing the other to assume the obligation, the veteran is not released from his or her basic responsibility for payment. In the event of default by the assuming party, the Administration will look to the veteran for payment.
2. The veteran who possesses the loan agrees to allow another veteran to assume the loan after qualifying. This arrangement relieves the original borrower of payment responsibilities.
3. VA loans made directly by the Veteran's Administration may or may not be assumable.

VA-insured properties are excellent buys for the investor. If assumable, the resale is greatly facilitated. The new buyer may assume the loan, or the investor can sell on contract while maintaining the original VA mortgage.

SEE ALSO: CERTIFICATE OF REASONABLE VALUE, and POINTS.

VACANCY FACTOR

The vacancy factor is the percentage of total available time that rental space is unoccupied in a rental facility.

INVESTOR ADVICE

The vacancy factor is calculated as space or unit vacancy times length of vacancy divided by total space-time available for the period considered.

EXAMPLE

Mr. R has an apartment house with 24 units, which are available 365 days a year. His total space-time available is:

$$365 \times 24 = 8{,}760 \text{ unit-days}$$

During the year, the following vacancies occurred for the reasons indicated:

Units Vacant	Time	Unit-Days Lost	Reason
2	5 days	10	Redecoration
4	7 days	28	Tenant moved
2	20 days	40	Fire damage
4	10 days	40	Eviction
Total Unit-days lost		= 118	

Vacancy Factor: $118/(365 \times 24) \times 100 = 1.3\%$ vacancy factor

A zero percent vacancy factor is almost impossible to obtain. Time will be required to redecorate between tenant occupancies and it will be virtually impossible to have one tenant move out and another in without some loss. Generally speaking, a 2%–3% vacancy factor is considered optimum. Small apartment houses with long-term leases may, however, achieve a lower vacancy factor.

SEE ALSO: GROSS RENT and NET RENT MULTIPLIER.

VALUABLE CONSIDERATION

This phrase is often cited in deeds where the exact amount paid is not to be revealed. This is a holdover from contractual law which requires a *consideration* to legalize the contract.

INVESTOR ADVICE

Where it is desirable to keep sales prices confidential, the deed often cites *"$1 and other good and valuable considerations."*

Thus, persons perusing the official records are unaware of the exact details of the sale. In many states, modern deeds no longer cite the consideration.

The attempt to keep the sales price private is defeated in those states which have a real estate transfer tax, requiring that revenue stamps be attached to the official document. One merely needs to determine the tax paid and the tax rate to have a very close estimate of the selling price.

A valuable consideration does not have to be money. It can be love and affection or anything considered to be valuable.

SEE ALSO: DEED, GRANTEE, GRANTOR.

VALUATION

Valuation is the act or process of estimating a specific type of value for an identifiable real property as of a stated date. The type of value can be:

- market value,

- insurance value,

- investment value, or

- any other interest which can be clearly defined to the evaluator.

INVESTOR ADVICE

There is a fine line between the terms *valuation* and *evaluation*. Whereas evaluation may involve various studies of real estate to establish feasibility or other economic considertions, valuation is a very precise process which narrows the process to:

- A specifically identified property;

- as of a specified date; and

- with the appraised interest clearly identified.

Most appraisal reports you review will be valuations that take into consideration the foregoing three considerations. In addition to these considerations, all recognized appraisal organizations require that their appraisers indicate the purpose of the appraisal, (i.e., fair market value, insurance value, etc.) together with the exact interest being appraised: fee, leasehold, life estate, and so forth.

SEE ALSO: FAIR MARKET VALUE.

VALUE

There are many types of value. In real estate parlance, many appraisers continue to define value as that promulagated by the California courts in 1909 in the case of *Sacramento Rail Road* v. *Heilbron*.[1] This definition states that fair market value is "the highest price estimated in terms of money which the land would bring if exposed for sale in the open market, with reasonable time allowed in which to find a purchaser, buying with knowledge of all of the uses and purposes to which it was adapted and for which it was capable of being used."

INVESTOR ADVICE

To have value to someone or anyone the object must have some utility or means of satisfying a human need. But utility is not enough to establish value. Air has utility— we all need it to live, but since it is abundant and free, it has no value. Value then is the product of the ability to satisfy a need *plus* some degree of scarcity to keep it from being free.

There is value unless there is a desire of someone to own and they have y to buy. Value varies with the individual. What has value to one may not necessarily have value to another. Real estate value is based on what the *average* buyer is willing to pay.

SEE ALSO: FAIR MARKET VALUE, UTILITY VALUE, and VALUE IN USE.

VALUE IN USE

The publication *Real Estate Appraisal Terminology* defines value in use as "A value concept which is based upon the productivity of an economic good to its owner-user. Value in use may be a valid substitute for market value, when the current use is so specialized that it has no demonstrable market and when the use is economic and likely to continue."[2]

INVESTOR ADVICE

An appraiser may be required to perform an analysis of a property in use where there is insufficient or no other rental data available. An example would be a motel in which the real estate is an asset contributing to a going operation. A value-in-use computation is generally appropriate when:

1. the property is fulfilling an economic need for the use it provides or which it shelters;
2. the property improvements are deemed to have a measurable or estimatable remaining economic life expectancy;
3. there is good ownership and adequate management;
4. a change of the property's use would not be deemed economically feasible.
5. there is ample evidence that the present use will continue by the current owners or that similar use appears economically practical; and
6. the appraiser has given due consideration to the property's functional utility in supporting its current usage.

SEE ALSO: FAIR MARKET VALUE, VALUATION, and VALUE.

VARIABLE EXPENSE

A variable expense is an expense of an operation whose value changes in accordance with some operational factor(s).

INVESTOR ADVICE

Many expenses of operating real estate are not fixed but tend to vary with certain criteria or circumstances. Heating costs vary with the amount of cold weather experienced. Electricity use tends to vary with the percent of the day in which darkness is encountered. Retirement expenses vary with the number of employees, their wage rates, and their time of service with the company.

Operational expenses are generally of two basic types: (a) fixed costs, such as property taxes, mortgage payments, and so forth; and (b) variable expenses, such as heat, lights, and advertising.

SEE ALSO: FIXED EXPENSES.

VARIABLE RATE MORTGAGE

A variable rate mortgage is a mortgage loan whose interest rate is not fixed but varies with some reference indicator such as the prime rate, cost of living, and so forth.

INVESTOR ADVICE

Since the lending institution's risk is less with a variable rate interest loan, it can usually set the rate at a lower level than if a fixed interest rate is desired. Thus, variable rate interest loans are more desirable as interest rates rise.

??????? What will happen if interest rates rise and there is a downturn in the economy?

Variable rate interest has a degree of uncertainty not encountered with fixed rate loans. If you feel that the future trend of interest rates is downward, the variable rate approach, with its lower initial premium, is the one for you. However, if you feel that interest rate are likely to rise, the fixed rate is the more prudent approach.

One alternative to high interest rates is consideration of a shorter term. This consideration assumes that the cash flow will support that alternative. Lenders are often able to quote lower rates where the term of risk is diminished. For instance, a 12% rate for a 30-year loan might be reduced to 11% if you are willing and able to reduce the pay-out term to 20 years.

SEE ALSO: FLOATING RATE INTEREST.

VENDOR'S LIEN

A vendor's lien is a lien placed on real estate for nonpayment of materials or supplies delivered to the construction site.

INVESTOR ADVICE

In the event that your contractor fails to pay for materials delivered to the job, his or her supplier has the right to place a vendor's lien on your property. To avoid this problem, insist that the contractor be bonded.

Similarly, you must be careful in closing on a new project that could have contractor, subcontractor, and vendor liens filed after the closing. Since most states allow 90 to 120 days after the last delivery of materials or work performed, it is possible for liens to appear after you have taken possession.

This latter problem can be handled in one of two ways:

1. Seller funds can be held in escrow until after the time allowed for filing of liens.
2. In some states, title insurance for protection against contractor, subcontractor, and vendor liens can be obtained, at an extra fee.

SEE ALSO: CONTRACTOR'S LIEN and SUBCONTRACTOR'S LIEN.

VERTICAL REVITALIZATION

Vertical revitalization is the rehabilitation of existing high-rise structures or the development of available air space above existing structures.

INVESTOR ADVICE

Vertical development or redevelopment in areas with very high land values is one of the best methods of obtaining additional rentable space at an affordable price.

You should search for buildings in use which are ideally located but showing signs of the approaching end of their useful life. Often a deal can be struck with these landowners to provide new custom-built space in return for the right to own and develop the remainder of the property to its highest and best potential.

Excellent examples of vertical revitalization are found in New York City where new structures were built over the Pennsylvania and Grand Central railroad terminals. Boston has also made excellent use of air rights over railroad yards. Building over existing structures is usually more expensive than just tearing down the old and building new; however, if the existing structures have historical or other significance, building over the old is the best alternative.

SEE ALSO: AIR RIGHTS and RECYCLED REAL ESTATE.

VISIBLE POSSESSION

Possession of property which is visible to the owner and the world in general—a necessity for an adverse possession claim.

INVESTOR ADVICE
In order for a person to obtain title by adverse possession, it must be shown that the property was in open and notorious possession by the claimant for the specified time required by state law. In Utah, that time period is seven years. Visible possession is adequate proof of that claim.
SEE ALSO: ADVERSE POSSESSION and COLOR OF TITLE.

VOID CONTRACT

This term refers to a contract that is no longer enforceable.

INVESTOR ADVICE
Contracts may become void for any number of reasons, some of which are:

* failure of one or more of the parties to perform in a timely manner;
* inability of the seller to provide clear title;
* mutual agreement between buyer and seller;
* failure of the buyer to acquire required financing, where the deal was made subject to this provision; and
* failure to close on time, where there is a time is of the essence provision in the contract to which both parties agreed.

You must be very careful in assuming that a contract is void—an assumption that can be very expensive if not true. Where you believe that a contract is void, it is best to get a written statement to that effect from the other party. This will assure that both parties are in full agreement.
In many states, it is the policy of realtors to write the following across an earnest money receipt and offer to purchase:

"Contract cancelled (date)."

Both buyer and seller are then asked to sign below the statement and copies are provided to all concerned. Where the earnest money is to be return or divided, this official record of contract cancelling can be accomplished by completion of the release of earnest money form, shown in Figure 54.
SEE ALSO: EARNEST MONEY DEPOSIT AND OFFER TO PURCHASE, RELEASE OF EARNEST MONEY, VOIDABLE CONTRACT.

VOIDABLE CONTRACT

A voidable contract is a contract that can be voided by one or both parties under conditions agreed to in the basic agreement.

INVESTOR ADVICE
Voidable contracts are often written as a means of protecting both the buyer and seller. Any offer to purchase which contains a subject-to provision would be classified as voidable. Similarly, contracts with provisions such as 24-hour contingency clauses are voidable under the stated contingency.
SEE ALSO: CONTRACT, EARNEST MONEY RECEIPT AND OFFER TO PURCHASE.

W

Warehouse
Warranty Deed
Water Rights
Water Master
Water Table
Well Permit

White Water Waste
Will
Will of Decent
Working Capital
Wraparound Mortgage
Writ of Eviction

W

WAREHOUSE

A warehouse is:
1. A structure designed for bulk storage of one or more types of materials.
2. A verb meaning to reserve or guarantee available financing for a project.

INVESTOR ADVICE

Warehouse structures are usually limited in height to about 40 feet, the maximum useful storage height. They may be at ground level or have raised floors to facilitate material loading and unloading. In high-density areas with associated high land costs, multistory warehouses may exist; however, the problems of moving materials by conveyors or elevators keep these buildings to a minimum.

Recent advances in computer technology have encouraged the introduction of mechanized warehouses which greatly improve the storage capacity of a building. Mechanized warehouses need aisles only wide enough to move the objects to be stored, whereas the standard warehouse requires aisles large enough for forklift operation.

Turning to the second definition of warehousing, developers who want to assure adequate funds for a long-term project can warehouse adequate funds through their mortgage banker or direct with sources such as insurance companies, pension funds, and commercial banks. This is a particularly good practice where an inordinate increase in interest rates or fund scarcity might tend to disrupt a project.

The cost of warehousing can be as little as 1 or 2 points or as much as 10 points. The cost may be considered good insurance when it assures the availability of mortgage money at a lower rate than the competition can offer, or when it guarantees the success of a project regardless of changes in economic conditions.

SEE ALSO: MORTGAGE COMMITMENT, NET LEASE, and TAKE-OUT LETTER.

WARRANTY DEED

This term refers to a deed in which the grantor covenants and guarantees that the title is free of defects and that it is unencumbered except as noted therein. In addition, the grantor agrees to protect the grantee against any loss by reason of any other title or interest at the time of transfer and not as excepted therein—also known as a *general warranty deed* or *full covenant deed*.

INVESTOR ADVICE

Figure 34 shows an example of a standard warranty deed. Figure 18 shows a special form of this deed which is used when the grantor is a corporation.

Although the guarantees contained in the deed are legally binding on the grantor, there is always the possibility of a defect being found at a time when the grantor is not financially able to make his or her promises good. Without exception, a buyer should demand title insurance to back up and guarantee these promises.

SEE ALSO: SPECIAL WARRANTY DEED.

WATER RIGHTS

Ownership of a specified amount of irrigation water or the right to tap an underground water source, evidenced by a certificate of ownership and registered with the secretary of the water association or governmental agency which controls the water source.

INVESTOR ADVICE
Irrigation water rights may be quantified in any of the following ways:

- specified number of acre-feet owned;

- specified number of second-feet of flow from a designated irrigation ditch;

- number of gallons/minute/day or other period allowed to be pumped from a well; and

- use of full flow from a designated size pipe connected to a pressurized irrigation system.

When you purchase land in the arid regions of the western United States, it is normal that water rights also be purchased and transferred with the land. Without water, land is of little value.

> **WARNING!** A statement of water ownership on a deed may not be adequate evidence of water right ownership.

Where the agreement of sale includes water, a notation on the deed is not always considered sufficient to effect a transfer of water rights. You should also demand that the owner's certificate of ownership be endorsed to you and the transfer registered with the secretary of the water organization. Water certificates are much like bearer bonds and can be sold by the owner, leaving you with only a claim against the former owner.

People unfamiliar with water rights have been known to buy a building lot after having determined that culinary water was available to the site. What they didn't determine is that a connection to that system will require forfeiture of one water share from a designated water source—a share that may not be available from any source at any price. Home construction in some localities is almost nonexistent due to a lack of available water.

Water rights are made available to property owners from federaly developed sources, state-developed sources, and private sources. When the state or federal government develops a water source, it is usually allocated to cities and other property owners on some equitable basis. These original allocations are then gradually subdivided into smaller rights as needs arise and owners are willing to sell.

SEE ALSO: CULINARY WATER, IRRIGATION WATER, and WELL PERMIT.

WATER MASTER

A water master is a person assigned the duty of directing water flow within an irrigation system.

INVESTOR ADVICE
The water master is responsible for clearing minor debriscanals, water gates and weirs. He or she also is responsible for opening and closing the gates which direct the water flow. The water master notifies all users of their allotted time on the ditch and the approximate time that water will arrive to the property. Time on the ditch is rotated so that all users have an equal share of day time use. During the irrigation season, it is not unusual for water to flow 24 hours per day, which means that many farmers must work their field at inconvenient times if they want their share.

SEE ALSO: IRRIGATION WATER, WATER RIGHTS.

WATER TABLE

The normal elevation of available underground water in a given area is called the water table.

INVESTOR ADVICE

Various governmental authorities are constantly measuring the height of the water tables to prevent overusage in periods of lower than normal rainfall. Where acute shortages develop, these governmental agencies are empowered to restrict the flow from the aquifer being used.

Overusage of available underground water can produce inflows of undesirable waters, such as seawater or contaminated waters and cause severe land subsidence such as that currently being experienced in the Los Angeles area.

The height of water tables varies. In Florida and the gulf coast of Texas, sweet water can often be obtained at a depth of less than 25 feet. In these high water table areas, there is little restriction on water use. In parts of the Southwest, significant amounts of water are often found but at depths of several hundreds of feet. These aquifers are very carefully protected.

SEE ALSO: IRRIGATION WATER, WATER RIGHTS, and WELL PERMIT.

WELL PERMIT

Authorization to drill a water well, issued by the federal or state authority which controls the use of groundwater.

INVESTOR ADVICE

CAUTION! A well permit is no assurance of the availability of usable water.

When you purchase property for development, you will ascertain that a well permit is included with the purchase or can be readily obtained from local authorities. You should also determine the level at which you can expect to find water and the type of water likely to be found. In some areas, a well will produce good usable water at expected depths and then another nearby well dug to the same depth will produce water unfit for human consumption.

Before you buy property in arid areas, check with local drillers to determine the probability of success in drilling a good well, the cost of drilling, and the cost of preparing the well for your use (to include casings and distribution facilities).

SEE ALSO: CULINARY WATER and WATER TABLE.

WHITE WATER WASTE

Water that has been used for human bathing and other washing activities is called *white water waste.*

INVESTOR ADVICE

The disposal of wastewater is strictly controlled by the health authorities in most localities. In those areas, constituting watersheds for the production of water for human consumption, particular attention must be paid to the disposal of all waste.

In these controlled watershed areas, wastewater is classified as two types: (a) white water, and (b) gray water, which contains untreated sewage. White water can be disposed of locally by approved septic system treatment. Gray water, on the other hand, must be piped to a treatment facility or held in holding tanks for shipment out of the watershed area.

SEE ALSO: GRAY WATER and SEPTIC SYSTEM.

WILL

A will is a properly executed written document that directs the disposition of one's assets after death.

INVESTOR ADVICE

No one should die without a written will, regardless of the size of their estate. To die intestate is to invoke the state's Will of Decent, which will dispose of your assets in accordance with state law rather than as you desire. It can also be expensive in administrative costs, time, and taxes payable.

In most states, a handwritten will (holographic) is legal. The excuse of the legal costs involved in preparing a will is thus unfounded. A properly prepared will is the only way to assure that your estate will be disposed of in accordance with your desires.

Holographic wills, unless acknowledged, must be proven in probate court through witnesses who will certify that the handwriting is indeed that of the deceased. Properly acknowledged instruments are said to be self-proving in that no proof of their legitimacy is required.

A will is only a part of proper estate planning. Good planning, accomplished with the advice of your accountant, attorney, and estate planner includes a will, establishment of trusts, planned giving, and other tax-saving procedures.

SEE ALSO: ADMINISTRATOR(IX), CODICIL, ESTATE PLANNING, EXECUTOR(IX), HOLO-GRAPHIC WILL, INTESTATE, and WILL OF DECENT.

WILL OF DECENT

This term refers to state laws that direct the disposition of the assets of a person that dies intestate.

INVESTOR ADVICE

State laws of decent vary from state to state but usually favor a surviving spouse, children of the deceased, and close relatives. The law varies considerably regarding those assets which go to a surviving spouse. This is particularly so in those states which utilize Old Spanish property laws, in which property is often divided into his, hers, and their community property.

Even though state laws vary, the general rule of distribution is one half to one third of the estate to the surviving spouse and the remainder to the children of the deceased. Where there are no children, first priority is to surviving parents, brothers and sisters and finally nieces and nephews. Where no relatives can be located, the estate goes to (escheats) to the state. Some states have particular laws applying to property which has been inherited, sometimes returning it to the nearest surviving blood relative from which the property was received.

The foregoing rules concerning state laws apply to real property in the state in which the property is located. Personal property is distributed in accordance with the laws in the state of residence.

SEE ALSO: ADMINISTRATOR(IX), ESCHEAT, EXECUTOR(IX), INTESTATE, WILL.

WORKING CAPITAL

In accounting, working capital is defined as current assets less current liabilities—cash and near cash available for operation of the company.

INVESTOR ADVICE

Insufficient working capital is the major cause of failure of businesses. It is very difficult for a business owner to realize that he or she must restrict business growth to that which can be supported by his working capital. The owner feels that as long as profits are rising, expansion can continue. What the owner doesn't understand is that an increase of business and profit usually is accompanied by larger inventories, larger receivables, and a decrease in working capital.

New business or sales require increased expenditures for inventories, work in progress, and accounts receivable. Even though the new business means increased profits, these profits cannot be used in the business until converted to working capital. The situation can be somewhat ameliorated by increasing and stretching out the accounts payable; however, there is a limit as to how far your creditors will allow you to go.

The best assurance of adequate working capital is an initial pro-forma cash flow analysis followed by periodic reviews against actual performance. This will assure adequate time for planning and corrective actions, which may include additional loans, additional capital infusion, or, if absolutely necessary, a reduction in operations.

Most new businesses rely on an established line of credit to supplement their retained earnings. This means a careful projection of future need, as shown by the pro-forma cash flow analysis, and a preapproved line of credit. To keep your banker happy, you should periodically furnish actual financial statements for comparison against the pro-forma needs. Where your actual figures closely follow your projected figures, no problems will result and your line of credit will remain in effect.

SEE ALSO: ACCOUNTS PAYABLE, ACCOUNTS RECEIVABLE, CASH FLOW, and PRO-FORMA ANALYSIS.

WRAPAROUND MORTGAGE

This term refers to a new second mortgage loan that advances additional funds over and above an existing loan.

INVESTOR ADVICE

If an existing loan is assumable, even though insufficient to finance a property, a wraparound mortgage may provide the best overall interest rate. Even though the second mortgage carries a higher interest rate than the first, the resultant overall interest may be significantly less than the interest an all-new loan.

EXAMPLE

A certain investor plans to buy an income property for $500,000. There is an existing assumable loan of $300,000 on the property which bears an 8% interest rate. The investor will be putting $100,000 down, which requires an additional $100,000 loan.

The investor reveals his plan to his local banker, who agrees to either refinance the property at the going rate of 12% or provide the additional $100,000 on a wraparound basis at 13%. The investor makes the following calculations:

$300,000 @ 8% $24,000
$100,000 @ 13%   13,000
    Total first-year interest $37,000
Effective interest rate: $37,000/$400,000 = 9.3%

The investor selects the wraparound alternative. His bank assumes the existing $300,000 loan and advances the additional $100,000 on a second mortgage basis. The investor makes only one payment each month—an amount sufficient to pay the original loan payments plus an additional amount required to amortize the second mortgage in the remaining term of the first mortgage.

SEE ALSO: ASSUMABLE MORTGAGE, SECOND MORTGAGE, and PIGGYBACK LOAN.

WRIT OF EVICTION

A writ of eviction is a court order, obtained by a landlord, which directs a tenant to vacate a rental property—usually due to nonpayment of rent or other failure to comply with the terms of a lease.

INVESTOR ADVICE

It is only good business to get rid of a tenant who will not comply with the terms of a lease, whether it be for nonpayment of rent or other valid reasons.

Personal contact with the offender is by far the best way of dealing with this type of situation, but where this fails it may be necessary to obtain a writ of eviction. Many states, such as Utah, do not allow a landlord to evict a tenant. The landlord must obtain a court order of eviction, and the sheriff is then directed to evict the tenant.

SEE ALSO: ESTATE AT SUFFERANCE, LANDLORD, LEASE, NOTORIOUS POSSESSION, and TENANT.

Y

Yield
Yield on Equity

Yield on Value

Y

YIELD

The return on capital invested—net income plus capital gains divided by amount invested.

INVESTOR ADVICE

The term *yield* is often confused with other terms, such as *overall return*—net income divided by fair market value. The effects of positive and negative leverage can produce a yield on equity greater or smaller than the return on the entire investment. Calculating yield includes all capital invested, the investor's equity and accumulated capital gains.

Although yield is important in any investment situation, there are other important considerations: (a) the holding period and (b) the timely return (recapture) of the invested equity.

SEE ALSO: LEVERAGE and OVERALL RATE OF RETURN.

YIELD ON EQUITY

Net income after debt service plus equity loan payments, divided by invested equity—also known as equity dividend rate.

INVESTOR ADVICE

The yield on equity is a short term look at the income derived from the operation (cash flow plus periodic equity loan payments) divided by the initial equity invested. It does not take into consideration possible tax savings through depreciation or appreciation through capital gains to be received when the property is sold. It says, "If I invest a certain amount, I will create an income flow equal to a percentage of my initial investment."

SEE ALSO: YIELD and YIELD ON VALUE.

YIELD ON VALUE

Net income divided by the current fair market value—may also be modified to consider income taxes paid—usually designated as overall return.

INVESTOR ADVICE

A common mistake made by many novice investors is to consider their return as being net income divided by price paid. They forget that they have unrealized capital gains invested as well as the initial investment.

One property owner was heard to say, "I'm getting a 50% return on my duplex. I get $12,500 a year in net income and I only paid $25,000 for the unit 20 years ago." What he failed to realize was

> **DON'T FORGET!** The capital gains yet to be realized are part of your investment.

that the property, if sold at that moment, would net $150,000 after sales costs. His return was thus $12,500 divided by the $150,000 or 8.3%. At that instant, tax-exempt bonds were yielding 12% on a taxable basis. He should have sold.

A proper consideration of the return should use a denominator which is the total investment, even though the capital gains have not been realized. Many investors like to consider the yield on value as the net income divided by the cash that would be generated by a current sale of the property.

If the return is less than that available through other investment media with the same risk, it is probably time to sell the property and recover your equity for reinvestment in a more profitable venture.

SEE ALSO: FAIR MARKET VALUE, OVERALL RETURN, and YIELD ON EQUITY.

Z

Zero Down Technique
Zero Lot LIne
Zoning

Zonaing Codes
Zoning Variances

Z

ZERO DOWN TECHNIQUE

A method of buying real estate with no money down—100% financing.

INVESTOR ADVICE

Various get-rich-quick artists and seminar leaders have suggested ways of buying real estate with no money down. These techniques are feasible in times of inflation and when real estate values are rapidly appreciating. The gains from such purchases are basically in the capital appreciation realized at the time of sale.

Without capital gains, the total return is likely to cover barely the debt service with little or nothing left over to compensate for the management effort required or the risk taken.

Most of the techniques described for getting rich quick involve seller financing or partial financing. Usually, it is suggested that the first mortgage be assumed and the seller asked to take back a second for the balance due. The seller is persuaded to accept this type of deal by a purchase offer which is higher than the going rate for the property.

A seller must be strongly motivated to sell under these types of arrangements. With nothing down, the seller pays for the title policy, closing costs, and realtor fees out of pocket. In addition, the seller is the only one who is taking a risk. If inflation continues, the seller will probably get his or her money. If the market stagnates or goes down, he or she is left holding the bag.

Another technique involves new financing for the maximum amount possible, with the seller taking a second mortgage for the balance due. Other techniques are based on the assumption that the property will appraise for significantly more than the selling price, allowing a first mortgage to cover the purchase costs.

Buyers who practice this type of investing usually have nothing to lose, since nothing has been risked. If the market turns down, the buyer lets the seller take back the property. When the seller sues to obtain a deficiency judgment, he or she finds that the buyer has taken bankruptcy or else has nothing to satisfy the claim.

SEE ALSO: CREATIVE FINANCING.

ZERO LOT LINE

A zoning provision allowing the construction of buildings on or approximately on the boundary line. Normal zoning has specified building-to-lot-line requirements.

INVESTOR ADVICE

In the recent past, zero lot lines were the standard practice in most cities. Today, this is true in only the most congested areas which are 100% commercial. Industrial parks now provide for building separations similar to residential.

Residential construction, which formerly called for building separation, has been relaxed in very expensive land areas to permit construction of row houses or other types of planned unit developments (PUDs).

Where allowed, zero lot line construction can permit maximum utilization of very expensive property. If zero lot line construction is planned, carefully check the local building ordinances and restrictions before buying undeveloped land.

SEE ALSO: BUILDING CODES, PLANNED UNIT DEVELOPMENTS (PUDS), RESTRICTIVE COVENANTS.

ZONING

Governmental agency control of the use of land under provisions of state police powers.

INVESTOR ADVICE

Any municipality or county of significant size and population has enacted zoning laws to promote the uniform use of available land. The zoning of particular parcels of land is in accordance with large area designations or individual decisions rendered through master planning and the rezoning process.

Zoning is generally designated by classes or codes, designated by abbreviations such as R-1, C-2, and so forth. Zoning may be absolute or conditional. If absolute, any authorized use of the land as authorized by that code can be made without reference to the zoning authorities. Where the zoning is conditional, it means that any use authorized by the code may be exercised after approval of the specific proposed use by the zoning authorities.

Exceptions to zoning laws are allowed under two conditions:

1. where the land was utilized for a specific legal use prior to a zoning change and continues to operate under the grandfather clause; and
2. where specifically authorized as nonconforming use by the zoning authorities.

A smart investor will be fully cognizant of the city's master planning. He or she can often purchase property with a less valuable current zoning and then have the property rezoned for a higher and better use. Rezoning alone can often double or triple the value of a parcel of property.

SEE ALSO: GRANDFATHER CLAUSE, MASTER PLAN, NONCONFORMING USE, PLOTTAGE, POLICE POWER, and ZONING CODES.

ZONING CODES

Abbreviated designations for authorized land use.

INVESTOR ADVICE

Zoning codes vary from authority to authority. It is not unusual to have many designations for a specified use in one metropolitan area containing several municipalities. For instance, R-2 may mean single-family housing in one area and duplex housing in another. Don't depend upon your own idea of what a designation means unless you have checked it out in the zoning regulations.

In general, the following meanings apply:

R—residential use,
C—commercial use,
M—manufacturing or storage use, and
A—agricultural use.

A letter followed by a number or other letters usually qualifies the zoning to specific use or uses within the larger general classifications.

SEE ALSO: MASTER PLAN, SPOT ZONING, and ZONING.

ZONING VARIANCES

Authorized use of land which does not conform to the specific zoning of the parcel or area.

INVESTOR ADVICE

Zoning variances are granted by those having the authority to enact zoning laws. Each zoning authority has specific procedures for the requesting of variances, but such variances are only granted for very compelling reasons of public good and benefit.

If you are proposing to purchase land which is not zoned for your intended use, you should make your offer subject to the required zoning variance or rezoning being granted.

SEE ALSO: MASTER PLAN, NONCONFORMING USE, SPOT ZONING, ZONING, and ZONING VARIANCES.